Books by George Santayana

ESSAYS IN LITERARY CRITICISM OF GEORGE SANTAYANA
THE LETTERS OF GEORGE SANTAYANA
THE LIFE OF REASON (one-volume edition)
THE POET'S TESTAMENT: POEMS AND TWO PLAYS
THE BACKGROUND OF MY LIFE: VOL. I OF PERSONS AND PLACES
THE MIDDLE SPAN: VOL. II OF PERSONS AND PLACES
MY HOST THE WORLD: VOL. III OF PERSONS AND PLACES
DOMINATIONS AND POWERS: REFLECTIONS ON LIBERTY, SOCIETY
    AND GOVERNMENT
THE IDEA OF CHRIST IN THE GOSPELS, OR GOD IN MAN
REALMS OF BEING
THE REALM OF SPIRIT
THE REALM OF TRUTH
THE PHILOSOPHY OF SANTAYANA: SELECTIONS FROM THE COMPLETE
    WORKS OF GEORGE SANTAYANA
OBITER SCRIPTA: LECTURES, ESSAYS AND REVIEWS
THE LAST PURITAN: A MEMOIR IN THE FORM OF A NOVEL
SOME TURNS OF THOUGHT IN MODERN PHILOSOPHY
THE GENTEEL TRADITION AT BAY
THE REALM OF ESSENCE
THE REALM OF MATTER
PLATONISM AND THE SPIRITUAL LIFE
DIALOGUES IN LIMBO
POEMS
SCEPTICISM AND ANIMAL FAITH
EGOTISM IN GERMAN PHILOSOPHY
SOLILOQUIES IN ENGLAND AND LATER SOLILOQUIES
CHARACTER AND OPINION IN THE UNITED STATES
THE SENSE OF BEAUTY
INTERPRETATIONS OF POETRY AND RELIGION
THE HERMIT OF CARMEL AND OTHER POEMS
WINDS OF DOCTRINE
THE LIFE OF REASON: OR THE PHASES OF HUMAN PROGRESS
    I. INTRODUCTION AND REASON IN COMMON SENSE
    II. REASON IN SOCIETY
    III. REASON IN RELIGION
    IV. REASON IN ART
    V. REASON IN SCIENCE
LITTLE ESSAYS DRAWN FROM THE WORKS OF GEORGE SANTAYANA
    By Logan Pearsall Smith, with the collaboration of the author

PERSONS AND PLACES

GEORGE SANTAYANA, AS DRAWN FROM LIFE
BY LINO S. LIPINSKY, IN ROME, 1950

PERSONS AND PLACES

GEORGE SANTAYANA

NEW YORK

CHARLES SCRIBNER'S SONS

INTRODUCTION

TO THE SINGLE-VOLUME EDITION OF
PERSONS AND PLACES

I N recent years there has been a great spawning of 'confessions' by literary shellfish basking in some ebb-tide of local interest. I doubt if Santayana would have had much sympathy with this current necessity to get rid of one's life before it had been completed by Nature. In the old days of our friendship he had always maintained that the appropriate time for an author to unveil his personal history was after his death. The fact that two volumes of his autobiography were published during his life was primarily due to the exigencies of the last war.

For back in 1942, Santayana was more or less isolated in a nursing-home in Rome. I knew that he had been working intermittently on his reminiscences, but I had been out of communication with him for some time. There was no telling then how long the war might continue. Under the circumstances, John Hall Wheelock of the House of Scribner felt that it was too risky to leave a valuable manuscript at the mercy of unpredictable events. So he consulted various diplomatic officials, and got together with the Irish poet Padraic Colum who had some influential contacts at the Vatican. After many devious threads of communication had been woven, and some mechanical wings of diplomatic immunity enlisted, the manuscript of volume one of *Persons and Places* landed out of the blue one summer day on his desk in Fifth Avenue.

It proved quite a task to groom a rather disorderly holograph for public appearance, but the eventual debut in 1944 was sensational. For the second time in his life Santayana hit the jackpot in the American publishing world: "The Background of My Life" became

—like his novel *The Last Puritan*—a Book-of-the-Month Club selection. It was recognized at once that here was an autobiography of
a very high order, and one harked back to *The Education of Henry
Adams,* or the subtle twilight reminiscences of Henry James, for
models of evaluation. If the criteria in question are the elevation of
a writer's style, the fullness of his story, or that enhancement of our
consciousness which is the touchstone of all outstanding literary
achievement, *Persons and Places* can stand on the same exclusive
shelf with those two American classics. But the adjective "American"
should make us pause. Santayana was born in Madrid just one
hundred years ago, and despite the fact that he was exported to
Boston at the age of nine, and later on taught philosophy at Harvard
with William James and Josiah Royce, he remained a Spanish
subject all his life. One of his last acts in 1952, when he was
eighty-eight years old, was to make a special visit to the Spanish
consulate in the heart of Rome in order to have his passport renewed. I would not labour these facts if it were not for the strange
tendency in certain circles in America to camouflage the truth—to
impose on Santayana an official American stamp. On the other
hand, he has admitted quite frankly that if he is to be remembered
as a poet, or a novelist, or a philosopher, or perhaps more faithfully,
as *un homme de lettres,* it must be as a writer in the English language, and—I might add—as a rather wayward flower of the New
England literary tradition. But to admit this is not to deny a fundamental Spanish psyche, or a loyalty to the country where he was
born and passed the first eight years of his life, and returned to
every summer in his later Harvard years to be "at home" with his
father in Avila. When we recall that all these facts have been so
fully delineated in *Persons and Places,* there is no legitimate excuse
for further misrepresentation.

To the end of his life, however, Santayana regretted the urgent
and partial publication of his autobiography, and he wrote to me
that he considered it to be a "mutilated victim of the war." No doubt
he had very mixed feelings that day in 1942 when an obscure
messenger from the Vatican knocked at his door in the nursing-

home of The Blue Sisters in Rome, and handed him a letter requesting the manuscript and explaining how it might be safely transferred to New York. In the first place, it was not yet completed; and
secondly, he had not originally meant to have it published until
after his death. Perhaps when he heard somewhat later what a
succès fou volume one had turned out to be, his sense of appro-
priateness was slightly modified. Several months before he died,
he told me that he dreamed of the day when his story might be
offered *as a whole* to the public. With the publication in his
centenary of a single-volume edition of *Persons and Places,* I feel
that to a certain extent his shade has been appeased, and his dream
fulfilled.

DANIEL CORY
Rome, 1963

THE BACKGROUND OF MY LIFE

.

THE
BACKGROUND
OF
MY LIFE

GEORGE
SANTAYANA

VOL. I * *Persons and Places*

CHARLES SCRIBNER'S SONS

CONTENTS

CHAPTER		PAGE
I.	Time, Place and Ancestry	1
II.	My Father	10
III.	My Mother	30
IV.	The Sturgises	56
V.	My Sister Susana	75
VI.	Avila	96
VII.	Early Memories	116
VIII.	I am Transported to America	130
IX.	No. 302 Beacon Street	140
X.	The Latin School	148
XI.	The Church of the Immaculate Conception	163
XII.	First Friends	178
XIII.	The Harvard Yard	186
XIV.	First Return to Spain	203
XV.	College Friends	224
XVI.	College Studies	238
	Index	255

THE BACKGROUND OF MY LIFE

CHAPTER I

TIME, PLACE AND ANCESTRY

A DOCUMENT in my possession testifies that in the parish church of San Marcos in Madrid, on the 1st of January, 1864, a male child, born on the 16th of the previous December, at nine o'clock in the evening, at No 69 Calle Ancha de San Bernardo, was solemnly christened; being the legitimate son of Don Agustín Ruiz de Santayana, native of Zamora, and of Doña Josefina Borrás, native of Glasgow; his paternal grandparents being Don Nicolás, native of Badumés, in the province of Santander, and Doña Maria Antonia Reboiro, native of Zamora, and his maternal grandparents being Don José, native of Reus, Catalonia, and Doña Teresa Carbonell, native of Barcelona. The names given him were Jorge Agustín Nicolás, his godparents being Don Nicolás Ruiz de Santayana and Doña Susana Sturgis; "whom I admonished," writes Don Joaquín Cabrasco, who signs the certificate with his legal *rúbrica* or flourish, "of their spiritual relationship and duties."

A shrewd fortune-teller would have spotted at once, in this densely Spanish document, the two English names, Glasgow and Sturgis. Where did they come from, what did they forebode? Might not seeds of my whole future lie buried there? And if the diviner had had preternatural powers, he might even have sniffed something important in those last, apparently so effete and perfunctory words, that Doña Susana Sturgis, who was my mother's daughter by a former marriage and then twelve years of age, had been forewarned of her spiritual relationship and duties: not that she should forbear marrying my godfather, my uncle Nicolás, who was a major in the Spanish army, with a wife and child, and

1

forty-five years old; that was canonical red-tape nothing to the purpose; but that she was called by Providence to be really my spiritual mother and to catechize my young mind. It was she that initiated me into theology, architecture and polite society.

With parents evidently Catalans of the Catalonians how did my mother come to be born in Glasgow, and how did she ever marry a Bostonian named Sturgis? These facts, taken separately, were accidents of travel, or rather of exile and of Colonial life; but accidents are accidents only to ignorance; in reality all physical events flow out of one another by a continuous intertwined derivation; and those odd foreign names, Sturgis and Glasgow, were in fact secretly allied and their presence here had a common source in my grandfather's character and circumstances and in the general thaw, so to speak, of that age: incongruous wreckage of a great inundation.

Not that I would nail the flag of fatalism to the mast at the beginning of this retrospective voyage. What we call the laws of nature are hasty generalizations; and even if some of them actually prevailed without exception or alloy, the fact that these laws and not others (or none) were found to be dominant would itself be groundless; so that nothing could be at bottom more arbitrary than what always happens, or more fatal than what happens but once or by absolute chance. Yet in the turbid stream of nature there are clear stretches, and traceable currents; and it is interesting to follow the beginnings and the developments of a run here and a whirlpool there, and to watch the silent glassy volume of water slip faster and faster towards the edge of some precipice. Now my little cockle-shell and the cockle-shells of the rest of my family, and of the whole middle and upper class (except the unsinkable politicians) were being borne along more or less merrily on the surface-currents of a treacherous social revolution; and the things that happened to us, and the things we did, with their pleasant and their hopeless sides, all belong to that general moral migration.

My grandfather, José Borrás y Bufurull, belonged to a well-established family of Reus, of the sort that possess a house in the town and a farm in the country. In this as in other ways many old towns near the Mediterranean preserve the character of ancient cities or *civitates,* and Reus in particular is a place of great dignity in the eyes of its inhabitants, who are reputed to speak habitually of "Reus, Paris and London." But José was a younger son, and the law of entail or *mayorazgo* still prevailed at that time in Catalonia, so that the house and land and an almost Roman authority as head of the family fell to his eldest brother. Yet dignity to the classic mind does not involve great wealth or much territory, and younger sons, even in Reus, had to seek their fortunes away from home. They might indeed expect hospitality or a little aid from their families in time of stress, but were well aware that in the ancestral estate and community there was no place or occupation for more than one household at a time. There was the Church always tempting them, if it tempted them; there were the other professions, and there was the New World, or at least Cuba and the Philippines. One of my grandfather's brothers had actually combined these opportunities, become a monk, and later been established as a parish priest in Montevideo or in Buenos Aires.* The ultimate resource, among all my Spanish acquaintance and relations, was some post under the government; and my grandfather might very well have sought his fortunes no further afield than Barcelona, or at most Madrid; but he went much further. Economic considerations were probably not uppermost in his mind; if they were, his career must have disheartened him. Those were unsettled and unsettling times, the repercussions of the French Revolution had not spent themselves, and emancipation of mind was sure to follow, if it had not preceded, being cast

* A history of the Borrás family of Reus has been published, but it contains hardly any information about my grandfather and none about my mother. In some respects the traditions recorded there diverge from those that my mother handed down; they may be more accurate, as my mother had no great interest or respect for the past. The exact facts in any case are not important, and I report the impressions that I have gathered.

loose upon the world. In any case we know that my grandfather, far from becoming a monk, like his brother, became a Deist, an ardent disciple of Rousseau, and I suspect a Freemason; and when a French army entered Spain, in 1823, to restore the shaken authority of Ferdinand VII and the absolute monarchy, José Borrás was compelled or thought it advisable to leave the country. The story goes that he fled first to Las Palmas, in the Balearic Islands, where he saw and wooed Teresa Carbonell, a stout blonde with very blue eyes (my mother's eyes were also blue and large); and that after a romantic marriage he persuaded her to follow him in his wanderings. In my certificate of baptism, however, Teresa Carbonell is set down as a native of Barcelona, which is not strictly incompatible with her living later at Las Palmas, or her family belonging there; but she and her whole history are wrapped in some obscurity, and suggest various problems that I have no means of solving.

One of these problems is why my grandfather should have chosen Glasgow for a place of refuge, and what he did there. Mahon, in the neighboring Minorca, had long been in British occupation, and occasions may have presented themselves to sail from there to Scotland, or perhaps to Lancashire; and he seems to have remained in those parts for some years, probably giving Spanish lessons and in any case learning English. This exile in poverty and obscurity, in so remote, cheerless, and industrial a scene, may not have been altogether unwelcome to him. Catalans are industrially and economically minded; novelty and distance allure them; and who knows how many utopias and ideologies, and what reflections on the missed opportunities of human government may not have kept his brain and heart warm in that chilly climate. All I can say is that his thirst for exploration or his longing for a simpler and more ideal society carried him eventually across the Atlantic, to rural, republican, distinguished, Jeffersonian Virginia. Here, if anywhere, mankind had turned over a new leaf, and in a clean new world, free from all absurd traditions and tyrant mortgages, was beginning to lead a pure life

TIME, PLACE AND ANCESTRY 5

of reason and virtue. With slavery? Perhaps that was only a temporary necessity, a kindly apprenticeship to instill into the simple
negro a love of labor and of civilized arts; and as the protection
of industries might be justified provisionally, until they could
become well-rooted, so domestic servitude might be justified provisionally, until the slaves were ripe for freedom.

Be that as it may, José Borrás either came well recommended
or ingratiated himself easily into the democracy of Winchester,
Virginia, becoming (as a florid testimonial averred) one of its
most honored and beloved citizens; so much so that as the years
revolved, and a change of government in the liberal direction had
occurred in Spain, his Winchester friends induced Andrew Jackson, then President of the United States, to appoint him American
Consul at Barcelona. Thus his cordial attachments in exile enabled him eventually to return home, not only safely but glori-
ously, and with some prospect of bread and butter.*

* THE PRESIDENT OF THE UNITED STATES OF AMERICA
to all who shall see these presents, greeting.

No ye, that reposing special trust and confidence in the abilities and the
integrity of Joseph Borras of Spain, I have nominated and by and with the
advice and consent of the Senate do appoint him consul of the United
States of America for the Port of Barcelona, in Spain, and for such other
parts as shall be nearer thereto than the residence of any other consul or
vice-consul of the United States within the same allegiance,—and do
authorize and empower him to have and to hold the said office and to
exercise and enjoy all the rights, preeminences, privileges, and authorities
to the same of right appertaining, during the pleasure of the President of
the United States for the time being; HE demanding and receiving no fees
or perquisites of office whatever, which shall not be expressly established by
some law of the United States. And I do hereby enjoin all captains, masters, and commanders of ships and other vessels, armed or un-armed, sailing
under the flag of the United States as well as all others of their citizens, to
acknowledge and consider him the said Joseph Borras accordingly. And I do
hereby pray and request Her Majesty, the Queen of Spain, Her governors
and officers to permit the said Joseph Borras fully and peaceably to enjoy
and exercise the said office without giving or suffering to be given unto him
any molestation or trouble, but on the contrary to afford him all proper

An element of mystery or mystification hangs about this home-coming. The date of my mother's birth, according to her official papers, was 1828, but there is reason to believe that in reality it was 1826. When she was brought to Spain in 1835 the shocking fact appeared that she had never been christened. Was there no Catholic priest in Glasgow in those days, and none in Winchester, Virginia? Had no travelling ecclesiastic been met with in all those wanderings? No doubt her father's enlightened principles made him regard all religious practices, morally and philosophically, as indifferent, while socially it was advisable that everyone should be affiliated to the religious customs prevalent in his country. But what was to be my mother's country? If it were to be Scotland or Virginia, she ought to be christened and brought up a Protestant: if it were to be Spain, it was imperative that she should be a Catholic. The matter therefore had to be suspended until the question of final residence was settled: although it may seem singular that my grandmother should have wholly acquiesced in this view and allowed her daughter to grow up, as they say in Spain, a Moor. Now, however, the matter had to be patched up as expeditiously and quietly as possible. Friends and relations, even clerical advisers, are very accommodating in Spain and very in-genious. The age of seven, the canonical age of reason, when one begins to sin of one's own accord, was the right age for confirma-tion; young Josefina was small for her age; let her official age be reduced to seven years, let a private christening, to supply the

---

countenance and assistance; I offering to do the same for all those who shall in like manner be recommended to me by Her said Majesty.

IN TESTIMONY WHEREOF I have caused these letters to be made patent, and the seal of the United States be hereunto affixed.

GIVEN under my hand at the City of Washington, the third day of March in the year of our Lord one thousand eight hundred and thirty-five, and of the Independence of the United States of America the fifty-ninth.

(Signed)   ANDREW JACKSON

By the President

(SEAL)   John Forsyth, *Secretary of State.*

place of the missing documents, be smuggled in before the confirmation, and then the child would be launched quite legally and
becomingly in her religious career, with confession and communion to follow immediately. This wealth of sacraments, raining
down on her unprepared and extraordinary self-reliant little soul,
seems not to have left much hunger for further means of grace.
My mother always spoke of such things as of troublesome and
empty social requirements; and even ordinary social requirements,
like visiting, rather annoyed her, as if they interfered with her
liberty and interrupted her peace.

On the whole, however, her ten years or more of girlhood in
Barcelona seem to have been gay and happy—the only frankly
happy period of her life. Without being robust, her health was
perfect, her needlework exquisite, her temper equable and calm;
she loved and was loved by her girl-friends; she read romantic
verses and select novels; above all, she danced. That was the
greatest pleasure in life for her: not for the sake of her partners—
those were surely only round dances, and the partners didn't
count; what counted was the joy of motion, the sense of treading
lightly, in perfect time, a sylph in spotless muslin, enriched with
a ribbon or a flower, playing discreetly with her fan, and sailing
through the air with feet that seemed scarcely to touch the ground.
Even in her old age my mother never walked, she stepped. And
she would say in her quaint, perhaps Virginian English: "Will
you step in?" She was not beautiful, and prematurely regarded
herself as an old woman, and put on a white lace cap; but she had
good points and made a favorable ideal impression, even if she
did not positively attract. I can imagine her in her young days,
agile of foot and hand, silent and enigmatic behind her large
sunken blue eyes, thin lips, and brown corkscrew curls, three on
a side, setting off her white complexion. If men did not often
make love to her, especially not the men who care specifically for
women, she amply took her revenge. Her real attachments, apart
from her devotion to her father, were to her women friends, not
to crowds of them, but to two or three and for life. To men as

men, even to her two husbands, she seems to have been cold, critical and sad, as if conscious of yielding to some inevitable but disappointing fatality.

I will translate a letter written to her by my father, dated Jan. 28, 1888, when I was in my second year at the University of Berlin, and it began to seem clear that I should drift into an academic life in America.

"My dear Josefina; I have had much pleasure in taking note of your kind letter and of the verses which, while thinking of me, you wrote twenty-five years ago. A volume would be requisite for me to recount the memories I have of our relations during now little less than a half a century. When we were married I felt as if it were written that I should be united with you, yielding to the force of destiny, although I saw plainly the difficulties that then surrounded such a union, apart from those that would not fail to arise later. Strange marriage, this of ours! So you say, and so it is in fact. I love you very much, and you too have cared for me, yet we do not live together. But it is necessary to keep in mind the circumstances peculiar to our case. I have always believed that the place in which it would be natural for you to live was Boston, in consequence of your first marriage which determined the course of your whole life. My position has offered and now offers no inducement, none, to balance the propriety or necessity of that arrangement. On my side, I could not then or later leave my own country for good, in order to live in Boston, when in view of my age and impediments it was impossible for me to learn to speak English well and to mix in that society. Here I have been a help to my family, and there I should only have been an encumbrance.

"I should have wished that Jorge should not have been separated from me, but I found myself compelled to take him in person and leave him in your charge and in that of his brother and sisters. Unhappy compulsion! Yet it was much better for him to be with you than with me, and I prefer his good to my pleasure."

How much in this was clearness of vision, how much was modesty, how much was love of quietness and independence? It is not a question for me to decide, but there was certainly something of all those motives. Education such as I received in Boston was steadier and my associations more regular and calmer than they would have been in Spain; but there was a terrible moral disinheritance involved, an emotional and intellectual chill, a pettiness and practicality of outlook and ambition, which I should not have encountered amid the complex passions and intrigues of a Spanish environment. From the point of view of learning, my education at the Boston Latin School and at Harvard College was not solid or thorough; it would not have been solid or thorough in Spain; yet what scraps of learning or ideas I might have gathered there would have been vital, the wind of politics and of poetry would have swelled them, and allied them with notions of honor. But then I should have become a different man; so that my father's decision was all for my good, if I was to be the person that I am now.

CHAPTER II

MY FATHER

THE name Santayana is derived by phonetic corruption from that of a small town in the Cantabrian hills, not far from the sea and from Santander. This name was originally Santa Juliana, doubtless that of some shrine or hermitage; but in Latin, as in Italian, *J* is only a double *i*, or *y*, the consonant, and the consonant *y* in Spanish is often confused with the stronger sound of *ll*, or the Italian *gl*; so that Santa Juliana could obviously yield in the vernacular to Santa Lliana, Santallana, Santayana, and Santillana. This last is the present name of that village; and on the other side of Santander, towards the Southeast, lies the village of Espinosa; so that my witty friend and translator, Don Antonio Marichalar, Marqués de Montesa (from whom I borrow the above etymology), half in banter and half in compliment finds in those seaside mountains, opposite one another, the native soil of Spinoza and of myself. But if I cannot be mentioned without a smile in the same breath with Spinoza for greatness of intellect, he cannot be compared with me for Spanish blood. He was a Jew: his ancestors could have found their way to Espinosa only as they did later to Amsterdam, or he himself to The Hague, or I to America; whereas if the reader will look back to the first page of this narrative, he will see that my grandfather was born in the province of Santander though not at Santillana, and that his wife and my father were born at Zamora, in Leon, my grandmother having the distinctly Portuguese or Galician surname of Reboiro: so that my ancestry on my father's side points distinctly to northwestern Spain, and Celt-Iberian blood; while my mother's origins were as unmistakably Catalonian and Balearic; rooted, that is, in those northeastern shores that look towards Provence and towards Italy and have linked Spain for many ages with the whole Mediterranean world.

The name Santayana is tolerably well known in Spain. My father had a book of the eighteenth century written by one of the family on the subject of international trade, advocating the Spartan policy of isolation and autarchy. My father didn't call it Spartan, but monkish; and it was based perhaps more on fear of heresy than on love of political independence; but the author was not an ecclesiastic, but a man of affairs. My two forlorn unmarried aunts, older than my father, used to tell me that our family was noble and allied to the house of a Marqués de Santayana then existing in Madrid; but they had no means of tracing the relationship, nor did my father give the least attention to questions of this kind; so that I know nothing of my ancestry beyond his own time. Moreover our family name is really Ruiz, a very common one; and perhaps the addition of de Santayana was as accidental in our family as the addition of de Espinosa must have been in a family of Amsterdam Jews. Dropping Ruiz and retaining only Santayana was my father's doing, and caused him some trouble in legalizing his abbreviated signature in formal documents. He loved simplicity, and thought plain Agustín Santayana as pompous a name as his modest position could carry. I sympathize with the motive; but why not drop the Santayana and keep the Ruiz, which was the true patronymic? Legally I still possess both; and the question has no further importance, since with me our branch of the family becomes extinct.

If I were looking for ancestors there is only one known to fame to whom I might attempt to attach myself, and he is Gil Blas, whose blood I should rather like imagining I had in my veins. I feel a natural sympathy with unprejudiced minds, or if you like with rogues. The picaresque world is the real world; and if lying and thievery and trickery are contemptible, it is because the game is not worth the candle, not because the method is unworthy of the prize. If you despise the world, and cheat it only to laugh at it, as the Spanish rascals seem to do, at least in fiction, the sin is already half forgiven. When the rogue tires of the game or is ruined by it, he may unfeignedly turn his free spirit towards higher things, or at least, like the good thief in Calvary, may recognize their existence. Those who lack the impudence and nimbleness of the rascal cannot help admiring his knowledge of things, and his quick eye; and the very meanness and triviality of his arts will keep him from thinking, as sinners do on a larger scale, that they are altogether heroes. Gil Blas doesn't become a saint— his biographer is a Frenchman—but becomes a good bourgeois, rich and happily married. It is a sort of redemption, though the Spanish spirit in him demanded another sort. The worthy solution would be found not in prosperity (too nearly what the unregenerate Gil Blas was pursuing) but rather in devotion, religious in its quality, even if not in its object: the solution that the poet Zorilla, a friend of my father's in their youth, puts into the mouth of the reformed Don Juan, reformed, that is, by love.

> ¿No es verdad, ángel de amor,
> que en esta apartada orilla
> la luna mas clara brilla
> y se respira mejor?
>
> Angel love, is it not true
> that on this sequestered shore
> the moon shines as ne'er before
> and to breathe is something new?

Gil Blas represents also the sort of spiritual democracy that is characteristically Spanish, Christian, or Oriental. An unprejudiced man will be ready and happy to live in any class of society; he will find there occasions enough for merriment, pleasure, and kindness. Only snobs are troubled by inequality, or by exclusion from something accidental, as all particular stations are. Why should I think it unjust that I am not an applauded singer nor a field-marshal nor a puppet king? I am rather sorry for them; I mean, for the spirit in them. Success and failure in the world are sprinkled over it like dew: it does not depend on the species of plant that receives it, save that the plant must exist and must spread its living texture to the elements. That is a great privilege, and a great danger. I would not multiply or inflate myself of my own accord. Even the punctilious honor of the Spanish gentleman is only an eloquent vanity, disdaining many advantages for the sake of a pose. Why assume so much dignity, if you have it not? And if you have it, what need have you of parading it? The base and sordid side of life must be confessed and endured humbly; the confession and the endurance will raise you enough above it.

The Spanish dignity in humility was most marked in my father. He lived when necessary and almost by preference like the poor, without the least comfort, variety, or entertainment. He was bred in poverty, not the standard poverty, so to speak, of the hereditary working classes, but in the cramped genteel poverty of those who find themselves poorer than they were, or than they have to seem. He was one of twelve children, imposing the strictest economy in the household of a minor official, with insecure tenure of office, such as his father was. For supper they had each a small bowl of garlic soup—something that my father loved in his old age, and that I also liked, especially if I might break a raw egg into it, as those twelve children were certainly never allowed to do. You fry some garlic in a pan with some olive oil; when crisp you remove the larger pieces of garlic, add hot water according to the size of the family, with thin little slices of bread, no matter how dry, *ad libitum*, and a little salt; and that is your supper. Or perhaps with a further piece of bread, you might receive a slice of cheese, cut so thin that the children would hold it up to the light, to admire its transparency, and to wink at one another through the frequent round holes.

That oil and water will not mix is disproved by this excellent garlic soup but also by a salad, *gazpacho*, that somewhat corresponded to it in the South. Bread, tomatoes and cucumbers, with oil and vinegar, and some slivers of raw onion, if you were not too refined, composed its substance, all floating in an abundance of water; so that if hunger was partly mocked, thirst at least was satisfied, and this is the more urgent need in a warm climate.

If supper at my grandfather's was only bread and water, with condiments, breakfast probably included a tiny cup of thick chocolate into which you might dip your bread, before you drank your water; for a glass of water after chocolate was *de rigueur* in all classes in old Spain. The difference between simplicity and luxury was only this: that the luxurious had an *azucarillo,* a large oblong piece of frosted sugar blown into a light spongy texture, and flavored with lemon, to be dissolved in a glass of water. At midday the daily food of all Spaniards was the *puchero* or *cocido,* as the dish is really called which foreigners know as the pot-pourri or *olla podrida.* This contains principally yellow chick-peas, with a little bacon, some potatoes or other vegetables and normally also small pieces of beef and sausage, all boiled in one pot at a very slow fire; the liquid of the same makes the substantial broth that is served first.

My father was educated at Valladolid, I don't know first under what schoolmaster, but eventually at the university there, where he studied law; and he at least learned Latin well enough to take pleasure in translating the tragedies of Seneca into Castilian blank verse; a pure work of love, since he could expect no advancement, perhaps rather the opposite, from such an exhibition of capricious industry. Nor was that his only taste; he also studied painting, and quite professionally, although he made no great progress in it. His feeling for the arts and sciences was extraordinarily different from that which prevailed in the 1880's in English-speaking circles. As to painting all in England was a matter of culture, of the pathos of distance, of sentimental religiosity, pre-Raphaelitism, and supercilious pose. Even the learned and gifted that I saw in Oxford were saturated with affectations. My friend Lionel Johnson was typical: although thirty years later, during the war, I had other distinguished friends in Oxford, Robert Bridges and Father Waggett, who were not in the least affected. But my father could not understand the English mind, greatly as he admired and respected the practical lordliness of Britain. Speaking once of Newman, he said he wondered why Newman broke with the Anglican establishment. Was it so as to wear a trailing red silk gown? I had some difficulty in making him admit that Newman could have been sincere; perhaps it was possible, if, as I said, Newman had never doubted the supernatural authority of the Church. But of inner unrest or faith suddenly born out of despair my father had absolutely no notion. Could he ever have read the Confessions of his patron saint, Saint Augustine? Was that not a natural sequel to the tragedies of Seneca?

As to painting, my father's ideas were absolutely those of the craftsman, the artisan, following his trade conscientiously with no thought or respect for the profane crowd of rich people who might be babbling about art in their ignorance. This jealous professionalism did not exclude speculation and criticism; but they were the speculation and criticism of the specialist, scientific and materialistic. He viewed the arts in the manner of Leonardo, whom probably he had never read. In talking about the pictures in the Prado, which I had seen for the first time, he approved of an observation I made about *El Pasmo de Sicilia,* that all the figures were brick-colored except that of Christ, which was whitish—a contrast that seemed artificial. He said I had been looking at the picture to some purpose. But he was disappointed when he questioned me about the Goyas, because I said nothing about the manner of painting, and only thought of the subjects, the ladies' fashions, and the sensuality of the eighteenth-century notion of happiness, coarser in Goya than in Watteau.

His methods were not less workmanlike than his thoughts. His easel, his colors, ground by himself with a glass pestle and carefully mixed with the oil, his palette and his brushes were objects of wonder to my childish heart. I was too young to catch the contagion and try to imitate him; but afterwards, when drawing became a pastime for me (as it still is) I wondered sometimes if my father's example and lessons would have helped me to make the progress in draughtsmanship which I have never made. And I doubt that they would have helped me. Because composition and ideal charm which are everything to me in all the arts seemed to be nothing to my father. I might have acquired a little more manual skill, and corrected a few bad mannerisms; but I should soon have broken away and turned to courses that he could not approve. Yet I think that he himself suffered in his painting, as in his life, from the absence of any ideal inspiration. He was arrested by the sheer mechanics of the art, as I was arrested by ignorance of them; and he remained an amateur all his life in his professionalism, because after measuring his drawing, and catching the likeness (since his paintings were all portraits) and laying on his first strata of color, he would become uncertain and discouraged, without a clear vision of what might render his picture living, distinctive, harmonious, and in a word *beautiful*.

When I once asked him, apropos of his liberal politics, the hollowness of which I already began to feel, what ideal of society he would approve, he said he had no *ideal*. "I don't know what I want, but I know what I don't want." We laughed, and the matter ended there, since discussion with him was rendered difficult by his extreme deafness; and few things seem worth saying when one has to reduce them first to a few words, and to make and impose an express effort in order to communicate them. But in my reflections afterwards it has often occurred to me that this position, knowing what you don't like but not knowing what you like, may be sincere enough emotionally, but not intellectually. Rejection is a form of self-assertion. You have only to look back upon yourself as a person who hates this or that to discover what it is that you secretly love. Hatred and love are imposed on the spirit by the psyche; and though the spirit may have no image of the end pursued, but only of jolts and obstacles on the way, there could be no jolts or obstacles if the life of the psyche had not a specific direction, a specific good demanded, which when discovered to the spirit will become an ideal. Not to know what one wants is simple absence of self-knowledge. It is abdication—my father was inclined to abdicate—and the insistence on *not* wanting this, or *not* wanting that, becomes an unamiable exhibition of the seamy side of your nature, the fair face of which you have turned downwards. Now my father hated shams, among which he placed religion, and hated complicated purposes or ambitions, with all the havoc they make; from which expressed dislikes it would be easy to infer that he loved the garden of Epicurus, with simple natural pleasures, quietness, and a bitter-sweet understanding of everything. This garden of Epicurus, though my father would have denied it, was really a vegetable garden, a convent garden; and it seemed strange to me that a man who had been so much at sea, and seen many remote countries, should take such a narrow and stifled view of human nature. He was tolerant and kindly towards the minor vices and the physical ills of mankind; he was tightly and ferociously closed against all higher follies. But is it not an initial folly to exclude all happy possibilities and condemn oneself to limp through life on one leg? If it be legitimate to live physically, why isn't it legitimate to live morally? I am afraid that my father, unlike my mother, was not brave.

In some directions, however, my father was docile and conservative. He had a great respect for authority in science or letters, and would quote Quintilian in support of his own preference for limited views: *Ad cognoscendum genus humanum sufficit una domus:* * *For exploring human nature one household is large enough.* Yet when authority made for boldness of thought or for ambitious aims, he mocked it. In the region of Avila, which is some 4000 feet above the sea level, the heath is strewn with many boulders, large and small, often fantastically piled one over another; and one day when we noticed a particularly capricious heap of them, I said what a pity it was that we hadn't a geologist at hand to tell us about the origin of this odd formation. "What would be the use of that?" said my father. "He would tell us his theory, but he wasn't there to see the fact." Hobbes had said the same thing: "No discourse whatsoever can end in absolute knowl-

* Probably a confused memory, mine or my father's, of Juvenal, Satire XIII, 159–60:

> Humani generis mores tibi nosse volenti
> Sufficit una domus.

edge of fact"; and I have made the *authority of things,* as against
the presumption of words or ideas, a principle of my philosophy.
Yet we materialists cannot consistently reject the evidence of analogy between one thing and another, since materialism itself is an
interpretation of appearance by certain analogies running through
things, and helping us to trace their derivation. There are glaciers
in movement today in other mountainous regions the effects of
which on the rocks they carry with them may be observed, as also
the effect of running streams and beating waves in rounding and
smoothing pebbles: so that those boulders on the skirts of the
Castilian mountains may be plausibly explained by analogy. But
my father feared to be cheated: and whenever he suggested anything a bit paradoxical, he would hasten to disown any personal
responsibility for it. "I haven't invented that myself," he would
say; "I have read it in a printed book, *en letras de molde.*" There
seemed to be a curious mixture in his mind of the primitive man's
awe for any scripture, with the skeptic's distrust of every theory
and every report. And yet this very distrust tempted him to odd
hypotheses at times to explain the motives behind what people
said or imagined. If a visiting lady told us something interesting,
which in my relative innocence I supposed might be true, it would
startle me to hear my father say, as soon as she had turned her
back: "I wonder *why* she said that."

Respect for authorities is fatal when the doctors disagree and
the pupil is not self-confident enough to give direction to this freedom. My father's style in painting, for instance, inclined to clear
shadows, pure outlines, and fidelity to the model, with little
thought of picturesque backgrounds or decorative patterns. Had
he had greater decision and dared to follow the ideal that he
denied he possessed; had he simplified his surfaces boldly and
emphasized characteristic features and attitudes without exaggerat-
ing them, he would have painted like Manet. But perhaps when
he was at work on a canvas that promised well, he would visit the
Prado, and some lurid figures by Ribera would catch his eye, or
the magic lights in darkness of Rembrandt, and he would come

home and spoil his picture by incongruously deepening the shadows. Stronger imaginations than his have been distracted and defeated by rival contagions; he at least was conscious of his defeat, and finished very few of his portraits; and he deputed even these to be finished when in reality they were scarcely begun.

He stopped halfway also in the law, which was his chosen profession, but for different reasons. Here he had not the blessed independence of the painter, consulting only his own inspiration. He had to think of tradition, of clients, of magistrates, of personal and political influences and intrigues; and his natural diffidence and dislike of rigmarole stood in his way. His family had no influential connections, and when still a very young man he accepted a post in the government service in the Philippine Islands. In this career, save for the effect of a tropical climate on his health, he did very well. Modesty combined with intelligence are prized in subordinates; and I had myself an opportunity, without any supernatural privilege of watching my father with his superiors in Manila before I was born, to see how he had behaved. My father's last post had been that of financial secretary to the "Captain General" or Governor General of the Philippines, who at that time had been General Pavía, Marqués de Novaliches. Now at the time of the revolution that dethroned Queen Isabella II, this general, then in Spain again, had been the only one to remain faithful to his sovereign, and actually to oppose Prim and Serrano in a battle at Alcolea, in which he was wounded and easily defeated. In 1871, when my father and I were living alone in Avila, my mother and sisters having gone to America, Novaliches and his lady came to live in Avila, in the palace that was later the Military Academy; and in their solitude and provincial retirement they seemed to relish the society of my father, with whom they had so many old memories in common. They had a carriage—the only one then in Avila—in which they took a daily drive along one *carretera* or another, or perhaps to the green hermitage of Sonsoles at the foot of the mountains opposite: a favorite walk of ours also. Sometimes they would send word, asking my father to accompany them; and as he and I were then the whole family, it was inevitable that I should go too.

Conversation on those occasions was naturally above my head, as I was seven years old; and after the first day I was promoted to a seat on the box beside the coachman, where I could watch the horses and the front wheels in motion to my heart's content. The landscape of that region has character, but no charming features such as a child might notice; indeed it is striking how entirely children and common people fail to see anything purely pictorial. Women and babies seem to them lovely, and animals attract their attention, as being human bodies curiously gone wrong or curiously over-endowed with odd organs or strength or agility; but the fact escapes them that light and shade or outlines in themselves are something. It was unusually mature of me, in ripe years, to re-discover *essences*—the only things people ever see and the last they notice. From that coachman's box my young mind saw nothing but the aesthetics of mechanism; yet my unconscious psyche kept a better watch, and I can now evoke images of impressions that meant nothing to me then but that had subtler significance. Now I can see how deferentially my father sat on the front seat of that carriage, listening to the General's thick voice: for he had been wounded in the jaw and tongue, so that he had an impediment in his speech and wore a black beard—of the sort I don't like —to conceal the scar. Every now and then he made a one-sided grimace that I still recall, as well as the serene silent figure of the Marquesa at his side, dressed in black, passive and amiable, but observant, and when she spoke saying something always kind and never silly. She had the air, so common in Spanish ladies, of having suffered, being resigned, and being surprised at nothing.

My father couldn't particularly have relished the General's talk which must have turned upon the politics of the hour, the intrigues of his rivals and his own wrongs; but my father had heard such talk all his life, and was not impatient. He liked to know and to read the opinions most opposed to his own. He actually preferred *El Siglo Futuro*, the Carlist and clerical newspaper, to the liberal sheets. I daresay it was written in purer Castilian, but that was not his chief reason for reading it: he wished to understand, he said, why Spain made so little progress. "Progress" of course meant material development and assimilation to England and France. I think that intellectually my father had no other political criterion; yet emotionally he remained a patriot, or at least, without considering what virtues were proper and possible for Spain, he suffered at the thought that his country should be inferior in anything.

We soon left for America, and Novaliches and his lady also left Avila on the return of the Bourbons, and resumed a place in the great world: not a leading place any longer, but a sort of grandfatherly place in the background of affairs. Once, some twelve years later, when I was to pass through Madrid, my father gave me a letter of reintroduction to the old General. I was then, 1883, in that appealing phase of youth when one's heart and intelligence are keenly active, but unpledged; and if Novaliches or the Marquesa should take a fancy to me, might they not still have enough influence to secure a place for me in the army, or at court, or in some government service, where my knowledge of foreign languages might be useful? English, my strong point, was as yet little studied in Spain, and even my elementary German might have seemed an accomplishment: unfortunately it was my Spanish that limped, although that defect would soon have been remedied had I remained in Spain. These illusions floated, I know, in my father's mind, and they tempted me also imaginatively; but practically, had it ever come to a choice, I should have dismissed them. They would have led me into a slippery and insecure path, full of commitments, personal obligations, and false promises, very different from the homely plank walk across the snow that was to open to me in America. I have never been adventurous; I need to be quiet in order to be free. I took my letter to the General's house, but he was out of town; and this little accident, which we might have foreseen, as it was midsummer, sufficed to discourage us. We took it instinctively for an omen, symbolizing the insurmountable difficulties in the way of our hopes. We had no money. We had no friends. My mother not only would not have helped, but would have regarded my action as an ungrateful rebellion against her and a desertion of my duty. The desertion, though excusable, was really hers, because nothing would have been more natural and proper than for her to return to Spain, being a Spanish subject, especially a few years later when for her daughters it then would have been a most welcome change. Only her son Robert, then thoroughly Americanized and planning marriage, would have been separated from her, not my father or my sisters or me. But her will was adamant, once it had taken shape: and without her aid—apart from the unpleasantness and responsibility of the quarrel—I could not have weathered the storms and the prolonged calms of such a voyage in Spanish waters. How her passionate will found expression in words may be seen in a letter, unusually rhetorical for her, that I will translate literally: it deals with this very point of a possible military career for me in Spain, although the essential question—sticking to her or sticking to my father and my country—is not mentioned.

No date (about 1880).

"I am glad that our son has no inclination to be a soldier. No career displeases me more, and if I were a man it would repel me less to be a hangman than a soldier, because the one is obliged to put to death only criminals sentenced by the law, but the other kills honest men who like himself bathe in innocent blood at the bidding of some superior. Barbarous customs that I hope will disappear when there are no Kings and no desire for conquest and when man has the world for his country and all his fellow-beings for brothers. You will say that I am dreaming. It may be so. Adieu."

In repeating the part of this letter about the hangman and the soldier, my father once observed, "I wonder in what novel your mother had read that." Perhaps it had been in a novel; but I suspect that the words may have come from her father's lips, or out of the book of maxims drawn from all sages, from Confucius to Benjamin Franklin, that my grandfather had collected and published, breathing the spirit of Locke, Rousseau, and *Nathan der Weise*. My father was as strong a liberal as my mother; but he had studied Roman law and looked upon government as an indispensable instrument for securing peace and prosperity. Arcadia and the state of nature were among the ideals that he refused to have. He had lived among the Malays in the Philippines, the most blameless of primitive peoples, and he spoke kindly of them; but the only Malays he respected were those that had become Mohammedan and warlike—pirates if you like—and had kept their independence. He was modest enough not to hate superiors, as my mother did; he admired them.

When I ask myself what it was that he admired, say in the English or in the Romans, and what he respected them for, I think it was not that he had any inner sympathy with their spirit. The English I know he didn't understand: their whole poetic, sporting, frank, gentle side was unknown to him. He thought them only stiff, determined, competent and formidable. They were all captains of frigates pacing the quarter deck. And they were all rich, oppressively rich; because in his respect and admiration for the English there was an undercurrent of contempt—as towards people who are too well dressed. If you wish to be thought a gentleman among the English, he would say, you must shave and change your linen every morning, and never eat with your knife. The only time I remember him to have been annoyed with me was during my first visit to him in 1883, when we had made an excursion to the Escurial, going third class at night from Avila, because in the morning, before we had breakfast, I wanted to wash my face and hands, and asked the waitress for some soap. "*¡Cuantos requisitos!*" he exclaimed. How many requirements!

As to the Romans, I am uncertain of his feelings. He often quoted them as great authorities, especially the line of Lucretius about *Tantum religio potuit suadere malorum*. But it was the thought, the political wisdom in them, that he cared for. He took their Greek refinements, as the true Romans took them, for mere accessories and matters of fashion. When I once wrote out for him (he had few books) the well-known little ode to Pyrrha in the first book of Horace, he was arrested at the word *uvida,* and remarked on the interweaving of the concordance between adjectives and nouns. Of the poetry, of the Epicurean *blasé* sentiment, he said nothing. If I had written out the first ode of the fourth book, through which so much pierces that is disquieting, what would he have said? He might have shrugged his shoulders at pagan corruption: societies are like human bodies, they all rot in the end, unless you burn them up in time. But he was no soldier, not merely no soldier temperamentally in that personally he shrank from conflicts, but no soldier morally or religiously in that he saw nothing worth fighting for. Of course, you fought for your life, if attacked: that was a mechanical reaction of the organism. But he could have felt no sympathy with the martial regimen and martial patriotism of an ancient city. There was something sporting about it, a club of big boys, only hereditary, sanctified, made eloquent and mysterious by religion. The Spaniard is an individualist; he can be devout mystically, because that is his own devotion to his own deity; but socially, externally, he distrusts everything and everybody, even his priests and his kings; and he would have distrusted the *Numina* of Romulus and Remus.

In his old age my father's eyes became so weak that it was almost impossible for him to read or write. Painting he had long since abandoned; and in order to while away the time he took to carpentering and to framing and polishing steel clothes-horses of which there was soon one in every room of the house. I think he was happier in these rude occupations than when he had been more occupied with politics and ideas. He felt better, and his mind could choose its own themes, rather than the unpleasant events of the moment. Nature is far kindlier than opinion. When one faculty perishes, the others inherit a modicum of energy, or at least forget gladly, now that they are free, that formerly they were subordinate. Anything suffices, if nothing else is demanded; and mankind, let us hope, will dwindle and die more contented than it ever was when it waxed and struggled. I at least have found that old age is the time for happiness, even for enjoying in retrospect the years of youth that were so distracted in their day; and I seem to detect a certain sardonic defiance, a sort of pride, in the whining old beggars that look so wretched as they stretch out a trembling hand for a penny. They are not dead yet; they can hold together in spite of everything; and they are not deceived about *you*, you well-dressed young person. Your new shoes pinch you, and you are secretly racked by hopeless desires.

The house in which my father spent his last years, and which afterwards fell to me and was the only property I ever had in Spain, was built by an Englishman named John Smith, who had come to Avila as a railway foreman or contractor when the main line from the French frontier to Madrid was constructed. He had settled in Avila and established the hotel—*la fonda del inglés*—opposite the cathedral, to which all foreigners stopping in Avila were compelled to go. I must have seen him, but have no clear memory of him; only of the stories told about his outrageous Spanish, and of his long friendly relations with my father. They were once in England together; it must have been in 1867 when my father took Robert to London, or in 1873, on his way back from Boston to Spain. Anyhow Smith conducted him to Grantham, his native town, and regaled him with an oxtail soup that in my father's estimation, was "fit to resurrect the dead." The relish of it I am sure confirmed him in his rooted admiration for England. The fundamentals are fundamental and in England they were solid. Who, on such oxtail soup, would not conquer the world? It seems that on some occasion—perhaps at that convivial moment—my father had lent Smith a considerable sum of money; which Smith naturally never found it quite convenient to pay back; on the other hand a little more ready cash, especially if you are establishing a hotel or moving out altogether from one country to another, is eminently useful; so that it was agreed that my father should buy Smith's house, who would thus cancel his debt and get a little ready money in addition.

This house, one of the first in the town as you come from the

Station, was opposite the Church and convent of Santa Ana, where above a stone cross and a modest row of trees, the rocky soil rises a little above the road and forms a sort of terrace or little square. It was a working-man's dwelling, what in England is called a cottage, but commodious; there was ample room for my father and aunt, and for me and Susana, and eventually for my other old aunt and my cousin Elvira. In the first place it was a whole house, not divided into apartments; and it possessed a walled space, called a garden, in the rear, with a low wing on one side, which with its kitchen formed a complete dwelling by itself. This "garden" contained an apricot tree and some bushes, and one accidentally picturesque feature, which perhaps I was alone in noticing. The back wall, of uncut stones and mortar, coincided with a private aqueduct belonging to another convent in the neighborhood, called popularly *Las Gordillas*; and between the top of our wall and a broad arch of this aqueduct, there remained a semicircular space, exactly like those filled by Raphael's frescoes in the *Stanze* at the Vatican; only that instead of the *School of Athens* or the *Dispute of the Sacrament*, nature here had painted a picture of the *Valle de Amblés*, to which Avila owes its existence, with the purple Sierra beyond: a picture everywhere visible to the pedestrian round about Avila, yet here concentrated and framed in by its stone setting into a perfect and striking composition.

The ground before this little house was neither town nor country: virgin earth with rock emerging in places, and preserving its irregular surface; but stone paths had been laid across it roughly, in the directions that people were likely to take, and served as stepping-stones in case of mud or pools of water; for there was no drainage. We had a well with an iron pump, in the house, so that only the water for cooking and drinking needed to be fetched from the public fountains. Sometimes in summer, when the purest water was desired, a donkey with four large jars in the pockets of a wicker saddle brought it from some reputed spring in the country. This primitiveness was rather pleasant and on the whole salubrious; we lived nearer to mother earth; nor was it exclusively

Spanish. At Harvard I used to bring up my coal and water daily from the cellar of Hollis Hall, or water in summer from the college pump opposite.

Going to the fountain (as it was called) was a chief occupation for servants in Avila, whether girls or men, and also a chief amusement as were the innumerable errands they were sent on; it gave them a breath of air, a little freedom from the mistress's eye, and a lovely occasion for gossip and for lovemaking. Without going to the fountain and without errands (since all messages were sent by word of mouth, never by written notes) the life of domestic servants would have been prison-labor. As it was they knew everybody, heard everything, and saw wonderful things.

John Smith had built his house in the style of the country, but on a plan more regular and symmetrical than usual. A passage paved in stone like the paths outside, and on the same level, led from the front door to the garden; and on each side were square sitting rooms with alcoves: every sitting room in Spain having such a whitewashed sleeping cubicle attached to it. I always occupied the room immediately to the left of the entrance; while my father had the back room upstairs (the other being the kitchen) because it was the only sunny room in the house. There had been an open veranda running outside this room, through the whole width of the house; but my father turned it into a glazed gallery, himself making and fitting all the woodwork necessary. This, with my father's room behind it, was the pleasantest place in the house, and we habitually sat there, and made it the dining room. There was little furniture of any sort: a table and a few chairs could be easily moved anywhere: only the bookcases and a *chaise longue* remained always in my room, which had been meant for the study: while the room over it, possessing a sofa, two armchairs with oval backs, and an oval mirror, suggested the ladies' parlor. Susana occupied it whenever she came to Avila, and on other occasions my cousin Elvira.

All this formed a meager, old-fashioned, almost indifferent stage-setting to my father's life: the real drama was his health. He was a wiry and (for a Spaniard) a tall man, and lived to the age of seventy-nine; and long walks and long sea-voyages in comfortless old sailing vessels were nothing to him. Yet he was a hypochondriac, always watching his symptoms, and fearing that death was at hand. Whether this was congenital or the effect of insidious ailments proper to tropical climates, I do not know: but the sense of impediment, of insecurity, was constant in him. It defeated any clear pleasure in any project, and mixed a certain bitterness with such real pleasures as he enjoyed. They were snatched, as it were, from the fire with a curious uneasiness, as if they were forbidden and likely to be punished. And this when theoretically he was absolutely rationalistic, materialistic, and free from moral or physical superstition. Perhaps, if a man's bowels are treacherous, he cannot trust anything else. Dysentery removes all the confidence that the will has in itself: the alien, the irresistibly dissolving, force is too much within you. Moreover, my father had other obvious discouragements to face: poverty, deafness, semi-blindness: yet these, if his digestion had been good and strong, I don't think would have cowed him. He had plenty of Castilian indifference to circumstances and to externals, plenty of independence and capacity to live content with little and quite alone. But the firmness of the inner man must not be undermined by a sour stomach: that, at least, seems to have been my father's experience. Intelligence and brave philosophy were mixed strangely with this discouragement. On one of the many occasions when he thought, or dreaded, that he might be on his deathbed, he felt a sudden desire for some boiled chicken, without in the least giving up his asseveration that he was dying; and as his deafness prevented him from properly modulating his voice, he cried out with a shout that resounded through the whole house: *¡La Unción y la gallina!* "Extreme Unction and a chicken!" Extreme Unction only, be it observed. That is the last Sacrament, to be received passively, without saying a word. It would put him to no inconvenience. To have asked for confession and communion would have implied much talking; he was too far gone for that. Extreme Unction would do perfectly to avoid all unpleasantness regarding his funeral and burial in holy ground. Nobody would need to be distressed about his soul. And meantime, since these were his last moments, and the consequences of any imprudence would make no difference, why not boldly indulge himself one last time, and have some boiled chicken? That, I am confident, was his thought. And he had the chicken. The last Sacrament, this time, was not required.

CHAPTER III

MY MOTHER

I HAVE already recorded my mother's parentage with what little I have gathered about her childhood; and in the sequel there will be occasions to mention many other events in which she was concerned. Yet the crucial turn in her life, her migration to Manila, and her first marriage, remain to be pictured: I say pictured, because the bare facts are nothing unless we see them in a dramatic perspective, and feel the effect they had on her character and the effect that her strong character had on them. Between her father's return to Barcelona, to act as American Consul there, and the time, thirty years later, when my own observations begin, I must interpolate a little historical romance: because my mother's history during those years, her sentiments, and even her second marriage were intensely romantic. Romantic in a stoical key, when the heroine is conscious of her virtue, her solitude, and her duty.

Those dancing years of girlhood, with their intense girl-friendships, their endless whisperings and confidences and discussion of toilets and tiffs and other people's love affairs, with their practice at the piano, their singing-lessons, and their lessons in the languages—for my mother could read and half-understand French, although she never spoke it—would have had a natural end in being courted and married; especially in Spain, where young people easily become *novios,* or acknowledged sweethearts without any formal engagement to be married. To go to the papa and make an express demand for the young lady's hand, and to obtain leave to visit the family daily, would be an ulterior step, on which the wedding would follow presently; but to have *relaciones* or to be *novios* is a free and indefinite courtship, permitting no liberties, and involving no blame, should the courtship be broken off by either party. It might be described in Anglo-Saxon terms as a trial engagement. Now this normal development seems not to have occurred in my mother's case; I never heard the least hint that she had ever had a *novio* either in Barcelona or in Manila. In her the first flower of youth did not bring its natural fruit; it was cut short by the pruning hook.

Whether my grandfather's appointment lapsed with the change of Presidents in the United States, or whether those strictly legal fees to be received by him were disappointing, or whether other difficulties arose, I do not know: but he was still a Spanish subject, and after a change of government in the liberal direction had occurred both in France and in Spain, his friends were able to obtain for him what promised to be a lucrative post in the Philippine Islands. This was further geographically than Virginia, but politically and socially much nearer home; and perhaps the oceanic distance and the idyllic state of nature of the natives in those unspoiled latitudes tempted his imagination, as much as the easy life and future pension tempted his advancing years. At any rate, he decided to go; and it was obvious that his daughter, who was devoted to him and was the apple of his eye, must accompany him. Distant lands were not unknown to her, nor colored people. Her first memories were about a "Grandmother Locke" in whose house they had lived in Virginia, and the darky children that ran half-naked about it. The sea had no terrors for her; perhaps she positively preferred the excitement of a real danger, with the sense of her own courage in facing it, to the fading trifles that had entertained her until now. The problem was her mother, who seems to have been less willing to leave her friends and country for the second time. They were really her friends and country, something that was not true in her daughter's case nor, in a moral sense, even in her husband's, because with his opinions a certain irritation at all things Spanish was hardly to be avoided. It is easy to acknowledge the backwardness or poverty of one's country, and to be happy there, when one thinks those things relative and unimportant, and the contrary advantages treacherous and vain. The Arab is not ashamed of his desert, where he is alone with Allah; but the pupil of the French Revolution, dreaming of multitudes all possessing a multitude of things, and of the same material things, cannot rest in a few old customs and a few simple goods. He has a bee in his bonnet; or rather his head is a veritable beehive, and the only question for him is in which direction to fly. My grandfather, though perhaps a little weary, was determined to launch forth again in pursuit of fortune: but my grandmother wouldn't go. She was very fat; she was not young; perhaps she felt that she had not much longer to live; perhaps she had a premonition that this adventurous project might go wrong, and that her husband and daughter might come back to her before they expected. If so, she would have been half right, as are the best premonitions. She died soon; her husband never returned; and new dawns opened before her daughter in which she counted for nothing.

The voyage from Cadiz to Manila, round the Cape of Good Hope, lasted six months, included the inevitable worst storm the Captain had ever encountered, with death yawning before the passengers in every hollow between the black waves; and it included also the corresponding invention of something to do in good weather. My mother then made the first of her bosom-friendships with a young lady I believe of Danish or Dutch extraction but Spanish breeding named Adelaida Keroll; she learned to play chess; and her father gave her lessons in English to brush up her Virginian baby-talk, which must have been rather forgotten during her ten years in Barcelona.

And what language, I may ask incidentally, would she have habitually heard or spoken in Barcelona between 1835 and 1845? Castilian, no doubt, officially and in good society; but surely Catalonian with the servants and in the streets; and was not Catalonian also the language that her parents spoke when alone together? Perhaps not. That was not yet an age when disaffected people were nationalists; they were humanitarian and cosmopolite: they were purists in politics and morals, theoretical Brutuses and Catos, inspired by universal ideals and categorical imperatives of pure reason. In any case I have only heard a very few words of Catalonian, bits of proverbs or old songs, from my mother's lips. Yet she may have spoken it fluently at one time. Had we not lived in America later, I might never have heard her say a word in English, which had been one of her first languages; even in America she never spoke it easily or if she could help it. Her Spanish, however, was far from perfect; and perhaps a certain confusion and insecurity in her language contributed to render her so prevailingly silent. The things she was likely to hear or able easily to express were of little interest to her; and it annoyed her to be troubled about them.

In the 1880's, when we lived in Roxbury (a decayed old suburb of Boston) a rich widow who lingered in a large house round the corner, and had intellectual pretensions, came to call and to invite my mother to join the Plato Club—all the very nicest ladies of the place—which met at her house once a fortnight in winter. My mother thanked her, and excused herself. The president and host of the Roxbury Plato Club would not take no for an answer. Might not my mother *develop* an interest in Plato? Would she not be interested in *meeting* all those superior ladies? In what then *was* she interested? What did she *do*? To this my mother, driven back to her fundamental Philippine habits, replied without smiling: "In winter I try to keep warm, and in summer I try to keep cool." Diogenes could not have sent the President of the Plato Club more curtly about her business.

I am convinced that this contempt of the world, this indifference and pride had a double root in my mother. Partly it was native independence, like that of the wild bird that refuses to be tamed; but partly also it was a second mind, a post-rational morality, induced in her by the one great sorrow and disappointment in her life, of which I shall speak presently. She put on a resigned despair, a profound indifference like widow's weeds or like a nun's veil and mantle, to mark herself off as a stricken soul, for whom the world had lost its savor. The sentiment was sincere enough and rendered easy to adopt by that native wildness and indolence of the bird soul in her which it seemed to justify rationally; yet her change of heart could not be complete. It was romantic, not religious. She kept intact her respect for the world in certain directions, and even a kind of negative snobbery. She could not forgive the shabby side of things for being shabby, or the weak side of people for being weak; while she sternly abdicated all ambition in herself to cultivate the brilliant side, or to hope for it in her children; and this renunciation was bitter, not liberating, because she still craved and needed that which she knew she had missed.

Was it only English that her father taught her during those six months out of sight of land? What better occasion for instilling true wisdom into a virgin mind, so ready to receive it? Just at the crisis, too, when frivolous amusements were being abandoned together with all familiar faces and ways, and a violently different climate, frequent earthquakes, torrential rains, a new race of human beings and a simpler more primitive order of society were to be encountered. I like to believe that during some of those starlight nights or lazy afternoons under an awning in the slow swell of a tropical sea, my mother must have imbibed those maxims of virtue and philosophy to which she always appealed: commonplace maxims of "the enlightenment" but taken by her, as by her father, for eternal truths. Pope's *Essay on Man* contains them all in crisp epigrams; and it was in this oracular form that my mother conceived them, as if self-evident and recommended by their luminous simplicity to every virtuous mind. All else was unnecessary in religion or morality. Nor was there any need of harping on these principles or of preaching them. Hold them, appeal to them in a crisis, and they would silently guide you in all your actions and judgments.

I never accepted these maxims in my own conscience, but I knew perfectly what they were, without being expressly taught them, as I was taught the catechism. They were implied in every one of my mother's few words and terrible glances. And she was almost right in thinking that, without much express admonition or direction from her, they would suffice to guide us safely in all circumstances; because they were not really confined to being "virtuous." We knew that it was equally obligatory to be "refined." To be a *persona fina* was to be all right: refinement, to her mind, excluded any real vices. Her notion of what was right, like the Greek notion, did not divide the good from the beautiful. And this had a curious reverse effect on the education of her children. We were expected to be refined, but that did not mean that we were to have any advantages or accomplishments. It was quite sufficient to be virtuous. Of course we were to be educated: enlightenment and virtue (again a Greek notion) were closely allied. It was not religion that made people safely good, it was reason. If she had not felt so poor, no doubt we should have been sent to the best schools or had the best private tutors, according to prevailing fashions. But the object, in her mind, would still have been to make us personally more virtuous and enlightened; it would not have been to widen our interests or our pleasures and to open the way for us to important actions or interesting friendships. Nor, in the case of the girls, would the reprehensible object have been that they should find distinguished rich husbands, or any husbands. They could be virtuous at home, where they belonged; and if they were virtuous, they ought to be happy. The result of this was that two of her children had little education and led narrow dull lives; while the other two, Susana and I, had to make our friends and pick our way through the world by our native wits, without adequate means or preparation, and without any sympathy on her side—quite the reverse. Our new interests —religion, for instance—separated us from her and from the things she trusted. We were not virtuous.

Whether or not the seeds of this stern philosophy were sown in my mother's mind during those six months at sea, the end of the voyage put that philosophy to a severe test. Not all vessels took so long, even going round the Cape of Good Hope; and there was also the overland route by Alexandria, and camelback to Suez. Despatches from Spain, sent after my grandfather's departure, had reached Manila before him; and he learned to his dismay that in Madrid there had been a change of ministers, and that the post promised to him had been given to somebody else. Yet as justice does not exclude mercy in God, so injustice does not always exclude it in men. The Captain General of the Philippines enjoyed some of the prerogatives of a viceroy, since distance from superiors always leaves some room for initiative in subordinates; and another post was found for my unfortunate grandfather, an absurdly modest one, yet sufficient to keep body and soul together. He was sent as Governor to a small island—I think it was Batang— where there were only natives, even the village priest being an Indian. Terrible disappointment, do you say? But was not this the very ideal realized? What a pity that Rousseau himself, so much more eloquent than poor José Borrás, could not have been sent instead to that perfect island, to learn the true nature of virtue and happiness!

I am not sure that Rousseau or my grandfather need have been disappointed with the moral condition of Batang: perhaps it was just what they would have desired. Or if there were any unnatural chains binding those blameless children of nature, the chief gaoler and tyrant in this case was happily the philosopher himself, who might devote his energies and his precepts to relaxing those bonds and might win the supreme reward of making himself superfluous. No: the real obstacle was not moral: perhaps the real obstacle never is moral. If it were, the surrender of some needless prejudice, a slight readjustment of some idle demand, might immediately solve it. Are those blameless children of nature, for instance, promiscuous in their loves? Instead of crying, How shocking! the moralist has only to familiarize himself with their view, sanctioned by the experience of ages, in order to recognize that promiscuity may be virtuous no less than a fidelity imposed by oaths and fertile in jealousy and discord. But here the physician and the historian may intervene, and explain the origin of exogamy, monogamy, and the cult of virginity. Perhaps, as a matter of fact, promiscuous tribes are weaker, more idiotic, easier to exterminate than those that take it into their heads, no doubt superstitiously, to observe all sorts of sexual taboos. Perhaps it was the ferociously patriarchal family that made the strength of the Jews and of the Romans. The force as well as the obstacle in nature is always physical. So it was with my unlucky grandfather, and so it would have been with Rousseau, had he ever found himself safe and sovereign in his ideal society. The state of nature presupposes a tropical climate. A tropical climate is fatal to the white race. The white race must live in the temperate zone, it must invent arts and governments, it must be warlike and industrious, or it cannot survive. This fatality of course is not absolute or immediate; white men may live in the tropics, protecting themselves by a special regimen, and returning home occasionally to recover their tone; but if they leave children in those torrid regions, the children will die out or be assimilated, in aspect and temperament, and probably also in blood, to the natives.

Now when my grandfather found himself relegated to Batang, he was not a young man; he was a battered and disappointed official, a man of sedentary habits, studious, visionary, and probably careless about his health. It was noticeable in Spain and Italy, until very recent times, how little most people seemed to sleep, how much they smoked, how they never bathed or took exercise, how yellow was their complexion, how haggard their eyes. I don't know that my grandfather carried this neglect of the body and abuse of its powers further than other people did; probably he was more continent and abstemious than the average. He was an enthusiastic moralist and idealist, and it is only fair to suppose that his life corresponded with his principles. But now, in the decline of his life, he was suddenly transferred to a tropical climate entirely new to him, without advice or such resources, medical or other, as even a tropical colony would have afforded in its capital city; and he succumbed. His wife also had meantime died in Barcelona; and my mother was left an orphan, without property or friends, alone at the age of twenty in a remote island peopled only by Indians.

It was at this crisis that she first gave proof of her remarkable courage and strength of character. With what ready money she could scrape together, and with her jewels for security, she bought or hired a small sailing vessel, engaged a native skipper and super-cargo, and began to send hemp for sale in Manila. If she was without friends in a social sense, the people round her were friendly. Two of her servants, her man cook and her maid, offered to remain with her without wages; and her skipper and agent proved faithful; so much so that in a short time a small fund was gathered, and she began to feel secure and independent in her singular position. She adopted the native dress: doubtless felt herself the lady-shepherdess as well as the romantic orphan. And she was not without friendly acquaintances and friends of her father's in Manila who were concerned at her misfortunes and invited her to come and live with them. In time, offers of pro-tection came from even greater distances. Her uncle, the monk, then in charge of a parish in Montevideo, wrote asking her to join him, and be his housekeeper. Although I have heard nothing, I cannot help thinking that her other uncle or cousins in Reus, and her mother's relations, would also have offered to take her in—such orphan cousins or wards are found in many a bourgeois Spanish family—if she had seemed to desire it. But she did not desire it; and I don't know how long her life according to nature, to virtue, and to Rousseau might have continued, but for an acci-dent that I almost blush to record, because it seems invented. Yet it was real, and is referred to in my father's letter of 1888, already quoted.

That solitude, at once tragic and protective, was one day dis-turbed by a fresh arrival. Batang had remained without a governor; but at last a new governor, a young man, was sent out from Manila. Now two white persons, a young man and a young lady without a chaperon, alone together on a tropical island formed an idyllic but dangerous picture; and it became necessary for that

young lady in order to avoid scandal to return to a corrupt civilization. Thus the life of pure virtue, as I might show if I were
Hegel, by its inner ironical dialectic transformed itself into conventional life; and fate laughed at the antithesis that prudence
and decorum opposed to its decrees: because, though my mother
proudly turned her back on that young intruder, and went to live
with friends in Manila, he nevertheless was destined, many years
later, to become her second husband and my father.

The friends with whom she took refuge were a Creole family
in Manila, for I think the head of it was not a government official
but a merchant or land owner long established independently in
the country. His name was Iparraguirre, a Basque name rich in
resounding r's, and carrying my fancy, I don't know by what
association, to the antipodal seafaring peoples of Carthage and of
Japan. The Basque element is an original but essential element
in the Spanish race; it is sound, it is needed; but divorced from
Castile it would lose itself like those other ancient peoples with
strange languages that are driven to the uttermost coasts of all
continents, to hibernate there without distinction or glory: Lap-
landers, North American Indians, Highlanders, Welshmen, Bre-
tons, and one might be tempted to add, Irishmen, Basques, and
Norwegians. Here a distinction seems to be requisite; for the
Norwegians may seem to be, geographically, a primitive people
driven to the uttermost verge of the habitable earth, yet biologi-
cally they are a fountainhead and source of population, rather
than a forlorn remnant. They multiply and migrate; and though
they are not great conquerors (for their home strength and perhaps their moral development is not firm enough for that) they
become a valuable ingredient in other countries and peoples.
This is or may be the case with the Scotch also, and with the
Irish; and I like to think that it is true of the Basques. I have
known South Americans of distinction who bore the names of
Irazusta and Irrarrázabal; as if something Magian or Carthaginian
could resound at the limits of the new world. However, if the
Basques are to propagate their virtues it must not be in the

tropics; and in the family of Iparraguirre there was only one child, Victorina, who became my mother's second intimate and lifelong friend; so much so that afterwards, in Madrid, where Doña Victorina had gone with her husband, Don Toribio de la Escalera, who had been an officer in the Spanish army, the two families lived together for a time; and we have always regarded Mercedes, Doña Victorina's only child, as one of our family.

As I remember Doña Victorina she was a diminutive wizened old woman so round-shouldered and sunken in front as to seem a hunchback; but it was not her spine that was bent but her shoulder-blades that were curved forward, making her little convex back rounded and hard like that of some black insect. My mother too had the right shoulder-blade somewhat bent forward and protruding a little behind, which she said was the effect of continually stretching the arm round the frame of her embroidery; but if that were the cause, Doña Victorina must have embroidered with both hands at once. Nevertheless this little dark lady made a pleasant impression; she was lively, witty, affectionate, interested in everything and everybody, and her bright eye and suggestion of a smile—never laughter—made you feel that she wished you well but had no illusions about you. I can understand that her vivacity in repose—for like my mother she never moved about or did anything—should have made her a perfect companion for my mother, a link with the gay world, as Susana was later, that never pulled you or attempted to drag you into it. Doña Victorina was entertaining, she knew everybody and had known everybody, whereas my mother, if left to herself was silent and sad.

It was Doña Victorina who received me when I first came into this world, and wrapped me in a soft brown shawl that she and Mercedes have often shown me, and which Mercedes still keeps at the foot of her bed, to be pulled up at night in case of need. They must be good shawls and good friends that have lasted in daily use for eighty years.

Doña Victorina was pious, and this, it might seem, would have proved an obstacle to such an intimate friendship with my mother yet it did not. There are many kinds of piety. I imagine that Doña Victorina's was of the ancient, unquestioning customary kind, remote from all argument or propaganda; emotional and sincerely felt, but only as the crises of life are felt emotionally, deaths, births, weddings, fêtes, and travels. So you went to Mass or to a novena, punctually and with the appropriate sentiment, in the appropriate dress (always black); and you returned to your other employments and thoughts with the same serenity and simplicity. It all was one woof; the appointed dutiful, watchful, shrewd, and passionate life of woman. My mother skipped the piety: it was not in her private tradition; but piety in others did not offend her, and the mere absence of it in her did not offend any one.

For the orphan living with the Iparraguirres dancing could hardly have been again the chief of social pleasures. It was too warm for much dancing in Manila; but people drove out in the late afternoon and went round and round the promenade, to look at one another and take the air. When the Angelus bell rang, all the carriages stopped, the men took off their hats and the ladies, if they liked, whispered an *Ave Maria.* But there were some houses where people gathered for a *tertulia,* a daily *salon* or reception; and I suppose there were occasional official balls. Anyhow, young people could make eyes at each other and marriages could be arranged. My mother always spoke contemptuously of love-making and match-making: yet she herself was twice married, and not by any simple concatenation of circumstances but in spite of serious obstacles. Passion may inspire determination in a Romeo and a Juliet; in my mother I think determination rather took passion's place. She decided what was best, and then defied all difficulties in doing it. Now it was certainly not best, or even possible to remain forever a guest of the Iparraguirres. Victorina any day might be married and what would the orphaned Josefina do then? Go to Montevideo to keep house for her uncle, the parish priest? Wouldn't it be wiser and more natural herself to marry? Certainly not any one of those Creole youths or Spanish officials who in the first place did not particularly court her, and in the second

place were not virtuous. However, there was one wholly exceptional young man in Manila, tall, blond, aquiline, blue-eyed, an
American, a Protestant, and unmistakably virtuous. And that
young man, probably as little passionate as herself, and as little
trustful of the Spanish young women as she was of the Spanish
young men, could not but be visited by kindred thoughts. Was
not this grave, silent, proud orphan wholly unlike the other young
girls? Was she not blue-eyed like himself? Did she not speak
English? Had she not lived in Virginia, which if not as reassuring
as Boston, still was in the United States? And as he found on
inquiry, if she was not a Protestant, at least she was no bigoted
Catholic, but a stern, philosophical, virtuous soul. Was she not
courage personified, and had she not suddenly found herself
alone and penniless and, like Benjamin Franklin, made her own
way in the world? Was she not a worthy, a safe, a suitable, even
an exceptionally noble and heroic person to marry? And was it
not safer, more suitable and more virtuous for a merchant in the
Far East to be married to a foreigner than not to be married at all?

Such convergent reflections found ways of expressing themselves, and the logical conclusion was easily drawn. A virtuous
marriage meant safety and peace for him in his old bonds, and
it meant safety and peace for her, who had no dread of novelty,
in new bonds rationally chosen. By all means, they would be married; but there was an obstacle. No legal marriage was then possible in Manila except in the Church; and the Church there had
not the privilege of granting dispensation for a marriage to a
non-Catholic. Everybody, including the Archbishop, was sympathetic and free from prejudice; but a petition would have to be
sent to Rome for a special license. This would involve long delay,
perhaps a year, and of course some expense; and much worse, I
am sure, from my mother's point of view, it would involve a conspicuous act of submission to ecclesiastical authority, such as her
pride and her liberal principles would never submit to. Yet it
would have been useless to take extreme measures, and to declare
that she was a non-Catholic herself; there was no non-Catholic

marriage possible within Spanish jurisdiction. I am not sure whether her free principles would have gone so far as to justify her in eloping, and going to live with George Sturgis unmarried. Perhaps not: whether such a course would have seemed to her nobly virtuous, or not virtuous at all, but disreputable, I cannot say. She was capable of taking either view. It was he, perhaps, who might have blushed at such an idea; not only a foreign but an illegitimate union to be reported to Boston! However, a brief voyage to China, not more than ten days, might have sufficed to make that union legitimate, and to remove all reproach or legal impediment from any possible children. But accident offered a simpler means of effecting this purpose. There happened at that time, April, 1849, to be a British man-of-war at anchor in Manila Bay. The deck of that ship was British territory, and of course there was a chaplain, who being a jolly tar, would not object to marrying a Unitarian to a Papist. Indeed, although the thing was not then fashionable, he might have contended that theologically he was a Catholic, that he stood in the true Apostolic succession, and was blessing a truly Catholic marriage. In any case, the ceremony and the certificate of marriage under British law were legal; and we may imagine the wedding party, the bride and bridegroom, all the Iparraguirres, all the members of the House of Russell and Sturgis, and the nearer friends of both, setting out in the ship's cutter, manned by its double row of sailors, and flying the white ensign, to the frigate, and cautiously but joyfully climbing the ladder up the great ship's side. And perhaps, if the Captain was jovial, as he doubtless was, there may have been a glass of wine, with a little speech, after the ceremony.

This important event—important even for me, since it set the background for my whole life—occurred on the 22nd of April, 1849, chosen by George Sturgis for being the thirty-second anniversary of his birth. This choice of his birthday for his wedding is characteristic; as was also his sanguine assertion, only half facetious, that his son Victor, because born in the Tremont House in Boston, would some day be President of the United States.

Such fancies are in the tone of the Sturgis mind, inclined to pleasantry that is too trivial to be so heartily enjoyed; and these jester's jests are apt to have some sad echo. That future President of the United States did not live to be two years old, and his confident father had preceded him to the grave.

When this double bereavement fell on my mother, eight years after her marriage, she was already deadened to sorrow and resigned to living on resolutely in a world that could no longer please her or wound her deeply. Ten months after the wedding she had given birth to a beautiful boy, blue-eyed like his parents, fair, and destined to have yellow hair though at first quite bald; and his nature at once showed itself no less engaging than his appearance; for when only fifteen months later he found he had a little sister, who sometimes couldn't help calling away their mother's attention to herself, he, far from being jealous, was most tolerant and kind, and would even give the baby his toys, although she was too small to appreciate them. The contrast between the two babies was marked, and had a lasting influence in our family. Susana, the second child, was in the first place only a girl, and although my mother had all due respect and affection for her own sex, and, as I have said, was more attached to her women friends, to one or two of them, than even to her two husbands, yet she had no artificial illusions about womenkind, their rights, or their virtues. They were, in most things, inferior to men; she would have preferred to be a man. So that the fact that Susana was only a girl while Pepín was a boy instituted the first point of inferiority in her. Then curiously, she didn't have blue eyes, like her parents, but only hazel eyes and a great lot of brown hair; as if nature had wished to mark the fact that she was not at all angelic, like her brother, but belonged to a lower, much lower, moral species. And as she grew up, she showed no signs of unselfishness, but on the contrary a lively desire to have her own way, and to take the lead in everything. Our mother actually had to defend the too self-sacrificing Pepín, and later the too self-sacrificing Josefina, from Susana's prepotency. Because the curious part of it was, that not only poor little Josefina later, but even Pepín seemed *to like* doing as Susana wished, and *to imitate* her; which was a dangerous tendency that would have to be suppressed. However, not much suppression of Susana was necessary in those years; the great occasion presented itself only many years later, in regard to me; for Josefina was so tepid and had so few resources and so little initiative, that in regard to her it was almost a blessing that Susana should be there to take the lead.

Until the age of two Pepín had seemed to be in perfect health, even if rather gentle and oldish for a baby; but at that age signs of fading away began to appear, and became slowly more pronounced. No remedies, no care, no change of residence could arrest them, and seven months later the perfect child died.

There is an oval miniature of Pepín in a low-neck green frock like a lady's; he appears wide awake, pale, with very thin fair hair. This miniature was set in a circle of pearls and worn in the old days by my mother as a brooch, to pin a lace shawl over her bosom.

Was the death of this child due only to the effects of a tropical climate? I am not in a position to judge: but none of his brothers and sisters had a strong constitution. Even Susana, who seemed to be the most vigorous, was not rightly put together; and Robert, who seemed normal and commonplace, had a latent contradiction in his nature. I may return to this subject later. If I am right in suspecting that, eugenically, my mother and her first husband were not well matched, and that there was something hybrid in all their children, that latent weakness would only have reinforced the often fatal effect of a tropical climate on children of European race. That little Victor should have succumbed also is not to be wondered at: born in Boston, he was subjected to a long sea voyage to Manila, to a season of that climate, and then to an agitated long journey by sea and land to London, where he decided that he had seen enough of this world, and escaped from it at the age of one year and seven months. Perhaps, on the other hand, these voyages and this speedy removal to a temperate if try-

ing climate—"bracing," Bostonians call it—may have saved the
other three children from a gradual decline or relaxation of fiber,
if not from an early death.

The loss of her first-born did not affect my mother as it would
any mother, especially a Spanish mother. There were no violent
fits of lamentation, no floods of tears, no exaggerated cult of the
grave or relics of the departed. Especially in a woman who has
or is expecting other children, as was the case here, such wild
sorrow has its period: the present and the future soon begin to
gain healthily upon the past. But with my mother this event was
crucial. It made a radical revolution in her heart. It established
there a reign of silent despair, permanent, devastating, ruffled perhaps by fresh events on the surface, but always dark and heavy
beneath, like the depths of the sea. Her husband, with his sanguine disposition and American optimism, couldn't understand it.
He wrote worried letters home, expressing his fears for her life
or her reason. He didn't see the strength of this coldness. Her
health was not affected. She continued to bear children at frequent
intervals—five in seven years. She did not neglect her appearance,
her embroidery, her friends, or her flowers. She spoke little, but
she never had been loquacious: and when, in a brief interval
between babies, he proposed a voyage to Boston, to present her and
the children to his family, she readily agreed. This marriage for
him had been extremely happy. He described his domestic bliss
in glowing terms in his letters. Was it not a happy marriage for
her also? Of course it was. Why then this deadly calm, this
strange indifference? Why these silent steps, grave bows, and few
words, such as people exchange at a funeral?

Many Spanish women live in this way the life of a Mater
Dolorosa, and are devout for that reason to Our Lady of the Seven
Sorrows, with seven swords fixed in her heart. They give a religious or pictorial turn to their despair; but at bottom they have the
same experience that my mother congealed into a stoical philosophy. She knew that her father's positivism and humanism and
thirst for progress had a black lining; and she had the courage to

wear his mantle with the black side out. Let the world see the truth of its own madness. She at least would not pretend not to see it.

However, let me not exaggerate. This second life, this mystic unmasking of the commonplace and the obvious, was not explicit in my mother. She didn't know what her real philosophy was: her verbal philosophy remained the most trite and superficial positivism. Her depth was entirely psychic, passionately dispassionate, intensely determined and cold; but her intelligence had no depth. It was borrowed, and borrowed not from the best sources, but from the intellectual fashions of her father's time. Therefore, in her outward life and actions, she showed a persistent attachment to persons and to principles that really meant very little to her. This paradox must be accepted and understood if we are to explain the two apparently contrary bonds with which now, in this first voyage to Boston, she outwardly bound herself. One was her attachment to the whole Sturgis family, much more hearty than her attachment to her husband personally, of whom she never spoke with enthusiasm or even with deference. The other was the unwilling but somehow inescapable bond with my father.

For by a second curious chance, or perhaps by an unconscious or even conscious attraction, my father was one of the passengers in the same clipper ship, *Fearless,* that took her and her husband with their little children Susana, Josefina, and Roberto, in the record time of ninety days from Manila to Boston. He was on his way to Spain on leave, for the sake of his health; and by taking this roundabout course not only had a chance of visiting New England, New York and Niagara Falls, but of getting a glimpse of England also, and yet reaching Spain no later than those who had set sail for it directly at the time of his departure from Manila. For from New York to Liverpool there was already a line of steamers.

There is an unusually enthusiastic letter of my father's describing the lovely scene in some genteel suburb of Boston—very likely the same Roxbury that seemed so shabby thirty years later, when we lived there. It was a Sunday morning, and under the arching trees between their neatly painted separate and comfortable wooden dwellings, the happy citizens and their well-dressed wives and children walked with a quiet dignity arm in arm to church. It seemed the perfection of human existence, at last realized on earth. Whether if my father had understood the spoken language and had followed those model citizens into their meeting-house, he would have been as much edified by their mentality as he was by their aspect, I do not know; but his impressions on his second visit to the United States were rather different. From 1856 to 1872, from a rural suburb to a half-built quarter of the town, from summer to winter, from the "flowering of New England" to its industrialization, from the prime of his own life to its decline, many things no doubt had changed to lower the key of his judgment. But I was surprised, knowing his earlier impressions, by something he said when, towards the end of his life, I showed him some comic verses I had just scrawled comparing America with England, in which I satirized the American man, but paid a gallant compliment to the ladies. And he said, "No. The women there are just as second-rate as the men." Did he—he was so apprehensive—take that passing compliment of mine too seriously and think that I might be in love and meditating marriage with an American? Or had his earlier view itself been colored by amorous sentiments awakened during that recent voyage in an American ship by an interesting young mother, seen and conversed with for ninety days on deck and at table? Perhaps it is rash to identify in any case the moral color of a memory with the moral color originally proper to the fact remembered. Sunday morning in Roxbury, by a lucky chance, may once have seemed ideal, and that impression, while warm, may have been recorded in a letter; and some decades later the memory of that same scene, qualified by later discoveries, may have looked mediocre or even ridiculous, like the clothes that were the fashion thirty years ago. Even if Roxbury and the Puritan Sunday had proved elevating to behold by the stranger, they might mean boredom in a slum to the native unable to escape from them. Which of these judgments shall we retain? My philosophy would retain both, each proper to the ideal essence then present to the spirit; but it would discount both, and smile at both, as absolute assertions about that poor, material, ever changing congeries of accidents which was Roxbury in fact, or those unrecoverable manifold feelings which truly echoed and re-echoed through the emptiness of a New England Sunday.

What Boston first thought of my mother or she of Boston I can only infer from their relations in later years; these relations were always friendly and theoretically cordial, but never close. Indeed, when she first arrived in Boston she was expecting another child. It was born there, in the hotel that stood in Tremont Street directly north of the graveyard adjoining the Park Street church. I remember this *Tremont House* clearly. It had rounded red-brick bay windows like bastions, and the glass in some of the square windowpanes had turned violet, a sign of venerable age. In 1856 it may have passed for a fashionable place, being near the rural Common yet not far from State Street and the center of business. The principal churches were scattered round it—the Park Street Church, the Old South, King's Chapel, and St. Paul's —while round the corner the eye was caught by the State House with its classic dome, model for all Capitols in the New World. And almost opposite was the theatre, called the Museum, because before entering it your cultured mind was refreshed by the sight of a choice collection of plaster antiques, including the Apollo Belvedere, as well as by cases of stuffed birds and mammals that surrounded the grand entrance hall.

Such was the enlightened center of Boston in the 1850's; and there were gentle lights really burning in some of those houses, with no exaggeration of their range or brilliance: Ticknors, Parkmans, Longfellows and Lowells with their various modest and mature minds. I came too late to gather much of that quiet spirit of colonial culture, that felt itself to be secondary and a bit remote from its sources, and yet was proud of this very remoteness,

which gave it the privilege of being universal and just. In my
time this spirit lingered only in Professor Norton, but saddened
by the sense of being a survival. I also knew Lowell, in his last
phase; I once shook hands with Longfellow at a garden party in
1881; and I often saw Dr. Holmes, who was our neighbor in
Beacon Street: but Emerson I never saw.

All this was nothing to my mother, who was too proud to pretend to care for what didn't concern her. That which she saw and
prized in Boston was only what the Sturgises represented: wealth,
kindness, honesty, and a general air of being competent and at
home in the world. They belonged to the aristocracy of commerce,
the only one my mother respected and identified with the aristocracy of virtue. The titular nobility of Spain and other European countries, which she knew only by hearsay, was only the
aristocracy of undeserved privilege and luxurious vice. It was de-
testable; it was also out of reach; and she felt doubly virtuous,
being cut off from it physically as well as morally. In Boston her
friends were at the top, where they deserved to be; and although
her friendship with them was little more than nominal, she was
content to be counted among them; and this feeling made her
heroic resolution to break away from all her associations and go to
live in America very much easier than it might have seemed.
Climatically, socially, intellectually she was moving into a strange
world, but morally she felt she was moving into her true sphere.
It was the sphere of her principles and her imagination. She soon
found that in practice she could play no part in it; but that did not
change her theoretical conviction that it was the *right* place to
live in. There the mighty had fallen from their seat, and the
righteous had been filled with good things.

A superstitious person might have been alarmed at the omens
and accompaniments of this first visit to Boston; for Old Nathaniel,
her father-in-law, whom they presumably went to see, died soon
after their arrival, and George Sturgis, her husband, died soon
after their return to Manila not only prematurely and unexpectedly, for he was scarcely forty, but in the midst of a disastrous

commercial venture, which left the widow with inadequate means. My mother, however, had not a vestige of superstition; and her courage and coolness, her quick and intrepid action, on this occasion contrasted oddly with the utter apathy and despair that had overcome her on the death of Pepín. The pathetic but not uncommon loss of an infant had paralyzed her; the loss of a young husband, the prospect of a complicated journey half round the world, alone with four little children, and the prospect of life in a strange society and a strange climate in reduced circumstances, seemed to revive her energies and to make her more alert and self-possessed than ever.

Yet such a crisis had occurred once before, on the death of her father, when she had no experience and no resources, which this time was not the case: for now she was not penniless: her brother-in-law Robert gave her a present of ten thousand dollars to help her over the crisis and she had recently made the acquaintance of the whole Sturgis family in Boston, where a share, one-eleventh, of her father-in-law's estate remained for her support. She would have to give up her easy colonial life with numerous servants and old friends, and with nothing exacted of her except the usual charities. Yet she was not in the least perturbed. I almost think that she was relieved, liberated, happy to abandon burdensome superfluities and reduce her life to the essentials; and as to the demands that her new environment would make on her, perhaps she did not foresee them, and in any case she had ample strength to resist them. The admiration she aroused at this time was well deserved but not very intelligent. People supposed her to be bearing up under a terrible sorrow and cutting herself off from the dearest ties, in order to do her duty by her children; but the fact was that the most tragic events now could not move her deeply, and the most radical outward changes could disturb her inner life and daily habits very little. She had undergone a veritable conversion, a sweeping surrender of all earthly demands or attachments; she retained her judgments and her standards, but without hope. I am confident of this, because at about the same age I underwent a similar transformation, less obviously, because in my case there were no outer events to occasion it, except the sheer passage of time, the end of youth and friendship, the sense of being harnessed for life like a beast of burden. It did not upset me, as the revolution in her circumstances did not upset my mother; but it separated the inner self from the outer, and rendered external things comparatively indifferent. I recorded this conversion in my Platonizing sonnets; my mother expressed it silently in the subsequent fifty years of her life.

If clearness about things produces a fundamental despair, a fundamental despair in turn produces a remarkable clearness or even playfulness about ordinary matters. That tragic journey of the young widow with her four little orphans to the antipodes was planned and carried out in rather a lordly way. She would not go again in that nasty little clipper ship *Fearless*, or the like of her, where the passengers were cooped up for three months like the poultry under the benches on deck; she would go grandly, overland, or when possible by steam packet. She believed in progress. On her way, she would visit her eldest and richest brother-in-law in London. And she would travel with two maids and quantities of luggage. When travel was still difficult it was still pompous. She carried not only all her personal belongings, shawls, laces, fans, fancy costumes, and family heirlooms, but chessmen and chessboards, Chinese lacquer tables, and models of native Philippine houses in glass cases, with their glass trees, fruits, animals, and human figures. She even took with her, to look after the baby, a little Chinese slave, *Juana la China*, whom she had bought and had had christened and of course liberated. She believed in progress, and she was making one.

The visit to her brother-in-law Russell in London no doubt left its mark on her mind. It set the standard of propriety and elegance for her in the way of living in Northern and Anglo-Saxon countries. It combined, with the tropical charms of Manila, to make Spain, for instance, seem to her most inferior. Possibly it set the standard too high: because after that heroic effort to settle down in Boston she does not seem to have taken root there; and three years later, at the outbreak of the American Civil War, she left Boston again for Spain. It was not to be more than a temporary visit; her Boston house was merely let, and she meant soon to return to it. Yet she was away for eight years. During those three years in Boston, 1858–1861, she had an English governess for the children, a Miss Drew, whose correct British locutions, such as "make haste" instead of "hurry up," I sometimes detected in my sisters, when they spoke English; she had a French maid for herself in addition to Juana, the Chinese girl: in spite of her hatred of priests and indifference to religion, she took a pew in the Catholic pro-Cathedral in Castle Street—an almost disreputable quarter for true Bostonians to be seen in; and she seems to have made only one personal friend, an old maiden lady who was a neighbor and sometimes sat with her over their fancy-work. In fine, I gather that from the first my mother lived in Boston as she did in my time, entrenched in her armchair in her corner between the window and the fire, with a novel or a piece of embroidery to occupy her mind, expecting no visits, receiving them formally and almost silently if they came, going out for a stroll in good weather to take the sun and air, watching our movements and the servants authoritatively but as it were, from a distance, and seldom interfering, and in all things preserving her dignity and also her leisure. Perhaps she resented the tendency, meant for kindness, to assimilate and absorb her, and she emphasized her separateness in self-defense, as I had to do afterwards in personal and intellectual matters. Boston was a nice place with very nice people in it; but it was an excellent point of vantage from which to start out, if you belonged there, rather than a desirable point to arrive at if you were born in some other place. It was a moral and intellectual nursery, always busy applying first principles to trifles.

Was my mother cloyed with too much Boston, was she really troubled by anti-slavery agitation and war, or was she merely attracted by the idea of seeing her friend Victorina again, who had followed her husband to Madrid? I confess that none of these reasons seem to me sufficient to explain, in so calm a person, such a disturbing and unnecessary journey. However, the journey took place; and in 1862 my mother and her three children were living in Madrid with Don Toribio, Doña Victorina and the little Mercedes, then five or six years old. I remember this joint household very well, as it was re-established some years later, when I had come into the world. In Spain Santa Claus is nobly and religiously replaced by the Three Kings or Wise Men of the East that brought presents to the Infant Jesus; and in the absence of chimneys (except in the kitchen) children hang out their stockings or place their shoes on the balcony with which every window not on the ground floor is provided. It was *el dia de reyes* and we had not forgotten to put out our shoes on the night before; the good Kings had taken the hint and left something for each of us; but what was our glee that Don Toribio who had foolishly put out his big shoe also, found nothing in it but a raw potato!

In Madrid there was naturally a circle of retired or transferred officials and military men who had served in the Philippines, and also liked to renew old acquaintance and recall common experiences. Among these retired officials, at that moment, was my father. Don Toribio and Doña Victorina of course knew "Santayana," as they always called him. Without being a society man, he was liked for his wit and for his well-informed conversation. He spoke little—he was very prudent—but he spoke well. It was inevitable that he and my mother should meet again. If I were writing a novel and not a history I should be tempted to invent here a whole series of incidents and conversations that might have occurred during those ninety days in the clipper ship *Fearless* six years before, and to indicate how the scattered little impulses then awakened, now, when all checks to free expression were removed, could gather head, combine their currents, and become an irrepressible force. But I have no evidence as to what really may have brought these two most rational persons, under no illusion about each other or their mutual position and commitments, to think of such an irrational marriage. It was so ill-advised a union that only passion would seem to justify it; yet passion was not the cause. I say so with assurance because there is not only the fact of their ages, nearly forty and nearly fifty, respectively, but there are my mother's verses, kept in secret and sent to my father twenty-five years later, when it was likely that the two would never meet again; and there are also certain expressions of my father's about love and marriage, which it would not be proper for me to repeat, but which show that my mother, a widow who had had five children, could not have been the object, for him, of an irresistible love. It was an irresistible *dæmonic* force, a drift of circumstances and propensities, as in one more throw at dice, or one more picture to paint. Things on the whole *drove* them to that action; but both he and she performed it unwillingly and with full prescience of the difficulties in store. My mother's verses are melancholy and sentimental, containing nothing specific, but the tone is that of renunciation. It is *impossible,* she feels, to entertain the idea that nevertheless has presented itself and has seemed tempting. The lines seem to have been written when her mind was still undecided, as if to encourage herself to resist and to give up the project. It still remains obscure what the irrational force was that nevertheless carried the day.

CHAPTER IV

THE STURGISES

OR my purposes the Sturgis family begins with the children of Nathaniel Russell Sturgis of Mount Vernon Street, Boston, who died in 1856. These children were twelve in number, like those of my paternal grandfather in Valladolid; but two died in childhood and five others had disappeared before I was taken to America; although their children often come into my story, and cast more or less reflected light on their departed parents. It is only by reflected light that I am able to picture the old gentleman, on a rainy Sunday afternoon, sitting far apart with his newspaper, while Susan Parkman his wife read the Bible aloud to the children; but the reflected ray comes from a sure source, from Sarah, the eighth of those children, afterwards Mrs. Francis George Shaw, mother of the Robert Gould Shaw, Colonel of a Negro regiment raised in Massachusetts, whose monument stands at the edge of the Common opposite the State House in Boston. She was aunt to my brother and sisters, and by a pleasant arrangement that at once was established I too called her "Aunt Sarah," and repeatedly stayed at her house in Staten Island or in New York. The family were Unitarian, but apparently with varying degrees of radicalness and fervor; and it was with a twinkling eye and great gusto that "Aunt Sarah," who was a woman of spirit and warm convictions, told me the story. Her mother, she said, was reading about Jonah and the Whale; and her father, whose people came from Cape Cod and who knew what's what about whaling, put down his paper—what political gazette or commercial bulletin could he have been perusing in 1825?—and said solemnly: "Susan, do you

expect the children to believe that nonsense?" "I thought," Aunt
Sarah confided to me, "I thought, George, that my father was a
wicked man."

If the father was wicked, at least the eldest son, whom we
called "Uncle Russell," was virtue personified—I don't mean
moral virtue only, but *virtù* of every description. Unfortunately
it is again only by reflected light that I ever saw him, although
several of his children or grandchildren were among my best
friends, and he was prominent among the lares and penates
worshipped in our own household. For both my father and my
mother seemed to think him the perfection of manhood, as
exalted as he was kind, a center of dazzling wealth and exquisite
benefactions. His career had begun in the East, in Manila and
China; but somehow from there he passed to England, and eventually became a partner, at one time I think senior partner, of
Baring Brothers in London. He was twice married and had two
distinct families, two sons and a daughter married to Bostonians
and honestly though gently American, and three other sons and
a daughter brought up and settled in England, and, although their
mother was American, perfectly English. I knew, more or less
intimately, all these seven establishments: in two of them, one in
England and one in America, I was a frequent guest; and as this
relation lasted for half a lifetime, I had the melancholy pleasure
of watching them in their early glory and in their gradual obscura-
tion, dispersion and decline. This theme will recur often: it has
become a *leit-motif* in my view of life; and the first great, slow,
tremendous variation upon it was made by the splendid Russell
Sturgis himself. Of his great days I have seen many traces; all
his children's households were at first prosperous, fresh, luxurious,
recognizable copies of the parental grandeur; but the reflection
paled, as the sun itself descended. Perhaps Russell Sturgis remained too long at his post, or perhaps other greater circumstances
altered the fortunes of Baring Brothers; but everybody knows
that after being for years, with the Rothschilds, the greatest banking house in the world, it got into difficulties, was rescued by the

goodwill of the Government, but sank into comparative obscurity. When I was first in London, in 1887, my mother had instructed me to pay my respects in her name to our great "Uncle Russell"; and after I had been there a week or two, learned the ropes, got suitable clothes, and found myself alone and at leisure, I called one afternoon, at the right hour, at the mansion in Carlton House Terrace where the old gentleman still lived. The air of the great house, even externally, was rather cold and abandoned, but after I had rung the bell twice, a dignified old butler opened the door a little. When I asked for Mr. Sturgis and offered my card, the man explained civilly, in a sort of sick-room whisper, that Mr. Sturgis didn't see anyone, that he was not very well, but that I might see Mr. Henry Sturgis. When I said I would see Mr. Henry Sturgis, the butler seemed surprised. Mr. Henry Sturgis didn't live there; and he gave me an address in Marylebone where I might call upon him.

That was the nearest I ever got to "Uncle Russell"; but I learned from discreet hints dropped by his son Henry, when I saw him some days later, that it was not simple old age or simple illness that kept his father in seclusion. The distinguished head of all the Sturgises, who had united great abilities to the good looks, affability, sound sense, and kindness common to the whole tribe, no longer possessed those abilities. He in whom the not too brilliant intellect of the family had been focused and concentrated, had lost it. It would be no pleasure now, his son had said, for him to see me or for me to see him. That was the melancholy report I had to send to my mother.

I am sorry, in opening this family picture gallery, to turn in this way my first and most imposing portrait to the wall: but they are all to be works of my own brush, not done by the fashionable painters or photographers of those old days; and no living image of Russell Sturgis is in my possession. But I can give him a name, in lieu of a portrait, and will call him and his generation the Great Merchants: a type that in America has since been replaced by that of great business men or millionaires, building up their fortunes at home; whereas it was part of the romance and tragedy of those Great Merchants that they amassed their fortunes abroad, in a poetic blue-water phase of commercial development that passed away with them, and made their careers and virtues impossible for their children.

Nathaniel's second son, Henry, repeated the success of his brother Russell on a smaller scale, and ended with a more decided reverse, which however he barely lived to experience. He had not been long dead when I first reached Boston in 1872, and his stately house, which I passed daily on the way to school, was pointed out to me with a certain funereal reverence. He was also far less fortunate than Russell in his children: most of them died before him; the ominous word dissipated was whispered, or positively hissed, by the ladies when they felt obliged to mention some of them. Only two survived, Fred, who was a doctor in New York and whom we seldom saw, and Nena, who on the contrary seemed more like one of us than any other of the Sturgises. Not that we saw her often, for she was an expatriate, having just enough money to live in decent pensions in Europe, like so many English and American spinsters: but that only increased our points of contact, which were initially numerous. Besides being a Sturgis she was, like my brother and sisters, an East Indian; lively, erratic, and as her name, Nena, suggests, with something pseudo-Spanish or Creole about her. Her mother had been born of British parents in India, and I believe had lived there most of her life; at any rate, she was exotic, and Nena too seemed exotic in Boston, like ourselves. She even pretended to know a little Spanish picked up from her father. He, like his brothers, had been at one time or another connected with the house of Russell and Sturgis in Manila, of which an uncle of theirs had been a co-founder; and they had taken kindly to the place and its lazy opulence, as had my mother also. Their easy Spanish exempted her from having to dig up her little old-fashioned English phrases, as she had to do in conversation with the other Sturgises. Nena was Spanish at least in having *dis-*

posición, the inclination to assume accomplishments without much training; she composed and sang and even published some "Songs of the Pyrenees," in a language which was certainly neither Spanish nor French. Eventually, at a mature age, she married a cultivated Englishman named Middlemore who wrote for the *Saturday Review.* They both loved Italy, ultimately became Catholics, and died romantically within a few days of each other. I stayed with them for a weekend in 1887 in a pleasant house they had taken in the English country; that was shortly before their conversion and death, for they put off pledging themselves about the other world until they were about to enter it, and discover whether they were right or wrong. From my room I heard them discussing in the passage whether I was so much of a Catholic as to require fish on Fridays. "No," said the intuitive Nena, "he is a *philosophe.*" Philosophical indifference she assumed in me also in another direction, when she had her legs massaged in the drawing room in my presence—and this in the nineteenth century. She was forty-three and I twenty-three, ages that might make such a liberty innocent, or very dangerous. In fine she was *corriente* and *despreocupada* (it seems as if only Spanish epithets could fit her); I mean that she had no nonsense about her, was a man's woman, and a good sort. With one degree more of beauty and several degrees more of wealth she might have cut a charming figure in society.

A curious thing was that, with this sympathy between us and Nena and with my mother's admiration for the Sturgis character and ethics, Nena's detested stepmother, the *bête-noire* and stage villain of the whole Sturgis comedy, should have been a special friend of ours. "Aunt Lizzie," as we called this formidable lady, was a tall strong woman of fifty or more, with black hair and bushy eyebrows that met over her nose, and a bass voice; in which it was impressive to hear her tell how her brother, an unemployed clergyman with whom she had a lawsuit, had attempted to poison her, all for the sake of the wretched pittance that remained to her. She had also attempted to break her admirable husband's will, but to no purpose; her reduced circumstances obliged her to live about in boarding houses or with poor relations, no doubt souring her high temper and making her a dangerous enemy. She was a native of Worcester, Mass., and not a self-restrained Bostonian. She seemed mysterious and sordid, like some gaunt ghostly figure from Hawthorne's desolate New England. My mother alone was able to retain her favor; so much so that our house was filled, if not beautified, by remnants of the pictures and furniture from "Uncle Henry's" dismantled house in Beacon Street. This loan was welcome to my mother who, without having any knowledge or taste in matters of fine art, was accustomed to a certain air of luxury in her surroundings; and it saved "Aunt Lizzie" the cost of storage. For it would have been against her principles to *sell* anything: everything that once was legally hers she held forever with a grasp of iron. She even hinted, or actually proposed, coming to live with us, of course as a paying-guest; but this was too much. My mother above all things loved liberty, self-government, and silence; things not to be preserved where "Aunt Lizzie" was enthroned. It would have been an offense to the other Sturgises, and a constraint to ourselves. We should have had to speak English at table, as if we were not at home. We should also have had to double up, at least my sisters would have had to share the same room; and our domestic economy, however modest otherwise, provided that each of us should possess his or her private room as a castle. It might be small, like my narrow one-windowed den at the top of the house, but it should be sacred. I doubt whether this practice is altogether wholesome in youth. Animals are born and bred in litters. Solitude grows blessed and peaceful only in old age.

This habit of privacy turned our house, quite unintentionally, into a little monastery. In a monastery there is strict community in externals, in hours, food, manners, and mode of dress, while in theory and sometimes in fact each member remains inwardly a hermit, and silent in his thoughts and affections. The system suited me perfectly, since nature had framed me for a recluse and only the contrary force of circumstances kept me for many years from complete retirement; but that system perhaps had an unfortunate influence on my brother and sisters who would have been happier and more truly themselves if they had been carried along, body and soul, by an irresistible social medium. They instinctively sought such a medium, perhaps thought they had found it, but were never really unified or inwardly content. They had not the requisite inner clearness and force, such as my mother and I had, to thrive on a deliberate moral independence and a profound solitude.

I think I half understood why my mother was faithful to that objectionable virago, our "Aunt Lizzie." My mother was faithful to everything she once accepted—faithful, that is, within limits, as she was even to my father. This was part of her fidelity to herself. She might seldom or never see her oldest and best friends; she didn't need them; but she always remembered and cherished them as they had first figured in her life, as they ought to prove, if they in their turn would only remain faithful to what she had believed them to be. Now she had deliberately and forever accepted all the Sturgises: not so much because they were her husband's family as because, being his family, they made her husband himself much more acceptable than he would have been individually: for individually the virtuous George Sturgis was rather negative. The simplicity of the Sturgis mind was decidedly marked in him; whereas in Henry, and of course in Russell, if it was present at all, it had assumed the noble characters of integrity, decision, and benevolence. Now "Aunt Lizzie" was Henry's widow; she belonged to the great generation; she had been once accepted, and she should never be disowned. How should the Sturgises be offended, when it was for their sake that she was treated decently? My mother never cooled towards any of them because they hated "Aunt Lizzie" and why should she cool towards "Aunt Lizzie" because she hated *them*? Besides, there was perhaps a certain bond between the sisters-in-law in their common poverty and isolation. For my mother, though she never had any lawsuits or quarrels and was no doubt esteemed by all her first husband's people, was inevitably neglected by them. They came to see her, if at all, once or twice a year, for a visit of ten minutes. It was not their fault. She had nothing to tell them, they had to make talk: how many children their children already had; how sad that so-and-so had died; what a pity that so-and-so had failed, and had been obliged to move to a smaller house; but how bravely and cheerfully everybody put up with everything. And so, good-bye, they must be off; and they were so glad to find her looking so well. With "Aunt Lizzie" conversation had more substance. There was a common background; and to hear long accounts of the misdeeds of one's relations and one's own trials was something to which my mother must have been accustomed in Spain and in Manila. It was the staple of feminine confabulations; and, given my mother's perfect passivity, it was like hearing a novel read aloud: and my mother read many novels. They helped to pass away the time, and required no answer. Anyhow, friends the two sisters-in-law remained to the end. In her will, the Dragon left all those terrible yet space-filling mid-Victorian pictures and sofas and stuffed little armchairs and Chinese dovetailing tea tables to my mother, to live with until death.

Rarest of our Sturgis visitors but most picturesque was "Uncle Samuel," third son of old Nathaniel of Mount Vernon Street, and of Susan Parkman, his wife. Perhaps he called only once, perhaps twice; the dear gentleman was not often let out from Somerville, where he resided in private apartments at the Insane Asylum.* Sound commonsense people, roseate optimists, as the Sturgises were, they were too Bostonian not to have at least one mad member, even in the Great Merchant generation; and "Uncle Samuel's" was an appropriately mild case. He seemed, in these lucid intervals when he was allowed to go visiting, most amiable, dignified, and even happy. Indeed, why should he not

* Later removed to Danvers.

have been secretly a philosopher, saner than any of us, like Hamlet laughing at all the world and pretending to be mad in order to be free to laugh at it unmolested? But no: such complexities, as I have already hinted, were far from the Sturgis mind. It was straightforward, believed in what it saw, and in what sounded right. It had just enough rope to go once round the intelligible world; to go round it twice, like a philosopher, was beyond the Sturgises. Had "Uncle Samuel" attempted such duplicity, I am sure he would have become much madder than he was. It was rather simplicity that perhaps he had carried a little too far; so far, that the moral comfort of not apprehending too much had passed into the practical inconvenience of apprehending too little. At any rate, he visibly took excellent care of his person, if not of his affairs. He was a tall, handsome, courtly old gentleman, beautifully dressed in the style of his first youth. The change in men's fashions had not been radical enough to render his figure ridiculous; I remember only one singular detail. His long-tailed coat, cut like what is now worn for full dress in the evening, was double breasted and buttoned in front; and a thin line of white waistcoat peeped out beneath it. Beau Brummel might have approved, but comment must have been caused in Beacon Street. In his conversation there was nothing especially queer. We smiled on one another; explained our state of health, remarked upon the beautiful weather, so summer-like for the season, till finally, smiling even more pleasantly, he rose, extended his hand to us all in the right order, said he was pleased to have found my mother looking so well, which compliment she of course returned amid our approving murmurs. She thanked him for his visit; my sisters and I accompanied him to the front door, and stood there while he went down the steps, and as he turned into the street beyond the little grass-plot, he once more elaborately took off his very tall top hat, and sent us a parting smile.

My mother certainly had reason to be flattered by the courtesy of such a visit. If her mad but punctilious brother-in-law had extended his unaccustomed walk to one of the last houses in the

Mill Dam, to pay his respects to the foreign and remarried widow of a younger brother whom he had hardly known, save as a young boy, was not this a proof of the esteem in which the Sturgis family had held her from the beginning? That esteem had surmounted a very just initial prejudice against foreign marriages; and the surprise of finding the Spanish stranger so firm and courageous and consistent in her actions, and in her independence, had survived in this shattered mind, as it might not have survived if overlaid by years of commonplace acquaintance.

I leave what more I may have to tell about these elder branches of the Sturgis tree until I come to the part some of them played in my own life; as I leave also the fruits that ripened on the ninth branch. This was that of "Papa George," as I might call my mother's first husband, father of my brother and sisters, who was, as it were, my stepfather by anticipation and after whom I was named. This rather odd fact was due to the original innocent sentiment of my sister Susana, who as the reader may remember was my godmother, and in that capacity had a nominal right to give me a name. She could just remember her father, having been six years old when he died, and it was she, apparently, who suggested that I should be called Jorge, a rather unusual but not unknown name in Spain. That my father should have smiled and made no objection, I can understand, in view of his modesty and ironical turn of mind. He thought his predecessor a good soul, but a simpleton; and somehow his expectation about me, perhaps in order not to count on too much and then be disappointed, seems to have been that I should be a simpleton too. He liked to aim low, not trusting his star, and perhaps calling me Jorge in memory of "Papa George" was a subtle sign of such resignation. When I first returned to Spain in 1883, and we went out together for our first walk, he pointed out to me the first donkeys we came across, and said: "¿Reconoces los compañeros de tu infancia? Do you recognize the companions of your infancy?" I recognized them. But it was not I that ever played with donkeys. It was my brother Robert, Robert *Sturgis*, who had once had a donkey for a pet in his childhood. I reminded my father of this, and we laughed about it.

A more puzzling point would be to ask why my mother saw no objection to calling me Jorge after her first husband. Might not my father resent it? No doubt he said he didn't in the least; but wasn't there some indelicacy on her own part? She was passive, very passive unless her path were crossed; and her path in the matter of children had been crossed once for all by the death of her first-born. I too might have been named José, after her own father, or *Pepín,* her pet-name for that lamented child. But no, that would have been sacrilege. I think in my early childhood she sometimes felt a certain analogy between her lost darling and me, who was her first-born by her second marriage, after five years of widowhood; but the illusion was soon dispelled. I was too inferior; and to institute any such comparison would have damned me at once. Why then establish this strange link with the past by calling me Jorge? Anyhow, Susana had her way—she often did—and there was something prophetic about this mingling of Sturgis traditions with my little person. Jorge, translated back into George, has become a part of my *nom de plume.*

I should hardly mention the tenth child of old Nathaniel at all, or her branch of the family tree, not a luxuriant one and unknown to me save for one sprout; but this one had a peculiarity that impressed my young mind. Her name was Amy White; a spare, active, intelligent spinster, a little older than my sisters, and like any other friendly spinster, save for a horrid secret about her: she had a red hand. She always wore a glove, of course (this was Boston), and I never was permitted to see the offending member: but my sisters had once seen it, when they were children, and Amy, to prove that she could be naughty if she liked, had pulled off her glove and driven away all the little girls playing in Boylston Place by brandishing her crimson hand in their faces. Of course, it was not other people's blood that had stained it, but only her own; it was an enormous birthmark; but the suggestion of gore remained, and a vague affinity to *The Scarlet Letter*. Poor Amy White had no other distinction; and though she lived to old age, we soon lost sight of her. Obscurity—we were obscure, too—hid us from one another. If she had been rich this matter of the red hand might have kept her an old maid, partly out of pride on her part, partly out of a slight disinclination in shallow wooers. There were many rich old maids in Boston; some of them remained single precisely because they were rich, and had no need of marriage to give them all the comforts and luxuries of a home; and they were little hunted for their money. A poor young man, vaguely amorous (for mad love was improbable), would rather turn to a helpful poor young woman who would be attached to him, than to a luxurious rich one, with her fine friends and family ethics, who would keep him in leash like a poodle. Had Amy been rich, I say, she might have remained single with a good grace. She could have become soft and gracious; she could have been surrounded by books, friends and flowers; she could have busied herself with charities or with some favorite learned specialty, like Miss Grace Norton with Montaigne. The red hand wouldn't have mattered then; the glove, properly varied and always clean, would even have seemed a mark of distinction, like the ribbon of an order. Red-handed and poor, however, she couldn't be an attractive figure or a happy woman. She was not perceptibly soured; yet a chill wind of difficulty, of misfortune, of solitude played about her, at least in the mind of other people.

James, eleventh and penultimate child of old Nathaniel, like all his brothers, except silly Samuel, was a man of business and though he belonged to the generation of the Great Merchants, he was not one of them. If he went a-fishing for to catch a whale, it was, like Simple Simon, in home waters; yet he was often wrecked, having no judgment, and remained as sanguine as ever, and unsinkable. He would have done better in a government office, if any self-respecting Bostonian in those days had ever thought of a government career. Not only the civil service was taboo, but also the army and navy (except of course during the

Civil War and temporarily); and it is significant that none of the Sturgises of that generation were professional men, lawyers, doctors, or clergymen. One of Russell's sons, John, of the American branch, became an architect under the sign of Ruskin; it was he who built the pseudo-Italian terracotta and brick Museum of Fine Art in Copley Square, never completed, and soon afterwards pulled down. A grandson of Russell's, Clipston, later adopted the same profession, as well as High Church Anglican sentiments; and two of his younger brothers were at one time or another masters at the Groton School: but all this was under strong English influence and in another phase of New England culture. Of Russell's English sons, one was occasionally a Gladstonian Member of Parliament, and the other two occasionally wrote novels, but they all were unmistakably gentlemen of leisure. The glamour of the Great Merchants was gone, in spite of their father's glory: the glory of a sunset, perhaps, and to be admired without being imitated. But in Boston, in the middle of the nineteenth century, no one who was ambitious, energetic, or even rich thought of anything but making a fortune; the glamour was all in that direction. The Adamses were not, and always said they were not, Bostonians; and the orators, clergymen and historians of the day, as well as the poets, though respected and admired, never dominated the community: they were ornaments and perhaps dangers. The great affair, the aristocratic path to success and power was business.

"Uncle James," whose head was full of projects, confidently took that path, and though he sometimes slipped and "failed," he never failed finally. He would start afresh and begin to make money; there was always some speculation that could help him to do that, and renew in him the sense of prosperity. He was not a mere Micawber; he really prospered at times. For safety, he had a nice home-keeping unfashionable wife with a small fortune of her own which evidently he was prevented from managing: and whenever he was bankrupt, they moved to a smaller house in some side street, and lived on the wife's income until business

looked up again, when the family would come out once more into
the social sunshine.

I bore "Uncle James" a grudge. In the first place I didn't like
him: and the world is rather sharply divided for me into the
people I like and the people I don't like. Philosophy and charity
counsel me to correct this caprice, and I don't theoretically build
on it; but it persists in my inner feeling, and it is not wholly arbitrary. I dislike the people I dislike for some reason; they offend
some natural ideal within me. For I do not either like or dislike
people interestedly but absolutely disinterestedly, artistically, erot-
ically: and thus their harmony or disharmony with my psychic
impulse has its human importance. After all I am a man: what
I like and dislike probably is, fundamentally, what any honest
reflective person would like or dislike. "Uncle James" never
offended me personally or did me any intentional harm; he would
have been kind to me, like all the Sturgises, if there had been
occasion; nevertheless I didn't like him. He had a full round
beard, and I cannot like that. A long white, or gray, or even yellow beard, especially if clean, forked or blown into strands, is
suitable for Michelangelo's Moses or Charon in his bark, or
even for God the Father: but a round short full beard like Saint
Peter's is vulgar. That keynote was taken up in "Uncle James"
by his commonplace talk, his hurry, his bustling unperceptive
manners. How inferior to "Uncle Samuel," who was so elegantly
mad! But no wonder; James was some fifteen years younger, the
world had grown commoner, and he had passed his life making
and losing money. Only success, great success, can ennoble that;
a success that debouches into something that is not money-getting.
Moreover, "Uncle James" was cordial. That is the well-meant
American substitute for being amiable; but it won't do. It is being
amiable on principle and about nothing in particular; whereas
true amiability presupposes discernment, tact, a sense for what
other people really feel and want. To be cordial is like roughing
a man's head to jolly him up, or kissing a child that doesn't ask
to be kissed. You are relieved when it's over.

However, all this may be silly prejudice on my part. My real grievance touches something more positive. "Uncle James" was the only Sturgis of the first generation surviving in Boston during the 1870's and 1880's. It was to him that my mother inevitably turned for advice in money matters. In domestic economy she was firmness personified, never miscalculated her resources or left a debt unpaid (as I never did); but about investments and general business she knew absolutely nothing. "Uncle James," on the contrary, thought he knew everything. Just before the panic of 1873 he was sure of a boom: real estate, especially in the Back Bay and on the water-side of Beacon Street, was rising and rising in value. Now the house in which my mother lived, and which James himself, very likely, had chosen for her in 1858, when she first went to live in Boston, was in the depths of Boylston Place. That spot, genteelly retired in the '50's, had become unsuitable for two young girls about to enter society; several of the houses had become boarding houses, or something even worse. On the other hand business was flooding Boylston Street, just at the head of Boylston Place, and could not fail to run down that little slope and flood Boylston Place also. Let my mother move from Boylston Place but not sell her house, No. 17, because what with the business flowing down (in his imagination) from the busy street above, and the boarding houses requiring just such central but retired spots to flourish in, that property would prove a bonanza: the rent could be increased with every new lease. It would be perfectly safe, therefore, to put a slight mortgage on that house, and with the ready money so secured—say $10,000—buy cheap for $25,000 a very nice new little house on the water-side of Beacon Street, just the place socially for the girls, even if it was one of the last houses on the Mill Dam, surrounded by empty, half-flooded lots, and swept all winter by icy winds. Of course this $25,000 house couldn't be bought for only $10,000; it would be necessary to put a little mortgage, say $15,000, on this house also. But that was only a momentary affair; when the value of the house had risen, it could be sold, and the mortgage on both houses paid off, leaving enough to buy a new and better house elsewhere. The girls would both be happily married then and something different, perhaps in Longwood, would then suit my mother best for her old age.

Why didn't my mother consult some wiser friend before agreeing to this transaction? How could she, so prudent in her own affairs, not shudder at the thought of that double mortgage? Apparently she was simply deceived; or perhaps she, too, was allured by the idea of greater elegance, or (more likely) by the sense of the *necessity or duty* of living where she ought to live for her children's welfare. Why else should she have come to Boston or to America at all? And wouldn't it be unthinkable that she should have left Spain, where with her income she could live very well, in the style of the country, and where Susana already had had several suitors, in order to live in a disreputable back alley in Boston? I call it disreputable dramatically, as my mother would have called it if she had understood: but it was simply Bohemian. Vercelli's Italian restaurant was there in my time, and the Tavern Club, the only club I ever belonged to in Boston; and I frequented both, until they became stuffy and tiresome, and I preferred the Napoli in the North End, which was more genuinely Italian. However, "Uncle James" was right in thinking that it was now a place where "nobody lived"; and this was a reason for selling the Boylston Place house, though not for mortgaging it, and much less for buying another that absorbed half my mother's capital and was an ugly comfortless narrow mean slice of a house, built for speculation.

In the year 1872 there was a great fire in Boston. I well remember the night in which my brother Robert—who was then clerk in "Uncle James's" office and had the keys to it—was called up in the small hours by "Uncle James" himself; they must rush in a cab to get all the papers out of the safe: the fire was gaining ground in the business quarter, the post office was in flames, State Street threatened; just look out of the window and see the glare. Robert, who was then nineteen years old, awoke

with difficulty, took some time to understand, but then got ready
in the twinkling of an eye, because like all American youths he
loved nothing better than "going to a fire." When he was gone,
I too got out of bed and looked out of the window. I could see
a suffused light in the night sky, but no real beautiful flames;
and I went back to bed philosophically. How much "Uncle
James" lost by the fire, I don't know. India Building in State
Street, in which my mother had a share and which now, if the
Boylston Street house were unlet, became the sole source of her
income, luckily was not burned; but the ravage was impressive,
and Robert took me to look at it, full of the contagious excitement
and even pride felt by the Bostonians at having had such a big
fire. People wouldn't speak of the London fire any more; they
would say the Boston fire. Unluckily for Boston, Chicago had
had an even bigger fire; and more unluckily in my opinion Boston
had no Wren to rebuild the town. That was the era of an architectural medley of styles imitated from picture-books by professional speculators and amateur artists.

It never rains but it pours, and that same year 1873 was
marked by one of those periodical crises that now are well known
and expected, but that then seemed an inexplicable cataclysm,
contrary to the certainty of perpetual progress and prosperity
proper to the nineteenth century and to America. It was a financial deluge. Everybody suddenly felt poor: business unexpectedly
shrank; Uncle Jameses failed in every family. Hard times came,
especially (with those two mortgages and the deflation increasing
their relative amount) to my mother and to us. The Beacon
Street house could not be sold or let until nine years later, and
the Boylston Place house, though usually well let, was even
longer on our hands. It was not sold until Robert, having ceased
to work in other people's offices, took to administering property,
which he did admirably, getting us all out of our penury into
gradually increasing comfort, as his son has continued to do by
the wisdom of his investments. But the predicament at first was
so serious for us that "Uncle James" (himself no doubt ruined)

evidently felt ashamed of having got my mother into such difficulties, and wrote to his brother Russell in London. Russell at
once responded to the appeal, and promised my mother an allowance of £100 a year, which he inserted in his will, so that she
enjoyed it until her death in 1912: a real benefit to us all and
particularly to me. This sum, my mother always regarded as her
own, not her first husband's or her children's; and later it came
to devolve upon me, as a regular allowance.

As none of the great generation were professional men or
government officials or political figures, so none were bachelors or
old maids—except merry Samuel, who I daresay would have married a dozen times had he been at liberty. This was patriarchal,
and characteristic of a prosperous, ambitious, enterprising race.
But now we come to a novel fact: "Uncle James" had two very
presentable sons, Charley and Frank, apparently in good health
and of good habits; yet they remained single until their deaths
at the age of sixty-four and sixty-nine. Why so? I can suggest
only one cause: poverty. Not pauperism of course: they were
always well-fed, well-dressed and well-lodged; and I suppose they
(with their sister) divided their mother's little fortune between
them in the end, and had just enough to live on in modest
bachelor apartments or some secondary club. But they were poor
for their class and for their friends. They couldn't establish a
household of the sort they would have liked. Yet that was
not all. They apparently had nothing to do. Whether perhaps
Frank, who certainly went to College, also studied law, I don't
know, but I never heard that he practised it and as to Charley,
his elder brother (who had a round beard like his father) he
never was known to do anything but potter about in the New
England back country and shoot birds. There was a distinct class
of these gentlemen tramps, young men no longer young, who
wouldn't settle down, who disliked polite society and the genteel
conventions, but hadn't enough intelligence or enough conceit to
think themselves transcendentalists or poets, in the style of Thor-
eau or of Walt Whitman. That is what they would have wished

to be, but they were too well-bred, too citified. Why didn't they go to live in Europe? Frank, especially, had a suggestion about him of being a possible artist or wit: why didn't he paint or write or do something? It was the failure of nerve, the sense of spent momentum, of being sons of Great Merchants, but without either need or opportunity for enterprise, and without money enough to be important men about town. Superfluous persons who felt themselves superfluous: dry branches of the green family tree.

Nothing withered, however, about their sister Susie, one of the five Susie Sturgises of that epoch, all handsome women, but none more agreeably handsome than this one, called Susie Mac-Burney and Susie Williams successively after her two husbands. When I knew her best she was a woman between fifty and sixty, stout, placid, intelligent, without an affectation or a prejudice, adding a grain of malice to the Sturgis affability, without meaning or doing the least unkindness. I felt that she had something of the Spanish feeling, so Catholic or so Moorish, that nothing in this world is of terrible importance. Everything happens, and we had better take it all as easily or as resignedly as possible. But this without a shadow of religion. Morally, therefore, she may not have been complete; but physically and socially she was completeness itself, and friendliness and understanding. She was not awed by Boston. Her first marriage was disapproved, her husband being an outsider and considered unreliable; but she weathered whatever domestic storms may have ensued, and didn't mind. Her second husband was like her father, a man with a checkered business career; but he too survived all storms, and seemed the healthier and happier for them. They appeared to be well enough off. In her motherliness there was something queenly, she moved well, she spoke well, and her freedom from prejudice never descended to vulgarity or loss of dignity. Her mother's modest solid nature had excluded in her the worst of her father's foibles, while the Sturgis warmth and amiability had been added to make her a charming woman.

CHAPTER V

MY SISTER SUSANA

I KNEW the Sturgis clan in two ways, first at home, since my half-brother and half-sisters were characteristic Sturgises in their different directions, and then as friends freely chosen for personal reasons, where our nominal relationship merely furnished an occasion for discovering some real affinity. Of my personal friends among the Sturgises I will speak as they turn up: for these were all social friendships with fixed periods and circumstances, not friendships of the spirit. But the Sturgis influence flooding me at home was primordial and I might almost say pre-natal. It imposed on me my Christian name, and it gave me my second mother or godmother, who, by virtue of her remarkable Sturgis warmth and initiative, was I think the greatest power, and certainly the strongest affection, in my life. This bond, added to the fact that she was my sister, makes any attempt to describe her embarrassing for me and perhaps unbecoming. Yet she must be described, else this narrative would miss its object. I intend my recollections to be fragmentary, but only by excluding things that are of no importance, or all-too-human and well-known to every one in his own person; not at all fragmentary in the sense of leaving out the bull's-eye from my target. Let me tell then the story of Susana's life and thereby allow her, as far as possible, to describe herself.

I have mentioned how, even in early childhood, when she had an older brother, she took the lead; and this became a matter of course when she was the eldest and also far more lively, wide-awake and competent than her brother and sister. In their lessons and in their games she ruled the roost. In Boylston Place, when she was from six to nine years of age, she was the Captain of

all the children that played in the street; and if this practice
seems not very genteel, we must remember that in Boston, local
society was both select and democratic, given an acceptable quarter of the town; and that, as Boylston Place ran downhill, it
afforded in winter an irresistible chance for "coasting," that is,
for tobogganing with single or even with double or longer sleds.
There were big boys in the neighborhood who naturally assumed
the duty of steering; but Susana remained the arbiter of what
should be done, and how. For a little Spanish girl, fresh from
tropical Manila, to command in this winter sport shows her easy
adaptability, her gift of inspiring confidence, and the willingness
with which people spontaneously caught her enthusiasms.

Her enthusiasms sometimes were rather extraordinary. It was not
only others that caught them from her, she herself caught them like
a disease and was greatly their victim; because they were all far
from expressing her whole nature, or even its fundamental needs.
Her religion was the chief instance of this; but the trait appeared
earlier. In the summer of 1863, when I had announced my intention to come into this world but had not yet made my appearance,
the family lodged at La Granja, the small imitation of Versailles
not far from the Escurial, where Queen Isabella and her Court
spent the season; and the public were not excluded from the
park where the Queen took her daily drive. Naturally when she
passed, people took off their hats or curtsied, and sometimes a
group might even raise a discreet cheer. Now for some inexplicable
reason, Susana was captivated by this little ceremony: she would
not for the world miss seeing the Queen drive by, and she would
be the first to run forward, wave her handkerchief, and cry: ¡Viva
la Reina! As this happened repeatedly, the Queen noticed it,
and inquired: ¿Quien es esta niña, que se ha enamorado de mí?
"Who is this child that has fallen in love with me?" Isabella was
not unaccustomed to have people, not children, protest that they
loved her; but one of Susana's Sturgis characteristics was that
she showed her feelings in her face often without knowing it;
and the élan of her movements and the light in her eye were

unmistakable evidences of her emotions. She *was* in love with the Queen. How and why was a mystery. Isabella was a stout and not beautiful woman with a bad complexion; but she was frank, amiable, hearty, and easygoing (like the Sturgises) and there was the glamour of her station, her coach, her guards, and her gracious smiles. Then there was a family in Don Toribio's circle who held some position at court: *Doña Primitiva,* widow of a General Orà who had been executed for some *pronunciamiento* or conspiracy, and her daughter *Milagros,* a young woman of bold spirit who smoked cigars and was said to go about at night dressed as a man, so as to see "life." These ladies naturally retailed much Court gossip, which Susana may have listened to, and they, being in favor with the Queen, would naturally tend to describe her generous and regal qualities rather than those that might have seemed too primitively human. At any rate, Susana's enthusiasm continued, until one day the Queen stopped her carriage, beckoned to Susana, asked her her name, and after a few amiable words, said good-bye with some vague reference to the future.

Nothing more occurred, I believe, at La Granja; but later in Madrid it was arranged that Doña Primitiva should take Susanà to the Palace to be formally received by the Queen. It would have been indispensable, in ordinary circumstances, that my mother should have accompanied her daughter and been received also; but my mother's state of health served as an excuse. For my mother never under any circumstances would have gone to kiss a Queen's hand, and such a Queen too, so little virtuous or stoical; and the odd thing is that she should have allowed Susana to go. But it was like my mother to let things take their course, provided she was not personally involved in the proceedings. She hated royalties as she hated priests, but it did not ruffle her, it rather entertained her, that her friends and even her daughter should be interested in such follies, and should have so much to tell about them. After all, it was more vivid than a printed novel, especially as Susana was a good mimic and would act out for us at home all that she might have seen and heard abroad.

This policy of *laissez-faire* had unpleasant consequences in this case, as in many others; for some years later, when we had moved to Avila, a virtual invitation came through the Marqués de Novaliches for Susana to become a lady-in-waiting to the Infanta Isabel, who was of the same age; and my mother was so enraged that she refused to see Novaliches at all, pretended to be ill, and left it to my poor father to explain and to make excuses: that for the moment Susana's mother was ill, that she was about to start with her daughters for the United States, and that the project of Susana's figuring at Court was incompatible with the plans of the family and with their modest resources. Susana, I presume, knew nothing of this proposal until long afterwards; and I never heard her express any regret that it was not accepted. But my father, who had dutiful feelings towards Novaliches, was placed in an awkward position; and my mother herself was embittered and made uncomfortable. This incident, as well as the attentions of several young men courting Susana, no doubt hastened my mother's resolve to escape to Boston, and fostered a certain distrust and resentment that was latent in her towards Susana. Susana, she felt, was not loyal to her; she preferred other people and other principles. Unluckily, escaping to Boston did not correct this disloyalty. From the snares of dissolute courts and undesirable lovers Susana fell into those of the Jesuits and of religious enthusiasm.

She had always warmed towards religious doctrines and practices, as she had warmed towards anything interesting and vivid, such as children's games, social pleasures, or a reigning Queen in her brilliant equipage. She was abundantly alive, and all these were spontaneous ways of giving shape to life and of enjoying it intensely. This enjoyment, in her case as in mine, always had in it a touch of comedy. In regard to Queen Isabella this touch of satire became conscious in time or even dominant, and while Susana never lost her sympathy with that Queen and with all royalties, she saw and admitted their weaknesses and laughed at her own pleasure in those vanities. Thus she rendered her pleasure double, and rendered it pure. But in respect to religion she fought against all dramatic insight or transcendental laughter. She felt the laughter coming round the corner, and she attempted to run away from it, to condemn it in herself as a diabolical temptation. It was a sad business to have to be absolutely solemn, convinced, and fanatical, against her nature and to the ruin of her possible happiness.

From the age of fifteen to eighteen, when we lived in Avila, Susana had rather a limited field in which to display her adaptability, but she seems to have dominated it easily, and to have been happy in it. There was a small, modest, and grave provincial society, Avila being the quietest and most unspoiled of provincial capitals. *Tertulias* gathered together the local worthies and officials, and the town contained half a dozen presentable young men. There was a Casino, with a café on the ground floor, and upstairs a billiard room and a dancing hall, with a small stage. Here an inner circle, called *El Chenique*, sometimes performed amateur plays. These plays and occasional dances seem to have been the principal amusement for the young people. Susana took a leading part in them; yet I should hardly have become aware of it by her own report, because she seemed to have forgotten those early years, but our sister Josefina remembered them vividly, could recall all the people's names, and could recite the greater portion of the plays they acted, which were in verse. Josefina, who was two years younger than Susana, and most timid and dull, took little or no part in those gaieties; but she was always present at them, as she couldn't be left alone at home, and her silent mind, having nothing else to occupy it, retained every detail of her sister's doings and sayings. She and I in after years could thus reconstruct whole farces, *La Casa de Campo* and *Las Hijas de Elena* in which Susana, who had completely forgotten them, had played the heroine. Yet the impressions of those years, though overlaid, were not destroyed. When life in America had proved a failure for her, in society, at home, and in the convent where she had been a novice, Susana returned instinctively to Avila, renewed old acquaintance with one or two quiet devout ladies of the place, lived in my father's poor man's house, and eventually married one of those presentable young men (now a widower with six children) whom she had danced with at *El Chenique*.

America affected Susana exactly as it affected me. The people, principally the admirably kind and civilized Bostonians who became our friends, excited our interest, attached our affection and won our complete confidence. We laughed with them and not at them, and we thought and judged as they did on current and social matters; but beneath and in the end there was a chasm. It was only with friends of the heart, chosen friends, friends who at bottom had the same religion or philosophy with ourselves, that this chasm could be bridged; and for Susana, in this direction, it was requisite that her friends should be Catholics. Now, when she found herself again in Boston at the age of eighteen, none of the Sturgises or their friends were Catholics; but at first that seemed not to matter, and she plunged heartily into that society, as it was in her nature to do. Yet her view of the Sturgis family and of Boston in general, as she unfolded it to us merrily at home, though friendly and kindly, was frankly comic; and none of her cousins, female or male, became intimate friends of hers or admirers. It took time—this was Boston—for the admirers and intimate friends to appear. There was a great obstacle to be surmounted: our comparative poverty. Susana couldn't dress or travel as the rest did; she couldn't invite anybody to the house. There were two sets of people, however, with whom this obstacle didn't count: the very rich and self-satisfied, who might even be attracted by an interesting young friend to help and protect; and the semi-foreign Catholic families that were discovered to exist even in polite Boston. To these two classes Susana's true and lasting friendships were confined.

Of the highly placed, patronizing and somewhat older friends the most important was Miss Sara Lowell. (It was essential to leave out the *h* in Sarah or rather to transfer it to the first syllable and to call the lady *Sahra*.) Her traditions and standards were of the highest, and as the youngest and favorite child of a rich father, alone with him at home, she was mistress of establishments both in town and country. With Susana she could discuss all her other friends freely, as to a fresh, uninformed, and sympathetic audience. The two would sleep in the same bed, so as to have perfect privacy and endless time for confabulation. And somehow the religious question, that must have arisen in passing conscientious and ultimate judgments on everything and everybody, seems never to have disturbed this unclouded intimacy. Miss Lowell was of course a Unitarian, and an ornament of King's Chapel; but she was a woman of the world; and I suspect that she smiled to herself a little about the proprieties, thought them expedient but not indispensable or eternal; and a few amiable pagan myths repeated, or devotions practised, by a younger and less well-educated companion far from displeasing her may have seemed to her engaging. They indicated the need of something beyond reason; a need that all reasonable people must end by feeling. Miss Lowell in the end felt their need in her own life; and when everybody had understood that she meant to remain single, being perfectly happy in her virgin state and finding nobody worthy of her hand, she suddenly announced her engagement to a widower as rich as herself. This widower had two sons, no longer little children; and the story reached me (the reader may imagine through what channel) that one day one of the boys by chance caught sight of his stepmother before the long glass in her dressing-room, and exclaimed—those being the days of exuberant bosoms and bustles—"But mama, you are all ups and downs!" And when the lady, who was short and plump, said he was unkind, he protested: "I am not unkind. I like it." From this domestic scene I gather that the accomplished Sara, being a sensible woman, valued the ups and downs in her person, as well as the ups, and never downs, in her fortune.

The foreign Catholic families that became Susana's closest friends in Boston were two in number, the Homers and the Iasigis. The language in both families was French, although English in evitably tended to intrude more and more into their conversation, as it did in our own house, until in the end, for instance, I always spoke English with my brother Robert, and sometimes with Susana, although never with my mother or with my sister Josefina. This was particularly true of the Homers, because the head of that family was a pure American, so that at table—apart from whisperings among the ladies—the official language was English. Susana and I often had luncheon or early dinner at the Homers on Sundays, and as a boy I knew that household very well. There were four daughters, the eldest a little younger than Susana, and the youngest a little younger than I, but no boys; and as Mr. Homer always disappeared when we rose from table, the atmosphere of the house was thoroughly feminine, Catholic, and foreign.

In *The Last Puritan*, the Boscovitz family is drawn in part after the Homers. Mrs. Homer was a native of Gibraltar where her father and later her brother held the practically hereditary post of American Consul; but her mother came from Marseilles and she herself had been educated in a French convent. She had been married off to "Homer" as she always called him in the French fashion, because he was well off, and had been carried away to Boston helplessly, where she lived like a lap-dog in a cushioned basket, with her brood of daughters, her little belongings, and her devotions to occupy her mind. She was a great comfort to Susana, a link with the genuine, human, Mediterranean non-hypocritical world; and Susana in turn must have been an enlivening influence in that too domestic circle.

In blood the Iasigis were far more exotic than the Homers, since the father was a Turk and the mother nominally a Greek, but in language, religion, aspect, and breeding entirely French. Her mother at least must have been a Frenchwoman somehow married in Smyrna, from which the family came. I was not at home among them. The ladies for the most part became pious old maids or pious mothers; only one came later within my range. She had married a young Bostonian who had dipped into Bohemian life in France and Germany, learned to speak those languages with a deceptive fluency, and studied a little music. He could well return to Boston as an art critic, and as a friend (since he was not rich enough to be a patron) of all artists, musicians, and actors. He and his good-natured agreeable wife held open house on Sunday evenings (when theatres and concert halls were closed); there was beer with pretzels, and all artistic or European-ized Boston from Mrs. Gardner down, frequented those easy re-ceptions. I remember speaking there with the prima donnas Sembrich and Emma Eames and with Madame Paderewska. I asked the latter about the fidelity of the men in Poland to the Church; and she said that they all *had* to remain good Catholics, because a soul lost to the Church meant a soul lost to Poland. This Eastern way of identifying religion with nationality gave me a useful hint for the interpretation of both.

These things befell after Susana's time in Boston. For her the Iasigis and the Homers were friendly households, nests of mar-riageable girls, where she could break away from the restraints of polite hypocrisy and could take comfort in feeling that her religion was no anomaly but perfectly natural, traditional, and a matter of course. It was the Bostonians who were eccentric and self-banished from the great human caravan. I found the same comfort in ancient literature and philosophy, which carried me beyond the Church and beneath its foundations. It is all a *Santa Maria sopra Minerva*. But towards Boston and Protestantism Su-sana and I had exactly the same feelings.

I recognize now that the ripest and most settled circles in Boston were difficult for us to move in because of our poverty and lack of early friendships in that society. It was a little like the aristocracy in England, shy and secluded from strangers, but immensely simple and gentle when once you were inside. It was very difficult, for instance, for Susana to go to "parties." She had hardly any suitable clothes; she had to incur each time a relatively large expense in hired carriages, gloves and hairdresser; and she was not as accomplished or as well informed about Boston history and people as were the leading families. Then, as she grew older, she had none of those political or artistic enthusiasms that might bring the older young ladies together. And as to the men—and one went to "parties" to be seen by the men—I suspect that Susana found them dull. She was accustomed to be made love to, and they didn't make love; not unless they deliberately intended to propose marriage. But very few, hardly any of them, intended to do that for the present. Society thus became a skirmish at very long range in a very wide field, with little danger of wounds, and no danger at all of death. Was it worth while?

I am not sure that in all those years in Beacon Street, when she was between twenty and thirty, she received a single express offer of marriage. She had admirers; but none of them such as she could seriously encourage. The best of them, a young architect terribly marked by the smallpox, was poor; and though matters went far enough for her to read Ruskin's *Stones of Venice* (which I profited by, and built my love of architecture upon) poverty on both sides made further progress impossible: and there would have been another difficulty to overcome, namely, the difference in religion. Religion was gaining on her with the fading of youth. Without having had, I believe, any serious disappointment in love—for she did not love men, she loved only their attentions—spinsterhood was certainly leaving her heart unemployed, and even her women friends were growing less communicative, less intimate, more preoccupied with their other affairs.

There was only religion to fill the void; and this had a disastrous effect in our household. Josefina had always followed Susana, up to a certain point, in this as in other things, but mechanically and without a spark of emotion. There was no danger in that quarter. But I was a boy, becoming adolescent, and I naturally inclined to live in the imagination. That I should catch Susana's interest in architecture, and spend my afternoons drawing plans of palaces and fronts of cathedrals, was all to the good; it occupied my young mind harmlessly; but that I should love images and church functions and the mysteries of theology was dangerous and morbid: and who was to blame for it but Susana? A conflict against Susana and against Catholicism thereupon filled our household, divided it, and ended by a separation of all parties, morally and even materially, and the separate entrenchment of each combatant in his own camp.

That Susana, being my godmother, deliberately took me in hand from the first day of my arrival in Boston, and in teaching me English and Mother Goose taught me also my prayers in English and my advanced catechism—for I already knew the elements of Christian Doctrine and Sacred History—is certain; but I think there was a complete blindness on my mother's part in supposing that any deep or permanent attachment to religious faith in my case, could be achieved by Susana: and that for the reason that Susana was herself without it. I understood what she taught me very much better than she did, and I had a much greater affinity than she to a religious life. She tried it and couldn't bear it; I could have borne it gladly if I had wished to try it.

There was another difference. She thought religion a matter of fact, like the geography of the Fiji Islands and the ways of the natives there; and as those were reported to be so grand and so captivating she was anxious to be convinced that the reports were true and that she might ultimately go and live in those Islands. Now I was aware, at first instinctively and soon quite clearly on historical and psychological grounds, that religion and all philosophy of that kind was *invented*. It was all conceived and worked out inwardly, imaginatively, for moral reasons; I could have invented or helped to invent it myself, if I had gone in for it; and I could have accepted it and enlarged it by my own insights if like all original religious souls I had fancied myself inspired. Such invention need not be dishonest, if it is taken for a revelation. But you can't go for the proof or confirmation of it to the Fiji Islands, or to any other part of the existing universe; you must place it, and live by it, on quite another plane. In a word, I was a spontaneous modernist in theology and philosophy: but not being pledged, either socially or superstitiously, to any sect or tradition, I was spared the torments of those poor Catholic priests or those limping Anglicans who think they can be at once modernists and believers. They can be only amateurs, at best connoisseurs, in religion. The rest for them will only be a belated masquerade.

Thus I, who was the nominal prize at stake, came out of this family quarrel without feeling a blow, and my mother, if a little hardened and embittered, was not much changed by it. But for Susana it was tragic; though perhaps not worse, perhaps more satisfactory on the whole, than it would have been to vegetate and wither, an impecunious old maid in self-satisfied Boston.

The crisis came on slowly, and was never sharply terminated. It did not leave a scar but an ailment; and it kept passing, to the end of Susana's long life, through various phases.

In 1876 "Uncle Robert," head of the Philadelphia Sturgises died; and the widow invited Susana to spend a few weeks with her, to cheer her up and keep her company. This was a somewhat unexpected proof of liking from a quarter that had never seemed sympathetic. While "Uncle Robert" showed a traditional good-will towards us (including me, for he gave me my first nice book, a well-illustrated copy of Robinson Crusoe), "Aunt Susie," his wife, seemed too much preoccupied with her clothes, her babies, and her gaieties to take more than a perfunctory notice of her husband's poor relations. But Susana had the gift of inspiring confidence; she was a Sturgis; she was young, available, and a person in need of being befriended. This visit to Philadelphia resulted in a lasting affection on Susana's part not so much towards her Aunt as to the youngest of the children, Maisie, with whom for years afterwards, from Spain, she carried on a desultory correspondence. And the visit had another consequence that helped, as it were, to color a little more pleasantly the sunset of Susana's day in Boston. "Aunt Susie" sent her two trunks full of her almost new dresses, rather gay dresses, useless for a widow in mourning; and these dresses, in lingering adaptations and transformations, helped to furnish Susana's wardrobe for several years. I remember them well to this day. The best was the salmon-colored dress, as we called it, although at night it seemed only a brilliant yellow; it was elaborate with a looped overskirt, yellow satin bow-knots and scalloped edges, and a wealth all over it of little lace flounces. There were other gowns, less ornate and good for daily use, that outlasted the fashions; and there were some that never were worn at all, because Susana's interest in society had begun to flag, and she had at best but little pleasure in dress. She wished to look well of course; but the how and why of it escaped her. Neither she nor Josefina was good at needlework. Had they resisted their mother's lessons and example, or had nothing been done to initiate them into these arts? I think both causes cooperated; and it was a pity in many ways.

The first five years that we lived in Roxbury, which included my undergraduate days at Harvard, were the darkest in Susana's life. She was between thirty and thirty-five years of age; her Boston sewing-circle, her Boston parties, were things of the past; there was sullen disunion and hostility at home; and there were no new interests. She read and re-read the works of Santa Teresa; she conceived plans of offering up her life in sacrifice for the salvation (which seemed unlikely) of the rest of the family: and she considered whether she might not have a vocation to tread in Santa Teresa's footsteps. Her confessor was Father Fulton, head of the Jesuit College attached to the Church of the Immaculate Conception, where we usually went to high mass on Sundays— Susana and I only, because Josefina, thoroughly frightened by our mother's intense hostility to the Church, had given up going. Father Fulton, who belonged, I believe, to a Maryland Catholic family, had a rather philosophical mind; a little sleepy, like his half-closed eyes, not perhaps quite healthy, as his sallow complexion and heavy cheeks were not quite healthy. He admired the metaphysics of Coleridge, and perhaps understood it better than he did the feminine heart. There is a curious cruelty mixed sometimes with American shrewdness and humor. The sharp mind finds things queer, crooked, perverse; it puns about them; and it doesn't see why they shouldn't be expected and commanded to be quite other than they are; but all this without much hope of mending them, and a sardonic grin. My old teacher Royce had something of this perverse idealism, and I suspect there was something of it in Father Fulton. Didn't he see that Susana's imaginary vocation was false? He probably saw no reason why, *a priori*, it should not have been true; and he didn't positively dissuade her from testing it. When the test was applied, he advised her not to persist; but this experiment had involved untold conflicts, doubts, vacillations, and disappointments, which might have been avoided by a little more wisdom.

I remember one day, coming home with Susana from church, I said I thought I was better fitted than she for the cloister; and she replied: "You have *one* of the things required. You are *detached*." This was her way of expressing the fact that she lacked this necessary element. She lacked it so completely that she was most unhappy in going to the Convent of her own free will, and quite happy (according to my mother) in coming out of it (against her will, according to her own account), by the advice or injunctions of her superiors. I accompanied her to Baltimore; there was no simplicity, no ease, in her way of entering the convent or of being received there. She was too old, thirty-four, and too full of old memories and attachments to be happy in a round of mystical devotions; she was tired, and became sleepless. She insisted in her letters, and in her talk to the end of her life, that she loved our mother very much. These protestations seemed to me very strange; she *couldn't* love our mother very much: only enough to suffer, as I did not, from her hostility. Perhaps this morbid love (for there was something cowed or cowardly about it) was hypnotic and allied to forgotten experiences; perhaps it was only a verbal cloak for Susana's love of people in general, and her craving to be loved. In any case, it was a symptom of her radical unfitness for an ascetic regimen.

She had been for three months in the convent as what they called a Postulant, dressed in her own clothes but following the routine of the community, and had grown much attached to the

Mother Superior and to the Mistress of the Novices, when she became a Novice herself, having her hair cut, and wearing the nun's habit with a white veil in lieu of the black one. Talking with my cousin Elvira and me some years later in Avila, she said that this attachment, especially to the Mistress of Novices (who acted, I suppose, as a sort of female confessor or spiritual director), was the strongest she had ever felt in her life; and this assertion, making due allowances for dramatic exaggeration, seems to me interesting. It shows that she had never been much in love with any of her admirers, nor with her future husband, who was then courting her once more; and that her love for our mother had never been spontaneous, but a sort of unwilling and resentful love, a sense of subjection to an irrational influence. I saw a letter or two written afterwards by this nun to Susana; they were commonplace, pious, motherly letters; but motherly affection was new to Susana, and especially a motherly affection extending to spiritual troubles and needs, and bringing spiritual consolation. If when a girl she could fall in love at sight with a commonplace Queen, for being motherly and amiable, it is intelligible that as an unhappy woman she should have fallen in love with a gentle nun, for being wise and motherly. It is a wonderful thing to come upon intelligence and a guiding hand in the realm of spirit.

In spite of these affectionate ties and precisely because of this intelligent guidance, before six months of novitiate were over it was agreed that Susana should leave the convent. Then our mother did a very kind thing such as her usual manner would not have led us to expect: she with Josefina left Robert alone in the house with one servant (I was at College) and went to spend the winter in a boarding house at Baltimore, so that Susana should not have to return home directly, and might have the relief of a wholly new scene and new faces.

When they came back to Boston I was on the point of leaving for Avila and for an indefinite student life in Germany. I could not observe Susana's conduct or moods; but I believe she lived almost in seclusion, saw none of her old friends, and during the next winter decided to return to Spain, at least for some years, where she could live with Doña Victorina and with my father, alternately. This was practicable, because when Robert reached his majority, the trust that my mother had established on the occasion of her second marriage terminated, and her Sturgis children came into their money. It was a most modest sum, at that time only a few hundred dollars a year; but this was enough to get on with in Spain, living with old friends, and contributing a little to the household expenses.

I went to meet her in September, 1887, at Gibraltar, and returned with her to Avila; and in the winter she joined Doña Victorina and Mercedes in Madrid. But she still had, as it were, one foot in the stirrup. Could she live on in this way, as paying guest at other people's houses, forever? Would she return to dreary Roxbury? Could she persuade our mother to move back to Spain and reunite the family? Only one circumstance was favorable. Robert had taken charge of the family property and was doing very well in his investments. Without venturing on what is called speculation, he bought and sold safe investments with excellent judgment. The Beacon Street house had long been sold. The houses in Boylston Place and India Building were sold at good prices, and the family income increased steadily, until it became ten times what it had been in the beginning. Had Susana foreseen this development, which would have enabled her to set up a comfortable establishment of her own in Spain, she might have been content to do so. She had friends enough, and would have made many more; and the current affairs of the world, political and social, would have kept her mind occupied and her wits sharp.

But how could this favorable turn of fortune be foreseen? She was simply a little better off, but still had only a slender income; and she was alone. Unfortunately, not being a Sturgis, I had no share in the family trust, and had to earn my living; otherwise Susana and I at that time, about 1890, could have joined forces and lived very happily together, by preference in Avila. There are nice old houses there, one of which we could have restored and turned into a dignified and peaceful residence: and both summer and winter there, in one's own house with a few modern conveniences, are pleasant and healthy.

But the gods otherwise decreed: and Susana decided to marry her old admirer, Celedonio Sastre, in spite of his crusty old provincial habits and his six children. Her married life forms another chapter, which I need not write separately. Glimpses enough of it will come in the course of my own visits: for Avila never ceased to be a place of frequent pilgrimage for me so long as Susana was alive.

Old age—she lived to be seventy-seven, as Josefina did also—changed her character very little: perhaps time did not change her at all, but only brought out more clearly—worldly respect and timidity being gone—her frank and sensible humanity. This had been veiled by untoward circumstances, and sophisticated intellectually. Poverty and religion had long constrained and misled her. I do not mean for a moment that it was incongruous for her to be a believing Catholic. It was not only congruous with her temperament, but essential to her breeding and background and to the place she filled in the world. Why else should her good American relations have turned to her and hugged her in their troubles? Catholicism is the most human of religions, if taken humanly: it is paganism spiritually transformed and made metaphysical. It corresponds most adequately to the various exigencies of moral life, with just the needed dose of wisdom, sublimity, and illusion. Only it should be accepted humanly, traditionally, as part of an unquestioned order, a moral heritage, like one's language and family life, leaving religious controversy to the synods and metaphysical speculation to the schools. The synods and the schools make enormous assumptions, and perhaps reason on them correctly: that is a question of art and technique with which the layman had better not meddle. But as to the need or importance of those assumptions each man and each society decides afresh, and instinctively; because the controversies that agitate the public are inevitably superficial, making contrary and hasty assumptions of their own, without knowing it.

Susana's misfortune was that her instinctive and ardent sympathy with Catholic and Spanish conventions was crossed by controversy and strained speculatively, when she had no capacity for speculation; so that instead of finding peace and a secret symbolic life in religion, she turned religion into a problem and a torment. She became fanatical against her natural good sense, and worried about the salvation of her friends and relations as if that were not in God's hands, and as if the salvation of souls were a physical event, like the saving or drowning of passengers in a shipwreck. That was exactly how the early Christians conceived it, so that her zeal was strictly orthodox; but this only shows how orthodoxy must be taken with a grain of salt, to keep it beneficent and prevent it from turning into madness. The pity was that both in religion and in family life circumstances should have suppressed and embittered the native warmth of her nature, her need of being impassioned. She needed to be carried away, to be ravished; and since the days of being ravished by irresistible bold men were gone, she dreamt of being ravished, like Santa Teresa, by sacrifice and prayer. But Susana was not made either for prayer or for sacrifice, but decidedly like the other Sturgises, for that natural joyous enthusiasm and kindness which are their own reward. Before sacrifice and prayer can be self-rewarding a revolution has to be worked in the soul; and though Susana knew of this, she never experienced it in her own person. It would have required her to key her nature up to a note that it was incapable of sustaining.

I have said nothing of Susana's appearance and physique, yet what is more important in life than our bodies or in the world than what we look like? And not only for a woman. The crusty old Hobbes observes that good looks are a power even in a man, since they predispose women and strangers in his favor. But women and strangers are not all fools; and there is something unprejudiced and disinterested in a first impression that runs deeper than any labored or conventional judgment. Body, character and mind are formed together by that single hereditary organizing power which the ancients called the psyche or soul; so that however much the mind or the body may be distorted by accidental influences, at bottom they must always correspond; and the innocent eye often catches this profound identity. We are arrested by a beautiful body because the sight of it quickens in ourselves the same vital principle that fashioned that body. And so too any deformity or distortion offends us in beings akin to ourselves, and ways of life contrary to ours seem to us monstrous even to look upon, like the wallowing hippopotamus opening a vast mouth half as large as himself. Chaos is fertile in monsters destroyed as soon as they appear; but definite species establish and perpetuate themselves unchanged where the seasons revolve steadily and the very enemies of life are so constant that means of defense may be prepared against them. In the human family it is an open question how far inbreeding will perfect or debilitate a type, and how far half-breeds may form new and healthy races.

I like to muse on this theory apropos of my brother and sisters and of the American melting-pot in general. My mother's first marriage seems not to have been eugenically a perfect match. Of five children two died in infancy and of the other three only Susana could be compared to her ancestors in vital fiber; and yet even in her an odd constitutional disharmony was visible to the eye. She had elements of pure beauty, but neither her face nor her figure was well composed. Most arresting were her large clear eyes, between hazel and green, and *à fleur de tête*, with delicately pencilled almost invisible eyebrows much higher up; and this effect of aristocratic innocence was reinforced by the high smooth forehead; so that when she was a young girl she could have posed in a *tableau vivant* for *La Belle Jardinière*. Yet those beautiful eyes were rather too close together, and that calm forehead was too narrow; the oval of the face, in time, became decidedly pear-shaped; and if the little mouth went perfectly with the eyes, the nose that intervened was too long and pointed, and too flat under the forehead. Altogether this countenance, when animated, arrested and held people's attention. In a Victorian epoch when ladies were not made up, it was conspicuous for a youthful white and ruddy complexion and a great liveliness, because those Madonna-like eyes surprised you by their subtle changes in expression, their involuntary unaffected confession of eagerness, intelligence, or fun. In conversation everything was fused into a vivid personality, but in repose you couldn't help wishing that so many good points had been combined differently.

It was especially in her figure that the disharmony was obvious. Above the waist Susana was slender, as if designed by the same hand as her eyebrows; but if the upper half of her figure imitated Raphael the lower half most successfully imitated Rubens. She had very small hands and feet, quite Spanish, with short fingers proper for a dumpy woman; yet she was tall, American in her movements, and entirely without our mother's deftness and grace. She and her sister would never dance: they were conscious of doing it so badly that they refused to do it. As Susana grew older her weight became too great for her small feet, walking tired her and soon grew painful. For a time after her marriage she had a small Victoria in which she could drive, but in the end she ceased to go out, even to church, and set up a chapel at home, where a Dominican from the great monastery of Santo Tomás, in the valley beneath her windows, might come to say Mass on Sundays and feast days, and give her Communion.

The imperfections I could not help seeing in Susana and the points—very few—on which we did not sympathize, were a source of unhappiness to me, for she occupied a niche in my pantheon where I could never place any other creature. I remember how seriously my father upset me one day, after Susana had returned to Spain and had lived with him for a season, when he said: "Ah, *Susanita,* whom we thought the world of, so exceptional, so sprightly, so perfect, now she has become a woman like any other woman." There was truth, I couldn't deny it, in this judgment, but there was no charity. Susana was still herself; we are always ourselves at bottom, however disfigured by the incrustations of life. She had been defeated by unhappy circumstances, forced out of her native element, denied the breathing space necessary to her nature; and charity will always judge a soul, not by what it has succeeded in fashioning externally, not by the body or the words or the works that are the wreckage of its voyage, but by the elements of light and love that this soul infused into that inevitable tragedy.

CHAPTER VI

AVILA *

AVILA became by chance the headquarters of my family in Spain; we had no hereditary bond with that ancient and noble town. The first of us to go there was my uncle Santiago, sent no doubt by his official superiors, as a sort of punishment, to the worst of government posts. I fear he was rather a merry and lazy fellow, given to drink, and not useful in the office; yet his chiefs had the virtues as well as the vices of nepotism; and if advancement went automatically to their relations and to persons recommended by the big-wigs, still room was made for the ne'er-do-wells also in the smallest and dullest of provincial capitals. My father lighted on Avila because his brother was there; and the place recommended itself on acquaintance for being in the Old Castile of his youth, healthy, tranquil, and cheap. My mother too was willing to go and live there when, in 1866, she agreed to postpone her return to America. At least the town was accessible, being on the main line between Madrid and Paris, habitable in summer as well as in winter, and safely remote from the Court, from fashion, and from corrupt society. After three years she was finally able to escape with her daughters; yet unsuspected associations remained in their young minds with unsuspected virtues in that place, so that both eventually returned to live and die there; and there they both are buried.

As for me, I was scarcely three years old when we moved to Avila and I was nearly seventy when it ceased to be the center of my deepest legal and affectionate ties. That these ties, albeit

* Pronounced *Ah'vilah,* from the Latin *Abŭla,* from which the official Spanish adjective, *abulense.*

the deepest, should have left me so remarkably free was a happy circumstance for my philosophy. It taught me to possess without being possessed, yet it gave me a most firm and distinctive station. For the freest spirit must have some birthplace, some *locus standi* from which to view the world and some innate passion by which to judge it. Spirit must always be the spirit of some body. Now the chance that made me an exiled Spaniard and linked me in particular to Avila (rather let us say than to Reus) was singularly fortunate. The austere inspiration of these mountains, these battlemented city walls and these dark churches could not have been more chivalrous or grander; yet the place was too old, shrunken, barren and high-and-dry to impose its limitations on a travelling mind: it was a mountain top and not a prison. Standing there, the spirit was situated, challenged, instructed; it was not controlled.

The same thing, by another happy chance, might be said of my other principal point of attachment, namely Boston and Harvard College. The extreme contrast between the two centers and the two influences became itself a blessing: it rendered flagrant the limitations and the contingency of both. Granted that I was to awake in Spain in the nineteenth century, I could have found myself in no place less degraded than Avila; and granted that I was to be educated in America and to earn my bread there, I could have fallen on no place friendlier than Harvard. In each of these places there was a maximum of air, of space, of suggestion; in each there was a minimum of deceptiveness and of the power to enslave. The dignity of Avila was too obsolete, too inopportune, to do more than stimulate an imagination already awakened, and lend reality to history; while at Harvard a wealth of books and much generous intellectual sincerity went with such spiritual penury and moral confusion as to offer nothing but a lottery ticket or a chance at the grab-bag to the orphan mind. You had to bring a firm soul to this World's Fair; you had to escape from this merry-go-round, if you would make sense of anything or come to know your own mind.

In quality Avila is essentially an *oppidum,* a walled city, a cathedral town, all grandeur and granite; yet it is so small as to seem in the country. Step out of one of the lofty gates and you are at once amid wheat fields or on rocky and windy moors. At this altitude primitive bald nature has coexisted for ages with the tightest and most fortified civilization, ecclesiastical and military. Here no one need hanker after *rus in urbe*; he has the opposite, which is almost an equivalent. He has what we might call *urbs ruri,* or rather *oppidum in agris. Urbs ruri* would be a good name for some great English country house with its park, and its sub-ject farms and villages; for in the mansion there would be all the social amenities and sophistication of London, and yet looking about the eye would see nothing but emerald lawns and blue horizons, while at the gates the thinly peopled country would lie open to all lordly sports, from hunting and shooting down to driving, walking and golf. Avila, on the contrary, is an instance of *oppidum in agris*; not a private seat to which the great retire for pleasure and quietness, but a defensible eminence, perhaps with an ancient place of pilgrimage in it, where the country peo-ple have collected and walled in their granaries, leaving an open space in the midst for their meetings and fairs. Here in time the surrounding landlords will build themselves town houses, and perhaps come habitually to live, without surrendering their farms or neglecting their farming interests. They will form the ruling class, the *patres conscripti,* of the little republic, the typical ancient town, with its local religion and its gradually developing political eloquence.

Very likely the original pre-Roman *Abula* was a town of this kind; but that native simplicity has not survived the passage of migrations and conquests armed with alien imperial force, or with the force of immensely contagious militant religions. After the Romans and the Visigoths, the Moors swept over this region, but have left no such traces of their arts as may be seen at the not very distant Toledo. The great walls, the glorious crown of Avila, might have looked much as they do now in the Moorish epoch, for they are such as prevailed during the whole Byzantine millennium, from the fourth to the fourteenth century; but in their present form they belong to Christian times. There is a sweep and unity in their plan that indicate royal government and national resources; this had become a stronghold of kings against rival kings. and with this two new features, foreign to the ancient city, impressed themselves on Avila, and still, in their decay, lend it its dominant character: the seats of the nobility and those of the clergy. In my day several great families still had houses in Avila, to which some of them sometimes returned. Oñate, Superunda, Santa Marta, Parcent; but aristocratic families from different provinces and kingdoms had long intermarried, so that each great title might go with estates scattered all over Spain; and estates in the province of Avila, or palaces in the town, were not likely to be those of most importance to the family or favorite places for them of residence. Many great houses were therefore neglected, or turned into public offices or private apartments. Better preserved even if somewhat shrunken and depopulated were the convents and churches. The former Jesuit College, built into the walls and replacing the upper part of them over the *Rastro,* had become the Bishop's Palace; and many monasteries and convents, rather hidden behind blank walls, occupied large mysterious spaces in the town or choice positions in the suburbs. Avila was a distinctly clerical town, with Santa Teresa for its native patron and chief glory.

Yet the fundamental realities are still in evidence. The town walls, for all their massiveness, do not shut out the country from the eye. At every turn, through one of the city gates, or over some bastion, the broad valley remains visible with its checker-board of ploughed fields and straggling poplars lining the straight roads, or clustered along the shallow pools by the river; and at night, in the not too distant mountains, the shepherds' fires twinkle like nether stars. Or if the townspeople are too busy and nearsighted to remember the country, the country every Friday morning invades the town, and fills the market place with rustics and rustic wares.

At dawn they ride in from their villages in groups, on their trembling little donkeys, the man or woman perched on the hind quarters, behind the four-pocketed wicker saddlebags brimming with
scarlet tomatoes, bright green and red peppers, lettuce and yellow
chick-peas or clod-colored potatoes. In my time the peasant costumes, though tending to disappear, were still prevalent: the men
in broad black hats, short jackets, bright sashes and leather greaves,
attached like armor over their knee-breeches and blue stockings;
and the women bell-like in their wealth of brilliant flannel petti-
coats, worn one over another, and the topmost on occasion pulled
up to serve as a shawl, and protect the many-colored kerchiefs covering their heads and shoulders. Nor was garden produce all that
these self-sufficing peasants brought to market: there were also
home-made garments in plenty, such as *alpargatas*, or canvas shoes
with rope soles, and country crockery, *botijos* and *cantaros*, shining
in their newness, and no less smooth and rotund than the gorgeous
melons and watermelons of midsummer.

No danger that such a town should think itself self-supporting
like a capitalist, or existing by divine right to rule and instruct the
world. The country has created the city, built it up at the crossroads between one threshing-ground and another, where the
bridge crossed the river, and the riding paths met, leading beyond
the valley to the neighboring market towns. From the country
each city still draws its wealth and sustenance, as well as the fresh
hands required for its multiplying trades, the servants for its great
houses, and the young soldiers to be enlisted, by force or by bribes,
in its feuds and conquests.

Markets and fairs were dwarfed at Avila, however, by the religious feasts, doubtless much decayed in my day, yet still imposing.
I remember the procession of Corpus Christi, wonderful in my
childish eyes. And this not at all on account of the *gigantones*,
grotesque cardboard and cambric giants that formed the comic part
of the show. These were monstrous primitive caricatures such as
the raw mind loves, originally no doubt often obscene, and were
still allowed to precede or to follow the religious pageant, like an

Aristophanic farce after three tragedies. No: farce and even obscenity fall flat in early childhood; it is lovely marvels that entrance. Yet it was hardly the theological mystery that impressed me, the Eucharist as a means of grace: that too requires experience to comprehend it, and a second mind. The lovely mystery glittered on its own spectacular plane, the wonder was intrinsic to it, like that of the stars. To have explained would have cheapened it. At the age of six or seven I could feel the happy excitement of this feast, without words to express it or ideas to justify it; but had words and ideas been at my command they would have been like those that come to the French writer Alain on such an occasion. The occasion creates emotion, and the emotion creates intuitions to focus it and to lend it form. Was not this the festival of the summer solstice? Did not the summer sun and the June roses fill it with light and fragrance? Was not everybody happy and gaily dressed? Did not tapestries and damasks hang from the balconies, or where they were lacking, at least some gay coverlet or shawl or tablecloth? Did not gold thread and tinsel shine everywhere from vestments and banners? Were not the sun's rays doubly reflected from the golden monstrance that seemed to imitate them? And as the Host approached, borne high in a silver shrine amid lights and flowers, did not doves let loose from some window soar and circle in the upper air, while handfuls of roseleaves fluttered down like snowflakes on the procession? And the Host itself, the mystic center of all this joy, what was it but the bread of life, white wheaten bread sublimated into the pure principle of eternal happiness? For although hidden from the eye, the red wine that can turn to blood was not absent from the heart, and every holiday influence seemed fused together in this sacrament of union.

All this might be conceived to be the latent burden of my childish wonder, if the eventual poet who gave form to it had no further experience and no contrary inspiration: it is all that Alain cares to note, whose philosophy is rich in casual intuitions, but without foundations or results. What a pagan satirist might recog-

nize in this pageant might be only the echo of some cult of the
sun and the harvest, of golden Apollo and golden Ceres, with some
reminiscences of Bacchus. We might even go a step further and
see here only a prelude to the *Pervigilium Veneris* with its unfor-
gettable refrain: *Cras amet qui nunquam amavit, quique amavit
cras amet.* But that would be to take a false turn in the reading of
history, a turn that, at the crossroads, history did not take. To
reach Corpus Christi moral evolution had to move in the opposite
direction. These little boys and little girls dressed in white, fresh
from their first communion, are not simply preparing to make love,
and tomorrow to sing *Little Roger Coming Home from the Fair.*
Very likely some of them will do so, but it will not be in continu-
ation of this ceremony: they will do it rebelliously, sullenly, or
sneakingly, perfectly aware of their change of front. This feast
commemorates the institution of the Eucharist on the eve of the
Passion. It was moved from Maundy Thursday only because too
much overshadowed there by Calvary still to come; whereas now,
after Pentecost, it could be celebrated joyfully, and be felt to be an
initiation into a happy but transfigured life; a sacrament of love,
indeed, but of a love made selfless by renunciation and sacrifice.
The sun, the banners, the rose-leaves, the young children, are not
out of place in this feast; they rhyme with the new joy and innocence to be achieved; the purity of nature harmonizing perfectly,
while it lasts, with a chastened purity of spirit.

Those to whom such things seem nonsense must be puzzled
at the vogue that the cult of the Sacrament has acquired in the
present conceited but distracted age: it seems incongruous with
dominant industrialism and with opinion controlled by the daily
press. Perhaps it is a safety valve, a self-defensive movement of the
human psyche, threatened with absolute servitude, like that of the
working ants.

The rich, the polite, the well-informed about everything, would
perhaps see more in the other feast that I chiefly remember at
Avila: an autumn feast, the apotheosis of a reforming and literary
woman. Santa Teresa is not buried there, her heart alone is kept

as a relic in the chapel built over the room in which she was
born; and her beautiful image, an image almost identified with her
now by local sentiment, stands or rather kneels over the same
altar. It is a wooden image, moveable and fit to be carried in procession: only the attitude and the face and hands manifest the
artist; the rest is dressed in the Carmelite habit, modified by a
gorgeous mantle, a golden nimbus and many jewels. Yet the
sculptor and the saint triumph over these accessories, and we see
the enraptured nun, pale and heroic, lifted from the earth by the
power of faith and love. Yet Santa Teresa was eminently sane;
she was considerate of circumstances, of particular cases, of human
weakness and the humors of fate; she was distinctly modern. She
can appeal to the pragmatist in the believer: a dangerous tendency,
it seems to me, that carries religion into politics and, almost inevitably, coarsens religion itself into a sort of celestial politics and
diplomacy. One world is enough to my feeling, and I should wish
religion to digest and transmute this life into ultimate spiritual
terms rather than commit us to fresh risks, ambitions, and love-
affairs in a life to come. But my impulsive half-American sister
was an ardent disciple of Santa Teresa; and something unsatisfactory in Susana's piety perhaps prejudices my judgment in respect
to the perfection of her model. Religion in Susana seemed to remain always strained, and did not sweeten her old age. Did she
perhaps doubt the truth of her faith, and did she assert it so
persistently precisely because, at heart, she doubted it? Santa
Teresa had no such secret unrest; but perhaps she would not have
escaped it had she breathed for twenty years an American atmosphere. Fixity of tradition, of custom, of language is perhaps a prerequisite to complete harmony in life and mind. Variety in these
matters is a lesson to the philosopher and drives him into the cold
arms of reason; but it confuses the poet and the saint, and
embitters society.

   In Avila, in these processions of Santa Teresa, there were charming survivals of popular naïveté, worthy of the middle ages. The
Saint was too great, the crowds too large, for everything to go on

in her own church: ten days before the feast she was borne to the Cathedral, where the image of the Virgin Mary was brought out from her chapel to welcome the pilgrim; and the two statues, one to the right and the other to the left of the high altar, presided over the ensuing Novena. When this was finished, another procession was formed to carry the Saint back to her own home; but such was her ascendency in heaven as well as on earth, that the Virgin Mary herself could not forbear to accompany her parting guest at least halfway on the journey. At the appointed place, an open square where the eye could extend for some distance, the procession halted. Santa Teresa, who preceded (ecclesiastical etiquette requiring that the greatest shall come last), then turned completely round, and made three deep obeisances to the Queen of Heaven, who amid the delighted whispers and gratified vanity of the crowd actually made an obeisance in return, and then majestically moved away towards the Cathedral; whereupon the Saint resumed her homeward progress. So much for popular piety: but the pious also have their little human dissensions. At another hour there was another procession, by a rival confraternity carrying a different newly bought image of Saint Teresa, in the style of Saint Sulpice. And why? Because the regular Confraternity of Santa Teresa, whose property the old venerable image was, was said to be in the hands of rich men and ecclesiastics; and the artisans had seceded and formed a different confraternity of their own, with a modern pink-and-white image, plain painted stucco without silks or jewels, that they liked better.

To confirmed pedestrians like my father and me the friendly if rugged visage of Avila appeared more in its environs than within its walls. Each time that, coming from Paris in the 1880's and 1890's after my second night in the train, the dawn warned me that I must be approaching my destination, it was always with a beating heart that I looked for the names of the last stations, Arévalo, then Mingorría; after which, at any moment, I might expect to see on the right, sloping down gently towards the bed of the invisible river, the perfect walls of Avila, every bastion shining clear in the level rays of the sun, with the cathedral tower in the midst rising only a little above the line of the battlements, and no less imperturbably solid and grave. The stone in that level sunlight took on a golden tint, beautiful and almost joyful against the blackish rocks and arid slopes of the descending hills, only relieved here and there by fringes of poplars or dark green oaks. The landscape near Avila (that, I suppose, of an extinct glacier) is too austere to be beautiful, too dry and barren; yet it reveals eloquently the stone skeleton of the earth; not a dead skeleton like the mountains of the moon but like the mountains of Greece, vivified at least by the atmosphere, and still rich in fountains and in hidden fields. After all, Castile is not so high and dry as Arabia, which also has its green spots; the whole Spanish table-land slopes gently westward and south-westward towards Portugal and the Atlantic, whence come its rains and where its rivers debouch without impediment. Avila sits on the very tip of a tongue of high land stretching in this direction; and its peculiar picturesqueness depends on the circumstance that, although situated among the northern foothills of the Castilian sierras, it does not look northward but southward towards those very mountains, from a parallel minor spur. Being more often cold than warm, it has turned its face and opened its windows to the sun. From the promenade of the Rastro or from my brother-in-law's house on the crest of the same southern slope, the eye consequently dominates the pleasanter and more humane aspect of the country. At one's feet lie the roofs of a picturesque suburb, not without its churches and belfries; in the fields beyond rises the great monastery of Santo Tomás; you see the long straight roads, sometimes lined with trees, that cross the broad valley, and you may even catch a glimpse of the river, although in summer it is little more than a string of pools, with a little water trickling from one to another, or hiding among heaps of stones and stretches of sand. Beyond all this, to close the vista, rise the sharp peaks of the Sierra de Avila, and the more distant and massive Sierra de Gredos, both alike purple to the eye, and as it were liquefied by excess of light.

In this direction there was an interesting goal for a long walk in
cool weather; and a walk is pleasanter when it is directed to some
specific spot, where one may stop, look about, and rest a little
before turning satisfied homewards. This was the Hermitage of
Our Lady of Sonsolès, a large stone chapel with a farmhouse
attached, built on an eminence at the foot of the sierras, with a
grove of trees before it, a fountain, and some stone benches. In my
father's day we seldom visited it, because my visits then fell in
midsummer, and the walk across the whole valley was long and
dusty in the sun; but later, when I could stay with my sister in
the autumn, I could walk there alone, or sometimes accompanied
by my brother-in-law, who however rode his mule, while I and
his son Rafael (my usual companion) went on foot.

Celedonio, middle-aged and heavy, didn't come on my account,
although he pretended to do so. He came on a religious pilgrimage.
My fondness for this excursion served only as a hint to his secret
conscience, that perhaps he had neglected Our Lady of Sonsolès
too long. On these occasions it was therefore in order to enter the
Chapel, and to kneel for a while in prayer, or as if praying, before
the miraculous image. My brother-in-law's piety was of a primitive, prudential and chthonic kind, not at all theological. He with
his whole family marched dutifully together to confession and
communion once a year, at the Easter season, according to the precept of the Church, and he went to Mass on Sundays, unless
something prevented; but he would have nothing to do with modern devotions, or the people who, as he said, *se comían a Dios*,
gobbled up God, every day. Religion to his mind was and ought to
be a formality, like calling on the authorities, respecting the
written law, and keeping up the ancient dignity of Church and
State. One mustn't offend the powers that be: and these powers,
according to his agricultural sense of cause and effect, were mysterious and multiform. Our Lady of Sonsolès was one of them.
He carried in his waistcoat pocket a small silver reproduction of
her image and as Sonsolès was visible from the windows of his
dining room, before sitting down at table, he invariably went to

the window, as if to examine the look of the weather, pulled the little image out of his pocket, lifted (as if to scratch his head) the cap he always wore in the house, muttered a word or two in the direction of Sonsolès, and kissed the tiny amulet before slipping it back into its hiding place. This was his private grace before meat, good for his whole household, well known to everybody, but never spoken of.

On occasion, however, Celedonio would tell us about the miracles worked by this particular *numen*. One was commemorated by the votive model of a seventeenth-century ship that we might all see hanging from the rafters of the Chapel at Sonsolès, and depicted in the large painting on one of the walls. Some one in a storm at sea had invoked the aid of Our Lady under this advocation and had been saved from shipwreck. Had I been quite at ease in Celedonio's company (as I never was) I might have asked him whether he thought that, if this mariner had invoked, say, Our Lady of the Pillar instead of Our Lady of Sonsolès, he would have been less likely to escape. And if he had hesitated, I then could have aired my own strictly orthodox theology and said that the intercession of the Virgin Mary would of course be equally efficacious under whatever name she was invoked; but that the prayer, in each person, might be more spontaneous and trustful, and therefore worthier of being heard, if it were associated with the favors and the cultus familiar to him at home. Celedonio would have (or should have) congratulated me on this explanation; but he would certainly have thought me a dangerous person if I had asked whether, if that mariner had invoked not the Virgin Mary but Castor and Pollux, he might have been no less earnest and no less worthy of his reward. Whatever name we may invoke, is not prayer always essentially addressed to whatsoever real power we may depend upon to liberate us from the troubles that pursue us? Superstition may variously deceive the fancy; it never changes the allegiance of the heart, which I suppose is all that matters from a spiritual point of view.

Celedonio's allegiance, at least in his old age, was solidly prudential, and such as befitted a farmer, a lawyer, an administrator, and a *pater familias*. Perhaps in his youth he had had dreams. He had been in love with Susana, a love apparently never quite extinguished; for he had hung opposite his desk, where he could see it whenever he looked up from his papers or stopped to light a cigarette, an oil painting of Susana, at the age of fifteen, holding me in her arms, done in those early days by my father, after a photograph; and there were certain romantic vistas in his mind concerning Spanish history, and in particular concerning this shrine of Sonsolès. He vouched personally for a modern miracle—proving its sanctity. A certain person, whom at first he named, but who later became vague and might ultimately have been identified by tradition with himself, was one day riding across the valley when he was overtaken by a violent thunderstorm, and imprudently took shelter under a solitary oak by the wayside. The oak was struck and riven by lightning; the horse was killed, and the rider's clothes burned: yet the man had raised his eyes towards Our Lady of Sonsolès, had invoked her protection, and had miraculously escaped.

Without counting on miraculous favors, I too felt a genuine sanctity, a pagan sanctity, hanging about Sonsolès. Nothing forbidding, nothing ominous, but a sort of invisible sympathy of all things with man, when he takes his place gladly among them. The sanctuary was old, simple, solid, nobly placed on the hillside, with an enclosed grove before it, and a stone fountain, from which the water flowed in paved channels among the trees, keeping the grass green in the shady places. Chapel, farmhouse, and barns were contiguous along one side of the enclosure, all equally familiar possessions, ancestral, and tended with equal prudence and care. Poultry, a dog and a cat, even a stray pig or two formed a happy family. Not useless near a temple, any more than the donkeys and sheep in the background; for this was a place of pilgrimage, travellers must be refreshed, and there was even a rude space serving as a bull-ring at the yearly feast when a fair was held, with great concourse from the neighboring villages. From these coarse pleasures and hubbub in the hot sunlight, and from these troubles of the poor, it was all the more grateful to slip for a moment into the darkness of the cool oratory, and visit the Virgin in her placid unearthly splendor. The universe, our own souls, then revealed to us another dimension, besides those of our labors and sorrows.

The chapel was a perfect little temple, dark and windowless save for some opening in the roof. No modern ceiling or plastered walls or wooden flooring, but only rough stone everywhere and bare rafters; yet the shrine was ornate, and the image of Our Lady of Sonsolès, rather less than life-size, stood magnificently dressed and crowned, her white and gold mantle and rich veil being piously worked and renewed on occasion by Celedonio's daughter and other young ladies of Avila. "Sonsolès" means, or may mean, *they are suns*; and the place has a coat of arms or at least an emblem, rudely sculptured here and there on the stone, representing three faces of Sol, encircled by rays, like so many monstrances; for such symbols have transferable applications, and what depicts visible radiance may also indicate the diffusion of divine grace.

At heart Avila itself only repeats on a grander scale this same religious and human theme; only that the rustic setting has disappeared, and repentant paganism has become more Byzantine, more mediæval, enclosed and overshadowed as it is by such high military and monastic bulwarks. The place in my time was in part ruinous and neglected, reduced to 6,000 inhabitants from the 30,000 it is said to have had in its day. Almost half the area that slopes down to the river from what might be called the upper town was deserted within its circle of battlements and towers; there appeared only heaps of rubbish, a few nondescript huts, and some enclosures where occasional stray pigs and poultry might be encountered. Even in the upper part many old mansions and chapels were closed; sometimes only the great door, with a wrought-iron balcony over it, attested their ancient dignity. Yet dignity was not absent from the good people that remained, leading a simple, serious, monotonous provincial life, narrowed by poverty and overhung more obviously than busier places seem to be by the

shadow of illness, sorrow, and death. Almost all the women appeared to be in mourning, and the older men also. There was
nothing forced or affected in this: people were simply resigned to
the realities of mother nature and of human nature; and in its
simplicity their existence was deeply civilized, not by modern
conveniences but by moral tradition. "It is the custom," they would
explain half apologetically, half proudly to the stranger when any
little ceremony or courtesy was mentioned peculiar to the place. If
things were not the custom, what reason could there be for doing
them? What reason could there be for living, if it were not the
custom to live, to suffer, and to die? Frankly, Avila was sad; but
for me it was a great relief to hear that things were the custom,
and not that they were right or necessary, or that I ought to do
them.

How much respect did these grave, disillusioned, limited people
of Avila have for their conventions, and in particular for their
religion? Not much, I think, at bottom; but nothing else was practically within their range; and if something else had been possible
for them, would it have been better? The more intelligent of them
would have doubted this, and resigned themselves to their daily
round. What they had and what they thought was at least "the
custom"; they could live and express themselves on those assumptions. Their inner man, in bowing to usage, could preserve its
dignity. In breaking away, as the demagogues and cheap intellectuals wished them to do, they would have fallen into mental
confusion and moral anarchy. Their lives would have been no
better, and their judgments much worse. They could never, at the
time when I knew them, have come to feel at home in a society
where nothing was any longer "the custom," either in opinion or
in conduct. Everything in Avila, the walls, the streets, the
churches, the language, still bore witness to a faded but abiding
civilization; and it was not impossible for me to heighten and
vivify the picture, as I projected it into the past, and turn it into a
proud, distinct and uncompromising power, such as a corrupt
world would have to respect and to fear.

Every tourist with a guide book may learn that in Avila the Cathedral, San Vicente, Santo Tomás, and the Chapel of Monsén Rubí are notable monuments in which the whole troubled history of Gothic architecture might be studied, if there were not elsewhere so many purer examples of each of those phases. Architecture, especially Gothic, was a passion of my youth, when I searched and analyzed everything of the kind that I spied anywhere, and a pinnacle or the tracery of a window arrested my eye as if it had promised to be Helen in all her glory. But that illusion is gone, and Avila was not a place to encourage it. On the contrary, it is a place where I have felt the profounder power of unintended harmonies, of accidents, not happy in themselves, that merge into a background for happiness—I speak of happiness for a philosopher who can live happy in the intellect, amid the lovely promise and quick ruin of all other happiness. Lovely promise and quick ruin are seen nowhere better than in Gothic architecture, all exuberance, freedom, and instability, "vaulting ambition" in stone, original sin thinking it could glorify repentance. Oriental luxury invaded classic art in Byzantium; and the purely aesthetic and geometrical glory of this art appears better when the Christian occasion for it does not exist, as among the Moslems. It could then supply a myriad of lovely settings for poetry, for love, and for unbridled imagination, all without imposing a moral on the arabesques of creation. And for religion it could leave the empty and silent dome, where the solitary mind might settle its account with the universe. Our Gothic on the contrary became insatiably lavish in ornament and in all sorts of distracting curiosities; and I like it best when the hand of time or of chastisement has intervened in that orgy, which tended to become tiresome, and has introduced a new style, a different taste, an imperious broom, sweeping away half those golden cobwebs. Sometimes the incongruous addition is more beautiful than the background on which it intrudes; and many a Gothic church would lose its charm if you removed the renaissance tombs or the baroque porches. After all, it was only by the force of its own restlessness that Gothic was superseded.

This irony of progress was illustrated in my time even in the Cathedral of Avila. There were formerly magnificent red damask hangings round the chancel and choir. They covered the wall beneath the triforium and the upper half of the arches into the aisles, the lower half being screened by the no less magnificent wrought-iron and brass railings. They made the whole inner space warm to the eye and nobly secluded to the heart. The sanctuary then seemed something like a throne room and audience chamber for the Most High. It was regal without loss of sublimity or mystical suggestion, since the vault still soared far above this earthly luxury, and vast somber spaces remained open in the direction of the nave and of either transept. Nor was the public cut off as in eastern churches from viewing the ceremonies. Room was left for them between the sanctuary and choir; for the Spanish practice of placing the choir west of the transepts allows the laity to flood the very center of the scene of worship. It is the favorite station for the officially devout, benches being sometimes provided there; while the unpretending Christian can still see and hear everything from the aisles, without being observed among the observers. These intimacies and charms of divine worship are missed by the superior critics who deplore such intrusion of the choir into the nave. That the tunnel of a long nave is thereby blocked seems to them an aesthetic sacrilege; but to me it seems a devotional advantage, and even a poetic one; because a partial veiling of beauty often enhances it, and the screens that enclose the choir, without interrupting the continuity of the clerestory and the vault, diversify the scene beneath, and supply appropriate places for monuments and altars. Therefore to a more Catholic age those red damask hangings seemed an appropriate ornament for a church, and they lent to the Cathedral of Avila, which is rather cold and severe, a special humanity and splendor. Nevertheless, some years ago, the Chapter sold the whole to an American for twenty thousand dollars. They said that the damask was rotting, that they needed the money for structural repairs in the fabric of the Cathe-

dral itself, and that without the damask the architecture of the
church would appear to more advantage.

These excuses seem to me as lamentable morally as the loss of
the hangings is æsthetically. No doubt those hangings needed over-
hauling; but if the silk were rotting, would any shrewd Chicago
millionaire or his careful wife want them in their bright new
home? No doubt the government architects that direct repairs in
national monuments did not always act as the Chapter would have
wished, if they acted at all; and no doubt twenty thousand dollars,
to be spent as they directed, was an unprecedented temptation to
the bishop and canons. But if any of them said that to remove so
great an ornament to the cultus would better reveal the beauties of
the edifice, he must have been a sad Catholic and a false lover of
the arts. Churches are built for prayer, not to exhibit the history
of architecture; and it was a sound instinct in Christian times to
assume that all richness and beauty might be laid at the foot of the
Cross. Nothing that man naturally loves need go unconsecrated, if
only it be sacrificed in part and in part redeemed. Moreover, it is
not true that the damask hid anything worth looking at. The
Cathedral of Avila is noble, but no part except the apse is particularly original or interesting. The student could examine every
detail sufficiently before, while to the poet the bare stone walls—
for there is much flat empty surface here without any riot of sculptured niches, windows, or galleries—seem now exposed to too
much light, common, comfortless, bleak and discouraging. The
vandalism that has devastated the interior of almost all churches
elsewhere had now begun to attack them even in Spain. They
were becoming sepulchres for the religion that built them.

This church, faded and neglected but still glorious, was the last
in which I have been able to hear mass with inward satisfaction.
For one thing, there was no sermon in the morning. To separate
the Mass from the sermon shows a genuine respect for both. The
liturgy and the eventual discourse are alike assumed to be worth
attending to, each for its own sake. Then, at the High Mass here,

the rite was performed honestly, simply, in less than an hour, as a traditional ceremony, without any affectation of personal devotion or unction. It was the ancient Church still living. The little acolytes scampered about as if at play, swung their heavy silver censers with gusto, and let the chains rattle and the great puffs of smoke escape at each high turn of the pendulum, as if pleasure and duty had never been better matched. The music was rough, gusty, and not very classical, but at least brief; and like all the rest it was not offered to the public for admiration but performed simply to conform, as well as might be or was usual, to the prescriptions of the liturgy. Here was ancient priestly religion, as acceptable to the truly intelligent as their native language or their accidental governments, not because miraculously right or perfect but because ingrained in all their traditions, part of the soil and substance of their only possible life, to be transmitted with the inevitable variations to the next generation, if this generation is not to be wholly disinherited and barbarous.

I did not feel at all disinherited, although never a partaker in those rites. I respect them, I like them, and I refuse to use them for any baser purpose. They celebrate inevitable human passions and joyful hopes; and I shed no tears if those hopes and passions in myself have had their day. Why envy illusions? Insight is not only calmer, but more sympathetic and charitable, because each passion or hope when alive sees hateful enemies in every other passion and hope, whereas insight sees in each the good to which it aspires. In pure religion and in art all these rival goods may be celebrated without contradiction or disloyalty; for after all it is only the profane that expect art and religion to serve their private passions. Those who have passed the *pons asinorum* in the inner life know that the function of art and religion is precisely to transfigure those private passions so that, far from being served, they may all serve religion and art.

It was not, however, for the High Mass on Sundays that I most often visited the Cathedral, or lingered there with the most pleasure. Any day at any hour, to make a short cut from street to street

or to escape from the sun at the hot hours, I could traverse the dark
cool aisles, or sit for a while in the transept, measuring the vaults
with the eye, and examining the rather nondescript stained glass
or the agreeable if somewhat obscure paintings in the great gilded
reredos, or the charming twin pulpits, or the sculptures in some old
altar or tomb. Enough scent of wax and of incense clung to the
walls to preserve the atmosphere of the cultus, and the focus of it,
where some old man or old woman might be seen kneeling in
prayer, was usually some modern shrine; this was still a living
church, not a museum or a ruin. That circumstance, like Avila
itself, pleased and consoled me. Everything profound, everything
beautiful had not yet vanished from the world.

CHAPTER VII

EARLY MEMORIES

O F EARLY childhood I have some stray images, detached
and undatable, called up occasionally for no reason,
after the fashion of dreams. Indeed, sometimes I suspect that they may be fragments of old dreams, and
not genuine recollections; but in that case, where did the old
dreams come from? For autobiography it might be no less pertinent, and even more telling, to report them if they were dreams
than if they were true memories, because they would show how
my young mind grew, what objects impressed it, and on what
themes it played its first variations.

These images are all visual. I remember the *sota de copas* or
knave of cups in the Spanish cards, with which I was playing on
the floor, when I got entangled in my little frock, which had a
pattern of white and blue checks; and I can see the corner of the
room, our *antesala,* where I was crawling, and the nurse who
helped me up. I also remember sitting in my mother's lap, rather
sleepy, and playing with a clasp that could run up and down the
two strands of her long gold chain, made of flexible scales; she
wore a large lace collar, and had on a silk gown which she called
el vestido de los seis colores, because the black background was
sprinkled with minute six-petalled flowers, each petal of a different
color, white, green, yellow, brown, red and blue. Clothes and colors
evidently had a great fascination for me: the emphasis may have
been partly borrowed and verbal, because I heard the women constantly talking *chiffons;* but the interest was congenial. I have
always been attentive to clothes, and careful about my own; and in
those days of innocence, it was by no means indifferent to me
whether with my white summer dress I wore the plain everyday

blue sash, which I despised, or the glossy and fresh silk tartan, that made me feel more like myself. Yet I retain a memory, that must have been much earlier, of quite another kind. One evening, before putting me to bed, my mother carried me to the window, sitting on her arm, and pulled back the *visillo* or lace curtain that hung close to the glass. Above the tower of the Oñate house opposite, one bright steady star was shining. My mother pointed it out to me, and said: *"Detrás de ese lucero está Pepín."* Pepín, her lamented first-born, was behind that star. At the time, this announcement neither surprised nor impressed me; but something about my mother's tone and manner must have fixed her words mechanically in my memory. She seldom spoke unnecessarily, and was never emotional; but here was some profound association with her past that, for a moment, had spread its aura about me.

Another set of memories can be dated as not later than my third year, because they introduce my brother Robert, who left Avila when I was three and he was twelve. We occupied the same little room behind our mother's and next to the schoolroom; and I remember our pillow fights, or rather games, because Robert had a tender heart and was nice to his baby-brother. He was forbidden to purloin any part of my food, but might stick out his tongue in the hope, not always disappointed, that with my fork I might delicately place a morsel upon it. It was a feat of equilibrium on my part, as well as of magnanimity, and I remember it for both reasons. Also the crisp potato omelette, fried in oil, that I had for supper, and that I still pine for and seldom obtain; and the napkin, white on the black and red table cover, on which the feast was spread. The first toy I can remember was also in Robert's time at Avila, for it was given me by his Alsatian tutor, Herr Schmidt: a velvety gray mouse that could be wound up to run across the floor. And finally I can remember distinctly the occasion of Robert's departure. We all went to the station to see him off; for my father was taking him as far as London, from where his cousin Russell Sturgis (the Evangelical major with the side-whiskers and shapely calves) was to convey him to America to be put to school. But it is not any emotion connected with leave-taking for an indefinite absence that remains in my mind: only the image of young Robert's back, walking before me at a particular corner where we had to go in single file. He wore a long gray coat with a braided mantlet or short cape covering the shoulders; above which I can still see his gray cap and the tightly curling brown hair escaping and bulging out under it. Whether I was actually walking too or was being carried does not appear from the picture. The self in these clear and fixed intuitions remains wholly transcendental and out of sight. It is doing its duty too well to be aware that it is doing it.

That Robert should have had an Alsatian tutor in Avila (who also taught the girls) may seem odd. It was one of those unstable and unsatisfactory compromises that were involved in the circumstances of my parents' marriage. For a time they lived in Madrid, in the flat where I was born: but Madrid has a bad climate, with great heat in summer and cold winds in winter; it made a second residence necessary for the hot months, and was expensive and, for my mother, socially distasteful. Moreover, she had to go back to Boston; my father knew it, but kept finding reasons for putting the thing off. Finally, very characteristically, my mother took the law into her own hands, secretly made all the arrangements and one afternoon escaped with all of us, save my father, in the express train for Paris. There my father's remonstrances reached her. They were so eloquent, or backed by such threats of action (since he had a right at least to retain *me*), that we all finally returned. It had been agreed that we should live in Avila. But what education could Robert or the girls receive there? None! Therefore a private tutor was imperative, and somehow a young Alsatian was found who seemed to possess all the requirements. French and German were native languages for him, he spoke a little English, and would soon learn Spanish. His demands were modest and his character apparently excellent. So Herr Schmidt was installed as a boarder with a poor widow who lived on the ground floor, and there were daily lessons in the sunny little room at the back of the house which became the schoolroom. I don't know what idealistic cobwebs the German Minerva might have spun there had not her labors been interrupted; but presently a German Cupid had flown in over the flowerpots in the open window, and tangled those learned threads. For although this was before the Franco-Prussian war, young Schmidt showed all the sentimentality and push of a pure German; he believed in discipline and thoroughness, and the duty of founding all instruction on German geography, in the native language; so that between the difficult and most clearly articulated names of *Harzgebirge* and *Riesengebirge* he would whisper in Susana's ear: *"Je vous aime avec rage."* She was hardly sixteen, and he had to be sent away, which no doubt he thought a great injustice; for he wrote a long letter explaining his worthiness to be Susana's husband, and his willingness to go to America and establish himself there—on nothing a year.

It was this collapse of superior international education at home that had made it urgent to send at least Robert at once to school in America, and that separated me from my elder brother for the next five years. Two more years elapsed before my mother and sisters also departed. I remember nothing of that interval; but after they went my uncle Santiago, with his wife Maria Josefa and his daughter Antoñita, came to live with us, and a new and distinct chapter begins in my experience. The scene, the persons, the events are still present to me most vividly. I didn't feel deeply or understand what was going on, but somehow the force of it impressed my young mind and established there a sort of criterion or standard of reality. That crowded, strained, disunited, and tragic family life remains for me the type of what life really is: something confused, hideous, and useless. I do not hate it or rebel against it, as people do who think they have been wronged. It caused me no suffering; I was a child carried along as in a baby-carriage through the crowd of strangers; I was neither much bothered nor seriously neglected; and my eyes and ears became accustomed to the unvarnished truth of the world, neither selected for my instruction nor hidden from me for my benefit.

My aunt Maria Josefa was frankly a woman of the people. She was most at home in her kitchen, in a large blue apron that covered most of her skirt; and I shall never forget the genuine fresh taste of the fried peppers and eggs, and the great soft cake or *torta* that came from her hands. She was a native of Jaen, with a strong but pleasant Andalusian accent and exaggerated rhetoric. Her every word was a diminutive or an augmentative, and her every passion flowed out in endless unrestrained litanies of sorrow or endearment. She could hardly read or write, and her simplicity or humility was so great that she would casually observe that her daughter Antoñita had been a *siete mesina* or seven-months child; from which any one could gather the reason for her marriage. For my uncle this marriage had been unintended and undesirable; he was much too young and she was much too common; but having got the poor girl into trouble he nobly made the *amende honorable*; and terrible as the sacrifice would have been if he had had much ability or ambition, as things were it rendered poverty perhaps easier to bear. Poverty was not the only misfortune they had to put up with: but when the worst was over, I found my aunt living in Granada with a brother who was a tanner. This was in the summer of 1893, when I had reached Spain via Gibraltar. My mother and I were in the habit of sending Maria Josefa a small allowance so that she was well received and respected in her brother's household. The tannery occupied the court of an old, possibly a Moorish, house; the skins hung drying from the gallery; and my aunt's brother, in order to do the honors of the city (as I had not been there before, or had no guide book), took me to see the University, which indeed it would not have occurred to me to visit. In the library there was a large globe; and in order to make talk, which rather ran dry between us, I said I would show him the voyage I had just made from America. I was doing so when he asked, "But which is Spain?—What, that little spot? I thought it was this," and he pointed to Africa. It occurred to me that some great wits before him had seen no difference between Africa and Spain; but I didn't go into the intricacies of that opinion. As to my aunt, of course she was then old, fat, and broken, but calm and strangely silent. She had protested enough, and this was the fifth act of her tragedy, all storms subdued and equalized in resignation. Yet one more trial awaited her. Her brother died before her, and she had to retire to her native village near Jaen, from which soon no more answers reached us to our letters.

Not the person, *tia Maria Josefa*, in whose hands my mother could have wished to leave me at the age of five! But my mother's mind was made up and inflexible; it was made up abstractly, in scorn of particulars and of consequences. She had put off her departure only too long, and now she *must* go. Besides, strange as it may seem, she was well disposed towards my father's relations, as they were not towards her. She seldom spoke of them, but when she did it was amiably, even sympathetically. She seems to have trusted Maria Josefa, as one might a devoted old nurse; and this trust was deserved, because in relation to me Maria Josefa behaved perfectly. Moreover there was Antoñita, who but for her love-affairs and marriage would have looked after me more playfully than her mother. Antoñita was a nice girl, a friend of Susana's, pretty and with a latent depth of feeling which made people think her not insignificant, in spite of her simplicity and lack of education. My mother had liked her, and helped her to get prettier clothes. But she was ripening into womanhood and preoccupied with love. I remember her first *novio*, or acknowledged lover, the youngest of the Paz brothers, who were among the leading bourgeois families of Avila; and I think there was more between him and Antoñita than the local conventions allowed to *novios*. He came to the house, which is contrary to the rules: *novios* should meet only in public places, in sight of their elders, or talk together at the window, the girl sitting inside the *reja*, or in the balcony, and the young man standing in the street. This was called *pelando la pava*, plucking the turkey, or conjugating the verb *amo*, I love. There was a great attic over a part of the house, accessible from my father's room or studio, where he painted; and from one of the big beams of the roof hung a trapeze, arranged, I suppose, for my benefit. Into that attic the lovers would wander alone, whether to admire my performance, or not suspecting that I might be swing· ing there, I didn't know. That something was brewing became evident on another occasion. We were sitting one evening or late afternoon in the *café del Inglés* (for the lamps were lighted) when suddenly my aunt got up, evidently very angry, bundled Antoñita and me out of a side door; and once in the adjoining *portal* or *porte cochère,* began violently beating Antoñita with fists and claws, with such a flood of imprecations as only my aunt was capable of. All I could gather was that the poor girl had been looking at somebody; no doubt, as I now conjecture, at young Paz, at another table, making love to another girl. Anyhow, my aunt had worked herself up to such a rage that, being subject to fits, she fell full length with a loud bang on the stone floor. She fell exactly as *prima donnas* and murdered heroes fall on the stage; and apparently as harmlessly, for I heard no more of the whole affair. Relations with Paz were evidently broken off; there were no more trips to the attic, where I did my swinging undisturbed; and presently a very different *novio,* this time meaning business, appeared on the scene.

What brought him to Avila I do not know; probably some great lawsuit, for he was a lawyer, and ostensibly an important person, *bellâtre,* with well-oiled curly black locks and silken side-whiskers and the beginnings of a paunch, on which a conspicuous gold chain with dangling seals marked the equator. He was a widower with two little girls, but still young, not over forty; for people spoke of his brilliant prospects rather than of his brilliant past, and he had a still beautiful mother whom my father and I once visited in Madrid. She received us in her boudoir, or rather in the alcove attached to it, for she was still in bed, but elaborately prepared to receive callers. There were great lace flounces to her sheets, over a red damask coverlet, and she wore a lovely fresh peignoir and little cap, from which two great black braids hung down over her two shoulders, ending in coquettish knots of blue ribbon. What she and my father were talking about I didn't understand, but I felt I had never been in such a luxurious nest before, so much carpeted, so much curtained, so softly upholstered, and so full of religious and other bric-à-brac.

With such a mother, Rafael Vegas must have begun life convinced that he was a distinguished and fashionable person, and that his clients, when he had them, should pay him handsome fees. Nor could he have helped being a ladykiller, having not only the requisite presence and airs, but the requisite temperament; for he was no vulgar libertine, but a genuine lover of the fair sex, who demanded to conquer and to possess his conquests exclusively. He might have liked a harem, but he despised a brothel. His success with the ladies, young and old, was immense and in one sense deserved, since his admiration for them was sincere. That he was truly subject to the tender passion was proved by his courting and marrying two of my pretty and penniless cousins, beginning with Antoñita. Nothing but love could have prompted him in these cases; but to them it seemed a dazzling match, that meant initiation into a higher social sphere, as well as into all the mysteries of untried passion.

The wedding took place secretly in the small hours of the night, because a rowdy custom subjected widowers, on their new bridal night, to a *cencerrada,* or derisive serenade of cow bells, if the date and place of those mysteries could be discovered. Everything was therefore kept as dark as possible; only the immediate family was summoned, and they at the last moment, and only a cup of chocolate offered afterwards to the sleepy company before the newly married pair vanished to some unknown hiding place. I was of course present, and impressed by the strangeness of going out at night into a dark street and a dark empty church, with a knot of people whispering and hastening, with much trepidation, as if on some criminal errand. We were in our ordinary clothes, the bride in black, with a lace mantilla. It was all over in a moment. I was bundled to bed again, and might have thought it a dream, but for the talk afterwards about everything. Rafael's emphatic personal dignity would have suffered sadly had he not escaped the *cence-*

rrada; and he managed it cleverly, by not going on any wedding trip (he may also have been short of money) but establishing himself at once in our house, with his two daughters, in the best front rooms left vacant by my mother and sisters, who were in America. For a day or two, however, bride and bridegroom occupied my bedroom, because it looked out on a tangle of little courts and walled gardens, quite shut off from any street. On the first morning I followed the housemaid there—after all, it was my room— when she took in their breakfast to the happy pair. The two cups of chocolate were on a particularly fresh and well-filled tray, with *azucarillos*; there was a bright brass bed, wholly unknown to me, and a gorgeous red damask coverlet, and great lace flounces to the sheets, like those, or the very same, that on that other occasion, in Madrid, I saw setting off the charms of Rafael's black-browed mother. Rafael and Antoñita lay smiling and rosy on quite separate pillows; they said good morning to the servant and me with unusual good humor, and people all day indulged in witticisms and veiled expressions which I didn't quite understand.

I now had playmates in the house, two well dressed little girls about my own age; but we didn't like one another. It was made clear in every direction that our house and our standard of living were not such as the Vegas expected, and they bore us a grudge for causing them to be lodged and fed so badly. Yet our double or triple *ménage* was kept up for a year or more until an event supervened that brought disaster to my uncle's family and eventually sent my father and me to America.

Antoñita was soon quite obviously in what was called an interesting condition. The place that children come from was no mystery to me, although I was only seven or eight years old. I was already a calm materialist; not that in another direction I was less knowing in theology; and if any one had made the mistake of telling me that babies came in bandboxes from Paris, I am sure I should have scornfully replied that God and not milliners had made me; and that as God was everywhere, it was just as easy for him to make babies in Madrid or even in Avila as in Paris. Yet

Antoñita's baby, that God was undoubtedly making in Avila, was very long in coming to light. She continued more and more strangely to enlarge, until her haggard and unseemly condition, and murmurs and consultations in the family, began to suggest that something was wrong. Perhaps the date for the expected event had been miscalculated; or perhaps some complication prevented nature from bringing it about. At last one evening there was much agitation in the house, with strangers coming in, and long consultations; and I began to hear from Antoñita's room (which was my mother's room back to back with mine, but with no communication) piercing cries and weeping invocations of all the heavenly powers. This presumably lasted all night, since it was still going on when I woke up in the morning; and then there were more consultations with strange doctors and exhibition of surgical instruments. At one moment I remember my aunt bursting into the passage, with a bundle of bloodstained linen in her hands and floods of joyful tears, crying "She is saved, she is saved!" Yet later we children were taken to our neighbor's on the second floor, where we didn't know the people; and on the way out I saw, in a small wooden box that might have held soap or candles, a dead child lying naked, pale yellowish green. Most beautiful, I thought him, and as large and perfectly formed as the Child Jesus in the pictures; except that where the navel ought to be he had a little mound like an acorn, with a long string hanging out of it.

The image of that child, as if made of green alabaster, has remained clear all my life, not as a ghastly object that ought to have been hidden from me, but as the most beautiful of statues, something too beautiful to be alive. And it has suggested to me a theory, doubtless fanciful, yet which I can't think wholly insignificant, concerning the formation of living things. They are all formed in the dark, automatically, protected from interference by what is called experience: experience which indeed would be impossible if there were not first a definite creature to receive it and to react upon it in ways consonant with its inherited nature. This nature has asserted itself in a seed, in an egg, in a womb,

where the world couldn't disturb its perfect evolution. Flowers and
butterflies come perfect to the light, and many animals are never
more beautiful, pure, and courageous than when they first confront the world. But man, and other unhappy mammals, are born
helpless and half-shapeless, like unbaked dough; they have not yet
become what they meant to be. The receptacle that held them
could not feed them long enough, or allow them to attain their
full size and strength. They must therefore be cast out into the
glare and the cold, to be defeated by a thousand accidents, de-
railed, distorted, taught and trained to be enemies to themselves,
and to prevent themselves from ever existing. No doubt they manage to survive for a time, halt, blind, and misshapen; and sometimes these suppressions or mutilations of what they meant to be
adapt them to special environments and give them technical
knowledge of many a thing that, if they had been free, they might
never have noticed, or observed only poetically, in a careless and
lordly way. But every living creature remains miserable and
vicious, so long as in serving other things it has to suppress itself:
and if that alien world must need be served, the only happy solution and one that nature often finds, would be for the unfit species
to perish outright—there is nothing ignoble in perishing—and for a
different species to appear whose freedom and happiness would lie
in contact with those particular circumstances and mastery over
them. I say to myself, therefore, that Antoñita's child was so exceptionally beautiful, and would doubtless have been exceptionally brave and intelligent, because he had profited longer than is
usual by the opportunity to grow undisturbed, as all children grow
in their sleep; but this advantage, allowed to butterflies and
flowers, and to some wild animals, is forbidden to mankind, and
he paid for it by his life and by that of his mother.

For she had not really been saved; only a false hope made my
aunt think so for a moment; and on Antoñita's death, it would
have seemed natural that Rafael and his two little girls should
have left us and gone to live elsewhere in their own more luxurious
way. But not at all. Primitive human nature in my aunt Maria

Josefa yielded absolutely to every passion in turn, put up with every trial, but survived and clung no less passionately to whatever was left. Her grief on this occasion was violent, but violent only by fits, as when each new visitor came to condole with her, and she had to repeat the whole story, with appropriate floods of tears, sobs and lamentations. She even said at times that now she knew there was no God, because, with all her prayers and vows, no God could have allowed her poor innocent daughter to suffer so horribly to no purpose. Her heart thus unburdened, however, she couldn't but take comfort in that splendid man, her son-in-law, and devote herself to his service and care for his little girls. Rafael therefore not only remained in our house, but became all-important in it, as if my father had not existed. Nor could I be looked after exclusively, when after all I had my own mother to love me, even if a thousand leagues away, and there were those two darlings to rescue from the shock of having lost their second Mama as well as their first one. Moreover my uncle Santiago, though he said little, was beginning to go daft. Not on account of his daughter's death. He used to say, when people expressed their sympathy, that his real loss had come when she was married. I don't think this observation in itself a sign of dementia; but it indicated a general despair and passivity that went with his taking refuge in drink, and finally in idiocy. For idiocy may begin by being partly acted, like Hamlet's madness, in order to mock the facts, until the mockery becomes an automatism, and the facts are lost altogether. Years afterwards, when he was at his worst, he would walk ceaselessly round and round the house, half singing, half moaning, always repeating the same sounds, and crushing a piece of paper in his hand. He had recovered the animal capacity—such an insult to the world!—of still doing his old trick, no matter what might be going on. The marvel is how many individuals and how many governments are able to survive on this system. Perhaps the universe is nothing but an equilibrium of idiocies.

My father was mildness itself on ordinary occasions, but sometimes could be aroused to reveal his hidden and unusually clear mind, when all his command of terse language and his contempt for the world would flow out in a surprising and devastating manner. I was not present, but I gathered from stray comments overheard afterwards, that he had had an explanation of this sort with Rafael and Maria Josefa. At any rate, they suddenly left us. My father and I remained in what seemed that vast house alone with one little maid servant. Such an arrangement could not be permanent and doubtless was not meant to be so; and presently we too said farewell to that house forever and to Avila, as far as I was concerned, for eleven years.

During the three years that I was separated from my mother I went more or less to school. It was a large darkish room on the ground floor in the public building directly opposite our house; but the entrance was not in our street, and I had to go round the Oñate tower into the lane at the back, where the school door was. We children stood in *corros* or circles round the teacher—I think sometimes only an older lad—and recited the lesson after him. I don't remember any individual questions or answers, nor any reading or writing, yet we did learn somehow to read and write. I had two books: the *cartilla*, with the alphabet and the different syllables, with easy words following; and the catechism, perhaps in a later year. This was itself divided into two parts, one Sacred History, with pictures in it, of which I remember only Moses striking the rock from which water gushed; and Christian Doctrine, of which I remember a great deal, virtually everything, because it was evidently an excellent catechism, so that after learning it I have been able all my life to distinguish at the first hearing the *sapor haereticus* of any dangerous doctrine. Especially present to me is the very philosophic dogma that God is everywhere, by his essence, by his presence and by his power: of which, however, the first clause has always remained obscure to me; for if God is everywhere by his essence, it would seem to follow that everything is essentially divine—a vulgar pantheism; so that the meaning must be something very recondite and highly qualified, which escapes me. But the other two clauses are luminous, and have taught me from the first to conceive omnificent power and eternal truth: inescapable conceptions in any case, quite apart from any doctrines of historical Judaism or Christianity. I have reasserted them, in my mature philosophy, in my notions of the realm of matter and the realm of truth: notions which I am happy to have imbibed in childhood by rote in the language of antiquity, and not to have set them up for myself in the Babel of modern speculation. They belong to human sanity, to human orthodoxy; I wish to cling to that, no matter from what source its expression may come, or encumbered with what myths. The myths dissolve: the presuppositions of intelligence remain and are necessarily confirmed by experience, since intelligence awoke precisely when sensibility began to grow relevant to external things.

CHAPTER VIII

I AM TRANSPORTED TO AMERICA

MY FIRST voyage—if I hadn't been deadly seasick— might have initiated me into the life of primitive mariners, for we sailed the high seas in an open boat. It was a little freight steamer plying from Bilbao to Cardiff, hardly more than a tug; and though it had a small bridge and a deck house aft, it was open to the sky forward, and visibly freighted with reddish earth, which I believed was iron ore. The Bay of Biscay in such a craft confirmed its bad reputation; but on the third day there was sunshine and smooth sparkling water, and I recovered instantly. A quick and complete recovery is characteristic of my ill turns in general, and particularly of seasickness, which purges the system of its poisons. If I could have secured this advantage without the horrid prolonged trials that produced it, I might have gladly become a sailor. I love moving water, I love ships, I love the sharp definition, the concentrated humanity, the sublime solitude of life at sea. The dangers of it only make present to us the peril inherent in all existence, which the stupid, ignorant, untravelled land-worm never discovers; and the art of it, so mathematical, so exact, so rewarding to intelligence, appeals to courage and clears the mind of superstition, while filling it with humility and true religion. Our world is a cockleshell in the midst of overwhelming forces and everlasting realities; but those forces are calculable and those realities helpful, if we can manage to understand and obey them.

We were in the Bristol Channel, in sight of the Welsh coast; smooth grassy hillsides, gray-green in the slight mist and dotted with little white houses. But there was something far more interesting for me to watch; several boats with white sails, probably small yachts, bending and tacking in the almost imperceptible breeze. A British note: a first hint to me of that brave, free, sporting side of the youthful Anglo-Saxon character which I was later to love so much. For if in most things it is contrast that makes me admire and trust the unspotted young Englishman, in one respect it is affinity; I too love the earth and hate the world. God made the first, and man, with his needs and his jealousies, has made the second.

On landing, an ungainly ridiculous side of this world, and especially of Britain, became suddenly present. We had plumped on a Sunday into a British non-conformist industrial town. Ugliness and desolation could not be more constitutional. Perhaps we lodged in a too modest quarter, too near the port; but nothing was in sight save rows of mean little brick houses all alike, a long straight street wet with the rain, and not a soul stirring. However, the rain ultimately ceased, and on going out for a stroll we came upon a forbidding castle wall, closely skirted by what evidently was the old High Street of the place; and we learned that this was the seat of the Marquis of Bute, the great landlord of that region. Another British note: the living survival of mediæval features, material and moral, in the midst of modern England.

The next day we travelled to Liverpool, where I remember nothing but the docks, with long inclined ways, paved with cobblestones, leading down between great warehouses to the water's edge. There we crept into a small rowboat, that was to convey us to our ship. Several large vessels were riding at anchor in the stream: my father pointed to the ugliest and most dwarfish of them and said that this would be ours. No help for it now, I reflected: but at once my eye was attracted by a line of little flags running from stem to stern, over the top of the two masts. What did that mean? My father explained that dressing the ship in that fashion, although a British vessel, was a compliment courteously paid to the United States, because most of the passengers were Americans, who on that day were celebrating the anniversary of their Declaration of Independence. This incident has fixed the

date of my first sailing to America unerringly in my mind: it was
the Fourth of July, 1872.

The Cunard Steamship *Samaria* of that date was a vessel of
3000 tons, with a squat red smokestack between two stumpy masts,
and a bowsprit like a sailing-ship. Sails were indeed often set, in
order, it was said, to steady her, but probably also to help her
along; for never was vessel more distinctly an old tub. She stood
high, black, and short above the water, looking rusty and almost
derelict; however she bore us safely, if not steadily, to Boston in
twelve days. I was again terribly seasick most of the time; and my
father, if not exactly seasick, being an old sailor, suffered from
severe and prolonged indigestion, which he said upset and discouraged him altogether, and spoilt his whole visit to the United
States. I, at least, had intervals when I was well and hungry. A
nice young woman, Irish she said, took pity on me and tried to
entertain me; but we couldn't talk. I didn't know a word of
English or she of Spanish; and my father, who read English perfectly, could neither pronounce it nor understand it when spoken;
so that with English-speaking people he was reduced to uttering
single words, if they could be recognized as he sounded them, or to
writing them on a piece of paper. His deafness added to the difficulty, and made it impossible for him to surmount it. Nevertheless
my young Irish friend and I got on well enough without a common language: the goodwill in what we might say was always
intelligible. I afterwards often saw her family, for they occupied
the pew immediately in front of the one in which my sisters and I
sat at the Church of the Immaculate Conception; but our acquaintance never went beyond an occasional bow and discreet
smile. My particular friend, the young lady, for some reason was
never there. I have a dreamy recollection of hearing that she was
the invisible contralto that sang with so charming and rich a voice
in the choir; I am not sure of it, but in any case I liked to think so.

The day of our arrival was very warm, with the damp suffocat-
ing heat of the New England summer; there was naturally some
confusion in landing, and everything seemed odd and unaccount-

able. It was a sordid scene. I saw no stone quays, such as I associated with ports, at Bilbao, at Portugálete, and lately on a grand scale at Liverpool. No docks; only a wooden pier raised precariously on slimy piles, with the stained sea water running under it; and on it a vast wooden shed, like a barn, filled with merchandise and strewn with rubbish. America was not yet rich, it was only growing rich; people worked feverishly for quick returns, and let the future build for the future. But along came my brother Robert. I shouldn't have recognized him, nor he me, after those five years: a youth not yet eighteen, of middle height, with a narrow chest and sloping shoulders, and a straw hat with a bright blue ribbon: yet the tightly curling brown hair, quite dry and brittle (we both grew prematurely bald) was unmistakably Robert's: besides, he spoke Spanish, and very soon I was quite at home with him. But I had never seen a man in a straw hat before, and the blue ribbon didn't please me. Of course I had no idea that blue ribbons might have a meaning: 'varsity blues, royal blues, the Garter, or the record in Atlantic crossings or choice champagnes: there was no question of any of those things in Robert's case. His ribbon was an accident, a caprice of the hat-makers, seconded by thoughtless taste in the buyer. I say thoughtless, not to say crude: because I nurse a sort of moral sense about colors, and in artificial objects a plain unmitigated blue seems to me vulgar. Robert had pale blue eyes, innocent and sometimes a little watery. To pale blue my color-sense makes no objection, nor to dark blue; these have separate moral qualities proper in their place; and the lightest blue eyes always possess a mysterious center and several shades in the iris. I could have positively liked the blueness of Robert's eyes, and even that of his ribbon, if it had matched them.

Once on terra firma, or rather on the rough planks of the Cunard wharf, in what resembled the baggage room of a large station, I looked about for the carriages and horses. Carriages—anything with wheels—had been my favorite toys. Mine had been little ones, that I could pull round and round the dining room table on a string; but more exciting, in Madrid, had been the real carriages, so smart and shining, with their gay red or yellow wheels, their high-stepping horses, their solemn coachman and groom, and the smiling ladies inside. But what did I see here? I daresay there were vehicles of various sorts; but just in front of me, what first caught and held my attention, was something like a large baby-carriage suspended high in air on four enormous skeleton wheels: Robert called it a buggy. The front wheels were almost as large as the back wheels, with the rims almost touching. Those front wheels were too high to slip under the body of the carriage; in turning, the near tire was apt to scrape against the side with an ominous and unpleasant sound, so that it was impossible for a buggy to face about sharply; this littlest of carriages could make only a great sweep, and was in danger of upsetting at every corner.

Here by chance my eye, at the first moment of my setting foot in the new world, was caught by symbols of Yankee ingenuity and Yankee haste which I couldn't in the least understand but which instinctively pleased and displeased me. I was fascinated by the play of those skeleton wheels, crossing one another like whirling fans in the air, and I was disgusted by such a dirty ramshackle pier for a great steamship line. I think now that the two things expressed the same mentality. That pier served its immediate purpose, for there we were landing safely at it; it hadn't required any great outlay of capital; and what did it matter if it was ugly and couldn't last long? It might last long enough to pay, and enable the Company to build a better one. As for the buggy, its extreme lightness economized force and made speed possible over sandy and ill-kept roads. The modest farmer could go about his errands in it, and the horsey man could race in it with his fast long-tailed pair. Never mind if in the end it turned out to be like some experimental and too ambitious species of insect, that develops an extraordinary organ securing an immediate advantage but leading into fatal dangers. Abstract ingenuity is a self-rewarding sport. The taste for it marks the independence of a shrewd mind not burdened by any too unyielding tradition except precisely this tradition of experimental liberty, making money and losing it, and being happy rather than ashamed of having always to begin afresh.

Robert somehow guided us and despatched our things to Beacon Street; it was a complicated process and a complicated journey, a ferry and two horse cars, besides three short walks, but it was economical, ten cents each for the trip, and twenty-five cents to send the trunk by express: whereas a "hack" (a hired landau) would have cost five dollars. The method of sending luggage by express seemed to us obscure and disquieting. How could we trust all our worldly goods to a stranger, paying him besides in advance, and meekly accept in exchange a coarse brass medal perforated with a number? There was a twin medal perforated with the same number, which the expressman kept; and Robert said he would attach this to our trunk, having taken a note of the address to which that number should be despatched; and the trunk was sure to arrive safely and speedily. Although my own scepticism was not yet fully developed, neither my father nor I were by nature inclined to faith in the unintelligible: however, being born travellers, we were ready in a new country to bow to a new logic and a new ethics; and we trusted Robert and the mysterious order of nature.

Our faith proved entirely justified: and though my father perhaps never felt at home in this system of trust and credit, fearing the confidence tricks of omnipresent rascals, I soon learned to swim happily with my eyes closed on this stream of business convention, which indeed at this moment is supplying me with a comfortable income coming, as far as my direct action or perception goes, from nowhere. But I have meditated on this point, and think I see the principle of it. Life, physical life, would be impossible without bold and risky presumptions about the future and without the opportune course of nature, coming to meet and to reward those presumptions. Millions of seeds, thousands of hopes, are frustrated: but there is enough adaptability in living beings, and enough constancy in things, for some arts to prosper. When these arts have been long established with little remembered change, people think it a matter of course that things should proceed in that way, and are shocked if any accident, as they call it, produces what they call an anomaly; and they never perceive that they are daily building on faith over a sleeping volcano. Now a commercial society at first knows very well the risks it is running; ships sent out never return; stores are burned or pillaged; coin must ring true before it is accepted; and treasure must be kept hidden at home and guarded night and day with fear and trembling. But this state of things is so wasteful that merchants can afford to pay highly for a government that can give them security: and governments supported by trade will then police the country and the sea in the interests of trade, subordinating all other interests. Faith, trust, credit, security are the lifeblood of trade: when strictly protected by courts and prisons, they will reduce the expense of business enormously, and enable the merchant not only to grow rich and remain rich, but to supply the public with endless commodities at reasonable prices. And this is why, on landing in Boston in 1872, my father and I were able safely to commit our trunk to the expressman (police, courts, and prison would have got him instantly if he had stolen it) and could be conveyed from East Boston to Beacon Street at the expense of fifty-five cents instead of five dollars. But we had not the lordly pleasure of driving in our private carriage, or the excitement of carrying swords and pistols, in case bandits should waylay us.

Events looked forward to with trepidation, when at length they occur, often fall flat. I was going to see my mother and sisters again after three years! Husband and wife were to be reunited! Well, when Robert said, "This is our house" and we walked up a little flight of stone steps to a half-open door in a row of doors, belonging to a narrow high house exactly like the house next to it, nobody seemed to inhabit the house or any of the others. It was the dead season, July 16th, and the whole street was deserted. However, before we got to the last step, a second door further in was opened; we were expected; there were faces peering out: Susana and Josefina in white dresses, and, much smaller, my mother wearing a cap and looking very grave. We kissed each other all round, and Susana cried. (We had forgotten to kiss Robert at the wharf.) Why did Susana cry? Was it mere excitement, nerves? Or was she already—she was twenty-one—secretly regretting Spain and her *beaux jours*? They took us into the dining room to show us the "beautiful view" from the back of the house—a great expanse of water, with a low line of nondescript sheds and wooden houses marking the opposite bank. It was Bostonian to show us the view first; but we noticed that this dining room was hung with many oil paintings, little Dutch or classic Italian landscapes, still life, and over the mantelpiece an old portrait: some Elizabethan worthy in a ruff and puffed sleeves, with a large ring on his fat forefinger. My father naturally had begun by examining these pictures, all copies, of course; and we learned that the Elizabethan gentleman was supposed to be Lord Burleigh, but that "Uncle Henry," whose pictures these had been, had bought it because he thought the personage looked like a Sturgis and might have been one of his ancestors. My father must have been amused at this, it was so typical of the Sturgises; but he never spoke of it. As for me, what interested me was to find the large sofa so soft when I sat on it. One might ride on the springs as if on horseback.

It was inevitably Susana who took me in tow and who began to teach me English. I learned some verses by rote, about a bird's nest, out of a brightly colored and highly moral book for young children. They ended, as I pronounced them, as follows:

> You mahsthnoth in play-ee
> Esteal the bords away-ee
> And grieve their mahther's breasth.

The moral of this was wasted on me—I was not a young child— and if I had had an impulse to steal any bird's nest or bird's eggs, or even to climb any tree, it would not have been these nursery rhymes that could have dissuaded me. But I had no such impulse, and no such opportunity, which made this moralizing, like all moralizing, ring hollow in my ears. The lady who said many years later that she envied me for not having a conscience, didn't altogether misread me.* Like my mother I have firmness of character; and I don't understand how a rational creature can be wrong in being or doing what he fundamentally wishes to be or do. He may make a mistake about it, or about the circumstances; or he may be imperfectly integrated, and tossed between contrary desires, not knowing his own nature or what he really wants. Experience and philosophy have taught me that perfect integrity is an ideal never fully realized, that nature is fluid and inwardly chaotic in the last resort, even in the most heroic soul; and I am ashamed and truly repentant if ever I find that I have been dazed and false to myself either in my conduct or in my opinions. In this sense I am not without a conscience; but I accept nobody's precepts traversing my moral freedom.

As to my pronunciation, it improved rapidly and unawares. I then had a good ear and a flexible tongue, and the fact that English was a foreign language to me positively helped me to learn it well and to speak it, for instance, much better than Susana or Robert, or most of the boys in my successive schools. For among our friends and my teachers there were some who spoke excellent English, traditionally or by careful chastening of the Yankee vernacular; and I could easily distinguish the better of my models from the worse. We were expressly taught pronunciation and declamation, and declamatory American speech, in the 1870's, though blatant and sometimes infected with the Calvinistic drawl, still was at bottom noble and pure. The irregularity of English sounds and their subtlety was an interesting challenge: far from irritating, it attracted me, and made me sensitive to its fine shades; so that even before I had heard an English voice or lived in England, my

* This incident is related, with variations, in the *Prologue* to *The Last Puritan*.

English was good. In 1887, Russell * once asked me to join him at his grandmother's, Lady Stanley of Alderley, a great and venerable personage; and after we had exchanged a few phrases, Lady Stanley said, "But how well you speak English!" That is a backhanded compliment that one ordinarily prefers not to hear, since it implies that one evidently speaks like a foreigner: but in this case, as I was considered a Spaniard, it was not rude; and I explained that I had been educated in Boston. "But you haven't an American accent," the lady insisted. I reminded her of the culture of Boston, and protested that all my English was American, as I had been but three days in London. "No," she admitted, "you haven't a *London* accent. You speak like Queen Victoria." Let this stand as early testimony to my English speech: I spoke like Queen Victoria.†

* The name *Russell* in these pages, unless otherwise indicated, designates John Francis Stanley, second Earl Russell. His brother Bertrand, who was also my friend, I venture to call "Bertie."

† At my nicest, perhaps, but not always. And didn't Queen Victoria have a German accent?

CHAPTER IX

NO. 302 BEACON STREET

THE house to which Robert had guided us, although the most commonplace of houses and meanly built for speculation, is perhaps worth describing. We passed the next nine years in it—all the later years of my boyhood; and its character and the life we led there are indelible not only in my memory but no doubt in my character and sentiment. I was unhappy there. At school nothing was imposed on me that I could complain of; there were no grinding tasks and no punishments; but until the last two or three years, when I formed close friendships and awoke to literature, it was all dead routine, and insufficient. A great void remained, which nothing at home could fill. The family was deeply disunited, and each member unhappy for a different reason. One of the boys at school, Davis, who had once come to lunch with us, said afterwards that we seemed to live as if in a boarding house. This was not true at bottom, or at first, because on our Spanish side we formed a true family; but life in America gradually dispersed our interests and our affections. I found my own center later, at Harvard: and then the bond with my mother's house, when Susana had returned to Spain and Robert was married, became pleasant and peaceful. Once or twice I spent a whole summer there, reading in the Public Library near by, and preparing my lectures. But that was no longer in Beacon Street; the scene was more retired, more modest, more suitable. There was no longer the pressure of poverty or of tiresome dissensions.

Our house was, at that time, one of the last on the waterside of Beacon Street, and there was still many a vacant lot east of it, where on passing in sharp wintry weather it was prudent to turn up one's coat collar against the icy blast from the river; as also, for the matter of that, at every cross-street. On the opposite side there were straggling groups of houses running further west along the Mill Dam, under which, at some points, the tide flowed in and out from the Back Bay, the shallow lagoon that originally extended to Boston Neck, turning the town almost into an island. The water in 1872 still came up to Dartmouth Street and to what is now Copley Square. Among the provisional features of this quarter were the frequent empty lots, ten or fifteen feet below the level of the street. These lots were usually enclosed by rough open fences, often broken down at the corners, from which a short cut could be made diagonally to the next street; and by this we school-boys were quick to profit, for a free run on rough ground amid weeds and heaps of rubbish. The architecture of these half-built streets was conventional and commercial; no house of more than five stories, no apartment houses, no fanciful architectural styles, only two or three churches, closed except at the hour for services on Sundays. To go to Mass we had to walk over the Dartmouth Street railway bridge and some distance beyond, into the South End. I liked the spire at the corner of Newbury and Berkeley Street, and often walked that way in order to see it. It looked to my eye, fed on copperplate views of English cathedrals, a bit of genuine Gothic: but the brick Italian Gothic introduced by Ruskin as well as Richardson's personal memories of Provence, left me quite cold, in spite of *The Stones of Venice*. They were indeed absurdly out of place, bastard, and theatrical.

Ours was one of two houses exactly alike; yet as they were only two, we could distinguish ours without looking at the number displayed in large figures on the semicircular glass panel over the front door: for ours was the house to the left, not the one to the right. The pair were a product of that "producer's economy," then beginning to prevail in America, which first creates articles and then attempts to create a demand for them; an economy that has flooded the country with breakfast foods, shaving soaps, poets,

and professors of philosophy. Our twin houses had been designed
to attract the buyer, who might sell his bargain again at a profit if
he didn't find it satisfactory; and this was precisely the ground on
which my mother was persuaded to buy her house, not expecting a
financial crisis and a sudden but prolonged disinclination on the
part of the consumer to buy anything that he didn't need. The
advantages in our house were in the first place social or snobbish,
that it was in Beacon Street and on the better or fashionable
waterside of that street; which also rendered every room initially
attractive, since it had either the sun if in the front, or the view if
in the rear. This view of a vast expanse of water reflecting the sky
was unmistakably impressive, especially when the summer sunset
lit up the scene, and darkness added to distance made the shabby
bank opposite inoffensive. Gorgeous these sunsets often were;
more gorgeous, good Bostonians believed, than any sunsets anywhere else in the world; and my limited experience does not belie
them. The illumination often had a kaleidoscopic quality, with
fiery reds and yellows; but at other hours and seasons the aerial
effects of the Charles River Basin were not remarkable. Moreover,
the grand attraction of the water view was marred by two counter-
effects discovered eventually by enthusiastic purchasers. One was
the immediate foreground, modified but not removed afterwards,
when the embankment was added. Under your nose was a mean
backyard, unpaved, with clothes or at least clotheslines stretched
across it; and mean plank fences divided it from other backyards
of the same description, with an occasional shed or stable to vary
the prospect. Under your nose too—and this was the second coun-
ter-effect—rose now and then the stench from mudflats and sewage
that the sluggish current of the Charles and the sluggish tides that
penetrated to the Basin did not avail to drain properly. However,
this was chiefly noticeable in summer, when Beacon Street people
were expected to be out of town; they made no loud complaints;
and the democracy in general was not yet aroused to the importance of town planning for its own sake. The age was still enam-
ored of *laissez-faire*; and its advantages were indeed undeniable.

For the Government it meant a minimum of work, and for the public it meant a minimum of government.

Our white elephant offered attractions also for the investor; the town was rapidly spreading in that direction, land-values were sure to go up, and the house would become every year more central and more desirable. Finally, it was a small house, with only two rooms on each of the principal floors: comfortable and cosy, therefore, for a rich spinster or for an ambitious young married couple; especially as with its reception room and large dining room on the ground floor, and its front and back parlors upstairs, it lent itself to entertaining on a moderate scale. That it had only two decent bedrooms, one bathroom, and no backstairs, wouldn't matter with a very small family.

But we happened to be a family of five, demanding five separate rooms. Entertaining of any description was out of the question for us, apart from the expense, since our mother didn't pay visits or go anywhere, or wish for any society; and at that moment she possessed neither the objects nor the money necessary to furnish decently those superfluous reception rooms. She therefore turned the front parlor into a bedroom for herself, while my sisters occupied the two good rooms on the second floor, and Robert, the cook, the housemaid and I had the four small cubicles in the mansard or French roof. At least, this was the ultimate and normal arrangement; but when my father and I arrived, the family prejudice against doubling up had to be overcome for the time being. Not, however, in the case of my father and mother; for she resigned the front parlor to him and moved to one of the rooms above, the two girls being crowded into the other, while I was tucked, as a waif new to the New World, not only into Robert's room but into his bed, which happened incongruously to be a large double one. My mother had taken on her furniture from previous tenants or from "Aunt Lizzie"; and the double beds, not being wanted, had a tendency to pass out of sight into the upper regions; one falling in this way to Robert's lot. But this cohabitation with my elder brother didn't last long; it was contrary to my mother's instinct and

habits; and soon a small bed was provided for me and I was moved
into the adjoining little room, as into my own castle.

The strip of land that our house occupied was nineteen feet
wide, and not far from ten times as long, since it stretched from
the edge of the public road over the "side-walk," broad and paved
with brick, which it was the tenant's duty to keep swept and reasonably free from snow; over the grass plot in front of the house;
and behind the house over a long back-yard, and the alley outside
to the water's edge. The brick façade was meager and graceless;
my architectural fancy often conceived how easily those twin
houses might have been rendered symmetrical, homelike, and even
pleasing, in the Dutch manner, if the two doors had been placed
together in the middle, and if the steps, the little upper platform,
and the steps on either side leading down to the basement had
been combined into one picturesque design. The sash or guillotine
windows too might at least have retained the square panes of the
colonial period, instead of the hideous plate glass that was thought
an "improvement." But the builder was no artist; he made one
drawing for one cheap house, and for economy built two of them,
his capital or his courage not permitting him to build a dozen.

To this unsuitable residence our habits adapted themselves as
well as might be. The small room beside the front door became our
family sitting room. It was sunny and cosy; on cold evenings when
the furnace proved insufficient, it could be at once warmed and
ventilated by lighting the fire; and by day it afforded us the feminine Spanish entertainment of looking out of the window and
watching, a little below our own level, the stray passers-by. It was
here that I sat, close by the window, doing my fancy drawing and
reading, which occupied me much more than my school lessons.
We had one study-hour out of the five at the school in the morning, and that sufficed for most of my preparation; but I took my
Latin book, and one or two others home, where I could read them
aloud to myself, of course in my bedroom, and gather a rhetorical
impression, with little profit to my scholarship.

The back wall of our family sitting room was covered by a large bookcase with glass doors, which contained the eighth edition of the Encyclopaedia Britannica, Lane's *Arabian Nights*, and a lot of old books that nobody opened. But we had a few Spanish books, and could get others from the Boston Public Library. In this way I read Oliver Optic's stories for boys, doting on the seafaring and the oceanic geography; also Abbot's *Lives*, of which I remember *Alexander the Great* and *Mary, Queen of Scots*. We also had Motley's and Prescott's pseudo-Spanish histories; but I knew enough to spew them out of my mouth at the first tasting. The sectarian politics and moralizing of most historians made history an impossible study for me for many years; not ancient history, of course, nor Plutarch's Lives, which we had at school to read from at sight, and not Gibbon, when I came to read him; because although Gibbon's bias is obvious, it is entertaining, and by the time I came to him I was willing to laugh at absurdities whether in Church or State or in philosophic opinion, without feeling that ultimate truth was in the least affected by such accidents or by the derision of worldly wits.

During the first years Susana and Robert would read aloud to us in the evening, at first in Spanish: *Don Quixote* in its entirety (save the *lunares*) * and *El Servilón y el Liberalito* by the pious lady-novelist "Fernan Caballero." Then, because our interesting Spanish books were exhausted, or because Robert, especially, found English easier, they shifted to Shakespeare, and read *Julius Caesar* and *Romeo and Juliet*, of which I remember liking the first and thinking the second inexpressibly silly. There the practice died out. We had no more reading aloud, but Susana and I often read the same books separately. When I became fond of poetry, I tried to interest her in it, but failed. She liked nothing I showed her except Byron's *Don Juan*, because, she said, it was as good as prose.

The walls of this little sitting room were hung exclusively with engravings, most of which had adorned "Uncle Henry's" house. There were official large portraits of Napoleon the Third and the

* Facetious name for the interspersed Tales: literally, *moles*.

Empress Eugénie in their regalia, theatrically posed and very pompous: also an affecting scene in an English churchyard, full of yew and weeping willow, and showing a brave little boy and a sweet little girl, sitting and holding hands on the edge of a newly made grave, strewn with wild flowers; while above their heads, a large white angel in muslin, the spirit of their departed mother, spread her hands and her great wings over them in protection and blessing. To take away the taste of this, like a savory after a milk pudding, there hung near it a framed collection of *Poor Richard's Proverbs,* with quaint little eighteenth-century illustrations for each maxim. I learned most of them by heart, but can remember only *Early to bed and early to rise Makes a man healthy and wealthy and wise* and *Three removes are as bad as a fire.* I wished Franklin had said something crushingly true and materialistic about the Angel Mother and about Napoleon the Third's corsets and waxed mustache; but I was willing to nurse illusions about the Empress Eugénie. She had been the queen of fashion in her day, she was Spanish, and she might be said to look a little like Susana idealized.

The article in our Encyclopaedia on architecture, which I studied persistently, was an excellent corrective to Ruskin, to Ferguson's *History of Architecture,* and to the taste of my time. The illustrations were all plans, elevations, and sections; and the only styles treated were the classic and the "Italian." There were no perspective views. I was thus introduced to the art professionally; and the structural interest became as great for me as the picturesque. Yet as I was never to build anything except in fancy, and even if I had become an architect could never have built great English country seats like those depicted in my text, I turned all these technicalities to imaginative uses. Here were the magnificent houses in which the English nobility lived; I had only to supply the landscape, the costumes, and the characters—and vivid representations of all these were accessible to me—in order to complete the picture, and bring it to life. English high life, before I had seen anything of it—and I have never seen much, except at Oxford and Cambridge—at once established itself in my regard side by side with ancient and with Catholic life as one of the high lights of history. The notion of belittling any one of them—or of belittling any other civilization, because less known to me—never crossed my mind: and as one style of architecture does not prevent the others from being equally beautiful and proper in their time and place; so the whole mental and moral civilization that flourished with that style must be accepted as right and honorable in its day. This principle is applicable to religions and philosophies, in so far as they too are local and temporary; but in so far as the universe and human nature are constant, it is evident that a single system of science will serve to describe them, although the images and language will constantly differ in which that system is expressed. In the last resort, all mutations must help to fill out a single history of things, that doubtless never will be finished or written. There is no vacillation in the truth about vacillations; and in this sense philosophic insight, if humble and sane, is as perennial as its object.

In regard, however, to rival forms of art or civilization, I was directed from the beginning towards impartiality, which does not imply omnivorousness or confusion. All beauties are to be honored, but only one embraced.

CHAPTER X

THE LATIN SCHOOL

WHEN I search my memory for events and feelings belonging to my earlier boyhood in America, from the age of eight to sixteen, I find for the most part a blank. There are only stray images, like those of early childhood, with no sense of any consecutive interest, any affections or sorrows. And yet I know that my feelings in those years were intense, that I was solitary and unhappy, out of humor with everything that surrounded me, and attached only to a persistent dream-life, fed on books of fiction, on architecture and on religion. I was not precocious; I may have had more ability than the average boy, but it was lavished on boyish thoughts; and a certain backwardness, or unwilling acceptance of reality, characterizes my whole life and philosophy, not indeed as a maxim but as a sentiment.

Why have I forgotten all those years? The causes are no doubt physical, but the effects may be expressed in literary terms. The past cannot be re-enacted except in the language and with the contrasts imposed by the present. The feelings of children, in particular, although intense, are not ordinarily long-lived or deeply rooted. We cry desperately or we silently hate, for not being allowed to do this or to have that; but these objects are trifles. If we remember those occasions they would seem to us indifferent; we should be ashamed to confess those feelings, or we should laugh at them with superior airs: as if the things that now preoccupy us, if we outgrew them, could seem to us more momentous. Thus vast portions of the past—almost all our dreams, almost all our particular thoughts and conversations—become unrecoverable. Our accepted, organized, practically compulsory habits shut them out. But these habits themselves will change more or less with time and with circumstances. Even what we still think we remember will be remembered differently; so that a man's memory may almost become the art of continually varying and misrepresenting his past, according to his interests in the present. This, when it is not intentional or dishonest, involves no deception. Things truly wear those aspects to one another. A point of view and a special lighting are not distortions. They are conditions of vision, and spirit can see nothing not focused in some living eye.

Something like this was in Goethe's mind when he entitled his essay on his life *Fiction and Truth* or *Truth and Poetry*; not that any facts were to be reported inaccurately or invented, but that his mature imagination, in which those facts were pictured, could not but veil them in an atmosphere of serenity, dignity, and justice, utterly foreign to his original romantic experience. I am no Goethe; the atmosphere of my aging mind is not Olympian, and in retrospect it cannot help lending to my insignificant contacts with the world some flavors that Goethe's wisdom had washed out, though they were not absent from his younger days: I mean salt, pepper, and pity for mankind.

Of Miss Welchman's Kindergarten in Chestnut Street, my first school in Boston, I remember only that we had cards with holes pricked in them, and colored worsted that we were invited to pass through the holes, making designs to suit our own fancy. I suppose this was calculated to develop artistic originality, not to convince us how trivial that originality is, and how helpless without traditional models. I remember also that I used to walk home with another boy, not so old as I, but also much older than the other children; that there were banks of snow on both sides of the path; and that one day—this must have been in spring for there was a bush with red flowers in his grass plot—he said something very strange as he left me, and ran up the steps into his house. I reported what he had said to Susana, who pronounced it *pantheism*: perhaps it was that those red flowers were opening because God was awakening in them. This shows how far my English had got in that Kindergarten and how we lisped metaphysics there.

The Brimmer School, where I went during the next winter, 1873–1874, was the public grammar school of our city district, although more than a mile from our house, in the depths of the South End. I had to walk the whole level length of Beacon Street, cross the Common, and go some distance downhill in Tremont Street to Common Street, where the school was situated, looking like a police station. It was a poor boys' free school, the roughest I was ever in, where the rattan played an important part, although usually behind the scenes, and where there was an atmosphere of rowdiness and ill-will, requiring all sorts of minor punishments, such as standing in the corner or being detained after school. I don't know what lessons we had, except that there were oral spelling-matches, in which naturally I didn't shine. A word spelt aloud (as some Americans like to do facetiously, instead of pronouncing it) still puzzles me and leaves me dumb. Nevertheless, partly because I was older and bigger than most of the boys, I soon became "monitor," and had my little desk beside the teacher's, a woman, facing the whole class. This distinction was invidious, and there were attempts at chasing me or hooting at me when we got out of school. Only once did it come to blows; and inexpert as I was at fisticuffs, or rather wrestling, I was taller, and managed to hold my own, and make my nasty little enemy sneak away sullenly. And I was not friendless. There was another boy from the West End, Bob Upham by name, with whom I usually crossed the Common; this was the danger-zone, since in the streets there were policemen who understood these things and would stop hostilities. On that occasion Bob Upham behaved according to the strictest rules of honor, standing by me sympathetically, but without interfering, and he afterwards said that the other boy had "Very nearly got me." But I hadn't been at all hurt, and never have had another opportunity to try my hand at the manly art, in which no doubt I should have been a miserable failure.

By a happy chance it was possible to transfer me the next year to a much better school, the historic Latin School, where from the earliest times until my day at least, all well-educated Bostonians had been prepared for College. The School Committee in the City government had that year decided to try an experiment, and establish a preparatory course of two years, to precede the six traditional classes. The experiment was not long continued, but I profited by it, and passed eight full years in the Latin School, thus being more of a Latin School boy than almost anybody else. We were not lodged during those preliminary years in the regular Schoolhouse, but at first in Harrison Avenue, and later in Mason Street. Both these places, as well as the Schoolhouse in Bedford Street, were in a central quarter of the town. I still had to cross the Common, but now to West Street, whence it was but a step to those schoolhouses.

More than once in my life I have crossed a desert in all that regards myself, my thoughts, or my happiness; so that when I look back over those years, I see objects, I see public events, I see *persons and places*, but I don't see myself. My inner life, as I recall it, seems to be concentrated in a few oases, in a few halting-places, *Green Inns*, or Sanctuaries, where the busy traveller stopped to rest, to think, and to be himself. I say the *busy* traveller, because those long stretches of spiritual emptiness were filled with daily actions and feelings, later in my case often with giving lectures and writing books: yet all was done under some mechanical stimulus, the college bell, the desk, the pen, or the chapter planned: old thoughts and old words flowing out duly from the reservoir, until the college bell rang again, and the water was turned off. Of myself in those years I have no recollection; it is as if I hadn't existed, or only as a mechanical sensorium and active apparatus, doing its work under my name. Somnambulistic periods, let me call them; and such a period now seems to begin and to last for two-thirds of my Latin School days.

Certain detached images, with the crude spectral coloring of a child's picture-book, remain from this first somnambulist season. At the school in Harrison Avenue I can see the yellow wainscoting

of the schoolroom, and the yellow desks; and especially I can see
the converging leaden sides of the sink, where on one winter morning the teacher—now a man—sent me to thaw out my ears, frozen
stiff on the way to school. I was to bathe them in cold water;
there was sharp pain and subsequently enormous blisters; but the
accident never recurred, although I resolutely refused all scarves,
pads, or ridiculous cloth rosettes, such as the women recommended
to protect those asinine organs. I found that a little pressure,
applied at the right moment, at once brought the warm blood
coursing back, and prevented trouble. Cold, rain, and wind, unless
there were dust, never spoilt my pleasure in the open air when I
was young; on the contrary, I liked them.

I remember also my first Headmaster at the Latin School, Mr.
Gardner by name: a tall, gaunt figure in some sort of flowing
long coat—of course not a gown—with a diminutive head like the
knob of a mannikin. The insignificant occiput was enlarged, however, as if by a halo, by a great crop of dusty brown hair. Was it
a wig? That suspicion seemed to my mocking young mind curiously comic and exciting. What if it were a wig and should fall
off? What if we hung a hook on an invisible wire over the door, to
catch it as he sailed out? One day on his rounds of inspection the
Headmaster found us having our French lesson. A headmaster
has to pretend to know everything, and the pretense soon becomes
a conviction. Mr. Gardner at once took over the duty of teaching
us his super-French. "The French word *bonne*," he said, "is pronounced in Paris—I have been in Paris myself—exactly as the English word *bun*." Now, I had heard a good deal of French out of
school. There had been the French *bonne* Justine, the Alsatian
tutor who loved *avec rage*, and the Catholic families in Boston
who chatted in French together. And hadn't I inherited from my
sisters *La Jeune Abeille du Parnasse Français* and couldn't I say by
heart:

> *Et ma plus belle couronne*
> *De lilas*
> *Sera à toi, ma bonne,*
> *Si tu me dis où Dieu n'est pas?*

If *bonne* sounds exactly like bun, would Mr. Gardner maintain that *couronne*, save for that first letter, sounds exactly like *you run?* I was sure that it was as ridiculous to call a *bonne* a bun as to call a bun a *bonne*. But apparently headmasters were like that; and I kept my phonetic science to myself with the immense satisfaction of feeling that I knew better than my teacher.

I may add that at that time our French master was not a Frenchman, but a Yankee farmer named Mr. Capen, whom we called Old Cudjo, and who had a physiological method of acquiring a Parisian accent without needing to accompany the Headmaster to Paris. He would open his mouth wide, like the hippopotamus at the Zoo, and would insert a pencil, to point out exactly what parts of the tongue, lips, palate or larynx we should contract or relax in order to emit the pure French sounds of *u, an, en, in, un,* and *on.* Nobody laughed. I think the boys were rather impressed for the moment by the depth of Mr. Capen's science, and the hopelessness of profiting by it. He was not a man to be trifled with. He had a most thunderous way of playing what he called Voluntaries on the piano; and rumor had it that he had stolen a march, under a heavy handicap of years, on his own son, by marrying the girl his son was engaged to.

Scraps of rude, quaint, grotesque humanity: bits of that Dickensian bohemia still surviving in my day in certain old-fashioned places, of which I shall have occasion to speak again. But the image that for me sets the key to them all appeared when we moved to the Bedford Street schoolhouse. It seemed a vast, rattling old shell of a building, bare, shabby, and forlorn to the point of squalor; not exactly dirty, but worn, shaky, and stained deeply in every part by time, weather, and merciless usage. The dingy red brick—and everything in that world was dingy red brick—had none of that plastic irregularity, those soft pink lights and mossy patina that make some old brick walls so beautiful: here all the surfaces remained stark and unyielding, thin and sharp, like impoverished old maids. This house was too modern to be as solid as the Hollis and Stoughton Halls that I afterwards lived in at Harvard; it had been built in a hurry, and not to last long. The windows were

much larger, but blank and somber; their cold, glassy expanse
with its slender divisions looked comfortless and insecure. When
up three or four worn granite steps you entered the door, the interior seemed musty and ill-lighted, but spacious, even mysterious.
Each room had four great windows, but the street and the courts
at the side and rear were narrow, and overshadowed by warehouses or office-buildings. No blackboard was black; all were in-
delibly clouded with ingrained layers of old chalk; the more you
rubbed it out, the more you rubbed it in. Every desk was stained
with generations of ink-spots, cut deeply with initials and scratched
drawings. What idle thoughts had been wandering for years
through all those empty heads in all those tedious school hours!
In the best schools, almost all schooltime is wasted. Now and then
something is learned that sticks fast; for the rest the boys are
merely given time to grow and are kept from too much mischief.

A ramshackle wooden staircase wound up through the heart of
the building to the fourth story, where the Hall was; and down
those steep and dangerous curves the avalanche of nail-hoofed boys
would come thundering, forty or eighty or two hundred together.
However short their legs might be, it was simpler and safer, if not
altogether inevitable, to rush down spontaneously with the herd
rather than to hold back and be pushed or fall out, or be tramped
upon or deserted.

And the teachers, though it is not possible for me now to distinguish them all in memory, were surely not out of keeping with
their surroundings: disappointed, shabby-genteel, picturesque old
Yankees, with a little bitter humor breaking through their constitutional fatigue. I daresay that for them as for me, and for all
the boys who were at all sensitive, the school was a familiar symbol of fatality. They hadn't chosen it, they hadn't wanted it, they
didn't particularly like it; they knew no reason why it should be
the sort of school it was: but there it stood, there they somehow
found themselves entangled; and there was nothing else practicable but to go on there, doing what was expected and imposed
upon them. You may say that for the teachers at least, in that age

of individual initiative and open careers, a thousand alternatives were, or had been, possible; and you may say that they could not have been altogether insensible of their high vocation and the high vocation of their country to create gradually and securely a better world, a world free from superstition, from needless hatreds, from unjust inequalities, and from devastating misery. Yes: but all that was negative; it consisted of things to be got rid of and avoided, and in America the more obvious of them had actually been escaped. Officially, especially now that slavery had been abolished, everything was all right. Everybody was free. Everybody was at work. Almost everybody could be well educated. Almost everybody was married. Therefore almost everybody was, or ought to be, perfectly happy. But were the teachers at the Latin School, perhaps the best of American schools, happy? Or were the boys? Ah, perhaps we should not ask whether they were happy, for they were not rich, but whether they were not enthusiastically conscious of a great work, an endless glorious struggle and perpetual victory, set before them in the world. And I reply, not for myself, since I don't count, being an alien, but in their name, that they decidedly were conscious of no such thing. They had heard of it; but in their daily lives they were conscious only of hard facts, meagerness, routine, petty commitments, and ideals too distant and vague to be worth mentioning.

Those teachers were stray individuals; they had not yet been standardized by educational departments and pedagogy. Some were like village schoolmasters or drudges; elderly men, like Mr. Capen, with crotchets, but good teachers, knowing their particular book and knowing how to keep order, and neither lax nor cruel. Others, especially Mr. Fiske, afterwards headmaster, and Mr. Groce, were younger, with a more modern education. They might have been college professors; they loved their subjects, Greek and English, and allowed them to color their minds out of school hours. In a word, they were *cultivated* men. I was an unprofitable though not unappreciative pupil to Mr. Fiske, because I didn't learn my Greek properly. That was not his fault. If I could have had him for a private tutor I should have become a good Grecian: it would have added immensely to my life and to my philosophy. But I was only one of forty; I was expected to study dryly, mechanically, without the side-lights and the stimulus of non-verbal interest attached to the words. In Latin, I could supply these side-lights and non-verbal interests out of my own store. Latin was the language of the Church, it was old Spanish. The roots were all my roots. But Greek roots were more often foreign and at first unmeaning; they had to be learned by hammering, to which my indolence was not inclined. And there was another difficulty. My apprehension of words is auricular; I must *hear* what I read. I knew, with small variations, what was the sound of Latin. I had heard it all my life; slovenly and corrupt as the Spanish pronunciation of it may be, at least it is something traditional. But what of Greek pronunciation? How should Homer sound? How should Sophocles? How should Xenophon or Plato? The artificial German Greek that we were taught—without even a proper *o*—was impossible. I tried many years later, when I was in Greece, to learn a little of the modern language, in hopes that it might react on my sense for the ancient texts and make me feel at home in them: but the time was too short, my opportunities limited, and I was too old to be quick in such a matter.

Even as it was, however, I learned a little Greek at School after my fashion, and one day surprised Mr. Fiske by reciting a long speech out of *Œdipus Tyrannus* for my ordinary declamation. He couldn't believe his ears, and afterwards privately congratulated me on my pronunciation of the *o*'s. But that didn't make me master of the Greek vocabulary or the Greek inflections. I didn't *study* enough. I learned and remembered well what I could learn from Mr. Fiske without studying. He was an exceedingly nervous, shy man; evidently suffered at having to address any one, or having to find words in which to express his feelings. His whole body would become tense, he would stand almost on tiptoe, with two or three fingers in the side pocket of his trousers, and the other two or three moving outside, as if reaching for the next word.

These extreme mannerisms occasioned no ridicule: the boys all saw that there was a clear mind and a goodwill behind them; and Mr. Fiske was universally liked and admired. This, although his language was as contorted as his gestures. He always seemed to be translating literally and laboriously from the Greek or the German. When he wished to fix in our minds the meaning of a Greek word he would say, for instance: "χάραδρα, a ravine, from which our word *character*, the deeply graven result of long-continued habit." Or "καταρρέω, to flow down, whence our word *catarrh*, copious down-flowings from the upper regions of the head." We didn't laugh, and we remembered.

Very different was dapper Mr. Groce, our teacher of English composition and literature, a little plump man, with a keen, dry, cheerful, yet irritable disposition, a sparkling bird-like eye, and a little black mustache and diminutive chin-beard. I suspect that he was too intelligent to put up patiently with all the conventions. Had he not been a public-school teacher, dependent on the demo-cratic hypocrisies of a government committee, he might have said unconventional things. This inner rebellion kept him from being sentimental, moralistic, or religious in respect to poetry; yet he *understood* perfectly the penumbra of emotion that good and bad poetry alike may drag after them in an untrained mind. He knew how to rescue the structural and rational beauties of a poem from that bog of private feeling. To me this was a timely lesson, for it was precisely sadness and religiosity and grandiloquence that first attracted me in poetry; and perhaps I owe to Mr. Groce the beginnings of a capacity to distinguish the musical and expressive charm of poetry from its moral appeal. At any rate, at sixteen, I composed my first longish poem, in Spenser's measure, after *Childe Harold* and *Adonais*, full of pessimistic, languid, Byronic senti-ments, describing the various kinds of superiority that Night has over Day. It got the prize.

That year I won several other prizes, and began to be a per-sonage in my own estimation, because other people, in my little world, began to take notice of me. At home I had never been petted or praised, and my conceit, which was rather disdain for other things than claims for myself, had had only itself to feed upon. Being noticed had a good effect on me in awakening my sympathy in return without, however, either establishing or much modifying my good opinion of myself. Neither praise nor blame has ever done so. On the contrary, if people praise me I almost always feel that they praise me for the wrong things, for things which they impute to me out of their preconceptions, and which are not in me; and the blame often, though not always, has the same source. Yet blame is apt to be more keen-scented than praise; praise is often silly; but blame, though it may be baseless objectively, probably indicates a true perception of divergence from the critic's standards: so that relatively to the critic, it is seldom mistaken.

I have mentioned declamation: that was another stimulus to vanity. Inwardly it was one more dramatic indulgence, one more occasion for fantastically playing a part, and •dreaming awake; as I did in making plans of vast palaces and imaginary islands, where I should one day be monarch, like Sancho Panza; and this slides into the sphere of my youthful religiosity, of which more presently. But, socially considered, declamation was an effort *de se faire valoir*, to make oneself count, to gain a momentary and fictitious ascendency over others. Momentary and fictitious, because our declamation was pure oratory. It had nothing of that political timeliness which characterizes young people's debates in England. With us, the subject matter was legendary, the language learned by rote, stilted and inflated, the thought platitudinous. Apart from the training in mere *elocution* (as indeed it was called) it was practice in feigning, in working up a verbal enthusiasm for any cause, and seeming to prophesy any event. Very useful, no doubt, for future lawyers, politicians, or clergymen—training for that reversible sophistry and propaganda that intoxicates the demagogue and misleads the people.

That prize-day in June, 1880, in the old Boston Music Hall, marked my emergence into public notice. It abolished, or seemed

to abolish, my shyness and love of solitude. I could now face any
public and speak before it; and this assurance never forsook me
afterwards, except when sometimes, in my unwritten lectures or
speeches, I found myself out of my element, had nothing to say,
or was weary of saying it. In reality I was always out of my element in teaching and in society, and was saying something forced.
The dramatic practice of accepting a brief, or developing an argument, helped me for a time. I could be sincere and spontaneous in
the logic of my theme, even if the ultimate issue were unreal or
problematical; and in reviewing the history of philosophy this
critical honesty is enough, and supplies the information and the
dialectical training that are officially required. Nevertheless, this
was not preaching a gospel. It did not come from the heart. It left
the pupil unguided and morally empty, and in the end the teacher
felt himself a drudge. My shyness came back in what Hegelians
would call a higher form: I was no longer timid or without resource, but rebellious against being roped in and made to play
some vulgar trick in a circus. My love of solitude reasserted itself,
not that I feared the world, but that I claimed my liberty and my
Lebensraum beyond it. In solitude it is possible to love mankind;
in the world, for one who knows the world, there can be nothing
but secret or open war. For those who love war the world is an
excellent field, but I am a born cleric or poet. I must see both
sides and take neither, in order, ideally, to embrace both, to sing
both, and love the different forms that the good and the beautiful
wear to different creatures. This comprehensiveness in sympathy
by no means implies that good and evil are indistinguishable or
dubious. Nature sets definite standards for every living being: the
good and the beautiful could not exist otherwise; and the failure
or lapse of natural perfection in each is an irreparable evil. But
it is, in every case, a ground of sorrow to the spirit, not of rage;
for such failure or lapse is fated and involuntary. This sorrow in
my case, however, has always been mitigated by the gift of
laughter. Laughter helped me both to perceive those defects and
to put up with them.

Between the laughing and the weeping philosopher there is no opposition: *the same facts* that make one laugh make one weep. No whole-hearted man, no sane art, can be limited to either mood. In me this combination seems to be readier and more pervasive than in most people. I laugh a great deal, laugh too much, my friends tell me; and those who don't understand me think that this merriment contradicts my disillusioned philosophy. *They*, apparently, would never laugh if they admitted that life is a dream, that men are animated automata, and that the forms of good and beautiful are as various and evanescent as the natural harmonies that produce them. They think they would collapse or turn to stone, or despair and commit suicide. But probably they would do no such thing: they would adapt themselves to the reality, and laugh. They might even feel a new zest in living, join in some bold adventure, become heroes, and think it glorious to die with a smile for the love of something beautiful. They do not perceive that this is exactly what national leaders and religious martyrs have always done, except that their warm imagination has probably deceived them about the material effects of what they were doing.

My lachrymose prize poem about the beauties of darkness was not my only effusion. The habit of scribbling mocking epigrams has accompanied me through life and invaded the margins of my most serious authors. Mockery is the first puerile form of wit, playing with surfaces without sympathy: I abounded in it. During the winter of 1880–1881 our class, then the second class, formed a society to meet once a week in the evening and have a debate. We hired a bare room in Tremont Street, opposite the Common, with a few benches or chairs in it; some one would propose a resolution or advance an opinion, and the discussion would follow. When my turn came, I read a little satire on all our teachers, in verse, saying very much what I have said about them above; only that my account was more complete, included them all, and treated them less kindly. It had a great success, and the boys wanted to have it printed. Printed it was, but not as it originally stood. "Holy Moses," for instance, which was the nickname current for our headmaster, Moses Merrill, was changed to the less irreverent and more exact phrase: "lordly Moses," and many other things were modified. Then the whole was enveloped in a tirade, of a sentimental sort, about the Bedford Street Schoolhouse, which was about to be abandoned for a new building in the South End. A lot of copies were printed, perhaps two or three hundred; and on the day of our Farewell Public Declamation in the Hall, the Headmaster somehow got wind of its existence, and said, "We hear that one of the boys has written a poem about leaving this old Schoolhouse: will he get up and read it." I had a copy in my pocket: I got up, and read the longish sentimental part and then sat down again, leaving out the personalities. For the moment all was well; but other boys and some outsiders got copies; and the disrespectful gibes at the teachers became public under their noses.

It was a day or two before Christmas, and the School was not to meet again for ten days or more: however, after consulting with the family at home, I went to see the Headmaster at his own house, and explained how everything had happened. He wasn't severe; I had been really very complimentary to him, and had come spontaneously to apologize. But he said I had better write to the various teachers, explaining that I had only intended the thing as a private joke, without any thought that it would become public; and that I must particularly apologize to Mr. Chadwick, whom I had spoken of unkindly, and who felt the blow. When School met again, Mr. Merrill made us a long speech; but nothing more happened, and official sentiment towards me was not unfavorably affected. This appeared at the opening of the next term. My class had to elect the Lieutenant Colonel of the Boston School Regiment, the Colonel that year coming from the English High School; and by a majority of one vote they elected Dick Smith, and then me unanimously for Major of our Battalion. But the Headmaster reversed the order, and appointed me Lieutenant Colonel and Dick Smith Major, without giving reasons, at which legal but arbitrary exhibition of favoritism on the Headmaster's part Dick Smith's father took him out of the School; and I became both

Lieutenant Colonel and Major, both offices being almost sine-
cures.

These incidents established me during my last year as, in a
sense, the leading boy in my school, far as I was from being the
head of my class: yet in my irregular way I was not bad at my
studies, and got six honorable mentions in my Harvard entrance
examinations. This capacity of mine to pass examinations and to
win prizes was doubtless what had caused Mr. Merrill to prefer
me to Dick Smith for the head of the School Battalion; because
Dick Smith was a clean manly boy and a gentleman, but not an
intellectual luminary. This sporadic brilliancy of mine seemed to
render me a better representative of the School as a whole—a surprising and only momentary phenomenon. In reality I remained
there, as I remained later at Harvard for twenty-five years, a
stranger at heart; and all the false appearances to the contrary
would not have misled anybody (as they did not mislead President
Eliot and the intelligent public at Harvard) if *athletics* had been
important at that time in the School. Now, although there was, I
believe, a baseball team, it was an obscure unofficial affair; else my
complete uselessness, either as a performer or as manager in such
sports, would have at once set me down for a stray individual of no
importance to the life of the place. Not that I had then, or ever,
any *ideal* hostility to sport or to polite society or even to politics or
trade. As customs, as institutions, as historical dramas, these things
interest and please me immensely and excite my imagination to
sympathy with this form of them or antipathy to that other form.
But I can truly live only in the reaction of the mind upon them
in religion, poetry, history, and friendship. If I take a practical
part, it is only by putting on a domino for the carnival. I am
capable of that impulse, I can feel the fun and the intoxication of
it; but the louder the rout the greater the frivolity, and the more
complete the relief of stripping off the motley, washing away the
paint, and returning to solitude, to silence, and to sincerity.

CHAPTER XI

THE CHURCH OF THE IMMACULATE CONCEPTION

WHEN I began, in this small way, to play a part in the world and to be absorbed in it, was I awaking from my childish daydreams—my imaginary architecture and geography and my imaginary religion—and entering into real life? Or was I being seduced and distracted from my natural vocation, and caught in the vortex of a foolish dance where I could neither shine as a reveller nor find satisfaction as a mind?

Now when at an advanced age I look back upon my whole career, I think I can reply to this question. At bottom there was no real change, no awakening and no apostasy. There was only a change in the subject matter on which my fancy worked. I had new materials for my dreams, and other terms in which to express my secret aspiration. Instead of being an ineffectual poet I became, at intervals, a mediocre player: in both directions I was simply the artist. There was ultimately no material issue, in either case: it all inevitably ended in nothing. But in both cases there was a passing music of ideas, a dramatic vision, a theme for dialectical insight and laughter; and to decipher that theme, that vision, and that music was my only possible life.

This is a book of memoirs, not of philosophical argument, and I have no wish to browbeat the reader into accepting my theory of myself or of anything else. Let me return at once to my narrative and let him judge the facts for himself.

In the Boston of my boyhood there were two churches served by the Jesuits. The more modest one was a parish church for the German-speaking population, in which the Jesuits were mission-

aries under the direct authority of the Archbishop. Here I used to
go sometimes to an early Mass on Sundays, always alone. Mass
was said in the basement, low, dark, flat-roofed, and perfectly bare,
except for the altar and the Stations of the Cross hung around the
walls. But it was filled with a devout, decent crowd, chiefly men;
and they sang in unison several German hymns, simply, gladly,
and unaffectedly, yet rather musically as if they were singing
glees. I thought that here must be the origin of the Protestant
practice of psalm-singing: they had knocked off most of the Mass,
but kept the popular German accompaniment of a general chorus,
as in the Greek tragedies. Yet what a difference between these
Catholic effusions, which were not substitutes for the ritual but a
private and spontaneous participation in it, and the perfunctory,
inaudible pretense at keeping up with the paid quartet that was
really performing; where the music was not good enough to be
listened to for a concert, and the words too crude and obsoletely
doctrinal to express anybody's feelings—at least not in those Unitarian churches which, at that time, I was being taken to against
my will. It was in order to find myself for a moment in a religious
atmosphere that I got up before dawn on those winter mornings,
and took that double walk at a great pace, perhaps over snow, in
any case through deserted streets in biting weather. But I liked
the communal spirit of those people, devout and unspoiled; I liked
their singing, without myself understanding the words; and
though the priest turned round after the Gospel and said something in German, it was not a sermon, only a few announcements
or admonitions for the coming week; and the strange language
lifted me out of time and place, into the universal fold of all pilgrim spirits. I also liked the long double walk, with its slight
tang of hardship, I who never had real hardships to bear: and
breakfast afterwards seemed better than usual. Walking has always
been my sole form of exercise; and then I never went out merely
to walk, but only to get to and from school; and here was the
same kind of errand, only more voluntary, done with a more
concentrated mind.

If later I was taken to some Unitarian Church, it didn't matter. It seemed a little ridiculous, all those good people in their Sunday clothes, so demure, so conscious of one another, not needing in the least to pray or to be prayed for, nor inclined to sing, but liking to flock together once a week, as people in Spain flock to the *paseo*, and glad to hear a sermon like the leading article in some superior newspaper, calculated to confirm the conviction already in them that their bourgeois virtues were quite sufficient and that perhaps in time poor backward races and nations might be led to acquire them.

The other church served by the Jesuits was entirely their own, being attached to their Boston College, and built and managed according to their taste and traditions. It was not a parish, but attracted unattached or inquiring people from any quarter. Jesuit policy did not forbid certain attractions not found in poorer churches. The edifice was not—as often happened in those days— a Protestant meetinghouse turned into a church; nor did it attempt to rival the picturesqueness of an ivy-clad village church in a shady churchyard. It was frankly urban and rectangular, like a hall or a temple without columns, and without tower or belfry. The custom of the country demanded that the interior should be filled with pews, so that there could be no freedom of movement and no true vistas; yet the double row of high Ionic columns was imposing, and there were square vaults over the aisles, and a tunnel vault in the nave, without a clerestory. The whole was plaster or stucco, in my time painted white: nevertheless the ground-glass windows subdued the light, and turned this interior, for the benevolent eye, into an inoffensive harmony in grays. There was florid music: organist and choir attempted the most pretentious masses, Bach, Mozart, Schubert, Verdi, and on occasions threw in Rossini's *Stabat Mater* and Gounod's *Ave Maria*. On the great feasts we even had an orchestra in addition. I liked this rococo music, and I still remember and sing it to myself with pleasure. It *transports*; the means may be at times inferior, but the end is attained. The end is to escape to another world, to live freely for a while in a medium made by us and fit for us to live in. Not all that is artificial is good, because the artifice may escape control and become stupid or even vicious; and much that is natural is good, because we are vitalized by it; but only the artificial can be good expressly.

The adjoining College naturally required a good many teachers, so that a number of priests were available for preaching in the church, some of them, however, not quite masters of the English language. One pale Italian in particular was admirable on difficult points in the religious life, as for instance on the words: *My God, my God, why hast thou abandoned me?* The spiritual aspiration to abandon oneself here corrected the Jesuit's tendency to view salvation as a matter of legal give and take between God and man. We couldn't be saved I know if we didn't exist, and in that sense we must coöperate in our salvation; but the point is to be saved from ourselves morally while physically retaining our personal being and limitations. Tradition, since Plato, calls this method *mortification;* and the secret of it sometimes pierces through the machinery of religious ethics. More frequent and noted preachers, however, were the two successive heads of the College, Father Fulton and Father O'Connor. The latter was a young and very oratorical Irishman, eloquently proclaiming Catholic Truth against all heresies. It is not difficult for a man with a ready tongue and a good memory to pluck moral and theological arguments from the patristic garden. St. Augustine alone will furnish flowers for a thousand good sermons. And this practice of repeating ancient authorities cannot be taxed with laziness. More diligence and more conscience are shown in ransacking the Fathers than in ventilating one's casual notions; and Catholic preachers at least are expected to preach the Gospel, and not some message new to the age. But the Gospel arouses different feelings and meets with different opposition in successive times; and a mind sensitive to these influences can therefore preach it more usefully than if he merely echoed the words of the Gospel itself. Father

Fulton, of whom I have said something as confessor to my sister, was not eloquent; he was not warm; but he could explore the dialectics not only of doctrine but of sentiment; and it was in unravelling the complexities of our divided allegiance that I found him an instructive guide.

There was a feature in the interior of this church that, in my empty head, led to much architectural theorizing. The sanctuary, which was square, had an ordinary double vault lower than that of the nave; so that we were forever faced by two round arches of the same span, one of them two or three yards above the other. The space between them was awkward, and the architect had done nothing to disguise or relieve it. I knew very well that in basilicas the apse is often much lower than the nave; but there the semi-circular apse was not a sanctuary meant to house the altar, but only the head of the choir, round which the clergy had their stalls, with the bishop's or superior's throne in the middle; while the altar stood out in front, under an architectural canopy, and was approached by the priest from his end, looking eastward over the altar, and over the people beyond it; for in the original Christian basilicas in Rome the entrance is at the east end. Moreover, the arch of that apse is not surmounted by another arch, since the nave has a wooden roof, either showing the rafters or closed with a flat ceiling. In either case the arch has a rectangular setting, like a triumphal arch, and the triangles in the corners are adorned with mosaics or frescoes, to which they are admirably adapted. But in chapels or later churches, where the altar is set against a wall, or, as in the Cathedrals, stands at the extreme *chevet* or east end of the choir, the vault is never lower over the chancel or choir than over the nave: on the contrary, it might well be higher—as for instance it is at Le Mans and at Carcassone—with excellent effect and significance; while at St. Peter's the altar with its immense *baldacchino* stands under the vault of Michelangelo's dome, five hundred feet high.

Our local architect, then, whatever his model or reasons, was guilty of a solecism in designing those two equal, closely super-posed arches, and that chancel vault lower than his nave: but I was ready to forgive him in view of the favorable atmosphere that his interior, as a whole, offered me for meditation. The reredos contained three paintings, and the side altars in the aisles two more, all warm in color and acceptable in design—very likely copies of late Italian masters; their white plaster setting, with grouped columns, was graceful and pleasantly touched with gold in the moldings and ornaments; and above was a sensational baroque, curved pediment, broken in two, with two ecstatic saints kneeling perilously, but divinely confident, on the inclined upper surface of the two separated fragments. It was symmetrical, it was deco-rative, it was full of motion and enthusiasm. It warned me that there are more things going on in oneself than are dreamt of in our too economical philosophy.

When you looked, however, a little higher up, you saw things depicted as going on in heaven which, whatever may go on there, should not be so depicted on earth. Art, like mind, has its own categories and grammar for symbolizing realities beyond it, and makes nonsense if it violates them. Our language cannot control its objects, yet could not even indicate them if it destroyed itself. What you saw above the reredos, filling the whole space under the vault, was a painting, a fresco, I suppose, of the Assumption. The figure of the Virgin Mary was at the very top, as in Titian's *Assumption*, foreshortened, and clothed in the same dark red and dark blue; a heavy, materialistic, unworthy conception of the sub-ject. Out of place here, too, since this church was not dedicated to the Assumption, but to the Immaculate Conception. The Assump-tion is an alleged event; it is conceived to have occurred on earth, at a particular place and time; so that a treatment like Titian's, with the foreshortening, and with the drama of wonder and sur-prise in the crowd of witnesses, is not unjustified; and there the artist had a superabundant technique to exhibit in painting a great variety of gesticulating figures, a landscape, and an Italian sky. The Immaculate Conception, on the contrary, is a theological idea,* the notion of a human soul created perfect and spotless, with a body subject, like a flower, to the direct, unconscious, unimpeded magic of that soul. Why, then, not have filled this space with the accepted representation of the Immaculate Conception, after the manner of Murillo? An ethereal, girlish, angelic Madonna, clothed with the sun (the image is based on a passage in the Apocalypse), with the moon at her feet and the stars encircling her head, would have filled the center of the composition. Her garments would have been, in texture and color, like the sky and the light clouds; she would have floated as the sun in mid-heaven, and everything would have been tinted and softened by the radiance of a pervasive yet hidden light that she seemed to shed. In that heaven, any number of seraphs and cherubs that the artist could paint or could draw might have flown or soared as in their native element.

Cherubs? Seraphs? No: half a dozen large young women in modest evening gowns (except that their feet were bare), one pure yellow, one sea-green, another terracotta, with correspondingly large wings, like the Angel Mother in our engraving at home, all yearned aesthetically upward: and the central ones seemed anxious

* The non-theological reader must not be misled into thinking that the "Immaculate Conception" refers to the *Incarnation of Christ* without an earthly father, or to what Anglicans improperly call the "Virgin Birth." There is indeed a Catholic doctrine of the *perpetual* virginity of Mary, the *birth* of Christ being no less miraculous than his incarnation; a doctrine that my first Spanish catechism beautifully expressed by saying that the Child Jesus passed from his mother's bosom into her arms as a ray of sunlight passes through a pane of glass, without breaking or staining it. This might properly be called the "Virgin Birth," and is entirely distinct from the doctrine of the Incarnation contained in the Creed, and a later refinement upon it. The doctrine of the "Immaculate Conception," on the other hand, asserts that *the soul of the Virgin Mary herself* (though she was begotten and born like other people, except that her parents were unusually old) *did not inherit original sin from Adam*, being exempted by prevenient grace, in view of the redemption to be worked by her Son. As an inscription on her monument in the Piazza di Spagna in Rome has it, *Sanctificavit tabernaculum suum Altissimus*, the Most High had sanctified his tabernacle.

to hold up the Madonna, as if she were not levitating of her own accord. I don't know what models, if any, this composition may have followed, but it didn't please me. I was glad when on feast days a canopy with red and white hangings was set up to hide it, and to turn the altar, with all its lights and flowers, into a sort of throne. Regal and priestly grandeur, even dimly suggested, has always impressed me. In Egypt, in those colossal temples and profound sanctuaries, I envied the priests that once officiated there, faithful to immemorial traditions, and learned in mysterious conventions. It was somnambulism, but in a noble setting, healthful, protective, capable of perpetuating itself for generations, and of rendering human life humanly better rather than worse.

If ever I complained to my sister of those female angels and wondered how learned Jesuits could countenance such a lapse, she would say that angels were sexless, so that if artists might represent them as young men or boys or infants, why not, on occasion, as women? Theologically this was correct; angels are sexless, since they have no bodies, and according to St. Thomas, are each the only member of its species; so that in them any complications connected with reproduction are excluded *a priori*.* But theology— especially in regard to angels!—is something secondary: vision, inspiration, tradition, and literature come first. A Christian painter is not called upon to invent some form in which pure spirits might appear, nor is he likely to have seen them himself. What concerns him is not what they may be in heaven, but what they look like when visiting the earth. Now imagination has its specific hereditary idioms, just as the senses have; and if the artist be a Christian working for a Christian people he will be spontaneously borne along by the same tradition that has inspired the doctrines and visions of his Church; otherwise he would falsify the poetic character and tone of the themes that he illustrates. This will not deprive him of originality; he can be stylistic, hieratic, or picturesque,

* I refer to Catholic theology. In the *Jewish Book of the Jubilees*, assigned to about 100 B.C., we are informed that the angels in heaven are circumcised.

according to his taste or training: but he will cease to be a religious artist if he contradicts the revelation he has inherited.

Now in what form have angels appeared? The angels that came to Abraham's tent and the one that wrestled with Jacob were certainly men; and in the Old Testament it often seems that angels were strangers or travellers that gave some warning or left a mysterious impression and only afterwards were recognized to have been "angels of the Lord," or vehicles for a divine oracle. The Angel that appeared to Mary is understood to have been the archangel Gabriel, certainly no less masculine, if less military, than his companion Michael; so much so that his figure, like that of St. Joseph, was avoided in early Christian art, until the idiom of faith had become native to the popula˘ imagination, and it could be left free without danger of becoming equivocal. Then those innumerable charming Annunciations could be designed, where Gabriel is a royal page, as deferential as he is smiling and beautifully attired, gracefully bending the knee, gracefully delivering his embarrassing but important message, and ready gracefully to retire, perfectly pleased with himself and with his performance.* Or if direct and strangely crude evidence on the sex of angels were required it might be found in Genesis, where the angels sent to warn Lot cause a most embarrassing commotion in Sodom. Graver ambassadors are the two "young men" in white raiment seen sitting by the empty tomb on Easter morning, who speak mystically of not looking for the living among the dead. It is as if the soldiers on guard had turned, in the Evangelist's fancy, into young priests. They come to bring tidings of martyrdom and of a transfigured life. Sex is not absent here, as it is not absent in the monk or the mystic; it is expressly mentioned; yet it appears only in the firmness with which it is suppressed.

---

* *Cf.* Saint Bernard in Dante:

> *Baldezza e leggiadria,*
> *Quanta esser puote in angelo ed in alma,*
> *Tutta è in lui: e sì volem che sia.*
>
> Par. XXXII, 109–111.

Such was the mechanism of logic or poetry in mere ideas that occupied my mind when a boy: not expressed, of course, as I now express it, but intensely felt by me to determine the only right or beautiful order possible for the universe. Existence could not be right or beautiful under other conditions. But was existence beautiful or right? Quite the opposite; according to my youthful heart, existence was profoundly ugly and wrong. The beautiful remained imaginary. My daily life had nothing to do with it. Reality meant a dull routine of getting up in the morning, walking to school, sitting there for five hours, walking home, eating not very palatable food, and going to bed again. I was bored. I hadn't enough to do or enough to learn. At school there was nothing but lessons; and lessons in a large class, with indulgent teachers and slack standards of accuracy, meant perpetual idleness. I could have learned twice as much in half the time, had a better pace been set for me and more matter. In the absence of matter, I dreamt on a hungry stomach. But those ideal universes in my head did not produce any firm convictions or actual duties. They had nothing to do with the wretched poverty-stricken real world in which I was condemned to live. That the real was rotten and only the imaginary at all interesting seemed to me axiomatic. That was too sweeping; yet allowing for the rash generalizations of youth, it is still what I think. My philosophy has never changed. It is by no means an artificial academic hypothesis; it doesn't appeal at all to the professors; it is a system of presuppositions and categories discovered already alive and at work within me willy-nilly, like existence itself, and virtually present not only in the boy but in the embryo.

I say "within me," because there I have finally deciphered it by analysis; but it was not peculiar to me. It was common then in certain circles and was called pessimism. Pessimism is an accidental moralistic name for it; because the philosophy in question is a system of cosmology, a view of nature and history; moral preferences or judgments are not central in it. Whether a particular man is pessimistic because he dislikes the truth, or likes the truth and feels optimistic, makes but a slight difference in that total truth;

and such a feeling, turned into a sentence pronounced on the universe, seems, either way, rather impertinent. We speak of the fair, says a Spanish proverb, as we fare in it: and our personal fortunes may justly color our philosophy only if they are typical and repeat the fortunes of all living beings. I am not ashamed of my childish pessimism; it was honest; and it showed my courage in not letting my preferences cloud my perceptions nor my perceptions abash my preferences. The clash between them was painful, but not unnatural, and was destined to grow less painful with time, and this without any loss either of realism or of honor.

In spite, then, of my religious and other daydreams, I was at bottom a young realist; I knew I was dreaming, and so was awake. A sure proof of this was that I was never *anxious* about what those dreams would have involved if they had been true. I never had the least touch of superstition. To follow the logic of dogma and keep the feasts, if not the fasts, of the Church, was a part of the game; and the whole allegorical pseudo-historical pageant passed through my mind unchallenged, because I felt intimately the dramatic logic that had inspired it. But no logic can upset the facts. Thus it never occurred to me to shudder at the doctrine of eternal damnation, as the innocent Unitarians did or to be overawed by it, as were the innocent Calvinists. Hell is set down in the bond, like Shylock's pound of flesh: the play requires it. Of course damnation must be eternal, because every loss and every pain is irremediable. The consolation or peace said to wipe evil away, cannot wipe it out: you may forget it, but if you say you have annulled it, you are lying. Nothing that has ever occurred can be annulled. That is what eternal damnation means, or might be said to mean by a thinking being. But if you suppose that in an Inferno like Dante's you may soon be jumping about naked in a fiery furnace, you are dreaming. You are confusing poetry with fact. Never had I the least fear of a material hell or desire for a material heaven. The images were so violent, so childish, as to be comic.

The force of images is equivocal, reversible, hard to recover in memory. Two of my earliest effusions in verse were entitled: *To the Moon* and *To the Host*. The images were similar, and the sentiment in both cases was similar. The Host, I said, was "clear in faith's divine moonlight." It was "my only friend," much as the moon, to Endymion, might be the only goddess. And I sighed that my faith was "too like despair." The last word, what I really aspired to, was "peace." For this purpose the machinery of the sacraments was not needed, I had no wish to go to confession and communion, else I should have done so. My faith was indeed so like despair that it wasn't faith at all; it was fondness, liking, what in Spanish is called *afición*; I indulged in it, but only north-northwest, and keeping my freedom. I heartily agreed with the Church about the world, yet I was ready to agree with the world about the Church; and I breathed more easily in the atmosphere of religion than in that of business, precisely because religion, like poetry, was more ideal, more freely imaginary, and in a material sense falser.

Those verses were written when I was fifteen or sixteen, and before my prize poem. Seven years later, when I had studied philosophy and travelled, the same position is described, more cynically in the Byronic manner. The lines are entitled *At the Church Door*; I will quote one stanza from memory.

> Ah, if salvation were a trick of reason
> How easily would all the world be saved!
> But roses bloom not in the winter season
> Nor hope of heaven in a heart enslaved.
> To break the bond with earth were easy treason
> If it were God alone the bosom craved;
> But we have chosen thrift and chosen rest
> And with our wings' plucked feathers built our nest.*

* A friend of mine who was a bird-fancier (I mean who liked shooting) observed that here I had hit on a true simile without knowing it; some birds did pluck their feathers in nest-building, but from their breasts. I believe I corrected my manuscript accordingly, spoiling the sense: because what I meant was that we sacrificed our capacity for flight, under pressure of blind commitments or in mere apathy.

Here the drama had become frankly subjective: the turn it would take depended on the weather. Ideal flights, reason, heaven and union with God did not compose another world or carry us there; they were methods, directions, or goals of thought, habits that the human spirit developed under favorable conditions, when it was free. But for the most part, and especially then (in the 1880's), the mind was wretchedly servile, vulgarized, and absorbed in instrumentalities. And the worst of it was that we had lost courage and foresworn our vocation. We were not like a good dog that, if compelled to cross a river, hurries to the other bank, and shakes the water vigorously from his skin as soon as he gets there; we wallowed in our muddy bath like pigs in a sty, pretended that we positively enjoyed it, and paid our philosophers in obsequiousness if not in money for telling us that at least we were doing our duty.

From the boy dreaming awake in the church of the Immaculate Conception, to the travelling student seeing the world in Germany, England, and Spain there had been no great change in sentiment. I was still "at the church door." Yet in belief, in the clarification of my opinions, I had taken an important step. I no longer wavered between alternate views of the world, to be put on or taken off like alternate plays at the theatre. I now saw that there was only one possible play, the actual history of nature and of mankind, although there might well be ghosts among the characters and soliloquies among the speeches. Religions, *all* religions, and idealistic philosophies, *all* idealistic philosophies, were the soliloquies and the ghosts. They might be eloquent and profound. Like Hamlet's soliloquy they might be excellently reflective criticisms of the play as a whole. Nevertheless they were only parts of it, and their value as criticisms lay entirely in their fidelity to the facts, and to the sentiments which those facts aroused in the critic.

Two other important steps remained to be taken before my philosophy was wholly clarified and complete: I shall speak of them when it comes to my successive books. Yet it may be well to mention those two points here, in order that the skein of my meditations at the Immaculate Conception may be seen unravelled. One step was to overcome moral and ideal provinciality, and to see that every form of life had its own perfection, which it was stupid and cruel to condemn for differing from some other form, by chance one's own. The other step, rising above the moral dissolution that might invade a man who cultivated an indiscriminate sympathy with every form of life, made it clear that sympathy and justice themselves are only relative virtues, good only in their place, for those lives or forms of life that thereby reach their perfection: so that integrity or self-definition is and remains first and fundamental in morals: and the right of alien natures to pursue their proper aims can never abolish our right to pursue ours.

Why, before taking these final steps, had I stood so long "at the church door," with regret at never having really lived inside? I might prefer ideally an imaginary Atlantis to any earthly island: but how puerile and helpless to languish after it and not at once to make the best of the real world! I think there was a congenital transcendentalism in me, long before I heard of transcendental philosophy or understood it. I had a spontaneous feeling that life is a dream. The scene might entirely disappear at any moment, or be entirely transformed. There could be no *a priori*, strictly even no empirical, presumption against anything whatsoever. The volume and solidity of one apparition, of one imposed world, could never insure its perpetuity, much less prevent the reality or perpetuity of a thousand other worlds.

Now this, I am still convinced, is an invincible intuition: yet this invincible intuition, in its absoluteness and purity, leaves the mind empty and rescinds all faith. If it were the principle of life (which it is not) it would condemn us to suspended animation and the sense of infinite potentiality unrealized: the crystal vision, umbilical contemplations, and my childish verses *To the Moon* and *To the Host*. The light of spirit is indeed pure and unprejudiced, open, like the young eye, to whatsoever there may be. But this light is kindled by something else and it must fall on something else, if it is to reveal anything. It is kindled in an animal psyche, in a living perishable heart; and it falls on the world in which that heart and that psyche have been formed, and is deeply dyed in their particular passions. If, then, we are to see or to believe in anything, it must be at the bidding of natural accidents, by what I call faith: and the alternatives open to pure spirit are not open to rational belief. Rational belief must have other guides than sheer imagination exploring infinite possibilities. Those guides can be, logically, nothing but accidents; but they have a compulsory presence and evoke an inescapable adhesion, confidence, and trust; which trust is fortified by experiment and found trustworthy.

My instinctive transcendentalism or solipsism was, as I think, quite right analytically; but I was confused in playing with it as a criterion or judge of beliefs. Beliefs have an earthly origin and can be sanctioned only by earthly events.

CHAPTER XII

FIRST FRIENDS

IT WAS also at the age of sixteen that I began to notice the characters and quality of the other boys, and to find my ideal affinities. I say ideal affinities, because I had always had instinctive or canine friends: boys or girls—for there were several girls—with whom I played or prattled, or danced at the dancing school. There, at about the age of ten, I had a sort of *amourette*: absolutely groundless and silent, but absolutely determined. I remember the child perfectly. She had a dark complexion and curly black hair, and stood very straight, but gracefully. She was the first example to me of that admirable virtue cultivated by French actresses; eloquent stillness. I don't think she ever said a word, and I very few: but we always took each other out to dance, and were partners for the cotillion. Her name was Alice White, and I have never seen or heard of her since then. It was the friendship of two genteel kittens, who played gravely with the same ball, and eschewed the rest of the litter.

A less enigmatic companionship of my boyhood was with Charlie Davis. He was a soft blond youth, a little older and taller than I, but mentally younger: our great pleasure was to laugh about everything, like silly girls. But in our daily walks from school we must have gabbled on many subjects, because after some years —he left school young to go into an office—he became a Catholic, and asked me to be his sponsor at his christening. I was; and I remember later his desire to enter a religious order, to which his previous incidental entanglements with the fair sex proved a fatal obstacle. Must all novices be virgins? Probably only in that (Paulist) order, and in America. Our friendship died out: but he con-

tinued all his life to write occasionally to my sister Susana, partly
on religious subjects and partly in a tone of amiable banter and
comic pessimism. Let us hope, if I didn't save my own soul, that
I saved the soul of Charlie Davis.

He was by no means my first friend. The first was Gorham
Hubbard, at Miss Welchman's Kindergarten; the next was Bob
Upham, at the Brimmer School: and in him I first tasted two of
the sweets of friendship, which have regaled me since in many a
"nice fellow"; guidance or good judgment in practical matters—
which it is always a pleasure for me to follow if I can trust the
guide—and the quality of simple gentleman, a clean upstanding
independence and a sureness in everything personal and moral.
My favorite young gentlemen haven't always turned out well; they
have often gone to the dogs; but that was on account of a virtue
which lent them a chivalrous and aristocratic charm, namely,
indifference to public opinion, and courage in running risks.

I had also had several fancy-friends—little more than dream
images of a foolish sentimental sort. The reality of their persons
mattered little; they were simply knobs on which to hang my own
reveries. But now, in my second class year, the manly note sounds
for the first time. A common intelligence, a common readiness—
spes animi credula mutui—allies two young men in the presence of
a common world.

My first real friend was Bentley Warren. We two with Dick
Smith (who afterwards took his mother's name Weston) formed
what we called the Triumvirate. Warren was the link between the
other two of us, who hadn't very much in common, except perhaps
a better breeding than most of the boys at the Latin School. This
school, being public (i.e. free), was naturally frequented by the
ambitious poor—Irish boys wishing to be priests, lawyers, or doctors,
Jews wishing to be professors, and native Americans, like Warren
and Smith, whose families were in reduced circumstances. It was
my mother's straitened means that caused her to send me there,
instead of to some private school; and I should perhaps have
seemed an entirely different person, and had an entirely different

life, if this genteel poverty and this education in a public day school, among children of humble parents, had not fortified me in the spirit of detachment and isolation. Not that the most luxurious of American surroundings—such as I afterwards had some contact with—would ever have made an American of me. America in those days made an exile and a foreigner of every native who had a temperament at all like mine.

Warren's father, who had recently died, had been a Democratic congressman, elected in an off year of public dissatisfaction in a suburb of Boston, usually Republican; but two years of life in Washington, together with inherited dissentient opinions, had given his son a freer intelligence and a more varied experience than little Bostonians were apt to have. I often went to Mrs. Warren's to tea on holidays; and Warren sometimes came to lunch at our house. His Democratic views—if he had them—were not rabid; his most intimate friends were Harry and Jim Garfield, sons of the future President of the United States; and he left school at the end of our second class year in order to enter Williams College with the Garfields, a year before the rest of us were expected to be ready for the university. Dick Smith, too, on account of the tiff his father had with the Headmaster, left school early during our last year; so that as far as friendship was concerned—so new to me but so important—the end of my school life might have been desolate.

Not that my relations with Warren were broken off: we wrote each other long letters; and four years later, in 1885, I went to Williamstown for the festivities at his graduation. I think it was my first journey undertaken merely for pleasure, and at my own expense. Ward Thoron had invited me to his grandfather's at Lenox, and I combined the two visits. I have been to Williams and to Lenox again: to read a lecture in the one (on Shelley) and to "Ja" Burden's wedding in the other. There had been intervals of twenty or twenty-five years: Harry Garfield was president of the College; we spoke of Bentley Warren and of the old days, but with how different a sentiment! For me those things had passed into the empyrean, into an eternal calm where their littleness or their greatness was nothing and their quality, their essence, everything; for him they were merely early unimportant phases of the business which occupied him now, and not to be regarded on their own account. When I mentioned Bentley Warren, Garfield said: "Oh, yes. He is one of the Trustees of our College." From this I gathered two things: that Warren had been "successful" and was now rich; and that for Garfield this fact was what counted in Warren rather than their early friendship. I expressed surprise that in their Faculty Room they had no portrait of his father—an old member of the College and a President of the United States: and he said it was not for him to suggest that. Why not? Because it might seem egotistical? But why didn't his Trustees or whoever governed behind him—for Presidents of Colleges are secondary powers—take a gentle hint or spontaneously attend to something so obviously proper? I suppose they were always thinking of the future. A portrait in the Faculty Room would hardly have been an advertisement; it would only have been an act of homage. Let the past paint its own pictures.

My school friends were gone; but just beyond school bounds a new friend appeared, Edward Bayley. I was Lieutenant Colonel of the Boston School Regiment, the Colonel that year being from the English High School which, back to back with the Latin School, was housed in the other half of the same new building. In some matter of vital importance to our forces it became necessary for me to consult my superior officer. We met by appointment, and found that the high questions of epaulettes or of buttons were soon disposed of; but that first interview made us fast friends. We happened to live in the same quarter of the town, the Back Bay, about a mile from our schools, and we at once established the custom of waiting, he for me or I for him, at the corner, so as to walk home together. Yet this did not last many weeks, because that winter my mother moved to Roxbury, having at last got rid of the dreadful burden of our Beacon Street house; so that I saw my new friend only occasionally, or by express appointment. But that made no difference. The bond was established, silently of course, but safely. Even the fact that he was not going to College, but directly into some place of business, so that as it actually came about, we never saw each other after that year, and hardly a letter passed between us, made no difference in our friendship, though it entirely separated our lives. Strange enchantment! Even today, the thought of that youthful comradeship, without incidents, without background, and without a sequel, warms the cockles of my heart like a glass of old port.

There is a sort of indifference to time, as there is a sort of silence, which goes with veritable sympathy. It springs from clear possession of that which is, from sureness about it. Those who are jealous, jealous of time, of rivals, of accidents, care for something vague that escapes them now, and that would always escape them; they are haunted souls, hunting for they know not what. Not so those who know what they love and rest in it, asking for nothing more. If circumstances had led Bayley and me to go through life together, we should have stuck to each other against any incidental danger or enemy; there would have been something to tell about our comradeship; but there would have been nothing new in our friendship. Clearness and depth in the heart, as in the intellect, transpose everything into the eternal.

Is that all? What did he do? What did he say? What did he stand for? I confess that after sixty years I have to invent a theory to account for this fact. I have to compare that sudden, isolated, brief attachment with other friendships of mine that had something of its quality, but were circumstantially more describable. We were eighteen years old, and there was nothing in us except ourselves. Now, in himself, apart from circumstances, Bayley was like Warwick Potter, only stronger. In Warwick the same type of character, weaker although at the time of our intimacy he was much older, was made describable by his social background and breeding. He had been brought up in the most select and superior way in which it was then possible to be brought up in America. Not through mere wealth or fashion, because his widowed mother was neither very rich nor very well connected. He and his brothers would point out with glee that their mother's relations were a little common. But their father had been a general in the Civil War, and their uncle was the Anglican Bishop of New York: pontiff, that is, to the cream of rich and fashionable America. Moreover, Warwick and his brothers had been among the very first pupils of Mr. Peabody, on founding the Groton School, so that they received the fresh imprint of all those high and amiable intentions, and all that personal paternal care and spiritual guidance which it was Mr. Peabody's ideal to supply. School had been a second home to Warwick, and a real home. For, more than his brothers, he was sensitive to this type of distinctively English, homelike, refined sentiment, by which religion was merged in romantic and artistic memories, as well as in political pride, and in the sheer love of nature and freedom; only the sporting and military side of this education had not yet been much developed. This was to come later, with a certain standardized mentality and political ambition. In the early 1890's the rich dreamt of culture rather than of leadership. Warwick, who was young for his age, was particularly open to new impressions, plastic, immensely amused, a little passive and feminine. It was hard to say what he would have turned into if he had lived. And yet the dominant trait in him, as in Bayley, was clear goodness, the absence of all contaminations, such as the very young are sometimes proud of. He was sure, in great things as in little, to prefer the better to the worse; he delighted in pleasant ways and people, and he was religious. Love of historic Christianity opened to him a wonderful world existing before and beyond America. He felt at home in England and in the Church. He was civilized.

Now, how did it happen that Bayley who had nothing of that breeding and education, nevertheless possessed the same or a deeper intelligence of spiritual things? Why did a strictly Puritan and inward religion in him, far from producing narrowness or fanaticism, produce charity and hospitality of mind? Not that he was in the least what was called liberal, that is, indifferent and vaguely contemptuous towards all definite doctrines or practices, and without any discipline of his own. On the contrary he was absolutely loyal to his own tradition, and master of it; he was made, finished, imposing in the precision of his affections. He had perfect integrity (where Warwick had only blamelessness), yet he had sweetness too, affection for what he excluded from his own sphere, justice to what he renounced, happiness in the joys of others that were not joys to him, so that his very limitations were turned into admirable virtues. Here was this manly boy, taller and stronger than I, firmly and contentedly rooted in his New England Congregationalism, yet accepting, respecting and even envying *me* for being everything that he was not and did not expect to be. There was no shadow of the pathos of distance in this; it was honest religious comprehension that there are many vintages in the Lord's vineyard, and many different things that are beautiful and good. Where did Bayley learn this?

In his spiritual heritage there were doubtless certain naturalistic maxims that may have struck him in sermons or in casual reading. There was Milton with his Latinity and his Italian sonnets; and there was the young Emerson, a sort of Puritan Goethe, the Emerson of *Nature*, before he had slipped into transcendentalism and moralism and complacency in mediocrity. I may be reading ideals of my own into that very young man, in whom nothing of the sort may ever have come to light; but potentially I cannot help thinking that in him there was something more that those great men never possessed: I mean humility and renunciation. A dumb inglorious Milton who was not a prig, an Emerson with warm blood, who was not proud or oracular or cosmographical, and never thought himself the center of the universe. Young Bayley was my first, perhaps my fundamental, model for *The Last Puritan*.

It was doubtless the discovery that we were both—but differently—religious, that made us so quickly sure of each other. Never was trust more instinctive, more complete, or more silent. It has lasted in silence, at least on my side, for sixty years. Not long ago

I asked a Boston friend who turned up at Cortina about these very first friends of mine, Warren and Bayley. Did he know them? Were they still living? What had become of them? And I was not surprised to hear the warmest eulogy of both, although my informant was a Lyman of the Lymans and a Lowell of the Lowells, while Warren and Bayley were not descendants of the Boston Brahmins. And I said to myself, "Oh, my prophetic soul!" My earliest friendships were not illusions.

CHAPTER XIII

THE HARVARD YARD

I F FORTUNE had been unkind to me in respect to my times
—except that for the intellectual epicure the 1890's were
enjoyable—in respect to places fortune has been most
friendly, setting me down not in any one center, where
things supposed to be important or exciting were happening, but
in various quiet places from which cross-vistas opened into the
world. Of these places the most familiar to me, after Avila, was
the Harvard Yard. I lived there for eleven years, first as an undergraduate, later as an instructor and proctor. No place, no rooms,
no mode of living could have been more suitable for a poor student and a free student, such as I was and as I wished to be. My
first room, on the ground floor in the northeast corner of Hollis,
was one of the cheapest to be had in Cambridge: the rent was
forty-four dollars a year. I had put it first for that reason on my list
of rooms, and I got my first choice. It was so cheap because it had
no bedroom, no water, and no heating; also the ground floor seems
to have been thought less desirable, perhaps because the cellar
below might increase the cold or the dampness. I don't think I was
ever cold there in a way to disturb me or affect my health. I kept
the hard-coal fire banked and burning all night, except from Saturday to Monday, when I slept at my mother's at Roxbury. An
undergraduate's room in any case is not a good place for study, unless it be at night, under pressure of some special task. At other
times, there are constant interruptions, or temptations to interrupt
oneself: recitations, lectures, meals, walks, meetings, and sports. I
soon found the Library the best place to work in. It was not
crowded; a particular alcove where there were philosophical books

at hand, and foreign periodicals, soon became my regular place for
reading. I could take my own books and notebooks there if necessary; but for the most part I browsed; and although my memory is
not specific, and I hardly know what I read, except that I never
missed *La Revue des Deux Mondes,* I don't think my time was
wasted. A great deal stuck to me, without my knowing its source,
and my mind became accustomed to large horizons and to cultivated judgments.

As to my lodging, I had to make up my sofa bed at night before
getting into it; in the morning I left the bedding to be aired, and
the "goody," whose services were included in the rent, put it
away when she came to dust or to sweep. I also had to fetch my
coal and water from the cellar, or the water in summer from the
College pump that stood directly in front of my door. This was
economy on my part, as I might have paid the janitor to do it for
me; perhaps also to black my boots, which I always did myself, as
I had done it at home. But my life was a miracle of economy. I had
an allowance from my mother of $750 a year to cover all expenses.
Tuition absorbed $150; rent, $44; board at Memorial Hall, with
a reduction for absence during the week-end, about $200; which
left less than one dollar a day for clothes, books, fares, subscrip-
tions, amusements, and pocket money. Sometimes, but very rarely,
I received a money-prize or a money-present; I had no protection or
encouragement from rich relations or persons of influence. The
Sturgises were no longer affluent, and as yet they hardly knew of
my existence. Later, when their natural generosity could (and
did) express itself, it did so in other ways, because I was already
independent and needed no help. Yet on my less than one dollar
a day I managed to dress decently, to belong to minor societies like
the Institute, the Pudding, and the O.K., where the fees were
moderate, to buy all necessary books, and even, in my Junior year,
to stay at rich people's houses, and to travel. Robert had given me
his old evening clothes, which fitted me well enough: otherwise
the rich people's houses could not have been visited.

Doing my "chores" was something I rather liked, as I still brush and pack my own clothes for pleasure, and shave myself, and walk everywhere rather than drive, circumstances permitting. A little manual work or physical exercise changes the stops agreeably, lengthens the focus and range of vision, reverts to the realm of matter which is the true matrix of mind, and generally brings judgment and feeling back into harmony with nature. I have never had a man servant and later when I lived in hotels I seldom called on the servants for any personal service not in their common routine. This trait is a heritage from the humble condition of my father's family and my mother's reduced circumstances during my boyhood. I had not an aristocratic breeding; not only was I not served, but I was taught no aristocratic accomplishments, not even riding or driving or shooting or dancing. What is a gentleman? A gentleman is a man with a valet: originally he also had a sword, but in my time that was obsolete except for officers in full uniform; a bank account could take its place. But having many servants, though it makes a man a master, does not make him a gentleman. He is not one because his wife may keep servant girls in the house; he is one only if he has a body servant of his own. This defines the Spanish gentleman as well as the English gentleman, yet differently. The relation in Spain is or was more confidential, more general, more moral: the man served his master in all his affairs. In England, it is more a matter of laying out all his master's things. However, I confess that the mere fop is not a complete gentleman, however dependent he may be on his valet. To be a complete gentleman he should also have a horse, and should ride it gallantly. Don Quixote, too, had a horse, as well as a servant.

Life in the Yard for me, during my second period of residence there, 1890–1896, had a different quality. I hadn't a horse or a valet, but could count on enough pocket-money, a varied circle of friends, clubs, and ladies' society in Boston and Cambridge, and the foreglow and afterglow of holidays spent in Europe. The first year, when I had only one foot in the stirrup and was not yet in the saddle as a Harvard teacher, I lived in Thayer; graceless quarters and the insecure stammering beginnings of a lecturer. The

THE HARVARD YARD 189

only thing I remember is the acquaintance I then made with my next-door neighbor, Fletcher, who was afterwards a professor of Comparative Literature and made a translation of the *Divina Commedia*. He was also a football player; and I remember one day when I was violently sick at my stomach—my digestion in those days being imperfect—he thought to help me by holding my head (a common illusion among helpful people) and his grasp was like a ring of iron. He was a very good fellow, with a richer nature than most philologists, and firm morals. We had long talks and discovered common tastes in literature and the arts; but he didn't remain at Harvard, and I lost sight of him. Even if he had been at hand, we should hardly have seen each other often: there were things in us fundamentally inaccessible to one another. Besides, though I became a professor myself, I never had a real friend who was a professor. Is it jealousy, as among women, and a secret unwillingness to be wholly pleased? Or is it the consciousness that a professor or a woman has to be partly a sham; whence a mixture of contempt and pity for such a poor victim of necessity? In Fletcher, and in the nobler professors, the shamming is not an effect of the profession, but rather, as in inspired clergymen, the profession is an effect of an innate passion for shamming. Nobody feels that passion more than I have felt it in poetry and in religion; but I never felt it in academic society or academic philosophy, and I gave up being a professor as soon as I could.

The next year I again had my pick of rooms in the Yard, securing No. 7 Stoughton, in the southeast corner of the first floor, where I stayed for six winters. Here there was a bedroom, and my coal and water were brought up for me by the janitor; on the other hand I often made my own breakfast—tea, boiled eggs, and biscuits—and always my tea in the afternoon, for I had now lived in England and learned the comforts of a bachelor in lodgings. Only —what would not have happened in England—I washed my own dishes and ordered my tea, eggs, milk and sugar from the grocers: domestic cares that pleased me, and that preserved my nice china— a present from Howard Cushing—during all those years. There was a round bathtub under my cot, and my sister's crucifix on the wall above it: only cold water, but the contents of the kettle boiling on the hearth served to take off the chill. I had also acquired a taste for fresh air, and my window was always a little open.

One day a new goody left the bathtub full of slops, explaining that she hadn't known what to do with it; it was the only bathtub in her entry. I had myself taken only recently to a daily sponge bath. When I was an undergraduate few ever took a bath in Cambridge; those who lodged in private houses might share one bathroom between them, and those who went to the Gymnasium might have a shower bath after exercise; but your pure "grind" never bathed, and I only when I went home for the week-end. In Little's Block I believe there was a bathroom on each floor; but Beck was the only luxurious dormitory where each room had its private bathroom. Habits, however, were rapidly changing. Violent exercise and fiercely contested sports were in the ascendant among the athletes; this involved baths, but not luxury. Yet luxury was in the ascendant too; and the polite ideal of one man one bathroom, and hot water always hot, was beginning to disguise luxury under the decent names of privacy and health.

My father used to say that the English had introduced baths into Christendom from India; but I suspect that it was luxury and the *femmes galantes* of the eighteenth century that did it. What could be more un-English than a languid female in a turban, not unattended, and not without a semi-transparent clinging garment, like that of a statue, getting in or out of a marble bath like an ancient sarcophagus, itself draped and lined with linen sheets? These were the refinements of luxury and mature coquetry. And the Christian background appears in the gown worn in the bath, according to the monastic precept of never being wholly naked. No such scruple exists in England, or among athletes. The tone there is masculine and hardy, with a preference for cold water and the open air. Robert Bridges, the most complete of Englishmen, at the age of eighty, used to take his cold bath every morning in the lounge-hall of his house, before a roaring wood fire. Here was Sparta rather than India transported to the chilly North.

In Spain, in those days, there were no baths in houses. My sister procured an immense zinc tub, in the middle of which, when it was full, a special stove had to be introduced to heat the water, which a special donkey laden with four earthen jars had to carry from the fountain; the thing didn't work, and I doubt that she took more than one or two baths. For me she got a manageable little hip bath which I found quite sufficient. Yet baths, medical baths, were not unknown in mediæval Avila. They were prescribed for certain ailments. You went to the establishment as to a pilgrimage; the water was that of a particular spring, mineral or miraculous, gushing forth at that spot; and you took always an odd number of baths, probably nineteen or twenty-one (never twenty!) according to some Pythagorean superstition of ancient medicine. When they were well the good people of Avila no more thought of bathing than of drinking tea; yet I never came across any decent person there who offended the nose. Complexions were seldom fresh or ruddy; but it is working people's clothes that smell; only the feet, head and hands gather dust and grime. The protected parts of the skin shed their excretions and become clean of themselves, if only the clothes are well washed and aired.

Hollis and Stoughton were twin red-brick buildings of the eighteenth century, solid, simple, symmetrical and not unpleasing. No effort had been made by the builders towards picturesqueness or novelty; they knew what decent lodgings for scholars were, and that there was true economy in building them well. The rectangular wooden window frames divided into many squares, flush with the walls, and painted white, served for a modest and even gay decoration. There was a classic cornice, and the windows immediately under it were square instead of oblong and suggested metopes, while the slope of the roof also was that of a temple, though without pediments at the ends. On the whole, it was the architecture of sturdy poverty, looking through thrift in the direction of wealth. It well matched the learning of early New England, traditionally staunch and narrow, yet also thrifty and tending to positivism; a learning destined as it widened to be undermined and to become, like the architecture, flimsy and rich. It had been founded on accurate Latin and a spellbound constant reading of the Bible: but in the Harvard of my day we had heard a little of everything, and nobody really knew his Latin or knew his Bible. You might say that the professor of Hebrew did know his Bible, and the professors of Latin their Latin. No doubt, in the sense that they could write technical articles on the little points of controversy at the moment among philologists; but neither Latin nor the Bible flowed through them and made their spiritual lives; they were not vehicles for anything great. They were grains in a quicksand, agents and patients in an anonymous moral migration that had not yet written its classics.

In both these old buildings I occupied corner rooms, ample, low, originally lighted by four windows, with window seats in the thickness of the wall, which a cushion could make comfortable for reading. Between the side windows the deep chimney stack projected far into the room, and no doubt at first showed its rough or glazed bricks, as the low ceiling probably showed its great beams. But an "improvement" had spoiled the dignity of these chambers. The rage for "closets" invaded America, why I am not antiquary enough to know. Was it that wardrobes and chests, with or without drawers, had become too heavy and cumbrous for an unsettled population? Or was it that a feminine demand for a seemly "bed-sitting room" had insisted on a place of hiding for one's belongings? Anyhow, in 19 Hollis both the side windows had been hidden by oblique partitions, going from the edges of the chimney stack to the front and back walls and enclosing the desired closets, not large enough for a bed, but capable of containing a washstand, trunks, and garments hanging on pegs. Luckily in 7 Stoughton this operation had mutilated only one angle, and left me one pleasant side window open to the South, and affording a glimpse of Holden Chapel and the vista then open over the grass towards Cambridge Common.

Yet it was the outlook to the east, from both rooms, that was most characteristic. The old elms in the Yard were then in all their glory, and in summer formed a grove of green giants, with arching and drooping branches, that swung like garlands in the breeze. This type of elm, though graceful and lofty, has a frail air, like tall young women in consumption. The foliage is nowhere thick, too many thin ribs and sinews are visible: and this transparency was unfortunate in the Harvard Yard, where the full charm depended on not seeing the background. In winter the place was ungainly and forlorn, and not only to the eye. The uneven undrained ground would be flooded with rain and half-melted dirty snow one day, and another day strewn with foul ashes over the icy pavements. This was a theme for unending grumbling and old jokes; but we were young and presumably possessed snow-boots called "arctics" or thick fisherman's boots warranted watertight. Anyhow we survived; and as bad going for pedestrians is made inevitable during winter and spring by the New England climate, the Yard was not much worse in this respect than the surrounding places.

Holworthy in my day was still nominally the "Seniors' Paradise," but not in reality: in reality those who could afford it lived in private houses, in Little's Block, or in Beck. Holworthy preserved, as it has sometimes recovered, only the charm of tradition. The two bedrooms to each study favored the pleasant custom of chumming; but as yet Holworthy had no baths, not even shower baths, and no central heating. Modern improvements seem to me in almost everything to be a blessing. Electricity, vacuum cleaning, and ladies' kitchens render life simpler and more decent; but central heating, in banishing fireplaces, except as an occasional luxury or affectation, has helped to destroy the charm of home. I don't mean merely the ancient and rustic sanctity of the hearth; I mean also the home-comforts of the modern bachelor. An obligatory fire was a useful and blessed thing. In northern climates it made the poetry of indoor life. Round it you sat, into it you looked, by it you read, in it you made a holocaust of impertinent letters and rejected poems. On the hob your kettle simmered, and the little leaping flames cheered your heart and ventilated your

den. Your fire absolved you from half your dependence on restaurants, cafés, and servants; it also had the moralizing function of
giving you a duty in life from which any distraction brought
instant punishment, and taught you the feminine virtues of nurse,
cook, and Vestal virgin. Sometimes, I confess, these cares became
annoying; the fire kept you company, but like all company it sometimes interrupted better things. At its best, a wood fire is the most
glorious; but unless the logs are of baronial dimensions, it dies
down too quickly, the reader or the writer is never at peace; while
a hard-coal fire (which also sometimes goes out) sleeps like a
prisoner behind its iron bars, without the liveliness of varied
flames. The ideal fire is soft coal, such as I had in England and
also in America when I chose; like true beauty in woman, it combines brilliancy with lastingness. I congratulate myself that in the
Harvard Yard I was never heated invisibly and willy-nilly by
public prescription, but always by my own cheerful fire, that made
solitude genial and brought many a genial friend who loved cheer-
fulness to sit by it with me, not rejecting in addition a drink and
a little poetry; no tedious epic, but perhaps one of Shakespeare's
sonnets or an ode of Keats, something fit to inspire conversation
and not to replace it.

The quality of the Harvard Yard, both in its architecture and
its manners, was then distinctly Bohemian: not of the Parisian description, since no *petite amie* or *grande amie* was in evidence, but
of the red-brick lodging, tavern and stable-yard Bohemia of Dickens
and Thackeray; yet being in a college, the arts and the intellect
were not absent from it altogether. I had not been many days a
Freshman when I had a glimpse of this. A note was slipped by
hand through my door, inviting me to go that evening to a room
in Holworthy, where two Seniors interested in things Spanish
would be glad to see me and talk about them. I went. The two
young men were commonplace and easy going. They didn't actually speak Spanish but had an idea that they loved gypsies and
Moors, the *Alhambra* of Washington Irving and the *Carmen* of
Mérimée. There was a mysterious curtain cutting off a corner of

their room; and the talk soon drifted from Spain to painting Venuses from the model. Was that done here, I wondered, and was the model about to emerge from behind the curtain? That would surely have been contrary to College discipline; did these bold Seniors not care about that, or was I the greenest of Freshmen and were they trying to impose upon me? I saw little or nothing of them after that evening; probably I was less Spanish or less Bohemian than they expected. But by chance they gave me a useful hint. If I myself drew a little, why didn't I draw something for the *Lampoon*; and one of them suggested a subject: a mother with two or three daughters mistaking "Holyoke House" for a hotel and arriving with luggage and asking for rooms there. I made the drawing and sent it to the appropriate address; and soon I received a visit from the "President" of the *Lampoon* Board, who said they accepted my drawing but wished to keep it for the Class Day number—nine months hence—and meantime wouldn't I send them something else. Naturally I did so; and was thereupon elected a member of the *Lampoon* Board.

This was a decisive event in my Harvard life. Two other Freshmen, Felton and Sanborn, had also been elected; and they asked me to come and sit at their table in Memorial Hall. Felton's chum, Baldwin, was also there, and some other friends; so I immediately found myself in a little circle of more or less lively wits that congregated every day at meals, apart from any personal sympathies. In time, the inner circle narrowed down to four, the three I have mentioned and myself. We kept up our comradeship at table for four years; and Sanborn and I became personal friends on intellectual grounds.

In those days Freshmen at Harvard were still at school. Courses were prescribed, and we sat in alphabetical order, to be marked present or absent. Sanborn and I were likely to sit next to each other: not always, because those who had passed in French had to take German, and vice versa, and in some subjects the two hundred and fifty Freshmen were divided into more or less advanced classes. But I remember in Natural History 4, where Professor Shaler set forth "all the geology necessary to a gentleman," sitting next to Sanborn. We had separate chairs but one running desk in front of us, so that we could easily overlook one another's notebooks; and we amused ourselves in matching triolets, not always on that "concatenation of phenomena" which Shaler was impressing upon us.

Sanborn was a poet of lyric and modest flights but genuine feeling, not naturally in harmony with the over-intellectualized transcendentalism of Concord, Massachusetts, where his father was a conspicuous member of the Emersonian circle. There was more of Chaucer in him than of Emerson or Wordsworth: even Shakespeare—except in the songs—he found too heavy and rhetorical. These exclusions were involuntary; he was not in the least conceited about them, but on the contrary felt that he was a misfit, shy, ungainly in appearance, and at a disadvantage in the give and take of conversation or action. These maladjustments, a few years later, led to a tragic end. His father had found him a place in the office of *The Springfield Republican*. That town offered little to keep up his spirits. He fell into rather undesirable company, as at College he had sometimes succumbed to drink—not often, yet ungracefully. I think I understand the secret of these failings, gross as they seem for a man of such delicate sensibility. He was unhappy, he was poor, he was helpless. The sparkle of a glass, the glitter of a smile, the magic of a touch could suddenly transport him out of this world, with all its stubborn hindrances and dreary conventions, into the *Auberge Verte*, the green paradise, of his dreams. Yet this escape from reality was necessarily short-lived, and the awakening bitter and remorseful. The strain was too much for Sanborn. His discouragement became melancholia and began to breed hallucinations. He knew only too much about madness, as everybody did in old New England, and he feared it. He cut his throat in his bath with a razor, and we buried him in Concord, in sight of the optimistic Emerson's grave, after a parlor funeral, with the corpse visible, at which his father read a few not very pertinent passages from the Upanishads and the Psalms.

The other *Lampoon* men were more normal and better adapted to their social medium. Felton and Baldwin were not New Englanders, rather Southern, without crotchets and with unaffected old-fashioned literary tastes, leaning towards the sentimental and the nobly moral; leanings likely to grow more pronounced in later years, under the sacred influences of home and of political eloquence. They loved Thackeray; and Felton would read aloud *"Wait till you come to forty-year."* Their room, No. 1 Thayer, was the reality under the literary fiction of a *Lampoon* "sanctum." We gathered there to compose our parts of the fortnightly edition; chiefly drawings, although sometimes the column of puns entitled *By the Way* was concocted by us cooperatively, in the midst of a thousand interruptions. I never wrote for the *Lampoon*; even the text for my sketches was usually supplied for me by the others, who knew the idioms required. My English was too literary, too ladylike, too correct for such a purpose; and I never acquired, or liked, the American art of perpetual joking. What we printed was a severe selection from what we uttered: it had to be local, new or fresh, and at least apparently decent. Speech in this circle, if not always decent, never became lewd. There was an atmosphere of respect for holy things, of respect for distant or future ladyloves, and also of self-respect. We were not very intimate friends. The *Lampoon*, the Yard, the College had brought us together; and when we scattered the comradeship ceased. I scarcely knew what became of Felton or Baldwin. In recent years I unexpectedly received a letter from Baldwin, not reawakening old interests or old friendship, but full of conventional cordiality and platform sentiments. I should have preferred silence: because the young Baldwin had been an engaging person, who inspired trust and affection, and I recall the circle in which we moved with the warmest pleasure.

The man who gave the tone to the *Lampoon* at that time was Ernest Thayer, not one of our group. He seemed a man apart, and his wit was not so much jocular as Mercutio-like, curious and whimsical, as if he saw the broken edges of things that appear whole. There was some obscurity in his play with words, and a feeling (which I shared) that the absurd side of things is pathetic. Probably nothing in his later performance may bear out what I have just said of him; because American life was then becoming unfavorable to idiosyncrasies of any sort, and the current smoothed and rounded out all the odd pebbles.

In our last year or two, the *Lampoon* possessed a business manager whose name is known everywhere, and who is identified, perhaps more than any one else, with that inexorable standardizing current, namely William R. Hearst. He was little esteemed in the College. The fact that his father was a millionaire and a Senator from California gave him an independence that displeased the undergraduate mind, and his long cigars were bad form in the Yard. Yet his budding powers as a newspaper owner and manager made him invaluable to the *Lampoon* in its financial difficulties.

He not only knew how to secure advertisements, but he presented us with a material sanctum, carpeted, warmed by a stove, and supplied with wooden armchairs and long tables at which all the illustrated comic papers in the world were displayed as exchanges for our little local and puerile *"Lampy."* How easily a little cool impudence can deceive mankind! Yet the enterprise of our business manager in this affair, was of little use to us. Two or three times two or three of us may have gone into that new sanctum (for we were also supplied with keys) and looked at those startling comic papers, most of them unintelligible and grossly colored; especially the *Vie Parisienne* and the other French sheets, so different in prevalent theme from our decent and child-like fun. I myself actually read some of the longer stories in the *Vie Parisienne*: there was a certain overtone there of satire and subtle humor, sometimes even of pathos, as in Guy de Maupassant and Théophile Gautier; and the conventionalized illustrations showed a giraffe-like ideal of feminine beauty, very unlike the dumpy realities, as if a taste for elegance were struggling against mere sensuality. Yet the thing was horribly monotonous, and had been done better in *La Maison Tellier* and *Mademoiselle de Mau-*

pin. We turned a cold shoulder on Hearst's munificence, and continued to meet and to bring forth our labored witticisms, not without laughter, in Felton and Baldwin's room.

To the Harvard Yard in spirit, though not topographically, may be assigned my other contacts with college life during those first four years. Athletics did not figure among them. I never took any exercise except walking, and I seldom went, as yet, even to watch the games, which in the case of football was then done as in England, standing at the side lines, the crowd being kept back only by a chalk mark or a rope. This "Harvard indifference" was not due to intense study on my part or to misanthropy. I played the leading lady in the Institute Theatricals of 1884, and two years later, though I no longer looked at all deceptive in feminine clothes, I was one of the ballet in the Hasty Pudding play. These amusements, with rehearsals and a noisy trip to New York as a theatrical company, involved a good deal of intimacy for the moment, and I remember the names and faces of some of my companions, and some of the tunes we sang, chiefly from *Martha*; but for the most part scenes and persons are completely erased. I have a very short memory, except for such things as I absorb and recast in my own mind; so I am a good observer and critic, but a bad historian: let the reader of this book take warning.

One figure, however, still stands clear before me out of that medley: Crosby Whitman, our musician and director, in whom as in many a person, I felt a true potential friendship behind a slight acquaintance. Besides the love of music and of Miss Mary Anderson, he had a kind of cosmopolitan competence or normality that I seem to have noticed in the best people of the American West. They moved swimmingly in the midst of all the current conventions and noises, but they seemed to make light of them, as your good Bostonian never could. They were not "taken in" by the tastes, opinions, and pleasures that they played with as in a carnival. Crosby Whitman was a man of the world.

More intellectual, at least nominally, were the literary groups or societies of which, for me, the O.K. and the *Harvard Monthly*, when that was founded, were the most important. The members of the two were largely the same, and included *Lampoon* men as well; but the O.K., which later gave excellent dinners, had the advantage of running over into the class of merely intelligent or even athletic leaders of the College. In a commercial civilization, these were likely to be much *better beings* than the professional scholars or intellectuals, *better beings* even than the future lawyers, though these might have more historical and rhetorical attainments. I liked to feel a spark of sympathy pass from those sound simple active heirs of the dominant class to my secret philosophy: and sometimes the spark did pass, and in both directions. It was at the O.K. dinners in the 1890's, that I read my *Athletic Ode* and *Six Wise Fools*. Helped by the champagne, these trifles caught fire. The play of ordinary wit and sentiment, with a light touch and a masculine note, appeals to a side of the heart not reached in the standard poets; it moves from convention to sincerity, where the standard poets move from sincerity to convention.

The *Harvard Monthly* was founded by A. B. Houghton, afterwards American Ambassador at Berlin and London. His literary quality was in marked contrast with Sanborn's, as was also his character and fate. Houghton was as rich as Sanborn was poor; he was ambitious and bitter, nominally preoccupied with socialism and pessimism, not, I think, in a clear speculative spirit, but rather as scandals and dangers that the leaders of liberalism and plutocracy must somehow overcome. His conscience and critical faculty were not at peace about the way in which his father made money: it was chiefly in a glass factory: and the son would ask himself how many glass blowers died each year from blowing into those furnaces. In the good old times they would have died of famine, the plague, drink, war or the gallows—not perhaps gentler ways of keeping down the population below the means of subsistence. But that was not the question. The question was, Is material civilization worth while? Is the dull anonymous unhappiness that it steadily diffuses more tolerable than the sudden and horrible scourges that fall upon primitive peoples? Or should the question

of happiness be ignored altogether, as German philosophy ignores
it, and should the criterion be placed in more and more complex
formal achievements? In the end Houghton would seem to have
adopted the latter alternative, if we may judge by his brilliant
career; but in his student days, at Harvard and in Germany, the
problem of human suffering dominated his judgments. In verse he
was scornful and revolutionary, with a good deal of verbal facility
and technical ingenuity, after the manner of Swinburne. His versification was not slovenly, even when it was empty or trite. This
was remarkable in America, and indicated a certain documentary
precision and authority in his mind, that doubtless contributed to
his subsequent official distinction.

I knew Houghton very well; we discussed all manner of subjects. In 1898 he unexpectedly made me a visit in Brattle Street.
He glanced about my quarters disapprovingly, sucked his enormous
cigar, and said magisterially that it was a sad mistake to try and
swim against the stream. I have never been aware of swimming
against any stream: I have merely stood on the bank or paddled
about in the quiet backwaters. From there I may have observed
that the torrent was carrying down more or less wreckage. My
philosophy throws no challenge to those who rush down the very
middle of the rapids and rejoice in their speed. However, the
monition addressed to me by the wise Houghton revealed the
dilemma in which he had found himself, and his own decision
never to swim against the current. I wonder if he was ultimately
satisfied with his career? Perhaps his success fell short of his
hopes, and perhaps his conscience about the way the world is run
was never quite at rest. Yet he was actively abetting the dominant
procedure, no doubt wishing to improve it in detail, but in any
case determined to keep it going full blast. Was it faith in a divine
direction of things and in the course of history as the Last Judgment? Or was it the force of vested interests and formed habits
drowning the still small voice of the spirit?

After this glance into the great world, taken from the Harvard
Yard, I will add nothing more about that place. It has lost its char-

acter and its importance. When President Lowell was planning his "Houses" to be built by the river, he very kindly urged me to remain and take part in the experiment. I could have lived very like a don at Oxford or Cambridge. But it was too late. My heart might have been in the thing twenty years earlier, and perhaps then the transformation of Harvard into a university of colleges might have been socially more successful. But by 1912 the non-collegiate additions had become too numerous and too important for such a reorganization. The community too had outgrown the instinct for a secluded life. Colleges were fundamentally conventual and religious; on which foundation specific precious traditions, social and sporting, might develop together with an exact but familiar and humanistic learning. Now looser, wider, more miscellaneous interests had invaded every mind. But I am not writing a history of Harvard University. I know very little about it. I knew only the Harvard Yard.

CHAPTER XIV

FIRST RETURN TO SPAIN

THE chief event of my Freshman year occurred towards the end of it. I received—what was unprecedented—a note from home, asking me to be in my room on the following evening, because my mother and sisters were coming to lay before me an important proposal. I guessed at once what it would be, although no hint had been dropped on the subject. I was to go to Spain that summer to see my father.

My mother evidently felt profoundly the recent relief to her finances, and wished to be generous. Sending me to College, even on my modest allowance, had already consumed perhaps a fourth of her income; yet she still had money to spare, and desired to do more. She had done nothing for my father during these ten years; in a certain sense she had done nothing for *me*; for giving me food and lodging and a hundred dollars a year for clothes, books and pocket-money, was something she owed to herself. She would not have allowed a child of hers to beg or go in rags; and even in sending me to College she was carrying out a plan of her own, and trying to make me into what she wished me to be, rather than into what my father or I secretly desired. But now in letting me go to see him, she was doing us an unselfish kindness, relenting as it were and letting us, for a moment, have our own way. Neither my father nor I had made any such suggestion; but it was impossible that he shouldn't wish to see his son grown up; and everybody knew at home how I longed to travel, to see again with my own eyes old towns, cathedrals, castles, and palaces, and also the classic landscape of Europe: because in America, at least in the parts I knew, nature as well as society seemed to lack contrast and definition, as if everything were half formed and groping after its essence.

Late in June I started accordingly on my first journey alone, and sailed from New York for Antwerp. Robert had looked up the various routes possible, and it had been decided that I should go and return by the Belgian or Red Star Line. The ship was decent as standards stood in those days, but second-rate, perhaps of 5,000 tons; and as usual I was dreadfully seasick; so much so that the doctor and the stewardess took pity on me, some ladies became interested (I was nineteen years old) and a bed was rigged up for me on deck, where as they said I should enjoy the sunshine and the air. The fresh air was indeed a relief but the glare an added nuisance; and the coming and going of people, and their talk, only intensified the general instability of everything. I was too ill for the moment to be ashamed of myself; but when I once got back to my cabin, although I wasn't alone even there, the feeling of shame came over me. They say dying animals go into hiding; and I could understand that instinct. There are phases of distress when help is neither possible nor desired. It is simpler, easier, more honest to be seasick alone, and to die alone. The trouble then seems something fated, not to be questioned, like life itself; and nature is built to face it and to see it out. Much as I suffered at sea, I was always ready to go to sea again: such a trial leaves the will unaffected, as nightmares do: you start afresh as you were, perhaps more merrily and with a deeper courage. The thing will pass, the ghosts will vanish. There is no reason for changing your purpose.

When I appeared on deck again, looking and feeling perfectly well, shaved and in fresh linen, I was congratulated. One particular lady of uncertain age, who now explained that she was Mrs. X. of Cincinnati, Ohio, had to be thanked for the kindness she had shown, or at least intended, on the day of that disgusting exhibition which I was heartily sorry to have made of myself. A young man should be hardier, and I had been sicker than any girl. Mrs. X. had brought me a raw egg in brandy, and insisted I should swallow it, which I had done with dire results: brandy on such occasions is a brutal remedy that my throat, not to say my stomach, abhors. Now, it was eleven o'clock in smooth sunny weather, there was no question of brandy, but only of a cup of broth and a biscuit, which we had together. I must come, she said, to sit in *their* chairs, and take a vacant place that was at *their* table. *They*, she explained, were her son (she had been married very young) and her niece, not *daughter*, who was sixteen. I had to say of course that a young girl of sixteen couldn't be her daughter. Even the boy seemed surprising. Yes, she said, he was very tall for his age; but she didn't tell me how old he was, because nice people mustn't lie.

A girl of sixteen might have seemed the natural affinity for a boy of nineteen: but not at all. The niece was to be regarded as a mere child, and my special friend was to be Mrs. X. herself. She certainly was more entertaining, deeply interested in all the higher subjects, very refined, and very religious. She spoke of "plumes," and embroidered the words *Holy, Holy, Holy* in gold upon altar-cloths. They were going all the way up the Rhine, it was such a beautiful trip, so romantic and so full of historic associations. Didn't it tempt me? It tempted me; but frankly I had no extra money for trips, and must go straight to Avila to see my father. It was too bad, she said, that I had no extra money; but it was nice that I should be going straight to see my old father, after such a long absence. Her husband too was old, too old to enjoy travelling, but he was happy in thinking how many interesting experiences the family were having, and it was wiser and pleasanter for him to remain at home, he so loved his dog and his garden and his beautiful books, all the English standard authors bound uniformly and making such a splendid decoration for his sunlit library wall. I must come some day to Cincinnati and see their delightful home. I should love it. And by the first of September they expected to be in Paris: perhaps I might be there at the same time, on my way back from Spain. We must try to arrange it.

We parted at Antwerp on these terms, having exchanged addresses, and promised to keep each other informed of our movements. I had just time to see the market place with the Cathedral spire, like a group of inverted icicles rising above it; and inside, besides the general splendor of a great living place of worship, I admired the two magnificent, if theatrical, pictures by Rubens at the head of the two aisles, especially the *Descent from the Cross*. Yet this is too classic, too Michelangelesque for Flanders; I could have wished to carry away some humbler and more intimate memories: but the gorgeousness of Rubens blotted out the rest.

In Paris I saw nothing, merely driving from one station to the other; but at the Gare d'Orléans I found myself in the sort of difficulty that inexperience will fall into. I was provided with just the amount of French money that I had calculated would be sufficient, leaving a decent margin for emergencies; and at the ticket-office I asked, as planned, for a second-class ticket to Avila. I could have a ticket to Avila, the man said, but only first class for the express: the ordinary trains, with second and third class, would take more than two whole days for the journey. I counted my money. I could take a first-class ticket and have fifteen francs left. Would that be enough for meals and tips on the journey? I would risk it. It was only thirty-six hours, two nights and one day; I could have a sandwich instead of a dinner. It wouldn't kill me.

During the next ten years I repeated this journey many times; the expense was about the same if I went first class without stopping, or second class with two or three stops on the way: a method that avoided long nights in the train, and enabled me, by varying my voyage and landing at Cherbourg or England, or even Gibraltar, to see the principal sights in all France and Spain, without making trips expressly for that purpose. My architectural passion was thus richly satisfied: it was only Italy that remained to be explored and lived in when I became relatively independent.

My fifteen francs, however, were just enough to pay my way on that first occasion; and I found at Irun that I had only a few coppers in my pocket and couldn't telegraph to my father, as had been agreed, that I was arriving at 5:30 the next morning. It was broad daylight, being early in July, and I recognized the walls and the Cathedral tower, touched by the rising sun, before we reached the station. But there was nobody to receive me, and no vehicle. Not even anybody to carry my valise. I left it with the guard, and started alone on foot, immensely happy, and remembering perfectly that station road and the place among the first houses to the left, opposite the church and convent of Santa Ana, where Don Juan the Englishman's house stood, which was now my father's. There it was, the middle one of three humble two-story buildings, not properly lined up, and painted in varying weather-worn yellows or grays, with red tiled roofs. I pounded the middle door with the knocker. No answer. Finally a neighbor, from a window over the bakery in the house to the left, put out her dishevelled head and said "Knock hard. They are all deaf in that house." I knocked harder; until the window over my door was opened also, and another head, evidently the housemaid's, peered out, and looked at me with an air of inquiry. *"Don Agustín* lives here, doesn't he? I am his son." She smiled, wished me a good arrival, and said they were expecting me but not that morning. *El Señor* was still in bed; *la Señora* (his sister Maria Ignacia) was in the garden. And presently the door was opened for me. At the end of the stone-paved passage running through the house, I could see the so-called garden, and my aged aunt standing there, stooping a little, with a watering pot in her hand. The maid tactfully ran ahead and announced me loudly, and after embracing my aunt, whom I had never seen before, I had some difficulty in making her hear and understand why I hadn't telegraphed. Then I was led up to my father's room, where the same embraces and the same explanations, under the same difficulties, were duly repeated. But it was all right now; and rather characteristic of a young son from half round the world to arrive home with just twopence in his pocket.

My father looked much as I remembered him. When middle-aged he had seemed to me simply old; now that he was really old, he seemed no older, only deafer; a disadvantage for me—besides the fact that my powers of expression in Spanish were limited, for I had read, and even now have read, hardly any Spanish books.

But deafness was almost an advantage for him in conversation. It gave him a free field, and I soon discovered how entertaining and witty his talk could be. His views were distinctly *views*, partial, definite, and humorous. They were not at all the fruit of scientific thinking. He was rather like an ancient sage, a satirist and proverb-maker; his wit lay in putting things in a nutshell—into which naturally they couldn't go in their entirety. When he talked about persons and events these miniatures were excellent; they caught the traits relevant to his purpose. It was only when given out as general truths that his summings up become sophistical and monotonous.

To be monotonous, sophistical, and utterly intolerant is the characteristic of the liberalism that he seemed to have adopted as final and absolute: I belong to the next turn of the tide. The fifty years between our ages thus made a perfect contrariety in our fundamental principles; but they made him all the more valuable for me, so to speak, as a classic, as a point of reference in thought; because the same principles, as they are found in English-speaking people, are not held so radically or intelligently but enveloped in various national, religious, commercial or sentimental interests that confuse the issue. In him the narrowing and desiccating force of this philosophy, helped no doubt by old age, became conspicuous; and I wondered how so penetrating a mind in regard to particular facts and persons, could be satisfied with such jejune second-hand theories. Anti-clericalism was the dominant crotchet: hatred of religion had acquired all the dogmatism and intolerance of religion, with none of its advantages. For it was noticeable in my father how comfortless (except for the assumption that things were improving and apparently were to go on improving forever)—I say how comfortless his philosophy was; whereas in the Anglo-Saxon world, it is all veiled and emotionalized by a sort of music, like the empty trite words by the swelling harmonies of an anthem.

This difference is capital. It makes the whole moral lesson and speculative interest of my many visits to my father, of which this was the first. And I think now I can distinguish wherein that dif-

ference lies. Liberalism, Protestantism, Judaism, positivism all have
the same ultimate aim and standard. It is prosperity, or as Lutheran
theologians put it, union with God at our level, not at God's level.
The thing all these schools detest is the ideal of union with God at
God's level, proper to asceticism, mysticism, Platonism, and pure
intelligence, which insist on seeing things under the form of truth
and of eternity. You must be content, they say, to see things under
the form of time, of appearance, and of feeling. Very well: yet the
question returns why my father's view, which doctrinally was the
same as the Anglo-Saxon, was morally and emotionally so different. And to this question I reply, that prosperity may be the
ideal of the poor, or it may be the ideal of the rich; and it may be
accompanied by domestic, national, and religious joys, or by
domestic, national, and religious bitterness. My father's was the
bitter poor man's liberalism; the liberalism of the dominant Anglo-
Saxon is that of the joyful rich man. This colors differently their
common ideal of prosperity; but prosperity remains the ultimate
ideal of both. For this reason Latins who are rich either in possessions or in sympathies can hardly be liberals. They love the
beautiful.

This point touches the heart of my intellectual relations with my
father, and also my judgment, very different from his, on English
and American civilization. Both the side of it that he admired and
the side of it that I admire and love, were foreshadowed in Bacon's
New Atlantis. Bacon was the prophet of the rich man's Utopia;
he had the liberal's worship of prosperity, and the pragmatic
esteem for science and dominion over matter as means to that end:
and when my father saw the partial realization of that prophecy in
England and America, he was filled with respect and envy for it,
and chagrin that his own country was so backward in those
profitable inventions and methods. But Bacon's ideal had another
side, the successful rich man's delight in nobility and splendor;
he was a courtier, and still nursed the classic ideal of a hierarchy of
the arts, with a magnificent pageant of virtues and dignities, like
the celestial choirs come down to earth. His New Atlantis was not

to be merely prosperous, but solemnly ordered, glorious, and beautiful. Now just as in Bacon's mind this Roman or Byzantine vesture clothed a pragmatic skeleton, so in England and even in the United States, the cult of splendor and aristocratic ways of living and feeling endured and in some circles entirely hid the commercial and industrial mechanism beneath it. There was an intense poetic, sporting, and religious life. Of this my father knew nothing, or shrugged his shoulders at it, as at vanities that may be forgiven in a society that, in more serious matters, is thoroughly sound and utilitarian. Now it was precisely this free, friendly, laughing side of Anglo-Saxon civilization that I liked and cultivated. It could not have existed, I know, without the material prosperity that supports it; at least it could not have existed in these special forms. Yet friendship, laughter, and freedom were not invented in the nineteenth century, and the modern forms of them are good only for re-enacting those ancient glories.

It was not at long range only, like Lucretius, that my father could observe the evils occasioned by religion. His only friend in Avila, who at once courteously came to salute me, was a clerical, and a sad wreck. Whether his ruin was due directly to clericalism might be doubted; it was due rather to cards; but indirectly cards might be due to indolence and boredom, these to lack of national prosperity, and this in turn notoriously to clericalism. So that Don Pelayo, for that was his name, was a victim of the system that he so perversely advocated. Here was a perpetual thorn in my father's side; and yet the prick was a stimulant. It enlivened him and kept his exasperation always pleasantly fresh and green.

Don Pelayo expressed himself well, even grandly. His Castilian, like my father's, was of the purest, only that he loved rhetoric, as my father did not. His rounded periods were often Ciceronian. His model among the living, however, was only Cánovas del Castillo, prime minister whenever the conservatives were in power, whom he called "el monstruo de la edad presente," the monster, meaning the marvel, of the present age. Cánovas was neither a monster nor a marvel, but a plausible intriguing politician who made the best of a bad job. Perhaps he was less pernicious than his rival, the liberal Sagasta. He allowed Spain to draw her natural breath and to change spontaneously; he did not attempt to destroy her life and character, and to turn her into a capitalist plutocracy with an industrial proletariat, things equally contrary to her nature; because the Spanish people is a poetic people and Spanish greatness is a chivalrous greatness.

Sagasta, on the contrary, and the forces he represented, were corrupt to the core. I remember what my brother-in-law, a wiser head than Don Pelayo, said about Sagasta in 1898, after the battle of Santiago. The better Spanish cruisers had been sent to Cuba without their heavy guns. Where were those guns? In the pocket of the Minister of Marine. "How," I asked, "can Sagasta not be ashamed of himself, and how can he remain in office?" "He would have died of shame," my brother-in-law said dryly, "if he were capable of the feeling." * Such was Spanish Government under a foreign parliamentary regime.

Don Pelayo had studied at the University of Salamanca, but learning was not his strong point. Even the astronomy of Ptolemy was unknown to him. One evening we were walking in the Paseo de San Roque (a rough terrace by a convent wall, with an open view) and admiring the stars, particularly numerous and brilliant in the rarified atmosphere of Avila. "They say," Don Pelayo meditated, "that the earth is suspended in the void without any support. That is impossible. If it had no support it would fall to the ground." Unfortunately his practice was no wiser than his theory. In his youth he had divided a small patrimony with his two sisters, but had soon dissipated his share, and had gone to live with them at their expense. Finding nothing else to do, he continued to play cards in small taverns with only copper coins for stakes. As he was very near-sighted and his companions unscrupulous, he would find, even if he won, that he had only false pennies in his pocket. He would bring them up one by one in

* The original was more terse: "*Se hubiera muerto de vergüenza, si la tuviera.*"

the light to his better eye, and exclaim sadly: "But all these coins are ignoble." He felt himself Job-like; there was verbal majesty in his misery. My father used to say, that in spite of his grandiloquence, Don Pelayo would sell all his religious and political principles for one peseta. I think he might have sold them, because he needed the peseta; but he would have cheated the devil in doing so, because his ideal allegiance to them would have remained unchanged.

I was told that in winter, when my father took his walk soon after his midday dinner, Don Pelayo would sometimes arrive just before dinner was served. "No, thank you," he would say, "I have dined already; but if I may I will have the pleasure of sitting at table with you, while you eat." A place would be made for him; a heaping plate of chick peas and the other ingredients of the *puchero* would be placed before him, and he would resign himself to taste it. *"Empalmo,"* he would say: "I make a connection, I catch the branch train." It was true that the poor man had already dined—the day before yesterday.

My stay in Avila that year, 1883, was not long. I made a tour to Catalonia in order to visit relations, and by the way I saw a good many impressive things. I have already mentioned that my father and I made an excursion to the Escurial: later I went alone to Madrid and to the Prado, to Saragossa, to Tarragona, to Barcelona, and finally to Lyons and Paris. It was a varied feast for my hungry eyes. Most of those places have become familiar to me in later years, but of Saragossa, which I have hardly revisited, my memories belong to that early time, and are vivid. There was *La Seo*, the Cathedral, Gothic in style but preserving the square plan of the mosque that it replaced: seven lofty aisles, with rows of chapels in addition, and with the rich choir and sanctuary making an enclosed island in the middle. To me, who love shrines and individual devotions and freedom of movement in sacred places, this arrangement seemed ideal. A Jewish friend whom I once took to see the Pantheon in Rome pronounced it the first *religious* place he had found there; and I can understand that feeling. It belongs to what Spengler calls *Magian* religion and art: it reappears in the Mosque of Omar—a Christian Church—and in many other mosques. At Saragossa it is combined, as at St. Sophia, with the Christian theme of salvation, in all its complexities, historical, personal, and eschatological. There are a thousand mediations, unknown to the pure Moslem; but they do not destroy the sublimity or the inwardness of a total surrender of man to God. In Saragossa there is also *La Lonja*, a picturesque hall with twisted columns, the mediæval Merchants' Exchange. We are in the Mediterranean World; might be at Pisa or Palermo, or even at Damascus. Finally, there is *La Virgen del Pilar*; but here the architecture is vast, dreary, modern, and when I saw it, hideously painted. The only interest, the only beauty, is devotional and centered in the glittering shrine of the Pillar itself. *El Pilar* is the sanctuary of Spanish patriotism and chivalry: it is the point, as Delphi was to the Greeks, of their conscious contact with fate and with eternity. It is therefore truly sacred. That the legend should be childish or the statue ordinary makes no difference: what matters is the range of human need and aspiration that has been focussed here. I therefore went to the back of the shrine, where the jasper pillar is accessible to the public through an oval opening in the wall; and I kissed the hollowed place that had been worn down by the kisses of generations. Not that I expected any wish of mine to be furthered by such a ceremony: I was only offering up all my wishes, to be sacrificed or fulfilled as the issue might determine. In any case, I was quickening in myself the sense of their precarious fortunes and eternal claims. I kissed at once the beauty of the beautiful and the rod that smote me and drove me from its presence.

The goal of my journey, however, was Tarragona: for there a cousin and contemporary of my father's, Don Nicolás Zabalgoitia, was a canon in the Cathedral. Spanish custom calls a parent's cousin an uncle; courtesy therefore compels me to speak of the Canon as *tío Nicolás*; but he is not to be confused with my real uncle Nicolás Santayana, my father's brother, a major and my godfather, from whom I took my third Christian name. The Canon, however, was not my only relation in Tarragona. My father's eldest sister, my aunt Mariquita, lived with him and had kept house for him all their lives; and with them, at that time, lodged my father's youngest brother, Manuel, with his wife and their two children. More than half my entire Spanish connection lived under that roof: so that my father, who was always loyal to his family bonds, thought I ought to accept the invitation of my *tio Nicolás*, and make the acquaintance of that whole household.

Towards *tio Nicolás* my father had an old affection, as for a brother; yet like all my father's affections it was mixed with bitterness. In their youth Nicolás had been put in a monastery and had become a monk: yet scarcely had he taken his vows, when all the monasteries in Spain (except for a few devoted to supplying missionaries for the Colonies) were suppressed by the Government, and the monks dispersed. In time, a place was found for the waif as parish priest in some village, where he had to keep house and needed a housekeeper. Now my grandmother, as I have already indicated, was punctilious and vehement in her piety, poor, and burdened with a family of twelve children, for whom places had to be found in the world. Unfortunately the two eldest were daughters, not inclined apparently to become nuns; yet their mother doubtless thought that life in a clerical atmosphere would be better for their temporal and eternal welfare than would some modest commonplace marriage. Now that the young priest, their cousin, needed a housekeeper, would not the eldest sister, Mariquita, be suitable for that office? Surely a great confidence was manifested here in divine grace, to put a young man and a young woman, practically strangers to each other, under one narrow roof, where they were compelled by their cousinship to live on equal terms, not as master and servant, for day after day all summer, and night after night all winter. A triumph of chastity over propinquity would surely have been admirable in such circumstances, but the contrary was more probable. Could not my experienced grandmother or her confessor foresee it? A child, called a niece, before long was seen playing in that village parsonage; and although for some reason no more children appeared, the constraint and forced mendacity in such a household, added to its poverty, were not pleasant to consider.

My father's affectionate tone and loyal conduct towards his family never varied, whatever at any moment might be his feelings. He sometimes quarrelled with them, and spoke of them sharply to other persons; but the quarrels were soon made up, and he reverted to his fundamental tolerance and even deference towards all mankind. It was characteristic of him to combine a kind of enthusiasm and extreme courtesy of manner with a total absence of illusions about the person so favored. It was so, I suspect, that he had courted my mother, as it were against his will. Fate had allied him to her as it had to his blood relations. In itself the conduct of my *tio Nicolás* had nothing to surprise anybody. Everybody would say of him what Mephistopheles said of Gretchen: He was not the first. That was what his ecclesiastical superiors must have said of him. The thing was unfortunate but had to be overlooked: and it didn't interfere with his continuance in the priesthood or his ultimately becoming a canon.

Yet irregularities breed irregularities, and the worst, from my father's point of view, was yet to come. He had managed to secure for his youngest brother Manuel, a small post in the Philippine Islands. It opened a career for the young man and could ultimately secure him a pension. Spain was not then a capitalist country. Nobody had "money." There were some great landlords, and some modest ones, like my brother-in-law; there were lawyers and doctors; and the rest of the middle class, including the engineers, professors, military men, and ecclesiastics, held their positions under the government and expected pensions, not only for their widows and minor children, but for their unmarried daughters for life. A post under the government, especially in the Colonies which had a separate and less political administration, was a virtual settlement: it gave a relative sense of security. What, then, was my father's chagrin, when his brother Manuel was leaving for Manila with the prospect of a decent career, to find that his cousin Nicolás and his sister Mariquita had married off their "niece" to the young Manuel, who thus sailed on his first voyage already burdened with a wife! It was an outrageous marriage. The girl was not only a cousin but also a niece of her husband's; and he, who as a young bachelor might have made his way in Manila in any society, was condemned to wallow (*acochinado,* my father said) in a tropical pigsty, poor, unknown, and without ambition. It was he, retired on a miserable pension, with his wife Hermenegilda and his two surviving children, Manuela and Juan, that I found living at Tarragona, with my *tio Nicolás* and my Aunt Mariquita.

An unattractive family, unpleasantly complicated, crowded in a modest ill-furnished flat: yet at once I had occasion to see the human necessity of that loyalty to one's blood, apart from one's inclinations, which my father practised, and to put it in practice in my turn. For I brought no blessing to that family. On the contrary, I involuntarily imposed upon them endless trouble and responsibility, which they faced bravely; and they placed me under a permanent obligation to acknowledge and to assist them.

It had been a hot journey to Tarragona: especially at the station in Lérida, where I had to wait several hours between trains, the heat had been oppressive. When I reached Tarragona, I easily singled out my *tio Nicolás,* by his clerical robes; a stout, sound, white-haired old gentleman, dignified and affable; and with him my uncle Manuel, passive, modest, limp, and insignificant. At the house, my two aunts and two cousins were duly embraced. I was feeling a little dazed, not at all well. They had prepared an elaborate supper. I could eat nothing; excused myself on the ground of fatigue and of the great heat. But finally my head began to swim. I was unmistakably very ill, and had to be put to bed. They told me afterwards that I had been delirious, talked sometimes in English, sometimes in Spanish, but about imaginary things, and that the doctor had spoken of a high gastric fever. But after a day or two an eruption appeared. They said they were relieved. I was better. It was "only smallpox," and a mild case.

It was nasty and for a time troublesome; but when the blisters dried up and the crusts fell off, I had rather a pleasant convalescence. They had told me not to scratch my face, as that would make the marks permanent; but I have no marks whatever on my body, where I was free to scratch, and a few, not very obvious, precisely on my nose. My father had come to Tarragona on hearing the news, and my mother had telegraphed asking for a bulletin by cable; and this could be brief and favorable, as by that time I was well, though the red spots remained visible for some months.

The Cathedral was directly opposite, and my father and I used to walk in the cloisters; we are both given to pacing a room, like a beast in a cage; but a continuous cloister has all the advantages of an enclosed smooth space with those of fresh air in addition. It was a nice cloister, with the dark gray castle-like Cathedral overshadowing it, and one immense slanting palm tree spreading its crown victoriously over all human obstructions in the direction of the sun. We were by the shores of the Mediterranean, and a short walk would take us to the ancient citadel, overhanging the nutshell port. It was my first glimpse of that sacred sea; but the foreground at that moment was more vividly in my mind than the distances, geographical and historical: only some years later, when I went by sea from Malaga to Gibraltar did the full sense of ploughing those Homeric waters come over me, of which I expressed something in the Ode written on that occasion. Here the accent fell on ancient Tarraco, with its Roman castle still standing, and its so Spanish mixture of Carthaginian and Celtic suggestions. This had been the capital of all northeastern Spain—how much more noble and Spanish than modern Barcelona!—and the archiepiscopal see still retained vestiges of its ancient preëminence. Its canons wore red silk cassocks, like cardinals, with purple stockings: and *tio Nicolás*, who had been a handsome man, looked very grand in his vestments.

He had a jovial temperament and carried his heavy burden, both of flesh and of responsibility, with a good grace. And he was no fool. When I heard him and my father talking together, though at least in my presence their conversation was discreet and general,

I couldn't help making comparisons and wondering which of them
had the sounder and riper mind. My father was far better informed and freer to express himself; yet *tio Nicolás* seemed to be
at home in a rich humanistic world of men, of affairs, of convention and of religion, on which my father had turned his back with
a strange hatred. I can sympathize with the preference for obscurity and solitude. I prefer them for myself also: but that does not
condemn the world in its own eyes, or in those of justice, or
remove the glory and inner interest of its adventures. I felt that
tio Nicolás liked all that was likable, without being deceived by
it; and this seemed a kindlier and wiser sentiment than constitutional derision of everything that one might have discarded in
one's own life. I could see why he had been made a canon. Without eminence for either learning or virtue, he had a certain native
elegance in speech and manners. His latinity, if not impeccable,
was familiar and pleasant, and he felt the full afflatus of theological poetry and wisdom, however qualified his faith might be.
Once when I complimented him on his robust health, he shook his
head with a smile, and said "*Senectus isa morbus;* do you understand that?" I certainly understood *senectus* and *morbus;* but what
was *isa?* Sounded like Greek for "equal," was it Latin? Yes, he
said; it meant "itself."—"Oh, *ipsa!* Old age is itself a disease."—Yes,
that was it; but they pronounced it *isa.* And we talked sometimes
of chants and church music. I knew only what I had heard at the
Church of the Immaculate Conception; but I used to sing parts
of the Mass and of Rossini's *Stabat Mater* about the house; something quite natural in that sort of family, where the housemaid
sings while she makes the beds. Spanish chants have no solemnity:
they are as precipitate and perfunctory as the recital of the Rosary;
which doesn't preclude a general devout posture of mind in the
process. It might even seem more religious only to indicate the
burden of a prayer rather than to mouth the words in order to
impress other people. Worship should be addressed to God, not to
an audience. Be that as it may, *tio Nicolás* was far from sancti-
monious; he liked sometimes to be a bit naughty. At three o'clock

he was obliged, in spite of the heat, to cross the street to the Cathedral, to be present at Vespers; for if a canon was absent, he was fined one peseta. Referring to this regulation, and smoothing his robe, he would recite as he went heavily down the stairs:

Cantemos del Señor las alabanzas,
para llenar nuestras panzas

"Let us sing the praises of the Lord, that we may fill our bellies." Pleasantry? Cynicism? I think a mixture of both. After all, the sentiment is not very different from the keynote of Hebrew piety; and the Psalter needs to be taken liturgically and very symbolically, if it is still to serve for spiritual expression. I don't wonder that the old canons should have found Vespers rather sleepy and useless, the music not having been raised, as in Anglican services, into an independent vehicle of sentiment, or stimulus for it.

What did *tio Nicolás* really think of his profession? I doubt that he knew himself, or much cared to ask. He was at home in the conventions, could not break away from them without ruining himself and his family, and had no inner desire to break away. It is not as if he had been a philosopher with a clear contrary system of beliefs. He was a man of the world without any contrary system. Your genuine and profound sceptic sees no reason to quarrel with any ruling orthodoxy. It is as plausible as any other capable of prevailing in the world. If you do not think so, it is simply because that orthodoxy is not familiar to you, or not congenial. In a different age, or with a different endowment, you would have rested peacefully in it like the rest of mankind. And from the point of view of happiness, decency, art, and imagination, you might have been better off. Such, I suspect, would have been the philosophy of *tio Nicolás*, if he had framed one for himself: but he was content to quote the approved answers to all puzzling questions, and to let the Church and the Fathers bear the responsibility. It was not our fault that we were born. Is it our fault that we believe what we believe? To be incurious and at peace in such matters might even be a mark of profound faith, if the intention were to conform to the divine order of things in courage and silence, without knowing what precisely this order may be.

The worst symptoms of infidelity that I saw in that family were in the women. Not unintelligibly. It was they who had suffered most from poverty, since there had always been enough to eat, but not enough to appear in the world as women like to appear. And it was they who had suffered most from the latent disgrace of their position, and the dread of gossip and insults. They owed society a grudge for making their life difficult. They had not sinned against nature, but the world had sinned against them by its cruel tyranny and injustice. They were therefore rebels, impotent rebels, against all the powers that be, celestial and earthly. My aunt Mariquita was smiling and silent; she smiled feebly, passively, equivocally at everything, even at death and illness, and hardly said anything. When *tio Nicolás* died and she came to live with us in Avila, she would lock herself up in her room, where she didn't allow even the servant to penetrate; and when she came out for meals, she would hardly eat, insisting on mixing vinegar with everything. These were crotchets of extreme old age; but what her secret thoughts must have been appeared in her "niece" Hermenegilda and in Manuela, Hermenegilda's daughter, who were loquacious, and betrayed their sentiments even when they didn't dare to express them frankly. They had a typical low-class esteem for small material advantages, with cynicism about all virtue and so-called higher interests. In the working classes, whose poverty does not come from decay, concern about little benefits and little losses is a sign of thrift: thrift that makes for a modest well-being and for mastery in some honest art. There is no mockery then about superior gifts or unselfish virtues; there is respect for them and ambition to cultivate them. There may be even great illusions about the superiority of superior people. From such illusions my female relations at Tarragona were scornfully free. They imagined that they knew perfectly the corrupt motives and morals of all the rich and famous. And yet they didn't love the poor or consent to be identified with them. Manuela, whose pension when she became an orphan was only forty pesetas or eight dollars a month, might have married a member of the *Guardia Civil* or Constabulary, who had courted her: but he was only a private or a non-commissioned officer, and she refused. She thereby became chiefly dependent on me, or on what I induced my sister Josefina to give her. I didn't dislike Manuela: her mind was common, and sometimes also her manners, but she was sincere and unprejudiced. You could talk with her as with a man, and though her judgments on people were ignorant and uncharitable, they were hypothetically penetrating: I mean, they showed what such people *might* be. Incidentally they revealed the quality of Manuela's education and character. She didn't belong to the Intelligentsia, because she had read nothing, but she belonged to the revolutionary party, to the Reds. Since we are all rascals, let us all be rascals at one level, with equal chances to worm our way to a false eminence.

These principles were not entirely theoretical. Before I left Tarragona, my father and I became aware that there was a plot afoot to marry me to Manuela. It was a repetition of the plot that had contrived the marriage of her father and mother. *Tio Nicolás* could not have been ignorant of this scheme, if not actually the author of it: something that rather lowered my esteem for him, and chilled a little my sense of the kind treatment I had received in his house. He may have thought: What is there wrong in mating these cousins? Why is young Manuela worse than any other girl that Jorge might marry? In the abstract there might seem to be nothing wrong; at their distance they could have no notion of my real circumstances in America, which made any marriage impossible. Perhaps they counted on keeping me in Spain: counted on my mother's help, without understanding her character.

Illness had prevented me from reaching Paris at the time when my steamer friend Mrs. X. of Cincinnati, Ohio, was to be there; but I had her address and wrote explaining what had happened, not disguising the disgusting and contagious nature of the illness but calling it smallpox in plain English. Having done the Rhine she was now going to do the Rhone; and as I was also passing that way, I suggested that we should meet in Lyons. Lyons turned out to be a lucky choice, and I spent a week there, not waiting for Mrs. X., but going every night to the theatre where Sarah Bernhardt happened to be performing. It was a great treat: *Phèdre, La Dame aux Camélias, Frou-frou, Adrienne Lecouvreur,* and *La Tosca.* The divine Sarah was still relatively young, serpent-like, with her "golden voice" fresh and not too monotonous; and while dramatically she seemed most adequate in *Frou-frou* and *La Dame aux Camélias,* poetically and verbally it was in *Phèdre,* and especially in the passage from *Phèdre* repeated in *Adrienne Lecouvreur* that she captivated me entirely: and I still repeat to myself at night, as if it were a prayer, that passage and others as nearly as I can after her fashion. It was liturgical: the text spoke as if it were an oracle, and the actress was a speaking statue, and her voice came, ideally, through a mask. In listening to *La Tosca,* on the contrary, in the scene where Mario is being tortured, I found the strain intolerable, and slipped out—being in the pit, near the door —for fear of fainting. This experience led me to understand that there is a limit to the acceptable terror and pity that tragedy may excite. They must be excited only speculatively, intellectually, religiously: if they are excited materially and deceptively, you are overcome and not exalted. The spectacle either drives you away, as it did me, or becomes a vice, an indulgence that adds to the evils of life rather than liberates from them. Sardou was not a tragedian; he was a contriver of sensational plays.

The rest of my journey is described briefly in one of my father's letters: it acknowledges one of mine from Antwerp, whence I was sailing on October 8th.

Avila, 9th of October, 1883.

. . . "I see with great pleasure that you have kept well, that the financial or cash question has been happily solved, and that you have nothing to complain of unless it be having missed your Conquest, who as appears from the letter that I enclose and that I opened to see if it shed any light on your whereabouts, has been playing with you at hide and seek. My cousin Nicolás had already maliciously guessed as much [*lo ha maliciado*], for being a priest he has a keen scent for everything that concerns women. He used to tell me he was sure that you would never find that lady, and attributed the fact to the smallpox. I think that you will not have been overmuch troubled at such a trifle, and that you will not go to look for her in Cincinnati, Ohio, but that you will wait tranquilly for her to send you that teacup, bought expressly for you, and the only one that was not broken, seeing that she has sworn not to let anyone use it but you."

The teacup never was sent and I never went to Cincinnati, Ohio, or had further correspondence with Mrs. X. Some ten years later, however, I received a visit from a beautifully dressed young clergyman who said he was the Reginald X. of Cincinnati, Ohio. Only an English military tailor who had been converted could have made a clerical coat look so like the smartest of officers' tunics. I remembered Mrs. X. saying how much she hoped that her son would become a "priest"; and putting two and two together I could imagine which way the wind blew in that young man's religious vocation. We talked of seasickness, of the sea, of the British Navy, of the Church. I spoke sorrowfully of the state of religion at Harvard, and hoped it was better in Cincinnati. Even the Episcopal Theological School in Cambridge was not traditional and Catholic enough for my taste; nevertheless on week days when their chapel was almost empty, I sometimes dropped in there for Vespers, if I got back early from my walk and it wasn't yet time for afternoon tea. He smiled and understood my banter perfectly; scoffers were half converted when they laughed at themselves; but when I asked about his mother, as I did repeatedly, his replies were curt and he changed the subject.

CHAPTER XV

COLLEGE FRIENDS

MY DEEPEST friendships were all individual. The bond was not due to belonging to the same circle or class or even nation. Chance having allowed us to discover each other, character, quality, and sympathy did the rest. Of such friendships I have mentioned only the two that I formed at school; they had little or no sequel, except in my inner mind. Now I come to others that, by chance, I formed at college: not like those friends I have described as figures in the Yard, where college life had brought us together. These chosen friends were picked out from that flowing mass precisely because they belonged elsewhere; the Yard where we happened to be did not unite us, nor does the memory of them take me back to the Yard.

First in time and very important, was my friendship with Charles Loeser. I came upon him by accident in another man's room, and he immediately took me into his own, which was next door, to show me his books and pictures. Pictures and books! That strikes the keynote to our companionship. At once I found that he spoke French well, and German presumably better, since if hurt he would swear in German. He had been at a good international school in Switzerland. He at once told me that he was a Jew, a rare and blessed frankness that cleared away a thousand pitfalls and insincerities. What a privilege there is in that distinction and in that misfortune! If the Jews were not worldly it would raise them above the world; but many of them court the world and wish to pass for ordinary Christians or ordinary atheists. Not so Loeser: he had no ambition to manage things for other people, or to worm himself into fashionable society. His father was the proprietor of a vast "dry-goods store" in Brooklyn, and rich—how rich I never knew, but rich enough and generous enough for his son always to have plenty of money and not to think of a profitable profession. Another blessed simplification, rarely avowed in America. There was a commercial presumption that a man is useless unless he makes money, and no vocation, only bad health, could excuse the son of a millionaire for not at least pretending to have an office or a studio. Loeser seemed unaware of this social duty. He showed me the nice books and pictures that he had already collected—the beginnings of that passion for possessing and even stroking *objets-d'art* that made the most unclouded joy of his life. Here was fresh subject matter and fresh information for my starved aestheticism—starved sensuously and not supported by much reading: for this was in my Freshman year, before my first return to Europe.

Loeser had a tremendous advance on me in these matters, which he maintained through life: he seemed to have seen everything, and to speak every language. Berenson had the same advantage, with a public reputation that Loeser, who wrote nothing, never acquired; but somehow I felt more secure under the sign of Loeser. He had perhaps more illusions, but also a more German simplicity and devotion to his subject. I felt that he loved the Italian renaissance and was not, as it were, merely displaying it. This was then in the future; for the moment it was only a question of reading a few books that he lent me, discussing them, and sometimes going together to the theatre—which was at his invitation. In those days there were foreign companies often playing for a week or two in Boston, French operetta, Salvini, Ristori, and grand opera. I saw everything, and in the first years it couldn't have been at my own expense. It might seem that all my life I have been "sponging" on my rich friends, or even that I have sought rich friends for that purpose. This was not the case: there were plenty of rich people about that I fled from. But with people with whom I was otherwise in sympathy, friendship was naturally more easily kept up and cemented if they had a house where they could ask me to stay, or could invite me to be their guest, partly or wholly, for trips or entertainments that I couldn't afford if left to my own resources. Loeser was my first Maecenas of this kind, and one of the most satisfactory. His invitations were specific, for particular occasions. Only once, when we were looking at some modern pictures, I stopped before one that I liked and said that it was painted as I should have wished to paint. "Why don't you do it," Loeser cried impulsively. "Why don't you stay in Paris and paint? I will help you." But I knew that this was an *ignis fatuus* in the case of both of us: I couldn't give up philosophy and an assured livelihood, and he couldn't commit himself to a responsibility that would have at once become a burden and a source of angry feelings. Ordinarily his favors were discreet, and made for his own pleasure. He never gave me money or presents, nor did any of my other friends. It was simply a question of making possible little plans that were beyond my unaided means. Thus when we travelled together in Italy, I contributed twenty gold francs a day to our expenses, and he, who knew the ropes and the language, made all the arrangements and paid all the bills. He might have been a sort of magic dragoman in my service, spiriting up the scenes and spiriting away the deficits.

At Harvard, Loeser was rather friendless. The fact that he was a Jew and that his father kept a "dry-goods store" cut him off, in democratic America, from the ruling society. To me, who was also an outsider, this seemed at first very strange, for Loeser was much more cultivated than the leaders of undergraduate fashion or athletics, and I saw nothing amiss in his person or manners. He was not good-looking, although he had a neat figure, of middle height, and nice hands: but his eyes were dead, his complexion muddy, and his features pinched, though not especially Jewish. On the other hand he was extremely well-spoken, and there was nothing about him in bad taste. To me he was always an agreeable companion, and if our friendship never became intimate, this was due rather to a certain defensive reserve in him than to any withdrawal on my part. Yet in the end, taking imaginatively the point of view of the native leading Americans, I came to see why Loeser could never gain their confidence. His heart was not with them, and his associations and standards were not theirs. He didn't join in their sports (as rich Jews have learned to do in England), he hadn't their religion, he had no roots in their native places or in their family circles. In America he floated on the surface, and really lived only in the international world of art, literature, and theory.

Yet there was something else at work: for, except for my connection with the Sturgises, all those things were true of me, with poverty added, yet I was never expressly excluded from anything in America. I was not isolated, except quite secretly in my own feelings, as any poetical or religious youth might have been anywhere. And I found afterwards, when Loeser lived in Florence, that while he knew the whole Anglo-American colony slightly, he seemed to have no friends. For a rich bachelor that was odd; and I suspect that he preferred to keep his gates shut, and prowled about, as if a little mad, in his own castle. There was usually a certain vagueness about his assertions and plans, as if he were afraid that people might interfere with him; and when he married, at fifty, a German Jewish pianist, the separation remained, except that his wife sometimes still performed, and with great power, in public or in private concerts. It surprised me, whenever I was at Strong's villa, that Loeser who had a good motor, never came to see me or asked me to go to his house, except once, to see his new tower. This made me doubt whether Loeser had ever had any affection for me, such as I had for him, and whether it was only *faute de mieux,* as a last resort in too much solitude, that in earlier years he had been so friendly. However, circumstances change, one changes as much as other people, and it would be unreasonable to act or feel in the same way when the circumstances are different. Loeser in any case had shown me Italy, initiated me into Italian ways, present and past, and made my life there in later years much richer than it would have been otherwise. Let him be thanked without any qualifications.

In the 1890's I saw him several times in London. He lived in

the Burlington Hotel, behind the Arcade, amid a great lot of
leather portmanteaux and hatboxes. He had become very English,
much to my taste; his alien but expert knowledge of how an English gentleman should dress, eat, talk, and travel amused and instructed me vastly; but he didn't seem to have real friends among
the English, other than Algar Thorold, son of the Bishop of Winchester, who (twice, I believe) had gone over to Rome. The first
time he had essayed to be a Carthusian; but being disappointed
and having a relapse, the second time he married and became an
ordinary lay Catholic. He lived in Italy, in a truly Italian villa,
where I was glad to hear him and his wife speak of Loeser with
affection. It helped to relieve the latent uneasiness I felt about my
friend. He had sometimes been so dark and inconsequential that
I suspected a touch of madness in his nature. He would say and
do things that might pass for jokes; but oddities when indulged
may become illusions. He maintained that he had two original
works of Michelangelo in his collection: one a rough ordinary
putto from some fountain or altar, the other a truly beautiful panel
in wax, a Madonna and Child (certainly after Michelangelo's
earlier work) with a St. Joseph perhaps less convincing. I am no
judge in the matter; but to have discovered two unknown and
genuine Michelangelos, and got them cheap, is certainly a collector's dream, and incredible.

It was with Loeser that I first went to Rome and to Venice: my
preference for these two cities, rather than for the Florence so dear
to English-speaking people, may be partly due to a first impression
gained under his auspices. His taste was selective. He dwelt on a
few things, with much knowledge, and did not confuse or fatigue
the mind. We reached Rome rather late at night. It had been raining, and the wet street and puddles reflected the lights fantastically. Loeser had a theory that architecture is best seen and admired at night. He proposed that we should walk to our hotel.
He had chosen the *Russie*, where as he said only Russian Grand
Dukes stayed, so that it was just the place for him and for me.
We walked by the *Quattro Fontane* and the *Piazza di Spagna—*

long walk: but I doubt that the first loud accents that I heard on arriving at the Hotel were those of a Russian Grand Duchess. She said simply: "Oh my!"

Some ten years later, in 1905, Loeser had a spacious apartment in an old palazzo near the *Uffizi* in Florence. He said he couldn't offer me a room, but had secured a choice one (*choice* was a favorite word of his) for me, quite cheap, in a tower in the *Via dei Bardi,* with a loggia where I might have my breakfast, and wave to him across the river; for he too slept in a tower and had his bath in the open loggia at the very top of it. My room was indeed in a tower; there were 149 stone steps with hardly a door to pass on the way up: my choice room did have a bed in it, but the loggia was bitterly cold on those sunless mornings. This didn't matter, however, since there was no breakfast. My woebegone landlady had no idea of coffee, milk, or rolls, and her tea, in an open broken old dish, was half dust. However, I managed. I got up late, and went to breakfast in a good café, read the papers, sunned myself on the *Lungarno,* and by half past twelve was at Loeser's place, where I was expected daily for luncheon. But he said he had no dinner, only a bite of something by the fire in his library. One evening, however, I was invited to this frugal supper, and warned that Mrs. Y., of whom he had spoken to me, would be there also. Mrs. Y. was the wife of a British officer serving in India, and I had been given to understand that she and Loeser were on the best of terms. "But my servant, Antonio," he had added, "doesn't approve of her. I asked him if he was shocked." "Chè," said Antonio, "she is too thin!" I found Mrs. Y. most amiable, a slender blonde dressed like Botticelli's *Primavera,* hatless, with a workbasket beside her and evidently quite at home. Dinner was ample, served pleasantly at a low table in front of the fire. Apparently Mrs. Y. dined there every evening, and I began to understand that practically, if not nominally, she lived in that house. That explained why there had been no room to offer me, and why Loeser never "dined." Why hadn't he simply told me the facts? Did he think I should be shocked like Antonio? Or was he protecting the lady's reputation? But then why let out the secret in the end? However, it was better to be inconsistently secretive than to be mad.

In an earlier year, when I had been free in the spring, Loeser proposed a walking tour across the Apennines. First we went to Ravenna, which I hadn't seen, and thence to Pesaro where we abandoned the railway and drove to Urbino. From there, sending our things ahead by rail, we walked to San Sepolcro and La Verna. It was travelling as in the Middle Ages, stopping at small inns or at monasteries. At La Verna we found the Franciscan community making a procession in their half-open cloister. The monks were evidently peasants, some of them young yokels fresh from the plough, no doubt ignorant and stupid; and Loeser's modern Jewish standards betrayed themselves in his utter scorn of those mere beasts, as he called them. I wondered if St. John the Baptist or Elijah might not also have seemed mere beasts; but I didn't say so. Being at once a beast and a spirit doesn't seem to me a contradiction. On the contrary, it is necessary to be a beast if one is ever to be a spirit. The modern Jew recognizes verbal intelligence, but not simple spirit. He doesn't admit anything deeper or freer than literature, science, and commerce.

When we were at the top of the pass, after deliciously drinking, like beasts on all fours, at a brook that ran down by the road, we looked about at the surrounding hilltops. They were but little above our own level, yet numerous, and suggested the top of the world. "What are you thinking of?" Loeser asked. I said: "Geography." "I," he retorted, "was thinking of God." So that Loeser would probably have reversed my judgment about not apprehending pure spirit, and would have said that the Latin or Catholic is hopelessly materialistic even in his religion, whereas the Jew hears the voice of an invisible God in the silence of nature. Very good: but why not hear that voice also in the silence of beasts or of monks? Perhaps the reason was that the mountains are the skeleton of that land which feeds and surrounds literature, science, and commerce. To the Jew the earth seems a promised land, suggesting the millennium, the triumph of God in the human world. Swine, epicureans, and monks, on the contrary, not being legally edible, seem not only useless for that purpose but positively unclean. This comes consistently enough of regarding God only as a power, the power that conditions our happiness. It is then no metaphor to say that God dwells in the mountains or in the whirlwind: their reality is his reality, and their work his work. In science, commerce, and literature you are tracing his ways. And the idea that all these vast and apparently dead forces secretly conspire to direct human history and to prepare the glory of Zion, becomes sublime. But if God were regarded rather as the *end* or the *good* in which happiness might be found, might he not seem to dwell far more directly and intimately in the monk and even in the beast than in commerce, literature, or science?

At the beginning of my Sophomore year, not in the Yard but in the Church of the Immaculate Conception, I made the acquaintance of Ward Thoron, destined to be my closest friend while we were undergraduates. He said in recent years that he was the original of Mario in my *Last Puritan,* and there is some truth in that assertion, especially in regard to his family relations; but I had other far more accomplished models for my young man, and gave him a different education, different motives, and a different career. Ward had not been educated at Eton, but at the Jesuit College in Fordham, New York. He had graduated there at seventeen; and on the strength of that degree he was mechanically and foolishly admitted to the Sophomore class at Harvard. We were in the same class, but he was three years younger than I, and younger than most Freshmen. This, together with his being a Catholic, gave me at once the feelings of an elder brother towards him, and a sort of mentor. Except that he was at home in scraps of Church Latin, he was utterly unprepared for the studies he was to take up; and not coming from any of the usual preparatory schools, he had no ready-made circle of acquaintances in the College, who might have adopted him and steered him more or less safely. Nevertheless, he had a social position much better than mine, and lived in

a private house full of boys of good families, with plenty of money
to spend. He was never lonely: and this was at once an advantage
and a danger.

His grandparents, Mr. and Mrs. "Sam" Ward, of New York,
were persons of high transcendental New England traditions, but
at the same time rich and fashionable. Mrs. Ward was an impressive old lady, dressed in obsolete but regal garments and speaking
in impassioned accents. "Ah," she would exclaim, "I could never
close my eyes if I hadn't first opened wide my window and gazed
at the stars!" In her youth she had been a colonist at Brook Farm
with the social utopians; then she had passed from one Evangelical
sect to another, until she finally landed in the Catholic Church.
There she found inner peace, but socially she remained militant.
She managed to convert her daughters and even her son, but her
husband, alas! held on to his heathen idealism and Germanic intuitions: for he too was an ardent spirit, modified by luxurious living and much shrewd knowledge of the world. His grandson sent
him an essay of mine on Free-Will, which had been printed in a
College paper: on which the old gentleman made the penetrating
observation that if I had anything to say I should be able to say it,
that I knew the stock arguments on the subject, and that there
were no others.

Not satisfied with converting her daughters, Mrs. Ward insisted
on marrying them safely to Catholics, which at that time in her
circle practically meant to foreigners. One of these, my friend's
father, was a Frenchman who had occupied some post in the
Levant; his wife had died; and their children had been adopted by
their American grandparents. Ward saw his father but seldom;
however, he could speak French easily, and took easily to his
Catholic education and his American surroundings. He needed to
sail before the wind. Rough seas and contrary blasts were not for
him: I think he had no clear object in view that could have justified him in facing them. But given an open course he was clever
enough to steer his festive voyage and enjoy himself thoroughly
in doing so.

He once wrote an essay—it was only an exercise in composition, so that the views advanced didn't matter—on the *Art of Lying*, in which he gathered such arguments as occurred to him to prove the advantages of concealing or misrepresenting the truth; and then added that equal advantages could be found in telling it. He felt that he was playing a farce, and there seemed to be nothing else for him to do. Fordham had been a farce, Harvard was a farce also: yet if everything is a farce, the one in which you find yourself acting acquires, for the time being, all the values of reality.

This philosophy, hidden in a boy of seventeen under verbal sparkle and easy manners, but breaking down under pressure into genuine Catholic humility, had everything to please me. It was not even then my own philosophy. I was as convinced as I am now of the steady march of cosmic forces that we may, in a measure, enlist in our service, and thereby win the prize of life in the process of living, without laying any claims to dominate the universe, either physically or morally. But this is a comparatively mature, though very ancient, conclusion; and it is as well to become aware in the first place of the uncertainty and blindness of human opinion.

Ward and I didn't move in the same circles; I didn't know his friends nor he mine. Yet there were hours, especially the late afternoon hours, when we were much together, when the crowd were at their sports, in which neither of us took part. In the evening his casual boon companions would carry him off on their larks, perhaps too often for his tender years. He fell ill; and during a long convalescence, when he was confined to his sofa, I used to keep him company. During those long winter afternoons we read aloud alternately the whole of Tolstoi's *War and Peace* in French. It was no school task; we could talk instead, if there were anything to talk about; and we talked more or less about everything.

A feeling that we had moved into different climates came over me some years later when after his marriage he invited me to stay with him in Washington. He was living at his mother-in-law's, presiding at the other end of the table, while his wife sat with her sisters at the side, as if they were still children. He took me to see

Mr. Henry Adams, with whom he was on very friendly terms. "So you are trying to teach philosophy at Harvard," Mr. Adams said, somewhat in the gentle but sad tone we knew in Professor Norton. "I once tried to teach history there, but it can't be done. It isn't really possible to teach anything." This may be true, if we give very exacting meanings to our terms; but it was not encouraging. Still, both Mr. Adams' house and that of Ward's new family were luxurious. I got the impression that, if most things were illusions, having money and spending money were great realities. I also gathered that Ward no longer called himself a Catholic, but was more or less affiliated to his mother-in-law's church.

I have never seen Ward after that visit to Washington. He remained there while I was in America, or in summer resorts that I didn't frequent, and he has never, to my knowledge, been in Europe in the later years. But this material separation was not indifferent; it symbolized a separation in our interests and aims. I recognize the perfect right of anybody to surrender his personal inopportune advantages for the sake of others more social and opportune. That is the path of material evolution. But the evolution I admire and appreciate is not of that kind, which transforms the character and the ideal pursued. The evolution that interests me is that of a given seed, towards its perfect manifestation. From what I have heard about my friend in his maturity and old age, I gather that he played his part well and had his reward: but it was the sort of success by adaptability in essentials that leaves me cold: so that perhaps nothing was lost to him or to me by our separation; and our affectionate relation in youth retains its intrinsic value all the more distinctly by not being followed, as in the case of some of my other friendships, by later contacts that might obscure it.

Three other men in the Harvard class of 1886 belonged in the front rank of my friends: Herbert Lyman, Frank Bullard, and Boylston Beal. All these were pure and intense Bostonians of the old school, yet with differences that mark the range of Boston "culture" at that time. "Culture," with religious and philosophical preoccupations, belonged especially to Bullard. He was a nephew of Professor Norton, and I might almost say in fortunately delicate health; fortunately, because if he had been thoroughly sound, strong, and athletic, he would have had to go into "business" or into a profession no less businesslike and absorbing, because according to the ruling code this would have been his duty to society. That was what Herbert Lyman (also potentially rich) was obliged to do all his life. Business, together with music and a semi-administrative interest in King's Chapel, formed the entirely orthodox themes of his moral harmony. This harmony was beautifully achieved; yet it had cost him some renunciations and some moments of difficulty. He would have liked to devote himself entirely to music; but he had neither the great voice nor the exceptional musical genius that would have justified him in becoming a professional musician. Later his health faltered; but he pulled through, to the good age of seventy-seven. Only two years earlier, he was kind enough to make me a visit at Cortina, and seemed to me little changed from the memorable days that, fifty-five years before, we had spent together at Dresden. Of these, and of him, I will speak again. I mention him here lest he should seem to be forgotten in my catalogue of College friends.

Bullard and I hardly knew each other when undergraduates; but ten or fifteen years later he took to studying philosophy and came to hear some of my lectures. We then established an active exchange of moral and intellectual ideas. The influence of his uncle had led him to collect prints, especially Turner prints. They were very beautiful, and on the frequent occasions when I was a guest at his mother's house, we used to go up after luncheon to his study and look over his treasures. He had also some pre-Raphaelite prints that I couldn't praise so much; but the Turners and the photographed drawings by the old masters found us equally appreciative. It is not true, by the way, that the aerial effects in Turner's landscapes are exaggerated and melodramatic. Nature in England and elsewhere—for instance in Venice—is often like that, or even more emphatic; and the delicacy with which Turner preserves the special character and melody of the parts in the midst of that violent ensemble, shows a sincere love of nature and life and a devout imagination.

Frank Bullard and his collections did much more to educate my taste than my lectures did to clarify his intellect. He was interested and unprejudiced but, as he said, "bird-witted." His flights were short and flurried. He came to no large clear conclusions; what survived was only an open and ardent spirit. Christianity and Puritanism had here debouched into a sensitive humanity; yet the natural aims of life remained for him miscellaneous and conflicting. The day of fresh decisions and sharp exclusions had not yet dawned.

With Boylston Beal, too, my friendship grew after we had left College. We lived in the same boarding house one winter in Berlin, and we were constantly together at Cambridge in the early 1890's, he being at the Law School and I a young instructor, and both frequenting the same club. Later he married a cousin of my family, which established another bond. He travelled everywhere and knew the principal languages, and was as much at home in England and in European high life as it is possible for an American to be. During the war of 1914–1918 and afterwards he was Honorary Counsellor to the American Embassy in London, telling the ladies what to wear, the men what to say and how to address royalties and persons possessing complicated titles, by law or courtesy. It was happiness to him to live in beautiful places, among refined people, with simple, graceful, and honest minds; and so it would have been to me if my lot had been more often cast among them. I did taste such happiness in obscure modest places where perhaps it ran deeper, if less sparklingly, than in official or fashionable society; but Beal saw the thing in its spectacular as well as in its intimate forms. The spectacular and official side is easier to describe and to talk about, it gives one a glimpse of political history; yet I am sure that it was the quiet and domestic side that he loved and that colored his mature judgments and opinions.

A proof of this appeared in his attachment to traditional religion

—not to his home traditions, but to the Catholic and Anglican. In Rome, where he liked to spend, when he could, a part of the winter, he sometimes would take me to some sequestered little church that he had discovered, where there was a devotional atmosphere. He was not offended by modern images and pictures and flower pots; he didn't mind if the good nuns furnished their chapels like boudoirs; he felt the pious intention: they gave their best. This is even more Spanish than Italian: a domestication of the mind and heart in religion, and being tender in small things, rather than coldly despising them and confining religion to morality or to great tragic and cosmological vistas.

In politics also Beal reacted against the denials and abstractions of the reforming zealot, and was a pronounced Tory. I sympathized with all the affections that such a position implied; but I like to open the windows of the mind wider, and to recognize not only the inevitableness of moral mutations, but their fertility. One good thing is destroyed, but another good thing may be made possible. I love Tory England and honor conservative Spain, but not with any dogmatic or prescriptive passion. If any community can become and desires to become communistic or democratic or anarchical I wish it joy from the bottom of my heart. I have only two qualms in this case: whether such ideals are realizable, and whether those who pursue them fancy them to be exclusively and universally right: an illusion pregnant with injustice, oppression, and war.

CHAPTER XVI

COLLEGE STUDIES

WITH my return to Harvard, a fortnight late, from the journey to Spain, my College studies may be said to have begun. They did not begin well. I had failed in one subject—a half course in algebra—which I was obliged to pass later, as Freshman work was prescribed and no substitutions were permitted. I had done well enough in the rest of the prescribed mathematics, analytic geometry, which I had had some grounding in at school, and also in the physics, which interested me immensely: and even in the algebra there were points that struck my imagination, as for instance the possibility and advantages of duo-decimal notation: our decimal system being founded only on the stupid reason that we have ten fingers and ten toes. If my teachers had begun by telling me that mathematics was pure play with presuppositions, and wholly in the air, I might have become a good mathematician, because I am happy enough in the realm of essence. But they were over-worked drudges, and I was largely inattentive, and inclined lazily to attribute to incapacity in myself or to a literary temperament that dullness which perhaps was due simply to lack of initiation. With a good speculative master I might have been an eager pupil and cried at once: *Introibo ad altare Dei.*

I began badly also in not having a fixed plan of study. President Eliot's elective system was then in the ascendant. We liked it, I liked it; it seemed to open a universal field to free individuality. But to be free and cultivate individuality one must first exist, one's nature must be functioning. What was I, what were my powers and my vocation? Before I had discovered that, all freedom could be nothing but frivolity. I had chosen to go on with Latin and Greek, but disregarded the requirements for second-year honors in the classics, because those requirements involved Greek composition, which I couldn't attempt. I consciously continued my reading as an amateur, not as a scholar, I wasn't going to *teach* Greek or Latin. In this way I illustrated the complementary vices of the elective system: I was a smatterer, because things were arranged for the benefit of professionals.

So superficial was my study that I hardly remember what Latin authors I read or who was the professor. I read Lucretius, in a pocket edition without notes given me by a friend, somewhat pathetically, because he was leaving College. I couldn't properly understand the text, many a word was new to me, and I had to pass on, reading as I did at odd moments, or in the horse cars. But the general drift was obvious, and I learned the great passages by heart. Even the physical and biological theories seemed instructive, not as scientific finalities, if science could be final, but as serving to dispel the notion that anything is non-natural or miraculous. If the theory suggested were false, another no less naturalistic would be true: and this presumption recommended itself to me and has become one of my first principles: not that a particular philosophy called naturalism must be true *a priori*, but that nature sets the standard of naturalness. The most miraculous world, if it were real, would subdue the teachable mind to its own habit, and would prove that miracles were—as they are in the Gospels—the most ordinary and most intelligible of events. It made me laugh afterwards to read in pedantic commentators that Lucretius abandoned his atomism whenever he was poetical, and contradicted himself in invoking Venus, when Epicurus maintains that the gods do not trouble about human affairs. On the contrary, Lucretius might perfectly well have invoked Jupiter or Fate (as Leopardi constantly invokes Fate); for Fate, Jupiter, or Venus are names for the whole or some part of the life of nature. There is no incompatibility in these various appellations, if they are understood sympathetically as the ancients understood them. They were not gaping phenomenalists, but knew that our senses, no less than our poetry and myth, clothe in human images the manifold processes of matter. By these hidden processes they lived, before them they trembled, the promise and potency of them they sought to prophesy. Matter was the ancient plastic substance of all the gods.

I also took a half course in Latin composition which I audaciously neglected, "cutting" all the lectures except the first, but doing the prescribed exercises and taking the examinations. I passed with a mark of ninety per cent.

In Greek I did as badly as at school. Here again this was not the teacher's fault. He was the amiable Louis Dyer, who had studied at Balliol, married a Miss Macmillan, and later lived in Oxford, where I often saw him. He gave me his *Gods of Greece,* nicely bound, a book that had a great influence over me. Perhaps Matthew Arnold moved in the background and inspired us. But I was thirsting for inspiration, and Greek grammar and prosody didn't hold my attention. We were supposed to read the *Ajax,* but though in this case I went to all the lectures, I didn't study the text. The *Bacchæ,* however, was a revelation. Here, before Nietzsche had pointed it out, the Dionysiac inspiration was explicitly opposed to the Apollonian; and although my tradition and manner are rather Apollonian, I unhesitatingly accept the Dionysiac inspiration as also divine. It comes from the elemental god, from the chaotic but fertile bosom of nature; Apollo is the god of measure, of perfection of humanism. He is more civilized, but more superficial, more highly conditioned. His worship seems classic and established forever, and it does last longer and is more often revived than any one form of Dionysiac frenzy: yet the frenzy represents the primitive wild soul, not at home in the world, not settled in itself, and merging again with the elements, half in helplessness and half in self-transcendence and mystic triumph.

I have taken for a motto a phrase out of one of Euripides' choruses: Τὸ σοφὸν οὐ σοφία. It was this phrase, in that year, 1884, that led me to write my first sonnet, printed a year or two later, and reappearing as Sonnet III in my *Poems*; the first two having been composed afterwards on purpose to frame in the earlier ones and bring the argument to a head. I translated the dictum of Euripides in the rather thin and prosaic line: "It is not wisdom to be only wise"; and then, given that sentiment and that rhyme, I built the whole sonnet round them. Even when I wrote it, this sonnet was belated. I was twenty years old, and that sentiment was what I had felt at sixteen. But I still recognized, as I recognize now at nearly eighty, the legitimacy of that feeling.

The chief difference is that when, at sixteen or even at twenty, I said "faith," I meant the Catholic faith; and when now I oppose "faith" to reason I mean faith in the existence and order of nature, a faith in the assumptions made inevitably in daily life; yet I see far more clearly than I did in my youth that pure reason, a reason that is not based on irrational postulates and presuppositions, is perfectly impotent. It is not "smoky" or indistinct: on the contrary, it is mathematically precise, but abstract and in the air. What I had in mind then when I spoke of "knowledge" was the common sense and science of the day, which in fact were uncritically based on animal faith and empirical presumption, and which I, with a solipsistic breath, could at once reduce to a dream, not to say a nightmare. For that reason I called them "smoky," at once ugly, obscure, and unsubstantial. But it was immature of me to wish, lackadaisically and hopelessly, to substitute a religious myth for that sensuous obsession. And the rest of those twenty youthful sonnets pointed out well enough where a mature solution might be found: in obedience to matter for the sake of freedom of mind.

As to William James on Taine's *De l'Intelligence,* I am not conscious of any intellectual residuum, only of a few graphic memories touching his aspects and ways, which at that time were distinctly medical. He was impatient of the things he didn't like in philosophy; his latent pragmatism appeared only in its negative germ, as scorn of everything remote or pretentious; and his love of lame ducks and neglected possibilities, which later took the form of charity and breadth of mind, then seemed rather the doctor's quick eye for bad symptoms, as if he had diagnosed people in a jiffy and cried: "Ah, *you* are a paranoiac! Ah, *you* have the pox!" I remember his views better in another set of lectures on Herbert Spencer, or rather against him. James detested any system of the universe that professed to enclose everything: we must never set up boundaries that exclude romantic surprises. He retained the primitive feeling that death *might* open new worlds to us—not at all what religions predict but something at once novel and natural; also the primitive feeling that invisible spirits *might* be floating about among us, and might suddenly do something to hurt or to help us. Spencer was intolerable for shutting out such possibilities: he was also intolerable for his verbose generalities and sweeping "principles." There were no "principles," except in men's heads: there were only facts. James did not stop to consider whether this assertion was not itself a principle that might describe a fact.

Herbert Spencer, I think, taught me nothing. I agreed with his naturalism or materialism, because that is what we all start with: the minimum presupposition of perception and action. But I agreed with James about Spencer's theory of evolution: It was a tangle of words, of loose generalities that some things might sometimes suggest to us, and that, said properly, it might have been *witty* to say, but that had absolutely no value as "laws" or "causes" of events. Such "principles" might serve an "objective idealist," not a naturalist or a scientific man. James was characteristically masculine and empirical in his wrath at the "scandalous vagueness" of Spencer's ideas. For instance, what did it mean to say that things passed from the indefinite to the definite? Nothing can be indefinite. Make a blot of ink at random on a piece of paper. The spot is not indefinite: it has precisely the outline that it has.* But James, though trenchant was short-winded in argument. He didn't go on, for instance to consider on this occasion how, if there be

---

* Here was a hint of my "essences" given by an unintended shot, that hit the bull's-eye without seeing it. Forms are infinite in multitude and each perfectly concrete. James's radical empiricism was undoubtedly a guide to me in this matter. Also Berkeley's nominalism.

nothing indefinite, the notion of the indefinite comes into existence. Suppose that having made a random blot, shapeless as we
call it in spite of its perfectly definite shape, I at once folded the
paper in two. The blot would become two symmetrical blots, or a
larger blot bilaterally symmetrical. It might resemble an oak leaf.
It would then cease to have a nameless shape, but would become
Platonically or humanly specific. We should say it had a definite
shape, one that we could recognize and reproduce. Spencer, if we
interpret him critically and progressively, was therefore saying that
things change from forms that for our senses and language would
not be recognizable or namable into forms that we can distinguish
and name. This happens sometimes not because things grow more
definite, but because our senses and imagination have a limited
range and can arrest one form of things rather than another; so
that the world grows definite *for us* when we are able to perceive
more parts of it and their relations. Nature thereby has changed
but only intelligence has advanced; change is called evolution
when sense and language are thereby enabled better to distinguish
their objects. The notion that nature first acquired form as an
animal mind may gradually grow less stupid, belongs to the age of
fable. Spencer, unlike Lucretius and Spinoza, had no speculative
power. He meant to be a naturalist, but language and the hypos-
tasized idea of progress turned him into an idealistic metaphysi-
cian.

I will not attempt to describe here the many lessons that I
learned in the study of Spinoza, lessons that in several respects laid
the foundation of my philosophy. I will only say that I learned
them from Spinoza himself, from his *ipsissima verba*, studied in
the original in all the crucial passages; as a guide and stimulus I
had Sir Frederick Pollock's sympathetic book, with good render-
ings, and not much modern interpretation. It was a work, as he
told me himself forty-five years later, at the Spinoza commemoration at the Hague, of his youth; and perhaps the science was emphasized at the expense of the religion. Yet that the object of this
religion was *Deus sive Natura*—the universe, whatever it may be,

of which we are a part—was never concealed or denaturalized. Royce himself seemed to suffer less from the plague of idealistic criticism in this case than usual; for instance, about the saying of Spinoza's that the mind of God resembled the mind of man as the Dog Star resembles the barking animal. Royce said only that this was too materialistic, without caring or daring to broach the question as to the diffusion or concentration of that cosmic "mind." The unified "universal thought" that Royce posited would not be a "cogitation" but only a truth, the total *system* of cogitations that may accompany the total movement of matter. If it were one actual intuition it would not *accompany* the movement of matter but either describe and command it from afar or merely imagine it. Royce had a powerful and learned mind, and it was always profitable, if not pleasant, to listen to him: not pleasant because his voice was harsh, his style heavy, repetitious and pedantic, and his monotonous preoccupation with his own system intolerable. To listen was profitable nevertheless because his comfortless dissatisfaction with every possible idea opened vistas and disturbed a too easy dogmatism: while the perversity and futility of his dialectic threw one back in the end on the great certainties and the great possibilities, such as made the minds of the great philosophers at once sublime and sane.

As I have said elsewhere, I regard Spinoza as the only modern philosopher in the line of orthodox physics, the line that begins with Thales and culminates, for Greek philosophy, in Democritus. Orthodox physics should inspire and support orthodox ethics; and perhaps the chief source of my enthusiasm for Spinoza has been the magnificent clearness of his orthodoxy on this point. Morality is something natural. It arises and varies, not only psychologically but prescriptively and justly, with the nature of the creature whose morality it is. Morality is something relative; not that its precepts in any case are optional or arbitrary; for each man they are defined by his innate character and possible forms of happiness and action. His momentary passions or judgments are partial expressions of his nature, but not adequate or infallible; and ignorance of the circumstances may mislead in practice, as ignorance of self may mislead in desire. But there is a fixed good relative to each species and each individual; so that in considering the moral ideal of any philosopher, two questions arise. First, does he, like Spinoza, understand the natural basis of morality, or is he confused and superstitious on the subject? Second, how humane and representative is his sense for the good, and how far, by his disposition or sympathetic intelligence, does he appreciate all the types of excellence towards which life may be directed?

James and Royce were then the "young" professors of philosophy, they represented the dangers and scandals of free thought, all the more disquieting in that their free thought enveloped religion. But Harvard possessed safe, sober old professors also and oldest of all, "Fanny" Bowen. He was so old that to be old, self-repeating, dogmatic, rheumatic, and querulous had become picturesque in him, and a part of his dramatic personage. He was a dear old thing, and an excellent teacher. Between his fits of coughing, and his invectives against all who were wrong and didn't agree with Sir William Hamilton, he would impress upon us many an axiom, many an argument belonging to the great traditions of philosophy: and when after spitting into the vast bandanna handkerchief that he carried for the purpose, he would drop it on the desk with a gesture of combined disgust and relief, he expressed vividly to the eye the spirit in which philosophic and religious sects have always refuted and denounced one another. History sat living before us in this teacher of history. Descartes, Leibniz and Spinoza would be quoted verbatim, and expounded (especially the first two) on their own presuppositions and in their own terms. It was not criticism but it was instruction. Spinoza was rather beyond Bowen's range; yet even here the words of the master would be repeated, and could be remembered in their terseness, while the professor's refutations would blow by like dead leaves. Unfortunately old Bowen did not always preach to his text. Sometimes he would wander into irrelevant invectives against John Stuart Mill, who in a footnote had once referred to

Bowen (who was then editor of a reputable review) as "an obscure American."

We had another right-thinking and edifying teacher, no less thoroughly well baked in all his opinions and mannerisms, but younger in years and following a later fashion in philosophy. Professor Palmer practised all the smooth oratorical arts of a liberal parson or headmaster; he conciliated opponents, plotted (always legally) with friends, and if things went against him, still smiled victoriously and seemed to be on the crest of the wave. He was the professor of ethics. His lectures were beautifully prepared, and exactly the same year after year. He had been professor of Greek also, and made anodyne translations from Homer and Sophocles in "rhymic" and sleepy prose. In his course on English moralists he brought out his selected authors in dialectical order; each successive view appeared fresh and plausible, but not sensational. They came in a subtle crescendo, everything good, and everything a little better than what went before, so that at the end you ought to have found yourself in the seventh heaven. Yet we, or at least I, didn't find ourselves there. I felt cheated. The method was Hegelian adapted to a Sunday School: all roses without thorns. All defects in doctrine (why not also in conduct?) were steppingstones to higher things. We began with pungent, mannish, violent theories: Hobbes and Mandeville. We passed onward to something more feminine and refined, to Shaftesbury. From this we dialectically reacted, landing in the apparently solid, liberal, political reformer, John Stuart Mill: but no, that was not our divine destination. A breath of higher philosophy somehow blew over us. We levitated; and we knew not how or why, utilitarianism dissolved, lost in the distant valleys beneath us, and we realized the providential utility of utilitarianism in carrying us so far above it. "Purring pussy Palmer," my sporting friend "Swelly" Bangs used to call him: yet Palmer was a benign influence. The crude, half-educated, conscientious, ambitious young men who wished to study ethics gained subtler and more elastic notions of what was good than they had ever dreamt of: and their notions of what was bad became correspondingly discriminating and fair. Palmer was like a father confessor, never shocked at sin, never despairing of sinners. There must be a little of everything in the Lord's vineyard. Palmer was a fountain of sweet reasonableness. That his methods were sophistical and his conclusions lame didn't really matter. It was not a question of discovering or deciding anything final: the point was to become more cultivated and more intelligent. You could then define your aims and your principles for yourself. I found the authors read in Palmer's course, especially Hobbes, valuable in themselves; and Palmer's methods of exposition and criticism, sly and treacherous as they were, gave me a lesson in dialectic, and a warning against it. I began to understand that the cogency of dialectic is merely verbal or ideal, and its application to facts, even to the evolution of ideas, entirely hypothetical and distorting. If ideas created themselves (which they don't) or succeeded one another in the mind or in history by logical derivation (as again they don't), evolution might be dialectical: but as it is, dialectic merely throws a verbal net into the sea, to draw a pattern over the fishes without catching any of them. It is an optical illusion.

Dialectic didn't show its other, its honest, side to me until many years later, when I read Plato and knew Bertie Russell. Honest logicians never apply dialectic to history, and only in play to cosmology. Events are derived from one another materially and contingently. This is no less true when events are mental than when they are physical. It is *external* insights and interests that transform one system of philosophy into another, Socrates into Plato, Locke into Berkeley, Kant into Schopenhauer and Hegel. Each system remains logically and morally stable, like a portrait of its author. A philosophy that is radical and consistent cannot evolve. That which evolves is only the immature, the self-contradictory; and if circumstances do not permit it to ripen according to its inner potentialities, it withers and dissolves into dust, leaving no progeny. Each fact, each group of ideas, in fusion with other facts, passes into a new natural form, not evolved from the previous forms dialectically, but created by nature out of their matter and occasion, at each juncture with a fresh result.

I also studied Locke, Berkeley, and Hume under William

James. Here there was as much honest humanity in the teacher as
in the texts, and I think I was not impervious to the wit and wisdom of any of them. Hume was the one I least appreciated: yet
Palmer once said that I had Hume in my bones. In reality,
whether through my immaturity only, or through James's be-
wilderment also, I seem to have gathered no clear lesson from
those authors or from James himself. Verbally I understood them
well enough; they were not superficially obscure; but critically, as
to their presuppositions, their categories and their places in history,
I understood nothing. Even when four years later I gave that very
course, I didn't advance beyond a friendly literary interpretation
of their meaning and of the psychological cosmos that they seemed
to posit. I hardly questioned their ambiguous units, their "perceptions" or "ideas," but accepted them, as James then accepted
them, as representing total scattered moments of "experience" or
"life." This was historically just. This philosophy is purely literary
and autobiographical. It sees "experience" as composed of the
high lights that language and memory find in it retrospectively. It
hypostasizes the description into the object. But such hypostasis
is an indefensible trick of memory, a poetical or mythical substitu-
tion of images for events and of verbal for dynamic elements. It is
as if I pretended, in writing this book, to have discovered the
fundamental reality and total composition of myself, of my family,
of Spain, America, Germany, England, and Italy. A monstrous
trick of verbal legerdemain, a sophistical curiosity.

The only solid foundation for all my play with this subject was
supplied by the sturdy but undeveloped materialism of Hobbes,
powerfully supported by the psychology of Spinoza and insecurely
by the early medical psychology of James: to which in Germany
my passing enthusiasm for Schopenhauer may be added, because
by that time I was able to discount the language of a system and
perceive from what direction it drew its inspiration. The "Will"
in Schopenhauer was a transparent mythological symbol for the
flux of matter. There was absolute equivalence between such a
system, in its purport and sense for reality, and the systems of
Spinoza and Lucretius. This was the element of ancient sanity

that kept me awake and conscious of the points of the compass in the subsequent wreck of psychologism. Such wrecks are not fatal. Psychologism lives, and must always live, in literature and history. In these pursuits we are living as we imagine others might have lived, and seeing things as they might have seen them. We are dramatically enlarging our experience. What was lost in that moral tempest was only the illusion that such play of imagination revealed any profound truth or dislodged Nature to put Experience in her place.

An event that had important consequences in the future course of my life occurred silently and almost unnoticed during my Senior year. A young man named Charles Augustus Strong—there was already something royal and German about that "Augustus" and that "Strong," though the youth was modesty and Puritanism personified—came from the university of his native Rochester, New York, to study philosophy for a year at Harvard. As I too was taking all the advanced courses in that subject, we found ourselves daily thrown together, gradually began to compare notes, and to discuss the professors and their opinions; and finally we founded a philosophical club, in order to discuss everything more thoroughly with the other embryonic philosophers in the place. Towards the end of the year we both became candidates for the Walker Fellowship, usually awarded to graduates who wished to study philosophy in Germany. This was a rivalry that I disliked and also feared; because, if I had the advantage of being a Harvard man and better known to the professors, and also of being more glib and more resourceful in examinations, he had the decisive advantage of inspiring professional confidence. When you learned that his father and his brother were Baptist clergymen, you recognized at once that he too was a Baptist clergyman by nature and habit, only that some untoward influence had crossed his path and deflected him from his vocation. He had lost his faith in revelation. Modernist compromises and ambiguities were abhorrent to his strict honesty and love of precision. You mustn't preach what you don't believe.

He turned therefore to the nearest thing to being a clergyman

that he could be sincerely, which was to be a professor of philosophy. He was already, in aspect, in manner, in speech, in spirit,
thoroughly professional. Moreover, for studying in Germany he
was far better prepared than I in that he spoke German perfectly.
He had been at school in Germany, in a Gymnasium at Gütersloh,
and had received that strict training in all subjects which was not
to be expected in free America. He was slow but accurate, and
his zeal in the pursuit of truth was unflagging. He had the
memory and solidity of the head boy of the class. Besides, when
you observed him afresh, you saw that he was very good-looking,
tall, firm, with curly black hair and noble features. It was only his
shyness, reserve, and lack of responsive sympathy that obscured
these advantages. Perhaps if he found his proper element and were
happy they would shine out again.

How about me? Was I professional? Should I ever make a professor of philosophy? Everybody doubted it. I not only doubted it
myself, but was repelled by the idea. What I wanted was to go on
being a student, and especially to be a travelling student. I loved
speculation for itself, as I loved poetry, not out of worldly respect
or anxiety lest I should be mistaken, but for the splendor of it, like
the splendor of the sea and the stars. And I knew I should love
living obscurely and freely in old towns, in strange countries, hearing all sorts of outlandish marvellous opinions. I could have made
a bargain with Mephistopheles, not for youth but for the appearance of youth, so that with its tastes but without its passions, I
might have been a wandering student all my life, at Salamanca,
at Bologna, in Oxford, in Paris, at Benares, in China, in Persia.
Germany would be a beginning. If I never became a professor, so
much the better. I should have seen the world, historical and intellectual: I should have been free in my best years.

Now my mother was going to assign me a permanent allowance
of $500 a year, the sum that she received from "Uncle Russell"
or that symbolically represented the $10,000 she had once received
from "Uncle Robert," which she retained and meant to leave to
me. The Walker Fellowship amounted to another $500. The two

would make a neat sum, yet I knew that in Europe I could easily get on with less. From things that Strong had dropped in conversation, I had gathered that he was much in the same case. His father was well off and he too had an allowance. Perhaps he didn't need the whole Fellowship. I therefore did a sly thing. I asked him if he would be willing to agree that whoever of us got the Fellowship should divide it with the other. Then we should both be sure of going to Germany for the next year. He consented at once. I think he liked the idea of having me with him. Our discussions enlivened him. I should serve as a useful pace-maker in the pursuit of absolute truth.

Nevertheless my conscience was a bit uneasy. I felt in my bones that Strong would get the appointment, and I was simply robbing him of half his stipend. So I made a second proposal. Before agreeing to this plan, let us lay it before Professor Palmer, professional moralist and Head of the Department, practically the man who would decide between us. Let us ask him if he thought well of it. We went to see him together. I acted as spokesman, having the readier tongue. I said we supposed we were the only likely candidates for the Fellowship, that we both wanted it very much, and that we both had small allowances from our families, so that we could get on with less than the whole amount of the Fellowship. Would it be a fair thing for us to agree, whoever got it, to divide it between us?

Professor Palmer bit his lips, thought for a moment, and decided to be sympathetic. He saw no objection. The action would be equally unselfish in both of us. I knew it was not unselfish in me, yet Palmer's cant set me at rest. They must have been undecided about the choice in the Committee, otherwise Palmer would not have agreed to the division. Now they would give the Fellowship to Strong, knowing that I was to get half the money; so that really they would be voting half the money to me. Not quite satisfactory this, but excusable and rather ingenious.

I think this is the only occasion in my life when I have done something a little too clever in order to get money. Yet the result might have encouraged a person inclined to trickery, because I not only got what I wanted, but in consequence made a great haul, not exactly in money, but precisely in what I cared for more than for money, in travel, in residence in foreign parts, in a well-paved path open to all sorts of intellectual pleasures. Strong, for a family reason that I shall mention later, gave up the Fellowship at the end of one year. It was then awarded to me for two successive years. Later, Strong went to live in Europe, in Paris, in Fiesole. He had got used to having me to talk with. I was often his guest for long periods; and that division of his $500 let me into a series of favors that I was positively begged to receive. Strong had become rich, he was married and had a young daughter: yet his life was strangely solitary. He was no less bored than when he was younger. He would actually have paid me, as he paid one or two others, to live near him so as to have stated hours for philosophical discussions. He once expressly offered to guarantee me an income of $2,500 if I would give up my professorship and go and live with him in Paris. I didn't accept that offer; I waited before retiring until I had money enough of my own to make me independent; but I did make his apartment in Paris my headquarters for some years; which for me at that time was a great convenience and economy. I had a lodging at will, gratis, and I paid for food and service only when I was alone in the apartment or when we dined in restaurants, as we did every evening. At first on these occasions each paid for both on alternate days; later each always paid for what he ordered. Our tastes were becoming more different.

There was always a latent tension between us, because our reasons for living together were mixed and not the same in both of us. In both there was real sympathy up to a point and a real interest in the same philosophical problems and political and social matters; and our views if not identical were cooperative. They played round the same facts in the same speculative spirit. Yet we were not intimate friends. We were more like partners in the same business. And our motive for forming this partnership was in neither of us personal affection but in both only private interest.

Strong wanted a philosophical friend to talk with; at first mainly for the sake of company and stimulation, later rather in the hope of forcing his views and confirming himself in them by convincing someone else of their truth. I, on the other hand, wanted a material pied-à-terre, a place and a person or persons that should take the place of a home; and Strong offered these in a most acceptable form, especially when he lived in Paris. He was free from almost all the bonds from which I wished to be free; he was less entangling socially and financially than such attachments as I might have found in Spain or in England. Besides, I lived with him only at certain seasons, seldom longer than for a month or two at a time; and there was no pledge that our arrangement should be permanent. In fact, I constantly went off by myself, to Spain, to Oxford, to Rome, or even to other lodgings in Paris: because I found writing difficult, both materially and psychologically, when we lived together. His hours were inflexible, also his determination to revert daily to the same discussions; the limitations that had become tyrannical over him became tyrannical over others also. In this way, while the friendly partnership originally formed by us in dividing the Walker Fellowship accompanied us through life, the mixed motives that had prompted it accompanied us also. Strong was always being cheated, and a victim that complained of not being victimized enough; and I was always being punished by a sense of unnecessary dependence and constraint, when it was freedom and independence that I had sought.

These observations anticipate events that lay far in the future. For the moment I was plunged in work, more wholeheartedly perhaps than ever again, because I saw my future and my studies in an undivided prospect: my whole inner life would be in those studies, while those studies in turn would determine my career. And my bad beginning as a student at Harvard was redeemed by an honorable end. I received my bachelor's degree *summa cum laude*. In spite of mediocre standing in some subjects, my teachers thought that my speculative vocation and my understanding of the great philosophers entitled me to a first place. This was a repetition with a difference, of my career at the Latin School. There I had, as a person, carried the day against a middling record as a pupil: now at Harvard I carried the day against the same handicap by force of personal abilities in a special half-artistic direction.

I didn't wait, however, to receive my degree in person at Commencement. Herbert Lyman took the parchment in charge and brought it to me in Germany. On taking my last examination, I had sailed without knowing what would be the result. I took a German ship, not that I was bound directly to Germany, but that it touched at Cherbourg whence second class this time, I could travel leisurely to Avila and see a lot of cathedral towns: Caen, Le Mans, Angers, Poitiers, Angoulême, Bordeaux, and Burgos. The expense, stopping one night at each place, was not greater than in going first class through Paris. I was to spend the summer quietly in Avila, and in the autumn to join Herbert Lyman in Dresden and Strong in Berlin.

The curtain drops here, to rise presently on those other scenes.

INDEX

INDEX

Abbott's *Lives*, 145
Adams, Henry, 234
Adamses, the, 68
Alain, 101
America, 48, 80, 87, 133, 140–1, 155, 180, 182–3, 192, 198, 201, 203–4, 209–10, 225–7
Anderson, Mary, 199
Anglo-Saxon, the, 131, 209–10
Apollo, 240
Assumption, by Titian, 168
At the Church Door, by George Santayana, 174
Avila, 17, 19–20, 25–7, 78–9, 90–1, 96–115, 191
Avila, Cathedral of, 112–5

Bacchae, the, 240
Bacon, Francis, *New Atlantis*, by, 209–10
Badumés, 1
Baldwin, — —, 195, 197
Bangs, "Swelly," 246
Barcelona, 1, 5, 7, 217
Baring Brothers, 57
Basques, the, 39
Batang Island, 36–8
Bayley, Edward, 181–5
Beacon Street (No. 302), 70, 72, 84, 90, 140–7, 181
Beal, Boylston, 234, 236–7
Beck Hall, 193
Bedford Street Schoolhouse, 153–4
Berenson, 225
Berkeley, 242 n.
Bernhardt, Sarah, 222
Bilbao, 133
Bishop's Palace, Avila, 99
Blas, Gil, 11–2
Borrás, José (y Bufurull, author's maternal grandfather), 1–6, 31–2, 34, 36–7, 46

Borrás, Josefina (author's mother), 1, 2, 6–8, 22–3, 30–55, 57, 60–6, 70–3, 77–8, 86–7, 89–90, 96, 116–21, 137–8, 143, 181, 203, 215, 217, 250
Borrás, Teresa Carbonell (author's maternal grandmother), 1, 4, 6, 31–2, 37
Boscovitz family, in *The Last Puritan*, 82
Boston, 49–50, 53, 66, 68, 70–1, 76, 80, 83, 86, 97, 132–4, 234
Boston fire (1873), 71–2
Boston Latin School. *See* Latin School, The
Boston Music Hall, 158
Bostonian, the, 72, 80, 83, 137, 142, 151, 199
Bowen, "Fanny," 245–6
Boylston Place house, Boston, 70–2, 75–6, 90
Bridges, Robert, 14, 190
Brimmer School, the, 150
Bullard, Frank, 234–6
Bute, Marquis of, 131
Byron, Lord, *Don Juan*, by, 145

Caballero, Fernan, *El Servilón y el Liberalito*, by, 145
Cabrasco, Joaquín, 1
Cambridge Common, 192
Cánovas del Castillo, 210
Capen, Mr., 153, 155
Carcassonne Church (in the citadel), 167
Chadwick, Mr., 161
Charles River, Mass., 142
Church of the Immaculate Conception, Boston, 87, 132, 163–77
Cushing, Howard, 189

Davis, Charles, 140, 178–9
De l'Intelligence, by Taine, 241
Democritus, 244
de Santayana. See Santayana
Dionysius, 240
Don Juan, by Lord Byron, 145
Don Quixote, by Cervantes, 145
Drew, Miss, 53
Dyer, Louis, 240

Eames, Emma, 83
El Chenique, 79–80
Eliot, Charles W., 162, 238
El Pasmo de Sicilia, 15
El Servilón y el Liberalito, by Fernan Caballero, 145
El Siglo Futuro, 20
Elvira, Cousin, 27, 89
Emerson, Ralph Waldo, 50, 184
England, 25, 48, 131, 190, 209–10, 235, 237
English, the, 23, 83, 131, 190
English High School, Boston, 181
Episcopal Theological School, Cambridge, Mass., 223
Escalera, Mercedes de la, 40, 54, 90
Escalera, Toribio de la, 40, 54, 77
Essay on Man, by Alexander Pope, 34
Euripides, 241

Fearless, S.S., 47
Felton, 195, 197
Ferdinand VII, 4
Fiction and Truth or Truth and Poetry, by Goethe, 149
Fiske, Arthur Irving, 155–7
Fletcher, Prof., 189
Florence, Italy, 228–9
Franklin, Benjamin, 146
Free-Will, essay by George Santayana, 232
Fulton, Father, 88, 166–7

Gardner, Mr., 152–3
Gardner, Mrs., 83
Gare d'Orléans, 206

Garfield, Harry, 180–1
Garfield, James, 180
Gautier, Théophile, 198
Gibbon, Edward, 145
Glasgow, 1, 2, 4
Gods of Greece, by Louis Dyer, 240
Goethe, 149
Goya, 15
Groce, Mr., 155–7
Groton School, 68, 183

Harvard University, 9, 97, 201–2, 223, 238, 245
Harvard Monthly, 199–200
Harvard Yard, The, 186–202
Hasty Pudding Club, 199
Hearst, William Randolph, 198–9
Hermitage of Our Lady of Sonsolès, Avila, 106–9
History of Architecture, by Ferguson, 146
Hobbes, 17, 92, 246–8
Holden Chapel, 192
Hollis Hall, 186, 191–2
Holmes, Dr. Oliver Wendell, 50
Holworthy Hall, 193
Homers, the, 81–3
Houghton, A. B., 200–1
Hubbard, Gorham, 179
Hume, 247–8

Iasigis, the, 81–3
Ignacia, Maria, 207
India Building, Boston, 72, 90
Institute Theatricals (of 1884), 199
Iparraguirre, 39
Iparraguirre, Victorina, 40–1, 53–4, 90
Irish, the, 39
Isabel, Infanta, 78
Isabella, Queen, 76–8
Italy, 227–30

Jackson, Andrew, 5–6
James, William, 241–3, 245, 248
Jesuit College, Avila, 99
Jesuits, the, 163–5, 170

Jewish Book of the Jubilees, 170 n.
Johnson, Lionel, 14
Julius Caesar, by Wm. Shakespeare, 145

Keroll, Adelaida, 32
King's Chapel, 81

la China, Juana, 52
La Granja, 76–7
La Lonja, 213
Lampoon, The, 195–9
La Seo, 212
Last Puritan, The, by George Santayana, 82, 138 n., 184, 231
Latin School, The, Boston, 9, 148–62, 179, 254
Latins, the, 209
La Verna, 230
La Virgen del Pilar, 213
Le Mans, 167
Little's Block, Cambridge, Mass., 193
Liverpool, 131, 133
"Locke, Grandmother," 31
Loeser, Charles, 224–30
Loeser, Mrs. Charles, 227
London, 98
Longfellow, Henry Wadsworth, 50
Lowell, Abbot Lawrence, 202
Lowell, James Russell, 50
Lowell, Sara, 80–1
Lucretius, 239
Lyman, Herbert, 234–5, 254
Lyons, 222

Macmillan, Miss, 240
Madrid, 1, 54, 133
Mandeville, 246
Manila, 42
Marichalar, Antonio (Marqués de Montesa), 10
Maupassant, Guy de, 198
Mediterranean, 217
Merrill, Moses, 161–2
Middlemore, Mr., 60
Mill, John Stuart, 245–6

Milton, John, 184
Monsén Rubí, Chapel of, 111
Mosque of Omar, 213
Motley's Spanish History, 145
Murillo, 168
Museum of Fine Art, Boston, 68
Museum Theatre, Boston, 49

Napoli, the, Boston, 71
New Atlantis, by Francis Bacon, 209–10
New England, 191–3, 196
Newman, John Henry, 15
Norton, Charles Eliot, 49, 234–5
Norton, Grace, 67
Norwegians, the, 39
Novaliches, General Pavía, Marqués de, 19–21, 78
Novaliches, Marquesa de, 20

O'Connor, Father, 166
O.K. Society, 199–200
Oñate, 99
Optic, Oliver, 145
Orà, General, 77
Orà, Milagros, 77
Orà, Primitiva, 77

Paderewska, Madame, 83
Palmer, George Herbert, 246–8, 251
Pantheon, the, 212
Parcent, 99
Paz brothers, the, 121–2
Peabody, Mr., 183
Pelayo, 210–2
Philippine Islands, 19
Plato, 247
Plutarch, 145
Poland, 83
Pollock, Sir Frederick, 243
Poor Richard's Proverbs, by Benjamin Franklin, 146
Pope, Alexander, *Essay on Man,* by. 34
Portugálete, 133
Potter, Warwick, 182–4
Prado, the, 15, 18

Prescott, William Hickling, 145
Prim, 19

Quintilian, **17**

Reus, 1, 3
Revue des Deux Mondes, La, 187
Romans, the, 23–4, 37
Rome, 228
Romeo and Juliet, by Wm. Shakespeare, 145
Rothschild, the, 57
Rousseau, Jean-Jacques, 36–8
Roxbury, 33, 48, 87
Roxbury Plato Club, 33
Royce, J., 88, 244
Ruiz (Santayana family name), 11
Ruskin, John, 141, 146
Russell, 2nd Earl, 139
Russell, Bertrand, 139 n., 247
Russell & Sturgis, 59
Russie, Hotel, 228–9

Sagasta, 211
St. Peter's, 167
St. Sophia, 213
St. Thomas, 170
Samaria, S.S., 132
Sanborn, 195–6, 200
San Marcos, Church of, 1
San Vicente Cathedral, 111
Santa Ana, Church and Convent of, 26
Santa Marta, 99
Santa Teresa, 87, 92, 99, 102–4
Santander, province of, 1, 10
Santayana, Augustín Ruiz de (author's father), 1, 8–29, 38–9, 47–8, 54–5, 57, 65–6, 94, 96, 108, 118, 127–8, 131–2, 135, 203, 207–10, 213–5, 217–8, 221–3
Santayana, derivation of the name, 10–11
Santayana, George, *passim*
Santayana, Juan (author's cousin), 216

Santayana, Manuel (author's uncle), 214–6
Santayana, Manuela (author's cousin), 216, 220–1
Santayana, Maria Antonia Reboiro Ruiz de (author's paternal grandmother), 1, 10, 214–5
Santayana, Mariquita (author's aunt), 214–6, 220
Santayana, Nicolás Ruiz de (author's paternal grandfather), 1, 10
Santayana, Nicolás Ruiz de (author's uncle), 1, 2, 213–4
Santiago (author's uncle), 96, 119, 127; Antoñita, daughter of, 119–26; Maria Josefa, wife of, 119–22, 125–8
Santo Tomás Monastery, 105, 111
Saragossa, 212–3
Sardou, Victorien, 222
Sastre, Caledonia (author's brother-in-law), 91, 105–8, 211, 215
Sastre, Rafael (author's nephew), 106
Schmidt, Herr, 117–9
Schopenhauer, 248
Scotch, the, 39
Sembrich, Marcella, 83
Serrano, 19
Shaftesbury, 246
Shakespeare, 145
•Shaler, Nathaniel, 196
Shaw, Mrs. Francis George (Aunt Sarah), 56
Shaw, Robert Gould, 56
Sièrra de Avila, 105
Sièrra de Gredos, 105
Smith, John, 25, 27
Smith, Robert Dickson, 161, 179–80
Songs of the Pyrenees, by Nena Sturgis, 60
Sonsoles, Hermitage of, 19
South Americans, the, 39
Spain, 12–4, 21, 30–1, 39, 54, 99, 191, 211, 213–5, 218, 237

Spaniard, the, 12-3, 20, 24, 211, 237
Spencer, Herbert, 242-3
Spengler, Oswald, 213
Spinoza, 10, 243-5
Stanley, Lady, of Alderley, 139
Stones of Venice, by John Ruskin, 141
Stoughton Hall, 189, 191-2
Strong, Charles Augustus, 249-53
Sturgis, Charles, 73-4
Sturgis, Clipston, 68
Sturgis, Frank, 73-4
Sturgis, Fred, 59
Sturgis, George (author's step-father), 42-4, 46-7, 50-1, 62, 65
Sturgis, Henry ("Uncle Henry"), 59, 62, 137
Sturgis, Mrs. Henry (the first), 59
Sturgis, Mrs. Henry ("Aunt Lizzie"), 60-3, 143
Sturgis, Henry (son of Russell Sturgis), 58
Sturgis, James ("Uncle James"), 67-73
Sturgis, John, 68
Sturgis, Josefina (author's half-sister), 44-5, 47, 79, 82, 84, 87, 89, 91, 137, 221
Sturgis, Maisie, 86
Sturgis, Nathaniel Russell, 50, 56-7, 59
Sturgis, Mrs. Nathaniel Russell (Susan Parkman), 56
Sturgis, Nena, 59-60
Sturgis, Pepín (author's half-brother), 44-5, 51, 66, 117
Sturgis, Robert ("Uncle Robert"), 51, 86
Sturgis, Mrs. Robert ("Aunt Susie"), 86
Sturgis, Robert (author's half-brother), 22, 25, 45, 47, 65, 71-2, 82, 89-90, 117-9, 133-6, 138, 140, 145

Sturgis, Russell ("Uncle Russell"), 52, 57-9, 62, 68, 73
Sturgis, Samuel ("Uncle Samuel"), 63-5, 69, 73
Sturgis, Susana (author's half-sister), 1, 27, 35, 44-5, 47, 65-6, 71, 75-95, 103, 108, 119, 137-8, 145-6, 170, 179
Sturgis, Victor (author's half-brother), 43-5
Sturgises, the, 1, 2, 44, 47, 50-1, 56-74, 80, 92, 187
Sturgises, the Susie, 74
Superunda, 99

Tarraco, 217
Tarragona, 213, 216-7
Tavern Club, Boston, 71
Thales, 244
Thayer, Ernest, 197
Thayer Hall, 188
Thorold, Algar, 228
Thorold, Mrs. Algar, 228
Thoron, Ward, 180, 231-4
Titian's *Assumption,* 168
To the Host, by George Santayana, 174
To the Moon, by George Santayana, 174
Tolstoy, Leo, *War and Peace,* by, 233
Tremont House, Boston, 49
Turner, J. M. W., 235

Upham, Robert, 150, 179

Valladolid, 14
Vegas, Mrs., 122-3
Vegas, Rafael, 122-4, 126-8
Venice, 228, 235
Vercelli's Italian Restaurant, Boston, 71
Vie Parisienne, 198

Waggett, Father, 14-5
Walker Fellowship, 249-52
War and Peace, by Leo Tolstoy, 233

Ward, Mrs. Samuel, 232
Ward, Samuel, 232
Warren, Bentley, 179–81, 185
Watteau, 15
Welchman's Kindergarten, Miss, 149
Weston, Robert. *See* Smith, Robert Dickson
White, Alice, 178
White, Amy, 66–7
Whitman, Crosby, 199
Winchester, Va., 5–6

"X," Mrs., 204–6, 221, 223
"X," Reginald, 223

"Y," Mrs., 229
Yankee, the, 134

Zabalgoitia, Hermenegilda (author's cousin), 216, 220
Zabalgoitia, Nicolás (author's cousin), 213–21, 223
Zamora, 1, 10
Zorilla, 12

THE MIDDLE SPAN

THE
MIDDLE
SPAN

GEORGE
SANTAYANA

VOL. II ✳ *Persons and Places*

NEW YORK

CHARLES SCRIBNER'S SONS

CONTENTS

CHAPTER		PAGE
I.	Germany	1
II.	London	17
III.	Russell	44
IV.	Changes in Avila	76
V.	Younger Harvard Friends	98
VI.	Boston Society	112
VII.	Americans in Europe	131
VIII.	Official Career at Harvard	152
	Index	183

THE MIDDLE SPAN

CHAPTER I

GERMANY

THE impulse that sent me to study in Germany came from America—something for which America is to be thanked; yet the failure of that adventure in my case was connected with its origin. I was too much enveloped in my American (and afterwards in my English) associations to lose myself in the German scene, to learn German properly, and to turn a copious German "spiritual" stream into my private channel. In my Germany there was, and there still is, too much of me and too little of Germany.

Some recommendation that I have forgotten led me in the early autumn of 1886 to Göttingen, with the idea of learning a little more German than the very little that I knew. I lived in a boarding-house kept by Frau Pastorin Schlote, whose elderly daughter —not the Irma of *The Last Puritan*, who is imaginary—knew English and gave the foreign boarders lessons in German. I learned enough to understand lectures and formal conversation from the first; but there was no one with whom I could begin to talk, and with my dislike of drudgery, I turned rather to deciphering for myself, with the help of a grammar and a dictionary, texts that were worth reading on their own account: *Deutsche Lyrik*, Heine and *Wilhelm Meister*. I made good progress of a sort, for my own ends, but without thoroughness; and my tongue remained torpid and my inflections inaccurate. "*Sie sprechen sehr nett*," the superior housekeeper said one day when I excused myself, "*die Endungen aber fehlen.*" Two or three months later in Berlin my landlady and her friends one day were discussing me, when her daughter observed that I was in my room and could hear them through the thin door. *"Der versteht ja nichts,"* her mother cried impatiently, and went on wondering at my solitary life, that I went out for a walk alone and all the rest of the day sat working in my room. I understood every word perfectly: but in conversation I was helpless; there were no people with whom I cared to talk; and my punishment was that I never learned to speak the language.

From Göttingen I went to Dresden where Herbert Lyman had invited me to join him. I say "invited" because although I paid for my lodging, breakfast and midday dinner, he paid everything else for both of us, our way of living being entirely beyond the means of a student on half a Fellowship. We took a daily German lesson, and a daily walk; and in the evening, or rather in the afternoon—for the performances began at five or half-past five o'clock—we went to the Royal Theatre, hearing an opera or a play on alternate nights. The play often was Shakespeare, in the excellent German version. I remember *Julius Cæsar* particularly, a play that is not often done in English, I suppose because it is hardly a play for a star, like *Hamlet* or *Othello;* but the dutiful German State Company performed it with zeal and good judgment. We had an ample feast of Wagner, with Gudehus and Malten: old stand-bys but still adequate, singing and acting with a devout enthusiasm that was contagious. And after the theatre we had another treat that must not go unrecorded: an enormous delicious sweet omelette or *Pfannkuchen,* hot and crisp at the edges in its great pewter platter, followed by bread and cheese and a flagon of beer.

Memorable and important for me were these Dresden impressions: and I should include the lesson in architecture taught me by the Zwinger, the Royal Palace, and the Katholische Kirche; a lesson reinforced many years later by the monuments at Nancy. Baroque and rococo cannot be foreign to a Spaniard. They are profoundly congenial and Quixotic, suspended as it were between two contrary insights: that in the service of love and imagination nothing can be too lavish, too sublime, or too festive; yet that all this passion is a caprice, a farce, a contortion, a comedy of illusions.

All these wonderful things, besides the *Madonna di San Sisto* and everything else in the picture gallery, I saw while I stood side by side with Herbert Lyman, an intelligent observer who knew much more than I about music, yet a typical Yankee, cold, shrewd and spare inwardly, smiling with a sort of insulated incredulity at everything passionate, as if he lived inside a green glass bottle, warranted an absolute non-conductor. He condemned nothing, yet nothing seemed to make any difference *in him*. Why was he such a devoted friend of mine? We had no special interests in common, and I should not have distinguished him particularly from other kind and correct Bostonians if he had not shown such a marked and constant friendliness towards me. The secret of this was perhaps revealed by his younger sister one day at table in their house *in Beacon Street, opposite the Common,* the place where perfect Bostonians ought to live. The conversation had turned on summer resorts, and I said that I went every year to Europe, because the heat in New England was intolerable. This was tactless of me, since the Lymans had a luxurious ancestral house in Waltham near Boston which it would have been a crime for them not to occupy in summer, no matter what heat they might suffer there. However, I had smiled as I spoke, as if I couldn't really mean what I said. "Oh, thank you," cried the younger Miss Lyman, "we can't say that ourselves, but it's such a relief to hear it!" I expect that I said a good many things that it was a relief for her brother to hear. I was an exciting, slightly dangerous friend, yet not exactly disreputable, since I was by way of becoming a professor at Harvard. I could be acknowledged and cultivated and invited to the house. Moreover I had Bostonian connections. My sister was an intimate friend of Miss Sara Lowell, Herbert Lyman's own aunt, his mother's sister! Possibly he had heard of me before he had seen me, and that made such a difference in Boston! If my half-foreign sister was all right, why shouldn't I, at least educated in Boston, be all right also? He had very simple tastes; he liked my comic verses and would sing them to popular airs; for silly as the words were they could be sung without offence in any drawing-room. Yes, the partiality of the excellent Herbert for me was explicable. Other Bostonians, though they might not share it, could understand it. I was such a relief!

He not only sang a little, but would have liked to devote himself entirely to music. How, in what capacity? As a composer, as a performer, or merely as a critic, like "Billy" Apthorp in the *Boston Transcript*? Music would be an acceptable profession if you could begin by being famous. It was not acceptable if you were to begin at the foot of the ladder, and perhaps remain there. Herbert, who hadn't a great voice or a precocious talent, must therefore go into business. Yet there was no hurry about it. He might go to Germany for a year or two and study music. He would enjoy the Boston Symphony concerts all the more intensely every Saturday evening for the rest of his life. And his German musical holiday might well begin at Dresden. Now I was going to Germany too, where term at the universities didn't begin until the middle of November. Why shouldn't I spend the interval at Dresden? We could then learn German together, and have a good time as well. We had a very good time, but I, at least, didn't learn much German; I learned only what sufficed for my secret purpose—secret I mean even to myself. The purpose on which my heart was naturally set. This was not at all to be proficient in languages or to be a professor of philosophy, but to see and to understand the world. For this purpose our month or six weeks in Dresden was not merely a good preparation. It was a culminating point, one of the happiest episodes in my whole life.

I used at that time to sum up my first impressions of Germany by saying that there were three good things there: the uniforms, the music, and the beer. The formula was playful, yet it might still serve to express my sentiments if its terms were taken symbolically. *Uniforms*—which at that time were ornate and many-coloured, some sky-blue and silver, others white and gold—would stand for discipline and the glory of discipline. *Music* would stand for idealism, understood to mean love of ideal and immaterial things, of pure science and free imagination, and not "idealism" about material things, concealing or falsifying the truth about them. Finally *Beer* would stand for *Gemütlichkeit*, for joy in hearty, fleshly, kindly, homely, droll little things. How very much these three German virtues, when not exaggerated into vices, redeem the human soul from disorder, from servitude, and from spleen!

Berlin after Dresden seemed big, modern and ugly; but modernness, ugliness and bigness were familiar to me. I could live my own life in the midst of them, and so I did here. There were morning lectures with an interval of an hour between them: which I spent at the Museum, or at the Café Bauer over the English papers and a coffee with whipped cream. There was then a full dinner at half past one o'clock, in a restaurant upstairs near the Friedrichstrasse. It was so copious that, although this was my only solid meal, I usually skipped the boiled meat and vegetables, contenting myself with soup, fish, roast meat with vegetables, compote, and salad, and a dessert; washed down with half-bottle of white wine. The whole expense was three marks, two for the dinner, fifty pfennig for the wine, twenty-five for the coffee and the same for the waiter. I always sat at the same table, being one of the first to arrive, was expected, well received, and came to feel quite at home. I had a small room up many flights in the Louisenplatz, with a porcelain stove like a tomb in which a few diminutive cubes of synthetic fuel were buried every twenty-four hours. They did not make the room warm, but kept it from being too cold to sit in, warmly dressed, with a rug over one's legs. My landlady supplied coffee and rolls in the morning, and bread and cheese with a bottle of beer in the evening: so that after a good walk in the Thiergarten I would go home and devote the rest of the day and evening to work, without fear of interruption. At lectures I often sat with Strong, and sometimes with Houghton: they were my only acquaintances that year.

Of the four professors to whom I listened Paulsen was the

most important, not in himself—he was simply an excellent professor—but important for me as a medium and as a model of judicious and sympathetic criticism. This semester he lectured on Greek Ethics and in the next winter semester on Spinoza. In both subjects he helped to settle my opinions for good. The Greek ethics wonderfully supplied that which was absent in Spinoza, a virile, military, organic view of human life, a civilised view, to keep the cosmic and religious imagination of Spinoza in its proper moral place. The Greeks knew what it was to have a country, a native religion, a beautiful noble way of living, to be defended to the death. They recognised heroically that which Spinoza recognised only descriptively or pietistically: that the power of nature infinitely exceeds and ultimately destroys the power of each of its parts. The Greeks were thereby saved from arrogance without condemning themselves to littleness. For what is greater than beauty, and what is more beautiful than courage to live and to die freely, in one's chosen way? The Jews, on the contrary, and even Spinoza with them, fell into both littleness and arrogance: into the littleness of being content with anything, with small gains and private safety; and into arrogance in proclaiming that, in their littleness they possessed the highest good, heard the voice of absolute truth, and were the favourites of heaven. Undoubtedly if you renounce everything you are master of everything in an ideal sense, since nothing can disturb you: but the Jews never renounced anything that was within reach; and it was rather the Greek hero who renounced half of what he might have possessed, in order that the other half should be perfect.

I was thus fully settled in my naturalist convictions; they revealed the real background, the true and safe foundation, for human courage, human reason, and human imagination. These might, then, fill the foreground *ad libitum* with their creations, political and poetic. Both the Greeks and Spinoza, by a spontaneous agreement, combined the two insights that for me were essential: naturalism as to the origin and history of mankind, and fidelity, in moral sentiment, to the inspiration of reason, by which the human mind conceives truth and eternity, and participates in them ideally.

Besides Paulsen I heard Ebbinghaus who even asked me to his house, showed me his first fat baby and talked about William James, of course eulogistically, but with fundamental reservations, as for instance, on the question of freewill and responsibility, on which he said *"Das hat er eigentlich nicht durchgedacht."* This seemed rather a scholastic judgment to pass on James. He had thought and thought on that subject, yet he hadn't thought himself out of his half impulsive, half traditional horror of determinism, not because he couldn't think the argument out, but because, like Bergson, he didn't trust argument where he had intuition. Of course Ebbinghaus, whose training was scientific, knew that intuition is not a guide to matters of fact. James, however, was no draught-horse patiently pulling the scientific barge along a placid academic canal; rather a Red Indian shooting the rapids with spasmodic skill and elemental emotions. To Ebbinghaus it seemed that a professor's business was to trudge along the governmental towpath with a legal cargo, and I agreed with him technically much more than with James; but he was less interesting as a man and less challenging as a thinker.

I don't know for what reason I heard some lectures and took a seminar of Gezycki's—doubtless some recommendation from America, because Gezycki, who was a cripple, evoked emotional sympathies in reforming and free religious quarters in the Anglo-Saxon world. He defended English ethics rather than explained them; and his seminar on Kant's *Critique of Practical Reason* had no historical or critical value, but merely the interest of a pathetic personal cult of human happiness clung to passionately by an unhappy man. He too spoke to me of William James and of William James's brother-in-law Salter, who was a lecturer for the Ethical Culture Society. He was interested in James on the moral side, yet without spiritualistic leanings; and perhaps I may have learned from Gezycki to see that it is not *moral* to be romantic. This fact, for Gezycki, refuted romanticism; but for me it merely proves that the afflatus of romanticism belongs to the gnostic religions. It is a vital impulse expressed in fantastic assertions about the world; not (what Gezycki's heart desired) a social and personal discipline scientifically warranted to increase human happiness and abolish suffering.

For me, at that time, all this was of little account. What counted was Greek ethics, summed up in the stories that Herodotus tells about Solon, explaining the nature of happiness to the benighted Croesus. A string of excited, fugitive, miscellaneous pleasures is not happiness; happiness resides in imaginative reflection and judgment, when the *pictur*e of one's life, or of human life, as it truly has been or is, satisfies the will, and is gladly accepted. Epicurus had a different notion of happiness from that of Solon, but it was just as much a form of wisdom, a choice among possible lives; in neither sage was it a calculus of quantitative pleasures and pains. Epicurus renounced most of the things called pleasures, for the sake of peace, equanimity, and intelligence, and Solon's heroes renounced life itself for the sake of a beautiful moment or a beautiful death. The extreme of classical heroism here becomes romantic; because the most romantic career, if deliberately chosen and accepted without illusion, would be a form of happiness: something in which a living will recognised its fulfilment and found its peace.

After that first semester the wind was taken out of my sails for study in Germany. Strong and I had gone to England for the holidays; but I stayed at Oxford, and he joined other friends in Paris, neither of us returning to Berlin for the second semester. This was not dereliction on our part: we both had something better to do. Why hadn't someone warned us not to go to Berlin, but to choose some smaller place where there might be more unity of spirit in the teaching and in student life? Was there no such place at that unlucky moment? Were there no inspired philosophers then in Germany? Was there no enthusiastic romanticism and no *Gemütlichkeit*? For me it was a source of eternal regret to have missed the enrichment and the lesson that fusion with

German life, in my youth, might have given me. Nobody gave me clear advice in the matter, nor did Strong, who needed it less, seem to have received it, or to feel the danger we ran of wasting our time. He gave up the Fellowship for private reasons, and I, to whom it was then assigned, knew of nothing to do but to return to Berlin. All was changed there for me. Instead of keen curiosity and expectation, instead of delight at the freedom of thought and breadth of sympathy shown by my new professors, I was absorbed in other impressions and attachments. I had found England infinitely more interesting and stimulating than Germany. I had been again in Spain, even to Gibraltar, to receive my sister and had left her at my father's in Avila. I see now that I ought to have made a fresh plunge, a bold decision, gone to Marburg or Jena or Heidelberg or Bonn, seen only Germans, compelled myself to master the language, and lived, as during my first semester, an austere poor student's life.

At the time, however, I was will-less. Beal persuaded me to go to the pension, kept by an Englishwoman, where he was living, and where everyone was English or American. Mechanically I went again to hear the same professors. Paulsen was lecturing on Spinoza: a great treat, but essentially not a new light. I dropped in to listen to other lecturers occasionally, in their public courses: Wagner on political economy, Lasson on Fichte, Deussen on Schopenhauer and the Indians. I took a course under Simmel on *Ten Different Interpretations of the Essence of Kant's Critique of Pure Reason;* a clever series of criticisms, producing at least in my mind nothing but amusement and confusion. I was living in Babel. I felt no special inspiration, no guiding purpose, except the engagement involved in holding the Fellowship. Not that inwardly my devotion to philosophy was impaired. It remained my one all-embracing interest, not indeed as a science, only as a balance of mind and temper, in which all the sciences and arts should compose as true a picture as possible of nature and human nature. My quandary was not inward, it didn't concern my philosophy; it concerned only my academic position and possible career. And from that point of view this German experiment had been a failure. I was wholly incapable of taking a Doctor's degree in Germany. The only thing for me to do was to return to Harvard and take my Doctor's degree there, where I was at home and sure of my ground. I knew German enough to write my thesis on a German subject, if I might write it in English. Then, unless a place as teacher were offered me somewhere—I hardly thought of Harvard itself—I could go to the Institute of Technology and study architecture.

I wrote to the Harvard authorities explaining my position, saying I was coming back, and asking to have my Fellowship renewed as for a resident graduate. There was some hesitation about this point, but in the end I got the appointment. It was not materially indispensable to me, as I meant to live at my mother's in any case, but gave me more leeway. I began that year to save, and to possess a little capital. In other words, I began to prepare for my retirement from teaching before I had begun to teach.

From ten to twenty years later I made several holiday visits to Germany. They were in part acts of contrition for my youthful waste of opportunities, yet I should hardly have made them simply with that idea. The last of these visits I called a Goethe pilgrimage, because I went expressly to Frankfort and to Weimar to visit the home of Goethe's childhood and that of his old age. I was then preparing my lectures on *Three Philosophical Poets* of whom Goethe was to be one. Even that, however, would probably not have induced me to revisit Germany had I not meantime formed a real friendship with a young German, Baron Albert von Westenholz.

Westenholz was one of my truest friends. Personal affection and intellectual sympathies were better balanced and fused between him and me than between me and any other person. I made three trips to Hamburg expressly to see him, and he once joined me in London and again at Amsterdam and in Brussels; but travelling ultimately became impracticable for him, on account of his health and hobbies, and I could never persuade him to come

to Italy, where we should have found so many themes for enthusiastic discussion. But we carried on a desultory correspondence, and he never lost his interest in my philosophy and in my
books. Not that he was in any sense my disciple or surrendered
his independence of judgment. His liberal Lutheran background
and many-sided studies gave him independent points of view, and
his attainments were in many ways wider than mine; so that,
for instance, when in the later years I began to read New Testament criticism, chiefly in Loisy, he guided me very usefully to
various German authorities on the subject. He always maintained
an "Evangelical" conception of Christ very different from mine,
which is Gnostic and free from all claims to be historical. He
was too dutifully *gebildet*, too indoctrinated, to be as sceptical as
I am; and that difference lent spice to our discussions, especially
as he, with his lingering illusions, was the younger man and I, the
mentor, was the cynic. When my young friends are "gooder" than
I, I respect and love them, but when they are less tender than I
towards tradition, I feel that they are uneducated and stupid. I
could never accuse Westenholz of being stupid or uneducated:
but I felt to the end how *German* he was, how immersed in
learning and inclined to follow a sect, without much capacity
for laughter.

His father had been a partner in a family banking house established in Frankfort and Vienna, originally perhaps Jewish: but
my friend's mother was the daughter of a burgomaster of Hamburg, with the most pronounced Hanseatic Lutheran traditions.
The bank had a branch in London, and young Westenholz had
served his apprenticeship there and learned to speak English perfectly. But he never entered the firm: his health was far from
good: he suffered from various forms of mental or half mental
derangement, sleeplessness, and obsessions, which, however, he
himself diagnosed with perfect scientific intelligence. By way of a
rest-cure, he was sent on long ocean voyages; was wrecked off the
coast of Brazil, and later turned up at Harvard where he was
brought to see me.

I was then, in 1900–1905, living at No. 60 Brattle Street, and had my walls covered with Arundel prints. These were the starting point for our first warm conversations. I saw at once that he was immensely educated and enthusiastic, and at the same time innocence personified; and he found me sufficiently responsive to his ardent views of history, poetry, religion and politics. He was very respectful, on account of my age and my professorship; and always continued to call me *lieber Professor* or *Professorchen*; but he would have made a much better professor than I, being far more assiduous in reading up all sorts of subjects and consulting expert authorities. Before he left Cambridge, it was decided that I should visit him in Hamburg: I was to stay for a night at their town mansion (in an extensive park facing the Alster) to pay my respects to his invalid mother and his sister—a good many years older than he; and then he would carry me off to a little hermitage he had for himself in the woods, absolutely solitary, without even a carriage-road leading up to it.

Hamburg was not an inconvenient place for me to reach, since in those days I often sailed in the Hamburg steamers because they were the first to have single cabins, deep in the centre of the vessel, and well ventilated, so that I could hope to avoid seasickness, and to enjoy privacy. With these things secured, I was glad of a longish voyage, and instead of landing at Cherbourg or Southampton, I could easily go on to Cuxhaven and Hamburg: and the same convenience naturally existed for the return voyage. Our friendship became intellectually closer in later years, without seeming to require personal contacts; and I never went to Germany again after those external conveniences ceased to make the journey easy and as it were optional.

As for him, his impediments were growing upon him. Fear of noise kept him awake, lest some sound should awake him; and he carried great thick curtains in his luggage to hang up on the windows and doors of his hotel bedrooms. At Volksdorf, his country hermitage, the floors were all covered with rubber matting, to deaden the footfalls of possible guests; and he would run down repeatedly, after having gone to bed, to make sure that he had locked the piano; because otherwise a burglar might come in and wake him up by sitting down to play on it! When I suggested that he might get over this absurd idea by simply defying it, and repeating to himself how utterly absurd it was, he admitted that he might succeed in overcoming it; but then he would develop some other obsession instead. It was hopeless: and all his intelligence and all his doctors and psychiatrists were not able to cure him. In his last days, as his friend Reichhardt told me, the great obsession was with bedding: he would spend half the night arranging and rearranging mattresses, pillows, blankets and sheets, for fear that he might not be able to sleep comfortably. And if ever he forgot this terrible problem, his mind would run over the more real and no less haunting difficulties involved in money matters. The curse was not that he lacked money, but that he had it, and must give an account of it to the Government as well as to God. And there were endless complications; for he was legally a Swiss citizen, and had funds in Switzerland, partly declared and partly secret, on which to pay taxes both in Switzerland and in Germany; and for years he had the burden of the house and park in Hamburg, gradually requisitioned by the city government, until finally he got rid of them, and went to live far north, in Holstein, with thoughts of perhaps migrating to Denmark. A nest of difficulties, a swarm of insoluble problems making life hideous, without counting the gnawing worm of religious uncertainty and scientific confusion.

The marvel was that with all these morbid preoccupations filling his days and nights Westenholz retained to the last his speculative freedom. Everything interested him, he could be just and even enthusiastic about impersonal things. I profited by this survival of clearness in his thought: he rejoiced in my philosophy, even if he could not assimilate it or live by it: but the mere idea of such a synthesis delighted him, and my *Realm of Truth* in particular aroused his intellectual enthusiasm. In his confusion he saw the possibility of clearness, and as his friend Reichhardt said, he became sympathetically *hell begeistert,* filled with inspired light.

If this cohabitation of profound moral troubles with speculative earnestness was characteristically German, so was the cohabitation of both with childish simplicity. I was told one morning that that day was Fräulein Mathilde's thirty-third birthday. Where should I go to get some flowers or bon-bons to offer her with my congratulations: embarrassed congratulations, because if she had completed another year of life and that were so much to the good, it was less so that she had already completed thirty-three of them. But no: it was Sunday, and all shops were closed. I was genuinely sorry, because I am naturally remiss at paying compliments and attentions and giving due presents, and when an occasion presents itself boldly, I am glad to be forced to do the right thing. "If you really want to give her a pleasant surprise, write her a birthday poem," said Westenholz, seeing my perplexity. So I retired for an hour to my room and produced some verses, in which I congratulated the poor, the Baroness, Albert, and their friends on the prospect of having the *good* Mathilde (for she wasn't beautiful) with them for another year. The verses were worthless, but they had enough foundation in truth to serve their purpose. Mathilde really was all goodness, as Albert was too, only that he had intellect and madness to complicate the goodness.

In the afternoon, after a solid early dinner at which the Baroness was wheeled in a hospital litter to the table (for she insisted that she was too ill to sit up), brother and sister put their heads together to decide how they should celebrate the occasion; and it was decided that we three should go to their old house in the city, and take the dolls and the doll-furniture out of the boxes, and arrange everything in the dolls' house just as it used to be. Their old house was that of their maternal grandfather, who had been Burgomaster of Hamburg, belonging now to an uncle who wasn't living there for the moment. It was in the old town, near one of the churches with a high green steeple, and itself lofty and gabled: but we hurried up many flights of stairs as if treading on

forbidden ground: I should have liked to see the rooms, but foresaw difficulties in opening windows and conciliating caretakers
that would be involved in a visit of inspection unauthorised by
the owner: so that I too hurried guilty-like to the garret, under a
vast pitched roof, where evidently we might forget that we were
interlopers. The boxes were opened; the dolls, the furniture, the
crockery, were all distributed among the rooms of the immense
dolls' house, each precisely where it belonged. The names of the
various dolls were recalled, and in rapid German that I wasn't
expected to listen to sundry comic incidents of childhood were
referred to and enjoyed for the hundredth time. Then, dutifully,
everything was buried again in the boxes, to be resurrected perhaps when Fräulein's thirty-three years should have become forty-
five.

This joy in simplicity, this nostalgia for childishness, in highly
educated, rich, and terribly virtuous people surely is thoroughly
German: and doesn't it make some radical false turn, some organic
impediment, in their history? But let me not generalise. Westenholz at any rate was avowedly morbid and abnormal; without
being deformed, he had all the pathos and intensity that go
with deformity; jealousy and vanity, in professing to judge and
to dominate everything from above; great intellectual ardour and
display of theory; with genuine delight in the simplest pleasures
beneath, and temptation to the crudest vices. It would be a false
diagnosis to call him an old child, a pedant whose brain had
grown like a pumpkin, and left the heart rudimentary. His heart
was not rudimentary, it was large and nobly developed; but the
intellectual life accompanying it was not developed out of it but
borrowed, foreign, imposed by alien circumstances and traditions;
and for this reason, there was relief and joy in reverting from it to
homely things. *Los von Rom* is a very different cry in Germany
from what *No popery* was in England. In England, the King, the
prelates and the nobles felt ripe to be their own popes. They
wished to graft their culture on their instincts, and their instincts
were mature enough to breed a native culture, admirable in those

matters that touched English life—the home, the feelings, sports, politics, and manners, trade also and colonial conquests; yet their instincts were crude and incoherent in speculative directions, precisely in proportion as they receded from the manly arts of the native man. But in Germany the expression of the native heart had remained rustic and violent; *los von Rom* was a disruptive cry, expressing in enthusiasts an anarchistic impulse, and a rebellion against all control; whereas the princes and theologians and learned men who restrained that rebellion, and imposed a strict discipline on the people, imposed something alien and artificial, imposed officialdom, pedantry, or insane vanity. The heart might be free from Rome, but was enslaved to something far poorer and more acrid: so that a return to the heart became a reversion to childhood or to rusticity.

CHAPTER II

LONDON

THE GERMANY of 1886 had liberated, it had not enamoured me: and at the age of twenty-three a young man needs to be enamoured. A siren, however, was not far off, across the North Sea. After our first semester at Berlin, Strong and I decided to spend our holiday in England, and took ship at Bremen for London. It was a nasty voyage in a smallish German Lloyd steamer, an excellent cathartic to clear away all obstructions and leave a clean and keen appetite for something new. Regarding England I had favourable preconceptions derived from my father. It was in his opinion the leading country, the model country, for the modern world; and although this eminence might be patriotically claimed by Americans for America, it was not yet possessed by their country even in material things of importance; while in literature and philosophy, as well as in the art of living, the autarchy of the New World was that of the log-cabin: you might like roughing it and camping in the woods, but that did not create a new civilisation.

In approaching England I felt the excitement of a child at the play, before the curtain rises. I was about to open my eyes on a scene in one sense familiar from having heard and read so much about it. There was keen intellectual curiosity to discover the fact and compare it with my anticipations. There was my youthful hunger, still unappeased, for architectural effects, and picturesque scenes in general; and there was a more recent interest, destined to grow gradually stronger, in discovering and understanding human types, original or charming persons. And where were these more likely to be found than in England?

On our second evening from Bremen we had anchored in the

Thames and were to go ashore at Tilbury in the morning. Mean-while, the customs officers came aboard to examine our papers and our luggage. We were almost the only first-class passengers; and it was without the least hurry, and almost in silence, that we laid our passports on the cabin table before the two quiet officials who had sat down there. Quiet they were, well spoken, laconic yet civil; half business-like and half deferential, as if in the first place they recognised us for gentlemen, and as if in general they were respectful towards other people's privacy and peace. Perfectly ordinary men like policemen; yet how different from any customs officials that I had ever come upon in Spain or America, in France or Germany! What *decent* officials! They didn't seem to suspect us of lying or cheating, and showed no tendency to brow-beat or deceive us with rigmarole and loudness. A national note, firmness beneath simplicity; a *decent* people, not very perceptive, a little stolid, decidedly limited, but sound, trained, running easily in the national harness. And this among the common people, when not misled. I was glad of this first impression; and it was curiously confirmed in my first journey to Oxford, in a third-class carriage. It happened to be full, five persons on a side, yet nobody said a word; or if any word passed from one to another, it was so brief, and so low in tone, as to disturb nobody else. Not genial, other nations might say, not friendly or human; but I felt that it was truly friendly, since it was considerate; it showed aptitude for get-ting on together, political aptitude, precisely because it let everyone alone, allowed them their place, and didn't blame them for exist-ing even if their existence were a bit inconvenient.

So much for public manners, the best in the world; but soon I had a glimpse of the private feelings that might go with those manners in humble and ordinary people. We went to a boarding-house that Strong had heard of in Notting Hill, a remote place for the sightseer, but correspondingly cheap and *decent*, besides having the incidental advantage of involving long drives on the top of busses, and often sitting (since we started at the start), only a little above and behind the driver's box, with whom a word might be exchanged occasionally, and whose powerful horses and skilful driving through the dense traffic might be admired. It was six miles, an hour's drive, to the Bank; and in that cool misty season with the sun high, but coppery and shining dubiously through the grey atmosphere, the swarming city, still moderately uniform in the character and the height of buildings, offered a scene of inexhaustible interest, justifying the humour of Dickens and Cruikshank, as well as the gentility of Thackeray. Everything seemed ready to be etched, from the broken-down old women in black bonnets selling matches at corners, to the black-and-white harmonies of St. Paul's and the churches in the Strand, poetic to see looming in the distance, and interesting to study on a nearer approach. Yet here doubts began to assail the mind, concerning the solidity of England in subtler matters of taste and allegiance, doubts confirmed by the then brand-new Law Courts. This Italian architecture of Wren's, this Ruskinian Gothic, were foreign here: they were whims, they were fashions, they were essentially shams. But the function of shams in English society is a large subject, and I shall revert to it often.

At table in Notting Hill one of the inevitable solitary elderly ladies explained to us how much they all loved Longfellow: he was a household poet in England no less than in America. I replied that I was not surprised to hear it; but that in America his vogue was beginning to pass away; at least we poets at Harvard never read anything written in America except our own compositions. As for English poets we admitted nobody less revolutionary than Swinburne or less pessimistic than Matthew Arnold. If the lady had been an American and younger she would have said I was horrid; being English and old she silently thought so, and merely repeated gently, that in England they loved Longfellow best.

There was also at table a modest, well-set-up young man, a clerk, who betrayed some interest in philosophy or, as I soon gathered, in religion. On that footing we became friends at once: I have always found it easy to form casual friendships, especially with

Englishmen. He said he belonged to the Church of the Apostles, commonly called Irvingites. Should I like to go to one of their services? Very much: and on the next Sunday he conducted me to a church like a Roman basilica, with an apse, quite orthodox mosaics, and a semi-circle of living apostles in stalls, wearing white smocks, and looking like a row of butchers, except that butchers seldom have long beards. The sermon informed us that it was not necessary to die. The Day of Judgment had long since come and people were constantly being caught up to heaven alive, perhaps as they walked in the streets, or through the chimney. My friend gave me no further evidence of this phenomenon; but I saw (which was what interested me) that for him these absurdities furnished a happy interlude in a drab life, a peep-hole into fairyland, a little secret, unsuspected by the world, to keep up his self-respect, and cast a ray of supernatural hope into that small room in the third floor back, which might prove any day a jumping off place for a flight to heaven. By some chance his need of faith had attached him to the Irvingites; had his connections and education been more fortunate he might have become a high Anglican or Catholic; and his case showed, as it were under the microscope, the mechanism of conversion in higher spheres.

After two or three weeks at Notting Hill, spent in seeing everything in London that the guidebook recommended, Strong unexpectedly announced that he was obliged to join some family friends in Paris. He had evidently fresh money to spend, or was invited: I was not able or inclined to accompany him. Paris suggested a different side of life, and greater expenses; besides, I was intent on continuing my explorations in England and extending them at least to Oxford. Strong had dutifully kept me in the straight path of the earnest sightseer, visiting historic spots and notable monuments in the order of their importance and instructiveness, from the Tower to Madame Tussaud's. But when I was left alone, I began to live on a different plan, which I have followed when possible in all my wanderings. I moved to lodgings in Jermyn Street, Saint James's, No. 87, a house to which I was faithful for more than twenty-five years, and abandoned only bowing to *force majeure*. First Miss Bennett, the genial motherly landlady died: then her younger sister, a widow, married Colonel Sandys, who had long occupied the first floor. On arriving one year I noticed a change in the aspect of the house. The front door was painted a well-varnished dark green, with shining brass knocker and door-knobs; there was a fresh thick doormat, and when I rang the bell, though the man was the same familiar valet, he seemed much more spruce, and even a bit embarrassed in his conspicuously clean linen. The same lady, he explained, still lived here, but the house was no longer an hotel. And he politely presented me, on a solid silver tray, the letters that had arrived for me. There was nothing to do but to look foolish, and say, "Oh, indeed—I see—thank you," and get again into my taxi—it was already the age of taxis—and vaguely tell the driver to go somewhere else—anywhere—to the British Hotel a few doors beyond. But neither at the British Hotel nor elsewhere did I ever feel at home again in London lodgings; and this circumstance contributed to make my stay there always shorter and shorter.

Miss Bennett's was not a luxurious house, and I never took more than a single room there, and breakfast; yet though not a very profitable guest, I was a constant one, and always seemed to be welcome. I would even leave a hat-box there from year to year, as a sort of pledge, to get rid of the useless burden of a top-hat in the rest of my journeys. The full savour of the London of my youth, in the 1880's and 1890's, clings to my memories of Jermyn Street. I usually came down at nine or half-past to breakfast in a small back room on the ground-floor, always on bacon and eggs and *The Morning Post*. Sometimes another lodger would be there too but not often; and then we politely ignored each other's presence, concentrating each on his own teapot and toast-rack and dish of marmalade, and on his own newspaper, which in the other man's case was likely to be *The Times*. In the early days I preferred *The Standard*, because it was the Anglican clerical paper, opening to me the side of English life that interested me most; and when *The Standard* stopped publication, I took up *The Morning Post,* until that too succumbed—to the flood of vulgar journalism. After that I subscribed to no English newspaper; the continental press could inform me sufficiently about gross events, and I could always procure single copies of *The Times,* if there was anything of special importance.

The fire in Miss Bennett's breakfast room was the only common interest between the other lodger and me. Neither of us would attempt to monopolise it; we both kept at the distance that good form required. It would have been beneath us to huddle up close to it, as if we were ignominiously suffering from cold; yet we took good care not to retreat to such a distance as to abdicate the right to the best place, if we had come early and secured it. The best place then exalted the person who occupied it, and to preserve his Rights had become his Duty. I was being initiated into the secret of British politics.

In those days Jermyn Street preserved the character of a quiet and correct street in the heart of Saint James's. No. 87 was directly opposite the pleasant red-brick church with its pleasant trees, that made a green landmark, and with the pleasant broad face and pleasant chimes of its clock, that told you the hours. At night, lying warm in bed with the window open, I also liked to hear the patter, as of a child's drum, on the probably wet asphalt, as each hansom-cab, noiseless as to its wheels but *quadrupedante sonitu* as to its horse's hoofs, drove up the street, and drove away again in a brisk diminuendo.

It was precisely to the inveterate stranger in me that London had mightily appealed. All those hollow principles and self-indulgent whims of a decadent age had merged in the English gentleman into good form and sly humour; and in the Cockney they were reflected in his goodnatured derision and comfortable jollity. The spirit of London seemed remarkably mellow and rich in experience; for that very reason leisurely, gently mocking, not miscellaneously eager and hurried, like New York, nor false, cynical and covetous, like Paris. Not that great things have happened in

London; it has no such memories as Rome or Florence; but being
a commercial city, a port and the centre of a colonial empire, it
has encyclopedic contacts, and means of knowing the world at a
distance without being very much disturbed by it in its own back-
parlour. There is therefore balance in its omniscience, and a wise
perspective in its interests. Experience fosters both affection and
unconcern; and we are lucky when the affection settles down
upon what is near, and the unconcern upon what is distant and
irremediable, with a subtle amusement at both. This seemed to me
to happen in the typical Londoner, and it made him an engaging
person.

London has always responded to a rather youthful interest of
mine, the interest in streets, in clothes, in manners, in curious
architecture; also to my pleasure in casual acquaintances and small
explorations. These human episodes enlivened the landscape and
made particular spots memorable that would otherwise have been
merged indistinguishably in the motley scene: yet it was the
aerial landscape, always evanescent and always picturesque, that
fed the spirit, as the cool moist air expanded the lungs. I loved
the Parks—St. James's with its suggestions of by-gone fashions
and a smaller town; Green Park, spacious and empty, like a
country common; and Hyde Park above all, with its fashionable
pedestrians and riders, its horses and carriages, and its band concerts; all easy to turn one's back on, for the sake of a long solitary
walk. Yet these pleasures presupposed summer and fine weather.
It was a setting for a holiday, not for a life. I never studied in
London or read in the British Museum (as I did in the Bodleian)
or gathered books, or made lasting friends. I visited nobody, not
even the Sturgis connection: I was, and I liked to remain, an
unrecognised wanderer.

Even the theatres seldom attracted me. British plays are anodyne, transparently moral or sentimental or intellectual; that is to
say, not spontaneous products of the imagination. I think it must
have been Protestantism that so completely extinguished Elizabethan genius. When the theatres were reopened at the Restora-

tion, writers and audiences were utterly cut off from the healthy current of national life, and from the great classic and poetic tradition. They cared only for wit and satire and the evil pleasure of scandal. Now the wish to be edified has been added; but that limits the already slight range of the plays, without infusing into them anything poetical. The acting, too, is awkward and uninspired; the players are interested in themselves and not in their parts, and so are the audiences. Everything is modish, affected, trivial, and amateurish. Earlier, in the days of Irving and Terry, the stage production had been an object in itself. Elaborate scenery and costumes were designed to bring some historic epoch to light. Taste was preraphaelite; the stage resembled the Arundel prints after Pinturicchio that I had had in my rooms in Brattle Street. That fashion had passed when I was much in London, but the taste had not died in me, when the Russian ballet made its appearance. Here imagination and passion had fallen back upon first principles. Aestheticism had become absolute and violent, the appeal to the exotic and dream-like scorned to be accurate or instructive and was content to be vivid. Nor was elegance excluded, but it figured only as one *genre* among many, just as it does in Shakespeare and in real life. Delicacy was cultivated in its place, yet the way was left open in every direction to strength, to passion, to nature and to fancy. I wonder if Shakespeare could not be turned into Russian ballets to advantage: or into a kind of opera-ballet, in which the more important speeches could be introduced in recitative into the music. Aristophanes also might lend himself to such treatment.

It was only on rare evenings in London that I dressed or dined with friends or went to any show. I tasted the specific quality of the place better when I strolled about alone, dined in some grill room or in some restaurant in Soho, or walked out over the bridges to watch the evening glow reflected on the river. England preserves the softness and verdure of the country even in the city; and London, the densest of Babylons, is everywhere turned into a landscape by the mist, by the cloudracks, by the docks and shipping towards the East, by the green reaches, the fields, the boating crowds towards the West. It thins out and becomes rural imperceptibly in its immense suburbs, and not always vulgarly; there are royal preserves and stately seats in all directions. Woolwich steps down grandly to the sea, and Kensington Palace and Hampton Court lead nobly towards Windsor Castle. This instinct to merge town and country in one limitless park, and never to lose sight of a green field, an overhanging tree, or an impenetrable hedgerow no doubt renounces architecture on the grand scale. The city remains a conglomeration of accidents, of incongruous whims and private rights huddled together. The roads turn and wind round the freehold cottages and jealously fenced gardens, and comfort is never sacrificed to symmetry. Yet in neglecting grandeur the Englishman remains jealous of his dignity, and also of his privacy. He plants his neighbours out, if he possibly can; the comforts he exacts are simple; too much luxury would be incompatible with quietness and liberty. Even in the great respect that he shows for wealth and station he honours freedom rather than power. Your rich man can do as he likes, and can live as he chooses. Then the liberty that is a sham in public becomes a reality in private.

To the classic mind landscapes are always landscapes with figures. Even the desert, the sea, or the stars draw all their magic from the solitude or sacred companionship that the soul feels in their presence. So the aspects of a town borrow their quality from the life that they suggest—market, temple, fortress, or garden. London is essentially a commercial city. Everything about it hangs upon that fact, even the golden mist and the black fog that makes its beauty and its monstrosity; for they are effects of occupying a watery place near the corner of an island; ideal for shipping and in the midst of sea routes, and of being able at the same time to burn prodigious quantities of soft coal. Civilisations and towns created by commerce may grow indefinitely, since they feed on a toll levied on everything transportable; yet they are secondary. However much they may collect and exhibit the riches of the

world they will not breed anything original. Their individuality
and excellence, no less in Venice than in London, will be the
fruit of accidents, of converging influences and borrowed traditions. If an Englishman set out to be a *great* man, a genius, a
saint, or a responsible monarch, the devil would soon pocket him.
It is only the rich Englishman that can truly prosper in England.
Like the Lord Mayor of London, he can dress up in a traditional
costume, and receive Royalty and all other grand people at his
feasts. He can repeat the consecrated platitudes, and drink the
approved wines; and in his hours of obscurity and thrift, labor;
he can revise accounts, poke his library fire, drink tea with his
buxom wife, and send his sons to Eton or Harrow. Commercial
communities in this way accumulate great treasures and hand
down admirable institutions; yet in them the whole exists only
for the sake of the parts and their greatness is only littleness
multiplied. They become museums, immense hostelries, perpetual
fairs. Society will be nowhere brisker or more various. Everything
that money can buy will be at the command of those that have
money. The dandies and snobs will lead the aristocracy; fashion
will nowhere be more splendid and more respected, and misery
nowhere more squalid. The metropolis will overflow with life
gathered from the four quarters of the heavens; it will never be
a fountain of life.

As to the fish swimming about in this whirlpool, I could infer
from my American experience of a society even more commercial
and casual, that they had individual souls and personal histories;
and I had learned in Dickens something about such souls in the
lower classes, the Sam Wellers and the Mrs. Gamps, and among
the merchants and lawyers, for whom London was all in all. These
are not classes in which a stray foreigner like me would be likely
to make acquaintances; and a metropolis is not like a ship or a college, where prolonged contact with the same persons discloses
their individualities even to the least sympathetic stranger. Yet in
the classes with which intercourse was easier for me, I did pick

up various acquaintances; and some of those figures have remained pleasantly painted in my memory.

One day in Jermyn Street, when I had breakfasted in bed and came down nicely dressed about noon, fat Miss Bennett, who was arranging the flowers in a row of little vases in the narrow entry, smiled in her motherly way as she made room for me to pass, and said, "You have been doing the young lady this morning, Sir." Yes; though I was no longer a young man (this was in 1901) I had had a momentary lapse into fashionable life, and was going to take a turn in the Park before lunching at Hatchett's; and I confided to her that the previous evening I had been dining at the Savoy with two young officers of the Guards. It had been as far as possible from a debauch—I will describe it presently—but it had thrown me back into the mood of 1897, when I had known a knot of young men about town, acquaintances made at Cambridge; not all English, for there was an Australian and a Frenchman, and for that reason all the more knowing and entertaining. At that time (in my holiday year at King's and in Italy) I had been wide awake; but now I had entered a somnambulist tunnel, where the engines worked and the wheels made a more furious noise than ever, but where the spirit was suspended on the thought: When shall we come out again into the light and air? The two Guardsmen brought a glimpse into the open, not promising but suggestive. They knew nobody in my world, I knew nobody in theirs. Yet I, at least, was never more in my element than when I was far from myself. How did I know them?

We were waiting on the pier at Southampton in the previous September for the German liner that was to convey us to America. Fog had kept her from making the port on time. In standing about the steamer-office, waiting for information, I noticed two young Englishmen, well dressed, good-naturedly accepting the accident of being sent to dine and to spend the night at a local hotel, and being correspondingly delayed in their arrival in New York. They evidently didn't care. They were not going to America on business: I wondered what they were going for. For nothing, perhaps, to spend the time, to see the Rocky Mountains, or to look for heiresses. There was an air about them of being thoroughly equipped, perfectly trained and hardened, thoroughly competent to do anything and not knowing what on earth to do.

The next day on board, when the chief steward had found a place for me in the dining-room, there were the two young men, directly opposite me at the same table. Their casual conversation was not audible to me: they were English. After a day or two, however, in passing the mustard or the salt, we began to exchange a few phrases, and gradually came to joining forces on deck or in the smoking-room. The smoking-room was my place of refuge in transatlantic steamers, when I was not walking on the lower deck, which was clear of chairs, nearer the water, and comparatively deserted, allowing freedom of movement as well as of mind. When I had taken my exercise, and wished to sit down, I looked for a comfortable corner in the smoking-room. The smoking-room was the one place sure to be well ventilated; there were deep leather chairs where I could read at ease or even write in a note-book. The crowd and the hubbub didn't in the least disturb me, since I wasn't asked to attend to it. Here I could have tea, and here sometimes my two new friends would join me, and would explain incidentally they were simply on a tour, curious about America and apparently entertained by what I said of it. They were eventually coming to Boston, and I rashly offered to show them the sights of Harvard.

Rashly, I say, because when they turned up a month or two later, it puzzled me to think what the sights of Harvard were. These young men didn't want to see the stadium (then a novelty) nor the glass flowers. The Yard was leafless, muddy and at its ugliest, and I no longer lived there but in Brattle Street, not in rooms worth showing. Nor had I any longer any interesting friends that I could have asked to meet them at tea. So I frankly confessed my predicament and took them to see Memorial Hall with the panorama (and smell) of a hundred tables and a thousand men at dinner—for it was already six o'clock. They said it looked like Sandhurst. Evening had already come and there was nothing to do but to walk back to Main Street and to the electric car that would take them back to Boston. By way of apology for this futile afternoon, I sent two books to their ship to entertain them on their homeward voyage: my *Interpretations of Poetry and Religion,* then just out, for A, the one who seemed more intellectual, and Flandrau's *Diary of a Freshman* for the other, B, who was apparently simpler and younger. I knew that the first book was too serious and the second too frivolous, but perhaps between them they might represent the winds blowing at Harvard.

When I dined with them the next summer in London, I felt that they had asked me to the Savoy because they were in much the same predicament that I had been when I took them to the gallery of Memorial Hall: they wanted to be civil to me, but they had to invent a way. The food was excellent—all cold, by a caprice of B's—and they spied well-known people at some other tables, whose names they whispered with smiles: but they might have dined more pleasantly and cheaply by themselves at the Guard's Club, to which strangers were not admitted. The evening was clear and they proposed walking back to Pall Mall, exactly what my instinct would have prompted me to do. This undercurrent of common tastes was what established pleasant relations between them and me, in spite of completely different backgrounds. When we reached Pall Mall, I knew they were making for their club; I therefore said good night and turned up through St. James's Square, reflecting on what a tax it is to entertain strangers, even for people enjoying every advantage in the heart of London. Besides, three, except among very intimate friends, is not a propitious number for conversation: it renders sympathies shy to show themselves and interesting subjects hard to follow up. To cement a new friendship, especially between foreigners or persons of a different social world, a spark with which both were secretly charged must fly from person to person, and cut across the accidents of place and time. No such spark had seemed to pass between these young men and me; and yet I was sure, especially in the case of B, that a latent sympathy existed unexpressed: and the proof of it appeared not many days later. B wrote asking me to dine with him again, without dressing, in the most singular of places for dining—in the Bank of England. He happened to be for the moment the officer commanding the guard at that place; and this officer had the privilege of inviting one person to dine with him, and of drinking one bottle of claret and one of port. Would I come?

It was raining hard on the appointed evening and when I told my cabby to go to the Bank—the Bank of England—the fellow almost laughed in my face, but in a moment recovered his professional gravity, and observed a bit quizzically, "Bank, Sir? Bank will be closed, Sir," evidently doubting whether I was a little mad, or excessively green. I said I knew it was closed to the public, but went there by special appointment; and I jumped in resolutely, and closed the doors. My man started, driving at first rather slowly, but being once in for it, gained courage, and drove smartly the rest of the way. When I had got out and paid him, I noticed that he lingered a moment. His curiosity wasn't satisfied, without seeing whether people ever got into the Bank of England at eight o'clock in the evening.

The policeman at the door, on the contrary, understood everything, said "This way, Sir," affably, and hurried me across the court faster than I could have wished, because the scene was wonderful. In those days the court you first entered was surrounded by pavilions no higher than the blank outer wall; various crosslights from archways, doors and windows were caught and reflected by the wet pavements and casual puddles, or lit up bright patches of scarlet or brass or shining white belts in the groups of soldiers, hard to distinguish under the black sky, who lounged in the doors or huddled for shelter under the eaves. I thought of Rembrandt's *Night Watch*; but this scene was more formless yet more alive. Here everything trembled, water trickled and sparkled over all; and in the darkness itself there was a sense of suspended animation among ambiguous shadows that would yield for a moment to recognisable reality, where a face lifted or an arm moved or a voice spoke some commonplace word.

The room into which I was ushered had a dingy Dickensian look of solidity grown old-fashioned and a bit shabby. There was a walnut mantelpiece with a small clock and two candlesticks without candles; heavy black walnut chairs, with horsehair bottoms, and a table set unpretentiously, with thick white plates and thick glasses. But there was a pleasant fire in the grate, and the rather superannuated butler served us an excellent absolutely English dinner: mock-turtle soup, boiled halibut with egg-sauce: roast mutton: gooseberry tart and cream, and anchovies on toast; together with the two bottles of wine already mentioned. Too much food, you might say; but in the English climate, distressing to the lazy but friendly to the active man, after a long day pacing the streets in rain and shine as if you were pacing a deck, all that food was appetising. The old butler knew that it was just right, whatever notions the young officers of to-day might have got into their heads. One had to put up with them; but he was conscious of the whole weight and authority of the Bank of England backing him up. Where would the Army be without the Bank? Nowhere.

The good claret and port were left entirely to me. My poor friend was under the doctor's care and could drink only milk. He seemed very young and very dejected, in his white flannel shirt and sporting jacket, while his red and gold tunic and his huge bearskin lay on a chair, waiting to be put on at eleven o'clock for the evening inspection, when I should have to leave. We had a friendly philosophic talk about the troubles of youth—the chief of them being that youth cannot last. This fatality casts its shadow before it and makes the young dissatisfied with youth, although what will follow will probably be no better. My two Guardsmen were apparently thinking of resigning their commissions; something that surprised me a little in the case of A who I knew had made a special study of gunnery. As for B, soldiering was what any obligation is for the vaguely young—a constraint with some compensations. He was bored in the Army; but the devil of it was, what to do afterwards. Pity he hadn't found an American heiress; he would have been quite happy as a country gentleman, with nice horses and nice children. Perhaps he would have preferred an English heiress, who wouldn't have wanted to rush back to New York every winter; or perhaps he was already in love with someone who was not an heiress, and who drove him to foolish adventures in the vain effort to forget her. I was sorry for the poor chap. Most enviable of men, I should have thought him, in his person and surroundings; yet for that very reason he seemed to have no future. The garden that had bred him, having seen him bloom, had no further use for him. It is indeed in the nature of existence to undermine its best products, and also its worst. This may be an acceptable reflection to the philosopher, who dwells in the eternal, but not for the fatted calf being led to the slaughter.

Our conversation was interrupted by a knock at the door. The sergeant came to report that one of the men had been taken ill. "Get a cab—a four-wheeler would be better"—my friend said thoughtfully, "take him to the barracks and bring back another man," and he gave the sergeant some money for the fares. "Doesn't the Government," I asked, "pay little items of this sort?" "Oh, I suppose I might charge it, but it's hardly worth while. It doesn't happen very often." He spoke in his habitual tone, half resignation, half amusement; but I suspected an impulse beneath to look after his men personally, and to let them feel that the imperturbable air of an officer didn't exclude a discerning good will towards his soldiers. The ethos of an aristocratic society, I perceived, is of a very high order. It involves imaginative sympathy with those who are not like oneself, loyalty, charity and self-knowledge.

It seemed a good moment to say good night, without waiting for the hour when I should be asked to leave. The rain had ceased; many of the lights in the court had been put out; the place seemed emptier and more ordinary than before. When the ponderous

doors had been closed after me, I looked at my watch. It was
half past ten. The pavement was wet, but I had on thick boots.
Why not walk back the whole length of Fleet Street and the
Strand? If I had melancholy thoughts, the cool moist air and the
pleasant exercise would transform them. Scattered lights revealed
only nebulous spaces, as the stars do in the sky, save where a few
stragglers loitered in the glare of the theatre entrances. Morally all
things are neutral in themselves. It is we that bathe them in whatever emotion may be passing through us. That singular evening at
the Bank of England remains for me a picturesque image, lurid,
cynical yet on the whole happy.

Thirteen years later, in July 1914, I was on my way for a short
visit to England with a return ticket to Paris in my pocket, good
for three months. As soon as I got into the boat at Calais, I
prudently hastened to have a bite in the cabin before we left the
dock; that, with a useful medicine that I had learned to take,
would help me to weather the passage. I was having my cold meat
and beer at one end of the empty table, when a steward came to
ask me if I was Mr. Santayana—or something that represented
that sound. The gentleman at the other end had sent him to
inquire. I looked up, and in spite of astigmatism and near-sighted-
ness in me and the ravages of ten years in him, I recognised my
young Guardsman. I nodded assent to him, and immediately
gulped down the rest of my beer and went over to say how-do-
you-do. But I couldn't stop; he knew I was a bad sailor; and I must
go and find a sheltered spot on deck. I would look for him there
later, weather permitting, or in any case at Dover. Yet I didn't look
for him: on the contrary I chose a nook on the lower deck, in the
second-class portion, wrapped myself up in a great-coat and rug,
and weathered the passage undisturbed and without accident. At
Dover, however, I found him standing before the train that was
to take us to Charing Cross. We exchanged a few words. He
was going home, he said, to rejoin his regiment. He was with
ladies. The ladies were already in the carriage, and looked as if
they might be his mother and sister or his wife and mother-in-

law. In any case, they would certainly prefer to travel by themselves, and I discreetly got into another compartment.

We had each other's addresses. Perhaps if I had known I was
to remain in England for five years, or if he had known that he
was to die in five months, it might have occurred to one of us to
write; but neither of us did so. It was better not to force a
renewal of our acquaintance. Our paths were divergent, neither of
us was any longer young, and it had been his youth and that very
divergence that for me had made our acquaintance interesting.
There would no longer be anything strange in his being unhappy.
He had lost his good looks and his mocking pleasure at the ways
of the world. Although still a soldierly figure and distinguished,
he was now yellow, battered and preoccupied. I rather suspect a
wife and children didn't exist; if they did, his end, for them, may
have been a tragedy. But for a bachelor tired of knocking about
and doing nothing in particular, a gallant death was a solution. It
placed him becomingly in the realm of truth and crowned the
nonchalance of his boyhood.

It was on this trip, in July 1914, that I found 87 Jermyn
Street, "no longer an hotel"; a trivial circumstance in itself that
still marked the end of my pleasant days in London. I was there
henceforth only on the wing, as at a centre from which to visit
my friends in the country, or to go for a season to Oxford or Cambridge. I was at Cambridge, at the Red Lion, in the first days of
that August, when war broke out; and I was again in London, at
rooms I often took afterwards at 3 Ryder Street, when one evening, as I was going to bed, I heard a great crash. They must have
dropped a heavy tray of dishes in the pantry, I thought: but
presently came another crash very like the first, and then other
detonations: it was the first Zeppelin raid. I put on again such
clothes as I had taken off, and went down into the streets. It was
not late, hardly eleven o'clock; and the people about were naturally
excited and communicative. I went as far as Piccadilly Circus,
from whence I could see, towards the east, the glare of distant
fires. One corner shop in the Circus had been smashed: I suppose

that was the first great noise that I had taken for broken crockery. The next evening many people waited late in Hyde Park, to see if there would be another raid; but nothing occurred. Nevertheless here was now another reason for not staying in town, and I soon moved to Oxford, favourably placed, from the point of view of safety, in the very middle of England, not yet an industrial town, and the proverbial seat of quietness, religion and study.

The moment when I lost my pleasure in London was the very moment when I was at last free and might have settled down there, as would be natural for an unattached man who writes in the English language. Moreover, unlike most foreigners, I was perfectly happy in the English climate and the English way of living. They were a great relief from America in softness and dignity, and from the Continent in comfort and privacy. Yet a somewhat mysterious contrary force prevented me from making the attempt. Perhaps it was my age. I was fifty, and the prospect backward had begun decidedly to gain on the prospect forward. For the future, I desired nothing fixed, no place in society, no circle of prescribed friends and engagements. Direct human relations, certainly, with whatever persons I might come across, which might include stray poets or philosophers, or agreeable ladies, for instance, like "Elisabeth." But they should come and go, and I should be free always to change the scene and to move into another sphere. For constant company I had enough, and too much, with myself. A routine had established itself in my day, which I could carry with me wherever I went; it gave me abundance of private hours, and for relief and refreshment, I liked solitude in crowds, meals in restaurants, walks in public parks, architectural rambles in noble cities. To have become simply an old bachelor in London would have been monotonous. Acquaintance with varied and distinguished people, which London might have afforded, didn't in the least tempt me. The intellectual world of my time alienated me intellectually. It was a Babel of false principles and blind cravings, a zoological garden of the mind, and I had no desire to be one of the beasts. I wished to remain a visitor, looking in at the cages. This could be better done by reading people's books than by frequenting their society.

With few exceptions, nobody of consequence in London knew of my existence. Even my publishers, except old Mr. Dent, remained unknown to me, as Scribner had remained unknown in New York. I can remember only one literary man that (through Loeser, I believe) became a sort of friend of mine: and then it was his wife rather than himself that was eventually well known to the international public: but my London friend was her husband, Arthur Strong. He was at that time librarian to the House of Lords and was believed to get up the facts for the speeches of the Prince of Wales, later King Edward VII. He had been originally librarian to the Duke of Devonshire, with whose house he was said to be somehow connected.

Mrs. Strong was a large woman, with bold pseudo-classic features like a late Roman statue of Niobe; and when I saw her in their house in London, she looked like a figure by Burne-Jones that had walked out of the canvas: great heavy eyes, a big nose, a short upper lip, and full, richly curving lips, over a conspicuous round chin. But the most characteristic thing about her was the neck, long, columnar, and extremely convex in the throat, as if she habitually yearned forwards and upwards at once. She was also, at that time, preraphaelite in dress. I remember her one day at luncheon in green cotton brocade, with a broad lace collar, like a bib drooping over it. She was silent, and let her husband talk. Perhaps her thoughts were far away from him and from me. She was destined to become a Catholic and an authority on the history of Christian art, especially Roman archeology of the early centuries: and when I came across her once at the Berensons' in Florence, she did not recognise me or seem to remember that I had several times been her guest in London.

With Arthur Strong's mind I felt a decided sympathy. He was very learned in important but remote matters, such as Arabic literature. His central but modest position in the great world gave him a satirical insight into affairs, and he summed up his inner solitude in pungent maxims. He reminded me of my father. Through the Moors he had good knowledge of Spain also: and he said something about the Spanish mind that has given me food for reflection. "The Spaniard," he said, "respects only one thing, and that is—", and he raised his forefinger, pointing to heaven. There is no power but Allah: he is omnificent, and all appearances and all wills are nought. It is quite true that no genuine or reflective person in Spain trusts anybody or is proud of himself. He may be vain and punctilious, but that is play-acting: he thinks that pose is set down for him in his rôle; but inwardly he knows that he is dust. This is the insight that I express by saying to myself that the only authority in existence is the *authority of things*: that since only *things* have any authority there is, *morally*, no authority at all, and the spirit is free in its affections. Is this what the Moslems really feel? At any rate something keeps them (and me) from hurrying and fussing and being surprised. It is better to put up with things than to be responsible for them. We may leave responsibility, like vengeance, to God who made us and made the world and seems not to be disturbed at the result.

There was another member of the intelligentsia in London with whom I sometimes discussed high subjects. Of late years he has explained himself very well in his memoirs, entitled *Unforgotten Years*. I came upon him from two sides: Bertie Russell had married one of his sisters, and Berenson eventually married the other. It was Bertie that first introduced me to the Smith family, Quakers from Philadelphia long resident in England. In the name of his parents-in-law he wrote asking me to come to Friday's Hill, a place they had taken in Haslemere. I went, and found myself in an odd society. Old Mr. Smith, prosperous and proprietor of a thriving factory, had been also a Quaker preacher, and no less successful in saving souls than in making money; but, alas, in the midst of his apostolate he had lost his faith, and was at a loss how to reply to his trustful converts when they came to him for further guidance along the narrow path. "Don't tell Mrs. Smith," he said to me while showing me his garden, "but I am not a Christian at all.

I am a Buddhist." And he pointed to what he called his Bo Tree, a great oak, in the midst of which he had had a glass house constructed. We climbed the ladder into it, a single small chamber with a black horsehair lounge and a small bookcase, filled with little old-fashioned American books, among which I spied *Prue and I*, a novel by our "Aunt Sarah's" son-in-law, George William Curtis. I had expected the Dhammapada or the Upanishads. Vain flight of the American puritan to softer climates! He carries his horizon with him, and remains rooted at home.

Mrs. Smith too had been a preacher, and she remained a Quaker inasmuch as she continued to advocate simplicity of life and to call her children "thee"; and although she had abandoned the belief in hell, she went on preaching and feeling the immense importance of rescuing oneself from perdition; for as she wisely thought, there were bad enough hells on earth from which people needed to be saved. However, with a resignation that had a touch of defiance and warning in it, she put up with the unregenerate views of her children, and of the world at large.

It was strange to see Bertie, and even his brother, who turned up one day for luncheon, in that American Quaker family, and to hear those young women speak of the elder brother as *Frank*, which I never heard any of his friends or his wives do. But the Russells never knew themselves or their proper place in the world: that was a part of their mixture of genius and folly. I myself felt out of my element in the Smith family, yet was destined to come upon them all my life long in various ways. They not unnaturally thought of me among their class of expatriate Americans and members of the intelligentsia: only Mrs. Berenson, who had motherly insights and had been married to an Irish Catholic, understood me a little, and perceived how unwillingly and deceptively I had come to fall under those categories. However, I have much to thank the Smiths for. They formed a lively band in the carnival, and led me into other bands in the masquerade, which I should hardly have joined of my own initiative.

At Haslemere, they took me to visit "Michael Field," whose

identity and whose poems I had never heard of. Michael Field was
a pseudonym for two ladies, aunt and niece, who were linked
together by the tenderest affection and by a common inspiration
of the classic Muse. They had been forewarned, they may have
read up my poetry expressly; in any case, they awaited me as if I
had been Orpheus approaching lyre in hand towards their bower.
The aunt stood at the door, serene but intense; dressed in rich
black lace: I noticed a preciously bound small volume in her hand
and pink roses in her bosom. The niece kept somewhat in the
shadow, as if too young to be more than silent and curious. On the
tea-table there were red and green apples in a golden basket, and
under the table a large dog, with a wonderful coat of long silken
bronze-coloured hair. Unfortunately the dog couldn't travel and
would die if they left him: for that reason they were prevented
from ever going to Italy and Greece. But what did that matter,
when they had Greece and Italy in their hearts? They didn't say
so in words, but words in such a case were superfluous. Everything
breathed inexpressible tenderness and silent passion.

Some years later the Smiths introduced me to a better-known
personage: Henry James. Bertie and his first wife had then been
divorced and she and her brother lived together in St. Leonard's
Terrace in Chelsea. By that time Logan Pearsall Smith had developed his amiable interest in my writings and the Berensons
also had shown me the greatest kindness. Now the brother and
sister asked me one day to lunch with Henry James. Those were
his last years and I never saw him again. Nevertheless in that
one interview he made me feel more at home and better understood than his brother William ever had done in the long years
of our acquaintance. Henry was calm, he liked to see things as
they are, and be free afterwards to imagine how they might have
been. We talked about different countries as places of residence.
He was of course subtle and bland, appreciative of all points of
view, and amused at their limitations. He told me an anecdote
about Prosper Mérimée wondering at him for choosing to live in
England, and finding that a good background for his inspiration.

"Vous vivez," he had said, *"parmi des gens moins fins que vous."*
All of us naturally felt the truth of this as applied to Henry
James, and each of us no doubt thought it true of himself also:
yet how well we all understood, notwithstanding, the incomparable charm of living in England!

As for me, apart from the climate and the language, both
entirely to my taste, there was the refinement, if not the *finesse*
of English people in all their ways. They were certainly less
disinterested than I, intellectually, morally and materially; and it
was not from them that I wished to draw my ideas. But I respected and loved the English psyche, and the primacy there of
the physical and moral nature over the intellectual. It was the
safer order of things, more vital, more manly than the reverse.
Man was not made to understand the world, but to live in it. Yet
nature, in some of us, lets out her secret; it spoils the game, but it
associates us with her own impartiality. We cannot abdicate that
privilege. It is final, ultimate, proper for the funeral oration over
the earth: but those who are destined to live in this world had
better not hear of it, or if they hear of it had better not take it
too much to heart.

Of the London suburbs, the only one where I have stayed for
any time is Richmond. I saw the old Star and Garter at its last
gasp; it was being sold and transformed: and while the dinner
there was good enough, there was an uncomfortable air of removal.
But during the year of the armistice I spent some weeks at the
Richmond Hill Hotel; I was waiting to obtain leave to return to
Paris. The French authorities made a great fuss about it. Why, if
I had lived in Paris, had I abandoned *La France* in the hour of
danger? The military official evidently suspected that I was not a
neutral or an elderly man, but a young coward or a secret enemy.
I might have retorted that if I had returned at the outbreak of
war, I should only have added another mouth to the population,
quite likely to be starved during another siege. But I never protest or argue with persons in authority: instead I produced a note
in a fashionable lady's handwriting. It was from Madame de

Fontenay, addressed to the Chancellor of the French Embassy, requesting him to facilitate my journey, and including her husband's card. She wrote because I was a friend of the Strongs who were great friends of hers; and they were great friends of hers because they were son-in-law and granddaughter of Rockefeller. Monsieur Rockefeller, she once said to me with decision, was like a king. Her perfumed little letter worked like magic; and I was immediately able to cross the Channel; it was on the very day of the signing of the peace of Versailles.

In Richmond I had not had the comfort of private lodgings, but had quiet and rather nice early Victorian rooms; and for going in to London, as I did often, I liked the top of the busses, now motor-busses, and the long drive over Fulham Heath. On other days Richmond Park was at hand for walks in almost complete solitude. The Terrace, the tea-rooms, the river, and the trippers entertained me after the fashion of the Paris boulevards.

One day I fell into conversation with a young man who was reading a French novel conspicuous in its yellow cover. They all knew French and Italian, he said, in the Navy. He had cruised all over the Mediterranean. Now he was on special leave because his father was on his way to England to try the Kaiser. His father was a Chief Justice in India—Watkins: I had of course seen the name. Yes: I had certainly seen the name somewhere: I didn't add, over the fishmonger's round the corner. And the Chief Justice and his gallant son were enjoying their holiday for nothing. They didn't after all hang the Kaiser. Such little casual acquaintances amused me in my travels.

I had been in Richmond once before on a much briefer, soberer, more exalted errand: to visit old Lady Russell at Pembroke Lodge. Bertie took me there to high tea one evening. There was a beefsteak, and a half bottle of claret, exclusively for me. The atmosphere was exactly that of old-fashioned Boston: only the voices and the subjects of conversation were different. Lady Russell at once asked me if I knew *The Bible in Spain*. I had heard of Borrow's book, but unfortunately hadn't read it, so that I was at a loss to make a suitable reply. Soon, however, I was put at my ease by not being questioned, and Lady Russell—her daughter Lady Agatha was present but didn't talk—began to speak about herself and her feelings. The world had moved away from what it was in other days: she never went to London now except to dine with Mr. Gladstone. In fine, a picture of self-confirming but melancholy old age, when the nebula of experience contracts into a single central sun, alone now visible or trusted, and destined soon to be extinguished in its turn.

This visit forms an interesting contrast to the one, already mentioned, which I had made some years before to the Russells' other grandmother, Lady Stanley of Alderley. There I had been taken by the elder brother, here tabooed. I had just returned to London from Oxford, and Russell had asked me to join him at his grandmother's, on the way to Teddington, where he then lived. It was a large house in Dover Street, now a club or hotel. The front door, at one end of the façade, opened directly into a large square hall, where I was received by two flunkeys in white silk stockings. When I asked for Lord Russell and gave my name, it was evident that I was expected, for the footman I spoke to said, "Yes, Sir. In a moment," and the other instantly disappeared. Presently I saw the youthful figure of Russell himself tripping down the red carpeted grand stairs, and I can see it still, silhouetted against the western sunlight that streamed from the opposite windows above the landing. He was in an amiable mood, seemed to approve of my new clothes and hat and discreet tie, and led me up in the most friendly manner into a long room like a gallery that evidently occupied the whole front of the house. There was a row of windows, with boxes of plants in front of them, running along one side, and opposite a row of cabinets and sofas against the wall, the whole floor between being clear, and with the parquet highly burnished and waxed, so that footing was a bit precarious. At the other end, however, there was a large rug spread, on which stood the tea-table, surrounded by three ladies, and two or three vacant chairs of comfortable and homelike appearance. Lady Stanley, fat, old, jolly, and monumental, was enthroned in the centre; on one side sat the Hon. Maud Stanley, her daughter, amiable and middle-aged, and on the other her granddaughter, Lady Griselda Ogilvie, charming in the latest fashion and smiling with an easy grace. Our visit was as short as it was agreeable, for Russell was always conscious of the due time for catching trains. But it sufficed to leave a permanent impression in my mind, since this is the only glimpse I ever had of a grand house and of good society in London.

The recollection will serve to bring my rambling narrative back to the year 1887, and to the most extraordinary of all my friends.

CHAPTER III

RUSSELL

BECAUSE the windows of my room in Hollis Hall looked out directly on the brick path that led from the Harvard Yard to Jervis field, then the college playground; or because, for an undergraduate, I was thought comparatively articulate; or because I was a foreigner and known to write verses; or because the guide to whom the young Earl Russell was entrusted was a good friend of mine,[1] that exceptional nobleman, grandson and heir of Lord John Russell, was brought to see me, when on being "sent down" from Oxford in 1886 he visited America in charge of a tutor. He was the first Englishman I had ever spoken to or that had ever spoken to me. That of itself would have made him notable in my eyes; but this Englishman was remarkable on his own account.

He was a tall young man of twenty, still lithe though large of bone, with abundant tawny hair, clear little steel-blue eyes, and a florid complexion. He moved deliberately, gracefully, stealthily, like a tiger well fed and with a broad margin of leisure for choosing his prey. There was precision in his indolence; and mild as he seemed, he suggested a latent capacity to leap, a latent astonishing celerity and strength, that could crush at one blow. Yet his speech was simple and suave, perfectly decided and strangely frank. He had some thoughts, he said, of becoming a clergyman. He seemed observant, meditative, as if comparing whatever he saw with something in his mind's eye. As he looked out of the window at the muddy paths and shabby grass, the elms standing scattered at equal intervals, the ugly factory-like buildings, and the loud-voiced youths passing by, dressed like shop-assistants, I

---
[1] Herbert Lyman.

44

could well conceive his thoughts, and I said apologetically that after Oxford all this must seem to him rather mean; and he replied curtly: "Yes, it does." I explained our manner of life, our social distinctions, our choice of studies, our sports, our food, our town amusements. He listened politely, obviously rather entertained and not displeased to find that, according to my description, all I described might be dismissed forever without further thought. Then he sat good-naturedly on the floor and began to look at my books—a rather meagre collection in some open shelves. He spied Swinburne's *Poems,* and took out the volume. Did I like Swinburne? Yes, perhaps he was rather verbose; but did I know the choruses in *Atalanta in Calydon?* No? Then he would read me one. And he read them all, rather liturgically, with a perfect precision and clearness, intoning them almost, in a sort of rhythmic chant, and letting the strong meaning shine through the steady processional march of the words. It seemed the more inspired and oracular for not being brought out by any human change of tone or of emphasis. I had not heard poetry read in this way before. I had not known that the English language could become, like stained glass, an object and a delight in itself.

He stayed a long time, until, the daylight having decidedly failed, he remembered that he was to dine at the Jameses'. My own dinner was long since cold. He was off the next day, he said; but I must look him up whenever I came to London. I saw no more of him at that time; but I received through the post a thin little book bound in white vellum, *The Bookbills of Narcissus,* by Richard Le Gallienne, inscribed "from R." And William James not long afterwards took occasion to interrupt himself, as his manner was, as if a sudden thought had struck him, and to say to me: "I hear you have seen this young grandson of Lord John Russell's. He talked about you; you seem to have made an impression." The impression I had made was that I was capable of receiving impressions. With young Russell, who completely ignored society and convention, this was the royal road to friendship.

When late in March of the following year, 1887, after the

winter semester at Berlin, I reached England for the holidays,
Russell was not in town, but wrote that he was bringing a boat
down from the engineers at Newbury to the boatbuilders in
London. They were merely patched up for the journey; it would
be a three days' trip, one on a canal and two on the Thames. He
feared he couldn't offer me much accommodation and I should
have to sleep ashore, but it would be a good chance of seeing the
river. It was finally arranged that I should join him on the second
day at Reading. Muddy and sordid streets led from the dismal
railway station to the Kennet Canal Office where Russell's small
yacht, the *Royal*, was to lie for the night. After various inquiries
I found my way over a shaky plank (very little to my taste) to a
narrow strip of deck surrounding the cabin skylight. There I
found my host in conversation with a workman. My arrival was
noticed, and I was asked if I had duly deposited my bag at the
inn. All being well, I was left to stand about, while the conversation with the workman continued. I stood by for a while and
listened; but seeing that the business gave no signs of coming to
an end, and was not very intelligible or interesting, I sat on the
edge of the cockpit and took to sketching the hulks, masts and
chimneys visible from the river. In those days I always carried a
note-book and pencil in my pocket for setting down sudden inspirations. I had full time for exhausting the dreary beauties of the
scene and my small skill in expressing them. At length the worthy
workman departed (I suppose his working hours were up) and
Russell called me, quite affectionately, slipped his arm into mine,
and took me to look at the cabin and the engine-room and the
galley, which was also the place where one washed. My ignorant
questions were answered briefly, clearly, with instant discernment
of what I knew and didn't know about ships. Then we went
ashore for tea.

Russell said he should not have been a peer but an engineer.
At the time I thought this a little joke, remembering him reading
the choruses in *Atalanta* and wishing to be a parson; but now I
see that there was a genuine feeling in it. When he died, one of

the notices in the newspapers referred to his "scientific training" and its value in his political career. What was this scientific training? Surely nothing that he acquired at Winchester or Oxford, but what he learned while refitting his steam-yacht and talking to workmen, as he had that afternoon. He took up each mechanical novelty as it arose, experimented, became more or less expert. He carved, drove and steered admirably; he would have made an excellent naval officer and gunner. When he lived at Broom Hall and had a private electric plant for charging his launch and supplying his light, I remember asking him what electricity was. And he said, "I will show you," and after making me leave my watch at a distance, he brought me close to the large magnet that formed part of the machinery, until I felt a strong pull; and then he said triumphantly, "That is what it is." In one sense, a scholastic and verbal answer; yet there was the scientific humility and peace in it that is satisfied with dark facts. And there was another side to his pleasure in engineering: the sense of mastery. Matter can be wooed, coaxed, and mastered like a woman, and this without being in the least understood sympathetically. On the contrary the keen edge of the pleasure comes from defiance. If matter can crush us when ignored, it can be played with and dragged about when once caught in its own meshes: and this skillful exercise of compulsion was dear to Russell. When he acted as Leader of the Opposition in the House of Lords he was not half so happy or in his element. The peers could not so easily be engineered.

At the inn he began to lavish endearments on the cat, who returned his advances disdainfully, and after purring a little when stroked found the thing a bore and scooted into parts unknown. The barmaid then had her turn for a moment, and would doubtless have proved more responsive; but the other servants had to be spoken to about the tea—the tea was very important—and the smiling barmaid and the ungrateful cat were alike forgotten. Tea was a wonderful sedative; and the post and the newspapers were brought in at the same time. Russell opened his letters with the tips of his strong fingers, without haste, without one needless movement or the least unnecessary force. A brief glance usually sufficed, and the letter was dropped, as if into eternal oblivion, upon the floor. But now and then something called for a comment, and then my presence seemed providential. I was invited to observe the stupidity of the correspondent or the folly of the government, or the outrage it was to have such prolonged bad weather. What did I think of the absurd language of the Scottish housekeeper who asked: "Will I light the fire?" And could I conceive anything more annoying than the position of a young man who hadn't yet come into his money and whose grandmother (Lady Russell, and not Lady Stanley) was a fool? In all this fault-finding there was nothing really troubled or querulous. It was all serene observation of the perversity of things, the just perceptions and judgments of a young god to whom wrongness was hateful on principle, but who was not in the least disturbed about it in his own person. Was it not his own choice to move in this ridiculous world, where there were imperfect inns and yachts to be refitted and untrustworthy tradesmen and faithless cats and silly, disappointed barmaids? What difference could such incidents of travel make to a transcendental spirit, fixed and inviolate in its own centre?

The next day early we started down the river in the *Royal*. She was a steam yacht of 100 tons, rigged at sea, I was told, as a schooner, but now mastless. There was a cockpit aft, with a seat round it, and the wheel in the middle; my ecclesiastical mind at once compared it to the apse of a primitive basilica, with its semi-circle of stalls and its bishop's throne in the centre, whence the pilot of souls might rise and lay his hands on the altar; in this case, the wheel. Two or three steep steps led below, from this cockpit, into the cabin, which occupied the whole width of the boat and perhaps a third of her length. There were some lockers on either side, and two broad bunks beyond, supplied with red plush mattresses and pillows. The table between had flaps that could be let down, leaving only a ledge some six inches wide running down its length; two other sleeping places could then be arranged on the floor between the table and the bunks; but we were never more than two when I was on board. The cabin was sealed at the end by a varnished yellow bulkhead, decorated with a large barometer and a small clock. To go forward it was necessary to skirt the cabin roof, with its row of square lights, along the edge of the deck. There was a cabin boy who cooked and served our meals quite properly and might well have been called a steward. The two or three other men of the crew I hardly ever saw during the three weeks I spent, the following year, on board the *Royal*.

At such close quarters I soon began to understand what was expected of me. I was liked, I was wanted, I was confided in, but only when my turn came, when other interests flagged and nothing urgent was to be done. I should not have been liked, or wanted, or confided in if I had interfered with other things or made myself a nuisance. But as a sympathetic figure in the background, to whom Olympian comments were always intelligible, I fitted in very well. Being an unpractical person, a foreigner, and a guest, I naturally accepted everything as it came; and being indolent but meditative, with eyes for the new scenes before me, I was never better entertained than when neglected, or busier than when idle. Moreover, I was left free and had my escapades. In later years Russell, who was no pedestrian, liked to plan my walks for me and did it very well. His topographical sense was excellent, and in driving or motoring about he noticed and remembered every nook and every prospect. When asked for directions he liked to give them; it was a pleasure to his executive mind. So the next morning, when we arrived at Windsor and were stopping for some supplies, I was allowed half an hour ashore, and advised to go up to the Castle terrace: but I mustn't loiter, for in all Russell's mighty movements punctuality was absolutely demanded.

In the lovely misty sunshine of that April morning, I climbed the outer Castle steps, not without profound emotion. I was treading the steps of Windsor Castle. The Thames valley stretched before me, green and rural, peopled and living. Eton lay at my feet: I could distinguish the great east window of the Chapel, and the wooden turrets. The fields, the trees, the river glittered mildly in the sun, as if all atremble with dew. What homeliness, what simplicity in this grandeur! How modest were these important places, how silent, how humbly faithful to the human scale! If such gentle discipline could conquer the world, why should it not conquer the heart? But I mustn't sentimentalise too long, or my rebellious friend below—horrible thought!—might be kept waiting. Strange that being the heir to so many privileges he should appreciate them so little, and should use the strength that he derived from tradition in deriding tradition and in destroying it.

My position as a familiar friend who was not a nuisance was not established without some preliminary slips. One was a slip in the literal sense of the word. Russell had at Hampton, where he then lived, an electric launch for scurrying at a surprising speed along the river. Electric launches were novelties in those days, and with his good steering and perfect serenity, he attracted the admiring attention of the good people in the boats or on the banks. But nature had endowed him with a more surprising ability of another kind. He could walk along the edges and ledges of roofs, and up inclined poles, like a cat. I suppose all boys, except me, have had a desire to do such things, and have tried their hand at them at a certain age, and then abandoned feline ambitions for things more human. But in Russell, for some reason, feline instincts survived, and developed into habits. He performed his acrobatic feats as a matter of course, without training and without comment. He never boasted of them; he only thought it a singular deficiency in others not to be able to do them. One Sunday afternoon we had landed at Richmond for tea, and on our return found the launch removed from the landing—there was naturally a crowd of trippers on that day—and it lay at a little distance from the sloping bank, which didn't allow it to come nearer. For Russell this created no problem. One long boathook was turned into a bridge from the launch to the shore, and seizing the other as a *picador* does his lance, and sticking the prong through the clear water into the sand, he walked calmly and quickly aboard. But how was I to get in? In the same way of course. In vain did I protest, like Rosencrantz and Guildenstern, that I hadn't the skill. Hamlet said it was as easy as lying. If I had insisted on making them turn about, and wait for their chance to come up to the landing so that I might step aboard easily, I should have been making myself a nuisance. Seeing my hesitation, Russell said encouragingly: "Come on. Try it. I'll lend you a hand." I knew I should fall in; but I might as well try it, since the only alternative was to wade across, and I must get wet in any case. The pole was rather steep, I had on ordinary boots, not tennis shoes like Russell, and no experience in walking the tight rope. So I took the boathook and gave Russell my other hand. The result was tragic, but not what either of us expected. I fell in, inevitably, but I pulled him in after me; and while I only got my legs wet, he fell in backwards head over heels, with a tremendous splash, which caused great laughter among the sundry trippers lined up on the shore. There was no danger, even in a complete immersion; two feet of water at most, and a warm summer afternoon. We both climbed in easily; but Russell flew into an indescribable rage. His language showed that the society of workingmen had not been wasted upon him; or rather that he must have overheard a good deal that no workingman would knowingly have said in his presence. Where? Or could nature have endowed him with Billingsgate as it had endowed him with somnambulism when awake? For that inexhaustible flow of foul words and blasphemous curses was somnambulistic: he didn't know what he was saying or why. It was an automatism let loose, as was his acrobatic instinct.

I thought at the time that what maddened him was having been baulked and made a fool of in public; but now that I know him better I believe that he had no idea that he was in the least to blame. He felt innocent and injured. It was all my fault for being such an incredible muff. I had ducked him in the Thames and was keeping him wet to the skin in the cool breeze all the way home. His memory for injuries, however—and he thought every-body injured him—was remarkably short. As soon as he got into dry clothes his wrath subsided. Still, he had been so outrageously abusive, and so persistent, that I was cut to the quick. Not that I minded his words, which I had hardly distinguished and couldn't remember; they had no real application to me and couldn't stick. What I feared was that the sting of his own folly had made him hate me, and that all might be over between us. But not in the least. He didn't understand why that evening I could hardly swallow my food, or why I was leaving the next morning.

There was some difficulty about getting my things to the station. It wasn't far, and I had only a bag, but it was rather heavy. "I'll carry it for you," he said; and he actually did so, most of the way. And he continued to send me little notes, inviting me to this or that so long as I remained in England; and before long, instead of signing them "yours sincerely," he began to sign them "yours ever." This was not meant for a mute apology, kindness vanquishing resentment. He behaved exactly in the same way with his worst enemies, such as Lady Scott: forgot terrible injuries, and reverted spontaneously to a deeper impulse, which events had obscured for a moment. I accepted all his invitations. My ego was no less absolute than his, and calmer. If he allowed me my inabilities, I could allow him his explosions. That the wild animal and the furious will should exist beneath his outwardly exact and critical intelligence was so much added, a double *virtù*. I liked it and I didn't fear it.

The astonishing thing about this incident was that Russell completely forgot it. Years after, when I once referred to having pulled him into the water at Richmond, he denied it, and didn't know what I was talking about. This again was not a case of legal oblivion, such as lawyers command a man to scatter over his past when he is about to give evidence: it was a genuine blank. A blank, that is, in his conscious memory; for in his inner man the thing must have left its trace, because he never afterwards urged me to do anything to which I was not inclined or taxed me with any defect. He respected my freedom •inconditionally and gladly, as I respected his. This was one of the reasons why our friendship lasted so many years, weathering all changes in our circumstances, in spite of the few points of contact between our characters and the utter diversity in our lives. Neither of us was ever a nuisance to the other.

When I was about to make my first visit to Oxford, I had received four notes of introduction, enclosed in the following letter:

Ferishtah, Hampton

21 Ap. 1887.

Dear Santayana,

I find that the number of my intimate friends actually at Oxford is much decreased. Natheless I send you 4 to: 1 Burke of Trinity, 2 Jepson of Balliol, 3 Johnson of New, 4 Davis of Balliol.

1 is a friend of 8 or 10 years standing, a good fellow but so terrible reserved that you'll get nothing out of him.

2 is a funny fellow of immoral tendencies and pessimistic affectation. Well worth your visit to make him show off.

3 is the man I most admire and—in the world, knows every book that is, transcendentalist, genius, and is called affected. The way for you to treat him is to take no notice when he tries (as he will) to shock you. If he discourses, listen: it will be worth while.

4 is a strictly moral Radical Positivist. You may label him with all the 'ists suitable to that combination. He will only talk politics to you but has more heart than he shows on the surface. Still of course he's a Philistine.

Eh voilà!

Yours sincerely,
RUSSELL.

Write to me in about a week.

Number One in this list was not number one by accident. Perhaps I got nothing out of him, but I liked him very much. He was sensitive and brave. You felt that in some way he must have suffered a great deal. Had it been bad health, family quarrels, love, or perhaps some disgrace? He was Irish, but Protestant, very Protestant in a profound, silent, unhappy way. Intense moral feeling, intense sense of the difference between the better and the worse. He had been with Russell at a private school, and had a good education, but felt very Irish, and perhaps regretted that his money came from a brewery—*Burke's Ales, Stout and Porter*. We talked chiefly about Russell, whom he cared for; but caring didn't modify his strict standards, and while he could forgive Russell's commonplace peccadilloes, when it came later to his treatment of the Billings girls, whom Burke knew, he became intractable, and broke with him. As I wasn't going to desert Russell for that, or for anything, Burke and I ceased to keep up our acquaintance.

I found Number Two in comfortable not very academic lodgings, the best available no doubt, yet hardly worthy of his ornamental person. He was not really good-looking, but his hair was yellow, parted in the middle and carefully waved, like a ploughed field. He said his life was devoted to the culture of it. Incidentally, however, he had accomplished a greater thing. He had already, at twenty, doubled human knowledge in one of the sciences, the science *de modis veneris*. There had been forty modes before, now there were eighty. He didn't show me the classic designs for those forty modes; they are probably not extant; nor did he reveal the secret of his new variations. I was sceptical, and Jepson didn't interest me.

Number Three was then in his first year at New College. He had rooms at the top of the new buildings overlooking Holywell. Over the roofs of the low houses opposite, the trees in the Parks were visible in places, as well as the country beyond: and pointing to the distant horizon Lionel Johnson said sadly: "Everything above that line is right, everything below it is wrong." These were almost the first words he spoke to me, and they formed an admirable preface to a religious conversion.

He was rather a little fellow, pale, with small sunken blinking eyes, a sensitive mouth, and lank pale brown hair. His child-like figure was crowned by a smooth head, like a large egg standing on its small end. His age was said to be sixteen, and I readily believed the report. His genius was the kind that may be precocious, being an inward protest against external evidence; and his aspect, though thoughtful, was very youthful: yet his real age seems to have been twenty, only a year and a half younger than Russell and three years younger than I. He said he lived on eggs in the morning and nothing but tea and cigarettes during the rest of the day. He seldom went out, but when he did, it was for a walk of twenty miles in the country: and on those days he dined. There was also conspicuous on a centre table a jug of Glengarry whiskey between two open books: *Les Fleurs du Mal* and *Leaves of Grass*. Two large portraits hung on the wall: Cardinal Newman and Cardinal Wiseman. When he was of age he intended to become a Catholic and a monk: at present his people, who were Welsh, objected. This intention he carried out in part; but instead of becoming a monk he became a Fenian; for at the same time that he was converted from a legal Protestant to a legal Catholic, he was mystically transformed from a Welshman into an Irishman. It was the same thing, he said, being Celtic. Perhaps, too, being Irish was closer to his inner man, and certainly more congruous with Catholicism and with whiskey.

Our acquaintance was never close, but it seemed to gain in interest, for both of us, as it receded. Some years later he honoured me with a poem *To a Spanish Friend*, beginning with the words "Exiled in America," and ending with an exhortation to return to Saint Theresa and her "holy Avila." I returned often, and should gladly have grown old in that atmosphere, yet not in order to indulge the impulse to dream awake: rather in order to remove the pressure of reality (of which I was only too well aware) and to leave my reflexion free to survey that reality fairly, at arm's length. Lionel Johnson lived only in his upper storey, in a loggia open to the sky; and he forgot that he had climbed there up a long flight of flinty steps, and that his *campanile* rested on the vulgar earth. The absence of all foundations, of all concreteness, of all distinction between fiction and truth, makes his poetry indigestible. I see that it is genuine poetry—an irresponsible flux of impassioned words: and his religion too was genuine religion, if we admit that religion must be essentially histrionic. Let everything that comes, it says, be to thee an Angel of the Lord; embroider upon it in that sense, and let the vulgar world recede into a distant background for an endless flapping of angelic wings and chanting of angelic voices. The age had given Lionel Johnson enough verbal culture and knowledge of literature to raise his effusions in that angelic choir to a certain level of refinement and fancy; but he was not a traditional Catholic, accepting good-naturedly a supernatural economy that happened to prevail in the universe, as political and domestic economy prevail in one's earthly fortunes. Nor was he a philosopher, enduring the truth. He was a spiritual rebel, a spiritual waif who couldn't endure the truth, but demanded a lovelier fiction to revel in, invented or accepted it, and called it revelation. In part like Shelley, in part like Rimbaud, he despised the world and adored the unreal.

Had that first saying of his to me, that everything above the horizon was right and everything below it wrong, represented his primary and constant mind, he might have become a monk as he had intended; because that is the foundation of Christianity. There is a divine world *surrounding us*; but there is sin and damnation *in us*. Lionel Johnson never seemed to me to feel this as, for instance, St. Paul and St. Augustine felt it. What he felt was rather the opposite, that everything within him was right, and everything outside wrong; and if he made an exception of the blank sky, this was only because he could fill it at will with his poetry. In other words, he was a transcendentalist and a humanist; for that reason he seemed a prophet to Russell; and at bottom nothing could be more contrary to Christian humility and to Catholic discipline. I know that an effort has been made to represent him as a saint, hushing the sad reality: it is part of the general practice of bluff, silence, and the *claque* in journalistic criticism. Let me give some grounds for a contrary opinion.

Russell, who was faithful to the inspired friend of his school days and completely ignored his conversion and Catholicism, published a collection of Johnson's letters from Winchester, written when he was seventeen or eighteen years old. Here are some extracts: "I do not love sensuality: I do not hate it: I do not love purity: I do not hate it; I regard both as artistic aspects of life."

"A man's life is not his acts of profession: drills, sermons, death-beds, stone-breaking are not life: the life is the sunsets we worship, the books we read, the faces we love."

"I tell you, be happy, for that is to know God; be sinful, for that is to feel God; be all things, for that is to be God."

"At my worst moments I see myself Archbishop and Poet Laureate, at my best I don't see myself at all, but merely God and other men and the world and my dear art."

"I think that my earlier scriptures were the spiritualised expression of my life-long faith—I adopted the language of convenient morality to apply it to the immoral doctrines of my personal gospel."

After two years of Oxford, Johnson had developed an element of banter, and favoured me with the following letter:

Hunter's Inn,

August 2nd (1888)   Hedder's Mouth, Barnstable.

My dear Santayana,

Forgive my not writing earlier: I have been for weeks a wanderer, with letters chasing me about the world in vain.

I wish I could be in Oxford in August; but only, be sure, for the sake of meeting you. Unhappily it is impossible. I am bound, hand and foot, to a "reading party" in an obscure corner of Devonshire; and see no prospect of escape. Can you not find your way to our pastoral retreat? or be in Oxford in October? You will not go back to our dear America just yet, mon ami?

Berenson charmed Oxford for a term, and vanished: leaving behind a memory of exotic epigrams and, so to speak, cynical music. It was a strangely curious time. He is something too misanthropic: but always adorable.

I missed Russell lately by four hours: you know we have not met for many a year, almost. I incline to think it time for his drama of life to become critical in some way: at least, beyond disregarding all unities of time and space he does not appear to progress. This morning is very hot; the sea sparkles; Plato is beautiful; the world very charming; but why go to America? Come to Oxford in October and learn of me how to live on nothing with nothing to do. I intend to teach Berenson: and neither of you shall set foot again in Boston, that Holy and self-satisfied city.

Do you read Shelley still, and have you renounced that stage devil, Byron, and all his works, except Don Juan? Kegan Paul, whom you met, asked me the question concerning you the other day. Ach! there is always Keats.

When next you hear from me you will probably hear that I am a Jesuit novice or a budding Carthusian or some such an one. Anyway, the Church will probably have claimed her own in me. But just now I am lazy and fond of life this side of death.

Will you let me know your movements? And pray think out ways and means to see us all before you go to the Land of the Lost, and leave us desolate!

Yours very sincerely,

Lionel Johnson.

This was written at the moment when the vogue of aestheticism, pessimism, preraphaelitism, and amateur Catholicism was at its height. The superior young mind was bound to share these affectations, but might save itself by a mental reservation and a pervasively weary, all-knowing and all-mocking tone. Was Lionel

Johnson laughing at Jesuits and Carthusians, at Plato, Shelley and Keats, no less than at Berenson and me? Or had something or somebody, Shelley perhaps or the Jesuits, really taken him in? I have no doubt that sincerity existed somewhere beneath all these poses, but the exact place of it is hard to discover. Russell at that moment, in the drama of his life, was making rapid progress in the direction of Byron's *Don Juan:* he had fallen into the clutches of a mature adventuress who was marrying him off to her daughter. In what direction was Lionel Johnson's sincere drama progressing?

I am not writing Johnson's life or Russell's or even my own, but only picking out such points as interest me now in my personal retrospect. I saw Lionel Johnson in later years only at long intervals and found him each time less accessible. My last glimpse of him was in the summer of 1897, in Russell's rooms in Temple Gardens. It was a tragic spectacle. He still looked very young, though he was thirty, but pale, haggard, and trembling. He stood by the fireplace, with a tall glass of whiskey and soda at his elbow, and talked wildly of persecution. The police, he said, were after him everywhere. Detectives who pretended to be friends of his friend Murphy or of his friend MacLaughlin had to be defied. Without a signed letter of introduction he could trust nobody. He had perpetually to sport his oak. As he spoke, he quivered with excitement, hatred, and imagined terrors. He seemed to be living in a dream; and when at last he found his glass empty, it was with uncertainty that his hat sat on his head as with sudden determination he made for the door, and left us without saying good night.

I never saw him again, but he still lived for five years, and there may have been important changes in him before the end. Nor do I profess to have fathomed his Celtic inspiration or his Celtic Catholicism. He says in his lines on *Wales:*

> *No alien hearts may know that magic, which acquaints*
> *Thy heart with splendid passion, a great fire of dreams;*

and I am willing to believe him. But to my prosaic apprehension he remains a child of premature genius and perpetual immaturity; and I cannot forget what Oscar Wilde is reported to have said of him, that any morning at eleven o'clock you might see him come out very drunk from the Café Royal, and hail the first passing perambulator. Yet I should be the last to deride the haze in which he lived, on the ground that Bacchus had something to do with it. Bacchus too was a god; and the material occasion of inspiration makes no difference if the spirit is thereby really liberated. Lionel Johnson lived in the spirit; but to my sense his spirituality was that of a transcendental poet, not that of a saint. His mind was subjective in its presuppositions or in the absence of all presuppositions; so that after reading him through you are aware of a great wind of passionate language, but not of what was said or of what it all was about. And this vagueness was hardly due to absorption in something higher, because it did not liberate him from everything lower. So at least he tells us in *The Dark Angel*.

> *Because of thee, no thought, no thing*
> *Abides for me undesecrate . . .*
> *Of two defeats, of two despairs;*
> *Less dread, a change to drifting dust,*
> *Than thine eternity of cares.*

And if we ask what the alternative to these two despairs may be, and what will issue from the triumph that he still hopes for, we find nothing positive, nothing specific, but only transcendental spirit, still open to every thought and to every torment:

> *Lonely, unto the Lone I go;*
> *Divine, to the Divinity.*

These words are the words of Plotinus and of Christian mystics; but here we do not feel them to be backed by either the Platonic or the Christian scheme of the universe: they are floating words. Even the firmness and constructive power of the Catholic faith could not *naturalise* Lionel Johnson in the Catholic world. The same emotional absolutism, the same hatred of everything not plastic to the fancy, which drove him from Victorian England into Celtic poetry and Catholic supernaturalism, kept him from accepting definition and limitation even there; he could not deny himself other dreams. As he writes in *Gwynedd*:

> *We will not wander from this land;* [Wales]
> *Here distress*
> *Dreams, and delight dreams: dreaming, we can fill*
> *All solitary haunts with prophecy,*
> *All heights with holiness and mystery;*
> *Our hearts with understanding, and our will*
> *With love of nature's law and loveliness.*

The last two lines may seem to contradict what I am saying but I quote them in order to be fair. Understanding, with love of nature's law, if it were real understanding of the true law of nature, would stop all that dreaming, or reduce it to wasted time and gratuitous trouble, as he himself says in *The Dark Angel*, already quoted:

> *Because of thee, the land of dreams*
> *Becomes a gathering-place of fears:*
> *Until tormented slumber seems*
> *One vehemence of useless tears.*

But the word nature, in a Celtic poet, does not mean what it meant to Lucretius, nor understanding what it meant to Aristotle, nor law what it meant to Newton. These words mean rather landscape, divination, and magic; as, in the line about Wales, where he says he will not leave *this land,* he means the *soul* of this land, which is the land of dreams.

The passionate need of sinking into these dreams, and defying the false world that pretended to be more real, seems to me to have been the secret of Lionel Johnson in all his phases. It was what made him a pagan or a Buddhist at Winchester, a Baude-lairean Catholic at Oxford, and a Fenian conspirator in London. In his verse he could modulate those dreams lyrically, but not logically, morally, and historically as the Church had modulated her original inspirations; and he dared to take them, as the Church did hers, for revelations of the truth. But his dreams had no such application to the facts and sorrows of life as had the Christian faith. Their passion remained dreamy, weak and verbal, and he perished not a martyr to his inspiration, but a victim of it.

Now to return to Russell. In their adolescence both he and Lionel Johnson had revelled in transcendental liberty: but Russell was strong, and exposed to the dangers and vices of strength, as Johnson to those of weakness. Russell had no gift of fancy: he had to be satisfied with the vulgar plots that real life furnishes willy-nilly to the spirit; and he sank into them desperately, without discrimination and without taste. Yet his strong intelligence, rather conventional in worldly matters, remained conscious that it was being deceived. This early transcendentalism was not apparent in him; his wives, I expect, never understood that it was there; yet I think it helped to make him reckless in choosing and in divorcing them. For him it was all a desperate and worthless gamble in any case. Any lust, any convenience, any enterprise, any stale moral or political nostrum would do to play with: the point was to dream your dream out, and to have your way in it.

This is my interpretation: but in a letter written a fortnight before his death—almost the last I received from him—he puts the matter in the following words:

"It is not really the case that Lionel lies in the limbo of almost incredible things. On the contrary, all that is the real part of me and my very extensive external activities are to me of the nature of Maya or illusion. They interest me, they are my job, and I do them, but they are not part of my real life. I am surprised that you should say that I minimise my friendship of Lionel, to all intimate friends I have always admitted that he was my dearest friend and the greatest influence in my life, but I seldom take the public into my confidence about my real feelings. I received two great shocks in my life; the first being when Jowett sent me down— My rage and mortification at being so wronged produced a bitterness and permanently injured my character. Finally, when Elizabeth left me I went completely dead and have never come alive again. She never realised how I worshipped and loved her, and how I idealised what is in essence a worthless character, and her light-hearted cruelty killed something in me which has never revived. Since 1918 I have had neither ambition, nor enthusiasm, nor interest nor will to live, and I ascribe my bad heart entirely to the year's anguish I suffered after she left me and her betrayal with a kiss of Judas. Still, as you say I obliterate my feelings so easily, no doubt you will not believe this."

No: I didn't believe *all* this; the words about Elisabeth didn't ring true in my ears. But I believed and believe what he says about Lionel Johnson, which is what concerns me here; and I can also credit his living "dead," precisely when he was a member of the Government, busy and rehabilitated officially and financially. It would have been an experience such as in my own case I call somnambulistic, under which I may be doing mechanically what some people think my best work. He had transcendental insight, acquired in his adolescence (the natural time for it) under the influence of Lionel Johnson: and this common spiritual challenge to the dream of life raised their friendship to a great height and made it constant in spite of all obstacles and external disparities. Neither Johnson's Catholicism and drink, nor Russell's matrimonial imbroglios did justice to their inner man; such commitments were accidents, as was their vulgar politics also; and both knew it. I also divined it in them, but from the outside, and I am glad to have this confession of Russell's, written almost on his deathbed, to buttress my divination. Transcendental rebellion, like that of Lucifer, lay at the bottom of his heart, but buried like a prehistoric civilisation under layer upon layer of ruins. Lionel Johnson could display this spirit lyrically and publish it to the puzzled world in his talk and in his poems; but poor Russell had only his ruins to display and to be judged by most unjustly, ruins of passions that had hounded him through life like a succession of nightmares, and had made the gossips call him "The Wicked Earl."

But let me return to the pleasant summer of 1887, when under his auspices I first felt the full charm of England. His last invitation before I left for Spain took me to Winchester. He was staying at his old Housemaster's for the School celebration of the Queen's Jubilee, and he took a room for me at an inn. In this way I had the advantage of being guided, introduced, and shown what there was to see, and also the advantage of being left alone so as to see it. This was my first acquaintance with an English public school. Externally the flint walls and low buildings prepared me for mediaeval austerity; but at the Commemoration service in the chapel it was the soul of modern England that stirred under those Gothic arches and windows, and knelt or sang in those monastic stalls. Deeply moving was the singing by the whole School in unison of *God Save the Queen,* all the verses, under the spell of restrained emotion: fifty years of safety and glory behind, and before, for those young spirits, the promise and the uncertainties of a broad future. This was more than ten years before the Boer War, before the first hint of difficulty and limitation in British dominion. Nothing as yet impaired the sense of a glorious heritage committed to the care of the rising generation, to be maintained and enriched indefinitely. The pride of earth merged delusively and overpoweringly with the will of heaven.

We lunched with one of the masters, Mr. Richardson, whose amiable wife seemed to have a mother's heart for all the boys, and among them for Russell. She perceived that I cared for him and instantly became friendly and confidential. Winchester was the only place where he was loved. Ten years later, when I went with him there again for a hearing connected with the trial of Lady Scott, Mrs. Dick, as she was called, said to me: "We would all perjure ourselves for him." The act was hardly necessary, but the readiness showed the right spirit. Justice is before the law, moral reality above moral shams; and in that trial everything was a sham, and yet substantial justice was done in the end. It is the English way.

In the evening I went again to the chapel. This time I was alone, and from my corner I drank in the memorable spectacle, more memorable for being something usual and the crown of every school day. The boys were less restless at that hour; fatigue and darkness cut off distractions; the spirit of the place, the language of the prayers, had a chance of attuning the senses to their ancient music. That everything external was perfunctory rather helped something internal to become dominant. I saw some boys bury their faces in their folded arms, not (it seemed to me) affectedly, but as if seeking solitude, as if fleeing to the wilderness, carried by a wave of juvenile devotion. How well I knew that plight! Adolescence, in its pregnant vagueness, casts about for some ineffable happiness in the fourth dimension. But how admirable here the setting to give a true pitch to those first notes! This simplicity in wealth protects from vulgarity, these classic poets, when grammar and ferrule are forgotten, leave a sediment of taste and soundness in the mind, and these reticent prayers, with their diplomatic dignity and courtesy, leave it for the heart to say the last word. It is all make-believe, as sports are: but in both those dramatic exercises there is excellent discipline, and the art of life is half learned when they have been practiced and outgrown. What has been learned is the right manner, the just sentiments. It remains to discover the real occasions and the real risks.

In Avila, late in September, I had word from Russell, at Toulouse, "the little 'Royal' is now not far from the Pyrenees . . . We shall be at Marseilles in a week or 10 days and stay there a fortnight. I should be only too pleased if you would join us there en route for Naples." His notions of travel and of foreign parts were those of the British naval man that he ought to have been. To go to Spain you took ship to Lisbon, and to get out you took ship at Barcelona for Marseilles. He was bringing the *Royal* over the *Canal du Midi* from Bordeaux to Narbonne, and back over the *Canal de Bourgogne* from Marseilles to Havre. The yacht was too small for the high seas, and her draught just not too great for those inland shallows. Naples and Sicily had been familiar to him in his childhood: he had spent long seasons there with his parents: but intervening places had little hold on his imagination. My way of travelling from one cathedral town to another he called "getting lost among the railways." Naturally, joining the *Royal* in the Mediterranean was impossible for me, living as I did on a Harvard Fellowship for study in Germany. But his lordship took another view of the matter. "What you say about reading sounds nonsense," he wrote in October. "I should say a 'travelling fellowship' meant *travel* and keep your eyes open, not settle down in a hole to mug." But before the end of November his own spirits had flagged. He was at Civitavecchia, and wrote: "We have had vile weather—rain, cold and lots of wind and sea: and tho' the little boat has behaved wonderfully, you would scarcely have appreciated it . . . Thynne left me at Savona, Roberts never came, Jepson leaves me here . . . I shall probably lay up the 'Royal' at Naples, and come home about the New Year." In May, however, he was back in Italy, coasting from port to port after the fashion of the ancients. "I wish you would join me at Marseilles for the canal journey thro' France," he wrote, "as I shall be quite alone, and it will be a trip than wh. there could not be [anything] more pleasant or more lotus eating."

By that time I had given up all hope of profiting by a longer stay in Germany and had decided to return to Harvard to complete my studies for the doctorate. I would spend my last summer at Avila; but on the way, why shouldn't I join Russell, not at Marseilles but somewhere on the Rhône, and go with him as far as Paris? This was arranged, and I met him at Valence, early in June.

It was an inland voyage of three weeks up and down innumerable locks, through a country wilder and more deserted than I should have thought existed in France. The rivers, whether flowing southward or northward, were wider and swifter than they seem when looked at from the banks, and seen as pictures, not felt as powers. The banks, too, for the most part, without being mountainous, looked strangely primitive and unkempt. Such they must have been when Cæsar and his Gaulish chieftains took them for boundaries, or forded them with warlike cries. In sympathy with those rude predecessors (or because my razors were dull and toilet on board difficult to manage) I let my beard grow: an experiment that I repeated twenty years later, much in the same spirit and ultimately with the same negative result. Being primitive and "natural" does very well when it is inevitable and unconscious; but it is a mistake and a perverse affectation when it is intentional. I shaved again that summer as soon as I got to Paris and to a decent barber; and I shaved again in 1912 when I left Harvard and began life afresh as an elderly gentleman of leisure.

Russell spoke French readily and not incorrectly, with a strong English accent, and when speaking it he put on an air of genial assurance (rather American, I thought) entirely absent from the quiet precision of his usual conversation; and he did the same when he spoke in England in public. It was the second thickness of the veil of Maya wrapping and smothering his transcendental self. The first layer of illusion or shamming plunged him into the business of this absurd world; the second turned him into a sort of Low Church Evangelist or middle-class Browningite or unscrupulous lawyer, smilingly and victoriously proving the truth of some palpable lie. He was said to be an excellent debater; but Lord Curzon was also said to be an eloquent speaker; and when once I heard him speak in the House of Lords, on an Indian question which he ought to have known at first hand, he was so platitudinous and partial in his matter and such a bad actor in his manner, that I could hardly believe my ears. One of the French Ministers under Clemenceau, at the end of the war, at a luncheon given by the de Fontenays, had the same incredibly vulgar way of repeating party slogans with a false intonation. I can explain it only by the degradation of taste and intelligence produced by partisan propaganda. People will shout under the spell of convention things they would shudder to hear in their rational moments.

Two men in their early twenties eating and sleeping for three weeks in the same cabin, seeing the same sights and living through the same incidents without one moment of boredom, without one touch of misunderstanding or displeasure, could not but become very good friends. But we were predestined friends before, in fact ever since our first acquaintance; and I don't think this trip through Burgundy made much difference. Friendship in any case didn't mean for Russell what it meant for me. There was no dramatic curiosity in it for him, no love of speculation and unanimity. He cared nothing about what other people might be in themselves or in their feelings and careers; nor did he have the least need of unbosoming himself. He was frank enough and didn't take pains to disguise facts in his own life, when the interest of the moment led him to refer to them. In that way, during his lawsuits, he told me many secrets by implication; but he never set out to relate his affairs, expressly, for the sake of communication and sympathy. On the contrary, I think he revelled in secrecy. By this time, in France, he already had secrets that he didn't tell me, which I think had not been the case in England the summer before. Thus he said once that he might try his luck at Monte Carlo *again*. I knew nothing of his having been there at all; but I now gathered that he had probably lost a good deal at the tables.

The atmosphere of mystery had become thick, however, when I joined him again in England in August. He had now taken what might be called a mansion, Broom Hall, Teddington, with great old trees and a spacious lawn sloping gently down to the water's edge. The dark red brick house at the top, also spacious without being large, had a quiet old-fashioned air. The place might have seemed a little sad; but Russell was then bent on boating in the Thames and despised fashionable society. For him it seemed to me perfect. It was dignified enough to make a home of, so long as he was a bachelor, where he could have his books and family heirlooms properly placed, and at the same time keep the *Royal* and the electric launch at hand in his private dock. This prospect pleased him, and I found him engrossed in putting in the electric light and other domestic arrangements.

In the afternoon we were to go out in the launch; I was a bit surprised that Jennie, the housemaid, seemed to be coming with us; but I knew she was one of the Billings children. Their mother had been Russell's nurse, and they had played together in their early days. That might be an explanation; but not for the presence of a second young woman, silent and dejected with all her hair loose, already sitting in the stern of the launch, next to the wheel, where Russell would certainly sit. "That is my sister Emma," said Jennie, observing my surprise. I asked if she was drying her hair. No, Lord Russell (Jennie didn't call him "His Lordship") liked her to have it like that. Zo! I said to myself (having been lately in Germany) and I discreetly went to sit with Jennie in the bow, leaving Russell with his dishevelled and rather mad-looking sweetheart in the stern. But how could he be carrying on such an intrigue in public? I thought of Steerforth and Little Emily. And what could be Jennie's position in the matter? An accomplice, a jealous rival, or perhaps a second mistress? For Jennie's eyes were very bright, and she moved about with the freedom of a member of the family, and with some coquetry as well. Accustomed though I was to the wild oats and the love-affairs of my friends, these complications at Broom Hall troubled me a little. It might not prove such a peaceful and dignified retreat as I had fancied. I sailed for America with vague misgivings, and even wrote some verses on Broom Hall that I soon destroyed; yet a phrase or two linger in my memory that seem to have been prophetic. I praised the aspect of the place, then added, *Worse follows better: the wreck of boyish faith and boyish love.*

The next summer I remained in America, preparing my first course of lectures at Harvard. There I received the following letter:

Broom Hall,
23 July 1889. Teddington.
Dear Santayana,

I am now replying to your letter of May because I have found an answer to your query when the state of lethargy would cease. It has ceased and for the most commonplace of reasons. I have met a young woman and fallen in love with her! and soon I shall be a married man. Could a happier eventuality have occurred? Did I not often say that marriage was my best hope of salvation, only the trouble was to come across anyone I cared about? . . .

Though no doubt the thing is common enough and may be seen every day, still the difference is that the touch of a warm human love has come to *me,* and swamps and sweeps away all cobwebs and ash-heaps in my brain. All my friends and relations say they would not know me. If I ever told you I was satisfied with my situation before, it was a lie and a mere vain attempt to deceive myself.

Write to me and let me know if you will ever be in England or if we must wait till we go to the States to meet you.

Ever yours,
RUSSELL

My appointment at Harvard having been renewed I took a fast steamer in the following June and was in London before the end of the month. There I found the following note awaiting me:

16 June 1890 Walton.
Dear Santayana,

I am so glad to hear you are coming over. I enclose my new address: I am just moving. I shall be so glad to see you and hope you can give me a whole week. . . . Name your own time as I must not miss seeing you. I am so sorry you have only a few days in England. Write me a line as soon as you get this.

Ever yours,
RUSSELL

His new address was Amberley Cottage, Maidenhead. Odd that a newly married man should not mention his wife and still say "I" and not "we"; but Russell was said to resemble Meredith's *Egoist* and perhaps this was a sign of it. When I reached Maidenhead I was met by a little cart with a white pony: here at last was the feminine touch. We drove into a region of newly built villas in small squares of land with young hedges and little trees in curlpapers, and stopped at a flimsy particoloured "cottage," with a shallow tin verandah and the look of never having been lived in. I regretted the lovely lawn and the stately symmetry of Broom Hall: but no doubt the new Lady Russell was "modern," found Teddington impossibly dull and unfashionable, and thought it better to remove Russell from his old associations. Yet why choose this vulgar place? No view, no privacy, no glimpse of the river: a colony of hen-coops in a waste field.

But where was the new Lady Russell? No sign of her in the house, which was almost unfurnished. Even Russell's "office" was bare and carpetless. I saw only a desk, two leather armchairs, and on the mantelpiece a single framed photograph: an oldish but strikingly handsome woman in a ball gown, with great eyes and other conspicuous charms: might have been an emotional actress or a prima donna. It could hardly be Russell's wife: he had spoken of a *young* woman. He noticed that I was examining the photograph attentively and said: "That is Lady Scott."

Lady Scott was his mother-in-law. As I gathered later piecemeal, during the various lawsuits that ensued, she was the daughter of a country parson and had run away to Paris, when still a girl, with a wild young baronet named Sir Claude Scott; they had been married but unhappy, and she had long been a grass widow, with an uncertain income, scouring the borderland between the *monde* and the *demi-monde*. She then lived at Bray and fished in the boating region of the Thames. When she learned that a young and unmarried earl had taken a house not very far from hers, she soon found the means of making his acquaintance. She had a daughter, Mabel Edith, not so handsome as herself but presentable, and brought up like a lapdog amid false luxury and false gaiety. Here was a chance of settling Mabel Edith for life.

If you should read Russell's letter of the previous July, quoted above, without any preconceptions, would you detect anything wrong or queer about it? I think I should have suspected the rhetoric about a warm human love that had made him a new man. But Russell had really undergone a change, "the touch of a warm human love"; only the object of it had not been Mabel Edith. It had been her mother. Or rather, not so much the object of love as the guide to love; for it had been the half-motherly and half-wifely love of a mature woman for a young man physically susceptible but morally crude and insensible. She had overwhelmed him—their letters prove it—in a torrent of effusive sympathy and affection. He had never known a mother's love: "Mrs. Dick's" had come the nearest; but now such a love enveloped him, mixed with all the arts of sensuous seduction and worldly-wise prattle of a woman that had been beautiful and was still appealing. It had been a feast of sincerity, of sympathy, of abounding endearments such as he had never known or dreamt of. Lady Scott persuaded Russell that the way to make him and her friends for life, and guardians of each other's happiness, was for him to marry Mabel Edith. Mabel Edith was insignificant, but she was not less attractive than the housemaids and the lady-secretaries that could so easily seduce him. He would marry her.

Persons of strict morals and limited experience might well cry: Scandalous, monstrous, impossible! What mother would so outrage and deceive her innocent child? Yet in this case the innocent child never complained of her mother: the two remained perfectly united in feeling and policy until death. To pass on Russell to Mabel Edith was, in the eyes of the latter, an act of foresight and love on her mother's part. Wasn't she marrying an important and attractive young man? Didn't she become a Countess? And if the match didn't turn out well, what marriage in the Scotts' social circle had ever turned out well? That would be bad luck, or other people's fault: and Mabel Edith could always sue for divorce, with a tidy alimony. Of course this match couldn't turn out well: and if Lady Scott didn't foresee it, I think her blindness could be due only to the fact that she was in love with Russell herself and in such a welter of emotion and excitement that she was incapable of clear observation or judgment. But poor Mabel Edith—I can't help being sorry for her—very soon discovered the mistake they had made. Russell as a husband, Russell in the domestic sphere, was simply impossible: excessively virtuous and incredibly tyrannical. He didn't allow her enough money or enough liberty. He was punctilious and unforgiving about hours, about truth-telling, about debts. He objected to her friends, her clothes, and borrowed jewels. Moreover, in their intimate relations he was exacting and annoying. She soon hated and feared him. One day she couldn't endure him any longer and ran home to her mother, crying like a frightened child. Her mother clasped her to her bosom, petted her, soothed her; and they began to consider, with their solicitors, how best to get money out of Russell. That loving a man passionately and getting money out of him should go together was no paradox to Lady Scott. It was her ideal of life.

Such were the events, at least as I conceive them, that had caused me to find my friend no longer in the pleasant retreat of Broom Hall, but camping out in an ugly half-furnished villa in a new jerry-built quarter of Maidenhead, without his bride, but with her mother's portrait on the mantelpiece. He was already threatened with two nasty lawsuits: one brought by Emma Billings for breach of promise of marriage, and the other by Mabel Edith for a legal separation on the charge of cruelty.

I had seen enough at Broom Hall to know that in the case of Emma Billings, Russell had something to hide: it was a common seduction, but aggravated by his old relations with the family and by the oddity of some of his demands. Russell was aware of this, and settled the matter out of court; yet a field remained open here where the Scotts might still sow rumours and insinuations. The Oxford scandal was another such field: and both, in a corrupt society, could be used to corroborate the charges of cruelty brought by Mabel Edith. These charges were ridiculous in themselves, except where they touched the intimate relations of the wife and husband: and here they were so embarrassing to describe, and so impossible to prove, that they could serve only to arouse prejudice.

Lady Scott had planned something heroic: to give Russell up as a lover, resign him to her daughter, and keep him only as a dear, dear son and as a source of income. When Mabel Edith spoilt everything by leaving him and declaring war to the knife, her mother's friendly relations with him were not interrupted. "Lady Scott," he wrote to me, "accompanied me to Winchester on a visit to Mrs. Dick and got rather pitched into by her." No wonder; but he seems to have regarded the two matrons as his two godmothers. Lady Scott, in fact, always hoped for a reconciliation, and both mother and daughter kept writing him begging letters. If he proved so heartless as to refuse them all funds, what could they do but threaten? Make peace with us, they said; give us an allowance, or we will ruin your reputation. You are driving us to this against our will, and you know what lovely cues you have given us. Lady Scott felt grievously injured that Russell shouldn't understand her or remember how much she had always loved him.

Thus Russell, at the age of twenty-five, found himself with his back to the wall, and obliged to defend himself in public against scandalous accusations. He was victorious in his two principal trials; but in the meantime he had dilapidated his fortune and forfeited his place in the polite world. This was a greater misfortune than he thought it, because whenever he found himself opposed by a ruling convention he comforted himself with the assertion that he was right and the convention wrong. This self-righteousness only made matters worse; he felt deeply injured, and alienated himself all the more from a world that was less offended than he, and would easily have taken him back. There is nothing sacred about convention: there is nothing sacred about primitive passions or whims; but the fact that a convention exists indicates that a way of living has been devised capable of maintaining itself. I had no more *respect* for the polite world than Russell had, and that was the ground of my sympathy with him: for if convention has the advantage of possessing the field, rebellion against convention has the advantage of springing afresh from the heart, the ultimate judge of everything worth having or doing. Yet a young man with a brilliant career open to him in the world is a fool to flout public opinion, even if he secretly despises it. Peace with the polite world is all-important for one's comfort and euphoria so long as one lives in the polite world.

Luckily Russell's rebellions were not total or radical. They were in fact hereditary, and those of a vast movement long afoot in modern times. He was therefore able to pass into what might be called the anti-polite world, and to play his part there. The Labour Party could take his sermons in gaol at their word, and the verdicts of Courts in his favour as final. They could regard him as morally rehabilitated, and could mend his fortunes by including him in the Government. But Russell was never more desperate than in those last years; British society is sustained by "created interests"; that is to say, by vain commitments into which people have been led unawares, but which it would be too disturbing now to abandon. The farce must be kept up, and it becomes a point of honour to drop dead at last upon the stage, in all one's paint and feathers.

CHAPTER IV

CHANGES IN AVILA

WHEN, after three years, in July, 1886, I returned for the second time to Avila, my arrival had been duly announced by letter for a suitable hour in the afternoon. My father and Don Pelayo were at the station to receive me, and everything at the house was as I had left it. There were no explanations to make. Even my old Aunt Maria Ignacia knew that I was going to Germany to study philosophy. I was to be a professor abroad, or if not a professor, an architect. There was no question any longer of a career in Spain; I was too old and too much expatriated by my English language and my American associations. On the other hand, I came to Avila with a sense of coming home and with the intention of always returning there. Official life would carry me out of Spain, as it had carried my father; but so long as he lived he would be my natural centre. While a student I should spend my longer holidays with him, and I vaguely foresaw, what has not proved altogether unlike the truth, that I should spend my old age, very much as he did, perhaps in Avila with another Don Pelayo for company.

The next day my father said we must go to see my cousin Elvira, daughter of his brother Nicolas, my godfather; she was now married and living in Avila. And married to whom? To Rafael Vegas, the same man who had been the husband of my other pretty cousin, the unfortunate Antoñita. In the interval of some fifteen years, naturally Rafael had not lived alone, but had married and buried his third wife. He was still the same peacock, though some of his plumes were now white, and when he wedded Elvira people shook their heads. He was a bluebeard and this poor young girl would die of childbirth within a year, like Antoñita, and leave the old libertine, with his taste for dainty morsels, to gobble up some fifth victim. But the gossips this time were wrong. They didn't suspect the equal capacity of the fair Elvira, as yet unrevealed, for shedding yearly husbands. I have never heard of such a wealth of legal couplings as there were in her matrimonial circle. She was the fourth wife of her first husband, the second wife of her second, and the third wife of her third. She would remain each time childless, quietly smiling, and readier than ever to marry again.

Though short and fat, Elvira had a pronounced feminine charm. There was something calm, friendly, and sound about her person. Her clear white skin and no less clear brown eyes and soft curly brown hair gave her an air of neatness. She was *simplex munditiis*; and in spite of domestic duties, even at the times when she was poorest, she was always scrupulously clean. Her small hands moved nimbly and touched pleasantly; and she had a way of folding a scarf or shawl round her exuberant bosom that expressed happiness, grace, and almost humour. It was in the breast that she was most developed; the rest of her figure, though plump, seemed in comparison well-turned and almost tapering. She moved well; and when she was prosperous and suitably dressed—her third and last husband was a banker—she had the free and sure air of a lady. She ought to have been a lady, being born the daughter of an army officer who ought to have been a gentleman; and her Andalusian mother, whose name was Engracia or Grace, also had some pretensions to breeding or at least to luxury. But this only made her the more dissatisfied with her lot, her skin the yellower and her voice the shriller; and my maiden aunts, who resented her superior airs, used to say of their brother: *"Engracia le ha caido en gracia, y se ha desgraciado,"* which might be translated theologically by saying that Grace fell upon him and he was lost. The lady no doubt had a bad temper and could not forgive herself for being less brilliant than a sister of hers who had gone on the stage, who sang in light opera, married a rich man, became a widow when still young and good-looking, and lived luxuriously with her four children in Malaga, in an apartment like a *bonbonnière*, where I visited her in 1887. These were Elvira's "rich" relations, from whom she got her ideals of elegance and coquetry; yet by nature, like her father and mine and all true Castilians, she possessed a rather detached and sceptical philosophy, one that teaches us that all conditions are bearable, all dignities trumpery, and wisdom simply the gift of making the best of whatever is thrust upon us.

Rafael always had lived from hand to mouth, apparently prosperous but without any roots. His unexpected death left Elvira penniless, and she had to go and live with my father, in his poor man's house; for in spite of his own very modest means he was the stay and refuge of his whole family. This was the young widow's hibernation, and lasted several years. Whenever I came to Avila, I found her established at my father's as one of the family, at times with Susana, usually alone. She seemed resigned, disillusioned and cheerful. It was not at this time that she thought of perhaps marrying me. I was too young, a mere student from Germany, insignificant in comparison with her late pompous husband, who always took the lead in any circle, and knew by heart all the tricks of a country lawyer and an elderly ladykiller. But we got on very well together. I perceived that a year's life with Rafael, while it had left her without a shred of innocence, had neither disgusted nor corrupted her. She took the whole concealed side of life calmly, sensibly, without horror or curiosity; she had instinctively seen how tiresome it is; and we were able to talk about everything satirically, like two old cronies for whom the world has only a speculative interest.

She was not in those days without an earnest suitor, though she never accepted him, even as a *novio*. He was an excellent person, about forty-five years of age, but common; a cavalry captain who had risen from the ranks, whose name was Don Cándido. He was riding-master to the small garrison of the town, and gave me—as an indirect attention to Elvira—the only riding-lessons I ever took. They were of little use to me; I am not built for dancing or riding, and a foretaste of my necessary clumsiness at such things makes me avoid them. If I could ever have become good at them it would only have been, as in the case also of mathematics, if I had found an intelligent master who should have begun by explaining to me the *principles* of the thing, not an empirical practitioner like honest, dull Don Cándido who could only tell me to stick to the saddle and to go ahead.

But sticking to the saddle is not enough to please the ladies, and he never got ahead with Elvira. Somehow, however, she attracted the notice of a retired shop-keeper—let us call him merchant—a worthy and childless widower, who asked her to become his wife, as she sensibly did, foreseeing that he would soon leave her a little money, enough to make her independent. This happened almost at once; and then she took a small flat, in an *entresol*, overlooking the busiest street in the town. Sitting by her balcony, she was little above the heads of the passers-by. Everybody saw and admired her demurely sewing between her flower-pots; and she saw everybody and everything that passed, and through her maid or her own explorations she could learn everything that happened. It was a pleasant nest; and when I occasionally went to see her there, although we could hardly have the long unintentional conversations of the days when we lived in the same house, I became aware that she was considering the possibility of marrying me. She had no notion of geography or of foreign languages or foreign life; and seeing that I was well dressed and travelled about comfortably, she imagined she might live pleasantly in "America," that is, in Habana, on fifteen hundred dollars a year, which was then my salary. Probably she supposed that my family were rich and that I should have a share in their fortune.

It was not necessary for me to undeceive her on these points; my stay in Avila was short; and when I returned in a later year, I found that a far more desirable suitor had presented himself and been gladly accepted. He was her neighbour, and doubtless, from his own balconies on the first floor over his banking-house, he had watched her agreeable face at her window, and had been assured of her simple and quiet life. His second wife had recently died, leaving an infant in arms, his only child. What better mother than Elvira could be provided for it, or more blooming partner for himself?

In October 1905, I was in Avila, having a year's leave of absence from Harvard, and being on my way to Egypt, Palestine and Greece. The procession of *la Santa* passed Elvira's new house, and I was invited to see it from her windows. Two agreeable nieces of her husband's also were living there; the husband himself was gracious and well-spoken; we discussed the King's English marriage, then just announced, and I duly admired the fat and rosy baby. It was a picture of domestic happiness, dignity, and peace. But letters reached me that winter while I was in the East, announcing a rather strange and melancholy coincidence. Elvira had mysteriously fallen ill, and her husband also, and lying in separate rooms the two had died on the same day.

Elvira was not religious or romantic. Such a sudden fall of the curtain on a scene of decent well-being fits well with her person, her character, and her ideas. Her life had been thoroughly reasonable, frank and mediocre. After a Chinese fashion it was philosophical and sufficient.

The great event for me in Spain occurred upon my third return in 1887, when after my memorable first sojourn in England, and a month or two at Avila with my father and Elvira, I went to Gibraltar to meet Susana. That Susana should henceforth be in Spain (for I was sure she would never return to America, although she sometimes spoke of doing so "for a visit") weighted that centre of gravity decisively in my planetary system. It gave me an added reason for returning there often, and solved the problem of residence whenever I returned. For her, however, it was not a sufficient solution. She needed to be enthusiastic and she needed to be comfortable, and Spain was neither. Not that she had any feeling but affection for Spain, and loyalty to it even in those unhappy days; but now she was herself unhappy, and Spain didn't help her. Still, on the religious side the change of atmosphere was a relief; it removed the sense of tension under which she had so cruelly suffered; and this not merely externally or socially. I think that slowly, by living in Spain, her personal religious life was normalised, reduced to its healthy human function, and cleared of anxiety and bitterness.

On the social side, Susana was adaptable, and always took a healthy interest in the present. When in America she hadn't missed Spain, and now again in Spain she didn't miss America. Her good spirits in Boston, in the earlier days, had flowed from fun and comfort. When now she spoke of Boston society, she laughed at it for being so full of false pretenses and of insignificant points of pride. These were things that her Catholic discipline had taught her to put away. The only American memories that she seemed to idealise touched little luxuries and creature comforts: warm houses, bathrooms, table manners, ventilation, and *silver* knives, as she credulously called them, for the fruit. Her constitution was soft and frail, in spite of her robust appearance, and she suffered disproportionately from minor irritants; tobacco smoke, lights in the eyes, the crude scent of mutton, sourness even in good strawberries. She was weary; these trifles disturbed her physical peace, and made her seem less amiable than she was by nature. For in regard to people, though retrospectively critical enough, she was spontaneously sympathetic. Strangers, especially ladies, who saw her for the first time or had only occasional interviews with her, almost invariably liked her very much; but the value of such sympathy was only social, and left her daily life empty and dull. The fundamental difficulty came neither from Spain nor from America, neither from her friends nor her family. It came from the fact that she was thirty-six years old, and unmarried.

Between my father and Susana there was an old mutual affection and they attempted for a while to live up to it. For instance, Susana wished to make a pilgrimage to the tomb of Santa Teresa; but Alba de Tormes, where the saint is buried, was almost inaccessible, except on horse-back or, rather, on mule-back. There was a road of sorts, but no public conveyance, and a private carriage would have involved too much expense. My father, being a good pedestrian, was willing to walk there and back; and for Susana he conceived the plan of hiring a country waggon, with a mule and a *mozo*; a mattress could be spread out in the cart, which had a round canvas top: and there Susana could sit or lie down during the longer stretches. It was rickety, hard, and not very restful, and they would have to spend one night in whatever *posada* they could find at Alba; but they managed it. The excursion remained a memorable jaunt for him, and an act of piety or of penance for her: and there were no unpleasant effects except that in Avila she acquired the nick-name *la pelegrina*, which became capable of unkind interpretations.

For a few days, old affection and present good intentions could carry off the comedy between step-father and step-daughter; but it couldn't be kept up permanently. He was too old, crotchety, and poor; she was too much wedded to those religious opinions which directly or indirectly he was always attacking. Nor was there any need of keeping the thing up. She hadn't come to Spain in order to live with him, but rather with Doña Victorina and Mercedes. They had a flat in Madrid and a little house by the seaside, near Vigo, for the summer. Here there was no religious quarrel. Doña Victorina was pious, and Mercedes was more than pious: not only daily Mass and Communion, but apostolic labours in evening schools for workingmen in Vigo. Mercedes also had social position and, like Susana, had basked in the smiles of royalty; often visited the Infanta Isabel, and sometimes Queen Maria Cristina and even Queen Victoria Eugénie. Nevertheless, although in speaking to me both sides were naturally discreet, I could feel that between Susana and Mercedes there was no real sympathy, not even in religion. Mercedes was immensely spontaneous, pagan, superstitious, overflowing with devout sentiments, in diplomatic relations with the court of heaven even closer than with the court of Madrid. Susana was theological, instructed, theoretical; she justified her sentiments first and then, perhaps, she felt them. Mercedes was all initiative. In religion Susana had no initiative; she had sympathy only with things already afoot. She was at once imitative and satirical; because after mimicking involuntarily something that others were doing, her own disposition and intelligence reasserted themselves; so that she, like me, played a double part in her tragedy: she was one of the characters and also the chorus. And, unlike me, she had executive impulses that must have clashed with those of Mercedes. When she joined a movement she wanted to manage it. When she joined a family, if it were not possible or proper for her to rule it, she couldn't rest there. Cohabitation with the Escaleras was therefore never a real solution. Susana said that Galicia in summer didn't agree with her: the verdure and dampness brought on her New England "hayfever." She preferred Avila. Yet Avila, secluded as it might seem, was a microcosm, with all the problems of a world. Besides the tension with my father, there was soon an open quarrel with Elvira. The two hadn't the same breeding; Elvira wasn't pious, she had been the wife of an old rake. Elvira on her side whispered things about Susana that oughtn't to be whispered and attributed motives that oughtn't to be attributed. It became impossible for my father's two guests to remain together. Elvira couldn't be sent away; she had nowhere to go, and no money. Her rich aunt in Malaga, on the first Christmas after Rafael's death, had sent a large box of raisins and other sweets to console her niece, who was so fortunate as to have a dear old uncle to live with in her widowhood; but on the second Christmas, when Elvira hoped to be invited by her dear rich aunt to go and live in Malaga, no present arrived and there was stony silence. It was therefore Susana, being independent, who had to leave. In winter, in any case, she was to join Doña Victorina and Mercedes in Madrid; the parting from my father had therefore nothing tragic about it; and Elvira automatically remained with him, uncriticised and blooming alone. But where should Susana spend the following summer? With Doña Victorina and Mercedes in Galicia, when she was a free American and preferred Avila? She wasn't going to allow an ill-bred, ill-natured woman like Elvira to upset her plan of life or control her movements. She would spend that following summer in Avila, in another house.

There were two quiet and agreeable elderly sisters, old friends of Susana's, whom we called *las de Madorell,* one of them a widow with two daughters. The elder daughter, Monserrat, had lately been married. They had room for Susana in their house and would be really glad of her company, much more entertaining than their own, and of the generous contribution she would make to their little budget. There was only one objection—a foolish one. *Las de Madorell* lived in the same street as Don Celedonio Sastre, an old flame of Susana's, now a widower. Evil tongues would say that she came to live in that street so that Don Celedonio should not be able to forget her existence and her proximity. Such nonsense had to be disregarded: but Providence had mysteriously designed the means of defeating such gossip before it arose. Monserrat unexpectedly died, leaving two little girls, one just born, the other a year older. Their grandmother, one of the Madorell sisters, would go to look after them, leaving still more room for Susana in the house, and would establish a sort of continuity, almost a union, between the Madorells' household and that of Monserrat's disconsolate husband.

This husband, now a widower, whose name was Bringas, thus became a second widower in Susana's immediate neighbourhood; and this to some purpose. Bringas was an army man and a professor in the Military Academy in Avila. Of the various Military Academies, this was the most modest, preparing cadets for the Commissariat; but this involved in the professors somewhat wider and more business-like knowledge than infantry or cavalry officers were expected in those days to imbibe: supplies and transport were at once scientific and commercial matters. Bringas accordingly had a rather wide acquaintance with international affairs, industrial as well as political; and from the first he had naturally found much to talk about with Susana, fresh as she was from twenty years' residence in the United States. I believe he was an intelligent as well as a kindly man; but all that I may have heard him say was obliterated in my mind by the image of his person and his extravagant gesticulation. He jumped about and waved his arms like a puppet on a wire: and he proved the absurdity of this, or the impossibility of that, with so much emphasis and victorious joy that you forgot entirely what the joy and demonstration were about. He was a thin, nervous man, I daresay very strong, with a thin black beard and bright black eyes: most lively, but most restless, and I should have thought most tiresome. Yet those who knew him well were greatly attached to him: and I think Susana liked him better, perhaps, than she did Celedonio, but also feared him more, and felt less secure in his presence. In Celedonio there were no possible surprises; he was older and thoroughly consolidated, in mind and body. Bringas was a jumping-jack, an electrical apparatus. Who could tell what he might do next?

The sympathy that grew up in these circumstances between Bringas and Susana was obvious to everybody: it was obvious to me whenever I saw them together: and it was known to Celedonio; so that the presence of Susana for one summer in his street, far from seeming an advance toward him on her part, proved a cause of jealousy. A passing cause: because before the next year Elvira had married her second husband; then Susana returned to live at my father's, and ultimately Bringas married his deceased wife's sister, who had always secretly cared for him. The storm in the Avila teapot had cleared, and Susana's future remained to be determined by undisturbed reason.

I call it reason because reason in my philosophy is only a harmony among irrational impulses; and the hesitating, much meditated, troubled course that Susana now took was rational only in that sense. She decided to marry Celedonio. In their difficult negotiations it was agreed that the wedding should take place *after* that of Celedonio's daughter, who was the eldest of his six children, and had been for some years at the head of his household. Obviously it would be unpleasant for her to be superseded there by a half foreign step-mother, with money of her own. The five boys wouldn't mind so much: they might even see the advantages of the change: they would have better food, more interesting talks, and perhaps a few lessons in English at home gratis. But Celedonio had the selfishness of lazy power. Without being ambitious or meddlesome, he was insensible to the desires of others. His daughter had a *novio* of whom he didn't approve. He desired her to marry another man whom she didn't like. He could not force her, of course; he was no tyrant; but he wouldn't allow her to marry the other man. His own marriage was therefore postponed or would have had to be given up; but that his dignity wouldn't permit. And he persuaded Susana to consent to their marriage *before* that of his daughter. If on trial, step-mother and step-daughter couldn't get on, that would be an added incentive for the girl to be reasonable and marry the man that pleased her father. And this wasn't the end of Celedonio's selfishness. Far from hastening his daughter's match when trouble began between the women at home, he put off any settlement. He liked to have his only daughter at home as well as his new wife. She could do him all sorts of little services, as of old, that were not to be expected of Susana; and she could look after the boys in the old slipshod economical way, and let Susana play the sultana, growing fat and indolent, in quite separate apartments. The result was that Celedonio found himself the master of two households, actually on two separate floors, his wife's and his daughter's. When definite disputes arose he settled them judicially, like a Roman father; and he pretended not to notice the daily friction, the estrangement, the grievances that grew worse every year. His daughter was condemned to die an old maid, and his wife never to feel identified with her new family or to secure their affection.

Only in the later years, after her stepdaughter had died and several of the boys were married, did Susana's position become less unpleasant. She had more money than at first and kept a part of it from her husband. This Yankee insistence on individual rights was a sort of revenge for not being accepted and appreciated as she deserved; but in the end it redounded to the advantage of Celedonio's family. In old age he became stingy, and he had always been insensible to his children's wishes and needs: the result was that they had hardly enough to live on. It was then Susana that came to the rescue; and the boys' wives were grateful. They called her *mamá*, as the boys had never been allowed to do by their sister: and they brought up the grandchildren to speak well of her and to respect her.

Celedonio was a landlord on a small scale, as well as a lawyer, and possessed a farm at easy riding distance from Avila, and a house in the town; but his chief occupation was to be agent for two or three greater landlords who had estates in the province and lived elsewhere. His house stood on the better side of the town, a little beyond the walls, and had a wide view over the *Valle de Amblés*. For me now it became a sort of summer home. Towns in these parts are cooler than the country. Thick stone walls and courtyards overhung with galleries protect from the merciless sun, while the keen mountain air blows through and keeps the lungs and the spirit fresh. Here my father's books, in their old bookcases, and various portraits painted by his hand, as well as odd things of my own, were collected in two little rooms to the left of the street entrance or *portal*; and this apartment was called *el cuarto de Jorge*. There I was entirely independent, with a door into the open court, and two barred windows on the square. To those bars sometimes in the early morning some passing peasant would tie his donkeys. I could hear the venders' cries, and the bells ringing not very melodiously for Mass, or tolling for the dead. I could also overhear various conversations of the passers-by, or of old women who stopped to gossip. I was in the old world; I might have been in the seventeenth century.

On the other side of the street entrance there was a large room, now a coach-house and lumber-room, that must have been originally the hall or countinghouse where the master sat and received his tenants or clients and carried on his business. In a restoration it would have made the best room in the house: an excellent library or billiard-room, according to the taste of the proprietor. Behind this lay the court, paved in large irregular stones and

stretching, on the ground floor, from wall to wall, the whole width
of the house; but the stone stairs, open to the air, led up on one
side to an overhanging gallery, supported by a few stone pilasters,
that ran round three sides of the court on the first floor, and left
only a central square open to the sky, with the tiled roof sloping
from all sides inward, so that during a heavy shower the water
came splashing and roaring down in four little cataracts upon the
stone pavement. This ground floor was not the ground floor at the
back: the sharp declivity of the land turned it into a second storey.
There was a central deep room, and two smaller rooms, one on
each side. The central one had a large alcove, with two beds,
where Celedonio and Susana slept: one of the smaller ones was his
office and the other her dressing-room. Upstairs the house was
again divided by the court into two distinct portions. In front,
looking out of the square, was a suite of five rooms, occupied by
Celedonio's daughter, and her aunt, her mother's maiden sister,
who had been left alone, and had become a member of this family.
She was a delicate, quiet person, and rather a blessing, since she
behaved well and kept her niece company. In the back part of this
floor were some new additions made by Celedonio: a large dining-
room with a splendid outlook, a kitchen, and several other rooms
for the boys and for the servants. We had breakfast—chocolate
and a large roll cut into long strips, and perhaps a glass of milk
in addition—each in his own room: and dinner was at two, or
whenever Celedonio had finished his business in his office. After
dinner the family dispersed immediately, and often Celedonio also
went downstairs to interview somebody who came on business.

Susana and I would usually sit for an hour or more *de sobre
mesa*, and if we were alone would sometimes drop into English.
But I didn't like this, unless reminiscences of Boston made it
appropriate. Susana's Spanish was better than mine, but her English was worse, partly because of disuse, partly because she had
adopted indiscriminately all the ways of speaking that she had
heard, and some of them were dreadful. The best conversations
we had, however, were in the evening after supper, in the earlier

years. Supper was normally at half-past nine, sometimes later, and Celedonio would immediately go to bed and fall asleep. The boys went to the Mercado Grande, where the élite of Avila walked and sat on summer evenings, sometimes to the primitive music of the town band. Then Susana and I could sit by the open balcony in the *sala* admiring the extraordinarily brilliant starry sky, enjoying the cool of the night air, and discussing the past, the present, and the future. On the eternal we seldom touched. Her religious zeal had become wiser, she let God look after His own interests, and didn't worry any longer about other people's salvation.

The only entertainments for me during these many seasons in Avila were my long afternoon walks. At first Rafael, one of the boys, used to accompany me. He was sensitive to poetry, to religion, and to the arts, without having much technical knowledge; but his feeling was genuine and uncontaminated by any passing fashion. In 1905–1906, when I was lecturing at the Sorbonne, I invited him to come and spend a month in Paris. He came: and I remember one day in the Louvre, when I pointed out some Luca della Robbia reliefs, his sudden interest, and the simplicity with which he took out a note-book and pencil, and made a sketch of one of the pieces, with a note of the colouring. "When I get back to Zorita" (his father's farm), he said, "I will make one like that." Later in Avila, however, I usually walked alone and reduced myself to modest elderly circuits. The shortest and most obvious was to go round the city walls, down by the Rastro to the river, then up the old road skirting the north wall closely as far as San Vicente and then home by the Cathedral apse and the Mercado Grande. This walk—a question of less than an hour—had something that especially recommends itself to my heart and lungs. The ups were all steep and short, the downs gradual and long drawn out. You were stimulated at moments to a little climbing, and you were insensibly propelled and aided in the long stretches. My father's favourite walk, up the *carretera* to the *alto de Vico* and back, had the disadvantage of a slight rise all the way out; also that of occasional dust and passing muleteers and pedestrians.

I preferred pristine solitude. Such was to be found by following the river downward, as far as the dam at the electric power station; it was a path amid great boulders, with varied effects of foreground and distance. But it meant coming uphill all the way home: and the same objection kept me from often choosing the road to Toledo, though the scene was pleasing and I came out into the country at once, without passing through the town. In the end I discovered something unexpected: that the foot-path along the railway line going toward Madrid made an excellent promenade. There were no trains either way at the hour when I went out; and the rocky slopes upward on one side, and the ravines downward on the other, gave you the sense of being in the mountains, as in fact you were. There were also more trees and grass than usual in these highland moors, where the earth is dressed prevalently, like the religious orders, in browns and greys. Avila, though it supports life, looks enough like a desert to symbolise the desert that the world is for the spirit, in spite of the crowd and the pressure there. In both you may come unexpectedly upon scattered flowers or herbs of the sweetest smell; and I treasured the double monition of that bare and austere landscape, and of those sombre yet glittering altars.

Those pleasant seasons in Avila were interrupted for me by the war; and when I returned in 1919, after five or six years' absence, though the places were the same, the persons were somewhat altered. We all were growing old. I in particular had been deeply affected, not only by the war but by a thorough review and digestion of all my English and American experience. I had written *Egotism in German Philosophy*, *Soliloquies in England* and *Character and Opinion in the United States*. Not being able to fix my thoughts on abstract matters I had read Dickens, and learned to love that humbler side of English sentiment and virtue. Without so much as asking for a reason my heart had been entirely on the English side during the war. At Avila, everybody's sympathies were entirely on the other side; and this antithesis rather disconcerted me. My Spanish too, from disuse, had become less fluent. There had been deaths in the family: the daughter, her aunt, and one of the sons. These things somewhat narrowed the field of talk and embittered it. I asked myself why I should still come here, if it were not to be a pleasure all round.

Yet there are attachments to persons and places that hold us even when they give us pain; and I found, at least the first year, a new pleasure here and a new attachment. Pepe, the youngest of the sons, had been married before the war and he now had two little boys, five and four years of age, who became my companions. Not for walks, naturally: but they would come into my room in the early afternoon and we would amuse ourselves painting pictures. When this vein was exhausted, I got a toy theatre, with various stage-settings and cardboard figures; and with my old box of water-colours at hand I was able to make other figures, and to reproduce one of the plays in which Susana had acted in her girlhood (our sister Josefina remembered the text) and also one or two Russian ballets that I had seen in Paris or London. We had one dress performance, to which the whole family was invited; and the preparations and rehearsals amused the little boys and amused me even more for days and days. These were not pastimes that could last long. When I returned in a later year the elder boy was not at home. He had been sent, probably for religious instruction, to an uncle, his mother's brother, who was a priest; and with the younger boy, Roberto, alone, we couldn't revive the old interest. But we read a book of Mother Goose, which they had; and although the child didn't learn much English, I learned sometimes how profound was the difference between modern English and Catholic breeding. Roberto was a sensitive and high-spirited boy; and when I translated for him the lines about Little Jack Horner and the Christmas pie, he felt the *fun* of it perfectly, until having stuck in his thumb and pulled out a plum, Jack Horner says, "What a good boy am I!" Instead of laughing at this, Roberto blushed, seemed a little embarrassed and doubtfully amused, as if he had heard something very improper. What a shocking, incredible thing, he thought, for anyone to say!

So deeply had the lesson of Christian humility penetrated into this society that it seemed scandalous even as a joke to imagine a greedy boy praising himself or congratulating himself. Even one's relations were never to be praised or boasted of. You might expatiate on how much you loved them: this was a source of care, a constant danger of great suffering, for you; it was not a virtue either in you or in those you loved. It was one of your trials, almost one of your sins. You were a bundle of imperfections. You might laugh or you might grieve; you never could have anything to boast of.

This boy Roberto had been so named after my brother, who had made at least two journeys into Spain, first with his whole family, then more wisely alone. He had been taken ill there; and stayed longer than he had intended. He had been with Mercedes to Galicia, and much delighted with her circle, in which, as I once counted it in Madrid, there were twenty-seven women and not one man. My brother Robert seemed a complete Yankee. He had no knowledge and no feeling of what Spain represents in history and in morals: but with Spanish women he returned, as it were, to a forgotten paradise. He was generically fond of the sex, of no matter what nationality, but Spanish women held him suspended in a special way between respect and desire; and far below his crude conscious level something in him responded to Spanish love and Spanish religion. This secret need—unknown even to himself—had inspired him with a great sympathy with Pepe, who wished to be married but was prevented by his father's opposition; and Robert succeeded in bringing Pepe's wedding about, partly by expostulating with Celedonio, going so far as to call him a tyrant, and partly by generous gifts of his own to help the young couple. It was in gratitude for this action of Robert's that they had named their second son Roberto.

My brother didn't live to see the destiny of his namesake; it was I who watched it from a distance with a special interest. Roberto was fond of books and all sorts of knowledge, reminding me of my boyish pleasure in geography and travels. He, like his brother, was also religious; they were among the first to catch the new wave of hope and enthusiasm for the moral regeneration of Spain. They joined the *Falange,* fought in the civil war, and Roberto, after being twice wounded, was killed at the end, within sight of victory. It is at once sad, bitter, and amusing to think how little my brother Robert, and the hundred million like him in America, could have understood this little tragedy, the fruit in one way of his overflowing good-will and kindness.

I watched all this, as I say, from a distance, because after Susana's death in 1928, there was little occasion or propriety in my imposing myself on Celedonio's family. I went that summer to Galicia, to see Mercedes and my sister Josefina; also to see something of that corner of Spain, which was new to me. I even passed through a corner of Portugal, taking the fast train from Paris to Oporto, and thence to Vigo by a secondary line; and on my way back I visited Santiago de Compostela, La Coruña, Leon and Palencia, studiously avoiding Avila, because I knew that the state of Celedonio's mind was unfavourable, and I wished to avoid unnecessary discussions. He was nearly ninety, full of crotchets, and bent on delaying the execution of Susana's will. He died, however, before the next summer; and then I did go to Avila, for the last time, to settle Josefina's affairs and also my own. This I managed without great difficulty. I gave my father's house, built by John Smith, to the Sastre brothers. For many years they had been collecting the rent of it for me, and this was only a small acknowledgment of their friendliness and of the prolonged hospitality of their family, which had been a cause of great joy to me. Besides, I persuaded Josefina to sign a letter—a formal will covering her American property had been signed in Vigo the preceding summer before the American Consul—asking her executors to give suitable legacies for life to Mercedes, the Sastre brothers, and some other friends of hers in Spain. Having thus burned my bridges and cleared my conscience in regard to business duties, I said farewell to Avila and to Spain, no doubt forever. I shed no tears. I retained within me all that I wanted or could ever now enjoy in Spain. I cut off only useless repetitions and disappointments.

My sister Josefina, who was seventy-seven years of age, died the next winter, peacefully, without pain, and without moral worries. She was not without a certain shrewdness in small matters, but vague and indifferent in most directions. After Susana's death, they found means of reconciling Josefina to the Church. Susana had been, curiously enough, the great obstacle to her sister's faith: Josefina didn't want to be dominated. But the ladies in Avila, who were pious without being aggressive or punctilious, won her over with soft words; and they told me that the Dominican who heard her confession said that he thought she had never committed a mortal sin in her life. Perhaps not. He saw that she was like a little child, docile or rebellious according to the tact of her elders, but irresponsible. Some lines from I don't know where stick in my mind for describing her perfectly:

> Elle est morte et n'a point vécu.
> Elle faisait semblant de vivre.
> De ses mains est tombé le livre
> Dans lequel elle n'a rien lu.

Susana, who had lived intensely and who had made brave, desperate ventures more than once in her day, could not hope for such a tranquil end. When time and death had solved the worst difficulties of her married life, and she might have expected to reach port in calm weather, a new and unforeseen trouble overtook her. Celedonio, who had never been considerate, became morose and intractable. At the same time, he became helpless. There arose a chronic resentment between them. The only comfort was that now his family was on her side; for it was the sons that suffered most from their father's obstinacy and niggardliness. Susana no longer slept in the other bed in Celedonio's alcove: one of his sons slept there, in case his father required help during the night. Susana had a bed in her dressing-room, which looked out into the broad country. She could sleep in a well-ventilated apartment. And she could keep her savings, as much as twenty thousand dollars, safe in a concealed drawer, unknown to her husband. And her thoughts could run—was it wicked to let them do so?—to the time when Celedonio would have disappeared, and she could restore the house next door—not this house, which had too many disturbing associations—to live in comfortably in her last days, with me and Josefina and the eldest of Celedonio's sons. Wouldn't he, I asked her, prefer to join one of his married brothers? No, said Susana, because in his brother's household he would have to pay his share of the expenses, while at his step-mother's he would get board and lodging for nothing.

Architectural dreams, as in our first days in Boston, again would bring us together. Should the court-yard have a glass roof? I said no. The duke of Valencia had put one into his restored palace because he was an Andalusian; and in Seville the *patio* was the family living-room in winter as well as summer, and they wished to be protected from the cold and rain. But in Avila no one would think of sitting in winter in a court-yard; the open air, on the south side of some great wall, was the place for sunning oneself: and a glass roof spoilt all the architectural effect and poetry of a *patio*. But Susana said the galleries would be terribly cold in winter for passing from one room to another. That, I retorted, could be prevented by glazing the upper galleries, leaving the court and lower gallery open to the sky. A glazed or even walled upper gallery was a characteristic and picturesque feature in mediæval houses. She might have that next door, and be both comfortably and artistically housed.

Celedonio must have surmised that, with various degrees of impatience, Susana, his sons and especially his sons' wives were waiting for him to die. Not a pleasing thought to hover over your pillow. And your retort in old age can hardly be to grow amiable and generous, so that everybody shall love you and wish you a long life. That is not feasible. The natural retort is to revenge oneself by growing more disagreeable and more miserly, and by straining every nerve to live longer than people expect. The sweetest triumph would be to survive all these younger people who wish to bury you. And Celedonio, as far as Susana was concerned, enjoyed this triumph. When I last said goodbye to him, "until next year," he shook his head, and muttered that he wouldn't survive that winter. He did survive it, but Susana, who was standing by and not thinking of dying so soon, did not survive it. She had never been really strong. At one time she grew enormously fat, then later lost flesh and seemed less unwieldy; but she suffered from physical and moral disharmonies in her nature, and never was or could be thoroughly resigned or content. The house next door was restored by one of her stepsons with her money; and the same pile of bank notes kept so secretly in her drawer served another stepson to restore the house she had lived in for thirty-five years, in comparative shabbiness and discomfort. She and I never had our architectural domicile together; and she never enjoyed the sense of having found her true place in the world and of having won the esteem and gratitude of those who surrounded her. The bar sinister, as it were, of divided allegiances and of incompatible demands always cut across her fairest prospects.

Susana was a Sturgis. Like many of the Sturgises she had good looks, good humour, enthusiasm, love of society, and love of fun; and like the best of them, like her Aunt Sarah, she had also an intrepid instinct of leadership and could direct her passionate interest to some ideal and public end, in her case, towards the Catholic Church. This was not an effect of special intellectual or mystical insight into religion; the Sturgises were not naturally religious. It was an effect of contagion: she easily caught any ambient enthusiasm, and held to it more innocently perhaps and longer than those from whom she caught it. At the same time, she needed social support and sympathy. It would have been agony for her to have been alone with Allah. In order to flourish she required benign and congenial influences. Had these been more prevalent in her life she would have been universally loved and admired. Her mind would have been enlarged and refined; whereas in her continually difficult position she could hardly avoid the irritability and the unjust judgments of the unsatisfied. Yet this ran counter to her nature; I, to whom she had always shown her best side, could feel the warm affection beneath her partisanship, and the comedy behind her illusions. She couldn't bear to let the good and the beautiful slip by unrealised. Hence her impulse to dominate and to manage. That which grieves me now in her destiny is not so much what she missed as what she suffered. It is a shame that she should have suffered, when she was created to love, to laugh, and to enjoy.

CHAPTER V

YOUNGER HARVARD FRIENDS

ONE EVENING in the autumn of 1889, when I was stammering my first lectures in philosophy, there was an unexpected knock at my door in Thayer Hall: and on opening, I saw before me a young man of middle height, with dark hair and a smiling mouth, who said: "My name is Barlow, and my mother has asked me to come and see you." Two simple facts, baldly stated, with an air betwixt sheepishness and mockery, and conveying everything that I needed to know. Here was a Sturgis. His mother, whom we called Nelly Barlow, was the prettiest of "Aunt Sarah's" four daughters, and had married a rough diamond, General Barlow, fresh from the Civil War. The young man was Bob, their eldest son. I don't remember the rest of our conversation that evening, but we had no lack of subjects, knowing perfectly who and what we both were, and being equally at home at Harvard. I perceived at once that Bob had an acute, realistic mind; he didn't mince matters; and his way of talking might have seemed brutal but for a certain background of refinement and indifference that kept it from being conceited or aggressive. We are all fools and poor devils, he seemed to be saying, and we might as well put up with that fact.

Some years later, I saw his father in their house in New York, where after looking at his son's head and at mine where the hair was getting thin, he observed dryly: "The trouble with you young men is that you are rotten before you are ripe." A conspicuously pretty mother and a conspicuously gruff father explained the character of their first born. Bob was a satirical lover of the frail sex and frequented all levels of female society, approaching the dear creatures with a cold eye but with gallant inclinations. He allowed himself no exclusive passions, and remained a bachelor all his life. He particularly liked Paris, the French language and the French stage, about which he knew more than does the ordinary tourist. He was rather well read, with a relish for the sayings of wits, rakes, and cynical philosophers. Boldness pleased him in thought and in war, no less than in love; any man of character had his respect who dared speak the truth and shame the hypocrites. With this taste, sharpened and fed by legal practice, for he became a lawyer, went a certain gentleness of aspect and manner, equable, lazy, and a bit sleepy. You saw in him the child of a beautiful woman who lived to be over ninety; and he himself, though not positively good-looking, had the placidity of a privileged person, round whom everything was expected to revolve without demanding from him any special effort. He led a life of pleasure with apparent indifference, not to say melancholy, and he might have appeared somewhat weak or disappointed had he stood alone.

But Bob Barlow never stood alone. He was one of a pair, like statuettes for the mantelpiece. His mate, however, was no shepherdess, but a big, heavy, jolly man named "Swelly" Bangs, once centre of the 'Varsity football squad, and later an imposing judge. Nobody spoke of Barlow and Bangs; everybody said Bangs and Barlow, as if they had been a firm of lawyers in Dickens, and Bangs the senior partner. But, though both lawyers, they were not partners, Barlow having lived at first with his parents in New York, while Bangs was faithful to Boston. Bangs was simply the greater weight, the more obvious presence, with the more emphatic voice and the more aggressive opinions. What in Barlow was an innuendo turned in Bangs into a crushing dictum, as if he were about to sentence the prisoner to the gallows. Both friends had the mentality of the eighteenth century, and Bangs might have reminded one of Dr. Johnson, save that he banged most softly, with an air of the fine gentleman; for "Swelly" was a man of fashion. My first sight of him was when I was sitting in my lecture-room, waiting for the usual seven minutes to elapse before beginning; and, the place being almost empty, I noticed a new person dressed in a yellow Norfolk-jacket with a large plaid come in and deliberately choose a seat at the back of the room. He then produced a small leather ink-stand and *a quill pen* for the improbable purpose of taking notes. I don't think he came again; but on mentioning the apparition, I was informed that "Oh, yes, he was well-known. It was Swelly Bangs." Neither he nor Barlow was especially my pupil, or much given to technical philosophy. The bond between them and me was of another kind. It was what I might call the sporting mind, unbiased intelligence, spreading freely from youthful curiosity to the interests of the world in general, including the adventures of the philosophers: a sporting mind found in the old wits, in Montaigne and Voltaire, in Hobbes and in Dr. Johnson, but seldom found anywhere nowadays, least of all in America.

Bangs and Barlow sometimes took me to supper at a club they belonged to called popularly *The Spee* and officially the Zeta Psi. The dining-room resembled an old-fashioned ship's cabin, narrow, low, with sides and ceiling all panelled in wood, and a cushioned bench running round the wall. A narrow long table occupied the space between, so that dishes had to be passed along from hand to hand till they got back to the lower end of the table: and I think there were nautical lanterns for the lights, and other little suggestions of the sea. A pleasant setting for my fancy: confinement and comradeship in the midst of a boundless wilderness, and freedom of mind without the peril of losing one's physical balance. The company, the tone, the yarns, and the songs, if not literally nautical, yet had the mannish character proper to a band of young spirits escaping, in sport or in earnest, from the conventional world to sea or into the wilds. Bangs himself used to recite a whaling story, always called for on these occasions, which proved how a ritual gains by repetition. Everybody knew it by heart, and sometimes recited it in chorus. It was called, "Cap'n Sims, thar she blows!" It was full of dialect and local colour; and I still remember Captain Sims' praises of salt pork. Other victuals, he said, leave you half hungry, but salt pork "lays there a-nourish-ing of you for days and days." The supper, however, didn't con-form to this ideal, but was apt to include scalloped oysters and a welsh rarebit, with excellent drinks, both hot and cold. It was a somewhat freer and rougher society than I had known in my own college days, but I liked it immensely and didn't feel out of place in it. Being a little older than the others and a teacher in the College, I wasn't expected to contribute to the entertainment, nor had I any gifts in that direction. I might sometimes say a *bon mot*, but I could never tell a good story. Nature thus helped me to be discreet in all my relations with the younger people, and to pre-serve a certain propriety of language which the youngsters re-spected, and didn't seem to dislike. At any rate, I was asked repeatedly to *The Spee*, where Bangs and Barlow were always my hosts. My position in these undergraduate circles was like that of the prefect in *"Le Monde ou l'on s'ennuie,"* then a well-known comedy, when the duchess, going in to dinner on the prefect's arm, sighs that he won't be able to tell tales about the government, and he replies, "No, Madame, but I may listen to them." So I was able to listen to "Cap'n Sims" and to much else, without either forgetting my status or spoiling the fun.

The Bangs family had a country house near Wareham, in the flat sandy region of Cape Cod, and during one Easter vacation "Swelly" had an angling party there, in which I was included; for though I had never held a rod in my hand, and never meant to, I was notoriously content with looking on; and the nominal duty was assigned to me of opening the baskets and laying out the food for the luncheon in the woods. The woods are rather meagre and scrubby in Cape Cod; but there was moss and rock enough by that sluggish little stream to sit down with comfort, and trees high enough to produce an illusion of being embowered. And we camped out pleasantly at the house, which was closed except for a caretaker, and cooked our own food by a roaring wood fire after our exhilarating day in the fresh air. It was on this occasion that I wrote some lines on *Cape Cod*, of which the poet William

Moody said that there for once I had been inspired. But that inspiration came only by the way, as on returning we skirted a beach in the gathering twilight. Cape Cod in general has the most cheerful associations in my mind.

For here too, at Cotuit, lived the Codmans; and it had been in the summer of 1889 that I had stayed there, forming an affectionate friendship with the whole family, and in particular with Julian, the youngest son. The mother, whom we called "cousin Lucy," was a daughter of the great Russell Sturgis of London, by his first marriage; and although she had married a Bostonian, a somewhat English atmosphere permeated the household, its habits, its speech, and its sentiments. The family were Episcopalians, though not yet Anglo-Catholics. This was not really backsliding towards superstition, as Old Boston might think; everybody knew that Bishop Brooks was as liberal as any Unitarian, only nicer; and Julian, though apparently merely a rather short but well-built and good-looking young man, with excellent unaffected manners, had imbibed secret religious feelings; not so secret, however, that I wasn't perfectly aware of them. I liked those feelings. They were ballast, good for a young man of family who might otherwise dance too lightly on the summer waves.

The always agreeable Julian also had a feeling for poetry, which (like me, if less speculatively) he merged in religion: poetry, especially of the Victorian sort, perspicuous, highly aesthetic, elevating, yet disillusioned. That disillusion should be elevating was nevertheless a mystery; because after all it wouldn't do not to play the game. Pessimism was allowed when it was sincere, but the matter simply remained in suspense for a solution to be found later. With this happy turn of mind, Julian became the life of my "poetry bees," as he called them, when half a dozen of his friends would come to my room in Stoughton in the evening, to beer or hot Scotch whisky, and poetry: most often Keats, but often also Shelley, or Shakespeare's sonnets and songs. Without Julian's tact and fidelity the others (except Warwick Potter) would hardly have proved constant: but he gave the thing such a good start and chose the participants with so much tact that the pleasant practice lasted for years. Harvard social distinctions, not founded on wealth, breeding or attainments, had to be understood and respected if anything of this kind were to be "a success." For instance, I had a friend who was himself a poet, exceptionally cultivated, and educated by his father (an unemployed teacher) to perfection: Joe, or, as he preferred to call himself, Trumbull Stickney. I once tried to introduce him into our readings; but no, it wouldn't do. Julian confidentially informed me that "the others didn't like him." Why not? Because he had mentioned the sunset and called it "gorgeous." I understood that he was too literary and ladylike for Harvard: and I myself found him more companionable later in Paris, where my memory prefers to place him.

Many years later, in 1910–1911, I revived these poetry readings, but almost as if they were a university "seminar." We met in the afternoon, regularly once a week, and read only Shelley from beginning to end, except *The Cenci*. Julian's mantle, on that occasion, had fallen on the worthy shoulders of Conrad Aiken. He was the soul of the party; and we were too sensible, and too intent on our poet, to note particularly who took part. Friendship was not a prerequisite or a necessary result: for me the thing had an ulterior use, in that it led me to write my essay on Shelley.

Julian was a great comfort to me in those earlier days; reconciled me to being again at Harvard without my old friends, and gave me fresh information, judicious and never uncharitable, about things and persons in that little world. He had no fads, no vices, no prejudices, no faults. A little negative, you might say: and description can hardly do him justice. He was amiable, but having no special gifts, he lost distinction as he lost his youth. To have remained at forty or fifty as socially perfect as he was at twenty would have required one artificial aid: plenty of money. He would have known how to combine, in a generous establishment, material, intellectual and social pleasures; his legal profession would not have left him without sufficient leisure and his house would have been a Mecca for all his friends. Even as things

were, I was always happy in his company. Our nominal relationship through the Sturgises covered a real affinity. He was a young
man of the world, and made no bones of differences in age, or
nationality. We laughed at the same things, and we liked the
same things. What more is needed for agreeable society?

On the same sandy coasts of Cape Cod I repeatedly visited
another young friend, Cameron Forbes, at Naushon, an island in
Buzzard's Bay that belonged to his grandfather, Mr. John Forbes,
a personage who had played an important part, financially, in the
remote times of the Mexican War and the annexation of Texas
and California. "Cam," as he was called, inherited from that grandfather, as well as a prospective fortune, an aptitude for affairs and
for public life. He was not a youth to waste his time lounging
in clubs, nor was he particularly absorbed in books; when he had
a free day he would escape from Cambridge to his family farm or
estate or settlement in Milton, where there were horses and woods
and crops and buildings to inspect and to look after. At Harvard
his most urgent occupation was football, not only the practice of
it but the theory, and he eventually became coach to the 'Varsity
eleven, which that year, by what seemed a miracle, won the Yale
Game.

All this sounds rather remote from my meditative idleness;
but Cam had another grandfather. He was also the grandson of
Emerson. That heritage was no less real in him, though less
apparent: or rather, it appeared in him negatively, as a saving
check or divine inhibition. It kept him absolutely removed from
playing the rich young man. Simplicity, rusticity, hard work,
and public duty held him fast bound; yet as with Emerson so in
him, this severity was practical more than imaginative. Imaginatively he could escape from business as gladly as, in life, he fled
from luxury. There was no moral hesitation, no temptation to be
soft: his whole life, in spite of uncertain health, was devoted to
affairs, to politics, to administration: he was at one time Governor
of the Philippine Islands; and I heard that in his old age, still a
bachelor, he lived in his grandfather Forbes' house in Naushon

surrounded by his brothers' families, and most affectionately playing the patriarch. Nevertheless, transcendentally, I think he was haunted by the suspicion that all this ado was terribly unnecessary, just as football, if you think of it, is terribly unnecessary; and instigated by that qualm, he would sometimes draw me aside, and talk about rather intimate matters. He was not one of my little circle: but trusted that my experience and philosophy would enable me to understand in him that which he himself hardly understood.

One day, for instance, he showed me some verses of his about a young man dreaming that two goddesses, Life and Death, appeared to him and offered him their respective gifts: a sort of Puritan Judgment of Paris. The young man listens to their respective boasts and respective promises, and then says: I will choose Life, but on one condition: that I may afterwards reverse my judgment, and choose Death.

The verses were not well composed, and I doubt that Cam has written any others; but the thought was so original, so wise, and so courageous, that nothing in Emerson has ever pleased me more. Think what an incubus life would be, if death were not destined to cancel it, as far as any fact can be cancelled. That is the very image of hell. But natural life, life with its ascending and descending curve, is a tempting adventure; it is an open path; curiosity and courage prompt us to try it. Moreover, the choice must have been made for us before it can be offered; we are already alive, and a whole world of creatures is alive, like us. The first question is therefore what this world may bring to light, for others and for ourselves, so long as it endures. Therefore the preference for life is, as Cam felt, a duty, as well as a natural sporting impulse; but it is a conditioned preference, and something deeper in us than any casual prompting transcends that preference and is fortified by being able to transcend it.

Various traits, major and minor, belonging to Cam Forbes were appropriated by me for the hero of *The Last Puritan*. In the first place, the relation to his father, the atavism of Puritan blood asserting itself, affectionately and kindly, but invincibly, against a rich father, a sportsman, and a man in whose life there was something vague and ineffectual. I didn't know Mr. William Forbes well, nor much about him; but he was present and played the host the first time I went to Naushon. We had champagne every day for dinner; something so entirely contrary to Cam's instincts or possibilities, that when I went to Naushon the second time, with a party of young men from Harvard, Cam commissioned one of us to provide the drinks: even to think of them or order them repelled him. Yet it was a purely private and inward protest: his conscience allowed him to pay for the drinks of others. But my Oliver is no portrait of Cam or of anyone else, although many of the details are drawn from life in various persons. I meant the divine vocation in Oliver, though unrecognised, to be radical and devastating; there was nothing so definite in Cam, who was able to live the expected life and to make a "success" of it. And I also gave Oliver a better education and more ability than Cam ever had, and a greater sensitiveness to the equal rightness of the gay world and the religious world from which his own destiny had cut him off.

Here are three young men (excluding Bangs) who were grandsons, not as we all are, but essentially, so that being grandsons dominated their characters and their whole lives. In other words, they illustrated the decline of an age—the age of the great merchants. They were in one sense its ripe fruits, but in another sense they marked the dissolution of that economy, its incapacity to maintain itself for more than three generations. Two of my friends never married—a rare and almost discreditable thing in their world—and the third died rather young and left, I believe, only one child. Either their fortune was inadequate, or their virtue was inadequate, or their health and stamina were inadequate. Gently, or sadly, or cynically, they had to bow themselves off the stage. But this decline regards only a phase of society, not the life of society as a whole, which in New England was growing richer and more vigorous as it passed out of the period of great merchants into that of "big business" and was merged in the vast American vortex. These grandsons, these essential descendants, couldn't merge in it. They were not hardy enough, not crude enough, too well aware of what they would miss. They were not Babbitts.

Apart from any possible affinity to Babbitt, good sense and good nature (as in Bangs) kept the majority of well-bred Bostonians from being merely grandsons; and in some there was pure individual spontaneity and the certainty of having a fixed vocation. This was the case at that time with another young friend of mine, Howard Cushing. When an undergraduate he was already a painter, and sure that he would never wish to be anything else. The whole world was there before him for a model and he would never tire of catching poses and distinguishing colours. He was not poor, he spoke French fluently (his mother belonged to an old French family in Louisiana), and he was at home in all countries, but never happier than in his own. He loved what he called the *fearless look* of Americans; and his nature was so aristocratic (like that of Thomas Jefferson) that he could feel and actually be perfectly free, even in a democracy. What the crowd did and what the crowd thought was a splendid subject to observe, if not to paint, like scenes from the French Revolution or the martyrdom of early Christians: it was all delightfully full of colour and character. Yet what in the end he painted with most pleasure was the wonderful golden-red hair of his young wife and of his little children. He was domestic, all affection and simplicity, and something of his painter's art seemed to overflow into his surroundings, wherever he might be, and turn them into a picture.

I should hardly have known these younger men, or known them so intimately, but for what we called "the club." In my undergraduate days three of my best friends, Ward Thoron, Herbert Lyman, and Boylston Beal, who ought to have been invited to join some club, such as that to which Bangs and Barlow later introduced me, found themselves left out in the cold; and it occurred to them to found a new club of a socially superior kind, less popular perhaps, and less athletic, but more distinguished. They invited me to join them; but clubs with assessments and inevitable incidental expenses were then beyond my slender means. That club had now amply fulfilled its promise; it had gathered together stray young gentlemen not duly appreciated by their contemporaries but interesting in themselves, some rich, others clever, still others simply agreeable. Julian Codman, Cam Forbes, and Howard Cushing belonged to this club. It then (1890) occupied a wooden house in Mount Auburn Street, and was called officially the Delta Phi, or more familiarly "The Gas House," because all its windows would be lighted up at once by the electricity that was then a novelty; so that it was called "The Gas House" because of the absence of gas. Yet the nickname stuck, and could be interpreted to refer to the brilliancy of the members' minds, or the vanity of their speech. My contemporary, Beal, who had spent some years in Europe, was still studying at the Law School, and came daily to this club; and I suspect that it was he that suggested that I might now be made an honorary member. This was done, and I soon became an *habitué*, and picked up many a stray meal there, not having a regular eating place. There was another graduate, besides Beal, to keep me in countenance, Billy Woodworth, who was an Assistant at the Agassiz Museum, and an excellent cook. He would sometimes preside at supper, producing a dish of his own invention, and his conversation opened to most of us new perspectives, scientific and social, for he was a Californian of the freest type.

It was at the club that I formed the most unclouded and heartfelt of my American friendships, that with Bob and Warwick Potter. Of Bob I will speak later; he was in the class of 1891, and in his last year at Harvard he was preoccupied with his future. He was as much an architect by vocation as Howard Cushing was a painter, and they were both full of the studies they were about to make in Paris, at the Beaux-Arts or at Julien's. But Warwick, who was in the class of 1893 and died at the end of that year, was for the two previous winters my constant companion, and also pupil; and it was at the club, during our poetry-readings in my room, and on our walks that I insensibly came to think of him as a younger brother and as a part of myself. I didn't know how much attached to him I was, until I heard the unexpected news that he had died on board Edgar Scott's yacht in the harbour of Brest. He had been terribly seasick, and the seasickness had provoked an attack of cholera that had proved fatal. It seemed a new kind of blow, not violent, not loud, but strangely transforming. A gradual change due to many converging causes was going on within me. A twelvemonth before, my sister Susana had been married; that summer, my father had died; and the death of Warwick now came to accentuate the effect of these mutations and to make me aware of their meaning for my spiritual life. I shall return later to this my *metanoia*. Nothing apparently was much changed in my surroundings, opinions or habits; yet the public world was retreating to a greater distance and taking on a new and more delicate colouring, as if by aerial perspective. I realised that it was not my world, but only the world of other people: of all those, at least, and they were the vast majority, who had never *understood*.

I have already said something about Warwick in comparing him to my early friend Bayley: they were both good, or rather loved and understood the Good; for they were both too young to have been tried in the furnace and proved to be pure gold. But I felt that they were pure gold. There was an important element in Warwick, however, that didn't appear in Bayley: Warwick was full of laughter. Now laughter, as I have come to see in my old age, is the innocent youthful side of repentance, of disillusion, of understanding. It liberates incidentally, as spiritual insight liberates radically and morally. Susana also was full of laughter; it was the deepest bond between us. By laughing together we could erase the traces of any divergence or failure of sympathy. At the same time, Susana, like Bayley and Warwick, was devout; this marked their sensitiveness to the Good, their capacity to

worship. These were the two prerequisites, in my conception, to
perfect friendship: capacity to worship and capacity to laugh.
They were the two windows through which the mind took flight
and morally escaped from this world.

Warwick was not clever or specially good at his lessons: had
he become a clergyman, as he rather expected, his scholarship
would have been his weak point, and his theological ideas would
have remained vague and verbal. Yet he was very well educated
after the manner of ladies (which was rather the Groton manner); he had heard of everything, knew the points of the compass
in morals and history, and had good taste in English literature.
He also had good taste in choosing his friends and in judging
them: and his intimates were not of his own type: they were not
good pious boys, but captains of crews and owners of yachts:
young men who had experience far beyond his own innocence.
He was not out of place in their society, as he was not in that
of his masters at Groton or in mine. Though young for his age in
experience, he was intellectually alert and without prejudice and
laughingly open to every interesting fact or idea—a trait that
youth ought to possess but that is really the sign of a rare
maturity. You could sit with him by the fire over a mild whiskey
and soda, until the early hours, discussing Falstaff and Prince
Henry, or the divinity and humanity in Christ, or the need of
arms to give strength to letters. Both are needed; and the whole
world is needed, and a complete view of life, to give light to
friendship.

These relations of mine with younger spirits were all cut short
by early separations. That was in the nature of things, because
friends should be contemporaries. But I was divided from my
contemporaries by initial divergences of race, country, religion,
and career; and in spite of those barriers, my old friends kept their
place in my affections and interest to the end. Modern life is not
made for friendship: common interests are not strong enough,
private interests too absorbing. Even in politics, colleagues are
seldom or never friends. Their ambition, being private and not

patriotic, divides instead of uniting them. Nevertheless, I continued to have young friends, very nice young friends, all my life: a little ghostly and evanescent, but agreeable. As widowers proverbially marry again, so a man with the habit of friendship always finds new friends. I had many more at Harvard: I will speak of some of them among Americans in Europe, since it was usually in Europe that our acquaintance could first become companionship; but it would be monotonous to repeat story after story, all with the same moral, and in the same landscape. Harvard had nothing essentially new to offer or to awaken within me, after I returned from King's College, in 1897: the following fifteen years that I remained a professor were a somnambulistic period, interrupted only by the waking dream of a journey to Egypt, Palestine and Greece. Persons yielded in interest to places; and having chosen a place for the time being, I lived as best I could with the human souls that inhabited it. Not at all in bitterness; not with any painful sense of disappointment. My old age judges more charitably and thinks better of mankind than my youth ever did. I discount idealisations, I forgive onesidedness, I see that it is essential to perfection of any kind. And in each person I catch the fleeting suggestion of something beautiful, and swear eternal friendship with that.

CHAPTER VI

BOSTON SOCIETY

WHEN in the year 1858 my mother heroically fulfilled her promise to her late husband and first went to live in Boston, she knew what she was doing, for she had spent some months there two years before and had made the acquaintance of all the Sturgises and their friends. And yet I think she had expectations that were never realised. If not for herself—since she had lost all interest in society —at least for her children, she pictured a perfect amalgamation with all that was best in Boston. This amalgamation never took place. I have described the difficult position that my sister Susana found herself in, and her ultimate return to Spain; and my brother Robert, though a thorough American in all externals, never made a place for himself in good Boston society. This society, in my time, was on the one hand clannish, and on the other highly moralised and highly cultivated. The clannishness was not one of blood: you might almost say that all the "old families" were new. It was a clannishness of social affinity and habit; you must live in certain places, follow certain professions, and maintain a certain tone. Any adaptable rich family could easily enter the charmed circle within one generation. Money was necessary, not in itself but as a means of living as everybody else did in good society; and those who became too poor fell out within one generation also. As to the other characteristic of being cultivated and high-principled, it was not indispensable for individuals already in the clan; but it was necessary to the clan as a whole, for a standard and a leaven. I suspect that the lack of those qualities may have dissolved the society that I speak of, and allowed it to become indistinguishable from the flowing mass of the rich and fashionable all the world over.

Conversation in society, for me at least, was almost exclusively with ladies; but whenever I found myself by chance among elderly men, as for a while after dinner, I became aware of living in a commercial community. Talk reverted from banter to business worries, if not to "funny stories." The leaders were "business men," and weight in the business world was what counted in their estimation. Of course there must be clergymen and doctors also, and even artists, but they remained parasites, and not persons with whom the bulwarks of society had any real sympathy. Lawyers were a little better, because business couldn't be safeguarded without lawyers, and they often were or became men of property themselves; but politicians were taboo, and military men in Boston non-existent. Such persons might be occasionally entertained, and lauded rhetorically in after-dinner speeches; but they remained strangers and foreigners to the inner circle, and disagreeable to the highly moralised and highly cultivated Bostonian.

My contacts with this society were neither those of a native nor those of a visiting foreigner; nor could they be compared with my relation to Harvard College, where I was as much at home as anybody, with a perfectly equal and legal status. In order to have slipped no less automatically and involuntarily into Boston society, I should have had to go to a fashionable school, and my family would have had to occupy the position that I imagine my mother had dreamt of. As it was, I skirmished on the borders of the polite world, and eventually limited myself to a few really friendly families. Yet at first my lot fell, as was natural, within the circles of the Sturgises, especially of the children and grandchildren of Russell Sturgis of London.

In the summer of 1889, when living at my mother's at Roxbury and preparing my first course of lectures, I received an invitation to spend a few days at Manchester-by-the-Sea, with Russell Sturgis, Jr., and his family. I had never seen this elderly cousin, or any of his younger children: only once, many years ago, his eldest son.[1]

From Susana's satirical gossip of years before I had learned something about her cousin Russell. He was very Evangelical, distributed tracts entitled "Do you love Jesus?" and would send us Christmas cards—he never came to see us—wishing us joy and "one more year of leaning upon Jesus' breast." There was always some religious motto printed on his note-paper, which once happened to be "Ye are bought with a price"; and he having inadvertently written to Judge Gray on that paper, his letter was returned as a libel by the insulted magistrate. Apart from his evangelical work "Cousin Russell" appeared to have no occupation; and he was known to have spent the winter at Manchester-by-the-Sea for economy, which precluded daily attendance to business, if he had any. He may also have thought that on moral grounds, as a discipline and a tonic, a winter in the bleak country might be a good thing. The "kindred points of heaven and home" might there seem more precious than ever. We are always so near the abyss, and the wintry ocean might remind him of it. But why suddenly ask me to stay at his house, when he had never seen me and there was no real bond between our families? Had he heard that I was about to begin teaching at Harvard? If I were the right sort, might I not prove a useful acquaintance for

---

[1] This had been in the year 1876, when I was twelve years old. Robert and I had gone to Philadelphia to see the Centennial Exhibition. I remember only two things seen in Philadelphia, both architectural: the Fine Arts Building and the odd features of the typical Philadelphia houses: the white wooden shutters outside, and the ingenious arrangement of the stairs, making a bridge between the body of the house and a long wing behind, entered from the landing. The stairs could be lighted through a large window at the side, and the wing would supply various rooms, the dining-room especially, half-way between one storey and another of the house proper. For some reason, on our return, Robert wished to stay in New York. Young Russell Sturgis, 3rd, then nineteen years old, offered to look after me on the way home. We travelled by the Sound Boat—another interesting discovery in construction—a vast flat-bottomed steamer with a hall in the middle, surrounded by galleries and rows of little doors to private cabins. If we had only been quadrupeds, we should have fancied ourselves in Noah's Ark.

his younger sons, who were younger than I? And if I were not the right sort, why shouldn't he prove a saving influence over me?

When I turned up, I don't know what his first impression may have been; he and the whole family were certainly very kind. They seemed to accept me as an adopted relative. But gradually my defects must have become evident. No, I didn't swim, and I'd rather not take a dip in the sea before breakfast, as he and the boys did every morning even in winter. I didn't say so, but it cost me an effort to be shaved and dressed in time for the inevitable family breakfast. Lazy, soft, luxurious young man, and a *poor* young man, too, which makes vice so much worse and so much less excusable! However, these thoughts were as yet only in embryo. I got down to breakfast in time—a very nice breakfast, all sorts of hot things, not unwelcome when one has got up early—but after it there was a strange, awkward silence; everyone was standing up and no one leaving the room except to move into the drawing-room, which was separated only by a screen. The servants now came in, and stood uncomfortably in a corner. There were to be family prayers! They were *after* breakfast, as "Cousin Russell" afterwards frankly explained, because if they had been *before* breakfast, everybody would have been late or would have missed prayers altogether; but after breakfast, there you had them all, and no escape. Filled and soothed as I was by that abundant oatmeal, I rather liked the idea of prayers. I should have a peaceful quarter of an hour, speculative, digestive and drowsy. Chairs, big and little, were arranged in a circle round the room. In lieu of ecclesiastical objects, the broad sea and sky were visible through the long open windows. We might enlarge our thoughts, while "Cousin Russell" read a chapter of the Bible, not at all in a clerical voice, but familiarly and dramatically, to bring out the good points, and make us feel how modern and secular it all really was. The book closed, he rose and we all rose automatically to attention—he had been a major in the Civil War—we executed a sharp right-about-face, fell on our knees, and buried our faces in the warm chairs where we had been sitting. He recited, and the rest half murmured, the Lord's Prayer, with some other short things from the Prayer-Book, and a benediction. Then we all rose again, the servants disappeared, and a programme of healthy pleasures was announced for the rest of us for the morning. In the afternoon there would be an excursion and in the evening (not preannounced) there were to be parlour-games.

Never having been in an army, in a nursery, or in an Evangelical family, I found all this rather odd and exacting; but I was out to learn something of the world, and this was a part of it. On that occasion, for two or three days, I tried to do my duty; but duty in my ethics means a debt, an obligation freely undertaken; and I saw at once that I was unfit to live under a free government where other people voted as to what I should do. My unfitness must have transpired, for I was never asked again to Manchester-by-the-Sea, nor should I have been tempted. When later I knew how the other children of "Uncle Russell" lived in England, although, as I was informed, all had equal fortunes, this family seemed to belong to a different social class. Among the truly noble, as for instance in Spain, there was grandeur without much luxury or comfort; under the plutocracy, in which "Cousin Russell's" English brothers lived, there was luxury without grandeur; and in the bourgeoisie, which "Cousin Russell" himself had joined, there was comfort without luxury. Comfort, in his case, was stiffened by Spartan and athletic austerities, yet in sentimental directions he was soft enough. He was pleased with his appearance, being well built, portly, with fair side-whiskers that flew backward as he marched about; and of a summer evening he and his wife would stand embraced by the window, gazing alternately at each other and at the sunset over the sea. I knew this was a form of evening prayer, a wordless *Angelus,* and I stood discreetly aside.

At about the same time I made a first visit to another of "Uncle Russell's" children, "Cousin Lucy Codman" and her family, at their country house at Cotuit on Cape Cod. It was a much softer, sandier, flatter, poorer region than the Massachusetts "North Shore," with few summer residents, and little but scrub pine woods, straggling farms, and ghostly, gaunt natives who "made remarks." On the other hand the Codmans, in spite of their name so appropriate to Cape Cod, seemed almost to be living in England, with all the freedom, largeness, and tact of good society. You were taken for granted, put at your ease, made materially and morally comfortable. Conversation was spontaneous, unpretending, intelligent; you could talk about what interested you— if you did so with discretion and briefly; and you were not asked for your opinion on things you cared nothing about. The house was agreeably furnished, not over-furnished: there were flowers, a little music, enough wit to make express entertainments unnecessary. The father and the two elder sons were away—kept in Boston by their work; but the youngest son, Julian, sometimes took me out sailing in a cat-boat in very smooth water, a peaceful somnolent amusement very much to my taste. He was destined to become the most confidential of all my young friends in the following years, and I have already described him, his career, and the perfect sympathy there was between us. Julian, with the cat-boat, comes under the head of friendship, not of Boston society: and it was not on his account that I was invited to Cotuit.

I had been expressly summoned in order that I might make the acquaintance of Howard Sturgis, "Cousin Lucy's" youngest brother, who might well have been her son, being then thirty-three years of age. Howard, too, comes properly under the head of friendship, since I began the next year to make him almost yearly visits, sometimes reduplicated, at his house in Windsor: but since I first saw him in America, and it was my Sturgis connection that established a kind of family intimacy between us, I will say something about him here.

He had come to America for a complete change of scene, hoping it might help to heal the wound that, in his excessively tender heart, had been left by the death of his mother. She had not been, from all I have gathered, at all a remarkable woman, but luxurious and affectionate, surrounded in London by a few rich American friends, especially the daughters of Motley, the historian, who were married to Englishmen, and surrounded beyond them, more by hearsay than acquaintance, by the whole British aristocracy. Howard had been her last and permanent baby. The dear child was sensitive and affectionate, with abundant golden hair, large blue eyes, and well-turned chubby arms and legs. Her boudoir became his nursery and his playroom. As if by miracle, for he was wonderfully imitative, he became, save for the accident of sex, which was not yet a serious encumbrance, a perfect young lady of the Victorian type. He acquired a good accent in French, German and Italian, and instinctively embraced the proper liberal humanitarian principles in politics and history. There was an absolutely right and an absolutely wrong side in every war and every election; only the wicked, selfish, and heartless still prevented the deserving from growing rich, and maintained an absurd and cruel ascendency of birth, superstition, and military power. These were the sentiments of the Great Merchants, economists and reformers of the early nineteenth century, and Howard would have embraced them in any case because they appealed to his heart, and his feminine nature would never have allowed his intellect, no matter how keen, to do anything but defend his emotions. When women's opinions waver, it means that their hearts are not at rest. Let them once settle their affections and see their interests, and theoretical doubt becomes impossible for them. Howard's affections and interests were inextricably bound up with the liberal epoch; and no evidence would ever have convinced him that this was the only ground for his liberal dogmatism.

This was not all that he imbibed from his mother's circle. He was not only imitative, but he also had a theory that there was nothing women did that a man couldn't do better. Pride therefore seconded inclination in making him vie with the ladies and surpass them. He learned to sew, to embroider, to knit, and to do crochet; these occupations were not only guiltless of any country's blood, but helped to pass away the empty hours. He became wedded to them, and all his life, whether he sat by the fire or in his garden, his work-basket stood by his low chair. His needlework was exquisite, and he not only executed gorgeous embroideries, but designed them, for he was clever also with the pencil. Imitation, or a sort of involuntary caricature, sometimes went further with him. He would emit little frightened cries, if the cab he was in turned too fast round a corner; and in crossing a muddy road he would pick up the edge of his short covert-coat, as the ladies in those days picked up their trailing skirts.

Some of these automatisms were so extreme and so ridiculous that I can't help suspecting that there was something hypnotic or somnambulistic about them. He was too intelligent and too satirical to have done such things if he could have helped it. There may have been some early fixation at work, probably to his mother, of the kind that induces dreams, and develops into grotesque exaggerations and symbolic fancies. He mimicked people, sometimes on purpose, but often involuntarily: and his imagination penetrated their motives and thoughts, as his novels show, not necessarily with truth, but plausibly and with an endless capacity for extensions. He may have been at times the victim of this dramatic fertility in his own person, and found himself playing a part that the real circumstances did not call for.

He had not yet written his best novels, only an ultra-pathetic story about a little boy "Tim"; but one morning we found him sitting in the porch outside the living-room, on one of the wicker chairs with red-cotton cushions that adorned it, and that he copied later in the addition made to Queen's Acre; and we found him armed, not with his usual work-basket, but with a red leather writing case. He had an absorbed and far-away air. He was writing poetry: verses about the loss of his mother. We asked him to read them: he would not have brought them downstairs if he wished them to bloom and die unseen. He read them very nicely, without self-consciousness or affectation: the sentiment was intimate, but the form restrained and tactful.

Courage and distinction will save a man in almost any predicament; and Howard had been at Eton, where he acquired distinction and showed remarkable courage. Sending him there must have been a last desperate measure insisted on by his brothers, to cure him of his girlishness. A cruel remedy, it might seem, as if he had been sent to sea before the mast. Why hadn't his father and mother corrected him sooner? His father's mind had been growing feeble, and his mother probably thought the lad sweeter as he was. After all, too, they were Bostonians; and would it have been *right* to correct dear little sweet Howard for girlishness, when girlishness wasn't *morally wrong*? Let him go to Eton, properly safeguarded, if his brothers thought it absolutely necessary. And this heroic remedy didn't prove in the least cruel, or in the least efficacious. Young Howard calmly defied all those school-boys with his feminine habits and arts, which he never dreamt of disguising. He was protected by his wit and intellectual assurance; while his tutor, Mr. Ainger, author of the *Carmen Etonense,* and the two Misses Ainger, adopted him and screened him from the rude mob. Besides, Howard attracted affection, and however astonished one might be at first, or even scornful, one was always won over in the end.

After Eton, Trinity College, Cambridge was plain sailing, and confirmed his humanitarian principles and aristocratic habits. His studies don't seem to have been serious; but he remembered what he had read of belles-lettres, just as ladies do. He had even dipped into Berkeley's philosophy and had laid it aside, not unwisely, as an academic curiosity. To see interesting people, or at least fashionable people, and to hear about them, made his chief entertainment later. Of course he had travelled abroad and seen everything that everybody should see; he remained old-fashioned, without preraphaelite affectations, in matters of art. His novels were exquisitely felt and observed, full of delicately satirical phrases, and not without an obvious moral aimed against domestic prejudice and social tyranny: but his writing had hardly force enough, either in style or in thought, to leave a lasting impression.

In what he felt to be his homeless plight, he had looked about

for a house, and had finally taken a small one, with a nice garden
on the outskirts of Windsor Park. Its name had been Queensmead,
but there was a Kingsmead next door, and seeing that the land
was little more than an acre—at least the part of it visible from
the house—he re-christened it Queen's Acre, familiarly and ironically abbreviated to Quaker. The nearness of Eton, and of the
Aingers, had attracted him, for as often happens, he retained a
much greater affection for his school than for his College or University. In those first years his garden and his table were often
enlivened by groups of Eton boys. To some of them he gave pet
names, such as The Lion, The Bear, or The Babe; this last being
Willie Haines Smith, a distant cousin of his, who became his
adopted younger brother and companion for life.

All this lay in the future, and in England. For the moment at
Cotuit, although Howard was the guest of honour, the ruling
spirits were the ladies. There were two daughters, both in the
early twenties. Something, I hardly know what, seemed to desig-
nate the one in whom I ought to be particularly interested. I liked
them both; but to choose a wife was the last thing that I was
thinking of; my friends knew it, and this delicate question, never
spoken of, was left hanging in mid-air, until years later, when
one day Julian deliberately asked me why I didn't marry. I replied
that I wished to be free and didn't intend to live always in
America. Whether Julian's mother had prompted him to ask that
question, I don't know, perhaps not, since she had no reason to
desire me for a son-in-law, and her daughters, on approaching
the age of thirty, made reasonable and more suitable marriages.
Yet, out of sheer kindness, she seems to have taken an interest
in my happiness, as she conceived it ought to be; for she took
pains to go and tell my mother, whom she seldom visited, *how
strongly she felt* about certain things one of which was the *sad
mistake* that a poor young man made sometimes in backing away
from a rich girl, simply because she was rich, when they sincerely
cared for each other. This arrow was of course aimed at a particular target, but couldn't regard "Cousin Lucy's" daughters,

since they were not rich: so far from rich, indeed, that a poor young man couldn't have married them, no matter how often he had popped the question and been accepted. It would have meant a long engagement, with an eventual descent into another level of society.

I think I know what "Cousin Lucy" had in mind. She was spinning a romance out of a nascent sympathy between a certain distinguished heiress and me; it never went beyond agreeable conversations about books, operas, plays, and travels, merely at dinners and other social functions. Had I been in love with her, and pressed my suit, she might have made the mistake of accepting me, to the consternation of her numerous relations; but I didn't allow myself to fathom the question whether I was in love with her or not. The barrier was not her person nor the fact that she was rich; this fact was precisely what might have encouraged me, because I should not have been imposing any material sacrifices upon her; but she would have been imposing upon me her whole background, her country, her family, her houses, her religion. Not that I had any fault to find with these things *for her*; but a *déraciné*, a man who has been torn up by the roots, cannot be replanted and should never propagate his kind. In the matter of religion, for instance, I found myself in this blind alley. I was not a believer in what my religion, or any religion, teaches dogmatically; yet I wouldn't for the world have had a wife or children dead to religion. Had I lived always in Spain, even with my present philosophy, I should have found no difficulty: my family would have been Catholic like every other family; and the philosophy of religion, if ever eventually discussed among us, would have been a subsequent private speculation, with no direct social consequences. But living in a Protestant country, the free-thinking Catholic is in a socially impossible position. He cannot demand that his wife and children be Catholics, since he is not, in a controversial sense, a Catholic himself; yet he cannot bear that they should be Protestants or freethinkers, without any Catholic tradition or feelings. They would not then be his wife or children except by accident: they would not belong to his people. I know that there are some who accept this consequence, even pretend to have become Protestants, and bury as deep as possible the fact that they were born Catholics or Jews. But I am not a man of that stamp. I have been involuntarily uprooted. I accept the intellectual advantages of that position, with its social and moral disqualifications. And I refuse to be annexed, to be abolished, or to be grafted onto any plant of a different species.

This feeling was absolutely fixed in me from the beginning, but didn't prevent me from liking the Boston ladies, though I never courted any of them. I liked the elegance, the banter, the wit and intelligence that often appeared in them. I liked to sit next to them at dinner, when conversation flowed more easily and became more civilised in the midst of lights and flowers, good food and good wines. The charm of the ladies was a part of that luxurious scene, of that polite intoxication: for me it was nothing more. But people didn't understand that this could be all: even my sister Susana didn't understand it and more or less seriously looked about for someone with whom to pair me off. This was when we were children; later when I began to find my real affinities, Susana had returned to Spain, and perhaps had seen that I had not thought of marrying anyone in Boston, not even among the Catholics.

My real affinities were with three or four elderly ladies, who never appeared off the social stage, and who like me were more or less spontaneously playing a part, as it were, in public, while their real and much less interesting life lay hidden beneath, like the water-supply, the drains, and the foundations of their houses. They were all childless, or had lost their children, and their husbands, when living, either didn't appear at all in the same scenes, or played a subordinate, comic, errand-boy part in them. The invisible husband might be, in his own world, an important person, esteemed as much or more than his wife in hers: but like royal spouses occupying opposite wings in a palace, they had their own exits and entrances, their own hours and their own friends. This was the case with two leading ladies in the Boston of

my time, Mrs. Gardner and Mrs. Whitman. Often as I lunched
and visited at Mrs. Gardner's, both in town and country, I hardly
ever saw her husband; and it was only after years of acquaintance
with Mrs. Whitman that once, at a week-end party by the sea, I
caught sight of Mr. Whitman: not that he was living in the house
or belonged to the house-party, but that he had come, as if by
chance, in his yacht, and had looked in upon us.

These two ladies had individual vocations; their husbands had
their own position, their own work, and their own friends, and
having ample separate means they amicably cultivated separate
gardens. Mrs. Gardner was not a Bostonian: her vocation was to
show Boston what it was missing. Instead of following the fashion, she undertook to set it. It wasn't followed; Boston doggedly
stuck to its old ways and its old people: yet it couldn't ignore
Mrs. Gardner; her husband was an old Bostonian and always
countenanced, supported, and (invisibly) stood by her; and she
had an indefatigable energy and perseverance that, in spite of all
murmurs and hesitations, carried the day. When she became a
widow and built her Venetian palace in The Fenway, as Egyptian
monarchs built their tombs and went to live in them, she became
an acknowledged public benefactor. Criticism was hushed: and
there was something moving in beholding this old lady, whose
pleasure it had been to shock, devoting herself more and more
modestly to preparing and completing her museum, to be left to
the town that she had startled when younger, that had long
looked at her askance, and that she was now endowing with all
her treasures.

What her inner life may have been, her religion (she was outwardly a very High Church Anglican) or her sentiments regarding Boston, her husband, or the child she had lost, and regarding
the works of art and the artists that she devoted herself to collecting, I do not know: but it is easy to perceive the figure that
she wished to cut in the world. She modelled herself on the great
ladies of French and Italian society, as she had seen them in her
travels or during her residence in Venice. She was far from

beautiful, but she knew that this was no obstacle to dressing magnificently and boldly, or being positively alluring: her clothes (for the evening) filled Boston with alarm and with envy. She was not of good family, although professedly related to the royal house of Stuart; but she gave Boston a lesson in being aristocratic, and surrounded herself with interesting people, strangers, artists, musicians, and anyone who was either distinguished or agreeable. If the old Bostonians didn't like it, they needn't come; but they came, if they were asked.

She followed the fashion of the 1890's in collecting real or alleged works of the Old Masters, and also of some modern painters; but here the state of society in the twentieth century and in America prevented her from collecting as an aristocrat might, for his own pleasure, to enhance the surroundings of his life and the heritage of his family. She collected to collect; and such collections can have only one end, a public museum. This fatality, imposed by circumstances, worked a slow and subtle change in her bearing and in her satisfactions. She became an agent for her own museum. At least, so she seemed in her public capicity, for by building her museum she became a public character: but her personality never was quite transformed. I may say that I have never really seen her collection; for she would insist on showing me everything, instead of letting me—as a true *grande dame* might have done—ramble about without her and study what caught my eye; and when she showed her treasures, she would tell something about them, where she found them, or their history, and there would always be the personal play of conversation between her and her guest: so that the guest had a charming half-hour with her, but never *saw* any of her things. I should have bought a ticket and gone to her museum on the days when it was open to the public; but I dislike museums and never did so, especially as I heard that sometimes she walked about even on public days and acted as cicerone. Her palace and her pictures had become the last costume and the last audacity by which she would vanquish old Boston.

Mrs. Gardner, though she defied prudery, practised the virtue most difficult for a brilliant woman in a hostile society: she spoke ill of nobody. She joined kindness to liberty; and she played the queen and the connoisseur with so much good nature that in her masquerade she was aware of no rival, while in the real world she scattered substantial favours.

More in the spirit of Boston, more conscientious and troubled, was Mrs. Whitman. Not content merely to love the fine arts, she became an artist and designed stained-glass windows. There were echoes in her of Transcendentalism, but no longer imageless nor countrified. It had become symbolic, ritualistic, luxurious. I remember the high wax candles, as on an altar, decorating her dinner table. She didn't make a point of entertaining itinerant artists or other celebrities; but devoted herself to instilling the higher spirit of the arts and crafts into the minds of working-girls. Our good works, alas, are often vainer than our vanities. "What did Mrs. Whitman talk to you about?" somebody asked after a lecture. And one of the girls replied: "She said that art was green." It is true that Mrs. Whitman was partial to that colour, and Mahomet expressed the same preference, for an easily assignable reason: but when we express preferences, though we may diffuse those preferences by mere suggestion or hypnosis, we incite others to express their contrary preferences, and to nurse every preference, instinctive or imposed, out of pure doggedness.

This is not an incitement to learn, but to be content without learning: the great temptation of freedom. Mrs. Whitman's lecture, in the case of that working-girl, was a complete failure. If she had reported the *explicable* fact that Mahomet thought green the most beautiful of colours, something might have been gained; because the working-girl's casual preference for pink or for blue would have been not merely challenged but undermined. For if Mahomet loved green, because he constantly travelled through deserts, looking for the palm trees of some oasis, what desert are you, poor working-girl, travelling through, that causes you to long for pink and blue ribbons? If you reflect upon that, the apparently

inane conclusion that art is green might acquire a pregnant meaning. Art would appeal to the mind in general as the colour green
appealed to the eye of Mahomet, and for similar reasons. We
must consider human nature and the radical predicaments of the
living arts if we are to recover definite taste or artistic power. The
aestheticism of the nineteenth century was a symptom of decay,
aggravated by the pathos of distance.

Mrs. Whitman was a great friend of William James. They had
similar impetuous perceptions and emotions, a similar unrest, and
a similar desire to penetrate to the hidden facts, the submerged
classes, the neglected ideas, unpleasing to the official world. The
generosity of all this was evident: less evident was the fruitful-
ness of it. The field was vague and so was the mind of the reformers. One day James asked me to come to a supper that he
was giving for his more advanced pupils, about thirty of them.
Mrs. Whitman was coming. He wished me to come too—without
dressing, of course—and help Mrs. Whitman to feel at home. And
I was placed at her right hand, James sitting opposite, in the·
middle of the other long side of the table. Neither Mrs. James
nor any other member of the family was present: it was to be a
philosophical conclave, a semi-religious semi-festive mystery. Why
did James conceive such a supper? Out of kindness, to be hospitable and fatherly towards his disciples. But why did he ask Mrs.
Whitman, or why did she wish to come? Mrs. James could have
been equally hospitable and kind. Perhaps it was not from the
young men's point of view, but from Mrs. Whitman's, that he
saw the desirability of inviting her. She was interested in diffusing
high aspirations among the people: here she would see a chosen
group of ambitious young men, and perhaps scatter some good
seed or get some hint or some encouragement in her work. The
young men were of course impressed, some of them no doubt
dazzled, by James in his own library, walled completely with
books, save for his father's portrait in oils over the mantelpiece,
and by the lordly supper—with a touch of the *Kneipe* about it,
for we all had beer, except Mrs. Whitman. For her a half-bottle

of champagne was provided, which, as James said, would not be good for the rest of us. Above all they must have retained a striking image of Mrs. Whitman, beautifully dressed, not in an evening gown, but in a green velvet bodice with long sleeves, delicately set off by gold braid, an ample white silk skirt, and a large bunch of violets. She was not particularly beautiful, nor the opposite (as Mrs. Gardner was) but she had that vivacity and intelligence, added to the discreet arts of the toilet, that keep French ladies from ever looking old. I doubt that she said anything that any of those young men would note or remember. I had been summoned expressly to entertain her, and spare her the effort of having to make talk with shy uncouth youths all the evening; for there were no speeches. In philanthropic and propagandist directions I doubt that anything was accomplished: but the feast was rather beautiful in itself, and certainly cannot have been forgotten by any of those who were there. It was an instance of the manner in which those two distinguished spirits, William James and Mrs. Whitman, failed to diffuse their intended influence, and yet succeeded while failing: for they added something pleasant and pure to the world.

As to the male element in Boston society, it would perhaps be better for me not to say anything. I knew few of them well, because most of my friends, even at Harvard, were not Bostonians, and those who were Bostonians were seldom seen at parties. The men went there to see the women, and were like fish out of water in regard to one another. Besides, Boston society was dominated by the very young, except in staid elderly circles that met only at dinners. Sometimes, being a conveniently unattached bachelor, I was honoured by an invitation to small parties of that sort, at houses where I was not intimate. On such occasions I might make the acquaintance of representative elderly men, or hear them talk, when conversation became general. One distinguished Bostonian that I came to know in this way was Judge Holmes. His wife never went anywhere, and he, still rather youngish with a sweeping blond moustache, would play the bachelor. One day—

this was at Mrs. Gray's, who had been a Boston "beauty"—he said he didn't like to walk in Beacon Street. Every door seemed to him the tombstone of a dead love. This was one direction in which the Justice unbent; but his mind was plastic also in speculation. Being an exceptionally successful man he could be pessimistic in philosophy, and being an old Bostonian he could disinterestedly advocate democratic reforms. After I had left America he surprised me by writing in high terms about my *Winds of Doctrine,* especially the first page in which there is nothing not commonplace except perhaps the tone in which moral and political revolutions are spoken of, as natural episodes in a transformation without end. It is or it was usual, especially in America, to regard the polity of which you happen to approve as sure to be presently established everywhere and to prevail forever after. To have escaped this moralistic obsession, at least for a moment, evidently was a pleasure to Judge Holmes. He had a really liberal, I mean a truly free, mind.

There was another local celebrity whom I once heard discourse about politics at a dinner, not in a set speech, but in ordinary conversation. Everybody else stopped talking in order to listen to him because, by a rare exception in his class, he had gone into politics and been Governor of Massachusetts. His name was Roger Wolcott, and in his young days he had been regarded as the handsomest man and the greatest beau in Boston. He was attacking the New York *Nation,* a weekly paper which I always read. Its politics were radical, but the book reviews were written by professors, often professors of foreign languages, about subjects that interested me. The views of the professorial class, or intelligentsia, are naturally literary and captious; Roger Wolcott, as a man and as a practical politician, detested them. He said *The Nation* had a very bad influence in the country, especially among the young men. It gave them a false idea of what government was and ought to be. It made them ignorantly critical, supercilious, unpatriotic. As far as I remember, Wolcott didn't go beyond bare denunciation; he was probably not speculative, like Judge Holmes;

and he might seem to have been guided merely by club spirit or esprit de corps like so many Lodges and Greek Letter Fraternities that flourished in America without representing any genuine public interests. On the other hand, his experience may have given him some true intuition of the fated movement and destiny of his country, and his "stalwart" politics may have been only a vulgar cover for something heroic: I mean, for the courage and pride of sharing the life of his country, in soul as well as in body.

CHAPTER VII

AMERICANS IN EUROPE

MORE than with any other class of people, fate has associated me with Americans in Europe. Even when I was still living in the United States, it was people at home in Europe, socially and morally, that most readily became my friends. Not that being at home in Europe or at home in America counted in itself in my true friendships. That which counted in that case was exclusively the individual man or woman, the body and the soul. A field of action and of thought was essential, but only as a language is essential for conveying a thought: for when the thought is absorbing, the language is not noticed, and seems indifferent. Yet a common language, a common social and moral idiom, becomes in itself a great bond when you are travelling in strange places, among people with whom you cannot communicate. The common language draws you together, even if what each will say may eventually not prove important or acceptable to the others.

Now with Americans in Europe I had a common field of experience, a common social and moral convention, and we were for the moment in the same boat. A travelling acquaintance may of course disclose a vital affinity: but I think this was not the case with any of my American friends in Europe: either no vital affinity existed or we had discovered it in America, and it was independent of all accidents of residence. With converts of any kind, with American women married to Englishmen, with expatriates, with aesthetic souls that fled from America because the voices there were too rough, I never had much sympathy. It was persons who were thoroughly European or thoroughly American that held the first place in my esteem. In my esteem, but not in my life. In my life the foreground was filled with Americans in Europe.

This appears emphatically in the case of Strong, the only person not of my kindred with whom I have lived, on and off, for years. I have described the origin of our friendship and its not altogether satisfactory result. Why did Strong live in Europe at all? It would require more knowledge than our life-long acquaintance has given me to answer this question properly: there are mysteries involved, and Strong was more than reserved, he was inhibited, in regard to his private affairs. I can only point to the gross facts: he had been at school in Germany; he very naturally wished to return to Germany to study philosophy; and, then, when from Germany we had gone to London for our holidays, in the spring of 1887, he one day announced that *it would be best* for him to leave me and go to Paris to join his father, who was there with a party of friends. This sounded dutiful and pious enough; it was not for me to ask any questions, nor did I suspect any mystery. But a month or two later, I received a letter, saying that he had been travelling with Mr. John D. Rockefeller and family, and that he was engaged to be married to the eldest daughter, Bessie; that they were all coming to England in June; and that Mr. Rockefeller invited me to join them, on the day of Queen Victoria's Jubilee, to view the procession from a room he had engaged in Buckingham Palace Road. Not a word more. Had the pious rogue been engaged all the time to this fabulously rich heiress, when he generously consented to divide the Walker Fellowship with me? I can hardly think so. It must all have been a machination behind his back. His father and Mr. Rockefeller, eminent Baptist elders, had thought *it would be best* to settle these young people safely and happily for life, before they got any foolish notions into their heads. Old Dr. Strong (who was himself becoming a financier, had a red nose, and liked good dinners with plenty of champagne) saw a brilliant future assured for his son; and this marriage would rivet Rockefeller even more tightly to himself and to all the Baptist institutions; while Rockefeller saw his daughter, his favourite child, whose future gave him some anxiety, safely settled with a good-looking, high-principled young man sure to make her happy, and with his studious habits and mild disposition never to separate her from her father, either in place of residence or in sound Christian sentiments. The young people were willing enough. Both were probably profoundly bored and with a blank future. To be married was a new idea. It gave them something almost exciting to think about and to do.

In his old age Strong sometimes amused himself by writing "poetry." The most interesting of these effusions recounts how he loved five times, and Bessie, his wife, is one of these lady-loves, but evidently not the one secretly preferred. From this and from other indications I gather that he *thought it would be best,* after having been obliged by his conscience to resist the higher Baptist powers in regard to his religious allegiance, not to resist them in this, that seemed a reasonable proposal. People would think it a piece of incredible good fortune, but somehow for him it was sad.

In Buckingham Palace Road, on the appointed day, I was duly introduced to the great millionaire, still a dapper, youngish man with cordial American manners, and to his daughter Bessie, not at all the blushing bride, but the image of vigorous health and good sense, nice-looking, frank, and with manlike college airs, for she was fresh from Vassar. Our conversation corresponded, and was nothing but commonplaces helped out by smiles. Little did I suspect that I should never have a chance to talk with her rationally again; for even when I stayed in later years at her house, I hardly ever saw her. She was always, as they put it, in delicate health, which was a euphemism for not being in her right mind. It was to be Strong's destiny to become a sort of guardian or watchman over his invalid wife. At Compiègne, during her last years, he would see her for ten minutes in the morning, and for ten minutes again in the evening, each time bringing her a picture post-card to talk about. He had a great collection of them in stock, and dealt them out, as if just discovered, two each day, for her to put in her album.

Ten years later, when I was at King's College, the Rockefellers invited me again to see the Queen's procession, when she drove to the service in front of St. Paul's in thanksgiving for her sixty years' reign. This time we were in a room in Piccadilly; and the sight so absorbed me, with its vast historic and political suggestions, that I don't remember Rockefeller being there at all or any of the other guests. On another occasion, however, when I went to spend a holiday with Strong at Lakewood, New Jersey, I had a capital opportunity of learning some of the great capitalist's characteristics; for the house was his, he had only lent it to his daughter and son-in-law, and at that time he was living in it, in order to be near his private golf-links, where his own larger house had been closed for the winter. I saw him only at table; but as Strong was a silent man, and his wife was ill upstairs, it was practically with me that Mr. Rockefeller had to talk. He played golf assiduously, always alone, matching his score on one day against his score on another; just what the saints do when they daily examine their conscience and consider whether they have developed any new sins, or been carried by the grace of God one step forward towards perfection. Such was probably also the interest dominating Rockefeller's chase after millions. He was beyond comparing himself with his competitors; he compared himself with himself.

One day when I had mentioned Spain, he asked me, after a little pause, what was the population of Spain. I said I believed it was then nineteen millions. There was another pause, this time rather longer, and then he said, half to himself: "I must tell them at the office that they don't sell enough oil in Spain. They must look the matter up."

I saw in my mind's eye the ideal of the monopolist. All nations must consume the same things, in proportion to their population. All mankind will then form a perfect democracy, supplied with rations from a single centre of administration, as is for their benefit; since they will then secure everything assigned to them at the lowest possible price. This was not a subject for me to broach with Rockefeller; but I ventured a hint in another direction, which I don't know whether he caught. In Avila, for I couldn't speak for the whole of Spain, we had passed from olive oil and candles almost directly to electricity. Gas we had never known, but petroleum had been used in cafés and shops, and perhaps in one room in each house, in a lamp over the centre table, under which burned the charcoal *brasero*; but even in Avila the electric bulb was beginning to supersede it. The world changed rapidly, when we once set it changing. Yet the Standard Oil Company had no cause for alarm. Motors were coming in, and petrol would be more in demand than ever.

Another day, in the act of sitting down at table, as if he had something important on his mind, Mr. Rockefeller formally addressed his son-in-law. "Charles, I heard that you had been buying a cord of wood, and I went down to the cellar to look at it. *That* isn't a cord of wood. When I was a young fellow I used to cut a cord of wood, and I know what it looks like. I don't need a tape-measure to measure it with. They are cheating you."

Poor Strong said nothing, and I, trying to be sympathetic, observed that sometimes, when values changed, dealers found it simpler to reduce the measure than to raise the price. As a baker's dozen is more than twelve, so a conventional cord of wood to-day at Lakewood might be less than a natural cord of wood in Mr. Rockefeller's boyhood. Besides, things come to seem smaller as we grow bigger; and wasn't it possible that a part of the wood might have been burned already? My wisdom, however, seemed to fall flat and we talked of something else.

Rockefeller himself had changed surprisingly to the eye. From looking much younger than he must have been in 1887, he now looked immeasurably old. He had lost all hair, eyebrows and eyelashes included, and wore a pepper and salt wig decidedly too small for him. His skin, too, was curiously wrinkled, and he was elaborately wrapped up for his long day on the golf-links. But I understood that he remained the active head of his Company, and had a private wire to his office for receiving information and giving orders.

Strong's marriage had been arranged in France, and after it, it was in France that he and his wife lingered. They learned French conscientiously, and to become perfectly fluent, they agreed always to speak French together at table. This habit grew upon Mrs. Strong, until she refused to speak English at all; and when I last saw her, both she and Margaret, then about ten years old, had French nurses and would speak nothing but French. This habit, and the habit of constantly returning to France, had not been adopted deliberately. Strong was as firmly convinced of the wisdom and duty of living in his own country as were his family and the Rockefellers: but the state of his wife's health and spirits seemed to demand a frequent season abroad, and later his own health and spirits seemed to demand it also. He had not given up his intended profession, and for one year was instructor in psychology at Cornell. Here his wife's health again interfered, and that position was given up. They would live at Lakewood, and he would become an associate professor—this could be easily arranged by Mr. Rockefeller—at Columbia. Nevertheless, they were almost always in France; and Strong became attached to a limited but well-chosen group of resorts, to which he introduced me: Versailles, Saint-Germain, Fontainebleau, Compiègne, Aix-les-Bains, and Glion in French Switzerland. To two of these, the first and the last, I often returned alone in later years, finding them quiet and inspiring.

After his wife's death, Strong made a heroic effort to settle down in New York. He took a flat in an apartment house with a general restaurant, on Fifth Avenue, and a governess for Margaret; and he undertook his proposed teaching at Columbia. In his eagerness to begin work, he arrived on the first morning rather early at his lecture room. As yet there was no one there. He would have a moment to rest, and to look over his notes, recalling the chief points to be made in due order, before the students began to come in. When he looked at his watch again, the appointed hour had arrived, but still no students. It was customary to allow five or ten minutes for them to straggle from one lecture room to another. Five minutes, ten minutes passed, and not a soul. Was nobody taking his course at all? He must not be precipitate. There might have been some mistake about the room. He would wait another five minutes. At a quarter past the hour, he resolutely gathered up his papers, put on his coat and hat, and thought of the Apostles bidden to shake the dust from their feet. But resentment and mortification, if he felt them, were soon buried deep among forgotten dreams. The feeling that rose to the surface was one of relief. He made his way to the College Office. There he explained to the clerk that he was Professor Strong. Could they inform him if anybody had elected his special course in psychology? They would see. They had a list of all elective courses, with the number of students that had chosen each. No: there was no tally against that special course in psychology. Perhaps it was rather a graduate course. They would let him know if there were inquiries about it.

On his way home the feeling of relief gained upon Strong. He had done his duty. His important but neglected theory of perception, more accurate and scientific than any other, could be better explained in a book than in lectures to beginners. Now he could devote the winter to that necessary task. For the sake of his work, he must be careful about his health. His mind always worked better in a mild climate. He would stop at the up-town office of the Italian Steamship Company and engage cabins on their first boat for Naples. That old convent above the road to Amalfi would be a place to suit him perfectly: quiet, sunny, simple and healthy.

Italian food and habits, however, proved less favourable for work than he had hoped. The demon that pursued Strong everywhere was *ennui*. In Paris, at least, he could, as he put it, "attend the Comédie Française"; and every day he could sit for an hour or two in front of a café, *la Régence, les Deux Magots,* or *la Closerie des Lilas.* That made a little change of scene; and sometimes American acquaintances would come and speak to him. Finally he took an apartment on the third floor at Number 9, Avenue de l'Observatoire. The place was clean and quiet, no passing, and nothing but sky and a wall of trees visible from the windows. The *salon* had been decorated in the style of Louis Seize, with silk panels, but Strong ordered the silk to be removed and the panels painted a dull white, to match the mouldings; and he "purchased" English furniture at Maples', of the sort usually covered with gay chintz, to which he was not accustomed. He had it covered instead with a strong reddish-gray stuff to match the curtains; and a great walnut bookcase was made to run along one whole wall. The room was brilliantly lighted by three large windows, yet somehow seemed sad and unfinished. Strong hadn't the secret of making himself comfortable, and here, as at Fiesole later, he was always thinking of going somewhere else for a change.

To tell his whole tragic history, and that of his daughter, would require volumes, with profound knowledge of families and circles that I have never frequented. It would carry me too far from the persons and places that have left vivid images in my mind. I therefore bequeath the subject to any novelist that it might tempt; for it would be a great subject. As a mere hint, however, of the perspectives to be disclosed I will describe a single episode that I happen to have witnessed.

Strong, and even more his daughter Margaret, were condemned to move within the magnetic field of the Rockefeller millions. Not a few roving atoms, positively electrified, circled and buzzed within it. Among Margaret's Parisian friends were the Marquise de Blanc-Blanc and her daughter. The Marquise had little money and only one son, already the Marquis and as yet unmarried. One day we had word that she was coming to see Monsieur Strong— he was laid up with paralysis of the legs—for an important consultation. Her daughter accompanied her, but at once carried Margaret off to some concert or to some dressmaker's, so as to leave the elderly people unembarrassed in discussing business.

Strong had expressly asked me to remain. When tea had been served, Madame de Blanc-Blanc, with a perceptible air of addressing the public, began to speak of her son. "We have," she said, "the most satisfactory reports of his work in Poland. You know, Messieurs, how much the government appreciated his services during the war. He is a young officer of intrepid character, with a quick temper and an iron will. He was invited to accept a very difficult, a very delicate post, the command of a company of criminals. His success with them was extraordinary. They became like sheep under him in camp, and like wolves in the battlefield. Men's energies, he thinks, should never be suppressed, no matter how violent. They must be turned into the right path. *Voilà tout!* What a lesson for his future wife, if she could only learn it! Now in Poland he has a task no less difficult, and he is meeting with equal success. Not criminals now, cadets. Cadets who have imbibed, under evil influences, wild notions of liberty. What is liberty? It is the right to do wrong whenever you choose. Yet my son inspires them with respect. He shows them the invincible order that God has established in the world. They learn to obey. They learn to command. Ah, he is a disciplinarian! Yet this severity in him goes with the tenderest heart, when once his heart has been touched. I, his mother, can assure you of it. He has been a good son. And they say a good son always makes a good husband."

Here Madame de Blanc-Blanc paused, sipped her cup of tea, nibbled the edge of a small cake, liked it, gobbled the rest of it, drank more tea, and proceeded.

"I regret that my son should have been called away before he could pay his respects to you, Monsieur, and to our dear Margaret. He knows through us how pretty, how simple, how charming, how exquisite and how appealing she is. A man of bold spirit and high temper, a man of action, especially loves gentleness and sweetness in women, and I think that a young girl like Margaret could not help admiring his soldierly qualities. Her tastes are as yet a little vague, and in the firmness of his character she would be relieved to find the natural solution to her indecision."

Here again the Marquise made a short pause, and then turned to me with evident premeditation.

"You, Monsieur," she said in a conciliatory tone, seeing that Strong hadn't at all melted, "being Spanish, must be a Catholic?"

"Yes, Madame, we are all still Catholics in Spain, at least nominally. But you know the character of this epoch. Most of us have lost our faith."

"Ah, I know it well. That is an effect of men's vices. It wears off. You will return to us some day." And glancing at me to estimate my age, she added, smiling, "You will return soon." Then, addressing Strong again, she went on.

"Ah, faith is so important! Without the faith, the family has no stability, no union, no security. No one recognises any obligation. Everyone is divorced. When public morality is so relaxed, there remains no law except within the Church. We must all be faithful children of the Church. Without that safeguard, no prudent man can venture to found a family."

At this point the bell rang. The young ladies returned from their outing, and almost immediately Madame de Blanc-Blanc and her daughter took their leave. No distinct proposal had been made. The lady hadn't come to ask for Margaret's hand, as we had expected. She had come to lay down a prior condition, namely, that Margaret should become a Catholic. This was not altogether a gratuitous suggestion. Margaret, when she had a Catholic governess, had shown a marked inclination to the Church, and still felt no hostility to it, only an incorrigible vagueness about everything. The whole affair lapsed; and it was well. Her proposed family, as I discovered by accident, were already making merciless fun of her behind her back.

I have mentioned that Bob Potter, when in the summer of 1892 I stayed with his family at Bar Harbor, was preoccupied with a love affair and with his approaching departure for Paris, to study at the Beaux-Arts. A little more than a year later, after the death

of Warwick, both matters were happily settled, and I went to
New York for his wedding. The bride's father, Mr. Nicholas Fish,
had been for years American Minister at Brussels, and there his
only daughter had been educated, learning to speak French and
German perfectly. With these accomplishments, with the outlook
that a diplomatic circle always opens out, and with her own
quick intelligence, she had become an unusually charming person;
and her ambitious parents expected that she should make a
brilliant match. But she fell in love with Bob Potter, quite intel-
ligibly, for he too was unusually *distingué* for a young New
Yorker; but alas the Fishes thought him penniless: he had only
just money enough to smoke good cigarettes. This, to the young
lady's romantic mind, seemed quite enough for their conjoint
happiness, and she threatened to run away with her lover to
Paris, if they refused to consent to her marriage. The matter was
compromised by arranging for a quiet wedding in the house with
no promise of an allowance from the Fishes for the future.

During the next few years, I saw the Bob Potters but rarely
in Paris, as I could be there only in transit; but these interviews
sufficed to show me that, in this case, the marriage of a friend,
far from being an obstacle to further good-fellowship, was an
aid to it, because Mrs. Potter proved to be as good a friend as
her husband. In 1897 we arranged to make a trip to Italy together; and Mrs. Potter secretly took Italian lessons, so as to be
able to rescue us helpless men in all our linguistic difficulties.
I had been in Italy two years earlier with Loeser; and this second
journey with the Potters, partly over the same ground, showed
me how important the human element is in our supposedly
abstract interests. I saw Venice and Rome, and the pictures
everywhere, in a new light. Bob was a professional architect, with
French training: he was dazzled by the picturesque and somewhat religiously moved by the primitives; that was his Anglo-
Saxon side; but he was shocked by the false façades of the
baroque churches; they were stage settings, allowed to exhibit
their shabby side. Yet in persons, as I would tell him, he appre-

ciated the charm and dignity of clothes, which were all *façades*
and *postiches*. Why shouldn't buildings, with their meagre material framework, expand also into decorative cloaks, ruffs, and
panaches? There was a kind of homage to the eye and to the ideal
in such a seemly masquerade. It presented what it would fain
be, and what it thought worthy of your attention. To seem less
grand would have been less courteous.

Bob taught me less about the arts than Loeser did; his knowledge was more limited. It was exclusively American and French.
But he taught me a great deal in matters of taste, because as
appeals to taste, as charming images, he appreciated all sorts of
perfection. The only difficulty here was the resulting sense of
frivolity and anarchy. The world became a carnival of butterflies.
Insight didn't penetrate to the organic, moral and physical energies that were expressed in each type of perfection, and that determined its rank and dignity in the real world. To have insisted
on this vital background, however, would have destroyed the
purity of taste, in its aristocratic independence; and there is a
subjective root to immediate pleasure in form and harmony just
as profound as the roots of the arts in the public world; more
profound, even, because the public world itself takes shape only in
obedience to the private capacities of the people that compose it.
The appeal, in a liberal mind, must ultimately be to pure taste, to
instinctive preference: and when Bob Potter, so very tall and thin,
so refined and so embarrassed, said *pfui!* or when he was religiously silent and evidently moved in the presence of something
exquisite, my own load was lifted, and I saw how instrumental
were all the labour and history of man, to be crowned, if crowned
at all, only in intuition.

In 1896–1897, when I was at King's College, some Harvard
friends studying at the Beaux-Arts asked me to spend the Christmas
holidays with them in Paris, at No. 3, Rue Soufflot. They could
offer me a room, and I might contribute my share to the common
cost of their table. It was a pleasant way of seeing something, and
hearing more, of student life in the Quartier Latin; and topo-

graphically and linguistically, it helped to make me feel at home when I went later to live there with Strong.

The young men at the Rue Soufflot were only club acquaintances; later I had a real friend, Lawrence Butler, also at the Beaux-Arts, whom I often saw and visited, before and after, in America, although always, as it were, in the character of an American in Europe. It was in mid-ocean, in June 1895, that I made his acquaintance, when he was perhaps nineteen years old. I heard that he had fallen down the steep and curving stairs that led below to the cabin and had sprained his ankle. When two or three days later, I crossed him in that very place, I spoke to him. He was getting on, he said, and could move about with a crutch. This was the beginning of a very long and very satisfactory friendship. He was a well-bred youth and always kept his place as a *young* friend even when no longer very young: and this discretion on his part turned the difference in our ages from a difficulty into a pleasure. He asked me to stay at his house, and introduced me to his family, especially to his mother and to his favourite aunt, wife of Stanford White, the architect. He became an architect himself, though somewhat casually as to the practice of his profession, and this was a double bond, because his knowledge fell in with my tastes and his leisure with my habits.

His interest in building was human, domestic, proprietary: he was always thinking of *living* in his houses and *praying* in his churches. For beneath the surface, which was a sort of helpless herd-instinct, there was natural piety in him. He was affectionate and he was religious. I could be happy in his company. I used to tell him, and he agreed, that he ought to have been an English country gentleman. In Long Island, where he lived and where his mother's family had a sort of estate (since Smithtown and Garden City had been originally their land) things were too changeful and urbanised. There was no room for a landlord: there was only a land company. Nevertheless he had an ample house in the midst of woods far from all others, and even a toy cathedral in Garden City, which he looked after with special care. And his somewhat inarticulate inner man had another outlet. He sang very well: at least, he had a good tenor voice that promised great things, and that he took pains to cultivate, as he took pains to study architecture. In Paris Jean de Reszke gave him lessons, telling him to sing out and to shout—which was exactly what he could have done well and heartily. But like my luckless hero—Oliver Alden, to whom he contributed this trait—he could sing only what he felt.

Falling short, which was almost universal among those of my friends that had artistic or intellectual pretensions, was not always due to the materialism of the age, or to other untoward circumstances; not always even to being smothered in circumstances ironically too favourable. The cause seemed sometimes to be innate: dreaminess or somnambulism in a soul too vegetative to resist transformation or to transform anything else into its own image. Is it the fog of the North? That is what Nordics seem to think when they flock to the South for inspiration. They are then initiated into southern sensuality, as if into a warmer mysticism; but that doesn't enable them to accomplish anything definite. Is it immaturity? Perhaps we might say so, in a complimentary sense. Externally, in action and learning, they may be more than competent, they may be Titanic; yet there may remain undeveloped resources and potentialities within them; so that they feel always unsatisfied, reject all finalities, and elude all discipline.

The most Nordic of my American friends was so Nordic that he seemed an American only by accident. When he went home, everything seemed to him unnecessary and inhuman; and he was content to live in Paris among poor artists and working people, with none of the comforts or social pleasures among which he had been bred. His father, Dr. Slade, was a well-known Boston physician; but his mother was a Fräulein Hensler; and whatever Scandinavian tallness, blondness, calmness, vagueness, and migratory instinct may have been latent in her must have been concentrated in her son Conrad. He was very good-looking in the expressionless, statuesque manner, rowed with the 'varsity crew and allowed himself to do as others did around him; but inwardly he was extraordinarily solitary and independent, as if he still lived among the fiords. He had warm poetic passions, very un-American; no scruples, no tipsy gregarious impulse about indulging them, and no ribaldry. It all seemed to him a wonderful work of nature, like the revolution of the stars; and leading afterwards what in Boston would have passed for a most irregular life, he preserved an air of perfect purity and serenity, his blue eyes as clear and his thoughts as speculative as ever.

For some instinctive reason that I won't attempt to fathom, he became attached to me, and told me his love-affairs, which were, as poetry should be, simple, sensuous, and short. He didn't move at all in Boston society. His lady-loves were mature prima-donnas, or country lasses, or city waifs. In Paris, where he went at once in the hope of becoming a sculptor, he grew comparatively domestic and monogamous, following the ancient dictates of nature. He wandered, when the spirit moved, through Italy and Greece, and southern France, always with the eye of an artist and a prophet, seeking to divine the secret of the beautiful. In time he became a devout admirer of Renoir, who he said was the greatest painter since Rubens: for he himself had dabbled in painting more than in sculpture, without visible results in either, but with much subjective deepening of sentiment and perception. He could never explain to me in words what was the merit of Renoir and the other moderns; the merits I could discern in them were evidently not to the point. About Greek art he did give me a hint, that my knowledge is too superficial for me to follow out or to test. It concerned the priority of the skeleton and the movement in figures: the visible detail, even the visible outline, was to *grow* out of the attitude, not merely to catch it, as in a modern caricature. In that sense, he made some designs in silver-point after Greek coins, which seemed to me truly classic in spirit. It is the dynamic symbol to the mind, conveyed by means as simple as possible, that works the miracle: as to the detail of the image, the eye itself is inattentive, and the artist wastes his science.

In later years Slade was an impressive figure, tall, calm, stately, bald, with a great curly yellow beard with grey hairs in it; he looked like Leonardo da Vinci. The only change in his mind was a new, natural, and fixed affection. He had a little boy, and was wrapped up in the child. Then step-motherly nature smote him in his tender spot. The boy developed a disease of the bones; the doctors said it might be cured. I was never told of the end, and heard only of the child being wheeled about in his bed from one sunny beach to another, in the hope that the rays of the sun might penetrate to his crumbling bones, and heal him.

Another American expatriate of marked personality, though not an expatriate in Europe, differed from most of my friends in being a Westerner, in having read my books, and in our acquaint-ance having been cemented not so much in youth as in mature years. Andrew Green had been my pupil in College, and I had once asked him, seeing how good he was at field sports, why he didn't go in for football or running. He replied that he cared nothing for sport of any kind, and only did his high jump and his broad jump for a private reason. Not then, but years later, he told me what that reason had been. He liked to belong to the athletic squad because at the training table he could see a particular friend of his every day, whereas otherwise they would never come across each other. This was because the friend was a leader in the College world and Green an outsider. I knew what that meant in College; and the interesting thing was Green's supreme contempt for such barriers and his deliberate way of surmounting them when he thought it worth while.

His self-reliance and clear will continued to show themselves later. He went into business in Chicago expressly to make money quickly and to escape from business, exactly as I went into teach-ing, but more successfully; for in a few years he had made his little pile, went alone to China, and hired a junk to live in, while he sailed leisurely up and down the great rivers and explored the wonders of that country. Moral contrasts, moral liberty: aesthetic contrasts, aesthetic potentiality *ad infinitum.* No wonder that he read my books and understood them! Yet that was only the critical side of my philosophy, which people in my day could appreciate, even if they didn't trust it. That which escaped them, and probably escaped Green, was the deeper presupposition, without which all criticism would be futile: the need of singleness of mind and complete loyalty to the particular virtue possible to each age and to each individual.

What monstrous selfishness, I hear the Bostonians saying, to drop your work, never to think of the needs of others, and to run away and hide and lead an empty life of idleness at the antipodes! Yes, Green and I were unmitigated egoists: we thought before acting. We asked what the needs of others really were, and whether we were doing them any good. Had we been conscious of doing great good, as the Bostonians were, that feeling would have filled us with reflected happiness and zeal, and we should have gone on doing it. But were business men in Chicago or professors of philosophy at Harvard working for the good of others? Weren't they working to earn money or to propagate their views? Weren't they invading the public aggressively, with their enterprise or their propaganda, to satisfy a private ambition? Philosophy is not a useful science, like mathematics, requisite for engineers. It is a remnant or an echo of prophetic inspirations launched in antiquity into an ignorant world, and it perpetuates the Babel there. And as to business, if this meant the exercise of a needful profession with the necessary moderate compensation, the business man might plod on like any other artisan under a just consumer's economy. But business enterprise and free speculation are not in that class; at best they are instances of the producer's economy, which by chance may launch something valuable, or reorganise economic machinery to the ultimate public advantage; but essentially they are private adventures prompted by private ambition.

With his strong satirical intelligence and his strong aesthetic sense, I have no doubt that Green's inland voyage in China was profitable to his mind. He needed a career; he was not an ornamental young man with an ornamental culture in an ornamental society. By way of settling down, he went to the British West Indies and undertook fruit-growing. Incidentally he found there an original solution to the problem of love and marriage. He formed an uncloudedly happy union—with a Negress. This was no mere tropical interlude of sensual captivity. The lady—he showed me her photograph—was a slight little thing, not darker than some white people, and he had the greatest respect for her native wisdom and even for her literary taste. He regretted not taking her with him on his travels, but she would not have been admitted to the hotels, not at least in the United States.

All was not well, however, in that tropical paradise. Green's fruit was exceptionally good, but couldn't find a market. The United Fruit Company with its steamers wouldn't accept it: there wasn't enough of it, and it wasn't packed in the popular way. The public preferred insipid standard fruit in great beds of cotton wool to luscious special fruits in smaller baskets. Here was the tyranny of the distributor's economy persecuting the independent American in his Eden.

I have commemorated many American friends, and not one man of letters, not one poet. The poets and the learned men remained, for the most part, in the category of acquaintances. There may have been a professional feminine jealousy between us that prevented a frank and hearty comradeship. Yet I have been keeping in reserve a learned friend and poet for whom I had a great admiration, although I am not sure that it was returned, except by a certain dutiful respect for my age and for the sphere of my interests. We lived in the same garden within the same wilderness, but not with the same emotions. I cared for the garden, and he respected the wilderness. I have mentioned him before, among my younger Harvard friends: Joe or (as he afterwards called himself) Trumbull Stickney.

It is not at Harvard, however, that I like to think of him, either when he was an undergraduate or when some ten years later he returned there to teach Greek. I remember him with more pleasure in Paris during that long interval when he bloomed freely under all sorts of influences stimulating to the spirit. In his nice lodgings overlooking the quiet side of the Luxembourg gardens, or in long walks along the Seine, he would reveal his gradual change of allegiance from classic antiquity to something more troubled and warmer, more charitable, closer to the groping mind of our day, to the common people, and to the problem of America. He had been privately educated; his Latin and Greek were not of the slovenly kind that passed muster at Harvard; he spoke and wrote French beautifully. Yet except for his friend Henri Hubert, who was an archeologist and very like a German, I don't think he felt in the French the sterling qualities of his own people, nor could he tolerate the English: he was too impatient and too subtle to put up with their slow mental tempo and their moral assurance. I could never bring him to do justice to Spartan or Roman virtue. He found it brutal and stupid. I think he distrusted me also for being a materialist, not so much in theory, for we never discussed that, but in my constant sense of the animal basis of spirit, and my disrespect for any claim on the part of spirit to govern the world. He feared me. I was a Mephistopheles masquerading as a conservative. I defended the past because once it had been victorious and had brought something beautiful to light; but I had no clear expectation of better things in the future. He saw looming behind me the dreadful spectres of truth and of death.

I wonder if Stickney suspected, when he shuddered thus at my philosophy, that he was helping to quicken in me the immense sympathy that he felt for the philosophy of India. When he died his friends very kindly asked me if there was any book of his that I should like as a memento. I had vivid mementoes already: a lovely edition of Virgil that he had given me and that has filled many a vacant half-hour, always with thanks to the giver; and also his own doctor's thesis on *Les Sentences dans la Poésie Grècque,* which was an attack on rhetoric, and gave me a constant warning of the dangers I ran in that direction. Still, for a further memento, I asked for his copy—which he had once lent me—of Gade's *Die Samkyaphilosophie.* The gist of these Indian studies was given also in one of Stickney's most interesting poems. A Hindu finds himself in ancient Athens, bewildered by the noise of trade, politics and war, elbowed aside by the rude youths, forsaken and starving. At last in a quiet lane he knocks at a modest door. It is opened by a venerable old man. The stranger is introduced into a walled garden, his bowl is filled with pure rice, and he is left alone to meditate by the trickling fountain. The old man was Epicurus.

Stickney died comparatively young. When he returned to Harvard I was expecting to leave, and perhaps less interested in the life of the place than I had been in the old days, while he was busier than in Paris and preoccupied with matters not within my horizon. In any case, we seldom saw each other. When by chance we met, I felt that my society disturbed him. This would not have troubled me in itself or on my own account. I was hardened to the eclipse of friendships, and observed it without bitterness. The sun and the planets have their times for shining: we mustn't expect them to be always in our hemisphere. Yet something else did distress me in Stickney, quite for his own sake. I felt that he was forcing himself to play a part, a painful part like that of a convert who tries to live up to his new faith and to forgive his new associates for unintentionally wounding him at every turn. It is tragic in such cases to look back to the lovely familiar world that one has abandoned for being false or wicked, and to seek in vain for compensations and equivalents in the strange system that one has decided to call good and true. So Newman must have suffered when he became a Catholic. When would the ivy mantle these new brick walls, or the voice modulate the Latin liturgy as it had done the English? In some such case I imagined Stickney to find himself, now that he was back in America. His conscience had compelled him to swear allegiance to his country and to his work; but he was not at home; he had always been an exotic, warmed and watered in a greenhouse; and the harsh air and tough weeds of his native heath tried him severely. But perhaps the suffering that he endured was not due to any such moral disharmony: this may be merely my supposition. It may have been simply overwork, and the beginnings of the tumor in the brain that was about to kill him. Still that tumor itself was a sign of maladaptation. The too delicate plant, that had already flowered, couldn't endure the change of soil and of temperature, and bred a parasite that choked it.

CHAPTER VIII

OFFICIAL CAREER AT HARVARD

ON MY return to America in 1888 I at once consulted
Royce as to my thesis for the doctorate, and suggested
for a subject the philosophy of Schopenhauer, because
Schopenhauer was the German author that I liked
most and knew best. The wise Royce shook his head. That might
do, he said, for a master of arts, not for a doctor of philosophy.
Instead, he proposed Lotze. I had read Lotze's *Microcosmos* and
liked a certain moderation and orthodoxy that pervaded it, without deeply respecting its principles or its conclusions. Lotze was
a higher form of Palmer. But Royce said that his other books
were more technical and his metaphysics rather Leibnitzian. That
sounded better. I agreed, procured the complete works of Lotze,
and set to work to read, digest and annotate them, composing a
running summary and commentary, out of which my thesis might
be afterwards drawn. It was a pleasant task, not at all brain-
racking. I was soon absorbed in it, living in complete retirement
at my mother's at Roxbury. For exercise I would walk to Boston
or to Cambridge. I went to weekly seminars, admirable stimulants,
given by James and Royce. James read to us from the manuscript,
chapter by chapter, his new *Principles of Psychology*; while with
Royce we read Hegel's *Phaenomenologie des Geistes*.

I wish now that my thesis might have been on Hegel; it would
have meant harder work, and it would have been more inadequate; yet it would have prepared me better for professional controversies and for understanding the mind of my time. Lotze was
stillborn, and I have forgotten everything that I then had to read
in him and to ponder. I liked Hegel's *Phaenomenologie*; it set me

planning my *Life of Reason;* and now I like even his *Logik,* not the dialectical sophistry in it, but the historical and critical lights that appear by the way. I could have written, even then, a critical thesis, say on *Logic, Sophistry, and Truth in Hegel's Philosophy.* This would have knit my own doctrine together at the beginning of my career, as I have scarcely had the chance of doing at the end. My warhorse would not have been so much blinded and hidden under his trappings.

My dull thesis on Lotze was duly accepted, and I was told that I was the most normal doctor of philosophy that they had ever created. Retrospectively I may have been, because most of the candidates had been lame ducks; but prospectively, as a doctor who teaches, I was to prove unsatisfactory and irregular. They may have suspected as much; but they were kind masters and not in a position to make great demands. They accepted me thankfully in spite of my lack of a vocation for teaching; and at once a place was made for me among them. James wished to relieve himself of his course on Locke, Berkeley, and Hume: I was invited to give it for him at a salary of $500. This was an opening, and in itself a boon. With my allowance I should have $1000 for the year. I could return to live in the Yard and (if the appointment were renewed) I could go to Europe for the summer.

On the second day that I met my class of three or four pupils, the door unexpectedly opened and in walked President Eliot, as straight and solemn as *Hamlet's* Ghost. I got up from my chair, confused but without saying audibly "Angels and ministers of grace, defend me." Eliot said dryly: "Professor Bowen has resigned. Only three students had elected his course on Descartes, Spinoza, and Leibnitz, but we don't like to suppress any course that has been announced in the elective pamphlet. I therefore have come to ask you if you would be able and willing to give that course also, in addition to this; and the payment would be the same, another $500." I replied, quite reassured: "Thank you very much. May I have until tomorrow morning to think the matter over, when I will call at your office and give you the answer?" He said that would do perfectly, and looking somewhat less ghostlike he took his leave.

I don't know how clear the rest of my lecture on the life of John Locke may have been; but somehow it came to an end: and it was easy for me, once alone and fortified with a little food, to decide that I could manage to give that other course also. I should have one lecture a day at a convenient hour in the morning. The professors whose place I was taking were old rogues and had chosen eleven o'clock, the best hour for teaching: because it gave you an hour or two before your lecture to think over your subject and look up any necessary point, and luncheon not long after. Personally that pleased me; but professionally—and I now had a competitive profession—it was disadvantageous, because that hour was occupied by half the favourite courses for under-graduates. However, a small class with graduate students in it was perhaps best for a beginning. It reduced the physical strain, as well as the already small distance between the teacher and the pupils. We could philosophise together. And financially I was set at ease. If things went on like that, I could satisfy all my tastes and requirements.

I am told that in my first years I was a very bad lecturer. Cer-tainly my talks were desultory, not rich in information and not well arranged for taking notes. My interest was never in facts or erudition, but always in persons and ideas. I wished to re-think the thoughts of those philosophers, to understand why they took the direction they took, and then to consider the consequences and implications of taking that direction. At bottom, I was always discovering and developing my own philosophy. This at first was inarticulate, latent in me but not consistently thought out; and I can well believe that my pupils didn't understand it, and gathered only vague notions of the authors I discussed: for I doubt that the texts were much studied directly in those days at Harvard. The undergraduates were thinking only of examinations and relied on summaries in the histories of philosophy and on lecture notes. Nevertheless, even at the beginning, my pupils were attentive and friendly; and eventually my way of thinking had some influence on some of them. If they had read the texts assigned, their time on the whole would not have been wasted.

I think, however, that lectures, like sermons, are usually unprofitable. Philosophy can be communicated only by being evoked: the pupil's mind must be engaged dialectically in the discussion. Otherwise all that can be taught is the literary history of philosophy, that is, the *phrases* that various philosopheres have rendered famous. To conceive what those phrases meant or could mean would require a philosophical imagination in the public which cannot be demanded. All that usually exists is familiarity with current phrases, and a shock, perhaps of pleased curiosity but more often of alarm and repulsion, due to the heterodoxy of any different phrases.

It may be conceit on my part but I think I was the only free and disinterested thinker among the Harvard philosophers. The others were looking in philosophy either for science or for religion. They were as tolerant as I, or more so, of differences in opinion; but only as you are tolerant of all the kinds and sizes of shoes in a shop window. You are willing to have all varieties of shoes offered for selection; but you look for a single pair of shoes to choose for yourself, to pay for, to own, to wear, and to wear out or to be buried in; and you examine that vast assortment anxiously, with an unquiet mind, lest you should choose the wrong pair. Those liberal minds were thirsting for a tyrant. I, being a materialist, cynic, and Tory in philosophy, never dreamt of rebelling against the despotism of nature; and I accepted having feet, ugly and insufficient as they might be, because it would be much worse not to have them. But as to shoes, I have and mean to keep a free mind, and would be willing to go barefoot if it were convenient or if it were the fashion. So I believe, compulsorily and satirically, in the existence of this absurd world; but as to the existence of a better world, or of hidden reasons in this one, I am incredulous, or rather, I am critically sceptical; because it is not difficult to see the familiar motives that lead men to invent such myths. So I survey all those high-heeled ladies' shoes and all those invalids' fur-lined slippers with a smile: I might have worn the first once in some masquerade, and may yet wear the second in my decrepitude; but they are accidental paraphernalia. So are all systems of philosophy, so are all logical languages, so are all allegories and images of sense. The study of them is a part of the humanities, initiating us into the history of human life and mind; it is not the pursuit of science or salvation.

This divergence between me and my environment was not merely one of opinion: it interfered with my career and with the natural growth of my mind. President Eliot, who was an anti-humanist, once said to me that we should teach the *facts*, not merely convey *ideas*. I might have replied that the only facts in philosophy were historical facts, namely, the fact that people had or had had certain ideas. But of course I only smiled and took note of *his idea*. The history of philosophy is the only philosophy that should be taught in a university. *Systems* of philosophy are taught only by sects or by individuals setting out to be prophets and to found a sect. I now have a system of philosophy which I hadn't dreamt of then, although the reasons for it lay all in me; but this system is not intended to found a sect and will never do so. It aspires to be only a contribution to the humanities, the expression of a reflective, selective, and free mind. But I was living among sects, or among individuals eager to found sects; and I should have seemed to them vague and useless if I had been merely a historian and critic in philosophy. I was expected and almost compelled to be "constructive" or "creative," or to pretend to be so. Or as they put it, I must take up some special subject, physiological psychology (supposed to be a science) or Greek philosophy, if I trained myself to write a history, like Zeller's. A man must have a "specialty."

I was a kind of poet, I was alive to architecture and the other arts, I was at home in several languages: "aesthetics" might be regarded as my specialty. Very well: although I didn't have, and haven't now, a clear notion of what "aesthetics" may be, I undertook to give a course in that subject. It would help to define my status. I gave it for one or two years and then I wrote out the substance of it in a little book: *The Sense of Beauty*. The manuscript of this book went from local publisher to publisher, and was rejected. I had given up all expectation of getting it published when Barrett Wendell, always friendly to me and the humanities, sent me word that he thought Scribner's would accept it. I sent it to Scribner's; it was printed and did not prove a financial loss to the publisher, although it had neither a large sale nor a warm reception from the critics. However, it was a book, *a fact*; and it established pleasant relations between me and Scribner's which have lasted for fifty years.

My sham course in "Aesthetics" had served its purpose and so had my little book. Although looked at askance by the President I was reappointed year by year, and then for three years at a time with a salary of $1500 and a seat in the Faculty, which I seldom occupied. My life and pleasures were still those of a student; I lived on intimate terms with a knot of undergraduates; I went to "parties," chiefly dinner parties in Boston. In time I undertook another "constructive" or "creative" course entitled "Philosophy of History": this title attracted larger numbers, perhaps thirty men, many of them Jews: and it prepared the ground for my *Life of Reason*. But what then most enticed me in philosophy was Plato, and I had always had a great respect for Aristotle, especially for his *Ethics* and *Politics*; and out of these, with the help of a glance at Bacon, Locke, Montesquieu, and Taine (authors that my pupils could be expected to read a little) I composed my lectures on the "philosophy of history," which for me meant no providential plan of creation or redemption, but merely retrospective politics; a study of what had formed the chief interests of mankind in various epochs. Religion—my strong point in history—naturally came in, and I treated it, I think, without giving offence in any quarter.

In the winter and spring of 1896 I became convinced that the time had come for calling a halt. I had been an instructor for seven years: should I ask for promotion or look for another place? In my private life too there had come a crisis: my young friends had become too young for me and I too old for them; I had made a private peace with all religions and philosophies; and I had grown profoundly weary of polite society and casual gaieties. Then it chanced that at the English Cambridge they had established a new category of "advanced students," and Lowes Dickinson and Nathaniel Wedd of King's College had suggested that I might be admitted there. Here was an opportunity to break away from my second college life, already too much prolonged, yet continue my academic career, study Greek philosophy, live a while in England, and in the holidays re-visit Italy more at leisure than in 1895. I therefore asked Eliot for a year's leave of absence without a salary, after which I would return to Harvard for one more year; and then, unless I were appointed assistant professor, I should look for a place elsewhere.

This project was carried out. When I returned to America in September 1897, I settled down at my mother's, now no longer at Roxbury but in Longwood, within walking distance of Harvard. Electric cars were also available. It was a most economical way of living, practically with no expense except for luncheon, fifty cents at the Colonial Club. My relations with undergraduates and with Boston society, although renewed, were renewed on a new basis. I no longer played the familiar companion or the young man about town. I was simply an elderly mentor or an occasional guest. I began to give a new course, Philosophy 12, on Plato and Aristotle in English, which remained my chief subject until almost the end. I lectured on the *Republic*, the *Phaedras*, the *Symposium*, the *Phaedo* and the *Nicomachaean Ethics*. These books were assigned to be read in translation; and the essays submitted to me upon them by my pupils, usually not twenty in number, were sometimes excellent. I have given an imaginary fragment of one of them in *The Last Puritan*.

Early in 1898 I was appointed assistant professor for five years, at $2000 a year. When this appointment expired, it was renewed on the usual terms; but actually it ran only for four years, when at last I was made a full professor, with a salary of $4000. Moreover, two of those four years, 1904–1906, I spent abroad: the first, a sabbatical year, in Italy and the East, the second at Paris as exchange professor at the Sorbonne. This second lap of my assistant professorship was therefore much pleasanter and more varied than the first: and the last lap of all, during the four and a half years of my active professorship, also passed imperceptibly: I knew they were the last lap, and the exhilaration of finishing the race, even if not with an outward victory, was an inward comfort.

My official career at Harvard was thus completed without a break. When I resigned my professorship my name had figured in the Harvard Catalogue, in one capacity or another, for thirty years. Yet that long career had been slow and insecure, made in an atmosphere of mingled favour and distrust. My relations with President Eliot and with other influential persons had always been strained. I had disregarded or defied public opinion by not becoming a specialist, but writing pessimistic, old-fashioned verses, continuing to range superficially over literature and philosophy, being indiscernibly a Catholic or an atheist, attacking Robert Browning, prophet of the half-educated and half-believing, avoiding administrative duties, neglecting the intelligentsia, frequenting the society of undergraduates and fashionable ladies, spending my holidays abroad, and even appearing as a witness in the disreputable Russell trial. At the same time, in private, I had breathed the pleasantest airs of sympathy and friendship. My philosophic colleagues had supported me, my old friends had been faithful, appreciative, and always hospitable, my new friends had multiplied in numbers and influence, my books, though received coldly at first, had attained a certain reputation. I was still disliked, but I was swallowed.

Harvard, in those the waning days of Eliot's administration, was getting out of hand. Instruction was every day more multifarious and more chaotic; athletics and college life developed vigorously as they chose, yet not always pleasantly; and the Graduate and associated Schools worked each in its own way, with only nominal or financial relations with Harvard College. In public opinion a reaction was beginning to appear; but it had not taken visible form before the change of Presidents. Government was monarchical; but a monarch can hardly decide everything on his own initiative; he depends on vested interests and traditional advisers for his policy, and on committees and agents for carrying it out. Eliot, autocrat as he was, depended on the Fellows, half a dozen business men in Boston who were the legal proprietors of Harvard, and especially on one of them, the Treasurer, who managed the vast investments of the Foundation. He was also somewhat controlled by the Board of Overseers, elected representatives of the graduates. All this formed an immense tangle of disconnected activities: the President was driving not a four but a forty-in-hand. Most numerous and stately, but tamest, in this working menagerie was the Faculty of Arts and Sciences. Although a member of it, I hardly knew what were its attributions or privileges. The most interesting and clearest business of the meetings was to hear what the President might tell us of the action or prospects of the moment; and it was from him that any likely measures emanated. Sometimes, very rarely, there was clear opposition or even a hostile vote. That might produce a postponement, but could hardly arrest the movement of reform that he had undertaken in the interest of democratic arrangements and quick returns. Education meant preparation for professional life. College, and all that occupied the time and mind of the College, and seemed to the College an end in itself, seemed to President Eliot only a means. The end was service in the world of business.

The Faculty meetings were an object lesson to me in the futility of parliamentary institutions. Those who spoke spoke badly, with imperfect knowledge of the matter in hand, and simply to air their prejudices. The rest hardly listened. If there was a vote, it revealed not the results of the debate, but the previous and settled sentiments of the voters. The uselessness and the poor quality of the whole performance were so evident that it surprised me to see that so many intelligent men—for they were intelligent when doing their special work—should tamely waste so much time in keeping up the farce. But parliamentary institutions have a secret function in the Anglo-Saxon world, like those important glands that seem useless to a superficial anatomy. There is an illusion of self-government, especially for members of the majority; there is a gregarious sense of safety and reassurance in being backed, or led, or even opposed by crowds of your equals under conventional safeguards and guarantees; and there is solace to the vague mind in letting an anonymous and irresponsible majority be responsible for everything. You grumble but you consent to put up with the course that things happen to take. It is not as if the ruling party had intended the result: they gave a little push, and evolution has done the rest.

The Harvard Faculty was not divided into parties. Being appointed by the President, who was the irremovable executive, they were more like officials, naturally respectful to their chief; but some of them had personal views on education and public policy which they couldn't refrain from airing in voting on the President's reforms. I seldom went to the meetings, and spoke only once, when asked a direct question touching a degree to be granted out of course to an absent undergraduate, Bayard Cutting, who had left college to be private secretary to the American Ambassador in London, and had written a thesis on David Hume as a substitute for his unfinished work. I had read the thesis, and gave my opinion on it. The degree was granted. Bayard Cutting had been one of my young friends at the time when, to my sense, they were birds of passage. He married Lady Sybil Cuffe, who after his death lived in the Villa Medici, close to Strong's villa at Fiesole. Their only child, Iris, who herself lost her only child, wrote a book on Leopardi, for which she asked me to supply a "Foreword." It is a strange sadness that hangs for me now over all that history. An international intelligentsia adrift amid unsuspected currents and wrecked one by one on the reefs of El Dorado.

Did the members of the Harvard Faculty form an intellectual society? Had they any common character or influence? I think not. In the first place they were too much overworked, too poor, too much tied up in their modest homes. Nor had they had, like old-fashioned English dons, a common education, and written Latin hexameters and pentameters. I believe there were some dinner clubs or supper clubs among the elder professors: but I never heard of any idea or movement springing up among them, or any literary fashion. It was an anonymous concourse of coral insects, each secreting one cell, and leaving that fossil legacy to enlarge the earth.

Beyond my philosophical colleagues I had hardly any acquaintances among the professors, except Professor Toy, because of his wife, who was a friend and frequent hostess of mine for many years. Even among the younger teachers I had few friends. One, however, stood in a position very much like mine, in that teaching at Harvard was for him a sort of expedient, rather than a chosen profession, and that his interests and the subject he taught touched European history and politics. "Archie" Coolidge, as he was called, had been booked for a diplomatic career, and was actually secretary to some Legation, I believe in Vienna, when for a private reason he threw up his post and returned to Boston. He had been engaged to be married, and the young lady, in his absence, had changed her mind. The poor man, who was deeply in love, lost his head completely, and thought that by personal protestations he could bring her round. Unfortunately, Archie's person was his weak point. He had family, money, intelligence, experience and accomplishments, spoke even Russian, and had travelled all over the world. When I once asked him why he was going to Kamchatka he replied, "I haven't yet been there." But in his physique and manner, though there was nothing markedly wrong, he seemed not quite normal, as if nature had put him together carelessly with insufficient materials, and had managed to make him go, but only by fits and jerks. And his mind, too, while well stocked and perfectly reasonable, seemed somehow thin, as if there were no central sun in it, no steady light and centre of gravity. Anyhow, his return only made matters worse: he had left his post without excuse or permission and couldn't resume it. To fill up his time and to try to distract his mind from his terrible disappointment, people suggested that he should teach for a while at Harvard. In these circumstances he came to live in Cambridge, ate at the Colonial Club, and gathered a circle of young friends about him who were often my friends too. In these ways we were thrown together. We had a common *milieu* at Harvard and a common outlook into the great world, and his wider information always lent interest to what he said; but whether because of diplomatic reserve or of having a purely documentary mind, he never betrayed his deeper allegiance in politics and morals. American diplomacy was as yet innocent, an entertaining sport or holiday for home politicians; at most a little commercial or missionary enterprise might be connected with it. My relations with Archie Coolidge therefore remained always pleasant and unimportant.

Of the older Harvard worthies I was on good terms with two, Charles Eliot Norton and William James. They were perhaps the most distinguished, but not the most trusted; they too had had to be swallowed. They too, although in my time their position was established, had seemed at first questionable and irregular. Norton, with ten generations of local magnates behind him, had his inspirations and sympathies far away. He worshipped Greek art, he worshipped Christian art, he loved refined English life. He spoke rarefied English. He loved Turner and Ruskin. His personal friends were Burne-Jones, Carlyle and Matthew Arnold. To me he showed the most exquisite paternal kindness. He encouraged and praised me whenever he could do so conscientiously: when he wished to warn or admonish me, he did it through his nephew, Frank Bullard, who was one of my best friends. He feared that I lived too much among dreams. When my extravagant drama, *Lucifer*, was published, I of course sent him a copy; and in thanking me he said that the value of it, in its substance, could not be known for the present, but that the versification was that of a master. This was flattery, but not absurd flattery, from an old man with Victorian standards in literature. "Versification" was the right word in this case, for mine is not what English-speaking people now call poetry: it is not a dissolution and fresh concretion of language. Verbally it is ordinary speech made rhythmical and harmonious. Where I break through convention, whether in verse or prose, is in my themes or sentiments, as here in *Lucifer*. Norton very modestly and prudently refused to judge on this point. He was not at home in metaphysics or religion; the dissolution of common sense and a fresh concretion of myths seemed to him, I suspect, a waste of time. Here he had the prejudices of a positivist; yet he was cultivated and courteous enough to conceal them when speaking to a young man, like me, who possessed imagination without trusting it to reveal truth. My scepticism reconciled him to my mythology, and made him more benevolent than he might have been to a fanatic; and he was always benevolent, even when grieved.

At the funeral of C. C. Everett, an old professor at the Harvard Divinity School, a Unitarian and a Fichtean, I happened to join Norton as we came out. "All this," he said with his usual sweetness, "must make a sad impression on you." I admitted that of course death was sad, but my acquaintance with Everett had been very slight, and it was not, at his age, a loss to our philosophical forces. "I don't mean the death of Dr. Everett. He was a good man, but he had no intellect-u-al power" (Norton pronounced with this extreme accuracy, but easily; and the habit sometimes gave a satirical force to his words). "What I meant," he continued, "was this survival of superstition among us. Mr. Cruthers has compared Dr. Everett to an eagle." Cruthers was the Unitarian minister in Cambridge and couldn't help being saturated with complacency and with unctuous flattery of everything mediocre: but he was hardly superstitious. To compare that old theological or anti-theological professor to St. John was absurd or, if you like, blasphemous: but the primary evil was the insensibility to St. John, not the obituary fulsomeness about Everett. Fulsomeness and complete lack of perspective had become habitual in American appreciation of Americans. There was a conspiracy of flattery; free lances were sometimes broken against it, but the phalanx might be expected to sweep the field, and to form public opinion. This, I think, was what made Norton sad.

Norton was president of the Tavern Club, which occasionally gave dinners in compliment to some person not a member. I recollect two such occasions on which Norton presided, and made the inevitable complimentary speech. Here he ran serious danger of falling into the "superstition" that saddened him in others. But he had a means of safety; he was not without wit, a mild irony that saved him from platitudes. One dinner was in honour of John Fiske, a local disciple of Herbert Spencer, who had passed from popular science to history, and published first a book on *Cosmic Evolution* and later a *History of the United States*. Norton, in his speech, after paddling about as usual in the backwaters of anecdote, said that Fiske had been an industrious author. "I wish his style had been a little chastened,[1] but the substance has been solid. He began by giving us a history of the universe; he proceeded to give us a history of the United States; and we may hope that in this upward progress he may end by giving us a history of Cambridge, Massachusetts." The distrust of speculative pretensions, the positivism, the love of home and country (which was profound in Norton, and the cause of his melancholy) were all expressed in these words, with which he ended his speech.

The other dinner was in honour of Rudyard Kipling. Hard luck for Norton, I thought at first; why hadn't he pretended to be ill and let someone else praise what must be odious to him? But not at all. Norton was quite happy, not in his remarks but in his mood. He had known and liked Kipling's mother, and he was prepared *a priori* to accept the bard of imperialism as a distinguished lover of humanity. Kipling sympathised with the Hindus; he was democratic; a glib prophet with warm feelings and popular

[1] Norton said "chassened," doubtless to indicate that the word means castigated and not made chaste.

rhythms; and Norton was so saturated with morality that when anything seemed to him morally right, he couldn't notice whether it was vulgar. That which seemed paramount in Norton, his fastidious retrospective nostalgia, was in reality secondary. Fundamental still was his fidelity to the conscience of his ancestors.

Concerning William James, I have made sundry scattered observations for the public without attempting a fair total portrayal of the man or of his philosophy: neither he nor his philosophy lent themselves to being summed up. But here, where I am portraying only my own impressions, I may add a word more about the feelings that he excited in me. I trusted his heart but I didn't respect his judgment. I admired his masculine directness, his impressionistic perceptions, and his picturesque words. I treasured his utterances on the medical side of things, such as that the best way to understanding the normal is to study the abnormal. All this belonged to his independent, radical, naturalistic temper, to his American sense of being just born into a world to be rediscovered. But he was really far from free, held back by old instincts, subject to old delusions, restless, spasmodic, self-interrupted: as if some impetuous bird kept flying aloft, but always stopped in mid-air, pulled back with a jerk by an invisible wire tethering him to a peg in the ground. The general agreement in America to praise him as a marvellous person, and to pass on, is justified by delight at the way he started, without caring where he went. In fact, he got nowhere; and for that reason his influence could be great and beneficent over those who knew him, but soon seemed to become untraceable in the confused currents of the world. I, for instance, was sure of his goodwill and kindness, of which I had many proofs; but I was also sure that he never understood me, and that when he talked to me there was a manikin in his head, called G. S. and entirely fantastic, which he was addressing. No doubt I profited materially by this illusion, because he would have liked me less if he had understood me better; but the sense of that illusion made spontaneous friendship impossible. I was uncomfortable in his presence. He was so extremely natural that there was no knowing what his nature was, or what to expect next; so that one was driven to behave and talk conventionally, as in the most artificial society. I found no foothold, I was soon fatigued, and it was a relief to be out again in the open, and alone.

The feeling of walking on quicksands became almost worse when what he said was in harmony with my feelings than when it was opposed to them. If he talked about ghosts, I didn't care what turn his fancy might take; he would surely be graphic if he described those ghosts dramatically, and he would not in the least disturb me if he suggested that they might now be stealthily gliding behind our chairs. When, on the contrary, he said something that seemed to corroborate my own sentiments, I feared a trap. Let me describe one instance. One afternoon in the autumn of 1898 we were standing in Palmer's library after a brief business meeting, and conversation turned on the terms of peace imposed by the United States on Spain after the Cuban war. James was terribly distressed. Addressing himself rather to Palmer, who was evidently enjoying the pleasant rays of the setting sun on his back, and the general spacious comfort of his library (he then lived in the old President's house at the corner of Quincy Street), James said he felt he had lost his country. Intervention in Cuba might be defended, on account of the perpetual bad government there and the sufferings of the natives. But the annexation of the Philippines, what could excuse that? What could be a more shameless betrayal of American principles? What could be a plainer symptom of greed, ambition, corruption and imperialism? Palmer smiled approvingly, yet he saw the other side. Every thesis has its antithesis: the synthesis would be ultimately for the general good, and the course of history was the true Judgment of God. Those were not his words, but his little vague commonplaces could be so interpreted by anyone behind the scenes.

As for me, I couldn't help resenting the schoolmaster's manner of the American government, walking switch in hand into a neighbour's garden to settle the children's quarrels there, and to make himself master of the place. Yet that has been the way of the world since the beginning of time, and if anything could be reasonably complained of, it was the manner of the intrusion rather than the fact of it. For me the tragedy lay in Spanish weakness rather than in American prepotency: Uncle Sam would have continued to regard all men as free and equal, if all other men had looked as strong as himself. Yet Spanish weakness comes only of Quixotic frailty, due to tragic and comic disproportion between the spirit and the flesh. The resources of the country and people would not be materially contemptible if they were wisely husbanded, and devoted to developing at home, under native inspiration, an austere, passionate and intelligent life for the soul. The Spanish empire overseas had been glorious enough, and the end, harshly as it grazed against my family memories, seemed to me almost a relief. I am not one of those who dream of a Spanish America subject in future to the influence of the mother country. Let Spanish America, I say, and let English America be as original as they can: what is best in Spain, as what is best in England, cannot migrate.

I was therefore much more at peace about this pathetic war than was William James, or than was "Aunt Sarah," whom I had visited in the previous June, on my way to Europe. She, the mother of the heroic Colonel Shaw of the Massachusetts coloured regiment, even before there was talk of the Philippines was scandalised at McKinley. A large American flag was hanging in the street opposite her windows. "I wish I could pull that down!" she cried, condescending a little perhaps to my Spanish sympathies, but chiefly moved by the betrayal, as she thought it, of true American principles. "No, no," I protested, "the thing is sad for Spain, but was inevitable sooner or later. McKinley is only yielding to *force majeure*." Nor was I alone in this feeling. When the armistice was announced, I ran down to Avila from Paris. As we approached the frontier a merry crowd of young trippers, well-dressed men and girls, filled the train with laughter and shrill cries; they were Spanish people on an excursion to San Sebastian for the bullfight. At Irun I was not even asked for my passport. And in Avila I found everybody as resigned and sadly philosophical as I, or as any ancient sage.

Why was William James so much upset by an event that the victims of it could take so calmly? Because he held a false moralistic view of history, attributing events to the conscious ideals and free will of individuals: whereas individuals, especially in governments, are creatures of circumstance and slaves to vested interests. These interests may be more or less noble, romantic, or sordid, but they inevitably entangle and subjugate men of action. The leaders couldn't act or maintain themselves at the head of affairs if they didn't engage the impulses at work in the mass, or in some part of it. Catastrophes come when some dominant institution, swollen like a soap-bubble and still standing without foundations, suddenly crumbles at the touch of what may seem a word or an idea, but is really some stronger material force. This force is partly that of changing circumstances, partly that of changing passions, but passions are themselves physical impulses, maturing in their season, and often epidemic, like contagious diseases. James, who was a physician and a pragmatist, might have been expected to perceive this, and did perceive it at moments: yet the overruling tradition in him was literary and theological, and he cried disconsolately that he had lost his country, when his country, just beginning to play its part in the history of the world, appeared to ignore an ideal that he had innocently expected would always guide it, because this ideal had been eloquently expressed in the Declaration of Independence. But the Declaration of Independence was a piece of literature, a salad of illusions. Admiration for the noble savage, for the ancient Romans (whose republic was founded on slavery and war), mixed with the quietistic maxims of the Sermon on the Mount, may inspire a Rousseau but it cannot guide a government. The American Colonies were rehearsing independence and were ready for it. That was what gave to the Declaration of Independence its timeliness and political weight. In 1898 the United States were rehearsing domination over tropical America and were ready to organise and to legalise it; it served their commercial and military interests and their imaginative passions. Such antecedents and such facilities made intervention sooner or later inevitable. Domination was the implicit aim, whatever might be the language or even the thoughts of individuals. William James had not lost his country; his country was in good health and just reaching the age of puberty. He had merely lost his way in its physiological history.

James's displeasure at the seizure of the Philippines was therefore, from my point of view, merely accidental. It did not indicate any sympathy with Spain, or with anything in history that interests and delights me. On the contrary, it was an expression of principles entirely opposed to mine; much more so than the impulses of young, ambitious, enterprising America. These impulses may ignore or even insult all that I most prize, but they please me nevertheless for their honest enthusiasm and vitality. James himself, like a good American, was full of honest enthusiasm and vitality, and besides was sensitive, learned, and a perfect gentleman. In him too I sympathised with the initial phases and moral promptings of his thoughts. The bird flew up bravely; but when my eye was able to follow his flight, I saw him flutter, and perch, as if he had lost his energy, on some casual bough. His inspiration, even in science, was that of romanticism.

Less distinguished than Norton or James were two or three stray souls in official Harvard with whom I inwardly sympathised, perhaps without much personal contact. They too were barely tolerated by the authorities; they had cut peep-holes, as it were, in the sacred tabernacle through which to view the natural landscape. One of these was Barrett Wendell. He belonged to a little group of free spirits, almost of wits, in the Harvard class of 1877, and had been one of the founders of the *Lampoon*. His affections were local and his ideals conservative. He allowed himself little eccentricities, had tricks of intonation mistaken by many for an attempt to speak like the English; he admired the airs of the early nineteenth century, cared for birth and good breeding, and in literature for mannishness and good form, "rum and de-corum," as he once put it, and for tenderness and distinction of feeling. Yet he had no real distinction himself; his mind and his attachments, like his speech, were explosive and confused; there was emotion, often deep emotion, but it broke out in ill-governed and uncouth ways. He was not at all an Anglomaniac: he ideal-ised only the old colonial proprieties and dignities: he longed for an American aristocracy, not of millionaires, but of local worthies, sportsmen, scholars and divines. The New England literary men and orators of fifty years before would have satisfied him in respect to their station and manners, but he detested the radical revolutionary turn of their minds. He hated the empty, cold self-sufficiency, as he thought it, of Emerson and his friends. They had desiccated and impoverished the heart; they had made the world less passionate and less interesting to live in. In a word, Wendell was a sentimentalist.

Had he been thoroughly educated and a good Latinist like Dr. Johnson, he might have expressed and propagated his ideals to better purpose; as it was, his force spent itself in foam. He was a good critic of undergraduate essays; but not a fair historian or a learned man; and his books were not worth writing. He was useful in the College as a pedagogue, and there was a certain moral stimulus in his original personality. He carried his little person jauntily; wore spats and a red beard; when walking he would brandish the stick that (like me) he always carried; he would perpetually twirl the signet at the end of his watch-chain. Some-thing admirable was wasted in him. The age made it impossible for him to do well what he would have loved to do.

Why should such a man ever dream of becoming a professor? His case, I imagine, was not unlike mine. He happened to have his pigeon-hole in Boston, he was not rich, he liked to browse upon belles-lettres; why not teach English composition and litera-ture at Harvard? But with science and President Eliot in control, would Harvard accept his services? It was long very much in doubt. With time, however, Wendell had become a familiar figure, an object of universal smiles and affection; and when the official guillotine was ready to fall, public sentiment couldn't allow it. Indeed, in what remained of the old-fashioned College, Wendell's was useful work. He devised and carried out the plan of reading and revising hundreds of "daily themes," each on a half-sheet of note-paper: a voluntary exercise in writing, feeling, and judging of all things like a gentleman. You learned nothing except what to think about what you happened to know. If the effects of this training could spread and assert themselves against the self-confidence of the illiterate, a great change would appear in the tone of American publications. A change of tone there has certainly been in the last thirty years; and who knows how much of it may not be due to Barrett Wendell?

I seldom came across Wendell in Boston, but he was an inevitable speaker at Harvard meetings and dinners. Yet I think that silently we essentially understood each other. We were on the same side of the barricade. More than once he took some step, quite without my knowledge, to do me a kindness. Perhaps the most tangible sign of this sympathy between us was our common affection for Harvard—for the College, not for the University. We knew that the traditional follies there present were the normal, boyish, almost desirable follies of youth; and that the *virtu* there fostered and admired was genuine *virtu*, not perhaps useful for anything further, but good and beautiful in itself. We both desired to screen those follies and to propagate that *virtu* against the steam-roller of industrial democracy. We were not asking much; for these were precisely the follies and the *virtu* that democracy, if liberated from the steam-roller, would cultivate of its own accord. What we deprecated was only that this spontaneous life of the people should be frustrated by the machinery of popular government and of incorporated private interests.

A more pathetic servant of popular joys, humbler than Barrett Wendell and more openly sentimental, was my neighbour for years in the Yard, and although I seldom saw him, I was always vaguely aware of his beneficent existence round the corner. He was known as Charley Copeland. An artist rather than a scholar, he was a public reader by profession, an elocutionist; he could move his audiences by declaiming, with disciplined voice and restrained emotion, all the most touching or thrilling popular selections from the Bible to Kipling. This was a spiritual debauch for the hungry souls of the many well-disposed waifs at Harvard living under difficult conditions: and these Copeland made his special friends. Apart from his readings, he took pains to thaw out the most timid and warm them at his fire, materially and morally. He was the poor boys' providential host and inspirer, doing for the forlorn and disinherited what Norton did for those who were, or ought to have been, already somewhat cultivated, or what Palmer did, more speculatively, for the intellectual proletariat. This task of attracting the mass into the vortex of public interests, which at Yale was done by college organisations, at Harvard was done in these discreet ways by individual philanthropists, more from above and more tenderly, but I fear less successfully: because these contacts, for the majority, left only stray memories without establishing permanent personal interests. Copeland was not left without his reward in the esteem and affection of a particular circle, and of scattered admirers, yet his charitable work for the College remained for years without official recognition. It was only under President Lowell that he was made a professor.

Somewhat on the margin of Harvard lingered also for a time my friend Pierre la Rose. He too was connected with the English Department; but he pieced out his work there by planning restorations of old houses, or decorating and refurnishing them. He had excellent taste, not too servile or pedantic about the style of any period; his joy, I think, would have been like mine, in bolder decorative effects such as we were regaled with later by the Russian ballet. He was expert none the less in distinguishing the merits of classic and severe styles, and of the corresponding literature, particularly the French. Unfortunately there was nothing classical or severe about his own figure; he was not looked on with favour by the undergraduates of his own time, except by other exceptional persons like Trumbull Stickney, with whom he used to play classical music, for he also had some talent in that direction; but later local prejudice against him was vanquished by his pleasant conversation, discretion and varied knowledge. I found him in my later Harvard years the most sympathetic of friends. We often sat at the same table in the small room at the Colonial Club, and if the food was negative, we had a bottle of claret, and not only Harvard, official and unofficial, but the whole literary and political world, for our intellectual bill of fare. He would have made an excellent permanent Tutor in a genuine college, not only in English composition, but in French and in comparative literature, as well as in the history of the fine arts: and had President Lowell's "Houses" existed in the 1890's, he would doubtless have made a place for himself there. He had a quiet, well-informed, unexaggerated devotion to all charming things, a devotion that teaches by contagion, and awakens a taste for what is worth loving.

I had a hearty academic friend also at Yale; and when I say that it was William Lyon Phelps, those who knew him will understand the reason, because he was the hearty friend of everybody. He had come to Harvard when a graduate student to study early English under Professors Child and Kittredge, not to speak of Barrett Wendell, whose hearty friend he instantly became, in spite of the contrast in their idiosyncrasies. My friendship with Phelps would not have become so warm, at least on my side, but for the place and moment in which it was cemented. In 1892, he had returned to Yale, became an instructor or professor there, married, and settled in a nice little house where he was immensely happy, and where there was a spare room for a guest; and knowing my recently acquired taste for contemplating athletic contests, he asked me to come and visit him and his wife for the Harvard-Yale game. I knew nothing of Yale, which for a Harvard man was a half-mythical, half-hostile invisible object. Here was a capital chance to unveil the mystery, and see something of Yale from the inside. And I didn't go alone. Warwick Potter, who had a

Groton friend at Yale, arranged to come with me; but we parted
on reaching New Haven, each being met and carried off by his
respective host; and we had entirely different aspects of Yale to
describe, as on the Sunday afternoon we travelled back to Cambridge.

That was at the high tide of my second College period. Teaching philosophy had become a decent means of livelihood, and was
not yet a burden; I was not pledged to it, and was writing nothing
but poetry. Yale, seen under the enthusiastic guidance of my
cicerone, seemed a most living, organic, distinctive, fortunate
place, a toy Sparta to match our toy Athens at Harvard. I liked
it very much: what is more, I *believed* in it. That was the direction in which the anonymous, gregarious mind of America could
be sympathetically brought to become distinct and integral. Harvard liberalism tended, on the contrary, to encourage dissolution,
intellectual and moral, under a thin veneer of miscellaneous
knowledge. Phelps was naturally pleased at seeing me so sympathetic. Not considering that I was fundamentally a Spaniard and
a Catholic, he thought he had converted me to muscular Christianity; and in fact he had converted me to something Christian,
namely, to charity even towards muscular Americanism.

The Yale that Phelps showed me was the official Yale, yet the
officials seemed to be of an extraordinarily informal, varied and
youthful type. Phelps himself had these characteristics; and his
wife added a gentle harmonising treble to his spontaneous bari-
tone. I was keyed up by them to such an appreciative mood that
I liked even the Y.M.C.A. I felt that it was not meddlesome, but
truly friendly and helpful; and this was not the only time that I
felt this among the Evangelicals. Mrs. Palmer, for instance (unlike her husband), inspired me with immediate confidence and
respect. I was sure that she was honestly a friend of life in others,
even when their life was not at all like hers; and when still at
school I had discovered the same gift of steady charity in the
much-loved Bayley. The great point was that these people should
not be themselves flabby or sentimental or followers of Rousseau;

then their charity might be a true virtue, not a licence for their pet vices.

Phelps was irresistible. His every word was a cocktail, or at least a temperance drink. He made you love everything. Even if you were not naturally genial you found you were his friend, almost his intimate friend, without having in the least expected it. Whether this mesmerisation should be altogether welcome to a moralist, I am not sure. I suppose (when Phelps was not present) the most hearty optimist might distinguish degrees of delight. He might say: I delight in bread, but I delight more in bread and butter, and still more in cake; and I delight in a *baba-au-rhum* even more than in dry cake. Yet if you allow yourself to make these odious comparisons, you cast a shadow of inferiority over all delights except the greatest. You might even suspect that the greatest might some day be overshadowed, and that you might mysteriously find yourself preferring not to eat anything. Life and the morality that regulates life seem to require discrimination. They would relax, they would positively dissolve, if delight were spread indiscriminately over an infinite miscellany of commonplaces and there were nothing that you didn't love, nothing that you invincibly hated. So that perhaps the irresistible Phelps would have been too much of a good thing for all the year round; but for an occasional visit to Yale, or an occasional afternoon in Paris (where he and his wife often turned up), he was all Browning in a nutshell, and better for that compression.

It is an error into which too much domestic luxury has led American taste that all bread should be buttered. When eaten alone, bread is improved by a little butter or a little cheese, to lend it softness or savour; but when bread itself is an accompaniment, butter is out of place. It only adds grease to the greasy sauces and cloys the meat that it might have saved from cloying. So with moral enthusiasm. Great, solid, fruitful excellence should provoke it, not mere existence. Existence is something haphazard, and a great risk: the possibility of something good with the peril of many evils. Phelps complained that in my *Last Puritan* there was not a single *good* person. I thought Oliver, the Vicar, Irma, and several of the minor characters decidedly good people, and many others good enough as this world goes; but none were *merely* good, because goodness is an attribute and not a substance. To be good morally you must first be distinct physically: you must not be an anonymous *it*. The trouble with the goodness that Phelps wanted and possessed was that it was not distinguished. It seemed to me at Yale as if enthusiasm were cultivated for its own sake, as flow of life, no matter in what direction. It meant intoxication, not choice. You were not taught to attain anything capable of being kept, a treasure to be laid up in heaven. You were trained merely to succeed. And in order to be sure to succeed, it was safer to let the drift of the times dictate your purposes. Make a strong pull and a long pull and a pull all together for the sake of togetherness. Then you will win the race. A young morality, a morality of preparation, of limbering up. "Come on, fellows," it cried. "Let's see who gets there first. Rah, rah, rah! Whoop-her-up! Onward, Christian Soldier!" Irresistible as Phelps was, my nature reacted against that summons. Before I cry onward, I would inquire where I am bound. Before I take up arms, I must know in what cause. Before I call myself a Christian, I must understand what Christianity is and what it would impose upon me. Does it cry to me, as at Yale, "Come on, fellows! Let's see who gets there first!" "There," for a Christian, used to mean yonder, above, *Jenseits*, heaven: but when this world has become so lovely, and effort and work are a crown in themselves, the struggle becomes a crab race, and the real winner is he who runs forever and never gets there at all. As Emerson said, "If God is anywhere, he is here," so this modern Christian should say, If heaven isn't here it's nowhere. A conclusion that in some sense I should be willing to accept, only that I shouldn't call it Christianity: rather Epicurean contentment in being an accident in an accident.

My visits to Yale were unofficial, but I was asked to give odd lectures at most of the other New England colleges, and always did so with pleasure. My hosts were kind, the places, with my early memories of the Latin School and of simple old Harvard, were pleasantly reminiscent, and the intellectual atmosphere was honest and unpretending. I also gave lectures at Columbia, where the professors of philosophy took a professional interest in my views, such as in general I expect nobody to take: only perhaps a momentary pleasure in some phrase or in some bit of literary criticism. This was what came to me, by way of incense, from the female audiences that I often addressed at Radcliffe, at Wellesley, and other women's colleges. At Bryn Mawr, a comparatively fashionable place where I spoke in the Chapel, I overheard, as I came in, a loud and disappointed whisper: "He is bald!" and at Berkeley, where the summer school seemed to have no men in it, a lady observed that I had "a mellifluous voice," but that she "didn't like my logic." In the Middle West I was more honoured, even giving once the Baccalaureate Address, and at Wisconsin being welcomed twice and receiving an honorary degree. The moral and intellectual atmosphere everywhere in the United States seemed to be uniform: earnest, meagre, vague, scattered, and hopeful. After I left America, however, I gather that a sharp change occurred, introducing more variety, more boldness and greater achievements.

My academic career also had an unexpected extension to Paris. At Harvard, during my last years, there was a rich and isolated student named Caleb Hyde, interested in French literature. On graduating he founded an exchange professorship between Harvard and the Sorbonne, lectures to be in English at Paris, and in French at Cambridge. Barrett Wendell was the first appointed at Paris; and when I was in the East, during 1905, I received an invitation to be his successor. It was most opportune, giving me two years' holiday instead of one; for being in training as a lecturer at that time, and counting on an intelligent audience in Paris, my work there would be easy, and three parts pleasure. So it proved. Never have I talked to so *open* a public—I mean in a course of lectures; singly, I have found an equal openness once or twice in England. Yet, after Wendell, I was a sad disappointment to Hyde and, I suspect, to all the officials concerned. For I avoided seeing anyone, presented none of the letters of introduction that Hyde had sent me by the dozen, and lived in my hotel just as quietly as if I had had no academic duties. I had a reason for this, besides my love of obscurity. The tendency to give a political colour to this lectureship repelled me for two reasons: one, that I was not an American, and was presenting myself, as it were, under false colours; the other, that the political propaganda desired was contrary to my sympathies.

In spite of my avoidance of contacts, I came involuntarily on various little manifestations of the sham and corruption that prevailed in the official world. The most simple avowal of it was made by the Rector of the University of Lille, when on the provincial tour that formed a part of the lecturer's programme, I presented myself and expressed my readiness to give, at his discretion, one or two lectures in English. He raised his hands to heaven, and said quickly: *"Une seule! Il ne faut pas abuser de la fidelité de l'auditoire."* It was fidelity enough in an audience to sit through one lecture without running away. In Paris, in fact, the doors were always open, and slamming, with people coming in late or going away early. I was told of a group of students that peeped in one afternoon. *"Tiens. C'est en Anglais. Filons!"* said the leader, and they all disappeared. This freedom was a little disturbing, yet served to emphasise the sense of security given by the little nucleus of listeners who always came early, smilingly stayed to the end, and evidently understood everything.

Before I set out on my tour of the provincial universities, I had a glimpse of French Government behind the scenes. A young man in a shining red motor burnished like sealing wax turned up at the Foyot, where I lived, and said they wished to speak to me at the Ministry of Public Instruction, and that he would drive me there. I was received by the director of some department, who rang the bell and said that Monsieur So-and-So would explain to me the nature of a request that they desired to make of me. I bowed, said *au revoir, Monsieur,* and followed the secretary into an inner room. This secretary was obsequious, yet in himself, had he been dressed in oriental garments, would have been impressive and almost beautiful. He had a pale complexion, large calm eyes and a long silky black beard falling in two strands. We sat down. He said, with an air of mystery, and perhaps some embarrassment, that in the list of universities that they had selected for me to visit, they had included Lille. Now, there was a special circumstance about Lille to which they wished beforehand to call my attention. At Lille there was also a Catholic Institute. If, going as I did under government direction, I should also address the Catholic Institute, it would cause comment which they desired to avoid. For that reason they had troubled me with this little matter; and they hoped I should understand the position in which they were placed.

I replied that I understood it perfectly, that I had never heard of the Catholic Institute at Lille, had no relations with French Catholic circles, and certainly would not repeat my lecture, at Lille or elsewhere, even if, as was most unlikely, I should be invited to do so. In fact, the Catholic Institute was as oblivious of me as I was of it. But these precautions of the Ministry, and the stealthy hushed tone of them, taught me something of the spirit of the French Government. It was not national, but sectarian. It was afraid that a foreign lecturer should repeat to Catholic students what he had been sent to say to Government students. Apparently —though they paid me nothing, for it was Hyde that paid—they felt that, while I was under their auspices, I was pledged to their policy. If I had known this, or had thought it more than an absurd pretension, I should never have stepped within the Sorbonne.

The last university I visited was that of Lyons, and there pomposity was the order of the day. Everyone was pining for the blessed moment when they should at last be transferred to Paris; but meantime they would pretend that Lyons was the light of the world. I was asked to dinner by the Rector; he said nothing about *sans cérémonie,* and luckily I dressed, for it was an official banquet, forty men, and only one lady, the Rector's wife, in full regalia, next to whom I sat, with the Rector opposite. At the end, with the champagne, my heart sank, for I foresaw that I had to make a speech—my first and last speech in French. Luckily the Rector was very eloquent about the twin republics across the sea, both enlightened, both humane, both progressive, both red-white-and-blue. I had time to think of something to say. I had been hearing and speaking more French than usual, and I managed, not without faults, but decently to express my thanks and to praise the young French universities—younger than Harvard—that I had been visiting. But I also said that, although I was not myself an American, I would convey the friendly sentiments expressed by the Rector to my friends at Harvard, who I knew were inspired by the same feelings. Having relieved my conscience and given them a lesson, I went on more sympathetically and ended without eloquence but with decency. *"Vous avez eu des phrases,"* said one of the guests to me afterwards, *"qui n'étaient pas d'un étranger."* Quite so: the accent may not have been Parisian, but the sentiment was not foreign, because it was human and sincere. We all move together when we pursue the truth.

The last echoes of my official career were posthumous: the professor was dead, the man revived, spoke in the professor's place, and spoke in England. These were all written lectures, and most of them were published in *Character and Opinion in the United States*. Together with *Egotism in German Philosophy* and *Soliloquies in England* they mark my emancipation from official control and professional pretensions. There was no occasion to change my subjects, to abandon even technical philosophy or my interest in academic life and the humanities. But all was now a voluntary study, a satirical survey, a free reconsideration: the point of view had become at once frankly personal and speculatively transcendental. A spirit, the spirit in a stray individual, was settling its accounts with the universe. My official career had happily come to an end.

INDEX

Agatha (Lady Agatha Russell), 42
Aiken, Conrad, 103
Ainger, Canon, *Carmen Etonense,*
by, 120
Aingers, the, 120-1
America, 1, 7, 19, 100, 107, 175-6
Americans in Europe, 131-51
Antoñita, Cousin, 76
Apthorp, "Billy," 4
Aristophanes, 24
Aristotle, 157-8
Arnold, Matthew, 19
Atalanta in Calydon, by Swinburne,
45-6
Avila, 76-97, 135, 168-9

Bangs, "Swelly," 99-101, 107
Bank of England, 30-3
Bayley, Edward, 109
Barlow, Bob, 98-101, 107
Barlow, Nelly, 98
Barlow, General, 98
Beal, Boylston, 9, 107-8
Bennett, Miss, 21-2, 27
Berenson, Bernard, 37-9, 58-9
Berenson, Mrs. Bernard, 38-9
Berkeley, Bishop, 178
Berlin, 1, 5, 8-9
Bible in Spain, The, by Borrow,
41
Billings, Emma, 69
Billings, Jennie, 69
Bookbills of Narcissus, The, by
Richard Le Gallienne, 45
Borrás, Josefina (author's mother),
112, 158
Borrow, *Bible in Spain,* by, 41
Boston society, 3, 81, 107, 112-30
Bowen, Professor, 153
Brattle Street, No. 60, 12

Bringas, 84-5
Brooks, Phillips, 102
Browning, Robert, 159
Bryn Mawr, 178
Bullard, Frank, 163
Burke, of Trinity, 53-4
Butler, Lawrence, 143-4

Cándido, 78-9
Cape Cod, 101-2, 104
Cape Cod, lines on, by George San-
tayana, 101-2
Carmen Etonense, by Ainger, 120
*Character and Opinion in the
United States,* by George San-
tayana, 90, 181
Child, Francis James, 174
Codman, "Cousin" Lucy, 102,
116-7, 121-2
Codman, Julian, 102-4, 108, 117,
121
Codmans, the, 116-7
Colonial Club, 158, 163, 174
Columbia University, 178
Coolidge, "Archie," 162-3
Copeland, Charles Townsend, 173
Cosmic Evolution, by John Fiske,
165
Critique of Practical Reason, by
Kant, 7
Cruikshank, George, 19
Cruthers, The Rev. Dr., 164
Cuba, 167
Cuffe, Lady Sybil, 161
Curtis, George William, *Prue and I,*
by, 38
Curzon, Lord, 67
Cushing, Howard, 107-8
Cutting, Bayard, 161
Cutting, Iris, 161

183

Dark Angel, The, by Lionel Johnson, 60
Davis, of Balliol, 53
Declaration of Independence, 169
de Fontenay, Madame, 40–1
de Fontenays, the, 67
Delta Phi ("The Gas House"), 108
de Madorell, Monserrat, 84
de Madorells, the, 84
Dent, J. M., 36
de Reszke, Jean, 144
Deussen, Professor, 9
Dickens, Charles, 19, 26
Dickinson, Lowes, 158
Dresden, 2, 4

Ebbinghaus, Professor, 7
Edward VII, 36
Egotism in German Philosophy, by
   George Santayana, 90, 181
Elvira, Cousin, 76–80, 83, 85
Eliot, Charles W., 153–4, 156–60,
   171
Emerson, 104–5, 171, 177
England, 9, 15, 16–43, 64
English, the, 18–9, 23, 26, 35, 40,
   65, 90
Engracia, Aunt, 77
Epicurus, 8
Escalera, Mercedes de la, 82–3, 92–3
Everett, C. C., 164

Fish, Nicholas, 141
Fiske, John, 165
Florence, 23
France, 66–7
Frankfort, 10
French Government, 179–80
Forbes, Cameron, 104–6, 108
Forbes, John, 104
Forbes, William, 105–6

Gardner, Mrs. "Jack," 124–6, 128
German State Company, 2
Germans, the, 11, 14–5
Germany, 1–17

Gezycki, Professor, 7, 8
Gladstone, William Ewart, 42
Goethe, 10
Göttingen, 1
Gray, Judge, 114
Gray, Mrs., 129
Green, Andrew, 146–8
Green Park, 23
Greek ethics, 6, 8
Greeks, the, 6
Groton, 110
Gudehus, 2
Gwynedd, by Lionel Johnson, 61

Hampton Court, 25
Hegel, 152–3
Harvard University, 10, 70, 98–111,
   113, 149, 152–81
Herodotus, 8
History of the United States, by
   John Fiske, 165
Hollis Hall, 44
Holmes, Oliver Wendell, Jr., 128–9
Houghton, A. B., 5
Hubert, Henri, 149
Hyde, Caleb, 178–80
Hyde Park, 23

Ignacia, Maria (author's aunt), 76
India, 149
Iparraguirre, Victorina, 82–3
Isabel, Infanta, 82

James, Henry, 39–40
James, William, 7, 39, 45, 127–8,
   152–3, 163, 166–70; *Principles of
   Psychology*, by, 152
Jepson, of Balliol, 53–4, 66
Jermyn Street, Saint James's [No.
   87], 20–2, 27, 34
Jews, the, 6
Johnson, Lionel, 53–63
Jowett, Benjamin, 63

Kant, 7
Katholische Kirche, 2

Kensington Palace, 25
Kipling, Rudyard, 165
Kipling's mother, 165
Kittredge, George Lyman, 174

Lampoon, The, 170
Lasson, Professor, 9
Last Puritan, The, by George Santayana, 1, 105–6, 144, 158, 176–7
Latin School, 178
Le Gallienne, Richard, *The Bookbills of Narcissus,* by, 45
Les Sentences dans la Poésie Grècque, by Trumbull Stickney, 149
Life of Reason, The, by George Santayana, 157
Lille University, 179–80'
Loeser, Charles, 36, 141–2
London, 17–43
Longfellow, Henry Wadsworth, 19
Lotze, 152–3
Lowell, A(bbott) Lawrence, 173–4
Lowell, Sara, 3
Lucifer, by George Santayana, 163–4
Lyman, Herbert, 2–4, 44 n., 107
Lyman, Miss, 3
Lyons, University of, 180

McKinley, President William, 168
Malten, 2
Maria Christina, Queen, 82
Mercado Grande, 89
Mérimée, Prosper, 39
"Michael Field," 39
Moody, William Vaughn, 101–2
Moslems, the, 37
Motleys, the (daughters of the historian), 118

Nation, The, 129
New England, 3, 106, 171
New York, 22
Norton, Charles Eliot, 163–6, 173
Notting Hill, 18–20

Ogilvie, Lady Griselda, 43
Oxford, 8, 18, 35

Palmer, George Herbert, 167, 173
Palmer, Mrs. George Herbert, 175
Paul, Kegan, 58
Paulsen, Friedrich, Professor, 5, 7, 9
Paris, 22
Pelayo, 76
Phelps, William Lyon, 174–7
Phelps, Mrs. William Lyon, 175–6
Philippines, 167–8, 170
Plato, 157–8
Potter, Bob, 108, 140–2
Potter, Mrs. Bob, 141
Potter, Warwick, 102, 108–10, 174–5
Principles of Psychology, by William James, 152
Prue and I, by George William Curtis, 38

Radcliffe, 178
Realm of Truth, The, by George Santayana, 13
Reichhardt, 13–4
Richardson, of Winchester, 64
Richardson, Mrs., 64
Richmond (London), 40–4, 50
Rockefeller, John D., 41, 132, 134–5
Rome, 23
Rose, Pierre la, 173–4
Royal Palace, 2
Royal Theatre, 2
Royce, Josiah, 152
Russell, Bertrand, 37–9, 41
Russell, Hon. Mrs. Bertrand, 39
Russell, 2nd Earl, 42–75, 159
Russell, Countess, 63
Russell, Frank, 38
Russell, Lady Agatha, 42
Russell, Lord John, 44–5
Russell, Lady, 41–2, 48
Ryder Street [No. 3], 34

St. James's Park, 23

Salter (William James' brother-in-law), 7
Santa Teresa, 81–2
Santayana, Agustín Ruiz de (author's father), 9, 17, 37, 76, 78, 80–3, 87, 89, 109
Santayana, George, passim
Santayana, Nicolás Ruiz de (author's uncle), 76
Sandys, Colonel, 21
Sandys, Mrs., 21
Sarah, Aunt, 38, 96, 98, 168
Sastre, Celedonia (author's brother-in-law), 84–9, 92, 94–6
Sastre, Pepe, 91–3
Sastre, Rafael, 89, 93
Sastre, Roberto, 91–3
Schlote, Frau Pastorin, 1
Scott, Edgar, 109
Scott, Mabel Edith, 71–4
Scott, Sir Claude, 71
Scott, Lady (Mrs. Dick), 52, 64, 71–4
Scribner's, 36, 157
Sense of Beauty, The, by George Santayana, 157
Shakespeare, 24
Shaw, Colonel, 168
Shelley, Percy Bysshe, 103
Simmel, Professor, 9
Slade, Conrad, 144–6
Slade, Mrs. Conrad, 144
Slade, Dr., 144
Smith, John, 93
Smith, Logan Pearsall, 37–9
Smith, Mrs. Logan Pearsall, 37–9
Smith, Willie Haines, 121
Soliloquies in England, by George Santayana, 90, 181
Sorbonne, the, 89, 159, 178, 180
Spain, 167–8, 170
Spaniard, the, 37
Spinoza, 6
Stanley, Hon. Maud, 43
Stanley of Alderley, Lady, 42–3, 48
Star and Garter, 40

Stickney, Trumbull, 103, 148–51, 174
Stoughton Hall, 102
Strong, Arthur, 36–7
Strong, Mrs. Arthur, 36
Strong, Charles Augustus, 5, 9, 17–20, 41, 132–40, 143
Strong, Mrs. Charles Augustus, 41, 132–5
Strong, Dr., 132
Strong, Margaret, 136, 138–40
Sturgis, Howard, 117–21
Sturgis, Josefina (author's half-sister), 91–5
Sturgis, Robert (author's half-brother), 92–3, 112, 114 n.
Sturgis, Susana (author's half-sister), 3, 9, 78, 80–8, 91, 93–7, 109, 112, 114, 123
Sturgis, Russell, 102, 113, 116
Sturgis, Russell, Jr., 113–6
Sturgis, Russell, 3rd, 114 n.
Sturgises, the, 96, 112
Swinburne, Algernon Charles, 19; Atalanta in Calydon, by, 45–6

Tavern Club, 165
Thackeray, William Makepeace, 19
Thoron, Ward, 107
Three Philosophical Poets, lectures by George Santayana, 10
To a Spanish Friend, by Lionel Johnson, 55
Toy, Prof. C. H., 162
Toy, Mrs. C. H., 162

Unforgotten Years, by Logan Pearsall Smith, 37
United States, the, 167–70, 178

Victoria Eugénia, Queen, 82
Vegas, Rafael, 76, 78
von Westenholz, Baron Albert, 10–5
von Westenholz, Fräulein Mathilde, 14–5
von Westenholz, Baroness, 14

Wagner, Richard, 9
Wales, lines on, by Lionel Johnson, 59
Watkins, Chief Justice of India, 41
Watkins (son of the Chief Justice), 41
Wedd, Nathaniel, 158
Weimar, 10
Wellesley College, 178
Wendell, Barrett, 157, 170–2, 174, 178–9
White, Mrs. Stanford, 143
Whitman, Mrs., 124, 126–8
Wilde, Oscar, 60

Winchester (the school), 64–5
Winds of Doctrine, by George Santayana, 129
Windsor Castle, 25, 49
Wisconsin, 178
Wolcott, Roger, 129
Woodworth, Billy, 108
Woolwich, 25
Wren, Sir Christopher, 19

Yale University, 104, 173–5, 177

Zeta Psi ("The Spee"), 100–1
Zwinger, the, 2

MY HOST THE WORLD

MY HOST THE WORLD

GEORGE SANTAYANA

VOL. III ✳ *Persons and Places*

NEW YORK

CHARLES SCRIBNER'S SONS

CONTENTS

CHAPTER   PAGE

I.   A Change of Heart   1

II.   King's College, Cambridge   16

III. Travels   33

IV.   On the South Downs   57

V.   Oxford Friends   78

VI.   Farewell to England   96

VII. Old Age in Italy   119

VIII. Epilogue: My Host the World   133

      Index   145

MY HOST THE WORLD

CHAPTER I

A CHANGE OF HEART

IF a man were a wild spirit without a body or a habitat his philosophy might harmlessly change at every moment, and he might well pride himself on changing it often and radically, so as to display fertility of spirit and enjoy an inexhaustibly rich experience. Being absolutely free and unfettered by circumstances, why should he stick to any particular principles or ideas and waste his time repeating himself like an idiot or a cuckoo?

It happened in my case, however, that I reached the age of reflection in Avila, a little walled city, where old people, old churches, and barren grey moors strewn with prehistoric boulders filled my mind from the first with a sense of antiquity. Nor did reflection later, in the New World, lead me seriously to think myself, or anyone else, a disembodied spirit. On the contrary, it seemed to me evident that no discoverable mind can ever have existed except in a body; so that by the presence and action of that body it might give signs and leave memorials of its passage. Then the past might be partly recalled on occasion, not as a vain dream, but as an experience and a lesson still applicable to a moderately stable world. Moreover, this stable world might contain other living bodies, similar to one's own; and their action and gestures, by mimicry, might instantly suggest to us desires and intentions animating those creatures, and rendering them sympathetic or hostile to ourselves; and so a moral world, practical and social, would become, for our imagination, the theatre of our action, and a roughly valid representation of the forces actually playing upon us and determining the weal and woe of our lives.

On the other hand, the true romantic genius who to-day cries to the West Wind "Be thou me, impetuous one!" will cry no less exultantly tomorrow to become the East Wind for a change: although in infinite vacancy it might be hard to find the difference. A truly free spirit will never repent; he cannot revert to his true self, since he has no particular self to revert to. He must simply go on, as transcendental spirit actually does, from one fresh incarnation to another, in and out forever of every living thing. He must will everything, do everything and suffer everything, but his spirit can never die: at least it can never prevent itself from being born again. It must lust forever after the Eternal Feminine, or to put it more crudely, after the female of every species.

As for me, not only my body but my rather special and difficult relations to persons and places seemed clearly imposed facts; and in that setting my personal tastes and feelings became early apparent, and caused me to feel that I lived in a kind of solitude, not transcendental and spiritual, but decidedly solitariness in a crowd and foreignness among very distinct people. My preferences were clearly marked and out of harmony with my surroundings and, as I soon felt, with my times. But conceit, or firmness of disposition, kept me from suspecting that I ought to change my allegiances, and think and feel, play and work, as did the majority. Nor did I feel any impulse to contradict them or blame them. I had nothing to complain of, but I preferred solitude.

There was therefore no occasion for me to suffer moral revolutions or undergo any radical change of heart. My interest in religion had never been agonising, only speculative and devotional. Nothing in me called for any conversion or *metanoia*. Time might transmute, without erasing, my first opinions and affections; I might wish to change my surroundings and my way of living; I never undertook to change myself. I regard my occupations and interests somewhat as an actor regards his various parts or a painter his subjects. That a man has preferences and can understand and do one thing better than another, follows from his inevitable limitations and definite gifts; but that which marks progress in his life is the purity of his art; I mean, the degree to which his art has become his life, so that the rest of his nature does not impede or corrupt his art, but only feeds it.

Now in my mental life there have been two great impediments, two congenital vices, two initial temptations; the temptation of the primitive poet to believe his fables, and the temptation of the spontaneous agent to lose himself in his world. The primitive poet falls into that first temptation inevitably; his inspiration is passive and not an art; he lends credence to his obsessions as to a higher kind of knowledge, and proclaims each new intuition to be a revelation of the truth. The Jews, says Spinoza, whenever they think something, say God told them. Prophets indeed do this explicitly and with full conviction, opposing their sudden intuitions to the current views of mankind. They are even more credulous and absorbed in life than are ordinary people, only in some extraordinary direction. Yet, unlike madmen, good prophets proclaim new ideas that the world can be led to take seriously and to weave into its conventions, at least for a time and in some sect; whence all traditional religions and moralities.

I am naturally incredulous and not a willing dupe of life in the world or in my own head; yet my imagination is not inactive. I am therefore a sort of prophet at second hand, appreciating the inspiration of others and enjoying it as my own; and for that reason the temptation to mistake it for revelation was in my case never invincible. I have said how my youthful piety was accompanied by an equal delight in geography and in architecture. I had little real contact with any of these things, but pure delight in the form and idea of them. All that I later clearly denied them was the assent due to matters of common knowledge or history: matters of fact important to get right in action, but not especially interesting to the imagination of a poet.

All her life my sister Susana was a little troubled because, as she said, she feared that I was "moving away from God." Yet at heart I was not *moving* at all. I was only *seeing* what a catastrophe the Christian *Weltanschauung* was pregnant with, if you took it for history and cosmology, and not for a symbolic myth. And this intellectual catastrophe would also involve a moral one, in that it implied the exhaustion of an inspiration, the decay of a *Kultur*. It would be comparable to the catastrophe of paganism and of the classic world, tragic but interesting. The idea of such a catastrophe caused no revolution in myself: it was more like a bereavement or a total change of surroundings. I had never *practised* my religion, or thought of it as a means of getting to heaven or avoiding hell, things that never caused me the least flutter. All that happened was that I became accustomed to a different *Weltanschauung*, to another system having the same rational function as religion: that of keeping me attentive to the lessons of life.

Each religion, by the help of more or less myth which it takes more or less seriously, proposes some method of fortifying the human soul and enabling it to make its peace with its destiny. A philosopher may perfectly well cultivate more than one *Weltanschauung*, if he has a vital philosophy of his own to qualify his adoption of each, so as to render them complementary and not contradictory. I had, and have, such a vital philosophy; and the movement of my mind among various systems of belief has tended merely to discover how far my vital philosophy could be expressed in each of them.

My variations therefore never involved rejecting any old affection, but only correcting such absoluteness or innocence as there may have been about it, and reducing it to its legitimate function. So in 1900 I published the result of the gradual transformation of my religious sentiments. Religion was poetry intervening in life. That insight had come to me twenty years before, though not expressed in those words; it had really been native to me and congenital. So when I first went to Germany and began to read Goethe, chiefly as a lesson in the language, my vital philosophy recognised itself at once in the lines:

> *Ich hab' mein Sach auf Nichts gestellt . . .*
> *Drum ist's so wohl mir in der Welt.*

This is perhaps more cavalier-like and jaunty than I was, even at that time; yet the title of this drinking-song is *Vanitas! vanitatum vanitas!* and the stanzas describe a gay fellow's discomfiture when he set his heart on money or women or foreign travel or reputation or war; so that when he repeats at the end:

> *Nun hab' ich mein Sach auf Nichts gestellt . . .*
> *Und mein gehört die ganze Welt,*

there is evidently an equivocation in his boast. The whole world belongs to me implicitly when I have given it all up, and am wedded to nothing particular in it; but for the same reason no part of it properly belongs to me as a possession, but all only in idea. Materially I might be the most insignificant of worms; spiritually I should be the spectator of all time and all existence. This implication touched the depth of my vital or congenital philosophy, and for that reason doubtless the refrain of this song became a sort of motto for me at that time. Yet more than ten years had to pass before that implication, on the emotional side, came to expression in my Platonising sonnets; while theoretically I came to clearness about it only in my old age, when I freed "essences" from the psychological net in which we catch them, and distinguished intuition from knowledge.

Clearer to me in those student days was another point. Goethe's old soldier urges us, if we want to be good fellows, to drown our disappointments in drink. But isn't drink also disappointing in the end? And if it be a solution to drink, in order to forget the vanity of life and incidentally the vanity of drinking, wouldn't it be a better and juster solution to live in general as the world lives, so as to forget the vanity of doing so? Didn't all my American friends endeavour, with a good conscience, to drown unhappiness in work? Wasn't there some intoxication also in wealth, in women, in travel, in fame, and in war? And if drink and comradeship have a good side, which makes them jolly even if vain, have not all those other vanities their good side also? To abuse them satirically, out of spite, because you had expected too much of them, would be merely childish or, if you like, romantic. It would prove you to be moody, ill-bred, and unphilosophical.

Being a philosopher, I couldn't accept a solution not based on the truth. If all is vanity—and I heartily agreed to that—the solution must be built on remembering that fact, not on forgetting it; and if drinking and comradeship have a good side—and I heartily agreed to that too—the solution must recognise the good side of drink, and also of wealth, women, travel, fame, and war. Not being an old campaigner with one leg, like Goethe's soldier, but a young man just beginning to see the sunny side of life, it was more the challenge to drink that appealed to me than the chagrin at having found that drinking didn't pay. I knew that it wouldn't pay, if you gave yourself up to it; I felt no temptation to do that; but without setting my heart on anything the point was to enjoy everything with a free mind.

This was a pretty programme, easy for a boy to draw up; and my antecedent pessimism and religiosity lent a certain reality to the pose. It lay in my nature to foresee disappointment, and never to bet on the issue of any event. Yet without experience of the world, this programmatic distrust remained itself empty and insecure. Genuine detachment presupposes attachment. What can it signify for you to say that you renounce everything, if as yet you have loved nothing? I had been childishly absorbed in religious ideas, and it was a true though bloodless sacrifice for me to wash them clean of all pretensions to historical or material truth; yet I was able to do so when quite young, readily and even gladly, because when I learned to conceive those myths as poetry, their meaning and beauty, far from being lost, seemed to me clearer and more profound than ever.

The problem was not so easily solved when it came to exorcising the world and freeing myself from all illusions about it. The world is not a myth, to be clarified by a little literary criticism. It envelops our substance with a kindred substance immensely more voluminous; it stimulates and feeds from every quarter the concupiscence of the flesh, the concupiscence of the eye, and the pride of life. What can the poor rush-light of spirit, kindled in the midst, do to clarify them? The aspiration and the desire must be accepted for the performance.

That nevertheless, as a sentiment, my eventual *metanoia* was sincere may be seen in the slow change that appeared in my way of living. Old age contributed to it; on the other hand, I had larger means and easier access to the great world, had I been in love with it. But I have ultimately become a sort of hermit, not from fear or horror of mankind, but by sheer preference for peace and obscurity. Fortune has become indifferent to me, except as fortune might allow me to despise fortune and to live simply in some beautiful place. I have cut off all artificial society, reducing it to the limits of sincere friendship or intellectual sympathy. Instead of collecting pictures and books, as I had a tendency to do in the early 1890's, I have distributed my few possessions, eschewed chattels of every kind, a fixed residence, servants, carriages, or anything that would pin me down materially or engulf me in engagements. I have indulged rather freely at certain times in good food and good drink; but I think the glamour of those pleasures was due almost entirely to conviviality, that is to say, to a momentary imitation of friendship. In themselves, when I was alone, food and drink were never important to me. I was almost happier when I could be frugal, as at my father's at Avila, in the Duval restaurants in Paris, in the teashops in London, or now, where I write these words, under the drastic restrictions of war, in the clinic of the Blue Sisters upon the Caelius. I am happy in solitude and confinement, and the furious factions into which the world is divided inspire hatred for none of them in my heart.

It should be normal, at least according to the ancients, for a philosopher to reach this moral settlement in old age; but why did the idea of it and the need of it come upon me powerfully at the age of thirty? There were various reasons. For a poet and a lover of youth the age of thirty is itself a ground for *metanoia*. Being a teacher had been forced upon me by the necessity of somehow earning my living; but being a student was my vocation, and I had been living among students, interesting myself in their sports and their pleasures, and loving their quick and unprejudiced minds. Still this second vicarious adolescence had a rift in it: my sympathy with the young and theirs with me had limits that were growing narrower and sharper. My young friends seemed to me every year younger and younger, more and more standardised and generic. They would no longer be my friends, but only boys at the school where I happened to be one of the masters. That chapter then had come to an end: yet youth, in the world and in the poet's eyes, is perpetual. The platonic transition was therefore at once spontaneous and inevitable, from the many to the one, from the existent but transitory to the ideal and eternal.

This transition may be called philosophic *metanoia*. Like the tragic catharsis, it turns disaster into a kind of rapture without those false comforts and delusions by which religious *metanoia* is often cheapened. This philosophic insight was now brought home to me by the unexpected death of Warwick Potter. Though seven years younger than I, he had been a real friend, and as I now felt, my *last* real friend. I have already mentioned that I was surprised by the effect that the news of his death had upon me. Why did it move me so much? Though he was a general favourite and a long procession of us walked behind the bier at his funeral, there was after all nothing extraordinary about him. The cause of my emotion was in myself. I was brimming over with the sense of parting, of being divided by fortune where at heart there was no division. I found myself, unwillingly and irreparably, separated from Spain, from England, from Europe, from my youth and from my religion. It was not good simple Warwick alone that inspired my verses about him. It was the thought of everything that was escaping me: the Good in all the modes of it that I might have caught a glimpse of and lost.

Another event that same year had helped to *disintoxicate* my mind: the death of my father. I had never before seen anyone die, and that in itself is an impressive and sobering experience.

We were not at best an affectionate family, and my father had not had severe suffering to endure, yet the circumstances were deeply pathetic. He was seventy-nine years old, deaf, half-blind, and poor; he had desired his own death and had attempted to hasten it. The fact that he was my father, whose character and destiny were strikingly repeated, with variations, in my own, called up a lurid image of what my life in the world was likely to be: solitary, obscure, trivial, and wasted. I must not look ahead. Ahead, after youth was gone, everything would grow sadder and sadder. I must look within or above. I must follow the counsel that Beatrice gives to Dante, when she sees him overcome with repentance for his vain life in the world:

Pon giù 'l seme del piangere, ed ascolta,*

Drop (false hopes) the seed of tears, and listen. Listen to reason. If the joys of youth and the vision of perfect love have faded from your world, will you allow any baser thing to fetter you there? Let your heart rather follow its true object where that object is gone, into eternity.

A third event, the year before, had struck perhaps even deeper into my conscience. I had seen the illusion in disillusion, the vanity of religious substitutes for earthly happiness. In recording "Changes in Avila" I have said something about my sister's marriage. "Marriage and death and division," said the coxcomb Swinburne, "make barren our lives." Marriage properly makes our lives the opposite of barren; but it was not in the spontaneous ardour of youth, with the prospect of helping to people the world, that my sister had married: she was forty-one years old, and her husband already had six children. Nor was marriage in her case going to separate her from anything or anybody: she had no satisfactory friends or relations, and it was from loneliness that she was taking refuge in the difficult position of stepmother. Nor did her marriage divide her materially from me. On the contrary, it gave me,

---

* Purgatorio, XXXI, 46, et seq.

just when my father's life was closing, a fresh and agreeable home in Avila, where I could make her and her new family long visits. Why then did her marriage displease and dishearten me? Because it seemed, in such unfavourable circumstances, an act of desperation on her part, a redoubled proof of her weakness. She explained it by saying that she needed affection; but a second, semi-foreign wife and stepmother would surely find more criticism than affection in her new family. It was not the sweetness of affection actually found that attached her to them, or the prospect of a peaceful home life. I couldn't help seeing that it was a craving for moral support and social backing in her religion and in her self-esteem: the backing of poor dear little old Avila! This thought distressed me. When she had entered her convent in Baltimore, little poetry or dignity as there might be there, I had admired her courage in showing what seemed such contempt of the world. The material separation between us would then have been complete, but the sense of spiritual sympathy more than outweighed it. Her leaving the convent later was no surprise; she had attempted too much and too late; but her marriage now proved more conclusively that she had no contempt of the world; that her religious enthusiasm itself had been something human and social, and that she, who had given the first impulse to my speculative life, had never had any speculative or mystical insight. She was a Sturgis; and her charm and her ascendancy over me had been founded only on her natural warmth, geniality and fun, themselves now less spontaneous and engaging than when she was younger. She still clung to the Church with an intense party spirit, which she developed also in politics; but she couldn't *live* her religion as I *lived* my philosophy. It was too unreal for her human nature.

This was a sad disillusionment for me in regard to the person to whom I was most attached; and it became also in some measure a disillusionment about Catholicism. Was Catholicism, in principle, much better than Judaism? Wasn't it still worldliness, transferred to a future world, and thereby doubly falsified? The Jews frankly cared for nothing but prosperity, and their delusion was only that they could make a short cut to prosperity by smashing the Golden Calf and being faithful to circumcision and Sabbaths, or alternately by charity towards widows and orphans. In Christianity the idea of prosperity is abandoned for that of salvation in the world to come; and incidentally there is much aspiration towards spiritual perfection and many a master of it; yet this spiritual discipline is in some sense esoteric; in spite of it the goal, as conceived by the materially pious, remains as with the Jews an impossible security amid impossible splendours. The incidental esoteric discipline, which is all that I respect in Catholicism, terminates in the same inward liberation and peace that ancient sages attained under all religions or under none. The question is whether the paraphernalia of salvation are not in all cases accidental, sometimes pleasing and poetical, sometimes dangerously superstitious; and whether they do not encumber the spirit with other-worldliness.

Here, then, were four thoughts merging their currents and carrying me irresistibly towards the same sea: youth was past, friendship had had its day, the future offered me nothing that I cared for, religion and social utopias proposed nothing that I respected. I was driven from the temporal to the eternal, not by any one crisis or conjunction of events, but by the very nature of existence, when this had been honestly faced and frankly admitted. The cry of Ecclesiastes, *Vanitas vanitatum*, could be re-echoed, and the motto from Goethe about setting my heart on nothing could be retained; but both in a new spirit. At twenty my empty spleen could make a clean sweep of the world beforehand, because nothing in it would last forever; it didn't occur to me to ask whether lasting forever would improve anything that was worthless while it lasted. But ten years later I had travelled. I had learned something of the pleasures and manners of mankind, and for myself I had made some progress in the primrose path of Epicurean wisdom. I had now forever in my fancy a lovely picture of ancient Greece and a lovely picture of modern England;

and having begun by fully admitting that all was vanity, I could not be angry with the primroses for fading or with the path for being short. I accepted them as vain but beautiful, transitory but perfect; and I was no less ready to enjoy them than to give them up. To give them up, I mean, as possessions, as enjoyments, as private hopes; I would never give them up as allegiances. Never should I esteem and love them less because they happened to pass out of my orbit.

In another field, not so strictly personal, I was compelled to accept a rather difficult renunciation. I was a teacher of philosophy in the place where philosophy was most modern, most deeply Protestant, most hopefully new!—the very things from which, in speculation, my *metanoia* turned me away. I could never be, I will not say a leader, but even a happy participator in the intellectual faith of my neighbours. Not that I had any hostility to that faith: it was as natural in its place and time as any other, and contained important elements of truth; but it could never be my faith. In the midst of the living, I could live only with the dead. It was a comfort, but a cold comfort, to say that I was living among the immortals.

Reacting now against all these closed doors, I found the moral of Goethe's drinking-song cheap and hollow. His old soldier *dishonours* his past, as if his present cynicism and rowdiness could be something better. This is only one more mood, one more incident, and a more vulgar one because there is less courage in it. There was vitality in those human adventures; there is also wit and good humour in laughing now at their seamy side; but it is dishonourable and self-contradictory to forswear your honest loves, past or present. They it is that reveal your true nature and its possible fulfilments; they are the Good, in the modes of it that you can appreciate and unfeignedly worship. There is therefore enthusiasm no less than resignation in an enlightened *metanoia*. You give up everything in the form of claims; you receive everything back in the form of a divine presence.

This final settlement of the moral problem involved no visible change in my mode of living. I went on teaching and writing, drinking and travelling and making friends; only that now, beforehand and explicitly, these occupations were marked for me with a cross: the sign on the one hand of death and on the other of consecration. Gradual and bloodless as the change was, there was a wrench in it, a passage through dark night. I had become aware that, as a spirit, I was not myself but pure spirit, to whom all selves are mere objects, and all their joys and sufferings so many animal vapours, to be endured courageously and no less courageously dismissed and wiped away. The truth of life could be seen only in the shadow of death; living and dying were simultaneous and inseparable. For, as Emerson has it,

> *This losing is true dying,*
> *This is lordly man's down-lying,*
> *This his true and sure declining,*
> *Star by star his world resigning.*

Yet this transit through darkness brought me quickly back into the light, into the pure starlight that transports without dazzling. No part of time is lost in eternity, only the haste and uncertainty of passing from one thing to another. I had not been ravaged by any hostile fate; my heart had simply uttered a warning against its own weakness. It had said to me: Cultivate imagination, love it, give it endless forms, but do not let it deceive you. Enjoy the world, travel over it, and learn its ways, but do not let it hold you. Do not suffer it to oppress you with craving or with regret for the images that you may form of it. You will do the least harm and find the greatest satisfactions if, being furnished as lightly as possible with possessions, you live freely among ideas. To possess things and persons in idea is the only pure good to be got out of them; to possess them physically or legally is a burden and a snare.

I know very well that this philosophic salvation is not such as nature or life looks for or can accept: it is only what the truth affords to the spirit. Life and nature do not ask to be saved from themselves: they ask only to run on at full tilt. It is the spirit that asks to be saved from that insane predicament. Yet spirit is an emanation of life, and it is more truly and naturally happy in the first phases of its career than in its final salvation. In the end, when it has understood and renounced everything, if you ask it whether it is happy, it can reply only as La Vallière replied to the friends who asked her if she were happy in the Carmelite convent to which she had retired: *Je ne suis pas heureuse; je suis contente.* Nature had been muted, but spirit had been freed. In that sense, and under the spell of that profound conviction, I composed the second sequence of my sonnets, using the traditional language and images of love which can render that sentiment best. They belong to a second-rate kind of poetry that in itself has no claim to attention; but here, considered as autobiography, they may be recalled. The key to the whole is given in the one line:

A perfect love is founded on despair

This paradox is condensed and rhetorical; to get at the truth in it we must expand it a little and ward off certain misunderstandings. It is not love simply, but only *perfect* love that includes despair. Love in itself includes hope, or at least a desire to preserve the object of it, to enshrine and defend it. And in regard to the object even perfect love retains this solicitude. It is only in regard to the lover, as a poor human being, that hope must be cut off, plucked up by the roots, if love is ever to become pure, happy, and immortal. The perfect lover must renounce pursuit and the hope of possession. His person and life must, in his own eyes, fall altogether out of the picture. Stendhal, in his book *De l'Amour* (which unlike his others pleases me very much) distinguishes four kinds of love, *l'amour physique, l'amour vanité, l'amour goût,* and *la grande passion.* The first two are obviously imperfect and impure: they include craving, jealousy, cruelty, fear, folly, and self-degradation. Yet the vital side of physical love cannot be dispensed with, since it is the root of the whole growth and most intense in the *grande passion*. In the great passion this vital impulse is often diverted from physical lust and jealousy to absolute devotion, heroism and suicide. It is therefore psychologically not only possible but normal for the passion of love to be self-forgetful, and to live on in the very act of sacrifice and personal despair. So transformed, the great passion becomes worship. And the *amour goût*, which is more playful, and turns the vital element into laughter and delight, also reaches perfection only when all thought of the self, all *amour vanité*, drops out of it, and it becomes wholly aesthetic, pure joy in beauty and charm. Combine these two elements, the tragic and the lyrical, and you have turned love into a rapture in adoration which seems to me its perfection. It presupposes the total abdication of physical, social or egotistical claims; yet these claims were instinctive in the psyche, and the spirit has either adopted them and repented, or at least felt and understood them in refusing to make them. The passion of love, sublimated, does not become bloodless, or free from bodily trepidation, as charity and philanthropy are. It is essentially the spiritual flame of a carnal fire that has turned all its fuel into light. The psyche is not thereby atrophied; on the contrary, the range of its reactions has been enlarged. It has learned to vibrate harmoniously to many things at once in a peace which is an orchestration of transcended sorrows.

CHAPTER II

KING'S COLLEGE, CAMBRIDGE

I FIRST went to Cambridge on a flying visit, being taken there by Russell to see his brother Bertie who, he said, was anxious to make my acquaintance. These circumstances mark, in my mind, the character of my whole connection with Cambridge, wholly different from my connection with Oxford. Bertie was then living in the new part of Trinity, small rooms in a falsely Gothic dormitory that might have been at Harvard. He was very busy; there was a knot of other friends, none of whom I remember distinctly; and I had no time to see the beauties of the place. To Oxford, on the contrary, I had gone in my first free flight, alone, and with eyes and mind open. I had at once made friends, and learned silently to thread that secluded labyrinth. Officially, I was unknown and a stray tourist; inwardly, I was perfectly at home. In Cambridge, my friends were all professional. Bertie at once became a Fellow and an intellectual leader.

Lapsley, a Harvard man of the class of 1893, later became also a Fellow of Trinity, having written a most learned work on the history of the See of Durham. He spent his life in that College, but kept up his American relations and sympathies with an admirable fidelity. To me he was most hospitable and friendly, although his intense Anglican piety acted sometimes as an ulterior barrier between us. Still, I could tell him whatever I had seen, in Spain or elsewhere, of the too human side of Catholics, and he would relish my naughtiness. Those *Romanists* were so *pagan* and their liturgy so *incorrect*! He was consumptive, and had never married. For that reason, perhaps, he was on terms of intense friendship with Mrs. Wharton and a host of other American

16

ladies. The doctors commanded him never to skip his daily walk; and he would sometimes come to fetch me in a pouring rain which I would intrepidly face in his company, although I was not myself a slave to any regimen of exercise or of fresh air, even if heaven fall. He wondered how I could drink wine at luncheon; he drank only in the evening. But I never worked in the afternoon, I only walked or read, which I was never too boozy to do; why then not spiritualise one's mid-day food with a little liquor? It was precisely in the evening that I liked to sit alone by my fire, and perhaps concentrate my mind on something in particular.

It was in a professional capacity, as being an instructor at Harvard, that I was admitted to King's College in 1896. I was *in statu pupillari,* an advanced student, wore a Master's gown (without strings, because not a Master of Arts of that university) and dined at the high table. Never have I eaten such good food consecutively anywhere else; but it was dinner only: the rest one had in one's rooms. My rooms were first at the corner of Silver Street, and then in Free School Lane: only in the long vacation term, when Wedd lent me his rooms in Gibbs, or the Fellows' Building, did I live in the College. But what a place that was! The front or east room looked out across the Quad towards King's Parade. Over the rather bastard stone screen, you saw a picturesque row of old houses, not decrepit or intentionally picturesque: just the honestly useful, respectable work of an age of burghers. Each house was individual, but each knew and kept its place with decorum. In the middle of the Quad was a rather diminutive monument of the unhappy founder, Henry VI, adorned with two subordinate figures: Science, as the local epigram had it, turning her back to the College, and Religion, turning her back to the Chapel.

From my front windows I could see the exterior of the Chapel in violent perspective, the buttresses standing in file, like soldiers with shields, lances, and banners, or like the statue-columns of Karnak. Only a corner of the windows was visible at the top; above which the rough grey wall was crowned with lovely per-

forated battlements and pinnacles. Away with the pedants who say
that battlements should not be perforated! Not, I grant, in a castle,
although even there they may be decoratively shaped; but in a
church not expected to stand a siege—the walls being all glass—
why should not the traditional edging of battlements be retained
for beauty's sake? And why shouldn't the compliment be paid to
beauty with a frank smile, by opening lights in those mock battlements, as if they were laughing children looking through their
fingers? What could be more charming and lovely than the perforated battlements and the eight pinnacles (one especially thick
at the corner where the stairs wind up) of the Magdalen tower
at Oxford? King's Chapel, however, has a grander air, on account
of its four solid and lofty turrets. They are almost towers, yet I
think more decorative than if they were towers, because more sub-
servient and integral to the nave of the church.

And what a church! A Gothic Parthenon in dignity, a chapel
only in having no aisles and only one altar; but that is the tradition proper to every temple. We can't have everything or be everything at once; the god of pantheism is a monster; and if we wish
to be something perfect we must banish regret for not being anything else. Here we must banish the romantic love of unrealisable
things; we mustn't ask for a forest of columns teasing us with
alternative irrecoverable vistas; we must renounce a multiplicity
of vaults, each higher than the other, and of galleries hanging
and looking down over us, as it were, from other worlds. We must
renounce the wayside shrine and the screened chapel for our
tombs and our special devotions. In a word, we mustn't dream of
cathedrals. This is a Gothic hall, a single chamber, and in that
respect like the Pantheon, St. Sophia and the Sistine Chapel. Yet
it is Gothic not only in decorative style but in structure and spirit.
It is narrow, long, lofty: it draws you on, towards the goal of
your pilgrimage, to the place where the altar ought to have been.
It is a throne room for the Risen Christ, to be present in the
Sacrament. Here concentration is perfect, the whole court drawn
up in order, waiting; only the monarch is late. Meantime the

arrangements continue to suggest his presence, and we may study them the more freely while we postpone our acts of homage.

In the first place, it was perhaps not altogether true that there are no side chapels. There are small chantries between the buttresses under each window, some now used as a vestry: they might have been intended to hold tombs, or even side altars. Yet these chambers are low and walled off, and may be overlooked. That which at once catches and holds the eye is the vault. It is held up, lifted up, as if it could move, like a baldachino over a procession; it is woven of intricate fan traceries, undulating slightly, without sharp arches, or heavy pendants; the fans open like palm trees from the piers, and then merge their branches in a chain of diamonds and circles down the flat central part. It is regal elegance, rather than religious mystery, that spreads this canopy over us; yet never was perspective more magnetic or vault more alive. We are in the presence of something magical, something sublime.

Nor is the Gothic charm of suggestion and interruption altogether wanting. Halfway down the nave there is a screen, with an elaborate organ above, separating us from the choir. This screen has been condemned by many critics, as interfering with the vista; but that seems to me a strange innocence. The *vista* is emphasised, almost created, by the screen: instead of one long monotonous tunnel we have a great vestibule and a great yet only partially visible sanctuary beyond. The vault is uninterrupted, the great series of windows goes round all the way, and we see the central one, with the crucifixion boldly designed, over the altar. But the altar itself, the choir stalls, and whatever else there may be in the chancel, we do not see clearly; and the aerial perspective itself is defined and the whole edifice prolonged, by the presence of that obstacle. I don't say that the organ screen in itself is suitable in style or in colour; I should have preferred a stone one with a great crucifix, as in the Cathedral at Avila; but the presence of a screen, and of a screen high, at least in the middle, is essential to the *living* beauty of the place. Pedants often hanker for a dead beauty.

The crowning glory of King's Chapel, however, is the stained glass. I believe the west window, to which one at first turns one's back, is modern, but it is not offensive: all the rest (and for once, they are complete!) belong to the period and are Flemish. Under their spell I once versified my emotion about them, and will not bore the reader by serving it up again cold. I have never studied them in detail, for their technique or the treatment of their subjects; I gazed at them only as luminous tapestry, as accompaniments and accessories: yet over their blue ground and green shadows, their heraldries, and labyrinthine figures, touched with jewel lights, my eye always travelled with pleasure. They served as a sort of opiate; yet the dreams they provoked were all of order, tenderness, grandeur, and peace.

The same qualities that appeared there in a hieratic monument, a relic of the past, appeared smiling and always young if I looked out of my windows on the other side towards the Backs. The rooms in Gibbs are the noble model humbly reproduced in Holworthy at Harvard; a large square room in front, for receiving, meeting pupils, and dining, and two narrower rooms behind, which in Wedd's apartment were one the bedroom and the other the study. This study was full of books, especially in Latin, which was Wedd's subject. But the chief attraction was the view: a vast velvet lawn, sloping gently down to the river—here more like a canal—with great avenues of trees and pretty stone bridges leading to the wooded bank and gardens on the other side. Nor was architecture absent in this prospect. To the right the lawn was bounded by the charming garden front of Clare, at once cheerful and stately, decorative and domestic. There was something, as I remember it, particularly warm and amber-like in the colour of its stone; probably the same stone that looked so granite-like in the lower parts of the Chapel, and whitened into silver towards the top. But with colour and aerial quality the English weather plays unending tricks; what you see once you may never see again, yet you may count on soon seeing something new and in some way lovely.

How was it that my heart was not anchored in King's College, where I had been lodged so grandly and so comfortably, in perfect seclusion yet with everything that I could care for within easy reach? Why have I rather clung to Oxford, where I was never an inmate? It may have been an accident. In 1897 I was not young enough to be assimilated and not old enough to count, or to become a centre for a knot of friends. I made few new acquaintances and remained generally unknown. Some of these circumstances were distinctly to my liking and others might have varied with time; yet my feeling when I was at King's was that the birds were not worthy of the cage.*

Who were the birds? The Provost—whose name I have forgotten—very civilly asked me to luncheon when I was first admitted to the College, and I never saw him afterwards. There was the antiquarian James—later, I believe Provost—from whom I might have learned many interesting things, but I never exchanged more than a few words with him. Finally, there was the notorious Oscar Browning. He openly flaunted the banners of gluttony and promiscuity, neither of them suitable for a teacher of youth; yet everybody laughed, and the authorities affected a calm indifference. He was obviously a good soul, and kind, but club-footed, fat, self-congratulatory, and licentious. His warm affections ranged from royalty to the lower decks of the Navy. He seemed to be rich; I heard that besides his Fellowship—which was permanent on the old basis—he acted as agent for wine-sellers and launched new brands of choice claret and champagne. The claret he tasted—gratis—every day at luncheon, with a mutton chop, vegetables, and a pudding. His breakfast was no less copious; and before breakfast he had bread and butter in bed with his early tea, and a special bottle of ale at 3 A.M. for which he was awakened by an alarm clock. Afternoon tea, for him, required solid accompaniments,

* The year 1896–7 seems to have been an unlucky one for finding genius at King's. Several literary lights, including R. C. Trevelyan, the poet, had just disappeared and several public celebrities, including Keynes, had not yet come up. I believe Bury, the historian, was in residence but I never came across him.

after hard daily tennis and a Turkish bath. It was he that introduced Turkish baths into Cambridge. Tea by no means took away his appetite for dinner in hall: always a choice of thick or clear soup, then fish, a joint, a hot sweet, a cold sweet, and a savoury, washed down with champagne; and he with Wedd and me were usually the only ones to have the traditional glass of port after dinner in the combination room on ordinary days; but many others joined us on Saturdays, when there were usually old King's men who came up from London. With all this burden to carry, the O.B., as he was called, seemed always in perfect health and in jovial spirits. Was it genuine happiness, or a bold front put up to hide a desperate misery? He was also, I should have said, an alleged historian; but this seemed to be of no importance.

At King's I had two personal friends, Wedd and Lowes Dickinson. Wedd, who was a friend of the Russells, was my particular mentor and guide. We sympathised in our pagan satirical view of life. His scholarship and wit were of the Johnsonian stamp. "There," he said once as we walked over the bridge to the Backs, "is where the married Dons have their breeding holes." I think he was of humble extraction, and accepted a position of Court Fool in the learned world, with licence to say the truth in figurative language. I often remembered Bangs and Barlow when I was with Wedd: it was the same humanism without fig-leaves. Wedd's learning was far wider and more classical, but in his person he was less a man of the world. A little thick-set fellow with a ferreting air, he resembled a woolly lap-dog, only black. His black hair fell over his black eyebrows, and he seemed a picture of prehistoric man. People abroad, he would say, couldn't believe that he was an Englishman. Once when he had mentioned his nationality to a fellow traveller in France, the Frenchman wouldn't credit it. Irishman, perhaps, or Welshman, but Englishman, *jamais de la vie*. "*Mais si, Monsieur*," Wedd protested in his perfect French, "*Anglais piu-ah!*" I didn't say so, because Wedd mightn't have liked it, but I think the Frenchman was virtually right. Wedd was no Teuton, no Angle or Saxon, or Dane or Norman; he must have been a pure descendant of the few remaining primitive Britons: a Mediterranean race! Hence our good mutual understanding.

The College was not kept open for residence throughout the long vacation; at a certain date in August I had to leave. One of the Dons very kindly gave me a list of towns with interesting churches in the Eastern Counties, beginning with Norwich and ending with Durham; a tour in that region, as yet unknown to me, would fill up my time, unless I preferred to return to Oxford where I had spent the previous summer; for paradoxically, being a member of the University of Cambridge I was not allowed to reside in Cambridge out of term, but I might reside in Oxford, term or no term. Wedd, however, had suggested that I might join him at a village near Wark-on-Tyne, by the Roman Wall, and among Roman roads, a good place for long walks; and this decided me to travel northwards, and see something of that part of England. Architecturally, the prevalence of the perpendicular was rather monotonous, even disheartening; because the Reformation seemed to have overtaken most of the Tudor churches before they had clothed their perpendicular bones with the vesture of worship, and they stand bleak and empty, like solitary dead trees. I had seen in King's Chapel the very best that the perpendicular can do, in its gorgeous intentions; it needed all the colour and all the rich accessories that the commercial wealth of the age could supply, to redeem its spiritual starkness. But at York and Durham, and especially at Lincoln, there were lovely relics of the earlier time, the castle-building age, when structure was varied, picturesque, and defiant in itself, without rejecting the splendour that heraldry and religion might introduce into it. Yet somehow the Eastern Counties, even Cambridge, have less of what I like in England, than have the South and West: they look the wrong way. They are open to the winds and to the thoughts that devastate rather than to those that fertilise and refine.

In Northumberland Wedd and I spent an austere fortnight, in a modest cottage, without baths, with food that only a good appetite could swallow, and long tramps, one day fully twenty miles, over open windswept undulating country. It is the thought of those Roman roads and fortifications, rather than the sight of them, that remains with me. The North is formless; it has spirit in it, wind, but no images that beg to be retained, sculptured, immortalised. Let the North, I say, digest its barren tempests; let it send us only its young men, the raw material of genius, for the South to instruct, to enamour, and to mature.

In sharp contrast with Wedd was my other friend at King's, Lowes Dickinson. His classicism was not of the rough, coarse, realistic Roman kind, but Greek, as attenuated and Platonised as possible, and seen through Quaker spectacles. I liked his *Greek View of Life*, but it wasn't Greek life as depicted by Aristophanes or by Plutarch; it was what a romantic Puritan of our time would wish Greek life to have been. War, lust, cruelty and confusion were washed out of it. Dickinson was super-sensitive, hard-working, unhappy, and misguided. His gift was for form; his privately printed poems seemed to me admirable; but his subject-matter was perverse, even in those poems, and much more, I think, in his philosophy and politics. He prayed, watched, and laboured to redeem human life, and began by refusing to understand what human life is. Too weak to face the truth, he set himself a task too great for Titans: to shatter this world to bits, and put it together again on a moralistic plan. If at least that plan had been beautiful, he might have consoled himself for his practical impotence by being an avowed poet; but his plan was incoherent, negative, sentimental. It was that no one should suffer, and that all should love one another: in other words, that no one should be alive or should distinguish what he loved from what he hated.

Poor Dickinson came once or twice to America, the first time to give some Lowell Lectures in Boston. It was winter, and he suffered from the cold, as well as from the largeness and noise of the town. I remember his horror when the electric car we were in got into the subway, and the noise became deafening; also his misery when one evening we walked across the Harvard bridge, and he murmured, shivering: "I have never been so cold in my life." The cocktail, he said, was the only good thing in America. He hated the real, bumptious, cordial democracy that he found there; he would have liked a silent, Franciscan, tender democracy, poor, clean, and inspired. If he could have visited New England sixty years earlier he might have found sympathetic souls at Concord or at Brook Farm. He wouldn't have liked them, reformers don't like one another; but at least he might have imagined that the world was moving towards something better. As it was, he found that it was sliding hellwards with a whoop of triumph.

More important for me, and also in themselves, were my friends at Trinity College. Although I was a member of King's, all my work was at Trinity, under Henry Jackson as Tutor, and with Bertie Russell, G. E. Moore and MacTaggart as philosophical friends. Jackson was an influential person, he might have been Master of Trinity, the greatest position in the British university world. He was courtly, magnificent in his ample stiff silk gown, hospitable, universally informed, and learned, with the English trick of fathering some childish hobby. He maintained that Plato's logic was the same as Mill's. He was tolerant and considerate about my bad Greek, which I had confessed at the beginning; and, as I needed a translation to help me in my reading, he recommended me to get the dialogues we were to read—the *Parmenides, Philebus, Sophist,* and *Politicus*—in a cheap edition in separate little volumes with the text and a German translation on opposite pages. These little books proved invaluable. They went easily into the pocket, and I could read them anywhere during my walks, or look up again at any time a passage that had arrested my attention. He had published an analysis of the hypotheses about Being that fill the long second part of the *Parmenides*. Without attributing any historical insight to this view, I found it a useful thread through that labyrinth; and it also had an important influence on my philosophy, because it helped me to see that Being, the One, the Many, *et cetera*, were names of categories, not of existent things, so that all cosmological theories relying on dialectic (such as that of Leibnitz) were sophistical. They played with essences, and thought they were disclosing facts. Facts are all accidents. They all might have been different. They all may become different. They all may collapse altogether.

Jackson had splendid rooms in the Cloisters, afterwards occupied by Lapsley, and one day he asked me to luncheon there, to meet Lord Acton. I am not an admirer of celebrities, or curious about them. Obscure people, if they are nice, interest me much more. However, under the circumstances, it was as well for me to go. Lord Acton was a Catholic and a German; I don't know how he came to be an Englishman. He was fat, ponderous, with a full grey beard and an apostolic heaviness. His theory of history was ultra-empirical: anything might happen, and all testimony was acceptable. Miracles abounded everywhere and the testimony for prophecy, second sight, *et cetera,* was overwhelming. But even non-miraculous details seemed to fill his mind and absorb his interest. Having heard that I was at Harvard, he suddenly turned to me and asked if I knew how a certain movement had been carried out in a certain battle (which I had never heard of) during the American Civil War. The question annoyed me for various reasons. As politely as I could I said that I was born in Spain during that war, that I had heard little talk about it when I went to America, and hadn't studied the history of it. He then went on to explain the point at issue among the various witnesses, and I escaped further interrogation. The vision, I might almost say the smell, of a mind stocked like an old trunk with remnants of faded finery and knickknacks, moved me to sadness not unmixed with aversion. Daily experience, all trivial incidents floating like wreckage in a sea of ignorance, is bad enough: but think of a distinguished mind, consecrated to history, which is one of the Muses, and still remaining in that chaotic state! No wonder that Lord Acton should have felt the need of remaining a Catholic, under no matter what difficulties and sorrows! Not having found any order in the real world, he had to invoke an imaginary world where order should be morally perfect. It is a vendetta of faith against intelligence that perpetuates hostilities.

Of all my friends, of all persons belonging at all to my world,

Bertrand Russell was the most distinguished. He had birth, genius, learning, indefatigable zeal and energy, brilliant intelligence, and absolute honesty and courage. His love of justice was as keen as his sense of humor. He was at home in mathematics, in natural science, and in history. He knew well all the more important languages and was well informed about everything going on in the world of politics and literature. He ought to have been a leader, a man of universal reputation and influence. He was indeed recognised to be a distinguished man, having made his mark in mathematics and logic, and largely inspired the new philosophical sect of "logical realists." Yet on the whole, relative to his capacities, he was a failure. He petered out. He squandered his time and energy, and even his money, on unworthy objects. He left no monument—unless it be the early *Principia Mathematica* written in collaboration with Whitehead—that does justice to his powers and gives him a place in history.

In his physique he was a complete contrast to his brother, a Russell while his brother was a Stanley. Bertie was small, dark, brisk, with a lively air and a hyena laugh. According to some people he was the ugliest man they had ever seen. But I didn't find him ugly, because his mask, though grotesque, was expressive and engaging. You saw that he was a kind monster, that if he spit fire, it was a *feu-de-joie*. For so violent, so merciless a satirist, he made a charming companion. I, at least, was never afraid of him; and he was benevolence itself to the most humble and hopeless intellectual waifs. Though his laughter was savage, it was fed by the subtlest intellectual lights; that was the chief charm of his conversation, added to the sense of security that his faultless memory and universal knowledge gave in regard to any information that he might give. This information, though accurate, was necessarily partial, and brought forward in a partisan argument; he couldn't know, he refused to consider, everything; so that his judgments, nominally based on that partial information, were really inspired by passionate prejudice and were always unfair and sometimes mad. He would say, for instance, that the bishops supported the war because they had money invested in munition works; or that the United States government had called out troops, not to fight the Germans, but to support capitalism against the strikers. It was for this libel that he was sent to prison; and this wasn't the worst consequence of such rash assertions. They alienated opinion in high quarters and ruined his official career. "I would go to the stake for that," he would cry sometimes in summing up a philosophical argument. But going only to Holloway, in the first division, hadn't the posthumous value of martyrdom; and the general feeling that his judgment was unsound and his allegiance misplaced defeated all his attempts to guide public opinion.

He had been beautifully educated by private tutors at Pembroke Lodge. After the dreadful experience she had had with her elder grandson, who would throw her letters unread into the fire, Lady Russell dreaded the fatal influence of schools: Bertie at least must be preserved, pure, religious, and affectionate; he must be fitted to take his grandfather's place as Prime Minister and continue the sacred work of Reform. Bertie showed me his schoolroom at Pembroke Lodge, and his old notebooks on the various subjects that he had studied. It was perfect princely education, but a little like cultivating tropical flowers under electric light in a steaming greenhouse. The instruction was well selected, competently given, and absorbed with intense thirst; but it was too good for the outdoor climate. Moreover, there were obstacles that far from being surmounted were built upon as cornerstones of righteousness and sources of superior light. One was the hereditary liberalism and Low Church piety of the family. Another was Bertie's microscopic intensity that narrowed each of his insights, no matter how varied these insights might be, lost the substance in the visible image, the sense in the logic of the words, and made him, though he might be many-sided, a many-sided fanatic.

Bertie, Stickney and Westenholz, the three best-educated persons I have known, never went to school. Bertie, however, did go to the University, and here he made those fruitful contacts that produced his best work and opened to him an academic career. Had he been an obscure and penniless person, such a career might have fulfilled his ambition and determined his path; but for him, destined by his grandmother to be Prime Minister and by himself to be an international Messiah, academic life was but a preparation or an interlude. His vocation was to reform radically the whole intellectual and social world.

I can imagine two ways in which Bertie might have proceeded to prove how great a man it was in him to be. One would have been to carry out his grandmother's plans, get early a safe seat in the House of Commons, moderate his zeal so far as not to denounce bishops, generals, admirals or even Tory ministers, unless he had proofs of their obliquity, and generally to identify himself (as he could well do emotionally) with the official interests of his country. He would not at once or always have been in office. These intervals of leisure would have sufficed for the intensive study and the literary work that were appropriate to a leader of reform; and when his party won an election, he would have been able to exert the power of government for the heroic purpose of diminishing that power. He might have prevented the collapse of the Liberal party, by transforming it into a labour party true to democratic, anti-military, anti-imperialistic, anti-clerical principles. He might have shown the world whether at least in England it were not possible for a modern civilisation to exist with a maximum of liberty and a minimum of government.

The other way in which Bertie might conceivably have become a great man would have been by emulating people like Bacon, Hobbes, Spinoza or Auguste Comte. I don't mean in their doctrines but in their ambition. He might have undertaken an *instauratio magna* of scientific philosophy. He could have done it better than Bacon, inasmuch as the science at his command was so much more advanced; and the *Principia Mathematica*, a title challenging comparison with Newton, seemed to foreshadow such a possibility. Why, then, didn't Bertie proceed in this course? Or why didn't he choose the other, the political path?

I can judge only superficially, and from a distance. I didn't know him as I knew his brother. But judging by the work that he has actually accomplished, I think that, penetrating as his analysis might be in particular cases, in fundamentals he could never shake himself free from his environment and from the miscellaneous currents of opinion in his day. Except in mathematics, he seemed to practise criticism only sporadically, caught and irresistibly excited by current discussions. His radical solutions were rendered vain by the conventionality of his problems. His outlook was universal, but his presuppositions were insular. In philosophy he couldn't entertain the hypothesis that Berkeley, Hume, and Mill might have been fundamentally wrong. He seemed one day astonished and horrified when I said that the image of the sun as a luminous disc, sometimes (if you squint) with rays round it, was as fictitious and imaginary as the idea of Phoebus Apollo with his golden hair and his arrows. The senses are poets; and a strange allegiance to these imaginary figments kept Bertie's philosophy always inconclusive and unstable. Autobiographically, aesthetically, logically they are ultimates: they are what you confront absolutely when you concentrate and purify your attention; and in a critical analysis of experience Bertie was quite right in distinguishing them and in sticking to them. But they are the fireworks of animal sensation, not the stars of heaven. To turn them into elements in a cosmology, or into a system of ethics and politics, seems a blunder of the first magnitude. Animal sensation is sheer dream; only animal faith can lead us to reality. You can't build science out of literature; and the English and Germans, who in their positive science serve material interests and show plenty of hard sense, when they come to interpret science philosophically are crossed by the Protestant and romantic tradition of subjectivism, and end with devout feeling, translating everything into sentimental literature. Bertie at least escaped the fabulous sort of idealism. He almost emerged from psychological physics by composing physics out of logical elements. This was the "logical realism" which he took a leading part in suggesting. But he couldn't carry his suggestion out, because it dies in solipsism of the passing datum; or if you inconsistently grant many data, it dissolves into a multitude of sparks with only logical relations to one another. The universe has become a dictionary of the terms in which we apprehend it.

Less absorbing at the time, but ultimately perhaps more satisfactory, was my philosophical contact with MacTaggart. He was then a very odd person, who sidled along the street sticking close to the wall and half looking sheepishly down; and his absolute Hegelian idealism at that time prejudiced me against him. He had had, I understood, a fantastic tender passion that made him embrace some foolish illusions. But he must have seen enough in me to wish to save my soul, for he unexpectedly proposed to read Hegel with me, he an adept and I an ill-disposed outsider. It was a great favour to me; and we had a few sittings in the long vacation. We read aloud and discussed the beginning of the minor Logic, in the *Encyclopaedie der Wissenschaften*. I was then refractory to the transcendental point of view, and would continually transfer the matter in hand to the naturalistic plane, which MacTaggart, with some contempt, called *psychological*. Nothing seemed to come of our effort, and we soon gave the thing up. He retained, however, a friendly attitude towards me (as Moore did not); and during my last visit to Cambridge, in 1923, he came one evening to sit next to me at dinner in hall, and I soon found, when we began to talk about philosophy, that he had discovered that, apart from technicalities, I could be as transcendental as he. Only for me transcendentalism was a deliberate pose, a way of speaking, expressing a subjective perspective; whereas for him it revealed the metaphysical structure of all reality. He pinned his faith and hope of salvation on what I played with as an optical illusion, rendered harmless by being understood. Why didn't this mockery in me disgust and offend him? I think he was almost content with my doctrines of essence and of truth: indeed, he ought to have been more than content, because I granted much more than he asked for, at least in the case of truth. That evening he quoted me a line from one of my sonnets:

Truth is a dream unless my dream is true

and said that this was philosophical poetry at its best. The compliment was excessive and most unexpected; but now, on rereading that effusion of my remote adolescence, I can see that probably I then looked to the truth for the sort of *justification of faith* which MacTaggart demanded from the truth now. My imagination had framed a highly poetic, humanistic, supernaturalistic picture of the universe. I felt that it was a fiction; but I said impulsively: "If that fiction isn't the truth revealed, truth can never be revealed to the human heart." Truth was therefore—not really a dream in itself, since no mind was ever to see it—but something which it was a vain dream to look for, or to think we possessed in our philosophy.

This is what I suspect I felt at the age of twenty: but if so, MacTaggart read into my sonnet something that had never been in my mind—a perfectly legitimate use to make of words that set one thinking. For his own sentiment was different. He was an absolute idealist and could admit truth only as an attribute of opinions, more or less true as they grew more voluminous and consistent. Every philosopher thus had the fountain of truth within himself, and his system would become absolutely true if he could only make it all-comprehensive and perfectly coherent. Learned egotism could not have a more congenial prospect: but in MacTaggart I think there was also another motive force, distinctly not egotistical. Every opinion, in positing a truth to be attained, would remain essentially nothing but a dream, yet each would move truthward if it reappeared enveloped in another dream more coherent and comprehensive than itself. German philosophy is contemptuous of realistic faith in regard to perception or dogma, and of naturalism in morals; but nature takes its ironical revenge, and idealists are often most innocently realistic about society, and domestic, not to say animal, in sentiment. This definition of truth as harmony in dreams is a metaphysical echo of human craving for sympathy and democratic comfort in agreeing with the majority. We go right enough, darling, if we go wrong together!

CHAPTER III

TRAVELS

ALL my life I have dreamt of travels, possible and impossible; travels in space and travels in time, travels into other bodies and into alien minds. Not having been suffered by fate to be more than an occasional tripper and tourist, I have taken my revenge in what might be called travels of the intellect, by admitting the opposite of all facts and of all beliefs to be equally possible and no more arbitrary. These travels of the intellect helped me in boyhood to overcome the hatred that I then felt for my times and my surroundings; and later they have helped me to overcome the rash impulse to claim an absolute rightness for the things I might have preferred. Ideals are relative to the will. A little change in me would have banished that hatred and reversed that preference. My intellectual travels therefore reconciled me in the end, at least in theory, to the home facts. I could forgive the world everything except the ignorance and arrogance of thinking its condition alone possible or alone right.

In spite of my longing for unexampled things, I have always been a realist about the facts and suspicious of all desiderata and utopias. Your sanguine man who sets forth enthusiastically for El Dorado nurses a secret passion for the happy home. For that reason he is restless in his accidental lodgings and risks everything in the hope of discovering other lodgings where he would enjoy forever an unclouded happiness. The born traveller, on the contrary, is not pining for a better cage. If ever he got to heaven, on the next day he would discover its boundaries, and on the third day he would make a little raid beyond them. Imagination is potentially infinite. Though actually we are limited to the types

of experience for which we possess organs, those organs are somewhat plastic. Opportunity will change their scope and even their
centre. The free spirit in us knows that whatsoever may be offered
to it is but a reversible accident, and though we are compelled to
be absorbed ignominiously in such accidents, yet the interesting
side of those accidents for the intellect is only their character and
their reversibility. The precision and variety of alien things fasci-
nate the traveller. He is aware that however much he may have
seen, more and greater things remain to be explored, at least
ideally; and he need never cease travelling, if he has a critical
mind.

How, being lazy and hating excitements and risks, could I develop this passion for travel? One incentive was aesthetic. I loved
picture-books, costumes, theatres, architectural vistas, dialectical
perspectives. The harmonies into which accidents could fall were
picturesque; they were also ridiculous, and a sense for the ludi-
crous, a love of laughter, was native to me. A kindred but less
innocent motive was satirical. It was not only I, in my silliness,
that was laughing at the world: it was the gods that were laughing at it. Its own substance mocked the forms that it took. Not
only were events and conventions mere episodes in an endless
flux, but they were mechanically produced by forces irrelevant to
our dramatic poses and pert egoisms: they were like patterns seen
in a kaleidoscope—a toy of which I was fond. There was a sort
of satirical magic in their existence, and the childish impulse was
strong in me to turn the crank and see what would come next. A
third motive might be found in the antecedents of my family. My
father and mother had lived in exotic places. I gathered in childhood that travel was normal and enlightening: it taught us the
variety of tastes and standards in the world. My parents were
nevertheless most dogmatic in their views and precise in their
habits; they rejected almost everything; but this was perhaps the
effect of their ill-luck. To me the existence of the things they
condemned, such as religion, monarchy, luxury and fashion, was
not at all disquieting. On the contrary those fancy things were

fascinating, and a great relief to hear about, in contrast to the dullness of home life. I was glad to allow others to keep their ideals of any sort, provided I was allowed to keep mine. At any rate in a world where the exotic so abounded, to ignore it would be ignominious intellectually and practically dangerous; because unless you understand and respect things foreign, you will never perceive the special character of things at home or of your own mind. You will make ridiculous claims and assumptions, and you will continually run up against stone walls. *Travel,* therefore, I said to myself, *travel* at least in thought, or else you are likely to live and die an ass.

So much for the enlightening uses of travel; yet in the philosophic traveller something else is presupposed, without which he would lapse into a frivolous sightseer and his mind into an album of snapshots and clippings. Ghastly are those autobiographies that contain nothing but old jokes and old anecdotes. Before he sets out, the traveller must possess fixed interests and faculties, to be served by travel. If he drifted aimlessly from country to country he would not *travel* but only wander, ramble or tramp. The traveller must be somebody and come from somewhere, so that his definite character and moral traditions may supply an organ and a point of comparison for his observations. He must not go nosing about like a pedlar for profit or like an emigrant for a vacant lot. Everywhere he should show the discretion and maintain the dignity of a guest. Everywhere he should remain a stranger no matter how benevolent, and a critic no matter how appreciative. Were he a mere sensorium, without his own purposes, moral categories and points of reference, he might as well have left those variegated natives to lead their lives undisturbed and unvisited. They would have gone on the more comfortably without him, and he the more inexpensively without them, at home. The traveller should be an artist recomposing what he sees; then he can carry away the picture and add it to a transmissible fund of wisdom, not as further miscellaneous experience but as a corrected view of the truth.

Perhaps if in youth I had been able to satisfy my desire to travel, the lack of a fixed background, material and moral, might have reduced me to a vain wanderer. Circumstances prevented. I was tethered, even when I began to cross and recross the Atlantic, to Avila and to Boston, and allowed only an occasional halt between. My real nucleus was this combination, not easily unified. By the time I was free, I was no longer young. The Mohammedan countries, India and China, no longer tempted me. If materially I was less attached than ever to any particular spot, morally my native sphere had become definite. I was a child of Christendom: my heritage was that of Greece, of Rome ancient and modern, and of the literature and philosophy of Europe. Christian history and art contained all my spiritual traditions, my intellectual and moral language. There would have been no danger, however far afield I had travelled, of losing my moorings; and foreign things had no meaning for me except as they offered interesting analogies or contrasts for deepening my sense of my ancestral world.

This fidelity of mine to my origins showed itself indirectly even before I was able to choose my way. When in 1887 I went to Gibraltar by sea from Malaga, and saw Mount Atlas, it was the idea rather than the image that arrested me, glorious as this image was; and when I returned there in 1891, this time from America, and crossed to Tangiers with some steamer acquaintances, this first glimpse of something beyond Christendom chilled rather than excited my desire for exploration. This is the more remarkable in that one of those acquaintances was the painter John Sargent. He was then at work preparing his decorations for the Boston Public Library, and intent on finding figures and especially costumes suitable for his Hebrew Prophets; and in Spain he wished to re-examine the dressed wooden images of the Mater Dolorosa, in view of a Madonna that he meant to introduce into his design for the other end of the same hall. His appreciation of these so Spanish images appealed to me. Without being a pre-Raphaelite, he had altogether outgrown Protestant shyness in religious art, and felt the deep passion in it. Neverthless, we saw nothing in Tangiers that was more than curious: like the customs officers, three venerable old men sitting cross-legged on a raised bench, like a counter, who, having been bribed by my friends' courier, grandly motioned for our valises to pass unexamined. We saw some Jewish houses, not being admitted into the Moslem ones; and while Sargent and the others bargained for all sorts of treasures, I bought a pink-and-gold cloak, that for years afterwards decorated my wall, and that Sargent said was Venetian stuff woven with half moons expressly for the Oriental market. Two other pictures only remained in my memory of sights in Tangiers, which was then in all its primitive squalour: the market place with men, asses, sheep, and camels all lying together on the bare earth, amid puddles and rubbish; and on a slight eminence not far off, a story-teller reciting, like Homer, his military legends (so I was informed) with great calmness and long pauses, to an audience of a few scattered individuals, no less calm and otiose than himself. Yes, here was the antique background to our civilisation, important to remember; but I was sure that if we reverted to it, even as mere students and historians, it would seem tedious, filthy and trivial. In any case, I would let others inquire, and trust to their reports. Therefore, when two years later, I was again at Gibraltar, I let my American fellow travellers go to Tangiers alone, and spent a meditative day or two seeing what was to be seen from the Rock.

It was only after ten more years of routine, filled with occupations that leave no memories, that I found myself with two clear summers and one winter before me, for my first real travels. I might have gone to India, China, and Japan, had I been younger and in the mood of the Arabian Nights; but I was middle-aged and in the mood of Gibbon; The Life of Reason was then in the press. What a pity that I couldn't have rested and travelled before writing that book! It would have been richer in substance and purer in form. At least, I could rest now, and hope that the impurities would evaporate from my mind in the fresh air and light of history. My journey would be only over beaten paths, leisurely, comfortable, solitary, towards the fountains of my own past. I would visit, as far as practicable, the scenes where that past took shape and see *in situ* the ruins that remain of it. Perhaps this might help me to distinguish the part of my heritage that is hopelessly dead from the part that still has the seeds of the future in it. European life surely has a hereditary skeleton, an indisputable structure, that must be reproduced, of course with variations, so long as moral continuity and progress remain possible in our world.

The first scene in this drama should properly be Egypt; and from there tradition would bifurcate, one stream running to Palestine and Western Asia, the source of our religion, and another stream running to Greece, the source of our art, literature, politics, and philosophy. But the exigencies of travel and of the seasons didn't allow me to take things in strictly historical order. Tourists were not conveyed to Egypt before mid-winter, and there were side-shows, derivative episodes nearer home, that might be taken by the way. From Paris, where I had finished and sent off my last batch of manuscript, I went straight to Naples. It was September, still summer, but not unpleasant for a lazy man; and in an upper room at Bertolini's, with a wide view, I spent a few weeks of pleasant repose. I saw what was then visible of Pompeii; nothing of Herculaneum except at the Museum; and only the very surface of life in the town. But the atmosphere was already more balmy, more unconstrained, more animal, than in the north: I had moved several degrees towards the equator of the moral sphere. And not merely by way of relaxation; for I went to Paestum, and there saw Doric temples for the first time, symbols of severity, simplicity, harmony, and strength. There was the pure vein to be traced in the quartz of Roman accumulations and grossness; and I followed that vein back to Sicily.

Doric purity is not a thing to be expected again in history, at least not yet. It indicates a people that knows its small place in the universe and yet asserts its dignity. In early Christian art there may be simplicity and *naïveté*, but never self-knowledge. The aspiration in it is childlike. For anything like Doric fortitude in the West we must look to the castles, not to the churches; and the castles are Christian only by association. Here then was an ultimate point of reference, a principle of manly purity, to mark one extreme in the moral scale of all human arts, and to give me the points of the compass in my travels. And by a curious chance, during this same excursion to Paestum, I came upon the opposite extreme of the moral scale also, in a form that I have never forgotten. The reader may think it trivial, but I assure him that to me it has the most serious, the most horrible significance.

At Paestum there was only the railway station and no hotel, but travellers might spend the night comfortably at La Cava, not far away. I had done so and in the morning was waiting at the station for the train to Naples. The only other persons on the platform were a short fat middle-aged man and a little girl, evidently his daughter. In the stillness of the country air I could hear their conversation. The child was asking questions about the railway buildings, the rails, and the switches. "Where does that other line go?" she asked as if the matter interested her greatly. "Oh, you can see," the father replied, slightly bored. "It runs into that warehouse." "It doesn't go beyond?" "No. It stops there." "And where does this line go?" "To Naples." "And does it end there?" "No, it never ends. It goes on forever." "*Non finisce mai?*" the girl repeated in a changed voice. "*Allora Iddio l'ha fatto?*" "No," said her father dryly, "God didn't make it. It was made by the hands of man. *Le braccia dell'uomo l'hanno fatto.*" And he puffed his cigar with a defiant resentful self-satisfaction as if he were addressing a meeting of conspirators.

I could understand the irritation of this vulgarian, disturbed in his secret thoughts by so many childish questions. He was some small official or tradesman of the Left, probably a Free Mason, and proud to utter the great truth that man had made the railway. God might have made the stars and the deserts and all other useless things, but everything good and progressive was the work of man. And it had been mere impatience that led him to say that the Naples line never ended. Of course it couldn't run on forever in a straight line. The child must have known that the earth is round, and that the continents are surrounded by water. The railways must stop at the sea, or come round in a circle. But the poor little girl's imagination had been excited and deranged by religious fables. When would such follies die out?

Commonplaces that had been dinned all my life into my ears: yet somehow this little scene shocked me. I saw the claw of Satan strike that child's soul and try to kill the idea of God in it. Why should I mind that? Was the idea of God alive at all in me? No: if you mean the traditional idea. But that was a symbol, vague, variable, mythical, anthropomorphic; the symbol for an overwhelming reality, a symbol that named and unified in human speech the incalculable powers on which our destiny depends. To observe, record, and measure the method by which these powers operate is not to banish the idea of God; it is what the Hebrews called meditating on his ways. The modern hatred of religion is not, like that of the Greek philosophers, a hatred of poetry, for which they wished to substitute cosmology, mathematics, or dialectic, still maintaining the reverence of man for what is superhuman. The modern hatred of religion is hatred of the truth, hatred of all sublimity, hatred of the laughter of the gods. It is puerile human vanity trying to justify itself by a lie. Here, then, most opportunely at the railway station returning from Paestum, where I had been admiring the courage and the dignity with which the Dorians recognised their place in nature, and filled it to perfection, I found the brutal expression of the opposite mood, the mood of impatience, conceit, low-minded ambition, mechanical inflation, and the worship of material comforts.

In saying this I don't forget that all phases of life are equally natural and spontaneous, and that some animals are furiously busy while others are calm and brave. Each has its troubles and dangers and each sometimes has its rewards. But I was setting out on my travels with a moral personal interest, not with a scientific one. I wished to clarify and intensify my sense of the humanly beautiful. I wished to measure the distance and the steps between rational life, lived in view of the truth, and blind miscellaneous living. The world has always been filled with the latter; but in classical antiquity collectively, and in modern times individually, there has been an aspiration to look before you live; and this aspiration has left traces of its passage in monuments and maxims that it is my particular desire to understand. These are the maxims and monuments of human wisdom. I had already studied the maxims; now I wished to have a glimpse of the monuments, and a hint of the conditions that had made them possible. On, then, to Sicily.

It was not yet the season for tourists and at Taormina, my first halt, I found no vehicle at the station, and when at last I got a lift in a local cart, with some difficulty I reached my hotel, where nobody was expected, and I was served with a part of my host's supper. Although the weather was good, somehow the place seemed desolate, and it was impossible to fall into the mood of luxurious enjoyment appropriate to the scene. Like Capri, where I have never been tempted to stay, Taormina seems rather a refuge for moral invalids, favourable for a long convalescence or for a slow death. I went on to Palermo. Very like a Spanish provincial city, no doubt with its special charm when you acquired a domicile and corresponding habits: but for me it proved merely the starting point for two excursions: one to Cefalù, for the sea and sunlight and the picturesque, the other to Monreale, for the Byzantine architecture and mosaics. I am no connoisseur or even amateur of the special luxurious arts, carpets, tapestry, carvings, mosaics, iron or silver work. I like it all, as I like stained glass, as an enrichment, as an element in the beauty of something greater; and such things seem to me to require the life to which they belonged, if they are not to seem mere relics, old finery looking a little childish as well as shabby in its neglected gorgeousness. Moreover, for me on this journey, the Byzantine should come at the end, in Santa Sophia.

I felt more joyful and breathed more freely, when I passed to the southern coast, and saw something Greek. Agrigentum, in its desolation, left much to the imagination, but stirred it deeply. Not so much the ruins as the magnificent site, as if all the seven hills of Rome had been linked together in a chain, doubled in height, and been made to overhang the forum and the lower town in a broad curve. That vast acropolis must have been a sublime thing. Outwards, on the convex side, it is a sheer precipice; inwards its horns descend to the plain and make it accessible. One of these horns is occupied by what remains of the town. I climbed to the top, partly by steps. There was a little square, with a café, but no vestiges of the temples that must have stood there: for a reward I saw some large white goats, apparently clean as lambs, browsing among the steep lanes or perched upon the stone enclosures that bordered them. These ancient fortresses, in the days of peace, must have been very domestic and country-like in the simplicity and monotony of their ways. Dull, except for the recurring festivals and the frequent wars, yet well fitted, in both aspects, to fix the character of tragedy and comedy, as the Greeks fixed it, limited, monotonous, liturgical, but intensely felt, profoundly human, wonderfully central and final.

Agrigentum was a colony, suddenly rich, like an American mushroom city, short-lived and ruined even more suddenly than it had grown up; but for its day it was enormous, and it gave birth to a great poet-philosopher, the literary model of Lucretius, and a grander personage, with his tragic end soon enveloped in legend. Both Lucretius and Empedocles are said to have killed themselves, or voluntarily become gods: in any case they saw the world as the gods would: that is to say, as we all should, if we could surmount our accidental humanity and let the pure spirit in us speak through our mouths. I wonder if a mushroom civilisation, by its very thinness and sudden brilliancy, like fire in straw, may not be easier for the spirit to profit by and to transcend than a more deeply rooted tradition.

My last halt in Sicily was at Syracuse, where I chanced upon a pleasant small hotel, with views towards the sea, and at once established a routine for the day, which I might have kept up indefinitely. It was already possible for me to lead my chosen life anywhere, provided the material conditions were favourable and unobtrusive. I could have stayed on at Syracuse all winter. I think it was there that I read and despatched the first proofs of *The Life of Reason*. My daily walk usually took me to the ruins of the Greek theatre, past what must have been the agora of the upper town in antiquity, where the principal temple remains turned into the cathedral. This transformation excited my architectural fancy. To turn a Greek temple into a Christian church all you need to do is to wall up the peristyle, leaving a window in the upper part of each space between the columns, and then pierce arches in the side walls of the cella. Your interior then occupies the whole or nearly the whole of the temple platform; place an altar where the statue of the god had stood, and you have a complete church: even a great church, if you are prudent enough to retain a narthex before the inner door, and an ambulatory behind the altar. This was not done as I could wish at Syracuse; but the great columns were not walled up so as to be wholly concealed, and the line of the pediment remained visible, if not uninterrupted. The transformation had not been the work of one artist, but of many bishops; yet it allows enough to subsist of the ancient temple to make evident the continuity of worship and the identity of civic function in this edifice for three thousand years.

What surprised me at Syracuse was the slight elevation above the sea of Ortygia, the old castle occupied by the modern town. I had imagined a much loftier citadel, a great marine acropolis; but the defences must have been mainly artificial. There must have been sea walls as at Tyre round most of the peninsula and great towers and gates upon the isthmus. But to-day in walking out towards the theatre or towards the northern quarters where Epipolae extended, you hardly felt any change in height or defensibility. Perhaps my expectations had been raised by the grandeur of the acropolis at Agrigentum; I had to revise my ideal of Syracuse, and remember that the site of Ortygia was chosen, like that of Tyre or of Venice, for being surrounded by water, not for being unscalable from the land: and I began a sonnet that never went beyond the first two lines, which contained all that I had to utter about these places:

> Renowned Ortygia, castle of the sea,
> And Agrigentum, castle of the air.

After this spell of solitude among ruins I returned to take ship at Naples and found myself in the social bosom of dear old Boston. Mrs. Beal, my friend's mother, was on board with a companion, and it was arranged that I should join the party. I was glad to do so. Mrs. Beal had always been friendly and confidential. I could stand for a while to her *in loco filii*; she, with her courier and maid and companion, would tell me all the facts about everything, and yet leave me free enough to observe them for myself.

We saw, during a calm voyage, the mountains of Crete, the birthplace of Zeus. Afterwards in Athens, I heard Evans, the archaeologist, talk at table about his discoveries there. Tempting from a distance, to explore those mountains and to study those ruins; yet though I felt the attraction strongly, I nursed no illusions about it and suffered only a theoretical pang at having to renounce it all. In reality, it would have been a terrible bore and far beyond my physical endurance and agility. Yet to read about prehistoric Crete excites me always, no matter how imaginative or untrustworthy the author may be. Spengler may dream what he chooses about unknown civilisations, and Racine may render mythology credible and courtly, like the myths in the tapestries of modern palaces. I like to ponder on the wonders of Crete. It was there that Plato, in the Laws, thought of founding his ideal city. In such sea-girt mountains I like to imagine it, and I repeat as an incantation, the words of Phèdre to the son of Theseus:

> Pourquoi, trop jeune encor, ne pûtes-vous alors
> Entrer dans le vaisseau qui le mit sur nos bords?
> Par vous aurait péri le monstre de la Crète
> Malgré tous les détours de sa vaste retraite.

But the monster, though he transforms his monstrosity, is perennial; and it is the pure hero, who might have extinguished monstrosity, who dies young, entangled in the monstrous luxuriance of nature, that pays no heed to perfection.

The insults with which time pursues its noblest creations appeared at once in the harbour of Port Said. I knew I was in Egypt, yet I saw nothing but huge iron freight steamers, higher than the shore, and the bustle and sordid confusion of a landing stage and a railway station. However, we were not booked to stay there, and soon found ourselves in a quiet hotel in Cairo. No distinction, no dominant character in that city; a mixture of incongruities. Only one impression, as usual architectural, remains of that week in what was and is a great focus of Mohammedan life: the one or two great mosques that we visited. It was a surprise to me, thinking of Cordova, to see them so high, so majestic. The memory of Babylon and Assyria, or the shadow of the ancient temples in Egypt itself, must have led the Moslem builders to enlarge their scale, and to be imposing; whereas the note I expected in a Mohammedan place of worship was rather that it should be secluded, exquisite and devotional. However, my acquaintance with the religious sentiment of Islam was very slight, and I procured a French translation of the Koran to read during our trip up and down the Nile.

The flat-bottomed river steamer in which I was to live for a month was comfortable, and the food satisfactory. My cabin was at the end of one of the verandahs, so that I could sit by my open door, which was also the window, and watch the river and the banks undisturbed. I made all the excursions as prescribed except one. We were to stop three nights at Luxor. On the first day I went with the rest to view the ruins at Karnak: but on the next day, when the party was conducted to the Tombs of the Kings— a particularly long donkey-ride with a picnic at the ruins—I seceded. The attraction at the Tombs of the Kings was then merely pictorial: the architecture was not important, while at Karnak I had seen one of the wonders of the world, and I wished to go again, alone and on foot, to see it at leisure. This was my best day in Egypt. I climbed the great pylon; I wandered among the ruins; I lingered in the great hall, trying to evoke an image of what it must have been in its glory; I admired the minor temple with its forecourt of colossal statues serving as columns; but most of all I felt the spell of the inner sanctuary, approached by a sort of labyrinth of passages interlocked, and lighted only by cracks left purposely here and there between the immense blocks of stone that formed the walls and the ceiling. In the inmost chamber there was now nothing: but I could imagine the glittering antique image that must have stood there (like the Virgin of the Pillar at Saragossa, only colossal) which the High Priest, barefoot and duly vested, may have approached with great ceremony perhaps once a year. From all other eyes this inner splendour would have been forever concealed. How profoundly appropriate, for all its grotesque animal worship and solar myths, this ancient worship was to the real status of man! How childish our metaphysical moralisms and psychologisms seem in comparison!

For beauty, apart from grandeur and significance, only two or three heads and the temple at Denderah remain in my memory. The treasures of the Kings' Tombs had not yet been unearthed, and in any case belong to decorative rather than to constructive art. Denderah, being late (and those heads also, perhaps), reflected Greek influence, and doubtless on that account were easier for me to appreciate. I am not ashamed of liking late styles. They ought to be the surest expression of human taste, since technique has been mastered and accidental mannerisms have been overcome; only the volume and seriousness of inspiration may be wanting, unless the artist is able to transcend and rebuke his epoch, as the tragedians and Socrates and Plato could do in Athens. Then we obtain the maturity of lateness with an early inspiration revived as philosophy or religion.

Of course we went to the Pyramids. The tourist talk and the tourist foreground dominated; the great question was whether we should ride or not ride a camel, ascend or not ascend the great pyramid, pulled up at each step (four feet high) by an acrobatic

Arab: and little grinning English Tommies were crawling over
the Sphinx. I said to myself: *Non raggionam di lor, ma guarda e
passa*. It was not altogether easy to look. Sand had half buried the
base of all these monuments, and we were there pert and self-
conscious pygmies, incapable of imagining or understanding what
they signified, and playing with their ruins like a child with his
rocking-horse. There remained only the vain traveller's satisfaction
in saying, yes, I have been there, I have seen the Pyramids; and
the fact of having seen them, however flightily, certainly leaves in
the psyche a material *point d'appui* for anything we may otherwise
learn about them. I have since read two or three books about
Egypt, and there have been notorious discoveries, so that nowadays
a young girl can't stand still in the street without reproducing the
outlines of the ancient Egyptians. This was probably not the
immortality for which they cared so much; but I am at a loss to
conceive what that immortality could have been. It is not a subject
to which anything in me responds. Let the dead, I say, bury their
dead; yet those who have no sense for eternity try to prolong
their existence by desiccating their bodies or disembodying their
souls. It is in either case a sham, ghastly or ghostly. Leaving that,
I thank the Egyptians for the standard they have set up for mankind in the solidity of their architecture. We may refine all we
like; unless we rival or surpass that solidity, that superhuman
permanence, those symbols of silent potentiality and eternal peace,
we shall always remain secondary, temporary, capricious, and
childish. We shall always be doing things that are partial failures,
that we must abandon at once for something different, and that
even when they are in fashion disquiet us more than they satisfy.

It was not as a pious pilgrim that I went to Palestine; nothing
that I could expect to find there would affect my personal religion or philosophy. I went as a sceptic, to visit the birthplace
of religion in others and if possible to understand that religion
better. These parched Semitic deserts have been the fountain
of inspiration to the whole modern West and to a great part of
the East: only pagan antiquity, India, and China have reflected

rationally upon the subject, and leaving inspiration to take the forms it likes, have naturalised it in a calm philosophy. Nor was the expression of religion in art, as in Europe and in Egypt, that which I looked for here. Here the chief art was religious eloquence and that can be studied more quietly by one's own fireside. The rest was barbarous and secondary. But the primitive condition of the country—then (1905) still under Turkish rule—the mixture of races, languages, and costumes, the religious feuds, the medley of ruins and shrines, and the petrified deathlike aspect of these ravines and river-beds without water, and these hills without verdure, formed an ominous theme for historical meditation.

I was now alone, having parted from Mrs. Beal at Assouan. She was bound further up the Nile; but with the first cataract, the great dam, and the half-submerged temple of Phylae my journey had come to its proper end. Nubia lay beyond my range: sun, sand and natives were nothing to my purpose. I had made for the Holy Land in the only way then practicable, by sea to Jaffa. The little port, which we entered in a row-boat by scooting on the top of a wave between two rocks, the little town clinging to the face of the cliffs, and the little railway climbing the mountains to Jerusalem, were much to my taste: small, indifferent material things, to be disregarded by souls full of great passions. And the country, not unlike Castile, all rock and moor, also preached frugality, austerity, reserve. It taught the overfed, overdressed child of the West how unnecessary were most of his burdens.

In Jerusalem I was in the hands of a guide assigned to me by Cook's Agency, a short middle-aged native who spoke English and had been converted to Anglicanism from his doubtless Jewish affiliations. He had no sense for the matters historical and artistic, that really interested me, and thought it his duty merely to point out sites and name names, none of which were worth remembering. I stayed three weeks in Jerusalem, waiting for the rain to stop, for I had planned to go by carriage through Samaria and Galilee to Damascus. It would have been a memorable trip; but the roads, people said, would be impassable, and I finally gave up the idea.

So long a stay rather taxed my poor guide's ingenuity to think of new sights to show me; but some of the last were among the best. For instance, he took me one day to a Greek monastery some miles away in the country: the drive was not uninteresting, and the glimpse of the religious life of the Orthodox, and of their persons, was just what I was looking for and seldom found. My guide, while not unknown or turned away, seemed not to be on very good terms with the natives of any persuasion: doubtless they thought him a renegade for not being converted to their own sect. I seemed to be an object of curiosity to these Greek monks, as much as they were to me. Unfortunately, I couldn't say anything to them directly; but we exchanged courtesies through the interpreter. Meantime I observed their aspect and ways. Nothing religious: a sort of childish animality: no trace of Greek features, except in some the very large, thick-lidded eyes. They were all rather small, and of course long-haired and bearded. One couldn't help thinking of Christ, who no doubt in the pictures had been made to look somewhat like them: but to me the assimilation was distinctly unpleasant. Christ should never be painted to look like a savage or like a woman. There should be the dazzling apparition of a god, breaking through an ascetic figure.

Another afternoon, on foot, we went to a Catholic monastery on the Mount of Olives. Here the trouble with my guide didn't matter. An Italian monk showed us the garden; I at once established friendly relations; and he explained to me that the ancient olive tree was not the same that had stood there in Christ's time, but was an offshoot of it; they had planted other offshoots near by, against the time when the present hollow contorted old stem should crumble altogether; and he gave me a few leaves of this, which I sent in a letter to Mercedes. I felt at home: my vocation to live in Italy began to show itself.

We had of course been to Jericho, and the shores of the Dead Sea. Geographically, this was of the highest interest. What a cleft in the crust of the earth, to prove how rotten it is inside! The view across the Dead Sea from the Mount of Olives, with the mountains of Moab opposite, shows the same cleft in a grander light: the rottenness is not felt, only the sublimity of the depths and the heights, the gamut of nature keyed up to that of the Hebrew prophets.

As to Christian associations, legendary or historical, my own ignorance and the insensibility of my guide completely smothered them. I saw everything, but without even a borrowed illusion of devotion, such as I could have caught easily from a pious Catholic. Turkish soldiers kept guard at the supposed birthplace of Christ, lest Christian sects should come to blows over it: and everywhere ecclesiastical quarrels and modern desecration vulgarised sacred and poetic things.

Of the Mussulmans I had a better opinion: they were openly warlike, openly sensual, proud, chivalrous, and capable of friendship. They were poetical and manly, bold and bravely resigned to the will of God. They didn't overestimate their own importance in the universe; but they despised a servile mind. All this, however, was a mere ideal, a fancy of my own: I had no means of verifying or disproving it. It would have required a youthful and adventurous courage to explore the East like a Doughty or a Charles de Foucault, and in the first place a sportsman's agility and endurance, with a perfect command of Arabic. I was reduced to catching glimpses here and there of men and manners, and filling in the rest with memories of the Arabian Nights. My reading of the Koran had not awakened me to anything new: the lyric parts were inferior to the Psalms, and the legends inferior to those in the Old Testament; whereas to compare with the parables and the maxims of the New Testament there was absolutely nothing. Ritual sublimity the Koran, in the original, may well possess. Eloquence and nobleness belong to speech even in Spain, and they have a quality that is not Roman, but must be Moorish.

As to the Arabian Nights, I had feasted on them recently with unexpected pleasure. What I had read of them in boyhood had inspired me with a priggish contempt. I thought the tales (as they are) chaotic and demoralising, although I read them in a drasti-

cally expurgated translation. But now Mrs. Berenson, who had
charitably received me at Settignano when I was ill with a bad
catarrh, had piled the sixteen volumes of the French version of
Mardrus upon the table by my bedside; and if they didn't cure me,
at least they reconciled me to being laid up. The view of life, like
the life reviewed, is still chaotic; and I can understand the dislike
expressed by pious Moslems at having them regarded as true
pictures of their family life. The pictures belong to the general
tradition of the whole East, India and China included: they are
satirical, summary, realistic, exquisite, and entertaining. The exaggeration, Gargantuan or love-sick, has irony in it; the popular
story-teller indulges our unrestrained dreams, and at the same time
laughs at them. The ribaldry renders all this more piquant and
joyous than it otherwise would be; also less narcotic and vainly
imaginary, because sensuality after all belongs to real life, and
experience can at once justify the interest in it and discount the
illusion. I don't find the Arabian Nights, unexpurgated, demoralising, as I did, expurgated, when I was a boy. I see now that they
are playful and how much they adorn and embroider the commonplaces that they play upon. There is indeed no moralising in them,
nothing by way of a lesson; wisdom and poetry only in scraps,
comedy only in episodes, tragedy hardly at all. Yet we have the
daily texture of life spread before us in its crudity and in its magic;
the experience and the imagination of an unabashed creature that
understands nothing, but meets everything with the strength and
cunning of a man and the impulses of a child.

In Damascus I remembered the judgment that my young friend
Duer Irving had passed on Seville. Seville was nothing unless you
had a horse and a love-affair, and then it was everything. The
horse and the love-affair being out of the question for me at
Damascus, the place threatened to mean nothing to me: yet that
was not altogether the case. The suk was the best I saw in the
East: there was also a most picturesque market or exchange or
caravansary, where merchants and travellers gathered, where the
merchandise was on view, and where the central fountain, under

the open sky, and the surrounding domes and cloisters, produced most wonderful effects of light and shade. Here leisure and business, profit and enchantment, were not divided. The suk was comparatively lofty and wide, like the nave of a church, with much the same effects of light, for it was covered partly by stone arches, partly by wooden roofs, and in places only by awnings, so that patches of sunlight shone out here and there, to dazzle the eye and deepen the grateful shadows of the rest. The ground was earth to be trodden by beasts of burden, led in familiarly without undue regard for pedestrians; and the booths on either side for the most part had no great depth, but displayed all their wares within reach of the hand. One of the booths especially attracted my attention, and as a stubborn client happened one day to be bargaining and making his choice for half an hour, I was able to watch the scene unmolested at a discreet distance. It was a carpet shop. There was a broad counter in front, at one end of which sat the venerable merchant, impassive and apparently indifferent, dressed in black, red, and white, with a long grey beard. Behind him were two rows of rugs rolled up and standing on their edges, like so many barrels. The quality, colours, and pattern of each were sufficiently visible to entice the eye, and provoke at request that the precious thing should be unfolded. Then the youthful assistant would leap up from the other end of the counter, pull the particular carpet down and spread it out over the counter or if need be on the ground outside. This agile young man was beautifully dressed and fit to represent any of the adolescents in the Arabian Nights. He wore a red fez, a white-and-green striped tunic reaching down to the ankles, with tight sleeves, but growing full at the bottom and held together at the waist by an ample sash, that served also for pockets, and was made of a yellow brocaded stuff: and he was shod with yellow babouches. After many rugs, some of them lovely, had been spread out and rolled up again, he had to bring down and extend the heaviest of all, a great red one that covered the whole width of the road; but I didn't stay to see whether the bargain was finally struck. A great camel was coming up the path: he couldn't be allowed to tread on that invaluable carpet, so up it had to come again in the twinkling of an eye; and I took advantage of the excitement to slip away. It is an awkward position for the curious not to wish to buy anything: if they look, the tradesman at once thinks he has a likely customer, and begins to exhibit and praise his wares. You feel like an intruder and have to hurry away. For this reason I have never been able to examine precious objects, even books, except in shop windows.

Of architectural beauties I found little in Damascus; it was at Baalbek, on the way back, that the imagination was stirred, if not with beauty, at least with wonder. The scale and extent of the monuments here rivalled the Egyptian, while the style and the religious inspiration remained Greek. Perhaps of all periods in history the Hellenistic, between Alexander and Caesar, corresponds best to my feeling. In reading Plutarch, who lived later himself, but most of whose heroes lived earlier, I am put out by his doctrinaire morality, as if all men and ages ought to follow the same model; also by the limitations of the older heroes' minds. They were wonderful, they were perfect, but they were slaves to local traditions and special passions. The full-grown human soul should respect all traditions and understand all passions; at the same time it should possess and embody a particular culture, without any unmanly relaxation or mystical neutrality. Justice is one thing, indecision is another, and weak. If you allow all men to live according to their genuine natures, you must assert your own genuine nature and live up to it. Now, with Alexander, a great part of the East in fact, and the whole world in prospect, were introduced into the sphere of the West, into the narrow military life of the ancient city: yet the gods of the city were not abandoned; but exalted into gods of the open rational philosophic mind, they were retained to preside over a universal empire. Heliopolis, the City of the Sun, seemed to me to represent this ideal fusion. It was immense like the East, but unlike the East it was not miscellaneous. The miscellaneous East very soon overwhelmed it, as the miscellaneous North overwhelmed the Western Empire. Yet ruins give ground for hope; for although nothing can last forever, now and then good seasons may return.

On the way from Beirut to Athens, we saw the coasts of Cyprus and Rhodes, and stopped at a small island and then at Samos. In these islands I first trod Hellenic ground, but without emotion: hardly a stone, hardly a head, reminded me of Hellas. Athens itself, for the most part, was uninspiring. I engaged a youngish man, a Cypriot journalist, as a guide and as a teacher of Greek; but in both respects, in my two months at Athens, I gathered little new knowledge. The social foreground was too cosmopolitan, and the material foreground too ugly and insignificant. We went on one excursion, intending to reach Delphi; but at Corinth we found that the steamer had been purloined by a private pleasure-party, and I had to be satisfied with a trip to Nauplia, for Tiryns and Mycenae, and to Epidaurus. This last, my most remote point, proved the most inspiring. Whether it was the light and the solitude, the steepness of the pit, the completeness of the theatre (except for the stage) or the sombre wooded hills above, somehow all the poetry of early Greece seemed to flood the place: small, heroic, silvan, open to sea and sky, lyric and divinely haunted.

In the Acropolis I had two or three unexpected intuitions. One regarded the vitality, the dash, the solidity of Greek architecture. The lion's head at the corner of the immensely projecting cornice in the Parthenon seemed to have all the picturesqueness of a gargoyle: and the entablature was not what its name and usual aspect imply, a wooden beam laid across posts: it was a great wall built up over a foundation of columns, like the wall of the Doge's palace in Venice, firmer if not so high. On the other hand, that bold cornice and those broad pediments lent it an even greater dignity. This effect, of the temple raised over the peristyle, was new to me, and important. It removed the reproach, that pursues buildings of one storey, of lacking weight and height and being set up on stilts, propped up, rather than built. Here the burden carried seemed sufficient to ennoble the bearers, and to justify their stoutness, their number and their fidelity to one model, like hoplites in a phalanx. This architecture was not merely utilitarian and economical; it was religious and martial.

Beautiful beyond words seemed to me the door and the Ionic

porch at the back of the Erechtheum. Byzantine, Saracenic, and Gothic cannot surpass such a thing in loveliness; their advantage lies only in allowing greater variety, so that in a larger and more complex world they could diffuse disparate beauties, more picturesque and romantic than those of Greek buildings.

I left Greece disappointed, not with Greece but with myself. I should have been young and adventurous, knowing the language well, both ancient and modern, and travelling alone, with infinite time before me. Then if the historic Ilyssus proved to be a rubbishy ditch in a dusty waste, I could have found another Ilyssus in some mountain gorge in which to bathe my feet like Socrates and Phaedrus and pass in dialectical thought from sham rhetoric to rational love. But the foreground was a dreadful impediment, and I was the worst of impediments, with my middle-aged ignorance, my academic ties, and my laziness. Hellas must remain for me an ideal, a thing to recompose, as the Evangelists recomposed their idea of Jesus, so as to individualise and replenish their ideal of Christ. The real Greece is dead, pulverised, irrecoverable. There remain only a few words and a few relics that may serve to suggest to us a rational ideal of human life.

With this the moral object of my journey was attained, or shown to be unattainable; but there remained one more scene to peruse, and I took ship from the Piraeus for Constantinople. Galata, where the hotels are, was nothing; but I could walk across the bridge, guided the first time, afterwards alone, to St. Sophia, the other mosques, and the stray sights of the old city. No exterior effects at St. Sophia, even from a distance. Remove the picturesque accident of the minarets, and you have a flat dome little more beautiful than that of the Pantheon in Rome; in character almost like the Baths of Diocletian. Was this dome intended to be a marvel externally, like that of the Mosque of Omar? In any case, it is a marvel internally: as if a tent held down by a dozen pegs had been lifted by the wind, and crystallised in mid-air. The eye, as it travels down over the great arches to the arcades of the galleries and aisles, is a little distracted by the oblique lines of the Mohammedan carpets and pulpit, and the hideous yellow discs hung high on the walls; but discounting this, and examining things more closely, wonder returns. What columns, what capitals, what walls! Roman luxury refined by Oriental taste, Roman grandeur of scale and mass spiritualised by mystic aspiration. This vast chamber is a sanctuary, regal in magnificence but open to the sky and air; this unity is infinitely rich in detail, this heaven has its hierarchy of dignities and beauties. A theocratic and imperial Church displays its poetry here, as it displays its pride at St. Peter's.

After this, at once surfeited and disappointed, I wanted to see nothing more, suppressed my love of new places, and stopped only to rest at Buda-Pesth and Vienna. I meant to leave Vienna, at least, for another occasion, when I might make a long stay, and see the Catholic, gay, and courtly elements of Germany, so utterly ignored in the view of Germany obtainable from America; but I have never been in Vienna again. In fact, I have never again travelled for the sake of travelling. My orbit has become narrower and narrower, dropping one loop-line after another: somewhat as the ball at the gaming-table runs round in smaller and smaller circles, more and more slowly, hesitates at the edge of each socket and then finally flops down and settles comfortably into the predestined resting-place. And the predestined socket in my case was Rome: *omnium urbis et orbis ecclesiarum,* says the inscription at the Lateran, *mater et caput.* Mother and head of my moral world, surely, and central enough even to-day: balmy also, humanly habitable at all seasons, full of ancient and modern and even of recent beauties, and inhabited by a people that more than any other resembles the civilised ancients. I could not be more at home anywhere, while preserving my essential character of stranger and traveller, with the philosophic freedom that this implies. Thus I renounce travel here, where I may still continually travel in thought to all ages and countries and enjoy the divine privilege of ubiquity without moving from my fated centre of gravity and equilibrium.

CHAPTER IV

ON THE SOUTH DOWNS

NOT far from Petersfield in Hampshire, just above the village of South Harting, a steep road climbs up the side of the Downs. The valley, as you ascend, begins to look more and more like a map, with its variegated patches of green fields, hedgerows and woods, and an occasional house that seems remarkably neat and toylike in the distance. At the top, the back of the Downs becomes rolling and bare, with rough heather and grass and here and there a copse in the hollows. The sweep of the horizon is unbroken all round, the wind blows fresh and invigorating, and in clear weather the sparkling line of the Channel is visible, and the Isle of Wight. The silence is primeval. Here sheltered in part by some high hedges that enclosed squares of grass as if for tennis courts or gardens, stood a little white pavilion with a flagstaff; the cottage for the man once in charge of the "semaphore" or signal service from London to Portsmouth. That form of communication was now obsolete, although bonfires were still occasionally lighted on the topmost knoll. I don't know by what chance this spot attracted Russell's attention, but it appealed to his love of space and of unchallenged dominion. There was not a house in sight, and a vast stretch of moor and woodland was available for purchase. He bought it, using it at first as a retreat for week-ends and holidays, but eventually enlarged it, put on another storey, a library in a wing, and even a tower, made roads, and turned it into his chief residence.

The natives for some reason had fallen into the habit of calling the place the telegraph house. Russell was not sensitive to the magic of names. He had consented, I suppose at the Scotts' suggestion, to call his ugly villa at Maidenhead *Amberley Cottage,*

Amberley being his second title, by which his father had been known; and now when he had a place of some character and potential beauty he adopted for it that absurd name, *Telegraph House*. Soon, however, in the jolly English way, the absurdity was domesticated, and everybody called the place T.H. It was comfortable, had no pretensions, and yet a magnificent position, a wild and varied domain, and the charm of solitude. I visited it repeatedly during thirty-two years, under its three mistresses, all three of whom I found hospitable and friendly, and of all places it is perhaps the place where I have breathed most freely.

When first Russell took me there, no road existed within the grounds, and the cart that met us at the nearest country station cut deep ruts in the grassy hillside as we wound and tilted, like a boat over the waves, up to the little house. I had expected that we should be alone there, in a sort of bungalow; but at the door we were welcomed by two modest-looking women, evidently mother and daughter, who smiled and spoke not exactly as servants would. Mrs. Turner, for so the mother was called, must be, I thought, a sort of landlady or housekeeper; and then I remembered, on hearing the daughter called Martha, that a Martha Turner had been the secretary at Swinburne and Co., Engineers, where Russell was a partner. When those ladies unhesitatingly sat down at table with us, I began to understand how matters stood. Martha Turner was now his private secretary. He was a married man unable to get a divorce, because Lady Scott, no less proper and more fashionable than Mrs. Turner, chaperoned her daughter everywhere, even to hotels where the young man of the moment occupied the adjoining room. Nevertheless, Russell was engaged to be married to Martha Turner prospectively, in case he should ever be free: and meantime he occupied the room next to hers and her mother's at T.H. To nonplus Mrs. Grundy, his identity was concealed from the servants and from people at the village; Mrs. Turner was the legal tenant, and all letters had to be addressed under cover to her. He was only Martha's young man who came for an occasional visit.

I never disliked Martha Turner. She was a clean honest young woman, reasonable, docile, with a good complexion and a copy-book hand. She was the absolute slave and adorer of her lord and master, and juster to him than his other lady-loves. It must not be supposed that in this case or in that of Emma Billings a promise of marriage was a treacherous means of seduction. There was no need of such a promise. Talk of marriage may have come in, in both cases as a vague ideal; but Martha Turner was honest enough to know that her love-affair was its own reward. The motive force had not been ambition to be a countess: it had been old, simple, irresistible human nature. She loved him truly and was too faithful to rebel at anything. A separation was inevitable. I don't know on what terms they managed it; but he never wholly deserted her as a friend or perhaps even as a lover. There was nothing in him of the poet or the Don Juan, nothing of the gallant, fanciful vola-tile lover. His ideal was the home, or several homes: in a polyg-amous way he was essentially the faithful husband, like Isaac and Jacob, or like Louis the Fourteenth. Had he been an Eastern potentate or a very rich man he might have managed better, keeping all his wives going at once in separate establishments. But in England that was inadmissible. He wanted each wife to be his legal spouse, as did Henry the Eighth; and they too de-manded it. Hence his embarrassments and their tears.

This idyll had a romantic setting, worthy of Rousseau; but the conversation at table was like that in a respectable boarding-house; and Russell was discretion personified, explaining nothing, and leaving me to gather my impressions undisturbed. That was in 1891; I saw and heard nothing of T.H. or Martha Turner for the next two years: but in July, 1894, when for various reasons I was lying low in America, a new chapter opened in this romance. "I was so glad," Russell wrote, "to get your cable and to know that I shall find you in Cambridge. . . . It would be so nice if you would get me lodgings in Cambridge or a room in an hotel— anyway so long as I am near where you are." Why he should so unexpectedly come to America was a mystery: but I knew that he liked long slow sea voyages, and was not surprised that he should choose the *Cephalonia*, the most Bostonian of Boston boats, for the trip. When people cable to you, and suddenly express an affectionate desire to be near where you are, though that place be Cambridge, Massachusetts, in August, it is a sure sign of trouble; and I was rather puzzled on my part how to find a suitable place where Russell might lodge. I was living at my mother's in Roxbury, where we couldn't ask him to stay; no hotel existed in Cambridge and no lodging of the English sort, with a sitting-room and food served separately. I could move, however, to my rooms in the Yard, and put him at the Colonial Club where the restaurant was in working order, and pleasantly deserted. Except for the extreme heat, this arrangement proved pleasant enough. My room was comparatively cool and comfortable, with an outlook on trees and grass, and not much noise, and I took my meals with him at the Club.

One day, when we were at luncheon, in walked William James, with his usual vivacity. "You remember Lord Russell," I explained, "who visited you here eight years ago." "Ah yes. You have put on flesh," James observed with a medical smile, as they shook hands. It was very true; and Russell's loose white flannels, with jacket ridiculously short, did nothing to disguise the fact. Nor was it a comic or jolly fatness. He was already suffering acutely from varicose veins. His air was preoccupied and at the same time a little vacant. He had too many things to think of, and none of them rewarded thought.

The mystery of his journey—he was on his way to California—was solved one day when he took two photographs out of his capacious breast pocket and asked me which of those two women I thought he had better marry. As he was legally married already and not likely to be free for years, the question was speculative, and for my speculative mind easy to answer. I replied at once, "Neither." One was Martha Turner, looking like a particularly tidy policeman or soldier, conscious of being photographed. She had no superfluous hair, or anything else superfluous. Russell said she was a brick, and I readily believed it. But why marry a brick? In the other lady, quite unknown to me, everything on the contrary seemed to be superfluous. Veronica (for I never saw her and that is all I know of her name), Veronica didn't look very young; rather battered, theatrical and unhealthy. No doubt she was appealing, being unhappy, and perhaps intelligent. Russell explained that she belonged to an Irish but prosperous family in San Francisco, had lived long in Europe, was a Catholic and called herself an artist. All this, in 1894, went very well with being at once fashionable and advanced. It was to her, I could see plainly, that Russell's heart inclined for the moment. He suffered at the thought of giving her up, and he might never have had the strength to do it. It was she who thought better of it, and broke off their relations.

That she had been greatly tempted, I can well believe. Imagine a woman of thirty, not particularly beautiful, frail, sensitive, thinking herself highly cultivated and a woman of the world, but idle and homeless: what a divine vocation, to capture a superman, to tame him, to save his soul and to become a British peeress, with a lovely home and a fixed nationality! But she seems to have had a shrewd elder brother who managed her property, and kept an eye on her generally; and I suspect that she also had an experienced confessor. Doubtless they warned her. Anyhow, Russell wrote from San Mateo: "I am thrown back rather than forward . . . and am rather upset again. . . . There will be an issue some day." And some months later from Maidenhead, "Veronica has retired into an inscrutable silence. . . . It was very painful and a blow to one's vanity, that abrupt breaking off: and yet the relief was immense . . . Veronica saved the situation by cutting the knot—what I regret is that fear and pique were the cause of the step. I wish I could attribute it to unselfish consideration of Martha's interests." So I discovered that Veronica had known all about Martha. The lady had been aware that she was being asked to promise to marry a man who not only had a legal wife but had promised to marry somebody else whenever he should be free!

When Russell says that being finally jilted by Veronica was a "great relief," but regrets that her action was not due to "unselfish consideration of Martha's interests" he reveals two sides of his character that afterwards reappeared on various occasions. One was a certain passivity or fatalism in his actions and feelings. He doesn't see the absurdity of asking one rival lady-love to sacrifice herself for the sake of another, while never thinking of making the sacrifice himself and cutting the knot in the beginning. That falling in love is often fatal and involuntary may be granted, although it can sometimes be headed off; but then reason and duty come in, in a strong soul, to suppress or sacrifice the passion. But what is reason or duty? Either another passion—the passion for harmony and integrity in the soul—or social conventions, expediencies and taboos. Against everything of the latter kind a transcendental free spirit rebels: and there I see the secret of tragic strength being often mixed with an extraordinary fatalistic weakness. You are tossed by every wave, and yet something in you observes your plight and fundamentally despises you. Most of the heroes and heroines in Racine suffered from this intellectual elevation in moral helplessness, Phèdre especially;* and if Titus in *Bérénice* masters his passion, he does it behind the scenes under political pressure and against his will, so that his exercise of freedom

* J'aime! Ne pense pas qu'en disant que je t'aime,
 Innocente à mes yeux, je m'approuve moi-même,
 Ni que du fol amour qui trouble ma raison
 Une lâche complaisance ait nourri le poison.
 Objet infortuné d'une vengeance céleste,
 Je m'abhorre encor plus que tu ne me déteste . . .
 Que dis-je? Cet aveu que je te viens de faire,
 Cet aveu si honteux, le crois-tu volontaire?
 Tremblante pour un fils que je n'osais trahir,
 Je te venais prier de ne le point hair:
 Vains projets d'un coeur trop plein de ce qu'il aime!
 Hélas je ne t'ai pu parler que de toi-même.
              Phèdre. Acte II.

seems but another instance of slavery. And it was this complete helplessness that Racine felt to be tragic: he wrote *Bérénice* because he found in Suetonius the phrase: *invitus invitam*. Now in Russell the passion for harmony and integrity was entirely absent: the transcendental spirit, though conscious of itself, had no representative on the stage, nor even a chorus to fill up the interludes; it was silent, and therefore, for the public, nonexistent. He explains this himself in an unusually reflective letter written during this visit to America.

"San Mateo, Cal.
"12 Aug. 1894.

"You will think I have been remiss in not writing to you before to thank you for the lovely time you gave me at Cambridge. It was very peaceful and very restful: just what I wanted . . . I don't think I ever took in your character before so distinctly as I did this time: we are opposed as entirely as possible. You are all for rest in the perfection of form with the negation of an end as either existent or important: I am all for the emotional strife and struggle, however vague and however formless, as being at least a reaching toward some end unknown, and seen only by faith as existing at all. Is not that so?" This he modifies two months later, writing from Paris, October 19th, 1894: "Why do you refer to me as loving strife for its own sake? . . . I desire peace and rest above all things now, I hate to be involved in a personal turmoil which invades and makes impossible a philosophic calm. Of course I may have said, and it is true, that strife does me good, braces me, and brings out my best qualities: but I don't welcome it."

Strife undoubtedly brought out his ability, his cleverness, wit, and gift of satire and invective; they say he was an excellent debater. But that was play-acting: it made him unfair and superficial. He had learned too well from cheap politicians and expensive lawyers to defend his brief and to close his eyes to truth and to justice. Nor does "reaching toward some end unknown, and seen only by faith"—an endless end, or the Eternal Feminine—seem his

best side to Platonists like Lionel Johnson and me. His best side
in our opinion was his intellectual freedom or transcendental detachment. In the midst of his shabby adventures, which whatever
he may have been reaching towards brought him nothing but
"expense of spirit in a waste of shame," this heroic spirit remained
alive, as in all romantic prodigals; it was proud and brave enough
not to be overwhelmed by any folly or any mischance. For this I
admired him to the end, as I do Byron, not for what he did or
thought, but for what he was.

This time, however, the well-advised Veronica saved him in
saving herself, and he made his trip to San Francisco to no purpose. I profited by it in having his company for a week at Cambridge and then receiving various confidential letters and a copy
of *Leaves of Grass,* as a memento of his visit. He had been patient
in the extreme heat of a Boston August, and had taken pains to
be civil; yet he was not at his best in a strange environment. He
was not adaptable, and found queer things wrong rather than
amusing. In England, where he freely found fault with everything, his satire was intelligent, his misrepresentations witty, and
his discomfort feigned. He still felt himself there the cock of the
walk, as in his first youth, and that pose became him. At first it
was justified enough by his intelligence, his physique, and his
title; it was dramatically proper and carried off with great effect,
even if destined in the end to become tragic. But now the pose of
moral high-mindedness seemed less becoming, as when, for instance, he wrote that he "feared" that Veronica acted from pique
and not from "unselfish consideration of Martha's interests." This
tone is an echo of his Low Church breeding. When he was in
prison for bigamy he composed a book of "Lay Sermons" and published it. Russell was not only an engineer, he was also a member
of the bar and had practised for years as an attorney. Applied
science naturally figures in the budget of the superman and the
enlightened despot: it developed Russell's *virtù*; but applied
sophistry, used in the service of any prejudice or passion, narrowed
and cheapened his mind. In these "Sermons," he preaches against

tradition and legal control, with crushing texts from the Gospels quoted maliciously by an unbeliever. It sounds like cant and hypocrisy; yet Russell was blurting out his sincerest convictions, like any poor man ranting in Hyde Park. Indignant dogmatism was another helpless passion that would invade him before he could stop to look and think: the more tart and feeble his maxims, the prouder he felt in defending them. His brother Bertie had the same satiric gift and the same temperamental fanaticism; but in him perverseness was partly redeemed by historical knowledge and speculative acumen. It seems to me a great pity that their sympathies in politics, as in love, should have been so ill-directed, and that both should wear the crown of martyrdom for such cheap delusions.

To speak of martyrdom is hardly a metaphor. The two brothers were not executed, but both were imprisoned, ostracised, ruined, and driven very largely to waste their talents. At the end some official amends were made to each of them, but too late and only when British standards of propriety had broken down, partly perhaps through their influence. Yet had they found no opposition, I doubt that their fate would have been happier.

That their own independent principles exposed them to singular delusions, quite apart from politics, may be proved in Russell's case by the change of mistress found at T.H. on my next visit there. I first got wind of something new in the realm of Venus when I was asked to "join a house-party" at Amberley Cottage. A house-party in Maidenhead? Who could the woman be? I didn't join the party because that year, 1895, I was but a short time in England; but I did spend a night or two at Amberley Cottage, and at tea one day the lady turned up: "Mollie" I will call her. She was a fat, florid, coarse Irishwoman of forty, with black curls, friendly manners and emotional opinions: a political agitator and a reformer. She took me aside at once and began to lament that Russell should be attached to "that dreadful dull stupid girl," Martha Turner. He must be rescued. I smiled intelligently, but found myself in rather an awkward position, treated at once as a confidential friend, when I had no right to betray Russell's confidence and no wish that he should jump from the frying-pan into the fire, such as this red-cheeked lady's heart would surely be. Nor could I as yet say: "Rescuing him is not for me to attempt: perhaps you might do it." I didn't think he wished to be rescued; and I knew nothing about her except what she had now revealed, which rather suggested that to be rescued from her would be more urgent than to be rescued by her. So I said nothing but discreet commonplaces, and we parted amiably; and amiably we always got on afterwards, during the many years when she was Russell's comfortable wife, and even later, when they had been divorced.

Mollie was a good soul. I think it was a relief to her to give up her politics and "social work"; she retained only a natural motherly kindness to servants and to village children, and to me also, for which I was grateful. She knew what poverty was, and didn't overdo acting the grand lady; remained simple and active, and ready, as it were, to lapse at any moment into her native paddydom without much minding it. She had been an orphan or a foundling, picked up and adopted by a small Irish official or tradesman, who married her later; and she had a grown-up son who bore his name. The old man had died, and now she had two small boys by a second husband, who had brought her to live in London and introduced her to politics and social reform. In those circles she had caught sight of Russell, and Cupid had done the rest.

What could Russell find in this old frump completely to upset him, to make him abandon poor Martha Turner (of whose interests he had been so unselfishly jealous) and to drive him into bigamy, and to a grand trial in the House of Lords, into prison, and into long years of placid married life? Was it intellectual or political sympathy? The absence of antipathy—an antipathy which he would have found in almost any lady—may have helped; but Mollie had no positive intelligence, no real concern about reform; she was simply kind and accustomed to move among social reformers. Could it be sexual attraction? I have not the means of knowing Russell's feelings on this point: he was never ribald or indiscreetly frank in such matters; but the affair with Lady Scott may have been more than an initiation; it may have established an inveterate leaning towards mature charms and motherly indulgence. Anyhow, Mollie's determination to extricate Russell, and his headlong propensity to be re-entangled, overcame every obstacle. She abandoned her two little boys and her husband, who duly divorced her; and she and Russell moved for six months to Reno, Nevada, where he too was divorced, and the two innocents were duly married. The British authorities would not recognise this divorce and remarriage and he was condemned for bigamy by the House of Lords and sentenced to three months in the first division. But this added nothing to his disgrace: on the contrary, it added a touch of antique dignity to his position. His speech in self-defence—duly censored by his lawyers—was excellent, and the only regrettable consequence of having been in prison was the book of Sermons that he wrote there.

What had become of Martha Turner? I was never informed, nor so far as I can remember was I at all curious about it. All those years after 1897 were a somnambulistic period for me, and now seem a blank. But in 1895, she had written me from Newnham, where he had evidently sent her to polish up her education and make her fit to be a countess: very like the Russells to think College a good preparation for wedded happiness! This move, however, had at least left the hermitage of T.H. empty, and ready after 1898 to welcome the blooming bride fresh from Reno, Nevada. For the next fifteen years I periodically found her presiding over that place, attached to it more and more, and as happy as an exacting husband and a dwindling income could allow her to be. She mollified the servants, when Russell had exasperated them; she knew how to control him; she toddled about in her loose tea-gowns with her pack of little white lap-dogs tumbling about her feet, and blinded by the hair in their hidden eyes; and she disappeared for long intervals to her hut or to her tower, for a little solitude, a little nap, or a little effort to rewrite some child's story that some publisher would at last consent to print. She had no religion, but was humble, prudent and resigned. I never heard her sigh as if she regretted her little boys; her troubles seemed to be about the present, about Russell's affairs and expenses. He had become a County Councillor in London, where they had taken a house in Gordon Square, and had card-parties. Bridge and motoring were his most obvious enjoyments and expenses; he took a boyish pleasure in them. He had been the first to apply for a motorist's licence, so that the number of his car was A1.

Sitting by him as he drove was an unmixed pleasure; he did it perfectly, with sureness and ease, and his casual observations, as the road opened up before us and various little scenes appeared, belonged to the original sphere of our friendship. This sphere was play of mind, intellectual light; not philosophy, not theory, but quick intelligence turned upon common things, inquiringly, fearlessly, and universally. Theory and philosophy would have crept in, had we pursued any subject very far; but we never did. I was no more professional at heart than he was, and didn't want to be entrapped by my thoughts. Ours were flying comments, made for the pleasure of making them; a purer pleasure than is to be found in the things on which the comments are made. Speed—never forced speed—and fresh air and the gentle homely charm of the English roads, winding in and out of clean villages, and respectfully skirting any hedged and private domain, made the hours pass gaily and without fatigue: and we had enough sense of things great and distant for these little passing things not to seem too important, and to be judged merrily. We never laughed much, but we were always laughing a little.

Between 1914 and 1919, having been stranded in England by the war, I was often at T.H. I didn't perceive it at the time, but now I suspect that although it was always Russell that wrote to me, it was always his wife, first Mollie and very soon Elizabeth, who really thought of asking me so many times to stay. Their husband was their problem, and they thought I might throw light upon it. Another thing that I then overlooked, and now perceive retrospectively, is that I was no longer young; my presence in itself could not give anybody pleasure; and as to what I might say, or my reputation as a writer, Russell was entirely indifferent. He too was much changed physically for the worse; but in his ways and spirit, at least towards me, he seemed exactly the same; only, being much preoccupied with matters unknown to me, he now had no impulse to unbosom himself as in our younger days. I had lapsed into an old but unimportant acquaintance in his eyes, while in mine he remained the most interesting of mortals. Mollie, being a woman of experience, must have felt this shift in her husband's relations with me, and instinctively made me her confidant, when I was no longer Russell's. The whiskey and water that she drank at meals— and between meals also, I imagine—comforted her a good deal; she wasn't hard to comfort; yet one day she confided to me that she was troubled about Russell. He was in love with somebody else. The truth is I had wondered that this hadn't happened before. More than ten years of contentment with fat old Mollie seemed miraculous. Naturally I couldn't put the matter to Mollie in these terms; but I suggested that Russell was still young, that his temperament was vehement, that he was polygamous without being inconstant, and that it would be wiser to overlook any passing infidelity on his part. They were very happily married and he would return to her.

"No," Mollie said rather gravely, "she wants to be his wife; she wants me to divorce him." Why? Did the silly woman wish to be a countess? No: she wasn't silly, and was a countess already. She was the Countess von Arnim, author of *Elizabeth and Her German Garden*. Russell was very much in love with her.

When I returned to Oxford I procured *Elizabeth and Her German Garden*, asked people about the authoress, and read other books of hers. They were charming, light, witty, showing love of flowers and of solitude, and full of delicate and satirical insight into character, without bitterness or false expectations. In *The Caravaners* she was hard on the Germans: fairer, with greater reason for resentment, in *The Pastor's Wife*. With such horror of

domestic tyranny, this extraordinary woman was going to marry
Russell! Truly, *la raison n'est pas ce qui règle l'amour.*

I was sorry for Mollie; she had made great sacrifices, almost
justified so far by the result. Adaptably she had become attached
to T.H. and had helped to render the place more comfortable and
homelike. There was a dell of which she was especially fond just
below the house: sloping grassy reaches under great trees, with
rabbits sitting alert, or galloping away, their white tails bobbing
in the air. Here you unexpectedly found deep shade and a sense
of being lost and hidden in a green wilderness; while the prevailing notes of that highland solitude were rather openness, buffet-
ing winds, an invitation to adventure, at least in thought, and the
freedom of wandering unattached between earth and heaven.
Mollie had also attempted a garden, but the site was too exposed,
the soil not very rich, and it proved pleasanter to sit indoors, or to
stroll through the wilder parts. What folly, after having found
a remote refuge and domestic peace with this good woman, and
tested the union for so many years, that he should now drive her
away, and not only launch upon a new and dangerous voyage, but
destroy his home port? As I had been on Martha Turner's side
against Mollie, so now I was on Mollie's side against Elizabeth.
Russell knew it; of course my external, cynical, Tory view of
human affections could make no difference in his conduct; nor did
it make any difference in my attachment to him, which had never
rested on being pleased with his actions or opinions, but entirely
on sympathy with his indomitable person and on admiration of his
powers. Naturally we both were silent on the subject of his new
love-affair, and events went on without my knowledge. Mollie
simply dropped out of the picture. I knew she had been bought
off: but this had to be concealed, because English law prohibited
divorce by collusion. Divorce might be granted to the injured
partner as a release, and as a punishment for the offender: but not
if the offender were going to be made happy by it. Such was the
wicked fact in this case, at least for the moment; but by some legal
machination the divorce was obtained, and Russell and Elizabeth

were married. I had no notice of the fact, nor invitation to the wedding, but found her installed at T.H. as a matter of course on my next visit.

By chance, however, I did see Mollie again. I had gone from Oxford to Brighton for a change of scene and air; and walking one afternoon along the Front, I perceived a bevy of little white dogs, like lumps of cotton-wool, moving about the pavement. I looked up, and there was Mollie, richly draped in furs, and rounder than ever. She greeted me amiably, and insisted that I should come up to her lodgings, which she had taken with friends for a week or two. Luckily I never played bridge, or cards of any sort: otherwise I should have found it impossible to avoid taking a hand. There were card-tables, glasses and bottles, and four or five men and women of easy-going manners. I escaped; and to clear my conscience wrote that same evening to Russell, relating briefly but accurately just what had happened. Nevertheless, it seems he was displeased. I suppose I ought not to have gone to Brighton, or ought not to have seen those little white dogs. He could not have expected me not to have recognised Mollie, who had been my very friendly hostess at his house for so many years. For my own part, I was rather glad to have come upon her and found her looking so well and so much in her element. Was she perhaps happier? No: her pride had been wounded; yet it was not the first wound; and now she was free, with a fixed income, and could grow old in peace. She could keep warm and comfortable, while mad wars raged in the world, with her lap-dogs, her cronies, her game of cards and her tipple.

When eventually one afternoon I arrived at Petersfield, on my next visit to T.H., and looked about for the car, I could see it nowhere. After waiting a moment, when the traps that had been there were gone, I asked the guard. No: he hadn't seen Lord Russell's car. "Yes," said another man; "that's it over there, with Lady Russell." Then I noticed a small grey motor, with what seemed to be a young girl at the wheel. I was accustomed enough to being a traveller and a foreigner everywhere not to doubt anything because it seemed odd; and as I ran up to the fair stranger, she waved to me. We had never before set eyes on each other. Russell had written as usual, without saying a word about her, yet here she was alone to meet me. Even at close quarters in the open air she seemed very young: a little thing with a little nose, little eyes, and a little innocent mouth. Yet she had three grown-up daughters and a son of fifteen at Eton. I got in, my things were placed somewhere behind, and we started. She explained at once that she wanted to speak to me before I saw Russell: yet I found that she had nothing in particular to tell me. Evidently it was only that she wished to conciliate me, and thought it would be easier in a *tête-à-tête*. And the reason for this manoeuvre, that seemed unnecessary, was a letter I had written to Russell, which he had shown her, when I first learned that he was divorcing Mollie and marrying somebody else. He ought not to have been displeased with that letter, in which I compared him with Henry the Eighth and with Goethe. Like Henry the Eighth he desired to *marry* all his lady-loves; but that only made him wish later to cut their heads off, that each might make room for the next. Goethe, less bigoted morally and calmer, had finally married only one, the humblest, of his women, who had been his mistress and housekeeper for years. Russell then found himself married in the same sensible way as Goethe. Mollie was used to all his ways, and kept his house economically and in good order. What a mistake to send her away and insist on marrying Frau von Stein! That he *loved* Elizabeth, Gräfin von Arnim, I could well believe; also that she loved him: but why marry? She was a widow, a novelist, and a freethinker. Surely she might accept him for a lover. But if she put herself in his power legally, there would be trouble. With his fixed habits, it would be difficult for a lady to live with him long.

All this was not put so clearly in my letter, but could be read between the lines; and it evidently caused some stir and possibly some alarm in their breasts. Russell protested in a perfunctory way, as a lover and as a Christian, which he thought he was; and

I knew only long after that she had seen the letter at all, when she admitted the profound truth of it. At first, however, she wished to demonstrate—and I was a sort of dummy audience to convince in lieu of the world and of her own conscience—that she was the first *decent* woman to take Russell in hand, and that she had character, intellect, charm, beauty, and sufficient youth to hold him permanently and make a new man of him; or rather, to make him himself again, because his associations, ever since he fell into Lady Scott's hands at the age of twenty-three, had smothered and degraded his true nature. Clever and experienced as she was, she felt that this would appeal to me; that I also *believed* in Russell, against all apparent evidence; and that I should retract the horrid immoral suggestions of my letter, and admit that she was the providential Frau von Stein destined to lift her happier Goethe into a great statesman and a man of the world.

And in spite of the fatal issue, there were elements of truth in her prognostications. She did hold his affections; he spoke of the "anguish" he suffered when she deserted him; protested that he still "loved and worshipped her," that his life was blighted, and that all had been wanton cruelty on her part, because she was incapable of loving anybody, even her own children. These reproaches were absurd; Elizabeth was a cool but tender person; they merely proved how much he was upset and exasperated by losing her. It was also true that he was worth saving: and a certain side of his real gifts actually came to public notice at the end, not especially under her influence, but in politics. Yet, as he knew and admitted, those external occupations didn't touch his heart; they were parts of Maya, traditional whirlpools in which birth plunges us, such as making money, making war, or making love. They compel us to care intensely, as in a dream, for things of no ultimate consequence: and this not merely because those things are transitory, but because the effects of our efforts are incalculable in the end, and we may be bringing about results that, could we foresee them, would appall us. I think that this conviction, perhaps unconsciously, encouraged Russell to let himself go and to plunge into irrational ventures. In him, however, these courses left their mark and became automatisms, soon impossible to withstand or to correct. Maya might be an illusion, but she held him tight.

The marvel was that so many women, by no means fools, thought they could manage him, and that each in her turn believed herself predestined to redeem him and anchor him in the safe haven of her arms. Martha Turner thought so, Lady Scott thought so, Mollie thought so, and now Elizabeth thought so: the simplest, the most battered, the most intelligent of women were alike in their infatuation and blindness. I suppose their vanity conspired with his persuasiveness to deceive them; and he was persuasive: very different as a lover, Elizabeth said, from what he was as a husband.

That his society was charming, his personality dominant, that there was nobody in whose good graces one would rather be, I knew by my own experience. But in friendship liability is limited; each preserves his privacy and freedom, and there is no occasion for jealousy or tyranny. Towards his women, once they were enveigled into an unlimited partnership, Russell was a tyrant. He imposed on them an infinity of petty habits and rules, with the gravity of a strict moralist, and laid down heavily the most puerile and hackneyed saws of politics and conduct as if self-evident. To me these absurdities were amusing and harmless. I knew them by heart; they were parts of his imperious personality, which I accepted merrily when I was with him. He never dreamt that I should accept them for myself. He left me abundantly alone: I was a *hors d'oeuvre* in his menu; so much so that he was genuinely puzzled when in the last years I wrote him that he had been very important in my life. Certainly he had had no influence on my career; but my career was not my life. Mine has been a life of reflection, which he couldn't understand; and he had given me much to think of, many pleasures and many lights. But his wives and his cats were his prisoners, condemned to be petted at pleasure. They had only secret hours for being fondled, and were

treated in public, and ordinarily in private, with a virtuous austerity. His ways of making love were said to be somewhat capricious and exacting: Elizabeth once called them sadistic. And
love-making for him was no laughing matter, no playfulness of a
mad moment. It was a loving wife's sworn duty to be obedient;
and if she rebelled and fled from her husband, he said she was
cruel.

Elizabeth in the beginning was simply the amiable hostess:
always prettily dressed, witty, full of little amusing anecdotes
about her life in Germany. She would walk with me in the dell,
and show me her knowledge of flowers and discriminating love
of them. It was only gradually that she became confidential. She
had money and furniture of her own—not much, as I suppose the
war had cut off whatever her first husband may have left her,
but enough for her to be somewhat independent; and with her
love of solitude, she had found it necessary to set up a bungalow
of her own, where no one was allowed to disturb her. It was a
spacious apartment, charmingly furnished with books, flowers,
and gaily coloured chintz. Here she retired to rest and work. This
was the first symptom of domestic division that came to my notice;
but ultimately she began frankly to confess the difficulties she
found in living with Russell. What they were in essence she made
public afterwards in her novel *Vera*. As she said to me, she began
by making the man in it quite unlike Russell: but as the theme
was her own domestic tragedy, he became more and more like
Russell as the story developed. It is not a good portrait because the
fundamental structure is wrong, if it were meant to represent
Russell; but many of the details are photographic: and I think it
may truly be called cruel to publish them during his life-time.
But he had driven her to desperation; and she developed the spite
of a hunted animal.

For me the scene closes on T.H. rather distressingly, as on
an interrupted performance. The place was materially much improved, the grounds developed, the hall panelled, the rooms fresh-
ened up and adorned; but Russell was preoccupied and silent,

Elizabeth hardly visible save at table, and a mysterious emptiness seemed to pervade the place where, in good Mollie's day, I had felt so free and happy. After the rupture, Elizabeth and I remained, or rather became, very good friends. She occasionally came to Italy; finally she took a house on the French Riviera where at last, she said, she had a garden after her own heart. But no garden can be paradise when all within is a desert. She was desolate and bitter in her old age, and pronounced life to be "a very bad joke."

It was there that she heard of Russell's death, which occurred at Marseilles, not very far from her: for he too had come to the Riviera for a little rest. One of his relations one day turned up at her place, and Elizabeth on recognising the approaching lady, waved a welcome to her, but noticed a strange solemnity in her manner. "Why are you so serious?" she asked. "Frank!" the lady gasped tragically. "What is *he* up to now?" Elizabeth inquired without emotion. "Dead and cremated!" cried the other: and closed the chapter of that love affair sardonically, in sympathy with its theme. For it had been, for both, a false and hollow revival of youth in old age.

After Elizabeth deserted it, T.H. passed for me, and I think for Russell also, into a sort of penumbra. I was living abroad and visited it only once again, in 1923.* At the time of my last trip to England, nine years later, Russell was already dead, and had bequeathed the place to his brother Bertie. Then it underwent a curious transformation. Bertie was temporarily married to his second wife, who had been a teacher at Girton: they had young children and advanced ideas on education. Wasn't T.H. an ideal oasis for an unimpeded experiment in liberty? They would turn the house into a school where children should do exactly as they liked until they found it unpleasant and should learn only what they felt like learning. I don't know what were the results; perhaps the experiment was interrupted prematurely; for before long Bertie and his wife were divorced and the school

* Cf. *Farewell to England*, towards the end of this book.

was merged and lost in that universal experiment in education which nature has always been making just on Bertie and Dora's simple and cruel principles. I have not heard, and hardly wish to hear, what has become of T.H. For me it belongs to the happy past, rescued by being past from being ever changed.

CHAPTER V

OXFORD FRIENDS

Y FIRST acquaintance with Oxford is recorded in the early chapter on Russell; it was memorable but ended in a blind alley. Russell himself I never saw there, nor had he any affection or respect for that place; and Lionel Johnson and the others who had been his Oxford friends soon vanished into the outer wilderness. My other visits there, except in 1896–7 and after 1911, necessarily fell in the long vacation, since during the working terms I was in America. The colleges were deserted and only married Dons, caged like canaries in suburban villas, could be expected to be in residence. It was my Oxford, therefore, that I first learned to know, not that of the Oxonians.

There was, however, Louis Dyer, my old professor of Greek at Harvard, who lived in Banbury Road, and through him I made the most useful and faithful of my Oxford friends. Like Dyer, he was a Balliol man but not a Don, and they sometimes met at dinner on feast days at the High Table. There I first saw him: a monkey-like creature with a pasty round face, fringed on all sides by patches of black hair; for some disease made it difficult for him either to shave properly or to grow a decent beard. He was a little man, unobtrusive yet always watching everything with a critical experienced eye. In summer he wore a short alpaca coat and grey trousers, and a little cloth hat with a limp brim curling up all round. His shirt was starched, with a corresponding evening waistcoat that left it uncovered; and often the one black stud, expected to keep the two halves together, would slip out and let them fly apart, revealing a hairy chest immediately beneath. With this he sported a very low turned-down collar, and a drooping black evening tie. At a distance he could be recognised by his meditative way of walking, with occasional stops at a crossing or at a shop window; for he lived to observe. His hands were habitually crossed behind his back, and trailed a loose umbrella. Everybody called him "Old Higgs."

Higgs was a private tutor in modern history. In his younger days, when asthma didn't keep him at home, he had travelled a great deal, often on foot, especially through the Baltic countries, and had a rich collection of photographs showing the picturesque aspects of the North. I liked his conversation; for without talking shop or showing any political bias or academic jealousies, he was full of curious information and credible gossip about men and events, recent and remote; and like the learned men of other times, he knew the identity of human nature in all ages, and felt no contempt for manners or ideas that have now gone out of fashion. His standards were those not of a pedant or of a reformer, but of a man of taste. His taste and his diction were thoroughly Oxonian and not more limited or local than anything has to be that is definite; they were pleasant to come upon and to profit by, not as models to be copied elsewhere but as attainments to be prized where they belonged.

Yet his great service to me was of another kind. He showed me all the possible walks about Oxford; after going over each of them two or three times under his guidance, I was able when alone to recognise every turning and every stile, where there was a right of way through a field; and he encouraged me to go rather further than I should have ventured alone, to Islip, for instance, or to Abingdon. His antiquarian lore helped to make the way seem shorter and the sights more individual; and when the distance was too great for a comfortable day's walk, I learned the possible ways of shortening it by taking a train or 'bus to some intermediate point. This Higgs wouldn't do, for economy; and tea also sometimes became a difficulty, because he didn't like to pay more than sixpence for it. Afterwards, during the war, when I started out in the morning, this experience, together with an ordnance-survey map, very much lengthened the radius of my excursions, and I could easily go to Radley and to Nuneham, or to Stanton Harcourt without fatigue. Tea, in winter, would be at a shop in Oxford on my return; but at any inn in the country I could have bread and cheese, with beer, for luncheon: eggs or cold meat the good people never could supply. Old Higgs's days were then over, yet invisibly he often guided my steps; and I may say that I have never seen so many lovely views as through his eyes, because he would not only point them out to me in the first instance, but would find some just epithet to describe them. These modest landscapes rather require a poet to appreciate them; the tourist and even the painter might think them commonplace; their delicacy is aerial, moral, and fugitive, and a happy phrase arrests them best.

I almost saw poor Higgs die. I have called his trouble asthma, but there was a complication of troubles; and while he looked much as usual—that is, very queer—I was startled one day, when strolling with him in the Cornmarket, to have him suddenly stop and stand still, like Socrates struck by epilepsy or by inspiration. He half recovered after a moment and made at once for his lodgings, which were near by, in the first house to the left in Market-Street: pleasant lodgings, sunny with a glimpse of town life from the corner windows, by which he sat and kept the fire going day and night all the year round. I never saw him after that day. A poor devil, no doubt: but I am sure I might easily have led a life like his, had I been less lucky and more studious; and I shouldn't have been unhappy. Unattached academic obscurity is rather a blessed condition, when it doesn't breed pedantry, envy, or ill-nature.

Of notabilities (for which in general I have no liking) the most distinguished who was my friend in Oxford was Robert Bridges. Our friendship began late and was entirely his doing. A friend of his, at the turn of the century, had shown him a copy of my *Interpretations of Poetry and Religion*, saying, "Here is somebody whose philosophy seems to be much like yours. Perhaps you might care to look into him." And in fact I received in America a very kind and appreciative letter on the subject. Still, I never looked Bridges up when I was in Oxford. He was Poet Laureate, I hadn't read him, and I prefer to remain free and perfectly unknown in the places where I am happy. Higgs was not a commitment; but a Poet Laureate . . .

However, when I was caught in England by the war and settled down in Oxford, I somewhere came across him, probably at Corpus. He was an imposing person, twenty years older than I, tall, a little too thin and spare for Olympian Zeus, but otherwise of the same noble and leonine aspect. His manners, however, and his conversation were of the most unpretending, easy, and charming kind, those of the simple, affable English gentleman who remains always young. Soon I began to go sometimes to Chilswell for my walk. Mrs. Bridges proved no less friendly than her husband. I suspect that she, too, had read something of mine and, dear lady, had thought it edifying. Fortunately the religion of that household was not controversial, and until the very end I succeeded in giving them no offence. With her, moreover, I had another point in my favour. When their only son, Edward, came back wounded from the war, I liked him very much, and felt at once, as I told them, as if I had known him all my life. Youth and experience together make a charming combination: the youthfulness secures plasticity, and the experience gives a ground to build upon securely.

Yet in some things my lack of discipline betrayed itself; I hadn't been brought up in an English nursery and an English Public School, nor served in any war. Once, only once, they asked me to spend the week-end at Chilswell. All went well until Sunday morning, when in order to be ready for breakfast downstairs I had to get up rather early. I opened my door, and there were my boots, but no hot water. No mention had been made of any bathroom, and not knowing what to do, I rang, and waited a moment with the door half open. Then I heard an agitated voice saying "He has rung!" Feeling guilty, I closed my door again. Presently there was a knock, and I said perfunctorily, "Come in," thinking it was the housemaid, recalled to her neglected duties. But no, no one came in, and I went to open the door myself. There stood Mrs. Bridges, ghostlike, and without her front hair. She gasped: "What is the matter?" "Nothing, nothing, I only rang to ask the maid for some hot water." "Hot water!" cried Mrs. Bridges, as if shocked. "Only a little, just for shaving," I said apologetically, realising that tubs were not in order, at least not lukewarm tubs. "The maids have gone to church," Mrs. Bridges explained more calmly. "I'll see if I can get you a little." I was really very sorry, and ashamed of myself: I ought to have brought my hot water with me in a thermos bottle, since I was such a sybarite as to require it; but never before in England had hot water not appeared of itself in the morning, wherever I had lodged, and before dinner also, wherever I was a guest. Abashed, I now accepted a small white china jug of hot water from my hostess's hand, and did the best I could with it, a hard beard, a tender skin, and not too sharp a razor. The blessed days of Gillette and of shaving creams had not dawned, and like Olympian Zeus, I should have let nature take her course and possessed a rich and curly beard. Yet Apollo, Hermes, and even Edward Bridges shaved, and also Mars, who needn't have been so young. It would be hard to go back to nature without going back to savagery. That priests and monks should shave, even their crowns, is no doubt a matter of hygiene and cleanliness in warm countries; perhaps, also, as in the case of a nun's hair, a surrender to personal emphasis and boasts. My own instinct would choose hairlessness, long straight robes, and hands hidden in one's sleeves: such an aspect standardises one's personality in the world, and concentrates and purifies it in oneself.

On quite another occasion Bridges, who was a medical man, inveighed against the use of hot water. So bad for the nails and for the hair! With his magnificent *chevelure* contrasting with my baldness, I was reduced to bashful silence in regard to hair; and I kept it also in regard to nails, although not without casting a furtive glance at his hands. They were large, thin, strong hands,

that had been used for doing miscellaneous things, and were not
dirty: but they hadn't the nursery-maid's pink cleanliness produced
by soap and hot water. The nails were grey and thick, like talons.
Admirable, no doubt, for certain purposes; but in ages when hot
water is available for the toilet, delving is no longer done with the
claws, and even jealous ladies do not attempt to scratch each
other's eyes out. This does not prove, I admit, that hot water is
not a luxury, and unheroic. Even cold water is abhorrent, for
external use, to lions and eagles. I admired Bridges' Spartan ablu-
tions, but prefer in this respect to remain a Sybarite. Different
animals and different nations cannot be models for one another.

Pleasant as Chilswell was, it was not Bridges at home that
showed the grounds of his interest in me. It was Bridges afloat in
Oxford. He would often come into the town in the morning;
sometimes he was detained, or had business of some kind to do in
the afternoon; and, then, knowing my habits, he would come to
my lodgings in Beaumont Street at about half-past twelve, when
I was finishing dressing, and go with me to lunch at *The George*.
Conviviality, for me, has been a great discoverer and cementer of
affinities, or at least a substitute for them. Luncheon at *The
George* was better than, under the stress of rations, it was likely
to be at home; and we habitually enlivened it with a bottle of
good burgundy. On these occasions Bridges became again a young
man. He had been long a bachelor; he had once spent a whole
season in Rome, delighted with riding about the campagna, and
no doubt composing verses; whereas when in later life he returned
to Rome, everything disgusted him, especially the churches. All
that to the free traveller had seemed romantic seemed now to
the elderly Anglican false and dead. He could not bear the contrast with the English landscape and with English religious music
and sentiment. So, reverting with me, even in familiar Oxford, to
the atmosphere of the wandering student and poet, he relaxed his
acquired habits of mind. It was for mocking English prejudices,
while adoring England, that he valued my writings; and though
we seldom or never discussed our respective works, I knew that

it was this liberating outlook, partly in the Catholic and partly in the naturalistic direction, that he cared for in me.

That he was influenced by my philosophy is not admissible. A thinker is seldom influenced by another much younger than himself, and Bridges besides did not *understand* my philosophy. His own position was not clear to me until, with reference to his *Testament of Beauty,* he asked me expressly to criticise it and then replied, in a long letter, to my criticisms. He agreed with me, or rather with Kant, as to the *necessarily original* form of the mind, in sensation no less than in religion; but he clung to the belief that this inevitable originality was inspired, and revealed a sympathetic moral spirit in nature at large. Now, my position excludes this belief; because morality and spirit, in my view, express specific and contrary vital interests, as in politics. To assert that one such political or vital interest, say the Jewish or the Anglo-Saxon, coincides with the total inspiration of the universe, is egotism *in excelsis,* and a plain illusion of animal vanity and egotism. Banish that illusion: the vital and political interest concerned remains standing, but only as one local and temporary movement of animal life on earth. It is its own excuse for being, but it leaves the speculative spirit free to transcend it and to admit equally, in their places, all the other vital and political interests that may arise. I would relax English prejudices in the Catholic and in the naturalistic direction by a single and consistent insight, not by casual contrary sympathies. Catholicism is paganism spiritualised: it is fundamentally naturalistic; and the transcendental spirit and the wise statesman may accept Catholicism, where it naturally arises, as a good poetic symbol for the forces and the issues of human life in that phase; not, however, as a scientific revelation of reality or a history of literal facts. Religion is valid poetry infused into common life. It is not a revelation truer than perception or than science. Nature, where it breeds life, is undoubtedly animated by a spirit kindred to man's and to human morality; hence the dramatic sympathy in us with all real or imagined vitality in the universe. Yet this sympathy should chasten rather than inflate us, because it reveals to us how accidental are the objects of our love.

At Christ Church, about 1895, there was a young American whose name I have forgotten, but whom I had known slightly at Harvard. He was pale, quiet, very well dressed, evidently rich but also aesthetic. He seemed always to have a bunch of violets in his buttonhole. It was not surprising that he should have found his way to Oxford, and in particular to Christ Church. There he had spacious but singularly placed rooms that had been occupied by Lord Rosebery. They were in the cellar, immediately to the left as you come through Canterbury Gate, with the windows in pits so far below the level of the pavement that they had large iron cages to protect them. On the other side, however, towards the garden and the meadows, the ground was lower, and there was sunshine and even, through the shrubbery, the suggestion of a view. I found myself there at a large luncheon with sporting youths most of whom I never saw again; I suspect they were all members of the Bullingdon Club. At least this was the case with the very blond modest young man who sat next to me and whom I might also have forgotten had he not taken the trouble to follow up our acquaintance. His name was Harold Fletcher. I had spoken of Oxford architecture, especially of the churches, defending the intrusion of the baroque amid the gothic, as in the lovely porch of St. Mary's. This, although I didn't say anything about religion, was also a defence of Catholic sentiment and practice, and happened to strike in Fletcher a sympathetic chord. This I discovered long afterwards, for he was as silent as he was sensitive; at the moment he only asked me if I should like to drive some morning to Dorchester and see the church there, which was an interesting one.

We started at the appointed time, with the best of weather, in a smart dog-cart, but came to a stop a little beyond Folly Bridge, I wondered why. It was only, Fletcher said, that they were not allowed to drive a tandem through the town, and the groom had to bring the leader down here, to be added on as an afterthought.

Unexpectedly for me, the drive now acquired a picturesque interest of its own, apart from the landscape and whatever was to be seen in Dorchester. It became a festive occasion. Fletcher drove as quietly and as modestly as he spoke, and as much to the purpose, for he seemed perfect master of his horses and of himself. I have always liked to put myself in the hands of skilful people, especially when I am absolutely ignorant of their art. That is a part of my confident faith in nature. Nature may be trusted to do her job even in living creatures, when they are clean-cut and docile, like Fletcher and his two beautiful horses. I afterwards learned, however, that driving with Fletcher was not without its risks, as trusting to nature is also. He was extremely near-sighted, and the story went that one day, when the leader in his tandem had turned completely round, he had gone on driving merrily with the wheeler in the opposite direction. But in my time he wore glasses, and never had the least accident.

When he had left the university and come into his money, being an orphan and much attached to Oxford, he bought the stables in Holywell Street and set up in the coaching business. More than once I had the honour of sitting on the box with him in the coach to Woodstock and Blenheim, and admiring his skill and precision as a whip. Those were public occasions, imposing on him a professional gravity, like that of a captain at sea. Jollier and freer was a trip that his brother and I made with him driving a newly bought four-in-hand, from Leicester to Oxford, fifty miles in one day. It was a lovely trip, taken leisurely, with a long halt for luncheon and rest. We drove into Oxford at a steady slow trot; and at the end, after inspecting the horses minutely, Fletcher came radiant out of the stable. "By Jove," he said, "fifty miles, and never turned a hair!"

So pleasant were these outings that I went with him—though this had to be by train—to the cattle fair at Bicester, and enjoyed the scene greatly, while he did his business. The English air and the English country, apart from mankind, were enough to satisfy me: but here I was entertained also by the country types and the show animals; and there is always a convivial side to such excursions, that brings us back to our chosen friends, to a roast joint and a gooseberry tart and a great mug of ale or of porter.

A simple horsey chap, Harold Fletcher, and ten years younger than I: how much out of my line! Yet everything in this world has an explanation, and there was another side to my friend; something that I should not have required in him, yet without it he would never have been so attentive to me. He was religious: he felt the presence of the invisible. Not that he spoke of such things, for he was sensitive and reserved, but a caricature of his feelings appeared openly in his brother, in many ways his opposite and yet of the same blood. The brother was short and dark, quick and voluble, wished to be an actor, and believed in second sight and in haunted places. He lived in London and knew the personages and gossip of Bohemia. In Harold the taste for the supernatural took the nobler form of an orthodoxy edifying and well-ordered. This feeling, held in reserve, gave a moral background to his ways and to his tastes, even about horses. Horses were made by God; if we saw them from that point of view, we should understand them. That is just what I felt about young men like Fletcher; they are to be approached from within, by way of their genesis and vital impulses, and not to be judged by their utility to other people. Nothing living is a means: all is automatic, spontaneous, justified by whatever it tends to and loves.

I began to see what Fletcher cared for on that first excursion to Dorchester. After visiting the Roman Camp, about which his knowledge was perfunctory (or at least seemed so to me, with my avidity for the setting of ancient life in all its details), we went to see the church, large and perpendicular. In one place a frescoed wall had been recently uncovered. To me it was not very clearly visible or specially interesting, a pastel imitation of stained glass, confused without being brilliant, but what could be made out of the figures sufficed to show the style and spirit of a religious art: quaintly realistic, naïve, and devout. This was evidently what interested Fletcher. His taste had worked back behind the Renais-

sance, to the sentiment of the Middle Ages, to the familiar supernatural, to Catholic piety. There was no pre-Raphaelite affectation in him: he was looking beyond boastful material realism and
theatricality to homely truth, to humble devotion, to revelations in
solitude and comfort in hardship. He was no collector or picture-
dealer; it was not the old clothes of mediaevalism that interested
him but the faith that had worn them.

Fletcher was indeed a devoted friend, perhaps a disciple or
penitent, of Father Waggett's. He asked me expressly to meet
Father Waggett at tea in his rooms; I found a most engaging
clergyman, still young, with no clerical absurdities or insolence,
but with the manners of the world and yet a frank expression of
his apostolic vocation. I was reminded of my *tio Nicolás,* the
Canon of Tarragona; only that Waggett was much younger and
less indolent. I think he may have seen my *Interpretations of
Poetry and Religion,* then recently published; for this was some
years after I had made Fletcher's acquaintance, and not the source
of it. Waggett talked of religion freely and familiarly, like a
Catholic; but it appeared that he was also a naturalist, a zoölogist,
and was writing something that Fletcher had already seen and
admired—I think concerning the instincts of birds. When I expressed a desire to see it, Waggett said he would be glad to come
the next day to Fletcher's again, and read it to me, for it was not
yet printed. I was delighted; but when next day came, I found
Fletcher alone. Father Waggett had sent word that he was very
sorry, but wasn't able to come. "Do you know," Fletcher observed,
"what has probably happened? Waggett, last night, in making his
examination of conscience, asked himself why he was coming here
to read that paper. Was it in the hope of converting you or making
you realise how compatible religion is with science? No: it was in
order to hear himself praised. He mustn't come."

Pleasant to see how shrewd the simple Fletcher could be in
spiritual matters. He was no fool in anything. Our friendship took
root, as if it had been an old family friendship; for instance he
and his brother, who were orphans, took me for a week-end to

visit a maiden aunt of theirs, Lady Mary Marsham, the sweetest of perfectly deaf old ladies in the neatest of country houses. I have seldom been happier than with these unexpected friends.

One Sunday Father Waggett invited Fletcher and me to the midday dinner at Cowley. The refectory was imposing: plain high white walls, with only a large crucifix over the Abbot's chair, and a long narrow table, with a white table-cloth, running to right and left of him along three sides of the room. The monks all sat with their backs to the wall, leaving the inside of the square empty, as in the pictures of the Last Supper; only two chairs, like that sometimes assigned to Judas, were placed inside, for Fletcher and me. Waggett, in this setting, was absolutely at his ease and like himself elsewhere. Had we been at a military mess or at a duchess's table, he would have been the same.

As I found in a conversation we had afterwards in the garden about immortality, he was an *original*: I mean, that he drew his convictions from his own inspiration, even when they were, in words, perfectly conventional. Immortality was presumable and according to nature, because spirit, the witness, is essentially independent of any world it may discover, prior to it, and in no way held down to that particular world. Admirable, I thought, if only he had brought in his natural history at this point, to explain the inevitably transcendental character of perception or thought, not because thought is existentially independent of animal life, but precisely because animal life, in interaction with its environment, has imposed such thought. Now this *originality* in Waggett's sentiments, rendered him a perfect man of the world, not to be put out or embarrassed by the oddity of his surroundings: he was ready for anything, because what was active in himself, spirit, could survive anything unscathed, even death. This is the transcendental principle of courage and of simplicity. It enabled him to put up, I suppose, with the extreme artificiality, self-consciousness, and affectation of everybody else in that monastery.

If I described all the poses and movements of those poor monks,

especially of the young ones, it would be thought a gross caricature. Even to me now it seems incredible that I actually should
have seen the idiotic manners that I saw; may I not have dreamt
the whole thing afterwards? Yet there was pathos in those absurdities, because these souls, in need of religion, were groping
for expression and for support in an age and in a Church that had
subordinated religion to national pride and to worldliness. They
had to rediscover or to imitate a cultus: but for discovery they had
no genius and for imitation no taste and no innocence. They therefore seemed fools or hypocrites, when they were sincerely groping
after spiritual rebirth. Not all, perhaps; because in the revival
of Catholicism in England, both Anglican and Roman, there was
also a silly aesthetic sensual side, all vanity and pose and ritualistic pedantry, as in Frederick Rolfe; and this may have contributed
something to the affectations of the Cowley monastery.

Father Waggett some years later went to America and lectured,
I believe, at the Episcopal Theological Seminary at Cambridge. I
went to hear him preach there one afternoon, but I was disappointed. He wasn't the man who, in the garden at Cowley, had
talked about immortality. He was commonplace, cautious, dry.
What wonder, when he found himself bound by politic ties to
people utterly alien to his insights and offensive to his tastes?

The last time I was in Oxford, in 1923, I saw Fletcher's name,
half washed out by the rain, still legible on the gates of the
stables in Holywell, which looked closed and abandoned. Very
likely his enterprise was not successful; such ventures seldom are,
and by that time the motor had dethroned the horse. But Fletcher
had also become a local politician and agent for the Conservative
Party; and seemed, when I last saw him, very pleasantly settled,
with his sister, at Wolvercote. I sent them a large brass knocker
for their new house; and saw it later, brightly burnished, decorating the door that led from the road to their walled garden. I
was leaving England, and didn't knock; but I hope that good
fortune and happiness have done so, and have found their way in.

During the war Oxford was not deserted even by the young:

there was a remnant of boys under military age with others re-turning wounded or unfit for service, not to speak of a host of privates become cadets and studying to pass examinations for a commission. Somehow, I don't remember how, I made the ac-quaintance of two sets of undergraduates, one at Balliol and one at Magdalen. Three of the Balliol men remain in my memory, and one at least has become a celebrity: Aldous Huxley. He was then apparently almost blind, with a great shock of curly black hair, and I had no occasion to talk with him. Later, I saw him again, already a popular novelist, with his wife and child at Cortina; but I think there was a latent antipathy in our natures and affections which prevented any spontaneous intercourse. More interesting at the time was Grattan Esmonde, an Irish Catholic already deep in politics and also devoted to painting in several incongruous styles at once, Byzantine and French. Affectation and enthusiasm were so combined in him with insularity, and this with scraps of exotic knowledge, that it was impossible for me to make out whether he could be taken seriously in any direction. If you took him seriously, he might have seemed a re-incarnation of Lionel Johnson, this time genuinely Irish and at home in the political world. If you took him for an intellectual ballet-dancer, he would turn into the Lord Basil Kilcoole in my *The Last Puritan*; except that Esmonde, when I knew him, was really young and handsome, although his elegance was not borne out by everything in his person, as it should be in a genuine beau. Beau Brummel would have shuddered at the sight of those hands.

More my friend was the third of these youths, and he seemed the youngest and least significant, Raymond Mortimer. He was affectionate and literary, read my books, and took me out in a punt to his favourite silvan resorts. He was an adoped child, perhaps a foundling, and there was a certain mystery or ambiguity about his whole person. He quoted to me the phrase "affected and dis-affected" as describing him; but though disaffected politically, a pacifist, and universal rebel, he was not affected: at least not more than a young man must be who picks up a great deal that he hadn't imbibed traditionally and without selecting it. Something of the waif, a prior grudge against everything, seemed to lurk in him, together with the assumption of universal competence: an attitude with which I have some sympathy, being myself something of a waif and a detached critic; but I see the inversion and folly in it, and its hollowness, because the order of nature is the contrary, and we must be true to ourselves before we can be just to other things, and consistently love our enemies. *The pure spirit* in us may safely cultivate universal sympathies; for it can have no grudge against anything and will be tender also to our accidental natural selves and our home world; but *the man* must remain loyal to himself and his traditions, or he will be morally a eunuch and a secret hater of all mankind.

I saw Mortimer later in Paris; and during a season I spent at the Hôtel du Palais Royal he would sometimes join me at ten in the evening at the Café de la Régence, where I usually had a *camomille* or a beer before turning in. France was perhaps more congenial to him than his own country: it was more of a universal vanity fair and intellectual market, where the surviving moral and national elements would be more hidden and less obstructive to a foreigner than they were in England. For this reason I too preferred to live in Paris and to read French books: not that, like Mortimer, I detested the old France or the old England, but because the new France afforded a more lucid medium through which to observe the dissolution of Christendom. This dissolution might be regretted; yet it was imperative to understand the forces and know the facts that were bringing it about. Harvard, also, if you were morally an outsider, afforded such a medium; but there, as in England, the intellectual grab-bag was offered by a missionary hand and with a single purpose, though perhaps an unconscious one: namely to equip everybody as well as possible in the service of national wealth and industrial dominance. The intellectual result, if you forgot that political purpose, was utter confusion; yet this chaos itself was welcome to the dilettante, the parasite, and the *viveur*. It enabled him to pick sweets out of the grab-bag at will, and to indulge all his impulses for the moment, yet sadly in the end: an intellectual brothel.

At Balliol those stray young men, with Urquhart and perhaps another Don or two, had formed an ephemeral club called the Thuliots which they asked me to join; and I had begun to scrawl a paper on ultimate things, to be read at the next meeting, when the wind that blew towards *Ultima Thule* seemed to die down. The term ended, and the next meeting never took place.

Like my first acquaintances at Oxford, so the last, were made through the Russells, pronounced anti-Oxonians. One day I received a telegram, signed *Russell,* asking me to come on a certain day to luncheon at a certain farm-house at Garsington. I replied accepting with pleasure, and unquestioningly addressed the telegram to Earl Russell; for I had no reason to expect such a message from Bertie. The next day a note came explaining that it was Bertie who had wired, and hoping I should come just the same. Of course I went, had to go; although it was a new excursion rather beyond my walking range, and involving a journey by the local line to a way station. I arrived duly; it was a real farm-house; and I found Bertie in a spacious upper chamber, with plank walls, and many books strewn about: but nothing about the landlady or the house seemed to forebode luncheon; and I had a good appetite. Presently Bertie said: "We'll go now to the Manor: I have my meals there." So we crossed the road and came to a renovated stone house, a bit below, which I hadn't noticed on arriving, and which proved to be a rather elaborate establishment, with a great garden. There, without previous explanation, I was introduced to a marvelous creature, very tall, very thin, in blue silk flounces, pearls, and black cross-garters (like Malvolio) over bright yellow stockings. She was Lady Ottoline Morrell, had an aristocratic nose, pale blue eyes, with dark straggling locks, and now appeared to be my hostess. She had a husband who I learned afterwards was a Liberal M.P. and a brother of my friend Mrs. Warren. Lady Ottoline had married the son of a brewer, and not an excessively rich one; but he was nice-looking, and her action, together with his politics, which came out at once in his talk, prepared me to understand how Bertie came to be there. Later I gathered that there was a very close old friendship, or perhaps a love-affair, between him and Lady Ottoline, which I know to subsist to this day. He was spending his holiday with the Morrells, but slept and worked at the farm-house for greater quietness and freedom.

I soon gathered that it was this lady, ostrich or tropical bird as she seemed, that had wished to discover me, and had caused Bertie to summon me. He and I have always been on pleasant terms, personally and intellectually; yet just as our philosophies are separate without being opposed, except in technicalities and in politics, so our lives and interests are separate, and we were never friends in the sense of looking each other up simply for pleasure or liking to live together. Lady Ottoline was an intellectual, and cultivated the society of intellectuals; it was in that capacity that she had heard of me, no doubt through Bertie or perhaps through Bridges, and thought of adding me to her collection.

If I had been younger and interested in forming acquaintances in England, I might have profited by her hospitality, and met various distinguished people at her house, such as Mr. Asquith, then Prime Minister. As it was, I came upon two notabilities worth mentioning: Lytton Strachey and Siegfried Sassoon. Strachey, who was then youngish, looked like a caricature of Christ; a limp cadaverous creature, moving feebly, with lank long brown hair and the beginnings of a beard much paler in colour, and spasmodic treble murmurs of a voice utterly weary and contemptuous. *Obscene* was the character written all over him; and his expertness in secret history and in satire expressed that character intellectually. That it was not merely intellectual appeared one day, when I found Lady Ottoline out, but expected, the maid said, to return shortly; and being left alone in the drawing room, I picked up a beautifully bound small book that lay at hand on the table. It was a French tale of the eighteenth century, and as obscene as possible. Naturally I read on in it, for I like obscenity well enough in its place, which is behind the scenes, or bursting out on occasion in a comic, rollicking, enormously hearty mood, as in Aristophanes; and when Lady Ottoline arrived, and found me reading it, she took pains to say it was not her book, but Mr. Strachey's. Certainly it wasn't likely to be her book; but he might have put it in his pocket, and not left it lying on the drawing-room table.

Siegfried Sassoon showed at first sight more of Siegfried than of Sassoon: a large blond young man sprawling in a large arm-chair, and saying little, as if he were dreaming of the mountains and the open fields. I saw him only once; but he obligingly drove me back to Oxford that afternoon, and from casual words he dropped and what I have seen of his poems, I daresay that the Sassoon side would soon have cropped out. He seemed to be swimming socially on the crest of every wave and to be universally informed, with moral chaos and bitterness beneath.

Lady Ottoline was most kind to me and I liked her the better the better I knew her; yet I resisted her invitations to stay at Garsington, and was repelled by the idea of nibbling the edges of her social and political world. It was the antithesis and the scornful enemy of the Oxford I could love. Unfortunately this lovable Oxford was imaginary or extinct or evanescent. It could be recaptured only in odd persons and stray glimpses. My bad scholarship, my Romanism, my connection with America and my friendship with the Russells made me unpalatable to the very people that I might have liked best. The conservatives and the poets had never heard of me, or wished they hadn't. Robert Bridges, Father Waggett, and Professor Stewart were the only exceptions; and I was not young enough to profit much by their friendliness. My path, thank God, had led me through Oxford, but it also, thank God, led me away from it.

CHAPTER VI

FAREWELL TO ENGLAND

IN the year 1919, when the peace of Versailles was being debated, Robert Bridges made a determined effort to induce me to settle for good in England. He said I had things to say that the English needed to hear. Save for the deference I always showed him, who was the only real friend I ever had much older than myself, I might have replied that it would be more becoming and more efficacious for *him* to say these things, if he thought them worth saying. He was poet laureate, official prophet to royalty, psalmist and vicar of King David. He knew the chords to strike and had the ear of the public; and if the public didn't pay much attention to him, what attention would they ever pay to me, a foreigner and a sceptic? Moreover, it was not my vocation to address the British public or any public, but to record as best I could the inwardness of things for a free spirit.

I loved England only too much. Living there I was in danger of losing my philosophical cruelty and independence. Omens of this contagion in sentiment, if not in doctrine, had already appeared in my little book on *Egotism in German Philosophy*; yet the English, far from being propitiated, only felt the more sharply the radical divergence of my mind from theirs. The reviewers accused me of debasing criticism into propaganda. That is what my position would have been in them, if they had assumed it: a philosophical inconsistency caused by political animus. They didn't understand, though they may have felt instinctively, that the egotism I attacked was far from being exclusively German, but was present in them and in the Americans whenever they turned their national ideal into something cosmic and eschatological, and felt themselves to be the chosen people. That if they did so they were themselves neither good philosophers nor good Christians was one of the things they needed to hear: but they wouldn't listen. Did Bridges himself understand it?

It was the net of Oxford that he spread in order to detain me. I had lived there off and on for five years, but absolutely unattached. The point now was to attach me, because I didn't conceal my intention of running away to Paris, to Spain, and to Italy. Now Bridges was a member of Corpus Christi College, and I had more than once been to luncheon there with him in the Senior Common Room; while F. C. S. Schiller, for many years, had asked me to dinner there in Hall, each time that I turned up at Oxford. Besides, a Boston acquaintance of mine, Edward Warren, was also living at Corpus; but he always invited me to his own rooms, where we might be tête-à-tête and freely discuss Boston and other delicate subjects. I was thus not unknown at Corpus; but now Bridges induced the Head of the College to ask me to luncheon, in order to inspect me. Apparently I passed muster. In those days I was thoroughly at home in the Oxford atmosphere of moderately comic anecdote—never roisterous—and sly hits at one another's heresies. A well-established Don, whose scholarship was impeccable, might like Conybeare cry across the table, if someone had asked what is orthodoxy, "Orthodoxy is reticence." But I knew better than to take such liberties. I smiled, and remembered the advice of Job to hold my peace, that peradventure I might be thought a wise man. At any rate a few days later Warren approached me with a confidential communication. He had been commissioned to sound me on the subject of residence in Oxford. Should I like to become, for life, a member of the High Table and Common Room at Corpus? For the moment, and during the war, they could let me have rooms in College, but in normal times all their rooms would be needed for undergraduates, and I should have to live in lodgings. When I politely shook my head, and gave merely civil reasons for declining, Warren asked—so little did he or the others understand me—whether I should prefer to teach. Oh, no: I had never wished to teach. I had nothing to *teach*. I wished only to learn, to be always the student, never the professor. And with being eternally a student went the idea of being free to move, to pass from one town and one country to another, at least while enough youth and energy remained for me to love exploration and to profit by it.

That was all true enough, but I had other far more decisive reasons for not accepting this invitation. Certainly it had a tempting side. I was happy in Oxford, and I needed a centre in which to keep my books and papers, and in which to hibernate and feel at home. The centre I had in Paris, and was about to return to, possessed certain advantages: it was cheap—as I was largely Strong's guest there—and it was convenient for Spain and Italy; yet rooms in an Oxford College, with the privileges of a Don, would have been far more comfortable and dignified. Had I had more money, I might have been seriously tempted to accept: but not at Corpus. Especially not ushered in there, as it were, by Warren, a Bostonian, and with Schiller every day at dinner, as my only other old friend. They were both individuals that a novelist might like to study, interesting cases; but to be sandwiched between them as if intellectually I were such another tramp (as externally indeed I was) would have been a perpetual mortification. Warren was unfortunate, yet I objected to him less than to Schiller, because I pitied him, and our connection with Boston was a true link; but Schiller, with the airs of a professed and shameless sophist, was an English Churchman, probably for that reason tolerated at Oxford where otherwise he might have been taboo. Perhaps it was his German blood that prevented him, in his simplicity, from seeing himself as others saw him. He earnestly presented himself as a candidate for *the professorship of logic in Oxford* and asked *me* to write a testimonial recommending him for that position!

Bridges, who understood me better, must have suspected that my refusal was based on reasons that I hadn't mentioned. Perhaps I didn't like Corpus, and should prefer another College. Now Bridges belonged also to New College, just the college to attract me: beautiful chapel, beautiful music, beautiful garden, old monastic cloisters, old city walls, classical traditions, High Church atmosphere, an undemolished statue of the Virgin still over the College Gate! It happens, that except Lionel Johnson and Bridges himself, I had never had a New College friend, while I have had so many at Balliol, Christ Church and Magdalen. But that would not have been an objection, if the present residents, masters and pupils, had proved sympathetic, as some of them surely would have done. Bridges on several occasions tried to introduce me to the Warden of New College, but I smelt a rat; perhaps I was afraid that I might be inveigled into some rash commitment. In any case I eluded all contacts in that direction, and so markedly, that I am afraid Bridges was a bit offended.

He said that my abandonment of England was "deplorable." Yet nothing was further from my thoughts than to "abandon" England. I hoped to return often, and I had never lived there except as a stranger and a guest. I was simply avoiding a misunderstanding, a false position. I could never abandon *my* England, because that was a part of myself, just as *my* America and *my* Spain are parts of myself: but these are not to be confused with the real, public, ever-changing England, Spain or America of geography and politics. My England was only the illusion with which the real England had inspired me. This illusion contained some truth; but it sprang from a few contacts, many of them indirect, and supplied by other poetic fictions. Shakespeare and Dickens were important sources, and especially Shakespeare's comedies and comic scenes in the histories and tragedies; for the histories officially depict mediaeval passions that are not English now, nor elements in my England. They are noisy. But in the songs, and in Shakespeare's wit and wistfulness everywhere, I find the spirit of my England purer than in any later poet. He was not puritan, he smacked of the country air and of young blood. I am well aware that the real England has many a virtue appreciable from points of view other than mine, virtues that are their own reward; but that is not my affair. It would have been treason to myself and a false profession of faith to have *wedded* the real England or the real America. They are variable material complexes; I could draw from them the pleasures and lessons of travel, but they are not ideal objects to which I would pledge my troth.

Mrs. Berenson once observed with feminine insight that my reasons for not living in England were not those which I gave out, such as my health, or the advantages of living with Strong in Paris or at Fiesole. My real reason, she said, was that England was too much like America. Not yet, perhaps, in 1920; but I felt in my bones, and divined everywhere, the tyrant flood of democracy in England and of commercial imperialism in America, visibly undermining my England in England, and swallowing up my America in America. I was protecting, by fleeing from both, the memory of them in myself.

In these same months a suggestion that might have enticed me twenty-five years earlier came to me from a different quarter: it was that I should go to live as a paying guest with Howard Sturgis and the Babe. But twenty-five years earlier, Howard was rich and would not have dreamt of making me such a proposal, while I was poor, and could not have accepted it. Now the tables, in some measure, were turned. He was old, desolate, ill, and hard up; and I was a friend of long standing, free, with a comfortable income, and beginning to be esteemed as a writer. Moreover, I had always been on pleasant terms with the Babe, liked him, and didn't despise him for not being intellectual or for letting Howard adopt him and support him. If anything it was the Babe that was making the greater sacrifice; which indeed Howard would not have demanded if his affection had been more heroic and his character less feminine. He could perfectly well have helped the Babe to find some comfortable post and to marry, and not have allowed him to grow old in an ambiguous dependence, and incidentally to waste Howard's fortune, not in riotous living but in foolish speculation. The Babe was certainly a minor personage, and feeble; but he kept his head and his spirits up in a difficult position, and was really the victim of the devotion that Howard insisted on showing him.

It was the Babe, on my last visit to them, who dropped a hint, evidently in consequence of confabulations that they had had together. Why didn't I settle down in England? Didn't I have a thousand pounds a year? No? Not so much? Anyhow, I could contribute a tidy sum, if I lived with friends who already had an establishment, but were suffering from the hard times. It would be so much more comfortable for me than living always in temporary quarters, in foreign countries, entirely alone.

How came Howard, with his knowledge of the world and of all his friends' weaknesses, to entertain such a project? He was living in the past. He saw himself, Queen's Acre, and me as we had been twenty-five years before. He knew how enchanting he and his circle had been to me then: a little Russian ballet in real life, great airs, extreme elegance in a diminutive setting, wide margins left on every side for glimpses of high life, of royalty, of politics, of poetry, of grotesque philosophy and grotesque morals; he himself a figurine, a voluntary caricature, sitting with his golden hair beautifully brushed, his small feet daintily crossed, in the middle of a square carpet on the emerald lawn, with his work-basket and menagerie of little dogs about him. His sparkling talk, while he embroidered some large design in gold thread, was alternately tender and merciless, mimicking and ridiculing everyone not present; yet he trembled, like a universal mother, at the mention of any illness, any death, any public disaster. And through all this a drift of charming relatives, guests, and casual visitors, all perfectly at home there, yet all in holiday mood, acting their various parts appropriately in the comedy and saying delicate things with a dancing mind.

The happy presence of reason in human life is perhaps better exemplified in comedy than in tragedy. In comedy we see no terrible sub-human or super-human fatality to render reason vain. Reason therefore can make its little runs and show its comic contradictions and clever solutions without disturbing the sound vegetative substance and free flowerings of human society. In comedy we laugh at our foolish errors, correct them with a word, and know no reason why we shouldn't be happy ever after.

Sparks of this free spirit of comedy flew constantly from Howard in his youth; but even then each spark threatened to be extinguished by a little suppressed gasp of compunction. Ridicule and pity seemed to chase each other in his mind. Where pity had the start, ridicule dropped out in despair; but when ridicule came first, as it usually did, pity was sure to overtake and smother it before the finish. Sentimental plays with comic relief do not make good comedy; and that was the trouble with Howard's life. He lacked genuine British stamina to keep him jolly in old age; and religion or genius would have been requisite to stiffen the sentimental side.

At Howard's the transformation had been gradual. Long before the war, during my summer visits, I had seen it approach. In 1890, when I first saw him at home, it seemed a bower of roses. He played by turns the fairy prince and the disconsolate Pierrot, now full of almost tearful affection, now sitting dressed in sky-blue silk at the head of his sparkling table, surrounded by young dandies and distinguished elderly dames; or when he drove his wagonette and high-stepping pair skilfully and festively, holding high the reins in his white-gloved hands, as if he were dancing a minuet.

Gradually all that joyfulness and gaiety had faded from the scene. First his fancy clothes were discarded: they had lost their freshness and perhaps they had got too tight, for he was no longer very slender. Anyhow masquerades at home were ridiculous and unsuitable. Then he gave up mimicking people, except involuntarily in little touches when he repeated what anyone had said. His imitations had been works of art, taking off not only voice and manner to perfection, but supplying diction and sentiments to suit, and only slightly exaggerated. But mockery, his aging conscience warned him, was unkind; and if he gave up being kind, what would remain of him?

The irony of fate would have it that now when he disciplined himself in kindness he was really far less kind than he had been when merry and ready to make fun of everybody; for just as he had loved lame little mongrel dogs for being lame and mongrel, so he had really loved us all in his youth for being absurd and full of little weaknesses; whereas now the merry sentimentalist had become a melancholy one, and sadly censorious. And while the freedom and light faded from his spirit, the sunshine seemed also to fade from his garden and the joyousness from his house. Anticipations had not been realised. The house had been enlarged, but seemed smaller, the furniture old-fashioned and worn, the once flowering garden grey and bald like our respective heads. The ribaldry had been expunged from conversation, but also the wit, the frankness, the variety. Any straggling guest like myself caused evident disturbance. I knew that some white wine had been ordered expressly on my arrival, so that it might not seem that there was nothing to drink. If I came to live with them I should be an expense, as well as a help: nor could it be an act of kindness on my part in other ways, because our views now clashed not in merriment any longer but in displeasure. People do not grow better when they grow older; they remain the same, but later circumstances cause them to exhibit their character sometimes in a minor key with the soft pedal, so that they seem to us grown sweeter, and sometimes more harshly and disagreeably, when we think them soured or depraved. No: we are no longer charmed by their virtues or interested in their vices.

With the lapse of years Howard and I had begun to see each other in this less favourable light. He thought I was abominably selfish. Certainly, I am profoundly selfish in the sense that I resist human contagion, except provisionally, on the surface, and in matters indifferent to me. For pleasure, and convivially, I like to share the life about me, and have often done it; but never so as, at heart, to surrender my independence. On the other hand, I am not selfish in a competitive way. I don't want to snatch money or position or pleasures from other people, nor do I attempt to dominate them, as an unselfish man would say, for their own good.

I sincerely wish them joy in their native ways of living, as if they were wild animals; but I decidedly refuse to hunt with them unless the probable result recommends itself to me independently.

To heartlessness of this kind I am ready to plead guilty, and see clearly that it is inhuman. Sympathy with nature, however, is the source of it, and not any aggressive selfishness. Every need or passion evokes dramatic sympathy; but the contrariety among the passions gives that sympathy pause and evokes reason. Now reason, confronted with the chaos and hell of all these conflicting passions and needs, often takes a Mephistophelian turn. Reason can never be malignant, because it is a complex of sympathies, but it may sometimes be cynical, when it shows how many needs are needless and how many passions artificial. I confess that I often like the sayings of Mephistopheles and Iago as much as I dislike the conduct of Othello and Faust. In those sayings there is light; but in the action of those heroes there is no light, only the blind will of protoplasm to stir and to move on, or the blind error of a bull fighting a shadow. As to the action of Mephistopheles or Iago, there is properly none. There is no human motive for it, only the traditions of a puppet show, with devils popping up to do the mischief. And this explains the inhumanity of these stage villains. They develop reasoning in the modern drama without possessing the generic animal needs and passions requisite to evoke reason in any creature. Reason can serve to control and harmonise such natural interests; it cannot take their place.

I happened to be at Queen's Acre in 1914 shortly after the outbreak of war, when Howard was suffering from a cruel sense of the folly of mankind. What could be more senseless than destruction, destruction, destruction? Yet in his intense liberalism he had applauded the destruction of ancient institutions and ways of life, because destruction there had made room for liberty. The destruction of modern works, on the contrary, would make for poverty; and like a true child of the Great Merchants, Howard was convinced that riches exalted worthy people and made them beneficent. Destruction is indeed cruel and odious when it is carried on for its own sake, malignantly or covetously, like the destruction of the monasteries during the Reformation and the revolutions still to-day malignant; but if we take a broad cosmic view of destruction it is only the shady side of progress. Like natural death it is inevitable; and though we regret it when premature or needlessly painful, there would be as much sentimental folly in disallowing it as in mourning the coming on of night or of autumn.

So the war of 1914–18 was intended by the Germans to be, for them and for the future of the world, a step in individual and political progress; and so too the next war, wickedly destructive and arrogant on both sides, was conceived, first again by the Germans, and then by all the combatants. The Great Merchants' wealth and the whole economic system of which they were the flower, proved in fact less beneficent and much less durable than the *ancien régime*. Howard himself was a pathetic victim of this system; he was generosity and refinement personified; but he couldn't help envying the dying aristocracy that he imitated and denounced; and the necessary soil to sustain his wealth, refinement, and generosity slipped visibly from under his feet.

During that first climacteric war, I heard that Howard had taken lodgings in London in order to do "War Work" by reading, censoring and readdressing German prisoners' correspondence. This was a marked sacrifice of his comfort and leisure; but solitary comfort with moral irritation and loneliness is not happiness; and the change of scene, the dutiful occupation, and the sense of helping to console mothers, sweethearts, and wives was surely some compensation, in spite of possible bombs. But there was a tragic background to this charitable act. Howard was beginning to suffer from a mortal illness, cancer in the bowels; and although he had been reprieved by one dangerous operation, another was destined to be necessary. Fortune proved faithless to him with a vengeance; but he showed a remarkable fortitude, not stoical but tender. The fountains of pleasure and gaiety, so sparkling in his youth, had run dry. It was not difficult to surrender the world, when the affections remained which alone need never be surrendered.

When months later, in Italy, I saw in *The Times* that Howard was dead, and on writing to the Babe received assurances that Howard had died peacefully, without pain, and nobly resigned, then the whole long and curious chapter of my friendship with him came up before me, much as I have recorded it here; and I was glad that the end, which had to be sad, at least had not been harrowing. If I had jumped at the chance of going to live at Queen's Acre, thinking I had found a home at last, my illusion would have been short-lived, and our brief life in common would not have been happy. Still, when I returned to England in 1923, I went to see the Babe where he was living with his father near Bath; but it was an unsatisfactory postscript. What ghastly pleasure this is, to pull the dead out of their graves! My morning tea was served me in a beautiful china cup, one of a familiar set in the old days at Howard's, now apparently the last survivor, glued and rivetted together in many places, like a mutilated veteran of the Guard. Was I sorry that Howard was dead? No: but I was glad that he had lived. And here I repeated the experience of my uncle Santiago on the death of his daughter. "I had already lost her," he said, "when she was married." I had already, gradually and insensibly lost Howard when he began to shed his rare self, with its inimitable honest mixture of effeminacy and courage, sensibility and wit, mockery and devoted love.

Meantime, a curiously similar cloud had obscured my other chief friendship, my other Mecca, in England. Russell too had become estranged and resentful; and here also, while there was no open breach, there could be no pleasure or simplicity in keeping up the old intimacy. I have described already the circumstances and the issue of this misunderstanding: if now I compare what happened there with what had happened to me with Howard Sturgis, I see a fundamental difference. With Howard the chief trouble was that we had both grown old, that the natural period of our intimacy was past, and could not be prolonged honestly. Howard complained of this, because he was motherly, tender, affectionate, and jealous. He would have wished the Babe to be always a babe, and me to be always the delighted young traveller. I made no such claims, and felt only the melancholy that pervades a world where everything is transitory. By that time I was inured to the cyclical character of all my friendships, that set a period to the best of them, sometimes a very brief one. For me this involved no estrangement, no disillusion; on the contrary, the limits of each friendship perfected that friendship, insured it against disaster, enshrined it in the eternal. Spirit can immortalise events without being able to prolong them; it can virtually survey all seasons at every season. That is what I am doing now to my love of England and of my English friends. My farewell to them, in so far as it was my doing, was only temporal; they belonged to my past; materially we had to separate; it was better and wiser to do so in time. In that way nothing need grow stale, nothing need lapse or contradict itself or confuse the affections.

With Russell the bond had little to do with externals, whether in our persons or in our circumstances. Conventionally, without the quickness and simplicity of youth, we should never have become friends; and many people always wondered how it could have happened. The affinity between us lay beneath the surface, and I, at least, felt it at once very strongly: and in two directions. There was physical or vital affinity, or rather attraction by contrast: I admired his fearlessness, agility, and skill in doing things entirely beyond my powers; and he found me sympathetic and calm. Then, intellectually, in independent and disinterested judgment, we coincided: but since this was only a transcendental identity, it could pass unobserved, and could seem to be destroyed by our contrary prejudices in concrete matters. Nevertheless this double affinity could hardly be affected by the lapse of time: and I think that if Russell had finished his career in the world as early as I did, before the age of fifty, we might have been ideal old cronies in our declining years, grumbling of course at each other, yet perfectly happy together. But before he was rid of his matrimonial embarrassments, he had plunged into the troubled waters of unsuccessful business and unsuccessful politics; and he succumbed, exhausted, in the heat of the day, without ever feeling the cool of the twilight. I on the contrary have been enjoying peace for thirty years, in the midst of prodigious wars. In regard to Russell, I had really been guilty of an indiscretion in questioning the wisdom of his change of wives, when his mind was probably made up. But my motive had been sympathy with his new love, not disapproval; and I feared that legal commitments towards both wives at once would lead to a catastrophe. Had he and Elizabeth retained their freedom, the episode might have ended in comparative peace. Undoubtedly, on the day when Elizabeth had come for me at the station, to win me for her cause, Russell could reasonably have said "Allow that you were a fool. You didn't know Elizabeth, and you couldn't conceive how happy she would be with me." But soon *she was not happy*; and her unhappiness led her to confide in me, and deepen the sympathy naturally inspired by her delicate mind and person. Russell perceived this, and disliked it; his displeasure even became a kind of jealousy. Not that he imagined for a moment that Elizabeth and I were making love; that would have been absurd; but we seemed to be more confidential and sympathetic about him than with him. This was unfortunately the case, entirely against our will and expectation. We were both interested only in him, and troubled about what threatened to cloud our relations with him or, in her case, to make them impossible. I couldn't help recognising her difficulties, and the qualities in him that could cause them: to me they were an old story and I had, as he knew, foreseen them and warned him of what would happen. That this should now irritate him, was only human; but here a confusion seems to have arisen in his mind. He thought that I too had become *hostile* to him; that I was *abandoning* him and becoming her ally. He was angry because I saw her once or twice in London after she had left him. He seemed to demand that I should break with her, and because I refused to do so, he said I was "disloyal."

There was a marked peculiarity in Russell's mind that helps to explain this misunderstanding. Perspectives for him were strictly limited: he saw only what, for the moment, touched the matter in hand. All the rest of the truth lapsed altogether. He used to say in the early years that he cared nothing for what his friends might do when he wasn't present. I noticed, for instance, even when he seemed glad to have me as a companion, that he never remembered that any such things existed as my family, my prospects, my opinions, or my books. I was nothing but what I was *for him*. Far from resenting this, I had liked it. It helped me also to shed my past and my future, and to live for the moment in another's life. I was being treated justly and generously in my capacity of friend available for that occasion; I was not meddled with, judged, or misrepresented in my other capacities.

It is characteristic of spontaneous friendship to take on trust, without enquiry and almost at first sight, the unseen doings and unspoken sentiments of our friends: the part known gives us evidence enough that the unknown parts cannot be much amiss. Nor does this imply that the unknown parts must be intelligible to us or after our own taste; on the contrary, it is almost better that they should extend into the inimitable. Friendship may then be touched at the edges with admiration and love. Russell knew that I was a being apart, dependent on him for nothing except the pleasure of his society; he was well aware that in politics my views were different from his: not contradictory but at another level. I never aired them; and I heartily enjoyed the satirical expositions he would make of English law, custom, and prejudice. I learned a lot from him, and was silently confirmed in my silent affections and philosophy. We never argued. If by chance our divergences came to the surface, he grunted and I laughed. I knew that English opinions had to grow like that, with the scent and the promise of fruit; they were instrumental or edifying opinions, and it would have been unprofitable for them to bother to be true. I on my side was allowed to remain ineffectual and negligible in my wise fool's paradise.

Russell's indifference to everything not involved in his present surroundings or sentiments produced odd lapses in his memory. I have mentioned his forgetting altogether that I had pulled him into the water at Richmond, something that at the time had infuriated him. This might conceivably have been suppressed by Freud's "Censor"; there were other cases of forgetfulness regarding inconvenient or regrettable facts that, in early days, he himself had told me of; and here the pressure of a later *parti pris* evidently had first ignored and then erased the contrary memory. Yet in general it was more what Bergson describes: urgent practical business absorbing attention and driving irrelevant ideas from consciousness. Russell's worries fatigued, distracted and harrowed his mind. A curious sign of this, in his last years, was that he repeatedly called me Sargeaunt. Sargeaunt was a Latin master at Westminster, the translator of Terence in *The Loeb Classics,* who no doubt had been a friend of Russell's at school or in Oxford, and who sometimes came for a week-end to T.H. They had nothing now in common save that old sense of familiarity. This was incidentally what, from his present point of view, Russell saw in me. Both Sargeaunt and I were obviously inoffensive, unimportant elderly persons shuffling about abstractedly: both teachers and old bachelors and old acquaintances, who knew his ways and were not nuisances, and whose names began with an S and had A's and N T's in them. Sargeaunt or Santayana, what difference did it make?

No doubt this was only a slip of the tongue, in moments of abstraction. A Freudian treatment would have elicited that I had been the only one of his old friends, besides his brother, to stick to him openly through thick and thin for thirty years; that I had been the witness or confidant of many of his love-affairs (though not all of them) and had given testimony for him in the most scandalous of his law-suits, without a thought of the possible risk to my own reputation and livelihood. But all this lay in the past, hidden by the fog of the present, and to be brought to light only at the Last Judgment. To see now only what counted now was a sign of being a man of action and a good politician. And in his life now I counted for very little; perhaps at last I had even become a nuisance.

Yet at the very time when he was confusing me with Sargeaunt, he was complaining that I was "disloyal" and this reproach presupposes allegiance. It asserts regal claims that only long years of fidelity could justify: so that the past remained virtually present *in him*, though banished from his conscious memory. Precisely because he knew that I was loyal, he was hurt to find that I understood Elizabeth's grievances and rebellion. *I* had no grievances, *I* was not deserting him; and in his last letter to me, dictated a week before his death, he crossed out the secretary's word "sincerely" at the end and wrote as usual, "Yours ever."

When I returned to England in 1923 I had written to him announcing my presence and asked if he wished me to go and see him. He replied "Do as you like." I went for a short week-end. He was alone, and spent his day, as he had always done, exactly as if I hadn't been there. I found him busy over the wires of his new radio—it was then a novelty—and in the evening, without dressing, we went to dine at a retired Admiral's in a neighbouring village, where Russell, with his radio, was to give a talk to the villagers at the church vestry or school-house. The radio didn't work very well; it refused to connect with Paris, as Russell had planned; but a fragment of a fragment of a music hall performance in London was heard with satisfaction and wonder. On Sunday we went for a long motor drive; I was not forewarned, but I found that we were bound to a particular cottage where an interesting widow was expecting us for tea. She and Russell afterwards strolled aside in earnest and somewhat troubled conversation. Evidently the course of true love here didn't run smooth. Five years had passed since the flight of Elizabeth and I ought to have expected to find a lady in the picture. No doubt he had a secretary or other companion in London; but that wasn't enough. He was haunted by the need of a happy home.

The next morning he took me back to town in his motor: and here there was a significant change. It was a closed motor, that is to say, it had a glass front and a roof, but Russell drove and I sat beside him as usual on the front seat. However, there was a chauffeur, something not known formerly; and Russell said that now he sometimes let him drive while he himself dozed on the back seat. He was tired. For thirty years he had lived a distracted life under high pressure and a forced draught, a life absorbed not in doing what he was fit to do but in getting rid of obstacles and wasting his energies on trifles and his affections on impossible women. He needed relaxation, yet couldn't relax. He never drank: a glass of wine would upset him. Continual discomfort had crept into his system; it would be soothed or forgotten only by the greater strain of fast motoring or playing cards, with stakes rather higher than he could afford. For he had become poor; law-suits and losses in business had nearly ruined him; he was kept going precariously by being director of various precarious companies. He had forgotten his youthful cultivated tastes; he had lost his old friends; he had repudiated his wives or been abandoned by them.

Luckily politics, his hereditary calling, came after a fashion to the rescue. He was elected to the London County Council, and afterwards played a useful if not distinguished part in the House of Lords and in the Government. But for me this was small comfort. I knew what a sham it all was, how unhappy it left him, how it buried the truly masterful side of him under a load of ridiculous servitudes. He thought life had to be like that; that it was a rough, fast game you must play; after which your ashes should be scattered to the winds. Peace would come soon enough in death. He could not conceive peace to be something positive, like laughter or intelligence, that lived in the midst of life and was the true triumph over it. Yet he had possessed that peace in his first youth most emphatically; and we had enjoyed it together.

Such, on the sentimental side, and in regard to my friends, was my farewell to England. I recognised that that chapter was closed. I yet expected to return often to England, and to revisit my old haunts there, and find other pleasant places. I might see them in an autumnal colouring; that would be a new beauty; it might almost be worth the old. I should stop in London only in transit, but revisit Oxford, Cambridge, Windsor, and perhaps even T.H. for the old solitary walks over fields and downs, or by quiet rivers.

All this was not to be, and I am glad of it. Materially, however, I did return to England twice, and for a tell-tale reason. I was invited to give lectures. The author, the professor went; the spirit did not accompany him. The first time was in 1923 when they asked me to give the Herbert Spencer lecture at Oxford. I was glad to accept; this was my first and last official connection with that University. The question might be what to say about Spencer, whom I had not read or thought of since my undergraduate days, when William James lectured about him. To have reread Spencer would have been too severe a penance; I chose *The Unknowable* for a subject, as admitting no investigation. I chose also the earliest possible date in October for my lecture, so as to get back to Italy before the winter set in. However, with my romantic notion of revisiting old haunts, and composing elegies about *La Chute des Feuilles*, I went, as I have already related, to see Russell; and Howard being dead I went to see the Babe, and then retired to lodgings in Cambridge in order to finish writing my lecture. There the always amiable Lapsley put me up at the High Table at Trinity, where I had pleasant conversations with Mac-Taggart and with Housman. But I was not well, persecuted by my bronchial catarrh, and without heart to re-evoke any Oxford ghosts.

There, I went to the Clarendon Hotel, walked one day to Iffley, and saw nobody except young Randolph Chetwynd, who was charming, but busy trying to argue I don't know what socialists back to liberalism. He lived in an old stable or coach-house in New College Lane which had been turned into chambers: the sloping roof was open to the eye, plastered, and made picturesque by beams painted black and by iron brackets and lanterns. He dined with me at my hotel and after dinner left me alone to sit by his fire, with a glass of port, and a book said to be interesting; but no, I couldn't feel at home. Nor was my age the only cause. Oxford also was not itself. I couldn't walk through New College Lane or Merton Lane without being startled, as by a cavalry charge, by troops of young women on bicycles, wearing caps and gowns. Was it worth while for Randolph to stem the tide of Socialism? Better let the flood come, I thought, and perhaps something genuine after its kind might emerge after the deluge.

As to my lecture, it was kindly received, but by the oddest of audiences in the oddest of places. I never felt less in Oxford at Oxford than on that occasion. I had been put in communication with a scientific Don, doubtless of the Committee for the Spencer Lectureship; and when I called at his house by appointment an hour before the time for the lecture, his wife said he was so sorry but he had been called away to receive 4000 butterflies that had just arrived from South America. He turned up later, however, and took me to the Natural History Museum, not to see the butterflies, but to read my lecture in a hall like an operating-theatre, with a deep pit, and great blackboards and maps on the walls. He wore no gown and instead of introducing me said simply, "Oh you might as well begin." The audience, sprinkled about the steep semi-circle of seats, comprised a good many Indians and Japanese, and a few ladies. I recognised only old Professor Stewart, always most kind to me, and F. C. S. Schiller. This audience, however, soon became sympathetic, perceived that they were expected to laugh, and applauded heartily at the end. Several dusky youths brought me books to be autographed. Did they feel that I was one of them at heart? We might have been in Singapore.

This occasion had been graceless externally, but morally it left a pleasant impression. I felt that my labour had not been wasted. Not so the evening before, when I had been invited to dine at Wadham and to read a paper before a philosophical club. I had nothing with me except the first chapter of *The Realm of Essence*, so I read that. There was no sympathy in the air, and I read without warmth. When it came to the discussion everybody seemed at sea, and caught at phrases or trifles that struck them as odd. Nobody had heard of *Scepticism and Animal Faith*, published not long before. Samuel of New College, Robert Bridges' son-in-law, but white-bearded like a Hebrew prophet, observed sarcastically that "there seemed to be a thing called substance."

Only one little chap, perhaps an Irishman or a Catholic, said something that showed comprehension. How glad I was not to be at New College with the Prophet Samuel and the Prophet Joachim! Wasn't I at heart more English than these "Englishmen" and more Oxonian than these Oxonians? How much at home I should have felt in fleeing from them to Harold Fletcher and Father Waggett, to old Higgs and Robert Bridges!

A thousand silent isolated wits, if I could have got at them, would not only have understood my philosophy but would have fortified my love of England and of mankind. But my lot was cast among the heretics and the radicals, and I seemed insignificant to the professional idealogues who had never had the courage to face the cruel truth about anything, much less to utter it.

There was then a through train direct from Oxford to Dover, passing through the pleasant hilly country south of the Thames and avoiding London. I took it the next morning and found it most comfortable and almost empty. Apparently it was not yet the season for continental travel from Liverpool and the North; but it was lovely autumnal weather, pleasant to the eyes and suitable for a timely but still affectionate farewell to England.

Nevertheless I returned nine years later for another visit. I had agreed to go in September, to the Spinoza Tercentennial meeting at the Hague, and had already finished my address for that occasion when I received an invitation from the Royal Society of Literature in Bloomsbury Square to speak to them about Locke, born, like Spinoza, in 1632. Holland is not far from England geographically or morally, and after my heavy work on Spinoza it would be entertaining to write something lighter about the English worthy. The meetings at the Domus Spinozana had pleased me: I had paid my homage to the *numen* of the place, I had learned something about my hero, namely, how *theological* his youth had been (just like mine) and I had breathed gladly again the air of the Netherlands, their vast horizons and their homely ways. I would risk crossing the North Sea, and would ask Cory, who was in London, to engage rooms for me somewhere at St.

James's, where I should feel at home. I didn't mean to leave town
or to revive any sentimental associations. Oxford was vulgarised,
Cambridge was stale, Russell was "dead and cremated." I would
devote the mornings to finishing my lecture, and get some book—
it happened to be Aldous Huxley's latest—to while away the evenings; Cory would come to lunch with me every day at Hatchett's,
and then I would go for a solitary walk in Hyde Park, and a
comfortable tea before turning in. I carried out this programme to
the letter. My rooms in St. James's Place were not like lodgings
in Jermyn Street of old: bad service, gas fires (at which I had to
finish toasting my toast in the morning, holding it with a fork)
and a dismal outlook over mews and chimney-pots. Besides I was
suffering from my bronchial catarrh, not severely, but enough to
mar the pleasure of mere existence. However, I should have ended
my visit in a neutral state of somnambulism, but for the disgusting experience of the day of my lecture.

This lecture was a *jeu d'esprit*, it was gay, it was addressed to
the free and unprejudiced mind. It also presupposed a certain
familiarity with the quality of modern ideologies, seen satirically.
I had counted on an audience like the blessed one at the British
Academy in 1918 who laughed merrily when they heard that, for
a pragmatist, the real past was the idea of the past that he would
have in the future. But I found a Bloomsbury audience that
didn't consent to smile. Nor was it intellectual opacity alone that
enveloped me. All the lights in the room were in my eyes and
none on the reading desk. I had purposely brought my own manuscript, written large and clear on alternate lines, but I couldn't
see to read it. What was I to do? Finally, by having the lights at
the rear of the room put out, I found that I could manage, though
with great difficulty and uncertainty. Sir Rennell Rodd (not yet
a peer), who had been Ambassador at Rome, pompous and vac-
uous, introduced me in a vague little speech, saying nothing
about Locke and repeatedly calling me a-a-a thinker and a-a-a
writer, fortunately not a-a-a professor. It was evident that he knew
nothing about me. Disgusted as I was about the lights, and chilled

by the chairman and the audience, I couldn't fall into the spirit of my paper, or assume the facile and confidential tone that it demanded. However, I pulled through somehow, and at the end I was surprised that they applauded with some persistence, as if to say: "Your lecture was a bit queer and disconcerting in places, and we haven't quite caught the drift of it; but we realise that it was a superior lecture, as lectures go." Even Sir Rennell Rodd, in his speech of thanks, had a happy thought. He observed, between two little pauses, that perhaps there was subtlety in what I had said. Yes, Sir Rennell; there were insinuations.

When we broke up, an Indian came to ask me some leading questions about Locke. He wished to be confirmed in thinking Locke superficial. When I explained that Locke was a pioneer, more important in his influence than in his insight, my dusky friend showed his white teeth. Yes, he said, Locke wasn't *profound*. A lady also came up who said that she was Mrs. Inge and that her husband had been sorry not to be able to come and hear me. When I spoke of my sympathy with the Dean's views on the history of religion, and my debt to his *Plotinus*, she shifted the subject at once, repeating how much he liked what I had written about *the English character*. Was it entirely as poetry, as description, as analysis that those words of mine in the *Soliloquies* were so often noticed? Are they juster than what I said of other things? I am afraid they were valued a little as testimonials. The English now had begun to relish praise even from an obscure foreigner! I am confirmed in this suspicion by the fact that Bertrand Russell, who retained the old British pride in Baconian England, its science, philosophy, and politics, actually resented my sentimentality about the *boyish* Englishman, and complained that I cared for nothing except undergraduates and the families they came from. Quite so: there I found human virtue pure and not distorted by any fanaticism, intellectual or moral, or by any shams.

After this unpleasant last visit, my farewell to England seemed almost an escape. It was a relief to feel that this chapter, rich as it had been, was closed forever. It was like burying a wife

long ago divorced: there was peace in the finality of it. No more
attempts to patch things up, no more fresh disappointments to
cloud the memory of old embraces. For I had once embraced
England with a deep and quiet pleasure. She had seemed perfect
in her simplicity, in her distinction, in the comfort of her ways.
How decent, how wise, how gentle these ways had been, how
beautiful her eyes and voice, how healthful her affections! And
although I was avowedly a wayfarer, not fit to be her acknowledged lover or husband, yet she had sometimes seemed to love
me a little. She had understood that I was to be trusted, that I saw
things as they were, and was not shocked at the truth. She had
felt that I loved her as a poet should love, without claims, without
flattery, and with an incurable pang in his unfeigned rapture.

CHAPTER VII

OLD AGE IN ITALY

WHEN at the threshold of old age I found myself free and looked about for a place of retirement and finally found it in Italy and particularly in Rome, I was not at all in search of an ideal society or even of a congenial one. I was looking only for suitable lodgings, where the climate, the scene, and the human ways of my neighbours might not impede but if possible inspire me in my projected work and where I might bring my life to a peaceful end. As to society, I was quite content with that which naturally surrounded me; for I still had my family and my friends in America, in England, and in Spain; while in Italy later the Anglo-American residents, with their fringe of distinguished Italian acquaintances, would have been accessible to me if I had cared to cultivate them more assiduously. But essentially I desired solitude and independence: not in the English form of quiet home life in the country, but rather after the fashion of ancient philosophers, often in exile, but always in sight of the market-place and the theatre.

Nor was I at first entirely adrift. Even my relations with Harvard were not suddenly severed. President Lowell had resisted my wish to resign and we had come to an agreement that, after eighteen months' leave, I should return for the first half of each year. I meant to carry out this plan so long as my mother lived; but she died soon after my departure, and my sister Josefina returned to live in Spain. I had henceforth no home in America. At the same time my income was somewhat increased, and I resigned my professorship by letter. The question of an official residence thus presented itself immediately, and remained more or less open during the next ten years.

My nominal headquarters, as well as my books, remained for some time at Strong's in the Avenue de l'Observatoire, and my passport was periodically renewed by the Spanish Consulate in Paris. But Strong and I were never there in winter, and he usually went in summer to see his parents. Sometimes I spent a season there alone, in a silence most favourable for concentration of mind. Then, in the evening, I could remember that all Paris lay at my feet, behind that screen of green trees, and I would go to the Boulevards or to the Champs Elysées for a stroll and for dinner.

There was evidently no finality, no sense of home, in such a *pied à terre*. Nor was Paris a place where, even if I had been younger and richer, I should have cared to live. It did very well for an occasional season of cosmopolitan pleasures, but even its intellectual and artistic movements, though they greatly attracted and rewarded attention, were episodes, fashions, and extravagances with which no one would wish to be identified. Even distinguished and philosophical persons that I came across never inspired any confidence in my mind. Three of these might be mentioned: Bergson, Boutroux, and Dr. Cazalis, who wrote under the name of Jean Lahore. None of these were Catholics, so that in them all there was a certain strain of self-consciousness, as of outsiders who always felt a little aggrieved and a little insincere in the French atmosphere. I have never had a French friend. In the most charming of them I felt something false, as if an evil spell bound them to some secret and sinister cause, and they were feigning all their amiability for an ulterior reason. They could never be disinterested, never detached. They had in their hearts a sort of covert intensity and stubborn nearsightedness that I could not endure. On the other hand I have fed with perpetual delight on the French way of putting things: everything was perceived by them, everything tolerated, nothing overdone, nothing insisted upon. The French mind is an exquisite medium for conveying such things as can be communicated in words. It is the unspoken things of which one feels the absence or mistrusts the quality.

During my first three years I instinctively turned to Spain, and besides long visits in Avila, I lived awhile with Mercedes in Madrid, in a circle composed of twenty-seven women and not one man. For partial relief, I then went with her and Josefina to Seville. After a while they were bored there, and left me to enjoy the air in the gardens, the Cathedral, the little plays at 10.30 at the *Teatro del Duque,* the bull-fights, and the processions of Holy Week. I even went sometimes to the music hall *Novedades* to see the local dancing and hear the local songs. It was well enough for once, or for the young natives who can enjoy it all gracefully, and escape to higher things. But for me, with my tastes and at my age, it was only a flimsy spectacle, a surface without volume or depth and with nothing to hold me. During another winter, being cold and bored in Madrid with Mercedes and her intimates, I made a trip to Valencia, Alicante, and Murcia. I saw some lovely spots along the coast, where a Spanish *Riviera* might exist; but the towns and the life were distinctly second-rate, and even the language, as far as Murcia, not Castilian. Avila, I perceived, was the only place in Spain where I might live happily. I kept that in reserve; for the moment I would look about elsewhere. Before long, however, war had broken out, and by chance had caught me in Cambridge at the *Red Lion;* and in England I remained for five years.

When I returned to Avila after the war I felt a distinct change in the moral climate. My long residence in England and the fact that my sympathies during the struggle had been strong on the English side, produced a chill towards me in my sister's family. Their sentiments had been, and continued always to be, inspired by clerical and nationalist Spanish opinion, which anticipated what it became during the second general war. At that time I didn't altogether appreciate the grounds of such violent Anglophobia. It was not founded on knowledge of England, as my feelings were. It arose indirectly, through traditional fear and hatred of English influence in other European countries; and to this was added the detestation of French influence in Spain both in politics and in religion. These good people did not suspect (although

the Pope did) that modern Germany was more anti-Catholic than
England or even than republican France, in that it preached an
enthusiastic return to heathenism; whereas England and France
were merely Erastian, worldly, greedy and money-loving, as the
Catholic soul of Castile certainly was not. The Latin peoples did
not preach a racial war based like the Teutonic claims on the
Jewish foundations of Christianity, nor propose to saddle a Nie-
tzschean morality on peaceful lands like Austria, Bavaria, and the
Rhineland that were traditionally Catholic.

Not that my own philosophy was partisan or afraid of Nietzsche. Neither tribal nor commercial morality inspired me with
particular horror. I knew that the first was brutal and the second
vulgar; but they both were intelligible phases in human civilisation, just as Catholicism was; and it was an accident of temperament or circumstances how far my sympathies were enlisted on
one or the other side. Essentially I could sympathise with them
all, but could identify myself with none. That I was a philosopher, that I could identify myself willingly only with intelligence
and with the truth, offended my friends in Avila, as it now seems
to offend some of my friends in other places.

The idea of eventually living in Avila, with one of my sisters
or with both, remained with me; but the moment had not arrived.
Meantime I would make trial of the Riviera, the common refuge
of the lazy in exile; and I took rooms with only first breakfast
served, first at Monte Carlo and then in Nice, going to Italian
restaurants for my other meals. I should have liked the old town
of Monaco, with its gardens overhanging the sea, but there was
no hotel there, and no likely lodgings. In Nice I had a bad attack
of my chronic catarrh, and moved to a clinic, where lying comfortably in bed by a wide open window, I had a pleasant convalescence spent reading Spengler's *Untergang des Abendlandes,*
all but the mathematical part, which I couldn't understand and
distrusted *a priori*; for it is a marvel that mathematics should
apply so well to the material world, and to apply it to history or
ideas is pure madness.

The atmosphere of the Riviera, physical and moral, didn't agree with me very well. And the same may be said of Florence, in spite of the presence there of some old friends, Strong, Loeser, and Berenson. They, Strong especially, with his new villa, caused me often to stop there, as I never did again on the Riviera; yet even in Fiesole I was never happy. All nationalities are better at home, where they are less conspicuous as special nationalities, and may pass for common humanity. When you transplant the species, it suffers constraint and becomes sickly or intrusive or both at once. I like to be a stranger myself, it was my destiny; but I wish to be the only stranger. For this reason I have been happiest among people of all nationalities who were not of my own age, class, or family circle; for then I was a single exceptional personage in their world, and they a complete harmonious milieu for me to drop into and live with for a season. Where there were other foreigners among whom I was classed, and with whom I was expected to be more at home than with the natives, I was ill at ease in both camps, and disliked each for not knowing how to live with the other. For this reason in America I avoided all foreigners, especially all Spanish people; and in England or Spain or even Italy, I suffered when I was with Americans. Only in Paris, a cosmopolitan caravansary in itself, did Americans and other foreigners fall nicely into the picture and spoil nothing in the charm of the place. This would probably not have been the case even there, if I had known the best French people: but I saw only persons already cultivating foreigners and making up to them for interested reasons; and it was not among such that I cared to move.

It might seem that I turned to Italy and especially to Rome as a last resort, but that was not the case. Italy and Rome were my first choice, my ideal point of vantage in thought, the one anthropological centre, where nature and art were most beautiful, and mankind least distorted from their complete character. But I had wished to look about first to see if my own country, or places more allied to my later associations, like England, would not be, for me, more desirable retreats: for it was a retreat I was looking for, not a field of action. No: upon trial I was sure that none of them would be better. Therefore I began to spend my winters in Rome in 1920, as I have done ever since. For the summer I still went to Paris, to Avila, sometimes to Glion over the lake of Geneva, a short walk to the clinic where Strong often took refuge. But I remembered the terms in which my poetic friend Stickney had eulogised Cortina, an ideal Tyrolese village in an emerald-green valley amid the mountains of the moon; and now, after the war, Cortina was in Italy. I tried it, going to the Hotel Cristallo high on a hillside. It was here, in a bare little bedroom on the top floor, that I wrote at one stretch, *Platonism and the Spiritual Life*. In that year (1926) the valley of Ampezzo was still green and rustic, with only a few roofs clustering about the church, with its noble spire. The peasants were ideal peasants and the strangers very few, and true lovers of nature.

Cortina had extraneous advantages for me as well; it could be easily reached, yet not so easily as by a night express direct from Rome. It was almost inevitable to stop in Venice; and I fell into the habit of stopping there for some weeks in each year, especially in September and October. The fashion in Venice had moved to the Lido, where I didn't follow it; and the sea front, the Piazza and the Piazzetta preserved an Italian rather than a cosmopolitan character. I found a book by an old-fashioned English resident on *Walks in Venice* with accurate little maps indicating the turns to take at each point in the labyrinth of lanes; and with this guide I walked all over Venice, without ever taking a gondola, except on my arrival and departure, when I had luggage. The eye was feasted in Venice as nowhere else on light and colour. The sea, most inhuman of elements, met in perfect friendship here with the soft and pleasure-loving side of man; and the mixed architec-ture of a by-gone plutocracy reconciled me to the experiments of to-day.

Here too the desire to be splendid is in evidence, rather than vital greatness betrayed by a splendour that was unintended. How different these palaces, so rich and ornamental outside, so evidently striving to outshine one another, from the severe grandeur of the palaces of Rome, each turned inwards, walled and barred like a castle or a monastery against the outer world, plain like a fortress or a prison, yet imposing by the scale of the monumental doors and spaced windows, the cliff-like walls and the defiant cornices! In Venice, originally on the human scale, all was pleasant loggias and balconies, where the gay inmates might crowd to see and to be seen. Business was not hidden; it might be transacted in the great Piazza or on the frequented Rialto; but Pleasure soon drove it indoors, into the secret cabinets of rich men, while the young and gallant paraded the squares or the Grand Canal, to display their finery and plot their amours. Venice would have been vulgar but for two blessed accidents, that made it inimitably beautiful. One was the magic of that lagoon on which it seemed to float, and that mesh of canals vivifying it as the veins vivify the body and everywhere mirroring a sky itself softened and dyed by the denser tints that earth and water have reflected back upon it. The other happy accident was the age in which Venice flourished and from which it borrowed its arts. The model at first was Byzantium, also a commercial city, although an oriental and hieratic one; so that everything, even nautical things, came to the Venetians already mellowed and refined by the traditions of many ages and many empires. These Venetians were *nouveaux riches*; they could never have developed their arts from within; but they had many contacts, such as other Christian nations generally lacked, and they could adopt and combine many fashions, not without a festive originality in combining them. So later, when it became the fashion in Italy to be classical, the Venetians again had models nobler than their own genius; yet these models gained a new charm and elegance when reproduced, on a smaller scale, in the incomparable stage-setting of Venice.

I lodged habitually at Danieli's, going out to Martini's by the *Teatro Fenice* for luncheon, because it was quiet and pleasant there at that hour, sitting under an awning in the well-paved square, with interesting facades before one, and not too much food, as happened then in good hotels. For dinner I usually went to the Olympia, where a table at the back was reserved for me; and when the band began to play at nine o'clock, I was ready to go and stand in the Piazza, or walk about in the upper end of it, where few people gathered. The public seems to think that to hear music is to see the musicians fiddle and blow. I preferred not to see them. Here, and on the Pincio in Rome, I had my only taste of instrumental music: shocking confession, no doubt, for a person supposed to relish the fine arts. But music bores me if I am sitting penned in among a crowd in a hot place, with bright artificial lights, and a general pretence at intelligent interest, whether such interest exists or not. It is too much like sitting through a service in a Protestant church. At the opera I can forget this discomfort because the impression, visual as well as auditory, is violent enough to hold my attention; but for pure music I desire the open air, solitude if possible, and liberty to move about and to go away. There is a wonderful sense of freedom in standing on one's two legs. It adds, in my feeling, to the sincere enjoyment of both nature and art. Music and landscape then come as a gift, not as a thing procured for a ticket that constitutes a promise and imposes a sort of pledge. I prefer that the beautiful should come upon me unannounced, and that it should leave me at liberty.*

At Danieli's my favourite room was a little one in the entresol, No. 8, close over the entrance, where I could sit during my writing hours in the morning and during my reading hours in the early afternoon, by my low-silled window, open but discreetly curtained, little above the level of the Riva degli Schiavoni. Here I was conscious of the life of the place but not disturbed by it, and refreshed, whenever I looked up, by the lovely picture of San Giorgio Maggiore across the Bacino di San Marco. If I stretched my neck a little, I could also see the Dogana and the domes and belfry of La Salute; but this, although more ornate, seemed to me

---

* Veniam subito, nec quisquam nuntiet ante,
  sed videar caelo missus adesse tibi.
          Tibullus, III, *ad finem*.

less beautiful than San Giorgio, less naturally perfect and individual; because the brick and marble harmonies of San Giorgio, with the green roof of the tower, were a happy gift of fortune. Doubtless the plutocratic rebuilders of the old convent and hospital would have liked to face everything with white marble; but the rich, on their lavish scale, are no less or even more hampered than the poor; and in this case they had the exquisite taste of Palladio to redeem and to glorify their comparative poverty. The new west front should be shining white, to be gilded and mellowed by the setting sun; while the walls, the dome, and the outlying low buildings should preserve their weathered pink with only touches of white and grey in the lintels and cornices. And fortune smiled again when the campanile was added, a slender and more graceful copy of that of Saint Mark's, *matre pulchra filia pulchrior*: for it completes the harmony of its church, as the great campanile does not, lends it height and unity, rhymes the same russet with the same white, and caps the whole, in the hood of the spire, with a touch of aerial green. So nature has blessed and adopted this work of art, as if it had descended like a vision from the clouds and remained suspended between the sparkling sea and the depths of air.

Once, in 1939–40, when the Hotel Bristol in Rome was closed and about to be rebuilt, I spent a whole winter in Venice, not a thing to be recommended; yet a pleasant walk had just been opened along the sea front uninterruptedly to the Public Gardens. There were nine little bridges, I counted some 400 steps, to go up and down on the way: but from each bridge there was a new vista, and the varied shipping carried the mind from ancient wars to the one then beginning, and from those placid lagoons to the Southern Seas.

In Rome fortune at first lent me a living guide, in the person of the Rev. Luciano Zampa of Gubbio, a modernist priest who had translated my *Egotism in German Philosophy*. It was with him that I first ventured into Italian conversation. He helped me without discouraging me by too many corrections; and I could always put in an English or Spanish or French or even Latin word if my Italian failed me. Besides, he could often guess what I wished to say before I quite said it; my later friend Michele Petrone used to do the same; and with these two I could even become eloquent in Italian, in spite of my insecure hold on the language. But the great service that Zampa did me was to show me the less obvious sights of Rome. Being a provincial priest—at first dressed as a lay-man, having been unfrocked for his modernism, but afterwards restored to his clerical privileges—he had a traditional admiration for all that was ecclesiastically important. Great ancient columns and rich marbles inspired him with respect, apart from their beauty: and this proprietory human esteem for the arts was a good corrective to the priggish aestheticism of my English-speaking artis-tic friends. Later some of these artistic friends—Geoffrey Scott, for instance, in Florence—abetted this ecclesiastical view in so far as they renounced pre-Raphaelism and learned to love the baroque; but that was an aesthetic fashion also, and corrupt; Aubrey Beardsley substituted for Burne-Jones; whereas my honest Zampa was simply impressed by the positive qualities of great size, rarity, cost or splendour.

In spite of these lessons, however, I soon retreated into my aesthetic, or rather my poetic, shell, and limited my diet of visual impressions to a few chosen sights. The central streets came in inevitably for a person who lives in them and frequents cafés; but my usual walk was to Trinità de' Monti, the Pincio and the Villa Borghese. On some days I would go instead to the Tiber, St. Peter's, and (when it was made) the admirable garden at Castel Sant'Angelo; or else to the Janiculum, San Pietro in Mon-torio and, above all, the Aqua Paola, where I always read the monumental inscription over the fountain, until finally I knew it by heart. And if any friends turned up, I would explain my aver-sion to museums and picture galleries, but would offer to take them, after luncheon, to see three things, the Pantheon, Michel-angelo's Moses, and the Forum from the top of the Capitoline, which included admiring the two pavilions of Michelangelo and the statue of Marcus Aurelius. Of these things I never tired; but of seeing more things or other things I had had enough. Fresher thought came and I could transmit more pleasure in recognising these old objects than in staring at new ones.

Yet when not compelled to talk or to avoid useless explorations, I took many other casual turns in the labyrinth of the old streets: sometimes purposely making little circuits in search of odd variations on the theme of doors and windows, not to speak of church fronts and of fountains. Sometimes lovely things turned up in this way: for instance the German burying ground by the Sacristy of St. Peter's, and the court of the hospital adjoining the church in the Borgo Santo Spirito, not far distant. Monte Cavallo, at the tip of the Quirinal, where also a band played, was another spot to loiter in at sunset, when the level light gilded the whole length of the Alta Semita as far as the Porta Pia, a caprice of Michelangelo. Many things depended on the time of day and the weather for their full effect, as landscape necessarily does; and great weathered works of architecture become part of the landscape and move the mind to poetry, not to pedantic criticism.

This for me, with my imperfect eyesight wrapping everything in a second often merciful atmosphere, applies even to interiors. With Spanish preconceptions of what a church should be—sombre, devotional, and rich in shrines—Italian interiors are apt to strike me as empty and cold; and even the great basilicas in Rome seem to lack a focus and to be too much like artist's models and too little like places of worship. But this may be due to personal prejudice, which a new personal experience may correct. Now (1942) that I live not far from the Lateran, I often cross San Giovanni, as I used to do the Cathedral of Avila, in order to avoid the hot sun on the rough pavement; and being old and fond of sitting upon public benches, I rest for a moment on one of the wooden seats that are found there (but not, alas, at St. Peter's); and in those calm moments my eye has learned to frame wonderful vistas in that great church, forward to the restored apse with its golden mosaics and its papal throne, or across aisles and aisles, into vast side chapels, each a church in itself. And then the whole place seems to lose its rigidity and its dead pomp, and to become a marvellous labyrinth, as if it were a work of nature or of fancy rather than of human art. The gigantic violent Apostles in the nave cease to seem monstrous; they become baroque works of nature, as if water by chance had molded the sides of a cliff into the likeness of Titans. And what might have disappointed in the mother of Cathedrals, the moderate height, becomes only the condition of unlimited breadth; and you cannot complain that in the centre you have a ceiling instead of a vault or a soaring dome, when you see beyond, quite subordinate to this rectangular space, soaring domes and vaults, enclosing other spaces and shedding variously coloured lights on other elaborate altars. Thus familiarity discloses the richness of what seemed bare at first glance, and you find amplitude, time, and silence intensely present in what you had passed by as insignificant.

It might seem that with age places gained upon persons in interest to my mind; and that my pleasure grew in intercourse with things rather than with ideas. Yet what held me in things was only their aspects, the picturesque or moral suggestions in them; for to things as material weights or forces I have never become attached. The old animal passion for fetishes, for hugging and hoarding particular objects because of their material identity, seems to have been entirely extinct in me; and it was precisely this indifference to physical identities that made me episodical in friendship and Platonising in love. I was far from inconsistent or variable in affection towards the *true* objects of my choice, but these were not the material things or persons that chance put in my way, in their necessarily mixed and changing composition. I saw only the gifts and virtues of which, perhaps for the first time, they gave me a clear idea. They become to that extent my local shrines or the saints for that day in my calendar; but never did the places or the persons turn into idols for my irrational worship. It was only the *numen* in them that I loved, who, as I passed by abstracted, whispered some immortal word in my ear.

It is true that persons, however changed in aspect, at least keep their memories. They may hark back to the scenes and the interests that may have bound them once to their old friends; and beneath memory there is also a soul, an innate disposition and character that may be recognised at moments in spite of all the incrustations of age, servitude and vice. And besides that, there are lessons of experience; acquirements and remunerations brought about by fortune, that sometimes transform the most commonplace persons, or the least prepossessing originally, into noble minds; and then the Holy Ghost, that is no respecter of persons, speaks to us through those so softened and pathetic masks. I would not nurse my animal aversions any more than my animal favouritisms. Without disowning in any way the bonds of blood or of comradeship or of social utility, I gladly recognise the good and the beautiful in unexpected quarters; and I am not in the least daunted in my cult of those divine essences when I find that they have disappeared from a place or a person that had once seemed to possess them.

Never have I enjoyed youth so thoroughly as I have in my old age. In writing *Dialogues in Limbo, The Last Puritan,* and now all these descriptions of the friends of my youth and the young friends of my middle age, I have drunk the pleasure of life more pure, more joyful, than it ever was when mingled with all the hidden anxieties and little annoyances of actual living. Nothing is inherently and invincibly young except spirit. And spirit can enter a human being perhaps better in the quiet of old age and dwell there more undisturbed than in the turmoil of adventure. But it must be in solitude. I do not need or desire to hob-nob artificially with other old men in order to revisit them in their salad days, and to renew my own. In Rome, in the Eternal City, I feel nearer to my own past, and to the whole past and future of the world, than I should in any cemetery or in any museum of relics. Old places and old persons in their turn, when spirit dwells in them, have an intrinsic vitality of which youth is incapable; precisely the balance and wisdom that comes from long perspectives and broad foundations. Everything shines then for the spirit by its own light in its own place and time; but not as it shone in its own restless eyes. For in its own eyes each person and each place was the centre of a universe full of threatening and tempting things; but old age, having less intensity at the centre has more clearness at the circumference, and knows that just because spirit, at each point, is a private centre for all things, no one point, no one phase of spirit is materially a public centre for all the rest. Thus recognition and honour flow out to all things, from the mind that conceives them justly and without egotism; and thus mind is reconciled to its own momentary existence and limited vision by the sense of the infinite supplements that embosom it on every side.

CHAPTER VIII

EPILOGUE: MY HOST THE WORLD

PERSONS and places people the world; they individuate its parts; and I have devoted this book to recording some of them that remain alive in my memory. Mine are insignificant recollections: for even when the themes happen to have some importance as persons and places in the great world, it is not at all in that capacity that I prize and describe them. I keep only some old miniature or some little perspective that caught my eye in passing, when the persons perhaps were young and the places empty and not dressed up to receive visitors, as are museums, libraries, ball-rooms and dinner-tables. Those were free glimpses of the world that I could love and could carry away. They were my consolations.

Yet the very contrast between these glimpses, all picturesque and aerial, and the vast obscure inexorable world from which they came, forced me gradually to form some notion of that material world also. Mine was a blue sea family: our world was that of colonial officials and great merchants. From the beginning I learned to think of the earth as a globe with its surface chiefly salt water, a barren treacherous and intractable waste for mankind, yet tempting and beautiful and swarming with primitive animals not possible to tame or humanise but sometimes good to eat. In fine, I opened my eyes on the world with the conviction that it was inhuman: not meant for man, but habitable by him, and possible to exploit, with prudence, in innumerable ways: a conviction that everything ever since has confirmed.

One peculiarity seemed common to all satisfactions: they brought something perfect, consummate, final. The sea, after no matter what storms, returned to its equilibrium and placidity; its

133

gamut was definite. Voyages all led to some port. The vastness and violence of nature, in challenging and often decimating mankind, by no means tend to dehumanise it. The quality of attainable goods may change with the conditions for attaining them; but the way is always open, at the right time, for the right sort of animal and for the right sort of mind. Arts have their dates; and the great question is not what age you live in or what art you pursue but what perfection you can achieve in that art under those circumstances.

The great master of sympathy with nature, in my education, was Lucretius. Romantic poets and philosophers, when they talk of nature, mean only landscape or other impressions due to aerial perspectives, sensuous harmonies of colour or form, or vital intoxications, such as those of riding, sea-faring, or mountain-climbing. Nature is loved for heightening self-consciousness and prized for ministering to human comfort and luxury, but is otherwise ignored as contemptible, dead, or non-existent. Or when people's temper is hardy and pugnacious, they may require nature as a buffer on which to rain their mighty blows and carve their important initials. Where human strength comes from or what ends human existence might serve, they neither know nor care.

The spirit in me felt itself cast upon this social and political world somewhat like Robinson Crusoe upon his island. We were both creatures of the same Great Nature; and my world, in its geography and astronomy, like Robinson Crusoe's island, had much more massive and ancient foundations than the small utterly insecure waif that had been wrecked upon it. In its social and political structure, however, my world was more like Crusoe's energetic person: for my island was densely inhabited: an ugly town, a stinted family, a common school; and the most troublesome and inescapable of its denizens was the particular body in which my spirit found itself rooted; so rooted that it became doubtful whether that body with its feelings and actions was not my true self, rather than this invisible spirit which they oppressed. I seemed to be both; and yet this compulsive and self-tormenting creature called "Me" was more odious and cruel to the "I" within than were the sea and sky, the woods and mountains, or the very cities and crowds of people that this animal "Me" moved among: for the spirit in me was happy and free ranging through that world, but troubled and captive in its close biological integument.

This is the double conflict, the social opposition and the moral agony, that spirit suffers by being incarnate; and yet if it were not incarnate it could not be individual, with a situation in space and time, a language and special perspective over nature and history: indeed, if not incarnate, spirit could not *exist* at all or be the inner light and perpetual witness of *life* in its dramatic vicissitudes.

If it be the fate of all spirit to live in a special body and a special age, and yet, for its vocation and proper life, to be addressed from that centre to all life and to all being, I can understand why I have been more sensible to this plight and to this mission than were most of my contemporaries. For by chance I was a foreigner where I was educated; and although the new language and customs interested me and gave me no serious trouble, yet speculatively and emotionally, especially in regard to religion, the world around me was utterly undigestible. The times also were moving, rapidly and exultingly, towards what for me was chaos and universal triviality. At first these discords sounded like distant thunder. Externally they were not yet violent; the world smiled in my eyes as I came to manhood, and the beauties and dignity of the past made the present unimportant. And as the feeling of being a stranger and an exile by nature as well as by accident grew upon me in time, it came to be almost a point of pride; some people may have thought it an affectation. It was not that; I have always admired the normal child of his age and country. My case was humanly unfortunate and involved many defects; yet it opened to me another vocation, not better (I admit no absolute standards) but more speculative, freer, juster, and for me happier.

I had always dreamt of travel, and it was oftenest in the voluntary, interested, appreciative rôle of the traveller that I felt myself most honest in my dealings with my environment. The world was My Host; I was a temporary guest in his busy and animated establishment. We met as strangers; yet each had generic and well-grounded ideas of what could be expected of the other. First impressions made these expectations more precise; the inn was habitable; the guest was presumably solvent. We might prove mutually useful. My Host and I could become friends, diplomatically; but we were not akin in either our interests or our powers. The normal economy of an innkeeper, though incidentally and in a measure it supplies the wants of his guests, knows nothing of their private moral economy. Their tastes in wines, in service, or in music may entirely outrun or contradict his long-established practice, which he will impose on his guests with all the authority of a landlord; and there may not be another inn in the place, or only worse ones. The guest has no right to demand what is not provided. He must be thankful for any little concessions that may be made to his personal tastes, if he is tactful and moderate in his requirements, pays his bills promptly and gives decent tips.

Such at least was the case in the nineteenth century when the world made itself pleasant to the traveller; and not to rich travellers only but to the most modest, and even to the very poor in their little purchases and popular feasts. Personal freedom produced a certain dignity and good humour even in bargaining; for to buy and sell, to patronise a shop or a boarding-house, was an act of kindness; and bills, at least in civilly commercial England, were always receipted "with thanks." Having lived a peaceful independent life, free from hardship or misfortune, I have found it easy to conform externally with the mechanism of society. Matter has been kind to me, and I am a lover of matter. Not only aesthetically but dynamically, as felt by Lucretius, nature to me is a welcome presence; and modern progress in mechanical invention and industrial luxury has excited joyously my materialistic imagination, as it did prophetically that of Bacon. Moreover, I inherited from my father a bond with matter which Bacon and Lucretius probably did not feel: the love of employing leisure in small mechanical occupations. I should never have read and written so much if the physical side of these employments had not been congenial to me and rich with a quiet happiness. Any common surroundings and any commonplace people pleased me well enough; it was only when sugary rapture was demanded about them or by them, as happened almost everywhere in my youth, that my stomach rose in radical protest. Then I discovered how much the human world of my time had become the enemy of spirit and therefore of its own light and peace.

How had this happened? Not at all as lovers of antiquity or of the middle ages seem to think, because of mechanical inventions or natural sciences or loss of Christian faith. These transformations might all have occurred in the normal growth of society. Variety in cultures is not due to aberrations any more than is the variety of animal species. But there may be aberration in any species or any culture when it becomes *vicious*; that is, when it forms habits destructive of its health and of its ability to prosper in its environment. Now modern sciences and inventions are not vicious in this sense; on the contrary, they bring notable additions to human *virtù*. And I think that the Renaissance, with the historical learning and humanism which it fostered, was also a great gain for human happiness and self-knowledge. Of this the surface of the modern world during my youth gave continual evidence, in spite of an undercurrent of unrest and disaffection sometimes heard rumbling below. "My Host's" establishment made a brave appearance; and I was particularly conscious of many new facilities of travel, breadth of information, and cosmopolitan convenience and luxury. Though there was no longer any dignity in manners, or much distinction in costume, fashion had not lost all its charm. In literature and the fine arts talent could give pleasure by its expertness, if not by its taste or savour. I have described how in Boston and in England I sometimes sipped at the rim of the plutocratic cup; and this was a real pleasure, because beneath the delicacy of the material feast there was a lot of shrewd experience in that society, and of placid kindness.

There was another cosmopolitan circle, however, less select and less worldly, but no less entertaining and no less subject to fashion and to ironical gossip, the Intellectuals, into whose company I was sometimes drawn. I was officially one of them, yet they felt in their bones that I might be secretly a traitor. "Ah, yes," cried a distinguished Jesuit recently when I was casually mentioned, "he is the *poetical* atheist." And an Italian professor, also a Catholic but tinged with German idealism, remarked of me: "the trouble with him is that he has never succeeded in outgrowing material-ism." Finally, a faithful diehard of British psychologism, asked why I was overlooked among contemporary philosophers, replied: "Because he has no originality. Everything in him is drawn from Plato and Leibnitz." This critical band is democratic in that it recognises no official authority and lets fluid public opinion carry the day; yet it is, on principle, in each man, private and inde-pendent in judgment. Few, however, have much time to read originals or to study facts. Leaders and busybodies must obey their momentum. A personal reaction on what other people say is so-cially sufficient; it will do for the press; and it will corroborate the critic's opinion in his own eyes.

I cannot overcome a settled distrust of merely intellectual accomplishment, militant in the void. I prefer common virtues and current beliefs, even if intellectually prejudiced and simple, when the great generative order of nature has bred them, and lent them its weight and honesty. For I do not rebel in the least at political and moral mutations when this same generative order brings them about spontaneously; for it is then on the side of change that clear intelligence discerns the lesser danger and the wider inter-ests. I should have loved the Gracchi; but not the belated Cato or the belated Brutus. All four were martyrs; but the first two spoke for the poor, for the suffering half of the people, oppressed by a shortsighted power that neglected its responsibilities; while the last two were conceited idealogues, jealous of their traditional rights, and utterly blind to destiny. If I were not too old and could venture to write in French, I should compose a short history of *Les Faux Pas de la Philosophie*; by which title I should not refer to *innocent* errors, with which all human speculation must be infected, nor to the symbolic or mythological form of the wisest wisdom, but only to militant heresies and self-contradictions due to wilful conceit, individual or tribal, verbal or moral; and there is little in European philosophy that is not infected with these *unnecessary* errors. Let the reader compose his own catalogue of these blind alleys explored by the ancients and by the moderns; since this is a biographical book, I will limit myself to the first and principal "faux pas" that the world has seemed to me to have taken in my time.

The contemporary world has turned its back on the attempt and even on the desire to live reasonably. The two great wars (so far) of the twentieth century were adventures in enthusiastic unreason. They were inspired by unnecessary and impracticable ambitions; and the "League" and the "United Nations," feebly set up by the victors, were so irrationally conceived that they at once reduced their victory to a stalemate. What is required for living rationally? I think the conditions may be reduced to two: First, self-knowledge, the Socratic key to wisdom; and second, sufficient knowledge of the world to perceive what alternatives are open to you and which of them are favourable to your true interests.

Now the contemporary world has plenty of knowledge of nature for its purposes, but its purposes show a positively insane abandonment of its true interests. You may say that the proletariat knows its interests perfectly; they are to work less and to earn more. Those are indeed its interests so long as it remains a proletariat: but to be a proletariat is an inhuman condition. Proletarians are human beings, and their first interest is to have a home, a family, a chosen trade, and freedom in practising it. And more particularly a man's true interest may exceptionally be not to have those things, but to wander alone like the rhinoceros; or perhaps to have a very special kind of home, family and occupation. There must be freedom of movement and vocation. There must be *Lebensraum* for the spirit.

There have always been beggars and paupers in the world, because there is bound to be a margin of the unfit, too bad or too good to keep in step with any well organised society; but that the great body of mankind should sink into a proletariat has been an unhappy effect of the monstrous growth of cities, made possible by the concentration of trade and the multiplication of industries, mechanised, and swelling into monopolies.

The natural state of mankind, before foreign conquerors dominate it or native ideologues reform it, is full of incidental evils; prophets have ample cause for special denunciations and warnings; yet there is, as in all animal economy, a certain nucleus of self-preserving instincts and habits, a normal constitution of society. Nature with its gods is the landlord of whose fields and woods they are local and temporary tenants; and with this invincible power they make prudent and far-seeing covenants. They know what is for their good and by what arts it might be secured. They live by agriculture, the hunting or breeding of animals, and such domestic arts as their climate and taste lead them to cultivate; and when a quarrel arises among them, or with strangers, they battle to preserve or to restore their free life, without more ambitious intentions. They are materially and morally rooted in the earth, bred in one land or one city. They are *civilised*. Wandering nations, with nothing of their own and working havoc wherever they go, are *barbarians*. Such "barbarians" were the proletariat of antiquity. When they occupied some civilised region without exterminating the natives, and established in the old strongholds a permanent foreign domination, they became half-civilised themselves, without shedding altogether the predatory and adventurous practices of their ancestors. This is the compound origin and nature of modern Western governments.

Varied, picturesque, and romantic mixtures of civilisation beneath and barbarism above have filled the history of Christendom, and produced beautiful transient arts, in which there was too little wisdom and too much fancy and fashion: think of Gothic architecture, or of manners, dress, poetry, and philosophy from the middle ages to our day. Civilisation had become more enterprising, plastic, and irresponsible, while barbarism seemed to retreat into sports, and into legal extravagances in thought and action. Intellectual chaos and political folly could thus come to co-exist strangely with an irresistible dominance of mechanical industry. The science that served this industrial progress by no means brought moral enlightenment. It merely enlarged acquaintance with phenomena and enabled clever inventors to construct all sorts of useful or superfluous machines. At first perhaps it was expected that science would make all mankind both rich and free from material cares (two contradictory hopes) and would at the same time enlighten them at last about the nature of things, including their own nature, so that adequate practical wisdom would be secured together with fabulous material well-being.

This is the dream of the moderns, on which I found My Host boastfully running his establishment. He expected his guests also to act accordingly and to befuddle and jollify one another, so that all should convince themselves that they were perfectly happy and should advertise their Host's business wherever they went. Such forced enterprise, forced confidence, and forced satisfaction would never have sprung from domestic arts or common knowledge spontaneously extended. It was all artificial and strained, marking the inhuman domination of some militant class or sect. This society lacked altogether that essential trait of rational living, to have a clear, sanctioned, ultimate aim. The cry was for vacant freedom and indeterminate progress: *Vorwärts! Avanti! Onward! Full speed ahead!* without asking whether directly before you was not a bottomless pit.

This has been the peculiar malady of my times. I saw the outbreak of it in my boyhood, and I have lived to see what seem clear symptoms of its end. The Great Merchants of my parents' youth had known nothing of it on their blue-sea voyages round Cape Horn or the Cape of Good Hope. Their good hope had been to amass a great fortune in fifteen or twenty years, and return home to bring up a blooming family in splendour and peace. They foresaw an orderly diffused well-being spreading out from them over all mankind. The fountains of happiness were ready to flow in every heart and mind if only people were suffered to have their own way materially and socially. That the masses would crowd out, exclude, indoctrinate, enslave, and destroy one another could not cross their genial and innocent minds, as they skimmed those immense oceans in their tight, strictly disciplined, white-sailed little craft.

Alas! The healthy growth of science and commerce had been crossed, long before the rise of the Great Merchants, by an insidious moral and political revolution. From the earliest times there have been militant spirits not content with inevitable changes and with occasional wars between neighbouring states, not usually wars of conquest or eternal hatred, but collisions in readjusting the political equilibrium between nations when their actual relations were no longer the same. Indeed, the tragic causes of conflict and ruin in civilizations are fundamentally internal to each society. A whole city or state may sometimes be destroyed, like Carthage: but history, then, comes to an end for that particular society, and the others continue their course as if their vanished rival had never existed. This course may be cut short, however, by internal disruption and suicidal revolutions. Every generation is born as ignorant and wilful as the first man; and when tradition has lost its obvious fitness or numinous authority, eager minds will revert without knowing it to every false hope and blind alley that had tempted their predecessors long since buried under layer upon layer of ruins. And these eager minds may easily become leaders; for society is never perfect; grievances and misfortunes perpetually breed rebellion in the oppressed heart; and the eloquent imagination of youth and of indignation will find the right words to blow the discontent, always smouldering, into sudden flame. Often things as they are become intolerable; there must be insurrection at any cost, as when the established order is not only casually oppressive, but ideally perverse and due to some previous epidemic of militant madness become constitutional. Against that domination, established in wilful indifference to the true good of man and to his possibilities, any political nostrum, proposed with the same rashness, will be accepted with the same faith. Thus the blind in extirpating the mad may plant a new madness.

That this is the present state of the world everyone can see by looking about him, or reading the newspapers; but I think that the elements in this crisis have been working in the body-politic for ages; ever since the Reformation, not to say since the age of the Greek Sophists and of Socrates. For the virulent cause of this long fever is subjectivism, egotism, conceit of mind. Not that culture of the conscience and even the logical refinements of dialectic are anything but good for the mind itself and for moral self-knowledge, which is one of the two conditions that I have assigned to political sanity; but the same logical arts are fatal if they are used to construct, by way of a moral fable, an anthropomorphic picture of the universe given out for scientific truth and imposed on mankind by propaganda, by threats, and by persecution. And this militant method of reforming mankind by misrepresenting their capacities and their place in the universe is no merely ancient or mediaeval delusion. It is the official and intolerant method of our most zealous contemporary prophets and reformers. Barbarism has adopted the weapons of flattery and prophecy. Merciless irrational ambition has borrowed the language of brotherly love.

The very fact, however, that these evils have deep roots and have long existed without destroying Western civilisation, but on the contrary have stimulated its contrary virtues and confused arts—this very fact seems to me to counsel calmness in contemplating the future. Those who look for a panacea will not find it. Those who advise resignation to a life of industrial slavery (because spiritual virtues may be cultivated by a slave, like Epictetus, more easily perhaps than by rich men) are surrendering the political future to an artificial militant regime that cannot last unaltered for a decade anywhere, and could hardly last a day, if by military force it were ever made universal. The fanaticism of all parties must be allowed to burn down to ashes, like a fire out of control. If it survives, it will be only because it will have humanised itself, reduced its dogmas to harmless metaphors, and sunk down a tap-root, to feed it, into the dark damp depths of mother earth. The economy of nature includes all particular movements, combines and transforms them all, but never diverts its wider processes to render them obedient to the prescriptions of human rhetoric. Things have their day, and their beauties in that day. It would be preposterous to expect any one civilisation to last forever.

Had it happened in my time (as by chance it did happen) that my landlord should give me notice that he was about to pull down his roof over my head, I might have been a little troubled for a moment; but presently I should have begun to look for other lodgings not without a certain curious pleasure, and probably should have found some (as I did, and better ones) in which to end my days. So, I am confident, will the travelling Spirit do—this ever-renewed witness, victim, and judge of existence, divine yet born of woman. Obediently it will learn other affections in other places, unite other friends, and divide other peoples; and the failure of over-exact hopes and overweening ambitions will not prevent spirit from continually turning the passing virtues and sorrows of nature into glimpses of eternal truth.

INDEX

INDEX

Acropolis, the, 54
Acton, Lord, 26
Agrigentum, 41–3
Arabian Nights, 37, 50–1, 52
Aristophanes, 95
Asquith, Herbert Henry, 1st Earl of Oxford and, 94
Athens, 44, 46, 54
Avila, 1, 7, 10, 19, 36, 121–2, 124

Baalbek, 53
Babe, the, 100–1, 106, 113
Bacon, Francis, 29, 136–7
Beal, Mrs., 44, 48
Bérénice, by Racine, 62–3
Berenson, Bernard, 123
Berenson, Mrs. Bernard, 51, 100
Bergson, 110, 120
Berkeley, George, 30
Billings, Emma, 59
Boston, 24, 36, 137
Brighton, 71
Boutroux, 120
Bridges, Edward, 81–2
Bridges, Mrs. Robert, 81–2
Bridges, Robert, 80–4, 94–9, 114, 115
Browning, Oscar, 21–2
Buda-Pesth, 56
Bury, 21 n.
Byron, Lord, 64

Cairo, 45
Cambridge, Mass., 59–60
Cambridge University, *See* Chapter II (pages 16–32) and 113, 116
Caravaners, The, by Countess von Arnim, 69
Catholicism, 10–11, 84, 90, 122
Cazalis, Dr., 120

Chetwynd, Randolph, 113–4
Comte, Auguste, 29
Constantinople, 55
Cortina, 124
Crete, 44

Damascus, 51–3
Dead Sea, the, 49
Denderah, 46
Dialogues in Limbo, 131
Dickens, 99
Dickinson, Lowes, 22, 24–5
Doughty, C. M., 50
Dyer, Louis, 78

Egotism in German Philosophy, 96, 127
Egypt, and various places in, 38, 45–7
Elizabeth and Her German Garden, by Countess von Arnim, 69
Emerson, Ralph Waldo, 13
Empedocles, 42
Encyclopaedie der Wissenschaften, by Hegel, 31
England, and various places in, 11, 23, 57, 79–80, 86–7, 96, 99–101, 106–7, 111–13, 117–18, 137. *Also see* Cambridge and Oxford.
English, the, 30, 96–7, 117
Epidaurus, 54
Escalera, Mercedes de la, 49, 121
Esmonde, Grattan, 91
Evans, Sir Arthur John, 44

Fletcher, Harold, 85–90, 115
Florence, 123
Foucault, Charles de, 50

Gibraltar, 36–7
Goethe, 4, 11, 72

147

Greece, 11, 36, 54-5
Greek View of Life, by Lowes Dickinson, 24

Harvard, 17, 20, 92, 119
Hegel, 31
Higgs, 78-81, 115
Hobbes, 29
Housman, 113
Hume, David, 30
Huxley, Aldous, 91, 116

Inge, W. R., 117
Inge, Mrs. W. R., 117
Interpretations of Poetry and Religion, 80, 88
Irving, Duer, 51
Italy, and various places in, 38-44, 49, 98, 113, 119, 123

Jackson, Henry, 25-6
Jaffa, 48
James, William, 60, 113
Jerusalem. *See* Palestine
Johnson, Lionel, 64, 78, 91, 99

Kant, 84
Karnak, 45-6
Keynes, John Maynard, 21 n.
King's Chapel (Cambridge), 17-20, 23
King's College (Cambridge), 16-17, 21 & n., 23, 31
Koran, the, 45, 50

Lahore, Jean. *See* Cazalis
Lapsley, 16-17, 26, 113
Last Puritan, The, 91, 131
Leaves of Grass, 64
Leibnitz, 25
Life of Reason, The, 37, 43
Loeser, Charles, 123
Lowell, Abbott Lawrence, 119
Lucretius, 42, 134, 136-7

MacTaggart, 25, 31-2, 113

Marsham, Lady Mary, 89
Mill, John Stuart, 30
Moore, G. E., 25, 31
Morrell, Lady Ottoline, 93-5
Mortimer, Raymond, 91-3
Mount of Olives, 49

Naples, 38-9, 44
Newton, 29

Ortygia, 43-4
Oxford, 16, 18, 21, 71, 78-95, 97-9, 113-6

Paestum, 38-40
Palestine, and various places in, 47-53
Paris, 7, 38, 92, 98, 100, 120, 123-4
Parmenides, by Plato, 25
Pastor's Wife, The, by Countess von Arnim, 69
Philebus, by Plato, 25
Plato, 44, 46
Platonism and the Spiritual Life, 124
Plotinus, edited by W. R. Inge, 117
Plutarch, 53
Politicus, by Plato, 25
Potter, Warwick, 8
Principia Mathematica, by Bertrand Russell in collaboration with Whitehead, 27, 29
Pyramids, the, 46-7

Racine, 44, 62-3
Realm of Essence, The, 114
Riviera, 122-3
Rodd, Sir Rennell, 116-17
Rolfe, Frederick, 90
Rome, 36, 56, 119, 123-131
Rousseau, 59
Russell, Bertrand, 16, 22, 25, 27-30, 65, 76-7, 93-5
Russell, Mrs. Bertrand (Dora), 76-7
Russell, Lady, 28

Russell, John Francis Stanley, 2nd
    Earl, 16, 22, 27, 29, 57–76, 78,
    93, 95, 106–13, 116
Russell, Countess Elizabeth, 68–76,
    108, 111
Russell, Countess Mollie, 65–72, 74,
    76

Santa Sophia, 18, 41, 55–6
Santayana, Agustín Ruiz de (au-
    thor's father), 8–9, 10, 34
Santayana, Josefina Borrás, y Bufu-
    rull de (author's mother), 34, 119
Santiago (author's uncle), 106
Sargent, John, 36–7
Sassoon, Siegfried, 94–5
Scepticism and Animal Faith, 114
Schiller, F. C. S., 97–8, 114
Scott, Lady, 58, 67, 73–4
Seville, 51, 121
Shakespeare, 99
Sicily, 38, 41–3
Socrates, 46, 55, 80, 143
Soliloquies in England, 117
Sophist, by Plato, 25
Spencer, Herbert, 113
Spengler, 44
Sphinx, the, 47
Spinoza, 3, 29, 115
De l'Amour, by Stendhal, 14
Stewart, Professor, 95, 114
Stickney, Trumbull, 28, 124
Strachey, Lytton, 94–5
Strong, Charles Augustus, 98, 100,
    120, 123–4

Sturgis, Howard, 100–6, 113
Sturgis, Josefina (author's half-sis-
    ter), 119, 121
Sturgis, Susana (author's half-sis-
    ter), 3, 9–10
Swinburne, 9
Syracuse, 42–3

Tangiers, 36–7
Testament of Beauty, by Robert
    Bridges, 84
Trevelyan, 21 n.
Trinity College (Cambridge), 25
Turner, Martha, 58–62, 65–7, 70,
    74
Turner, Mrs., 58

Unknowable, The, 113
Untergang des Abendlandes, by
    Spengler, 122

Venice, 43, 54, 124–7
Vera, by Countess von Arnim, 75
Veronica, 61–2, 64
Vienna, 56

Waggett, Father, 88–90, 95, 115
Warren, Edward, 97–8
Warren, Mrs., 93
Wedd, 17, 20–4
Westenholz, 28
Wharton, Mrs., 16

Zampa, Rev. Luciano, 127–8